THEGREENGUIDE
San Francisco

Golden Gate Bridge viewed from Baker Beach at sunset / © Stephan Hoerold / iStockphoto.com

MICHELIN

THEGREENGUIDE **SAN FRANCISCO**

Editorial Director	Cynthia Clayton Ochterbeck
Edited & Produced by	Jonathan P. Gilbert, Azalay Media
Principal Writer	Barbara Rockwell
Production Manager	Natasha G. George
Cartography	Peter Wrenn
Photo Editor	Sean Sachon
Interior Design	Chris Bell
Layout	Michelin Travel Partner, Natasha G. George
Cover Design	Chris Bell, Christelle Le Déan
Cover Layout	Natasha G. George

Contact Us	Michelin Travel and Lifestyle North America
	One Parkway South
	Greenville, SC 29615
	USA
	travel.lifestyle@us.michelin.com
	www.michelintravel.com
	Michelin Travel Partner
	Hannay House
	39 Clarendon Road
	Watford, Herts WD17 1JA
	UK
	✐01923 205240
	travelpubsales@uk.michelin.com
	www.ViaMichelin.com
Special Sales	For information regarding bulk sales, customized editions and premium sales, please contact us at:
	travel.lifestyle@us.michelin.com
	www.michelintravel.com

HOW TO USE THIS GUIDE

PLANNING YOUR TRIP

The blue-tabbed PLANNING YOUR TRIP section gives you **ideas for your trip** and **practical information** to help you organize it. You'll find tours, practical information, a host of outdoor activities, a calendar of events, information on shopping, sightseeing, kids' activities and more.

INTRODUCTION

The orange-tabbed INTRODUCTION section explores San Francisco's **Nature** and geology. The **History** section spans from the Gold Rush to the 20C rise of progressive politics. The **Art and Culture** section covers architecture, art, literature and music, while **The City Today** delves into the modern region.

DISCOVERING

The green-tabbed DISCOVERING section features Principal Sights by region, featuring the most interesting local **Sights**, **Walking Tours**, nearby **Excursions**, and detailed **Driving Tours**. Admission prices shown are normally for a single adult.

ADDRESSES

We've selected the best hotels, restaurants, cafes, shops, nightlife and entertainment to fit all budgets. See the Legend on the cover flap for an explanation of the price categories. See the back of the guide for an index of hotels and restaurants.

Sidebars

Throughout the guide you will find blue, orange and green-colored text boxes with lively anecdotes, detailed history and background information.

😊 A Bit of Advice 😊

Green advice boxes found in this guide contain practical tips and handy information relevant to your visit or sight in the Discovering section.

STAR RATINGS★★★

Michelin has given star ratings for more than 100 years. If you're pressed for time, we recommend you visit the ★★★ or ★★ sights first:

★★★ **Highly recommended**

★★ **Recommended**

★ **Interesting**

MAPS

😊 Regional Driving Tours map, Places to Stay map and Sights map.

😊 Region maps.

😊 Maps for major cities and villages.

😊 Local tour maps.

All maps in this guide are oriented north, unless otherwise indicated by a directional arrow. The term "Local Map" refers to a map within the chapter or Tourism Region. A complete list of the maps found in the guide appears at the back of this book.

© Nils Kahle - 4FR Photography / iStockphoto

© Andrew Zarivny / iStockphoto.com

PLANNING YOUR TRIP

INTRODUCTION TO SAN FRANCISCO

CONTENTS

DISCOVERING SAN FRANCISCO

© Ray Laskowitz/Tips Images

YOUR STAY IN SAN FRANCISCO

Welcome to San Francisco

Globally recognized as a center of high technology and finance, the San Francisco Bay Area also boasts world-class cuisine, diverse cultural offerings, and a well-deserved eco-friendly reputation, not to mention an agreeable climate and incomparable geographic setting; all of which make the vibrant "City by the Bay" a most desirable place to live and an unparalleled destination for visitors.

DOWNTOWN *(pp62–109)*

Filling the northeast corner of the city, San Francisco's bustling downtown encompasses the city's major financial, retail and civic centers: the skyscraper-filled Financial District, the fashionista-beloved Union Square and Beaux Arts-style Civic Center. Also downtown are vastly diverse historic neighborhoods. North Beach recalls its early heritage with Italian restaurants, bakeries and cafes, while Nob Hill retains an upper-class cachet from the late 19C, housing many of the city's most grand hotels. To the east, Cantonese chattering and the smells fresh dumplings fill the air in colorful Chinatown.

BAYSHORE *(pp110–147)*

The Bayshore is home to several of San Francisco's most popular attractions. Fisherman's Wharf draws throngs to its colorful array of piers, docks, carnival amusements and seafood eateries. The Embarcadero offers a 3mi waterfront promenade from Fisherman's Wharf to AT&T Park, with expansive bay views, public art and the Ferry Building. West of Fisherman's Wharf, the Marina District is home to Fort Mason, the Exploratorium and dozens of trendy boutiques and restaurants. Farther west is the Presidio, a 1480-acre former military base with trails and great views of the Golden Gate and San Francisco Bay. Of course, the Golden Gate Bridge itself is a prime Bayshore attraction as well.

CENTRAL NEIGHBORHOODS *(pp148–169)*

San Francisco's central districts are anchored by the sprawling Golden Gate Park, which stretches 52 blocks from the Pacific Ocean to the Haight-Ashbury district, and houses the California Academy of Sciences, the de Young museum, and the Conservatory of Flowers. To the north, Pacific Heights has been San Francisco's most fashionable residential neighborhoods for more than a century. Nearby Japantown is a compact neighborhood centered on the Japan Center, a shopping, hotel, and restaurant complex.

SOUTHERN NEIGHBORHOODS *(pp170–189)*

The lively Castro District forms the heart of San Francisco's gay community. Bars, restaurants and boutiques crowd along Castro, Market and 18th Streets, while residential side streets are lined with refurbished Victorians. To the east, the sunny Mission District is both a Latino enclave and a magnet for the city's arty, hipster crowd. Farther east, SoMa is dominated by warehouses and office buildings, but is also a prime cultural and nightlife district, thanks to the museum-filled Yerba Buena

Queen Anne, Victorians

© Craig Buchanan / SFCVB

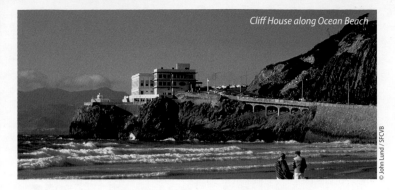
Cliff House along Ocean Beach

© John Lund / SFCVB

Gardens redevelopment and an influx of bars and nightclubs in former warehouse spaces.

OCEANFRONT *(pp190–201)*

Where the Richmond and Sunset districts meet the ocean, sit the San Francisco Zoo, the Cliff House, the ruins of Sutro Baths, and the Legion of Honor museum. Follow the Coastal Trail along the shoreline for spectacular views of the Golden Gate Bridge and Marin Headlands, or head to Fort Funston to watch hang-gliders. South of the Sunset District, Lake Merced and Sigmund Stern Grove offer further opportunities for various recreation activities.

EAST BAY *(pp204–231)*

The dynamic university city of Berkeley has an unending appetite for political activism, energetic intellectualism and cultural diversity. Up in the Berkeley Hills, the city boasts beautiful neighborhoods with stunning views of San Francisco. Oakland, Berkeley's neighbor to the south, boasts revitalized waterfront and civic center districts, an exceptional museum, and ambitiously restored mid-19C to 20C residential and commercial buildings.

MARIN COUNTY *(pp232–55)*

Marin County combines the sophisticated charm of Sausalito and the breezy maritime ambience of Tiburon with the ancient redwoods of Muir Woods and the rugged seascapes of Point Reyes and the Marin Headlands. While some 255,000 suburbanites reside in this county, most settlement is on the eastern side of Mt. Tamalpais, leaving the coastal precincts in a largely natural state.

WINE COUNTRY *(pp256–281)*

Lying within an hour's drive north and northeast of San Francisco, the hills and vales of Sonoma County and Napa Valley thrive on the abundant sunshine and fertile soil that produce grapes for some of North America's finest wines. The temperate climate, varied natural beauty and acclaimed wineries make the Wine Country one of California's foremost tourist destinations.

SOUTH BAY AND PENINSULA *(pp282–299)*

Located in the Santa Clara Valley, along Coyote Creek and the Guadalupe River, San Jose is now California's third-largest city. The self-proclaimed capital of Silicon Valley bustles with high-tech prosperity and offers a wealth of cultural attractions, from the downtown historic district to the Tech Museum of Innovation. Farther north, Palo Alto is home to Stanford University, while neighboring towns house the Stanford Linear Accelerator Center, the NASA Ames Research Center and the historic Filoli Mansion and gardens.

When and Where to Go

WHEN TO GO

The San Francisco Bay Area enjoys a temperate climate year-round. Although temperature variation from season to season is slight, weather conditions can change quite suddenly in the course of a day, and from area to area. Inland temperatures are usually higher than those along the bayshore and especially the oceanfront. Nighttime lows tend to stay between 45° and 55°F.

The key to comfort when visiting the region is dressing in layers. Shorts and other light clothing are rarely practical. In the **spring** and **summer**, daytime highs average in the 60s, although the infrequent fog-free day can bring sunny skies and temperatures in the 80s. July and August generally bring the busiest tourist season; visitors should make advance reservations whenever possible and expect long lines for the more popular attractions. The region's glorious views are at their finest during the clear days of **fall**, when daytime temperatures in the 70s make exploring the area quite comfortable. Rain is the norm during the **winter** months; 80 percent of the annual precipitation occurs between November and April, and temperatures hover between 45° and 60°F throughout the day.

Fog is an important weather determinant: its presence causes temperatures to drop, making a sweater or jacket necessary. Spring fogs occur in the early morning and generally lift by mid-day. Fog persists throughout the day in coastal areas during summer, though it may burn off over inland areas before returning in the evening. Fall days are relatively fog-free. Winter fogs usually occur inland, leaving coastal areas clear.

WHERE TO GO
SUGGESTED TWO-DAY ITINERARY
FIRST DAY

Fisherman's Wharf and Chinatown
Morning – Ride the Powell-Hyde cable car to **Fisherman's Wharf★★★**. Have an Irish coffee at the Buena Vista Café. Visit historic ships at **Hyde Street Pier★★** or rent a bicycle and bike the **Bay Trail★★** over the **Golden Gate Bridge★★★** to **Sausalito★**, returning to Fisherman's Wharf on the ferry.
Lunch – Dungeness crab or clam chowder at Fisherman's Wharf.
Afternoon – Walk down **Lombard Street★★★**, "the world's crookedest street"; view the Depression-era murals at **Coit Tower★★★**; then have a cappuccino and cannoli at an Italian cafe in **North Beach★★**. Browse the beat poetry section at **City Lights Bookstore**. Shop in **Chinatown★★★**.
Evening – Dine in Chinatown and see a show in the **Theater District**.

de Young Museum

© Gregory Bertolini / Fine Arts Museums of San Francisco

Yerba Buena Center for the Arts

© Rafael Ramirez Lee / Dreamstime.com

SECOND DAY
Alcatraz, Union Square and SoMa
Morning – Take a morning ferry to
Alcatraz★★★ (be sure to reserve
ahead). On returning, take the
F-Market streetcar line along the
Embarcadero to the **Ferry Building**
for some **shopping★★**.
Lunch – At the Ferry Building.
Afternoon – Explore South of Market,
including the **Museum of Modern
Art★★** and the **Yerba Buena Center
for the Arts★** (take kids to the
Rooftop at Yerba Buena Center for the
Arts★★). Shop in **Union Square★★★**.
Evening – Dine in the **Union Square**
area. Have a cocktail with a **view★★★**
at the **Top of the Mark** in Nob Hill
or go dancing at **Harry Denton's
Starlight Room**.

IF YOU HAVE FIVE DAYS...
THIRD DAY
Golden Gate Park and Ocean Beach
Morning – Grab a coffee, then head
out to **Cole Valley** for a French

breakfast at **Zazie**. Stop by **Haight-
Ashbury** before going to the
California Academy of Sciences★★
or the **de Young★★★** in **Golden Gate
Park★★★**.
Lunch – At the de Young museum.
Afternoon – Visit the **Japanese Tea
Garden★★** and the **Conservatory of
Flowers★★**, then rent a paddle boat
at **Stow Lake★**.
Continue out to **Ocean Beach**,
stopping by the buffalo paddock and
the Dutch windmills. Enjoy the sunset
from the **Beach Chalet** or the restored
Cliff House★★.
Evening – Dine in the **Castro
District★** or the **Mission District★★**,
then see a movie at the historic **Castro
Theatre★**.

FOURTH DAY
Presidio and Legion of Honor
Morning – Take breakfast on
Chestnut Street in the **Marina
District★**, then visit the **Palace of Fine
Arts★★** and the **Exploratorium★★**.

SAN FRANCISCO TEMPERATURE CHART			
(recorded at San Francisco International Airport)			
Month	avg. high	avg. low	Precipitation
Jan	56˚F (13˚C)	41˚F (5˚C)	4.6in (11.7cm)
Apr	63˚F (17˚C)	47˚F (8˚C)	1.5in (3.8cm)
Jul	71˚F (21˚C)	53˚F (12˚C)	0.04in (0.1cm)
Oct	70˚F (21˚C)	51˚F (10˚C)	1.0in (2.5cm)

Fog over San Francisco Bay

© Regis Lefebure / SFCVB

Lunch – Grab a light lunch at the **Crissy Field Center** in **The Presidio★★**. **Afternoon** – Visit the **Legion of Honor★★★**; walk the **Coastal Trail★★** to the **Sutro Baths Ruins★**. Have a late-afternoon snack at the **Cliff House★★**, enjoying the expansive views. **Evening** – Dine in **Hayes Valley**; attend an opera, play, symphony, dance or ballet performance at the vast **War Memorial** and **Performing Arts Center★★**.

FIFTH DAY
Civic Center & Pacific Heights
Morning – Visit the splendid **Asian Art Museum★★★** and **City Hall★★**. **Lunch** – In Hayes Valley. **Afternoon** – Shop in **Hayes Valley** and **Pacific Heights★★**; take a walk in Pacific Heights to see the stately mansions. Proceed south to **Alamo Square** for a photo of **Postcard Row★★★**. **Evening** – Dine in **Japantown**, see an art film at the **Kabuki Theatre**, roots

music at the **Boom Boom Room**, jazz at **Yoshi's**, or rock 'n' roll at the **Fillmore**.

IF YOU HAVE A CAR

In the Bay Area there are many outstanding scenic excursions and driving tours. *☾See the Principal Sights Map on the inside back cover.* Listed below are the sights within the *Excursions* section of the guide, where you can find directions from the city and local driving tours.

- ◆ **East Bay Area**
- ◆ **Marin Headlands**
- ◆ **Mount Tamalpais**
- ◆ **Point Reyes National Seashore**
- ◆ **Sausilito**
- ◆ **Tiburon**
- ◆ **Napa Valley**
- ◆ **Sonama Valley**
- ◆ **Upper Sonoma- Russian River Region**
- ◆ **Palo Alto**
- ◆ **San Jose**
- ◆ **San Mateo County Coast**

☺ Guided Tours ☺

If your schedule permits, a **guided tour** is a good way to get an in-depth look at a specific area of the city that piques your interest. Knowledgeable guides can illuminate the mysteries of Chinatown, the colorful history of the Castro District, the tastes and aromas of North Beach or the bustling waterfront. *☾See Sightseeing in What to See and Do* or check the San Francisco Convention & Visitors Bureau website (*www.onlyinsanfrancisco.com*) for information on themed tours and walking tours in San Francisco and the Bay Area.

What to See and Do

OUTDOOR FUN

A mild climate promotes recreational opportunities year-round, most in the city or within an hour's drive of its limits. Hikers, bikers and equestrians avail themselves of trails throughout Marin County, the East Bay and the San Francisco Peninsula. Lovers of water sports take to the waves for surfing, windsurfing and sea kayaking, though swimming in most places is unsafe. Jogging, roller-blading, hang-gliding, kite-flying and sportfishing are other recreational possibilities. Golden Gate Park, Marin County and units of the Golden Gate National Recreation Area (GGNRA) are good places to start when seeking outdoor recreation information. Trail maps, facility hours and other information are available at the **San Francisco Recreation & Park Department** *(McLaren Lodge, 501 Stanyan St.; ☎415-831-2700; www.sfrecpark.org)* and the **GGNRA** *(Fort Mason, Building 201; ☎415-561-4700; www.nps.gov/goga).* The **Marin County Visitors Bureau** *(1 Mitchell Blvd. Ste. B, San Rafael, CA 94903; ☎415-925-2060; www.visit marin.org)* also provides maps and information.

Hiking – The Bay Area is a hiker's paradise, with extensive trails exploring its valleys, scaling its peaks, tracing its coastlines and penetrating its forests. Contact the GGNRA or the San Francisco Recreation & Park Department *(above)* for trail maps and information. Within the city, the **Golden Gate Promenade** (3.5mi) from Aquatic Park to Fort Point below the Golden Gate Bridge, and the **Coastal Trail** (9mi) from the Golden Gate Bridge to Fort Funston, afford lovely ocean and cityscape views.

Biking – Mountain biking is an especially popular sport among the hills and valleys of Marin County and in the Presidio and Land's End areas of San Francisco. Most trails are accessible to both hikers and bikers, though some are restricted to hikers only. Routes within San Francisco include the Golden Gate Promenade and the Coastal Trail *(left)*. In addition, many streets have designated bike lanes. Shops offering rentals and trail information include:

- **Avenue Cyclery:** Bikes: 756 Stanyan St. at Waller St. ☎415-387-3155. www.avenue cyclery.com.
- **Bike and Roll:** Bikes, tandems, skates: five locations including 899 Columbus Ave., North Beach. ☎415-229-2000. www.bikethegoldengate.com.
- **Blazing Saddles Bike Rentals:** Bikes, tandems: six locations including 465 Jefferson St. at Hyde St., Fisherman's Wharf. ☎415-202-8888. www.blazingsaddles.com.

Golf – There are several public courses within the city of San Francisco; all rent out clubs and other equipment. You'll find others throughout the area.

- **Lincoln Park**, *Open daily dawn–dusk,* 34th Ave. & Clement St., Outer Richmond. ☎415-221-9911. ☎415-750-4653 to reserve tee times. www.lincolnpark gc.com.
- **Golden Gate Park Golf Course**, *Open daily dawn–dusk,* 47th Ave. & Fulton St. ☎415-751-8987. www.goldengateparkgolf.com.
- **Presidio Golf Course**, *daily dawn–dusk,* 300 Arguello Blvd., the Presidio. ☎415-561-4661. www.presidiogolf.com.

Windsurfing – Consistent westerly winds from March to October make San Francisco Bay a prime spot for windsurfing and kiteboarding, particularly at Crissy Field, Candlestick Point, and Lake Merced. A few organizations offer instruction and rental equipment, including the **Boardsports School** *(Mar–Sept only; San Francisco, San Mateo and*

SELECTED BAY AREA BEACHES	Price	Swimming	First Aid	Camping	Wheel	Beachwalking
Aquatic Park Beach		≋			♿	
Baker Beach						🏄
Bolinas Beach		≋				🏄
China Beach		≋	✚	⚠		🏄
Drakes Beach		≋			♿	
Fort Funston		≋				🏄
Kehoe Beach		≋				🏄
Land's End		≋				
Lighthouse Field State Beach					♿	🏄
Limantour Beach		≋			♿	
McClures Beach		≋				
Montana State Beach		≋				
Muir Beach		≋			♿	
North Beach & South Beach	👓			⚠		
Ocean Beach					♿	🏄
Rodeo Beach					♿	🏄
Stinson Beach		≋	✚		♿	🏄
Tomales Bay State Park	👓	≋		⚠	♿	

Alameda; ☏415-385-1224; www. boardsportsschool.com). Note that certification is required to rent windsurfing equipment; contact the **San Francisco Boardsailing Association** (www.sfba.org) for additional information.

Swimming and Beachwalking – Waters of the Pacific shore and Golden Gate can be dangerous. Tides sweep in suddenly and powerfully and "sneaker waves" may appear without warning. Never turn your back to the ocean. Avoid walking along coastal cliffs; keep to established trails. Rip tides (strong, narrow seaward flows), sudden dropoffs and strong currents make most areas dangerous for swimming and even wading. Besides,

water temperatures average a chilly 55°F (13°C) year-round. Exercise caution when swimming at all times, and obey posted warnings. Symbols on the chart above indicate: 👓admission/parking fee; ≋swimming; ✚lifeguard; ⚠camping; ♿disabled facilities; 🏄surfing.

Sportfishing – The cold, upwelling waters off the coastal shelf north and south of San Francisco bring salmon, tuna, sturgeon, halibut and various types of rockfish near shore. Charter boats abound for both experienced and novice fishers; many provide equipment and tackle, and sell fishing licenses.
For information and recommendations, visit www.sfsportfishing.com.

Good ones to try: the **Salty Lady** (*☎415-674-3474; www.saltylady.com*) or the **Blue Runner** (*☎415-458-8700; www.bluerunnercharters.com*).

Horseback Riding – Currently there are no public stables in the city, although plans are in progress to rebuild the historic stables at Golden Gate Park. But stables and ranches throughout the Bay Area cater to riders of every experience level, with lessons, horse rentals and organized trail rides. Contact **Bay Area Equestrian Network** (*☎925-484-0395; www.bayequest.com*) for information. **Miwok Livery Stables** (*701 Tennessee Valley Rd., Mill Valley; ☎415-383-8048; www.miwokstables.com*) offers public riding on GGNRA lands.

Hang-gliding – The cliffs of Fort Funston rank among the finest hang-gliding sites in the US (*main season Mar–Oct*). Several hang-gliding shops, located near the fort, offer rentals and instruction. Contact the **San Francisco Bay Area Paragliding Association** for a list of shops, current conditions and hang-gliding events (*www.sfbapa.org*).

ACTIVITIES FOR KIDS 👫
With cable cars and boats to ride, barking seals to visit, beaches to run on, bridges to cross, towers to climb and whales to watch, to say nothing of excellent museums and attractions to entice youngsters' interest, San Francisco is a giant funhouse for kids. Most attractions offer discounted admission for visitors under the age of 18, and some restaurants offer special kids menus. The family-oriented websites www.redtri.com/san-francisco-kids and www.sfkids.org are packed with tips, restaurant recommendations, special events and activities for young visitors. Throughout this guide, sights of particular interest to kids are indicated with a 👫 symbol.

SIGHTSEEING
The free publication *Where San Francisco* offers information on events, attractions, shopping and dining. It's available at hotels and visitor kiosks. In addition, the **San Francisco Convention & Visitors Bureau** publishes the free *San Francisco Visitors Planning Guide;* order one online at www.sanfrancisco.travel or pick one up at the Bureau's **Visitor Information Center**, located on the lower level of Hallidie Plaza (*Market & Powell Sts.; open year-round Mon–Fri 9am–5pm, Sat–Sun 9am–3pm, closed Sun Nov–Apr; ☎415-391-2000; www.sanfrancisco.travel*). The center has helpful multilingual staff and stocks brochures for restaurants, hotels, clubs and attractions. It also sells Muni maps and passes.

TOURS
CITY AND BAY AREA TOURS
Several operators tour the main attractions of San Francisco and the surrounding Bay Area by mid-size coach. Pickup and foreign-language tours are available; reservations may be required.

+ **Gray Line Deluxe City Tour:** 🕐*Open year-round daily 9.15am, 11.15am, 2.15pm. 3hrs 30min.* 🎫*$49.* ♿ *☎415-434-8687. www.sanfranciscosightseeing.com.*
+ **Great Pacific Tour Co.:** 🕐*Open year-round daily 9am, 11am, 2pm. 3hrs 30min.* 🎫*$49.* ♿ *☎415-626-7073. www.greatpacifictour.com.*
+ **Tower Tours:** 🕐*Open year-round daily 9am, 11am, 2pm. 3hrs 30min.* 🎫*$51.* ♿ *☎415-345-8687. www.towertours.com.*

HISTORICAL & ARCHITECTURAL TOURS
San Francisco City Guides, organized by the San Francisco Public Library, offers dozens of free walking tours led by volunteer docents (*year-round daily, starting between 9.30am & 2pm; check website for schedule & departure points.* ♿ *☎415-557-4266; www.sfcityguides.org*).

The **San Francisco Museum and Historical Society** offers free walking tours of the Financial District, Nob Hill, Civic Center, Golden Gate Park, Mission Dolores and Bernal Heights on a rotating basis most Saturdays. Most popular is the Barbary Coast Trail tour *(2hrs; reservations required; $15; call or consult website for schedule and departure points.* & *415-775-1105; www.sfhistory.org).*

The **Victorian Home Walk** unveils the city's past through the treasured "painted lady" architecture of Pacific Heights. Depart from the corner of Powell and Post streets in Union Square (*open year-round daily 11am; 2hrs 30min; $25; *415-252-9485; www.victorianhomewalk.com).*

NEIGHBORHOOD TOURS

All About Chinatown Walking Tours depart from Old St. Mary's Cathedral *(660 California St. at Grant Ave.; open year-round daily 10am; 2hrs; reservations required; $30 tour; $50 including dim sum lunch noon– 1pm;* & *415-982-8839; www.allaboutchinatown.com).*

Cruisin' the Castro walking tours highlight San Francisco's gay and lesbian community. Tours depart from Harvey Milk Plaza at Castro and Market Sts. (*open year-round Mon–Sat 10am or by appointment; 2hrs; reservations required; $30,* & *415-255-1821; www.cruisinthecastro.com).*

The **Haight-Ashbury Flower Power Walking Tour** departs from Stanyan & Waller Sts. (*open year-round Tue & Sat 10.30am, Thu 2pm, Fri 11am; 2hrs 30min; $20; *415-863-1621; www.haightashburytour.com).*

The **Precita Eyes Mural Arts Center** lead tours that explore **70 murals in a six-block walk** of Mission District *(depart from 2981 24th St. near Harrison St., open year-round Sat–Sun 1.30pm; 2hrs; $15; *415-285-2287; www.precita eyes.org).*

HobNob Walking Tours explore the robber-baron legacy of Nob Hill; they depart from the Fairmont Hotel (*open year-round Mon–Sat 10am &*

*1.30pm, Sun 9.30am; 2hrs; reservations required; $30; *650-814-6303; www.hobnobtours.com).*

The **Pacific Heights Walking Tour** is offered by San Francisco Architectural Heritage. It departs from Haas-Lilienthal House, 2007 Franklin St. (*open year-round Sun 12.30pm; 2hrs; $8; *415-441-3004; www.sfheritage.org).*

SCENIC CRUISES & FERRIES

Bay cruises offer views of the skyline, Golden Gate Bridge, Alcatraz, and the hills of Marin County and the East Bay. Some companies offer evening and dinner/dance cruises. Following are some popular cruises; for additional ferry information, *see By Ferry in Getting There and Getting Around.*

Blue & Gold Fleet Bay Cruise: frequent departures from Pier 39. Check website for schedule *(1hr; $24;* × & *415-705-8200; www.blueandgoldfleet.com).*

Red & White Fleet Golden Gate Bay Cruise: frequent departures from Pier 43½. Check website for schedule *(round trip 1hr; commentary; $26;* × & P *415-673-2900; www.redandwhite.com).*

Alameda/Oakland Ferry: runs between Jack London Square (Oakland), Alameda, Pier 41 and the Ferry Building as well as to Angel Island *(frequent departures year-round; no service Jan 1, President's Day, Thanksgiving Day, Dec 25; 30min one-way; $6.25;* × & P *415-705-8291; www.sanfranciscobayferry.com).*

BOOKS
See also Introduction to San Francisco

REFERENCE

San Francisco Architecture. Sally B. Woodbridge, John M. Woodbridge and Chuck Byrne (2005).
    Comprehensive and portable guide to the city's built

environment by recognized experts in the field.

San Francisco Secrets. John Synder. (1999). Compendium of history, trivia and stories that debunks popular San Francisco myths.

LITERATURE

San Francisco Stories. John Miller, ed. (2004). Vivid accounts of life in the city by 25 well-known literary lights including Mark Twain, Jack London and Tom Wolf.

The World of Herb Caen: 1938–1997. Barnaby Conrad (1999).
Recent history of the city as seen through the life and times of the SF *Chronicle's* beloved columnist.

FILMS

&See also Introduction to San Francisco

The Graduate. (1967).
Social commentary laces this coming-of-age comedy about a young man in need of direction and the women who provide it.

Vertigo (1967). Alfred Hitchcock murder mystery about an alcoholic detective in pursuit of a glamorous socialite with something to hide.

Harold and Maude (1971).
Cult classic rife with black humor about a morbid young man and his redemptive relationship with a life-loving woman in her 70s.

Mrs. Doubtfire (1993).
Zany comedy about a man who impersonates a British nanny to gain access to his estranged children.

The Rock (1996).
An Oscar-nominated thriller about a criminal plot to seize Alcatraz and threaten San Francisco with biological weapons.

Calendar of Events

Listed below is a selection of popular annual events in the Bay Area; some dates may vary from year to year. For more information about special events, contact the **San Francisco Convention and Visitors Bureau** (&415-391-2000; *www.sanfrancisco.travel*).

JANUARY

late-Jan
San Francisco Film Noir Festival
Castro Theatre.
www.noircity.com.
late Jan–Feb *(date varies)*
Chinese New Year Festival & Parade
Chinatown.
&415-340-3055.
www.chineseparade.com.

FEBRUARY

mid-Feb
Valentine's Day Woo at the Zoo
San Francisco Zoo. &415-753-7080. www.sfzoo.org.
late Feb–Mar
Pacific Orchid Exposition
Fort Mason Center.
www.orchidsanfrancisco.org.

MARCH

2nd or 3rd Sun in Mar
St. Patrick's Day Parade
Embarcadero to Civic Center.
www.sfstpatricksdayparade.com.
Mar
San Francisco International Asian American Film Festival
various Bay Area theaters.
www.festival.caamedia.org.

APRIL

Easter Sunday
Union Street Easter Parade & Spring Celebration
Union St. between Gough & Steiner Sts. ℘800-310-6563. www.sresproductions.com.

late Apr
Cherry Blossom Festival
Civic Center & Japantown. ℘415-563-2313. www.sfcherryblossom.org.

late Apr–early May
San Francisco International Film Festival
various locations. ℘415-561-5000. www.sffs.org.

MAY

Sun closest to May 5
Cinco de Mayo Festival
Mission District. www.sfcincodemayo.com.

3rd Sun in May
Bay to Breakers
Embarcadero to Ocean Beach. ℘415-864-3432. www.zazzlebaytobreakers.com.

last Mon in May
Carnaval San Francisco
Mission District. ℘415-857-3786. www.sfcatcarnaval.com.

Union Street Easter Parade & Spring Celebration

© Steven Restivo Event Services, LLC

JUNE

1st weekend in Jun
Union Street Arts Festival
Cow Hollow. ℘800-310-6563. www.unionstreetfestival.com.

2nd Sunday in Jun
Haight-Ashbury Street Fair
Haight-Ashbury. www.haightashburystreetfair.org.

3rd weekend in Jun
North Beach Festival
Washington Square Park. ℘800-310-6563 www.sresproductions.com.

mid-Jun–mid-Aug
Stern Grove Festival
19th Ave. & Sloat Blvd. ℘415-252-6252. www.sterngrove.org.

last weekend in Jun
San Francisco Pride Celebration
Civic Center. ℘415-864-0831. www.sfpride.org.

JULY

1st Weekend in July
Fillmore Jazz Festival
Fillmore District. ℘800-310-6563. www.fillmorejazzfestival.com.

July 4
Fourth of July Waterfront Celebration Fisherman's Wharf. www.pier39.com.

late July
Midsummer Mozart Festival
San Francisco Conservatory of Music. ℘415-627-9141. www.midsummermozart.org.

Jul-Aug
Summer Music Festival
Robert Mondavi Winery, Oakville (Napa Valley). ℘888-766-6328. www.robertmondavi.com.

AUGUST

early-Aug
American Craft Council Show
Fort Mason Center. ℘800-836-3470. www.craftcouncil.org.

Autumn Moon Festival, Chinatown

© Wing Cheng / SF Chinatown Merchants Association

SEPTEMBER
Labor Day weekend
Sausalito Art Festival
Marinship Park, Sausalito.
☎415-332-3555.
www.sausalitoartfestival.org.
Sunday after Labor Day
Opera in the Park
Golden Gate Park.
☎415-861-4008.
www.sfopera.com.
Sept
Chocolate Festival
Ghirardelli Square.
www.ghirardellisq.com.
next to last weekend in Sept
Autumn Moon Festival
Chinatown. ☎415-982-6306.
www.moonfestival.org.
late Sept
Folsom Street Fair
SoMa. ☎415-777-3247.
www.folsomstreetfair.org.

OCTOBER
early-Oct
Litquake
Various locations. ☎415-440-4177.
www.litquake.org.
1st weekend in Oct
Hardly Strictly Bluegrass
Golden Gate Park.
www.strictlybluegrass.com.

1st Sun in Oct
Castro Street Fair
Castro District. ☎415-841-1824.
www.castrostreetfair.org.
2nd weekend in Oct
Fleet Week
Embarcadero & Fisherman's Wharf.
☎650-599-5057.
www.fleetweek.us.
2nd Sun in Oct
Italian Heritage Parade & Festival
Fisherman's Wharf & North Beach.
Oct
ArtSpan Open Studios
Various locations. ☎415-861-9838.
www.artspan.org.
mid-Oct–mid-Nov
San Francisco Jazz Festival
Various locations.
☎866-920-5299. www.sfjazz.org.

NOVEMBER
Nov
Dia de los Muertos
Mission District.
www.dayofthedeadsf.org.

DECEMBER
Dec
San Francisco Ballet's Nutcracker
War Memorial Opera House.
☎415-865-2000.
www.sfballet.org.

Know Before You Go

USEFUL WEBSITES

www.onlyinsanfrancisco.com
The official site of the San Francisco Convention & Visitors Bureau is packed with information about hotels, dining, tours, shopping, events, etc.

www.sfgate.com
The *San Francisco Chronicle* site has sections describing neighborhoods and nightlife, plus restaurant reviews, news, weather and traffic information.

www.sfbg.com
Online version of the progressive weekly *San Francisco Bay Guardian*, with articles on the arts, nightlife and an annual Best of the Bay section.

www.sfweekly.com
Articles about offbeat and underground happenings in the city. Includes an extensive list of blog links.

www.sf.eater.com and www.tablehopper.com
San Francisco restaurant news.

sf.funcheap.com
Current listing of free and cheap things to do in the San Francisco Bay Area.

www.yelp.com
Reviews of local businesses, including restaurants.

LOCAL TOURIST OFFICES

Visitors may contact the following agencies to obtain maps and information on points of interest, accommodations and seasonal events.

- **San Francisco Convention & Visitors Bureau**
  900 Market St.
  San Francisco CA 94102
  ☏415-391-2000.
  www.onlyinsanfrancisco.com
- **Berkeley Convention & Visitors Bureau**
  2030 Addison St., Berkeley CA 94704. ☏510-549-7040.
  www.visitberkeley.com
- **Marin County Visitors Bureau**
  1 Mitchell Blvd. Ste B, San Rafael CA 94303, ☏415-925-2060
  www.visitmarin.org
- **Napa Valley Conference & Visitors Bureau**
  1310 Napa Town Center, Napa CA 94559. ☏707-226-5813.
  www.napavalley.com
- **Oakland Convention & Visitors Bureau**
  463 11th St., Oakland CA 94607.
  ☏510-839-9000.
  www.oaklandcvb.com
- **San Jose Convention & Visitors Bureau**
  408 Almaden Blvd., San Jose CA 95110. ☏408-295-9600.
  www.sanjose.org

INTERNATIONAL VISITORS

In addition to the agencies listed here, visitors from outside the US can contact the San Francisco Convention & Visitors Bureau's foreign-language event lines (**Français** *☏415-391-2003;* **Deutsch** *☏415-391-2004;* **Español** *☏415-391-2122;* **Italiano** *☏415-391-2002;* **Japanese** *☏415-391-2101)* or visit the bureau's seven foreign-language pages (French, German, Italian, Korean, Spanish, Mandarin and Japanese).

Embassies and Consulates

Visitors from outside the US can obtain information by contacting the San Francisco Convention & Visitors Bureau (*☏415-391-2000; www.onlyinsanfrancisco.com*) or the US embassy or consulate in their country of residence. Major international consulates in San Francisco include:

- **Australia** 575 Market St.
  ☏415-536-1970
- **Canada** 580 California St.
  ☏415-834-3180
- **China** 1450 Laguna St.
  ☏415-674-2900
- **France** 540 Bush St.
  ☏415-397-4330

- **Germany** 1960 Jackson St. ☎415-775-1061.
- **Japan** 50 Fremont St. ☎415-777-3533.
- **Mexico** 532 Folsom St. ☎415-354-1700.
- **United Kingdom** 1 Sansome St., Ste. 850. ☎415-617-1300.

ENTRY REQUIREMENTS

Citizens of countries participating in the **Visa Waiver Program** (VWPP) are not required to obtain a visa to enter the US for visits of fewer than 90 days, but must present a machine-readable passport upon arrival. Residents of visa-waiver countries must apply ahead for travel authorization online through the **ESTA program;** *www.cbp.gov/esta.* Travelers may apply any time ahead of their travel; at least three days before departure is strongly recommended. Beware private sites charging extravagant fees which are not affiliated with the US government. Upon entry, nonresident foreign visitors must present a valid passport, a visitor's visa and round-trip transportation ticket. Canadian citizens need a passport to enter the US. All travelers (including infants and children) entering the US from countries participating in the **Western Hemisphere Travel Initiative** (Canada, Mexico, Bermuda and the 17 Caribbean regions) must carry a passport if traveling by air. US citizens entering the US from WHTI countries by any means must present a passport, passport card or another WHTI-compliant document. For information on entry requirements, see **http://travel. state.gov** or contact the US consulate in your country of residence.

CUSTOMS REGULATIONS

All articles brought into the US must be declared at the time of entry. Items **exempt** from customs regulations are: personal effects; one liter of alcoholic beverages; either 200 cigarettes, 50 cigars or 2 kilograms of smoking tobacco; gifts not exceeding $100 in value. **Prohibited items** include plant material; firearms and ammunition; meat or poultry products. For further information, contact the US embassy or consulate before departing or go to the US Customs and Border Protection website: www.cbp.gov.

HEALTH

The United States does not have a national health program. Before departing, visitors from abroad should check with their insurance company to determine if their medical insurance covers doctors' visits, medication and hospitalization in the US, and to purchase private insurance if necessary. The European Health Insurance Card is not valid in the US. Prescription drugs should be identified and accompanied by a copy of the prescription.

ACCESSIBILITY

Throughout this guide, full wheelchair accessibility is indicated in sight descriptions by a ♿ symbol. All **BART** trains and stations and all **Muni** lines are wheelchair-accessible. The *Muni Access Guide* gives helpful hints for disabled persons using the system *(free from Muni Accessible Services, 1 South Van Ness Ave., 3rd Floor, San Francisco CA 94103; ☎415-701-4485, TTY 415-701-4730; www.sfmta.com/access).*

San Francisco Paratransit provides door-to-door van and taxi service for the disabled *(www.sfparatransit.com).* Other useful publications include Access Northern California (ANC, *1427 Grant St., Berkeley, CA 94703; t510-524-2026; www.accessnca.com) and San Francisco Access Guide (San Francisco Convention & Visitors Bureau; t415-391-2000 or 415-392-0328 TDD; www. onlyinsanfrancisco.com).* The Mayor's Office on Disability has resources at www.sfgov.org. You can also contact the Society for Accessible Travel and Hospitality, 347 Fifth Ave., Suite 605, New York NY 10016 *(☎212-447-7284; www.sath.org).*

Getting There and Getting Around

BY PLANE

San Francisco is served by two major airports, one south of downtown and one in Oakland. Plan to arrive at the airport two hours before departure time for domestic flights and three hours ahead for international flights. As airport security and baggage regulations change frequently, it is always advisable to check the rules before you fly. Visit www.tsa.gov for more information on what not to carry. Airlines serving Bay Area airports include:

Air Canada www.aircanada.com
Air France www.airfrance.com
American Airlines www.aa.com
British Airways:
www.britishairways.com
Delta Airlines www.delta.com
Southwest Airlines
www.southwest.com
United Airlines www.united.com

SAN FRANCISCO INTERNATIONAL AIRPORT (SFO)

13.5mi south of San Francisco via Rte. 101. ℰ650-821-8211. www.flysfo.com. Most international and domestic flights arrive and depart the Bay Area from SFO. The airport's **Travel Agency** *(◷open daily 7am–11pm)* is located in the International Terminal's main hall. **Airport Information Booths** are located throughout all terminals, both before and after security. A **medical clinic** is located in the main hall of the International Terminal *(◷open Mon–Fri 8.30am–5pm; Sat 9am–1pm; ℰ650-821-5601).*

OAKLAND INTERNATIONAL AIRPORT (OAK)

www.flyoakland.com. ℰ510-563-3300. 7.5mi south of downtown Oakland; 17mi southeast of downtown San Francisco via I-880 and I-80. This smaller, easy-to-navigate airport handles both domestic and international flights. **Information booths** are located near main entrances. If you're driving from San Francisco, allow at least 1hr, especially during rush hours.

AIRPORT TRANSFERS

Visitors have a variety of public and private transportation options for getting to and from San Francisco and the airports. Taxis, buses, and shuttles depart from outside the baggage-claim areas; for information, call 511 or log on to www.511.org, which provides consolidated transit information for the entire Bay Area.

BY SUBWAY

The most popular means of getting to and from the airports via public transportation is **BART (Bay Area Rapid Transit)**, the commuter rail system that links San Francisco with cities in the East Bay and South Bay. The trip from SFO to downtown San Francisco costs $8.25 and takes about 35min; it's a 30min, $6.85 (including shuttle bus) trip from OAK. At SFO, you can take a free AirTrain people mover from the terminal to the BART station; in Oakland, you must take the AirBART bus *(runs Mon–Sat 5am– midnight every 10min, Sun from 8am ; $3 exact change required)* from the center island outside the baggage claim areas to the Coliseum/Oakland International Airport BART station.

BY TAXI

There are taxi stands outside the baggage claim areas at both airports. Taxi service to downtown San Francisco from SFO takes approximately 20–30min and costs around $45; from OAK the ride takes around 45min and costs roughly $75.

BY SHUTTLE

Numerous companies offer door-to-door van service between SFO and OAK and private residences and hotels all over the Bay Area. Service is available on a walk-up basis, but it's best to make reservations if you are arriving after 11pm. Try **Airport Express** (℘415-775-5121; www.airportexpresssf.com) or **Super Shuttle** (℘800-258-3826; www.supershuttle.com). Cost to downtown San Francisco is about $17 from SFO and $27 (with Super Shuttle) from Oakland.

BY RENTAL CAR

♿See also By Car.
At SFO, rental-car agency service counters are located on the lower level of each terminal.
At Oakland, buses leave baggage claim area every 10min for the Rental Car Center, where agencies serving the airport have counters.

BY FERRY

♿See Sightseeing in What to See and Do.
Several commuter ferry services link San Francisco with Marin County, East Bay and North Bay cities. Most depart from the Ferry Building and Pier 41, offer free or discounted parking near terminals, accept bicycles, and provide discounted fares for children, seniors and disabled passengers.

Blue and Gold Fleet (℘415-705-8200; www.blueandgoldfleet.com) serves San Francisco and Sausalito (30min; $10.50), Vallejo (1hr; $13), Tiburon (30min; $10.50) and Oakland/Alameda (45min; $6.25).

Baylink Ferries (℘877-643-3779; www.baylinkferry.com) serve San Francisco and Vallejo (60min; $13).

Golden Gate Ferries (℘415-455-2000; www.goldengateferry.org) serve San Francisco and Larkspur (35min; $9) and Sausalito (25min; $9.75).

BY TRAIN

The **Amtrak** rail network serves the East Bay city of Emeryville; a free shuttle bus (20min) transports passengers to downtown San Francisco. Passengers can choose from first-class, coach, sleeping cars and glass-domed cars. Fares are comparable to air travel.
The **California Rail Pass** ($159) allows seven days of unlimited rail travel in the state during a consecutive 21-day period. A **USA RailPass** allows 15 or 30 days of unlimited travel within designated regions. Advance reservations are required for passholders. Schedule and route information: ℘800-872-7245; www.amtrak.com.
CalTrain offers service between San Francisco and San Jose. Schedule and route information: ℘888-500-4636; www.caltrain.com.

BY BUS

Greyhound buses arrive at and depart from the Transbay Temporary Terminal, (200 Folsom St.). Fares are generally lower than other forms of long-distance transportation. Advance reservations suggested. Schedule, fare and route information: ℘800-231-2222; www.greyhound.com.

BY CAR

Major interstate highways into San Francisco include US-101 and I-280 from the south; I-80 from the east across the Bay Bridge ($6 bridge toll for westbound traffic only); and US-101 from the north, across the Golden Gate Bridge ($6 bridge toll for southbound traffic only).
Visitors bearing valid driver's licenses are not required to obtain an International Driver's License to drive in the US. Drivers must carry vehicle registration and/or rental contract, and proof of automobile insurance at all times. Vehicles are driven on the right-hand side of the road in the US. Distances are posted in miles (1mi=1.62km); gasoline is sold by the gallon (1 gal=3.8 liters).

DRIVING IN SAN FRANCISCO

San Francisco Road Conditions: ℘511. Given the efficiency of public transportation, a car is not necessary in San Francisco. Public parking lots are expensive and street parking

CAR RENTAL

Rental Company	Reservations	Website
Alamo	800-462-5266	www.alamo.com
Avis	800-230-4898	www.avis.com
Budget	800-527-0700	www.budget.com
Dollar	800-800-4000	www.dollar.com
Enterprise	800-736-8222	www.enterprise.com
Hertz	800-654-3131	www.hertz.com
National	800-227-7368	www.nationalcar.com
Thrifty	800-847-4389	www.thrifty.com

(Toll-free numbers may not be accessible outside of North America.)

requires strict attention to posted curb colors and correctly curbed tires. **Rush hours**, the peak transit times for business commuters, occur weekdays 7.30am–9am and 4pm–6pm.

ROAD REGULATIONS

The maximum **speed limit** on most major expressways is 65mph in rural areas and 55mph in and around cities. Speed limits within the city range from 25mph in residential areas to 35mph on major streets. Use of **seat belts** is mandatory for driver and passengers. Child safety seats are required for children under 4 years old or weighing less than 40 pounds (seats available from most rental car agencies). Drivers must always yield the **right of way** to cable cars and pedestrians.

PARKING

When parking on a hill, drivers must block front wheels against the curb (facing downhill turn wheels *toward* curb, facing uphill turn wheels *away* from curb); use of parking brake is mandatory. Restricted parking is indicated by the color of curb: **red** (no standing or parking), **yellow** (loading zone), **white** (limited to 5min), **green** (limited to 10min), **blue** (reserved for the disabled). Check street signs carefully. Parking is prohibited during posted street-cleaning times.

RENTAL CARS

Major rental-car agencies maintain locations downtown and at San Francisco and Oakland airports. Most agencies rent only to persons at least 25 years old. A major credit card and valid driver's license are required. The average daily rate for a car ranges from $70–$150. Sales tax on car rentals is 8.5%.

BY PUBLIC TRANSPORTATION

Information on routes and fares for all transportation systems in the San Francisco Bay Area, including traffic conditions, is available free at 511 (*511 or 415-817-1717; www.511.org*). The online Trip Planner is useful. Public transportation carriers within San Francisco include **San Francisco Municipal Railway (Muni)** (*see below*); and **Bay Area Rapid Transit** (*see right*). Bus service to other areas is provided by **Golden Gate Transit** (*415-455-2000; www. goldengatetransit.org*), serving Marin, Contra Costa and Sonoma Counties; **SamTrans** (*888-500-4636; www. samtrans.org*), serving San Mateo County; and **AC Transit** (*511; www. actransit.org*), serving Alameda and Contra Costa Counties. **CalTrain** (*888-500-4636; www.caltrain.com*) provides rail service between San Francisco and San Jose.

SAN FRANCISCO MUNICIPAL TRANSPORTATION (MUNI)

☎415-701-2311; www.sfmta.com.
Muni operates an extensive network of transportation lines using buses, light-rail streetcars and cable cars. System maps *($3)* are sold at newsstands, map shops, City Hall and at the three cable car ticket offices (Powell & Market Sts., Hyde & Beach Sts. and Bay & Taylor Sts.); they may also be downloaded from the website. In this guide, recommended transit lines are indicated with the ᴍᴜɴɪ symbol.

Buses – Muni buses generally operate daily 5.30am–12.30am, every 4–20min; some routes on major corridors run 24hrs/day (**owl service** *designates late-night schedule*). Route maps are posted in bus shelters. All Muni bus services are accessible to riders with disabilities via wheelchair lifts, ramps and kneelers *(Muni Accessible Services ☎415-701-4485).*

Metro Streetcars – Muni's six-line light-rail system includes The J-Church, K-Ingleside, M-Oceanview and T-Third Street lines (daily 5.30am–12.30am) and the L-Taraval and N-Judah lines (24hrs/day; buses provide owl service) with service every 5–15min weekdays and every 10–20min evenings and weekends.

Cable cars – *see NOB HILL.* Cable cars are a fun way to get to many attractions, including Chinatown and Fisherman's Wharf. Three lines operate daily 6am-12.30am. The **Powell-Hyde** (PH) and **Powell-Mason** (PM) lines zigzag from Powell and Market Streets in the Union Square Area over Nob Hill to Fisherman's Wharf. The **California** (C) line runs along California Street through Chinatown from Market Street to Van Ness Avenue. Brown-and-white signs along the route indicate stops.

Historic Streetcars – Muni operates a fleet of 17 streetcars dating from the 1940s. The F-Market line, as it is called, runs along Market Street from the Castro District to the Ferry Building, then along the Embarcadero to Fisherman's Wharf.

Fares – Bus and streetcar fares are $2 (exact fare required), cable cars $6. Be sure to ask for bus and streetcar transfers *(free)*, good for transfers within 90min. The **Muni Passport** allows unlimited rides on all Muni vehicles, including cable cars, for one day *($14)*, 3 days *($22)*, or 7 days *($28)*. Muni Passports can be purchased at Hyde and Beach Streets (near Ghirardelli Square), SFMTA Customer Service Center, 11 South Van Ness Avenue at Market, at the information booths San Francisco International Airport, at the Visitor Information Center or online at www.sfmta.com/cms/mfares/passports.htm. The 7-day $69 *($39 kids)* CityPASS includes all Muni Passport priivileges as well as free general admission to five San Francisco attractions *(www.citypass.com/san-francisco).*

BAY AREA RAPID TRANSIT (BART)

☎415-989-2278 or 510-465-2278. www.bart.gov.
This fast commuter rail system links San Francisco with East Bay cities and San Francisco International Airport. It also provides subway service between the Mission District and the Embarcadero. BART runs Mon–Fri 4am–midnight, Sat 6am–midnight and Sun 8am–midnight. Route maps and schedules are available at stations. Ticket machines are located in each station. Fares are determined on a per-mile basis; be sure to keep your ticket handy, as it must be swiped both before and after every ride. In this guide, recommended stations are indicated with the ʙᴀʀᴛ symbol.

BY TAXI

All San Francisco taxis charge $3.50 for the first fifth of a mile and 55 cents each additional fifth of a mile. The major cab companies in San Francisco are **Yellow Cab** *☎415-333-3333,* **Veterans** *☎415-648-4444* and **Luxor** *☎415-282-4141.*

Basic Information

BUSINESS HOURS
Most businesses operate Mon–Fri 10am–6pm. Banks are usually open Mon–Fri 9am–6pm. Department stores and shopping centers operate Mon–Sat 9.30am–8pm, Sun 11am–6pm; many extend their hours between Thanksgiving and Christmas. Stores near Fisherman's Wharf have longer summer hours. Smaller shops and stores (except in Chinatown) may be closed on Sundays or Mondays.

DISCOUNTS
Most public transportation providers (Muni, BART, ferry companies) offer discounted fares of up to 50% for seniors, youth and disabled riders. Many museums and other attractions also offer reduced admission fees for children, students and seniors.

ELECTRICITY
Voltage in the US is 120 volts AC, 60 Hz. Foreign-made appliances may need AC adapters and North American flat-blade plugs.

EMERGENCIES
In the event of injury or emergency, telephone the police, ambulance or fire department by dialing 911. Visitors should immediately report a lost wallet or passport to the local police, then contact banks and credit card issuers (see Money) to prevent unauthorized access to credit or personal information. Lost passports should be reported to the nearest embassy or consulate of the country of residence.

EARTHQUAKE PRECAUTIONS
Although severe earthquakes are infrequent, they are also unpredictable. If an earthquake strikes when you are outside, move away from trees, buildings or power lines. If you are in a vehicle, pull to the side of the road and stop. Do not park on or under bridges; sit on the floor of the vehicle if possible. If you are in a building, stand within a doorway or sit under a table. Stay away from outside walls and be prepared for aftershocks.

LIQUOR LAW
The legal minimum age for purchase and consumption of alcoholic beverages is 21. Proof of age is normally required. Almost all packaged-goods stores sell beer, wine and liquor; legal hours of sale are 6am–2am.

MAIL/POST
Post offices located throughout the San Francisco Bay Area operate Monday–Friday 8am–5pm (some have extended weekday and Saturday hours). First-class rates within the US: letter 42¢ (1oz), postcard 27¢. Overseas: letter, postcard or

IMPORTANT NUMBERS	
Police/Ambulance/Fire (emergency, 24hrs)	☎**911**
Police (non-emergency, 24hrs)	☎415-553-0123
Physician Referrals (24hrs)	☎415-353-6566
Dental Emergencies (24hrs)	☎415-421-1435
Medical Emergencies (24hrs)	☎4 15-981-1102
24hr Pharmacies	
Walgreens 3201 Divisadero St. (Marina District)	☎415-931-6415
Walgreens 498 Castro St. (Castro District)	☎415-861-6276
Weather	☎831-656-1725

aerogramme generally 94¢ (1oz). Stamps and packing material may be purchased at many convenience and drugstores, and at post offices. Businesses offering postal and express shipping services are located throughout the city (◖*see Yellow Pages of phone directory under Mailing Services or www.yp.com*). Postal Service Information Line (*Mon–Fri 8am–6pm; ℰ800-725-2161; www.usps.com*).

MEDIA
NEWSPAPERS AND MAGAZINES

San Francisco's main daily newspapers are the *San Francisco Chronicle* and the *San Francisco Examiner* (free). The Sunday and Thursday *Chronicle* features an extensive arts-and-entertainment supplement. Two free weekly papers, the *San Francisco Bay Guardian* and the *SF Weekly*, feature diverse and comprehensive entertainment sections and are available in newspaper boxes and cafes. The *Bay Area Reporter* and the *San Francisco Bay Times* cater to the gay community.

MONEY

The American dollar is divided into 100 cents:
a penny = 1 cent
a nickel = 5 cents
a dime = 10 cents
a quarter = 25 cents

CURRENCY EXCHANGE

Most Financial District and downtown branches of Bank of America (*1 Powell St., t415-622-4481; www.bofa.com*) and Wells Fargo Bank (*1 California St.; ℰ415-396-2779; www.wellsfargo.com*) offer foreign currency exchange. Visitors can also exchange currency at Travelex (*www.travelex.com*) branches throughout San Francisco and at the airport (International Terminal).

BANKING

Most banks are members of the network of Automatic Teller Machines (ATMs), allowing visitors to withdraw cash using bank cards and major credit

MAJOR TV NETWORKS	
ABC	Channel 7
FOX	Channel 2
CBS	Channel 5
NBC	Channel 4
CNN	Channel 3
PBS	Channel 9
MAJOR RADIO STATIONS	
88.5 FM	Public Radio
102.1 FM	Classical
680 AM	Sports/talk
93.3 FM	Country
103.7 FM	Jazz
810 AM	News/talk
97.3 FM	Rock
104.5 FM	Alternative
1550 AM	News/talk

cards 24hrs a day. ATMs can be found at banks, airports, grocery stores and malls. Networks (Cirrus, Star, Plus) serviced by the **ATM** are indicated on the machine. For cash transfers, **Western Union** (*ℰ800-325-6000; www.westernunion.com*) has agents throughout the Bay Area.

CREDIT CARDS, TRAVELERS CHECKS

Banks, most stores, restaurants and hotels accept **travelers checks** with picture identification. **American Express Travel** is located at 455 Market St. (*ℰ415-536-2600*).
To report a **lost or stolen credit card**: American Express *ℰ800-528-4800*; Diners Club *ℰ800-234-6377*; MasterCard *ℰ800-307-7309*; Visa *ℰ800-336-8472*.

TAXES

Prices displayed or quoted in the US do not include sales tax (8.5% in California). Hotel tax is 14% (not included in quoted hotel rates). Tax percentages in other areas may vary.

PUBLIC HOLIDAYS

Most banks and government offices in the San Francisco area are closed on the following legal holidays:

January 1	New Year's Day
3rd Monday in January	Martin Luther King Jr.'s Birthday*
3rd Monday in February	Presidents' Day*
Last Monday in May	Memorial Day
July 4	Independence Day
1st Monday in September	Labor Day*
2nd Monday in October	Columbus Day*
November 11	Veterans Day*
4th Thursday in November	Thanksgiving Day
December 25	Christmas Day

Many retail stores and most restaurants stay open on these days.

SMOKING

California law prohibits smoking in enclosed spaces, including bars and restaurants. In addition, San Francisco ordinance prohibits smoking outdoors in city-owned parks and public spaces.

TELEPHONES

Local calls from a pay phone cost 50¢. Some public telephones accept credit cards, and all will accept long-distance calling cards. Most hotels add hefty surcharges for telephone calls. For long-distance calls in the

AREA CODES	
San Francisco (including Marin County)	☏415
Peninsula cities (including San Mateo County)	☏650
East Bay (including Berkeley and Oakland)	☏510
East Bay (including Contra Costa County)	☏925
Wine Country	☏707

US and Canada, dial 1 + area code + number. To place an international call, dial 011 + country code + area code + number. You'll find a list of country codes in the local phone directory. Unless otherwise indicated, telephone numbers that start with 800, 866, 877 or 888 are toll-free in the US only. Visitors using mobile phones compatible with GSM networks can avoid roaming charges by purchasing a prepaid local SIM card for use in their phones. SIM cards are available online and at service-provider outlets; you can buy vouchers to add minutes to your account at most newsstands and convenience stores. Another option for mobile calling is a pay-as-you-go phone, available from many local service-provider outlets.

TIME

San Francisco is on Pacific Standard Time (PST), 3hrs behind Eastern Standard Time (EST) and 8hrs behind Greenwich Mean Time (GMT). Daylight Savings Time (clocks advanced 1hr) is in effect for most of the US from the second Sunday in March until the first Sunday in November.

TIPPING

In restaurants, it is customary to tip the server 18–20% of the bill. At hotels, porters should be tipped $1 per suitcase and hotel maids $1 per day. Taxi drivers are tipped 15% of the fare.

© Peter Wrenn / Michelin

Cable car, Civic Center

CONVERSION TABLES

Weights and Measures

1 kilogram (kg) 6.35 kilograms 0.45 kilograms **1 metric ton (tn)**	**2.2 pounds (lb)** 14 pounds 16 ounces (oz) **1.1 tons**	**2.2 pounds** 1 stone (st) 16 ounces **1.1 tons**	*To convert kilograms to pounds, multiply by 2.2*
1 litre (l) 3.79 litres 4.55 litres	**2.11 pints (pt)** 1 gallon (gal) 1.20 gallon	**1.76 pints** 0.83 gallon 1 gallon	*To convert litres to gallons, multiply by 0.26 (US) or 0.22 (UK)*
1 hectare (ha) **1 sq kilometre (km²)**	**2.47 acres** 0.38 sq. miles (sq mi)	**2.47 acres** 0.38 sq. miles	*To convert hectares to acres, multiply by 2.4*
1 centimetre (cm) **1 metre (m)**	**0.39 inches (in)** 3.28 feet (ft) or 39.37 inches or 1.09 yards (yd)	**0.39 inches**	*To convert metres to feet, multiply by 3.28; for kilometres to miles, multiply by 0.6*
1 kilometre (km)	**0.62 miles (mi)**	**0.62 miles**	

Clothing

Women	○	US	UK
	35	4	2½
	36	5	3½
	37	6	4½
Shoes	38	7	5½
	39	8	6½
	40	9	7½
	41	10	8½
	36	6	8
	38	8	10
Dresses	40	10	12
& suits	42	12	14
	44	14	16
	46	16	18
	36	6	30
	38	8	32
Blouses &	40	10	34
sweaters	42	12	36
	44	14	38
	46	16	40

Men	○	US	UK
	40	7½	7
	41	8½	8
	42	9½	9
Shoes	43	10½	10
	44	11½	11
	45	12½	12
	46	13½	13
	46	36	36
	48	38	38
Suits	50	40	40
	52	42	42
	54	44	44
	56	46	48
	37	14½	14½
	38	15	15
Shirts	39	15½	15½
	40	15¾	15¾
	41	16	16
	42	16½	16½

Sizes often vary depending on the designer. These equivalents are given for guidance only.

Speed

KPH	10	30	50	70	80	90	100	110	120	130
MPH	6	19	31	43	50	56	62	68	75	81

Temperature

Celsius (°C)	0°	5°	10°	15°	20°	25°	30°	40°	60°	80°	100°
Fahrenheit (°F)	32°	41°	50°	59°	68°	77°	86°	104°	140°	176°	212°

To convert Celsius into Fahrenheit, multiply °C by 9, divide by 5, and add 32.
To convert Fahrenheit into Celsius, subtract 32 from °F, multiply by 5, and divide by 9.
NB: Conversion factors on this page are approximate.

Japanese Tea Garden, Golden Gate Park
© Andrew Zarivny / iStockphoto.com

The City Today

Ethnically diverse, well-educated, tech-savvy, food-loving San Francisco is one of North America's most desirable cities.

COSMOPOLITAN SAN FRANCISCO
AN ECCENTRIC, ENCHANTING PLACE

With much of its economy dependent on tourism and finance, San Francisco attracts and nurtures a diverse, largely well-educated population with strong interests in the arts, social experimentation and good living. About half of the city's residents are single, while over 40 percent of residents over the age of 25 have attended college. The arts thrive at all levels of society, from grand opera productions to neighborhood cultural centers. Eating well is a passion for San Franciscans, who are forever on a quest for new cuisines and creative restaurants, yet well-disposed toward traditional regional specialties. They enjoy working off their calories with outdoor exercise; weekends find them by the thousands jogging, hiking, biking and sailing, taking advantage of the waters and parklands surrounding their city.

San Franciscans actively guard their architectural heritage, subsidizing the archaic cable-car system and fiercely supporting zoning restrictions and retrofitting projects that preserve buildings. Strong supporters of the conservation movement, they have preserved an unparalleled system of parklands in and around the city. Though a reputation for tolerance holds sway, San Franciscans value individualism over universality, and residents are notorious throughout the Bay Area (as the surrounding region is known) for their stubborn political coalitions, special-interest groups that make consensus difficult, and neighborhoods that trenchantly guard their ethnic or cultural flavor.

Despite their preservationist attitudes, city denizens pride themselves for being at the forefront—though others might call it a sideline—of American social experimentation. Set in motion perhaps by its eccentric birth and history, the city's penchant for flamboyant eccentricity attracts an eclectic mix of people and ideas. Free-thinkers, poets, artists, counterculture gurus and revolutionaries have always thrived here. Following the same impulse, though on more established footing, are the many idealistic civic organizations that have taken root, such as the Sierra Club and Glide Memorial Church in the downtrodden Tenderloin district.

PEOPLE AND POPULATION

With a population of 812,836 (2011 estimate) inhabiting an area of only 46.9 square miles confined on the tip of a peninsula, San Francisco has the second highest population density in the U.S. after New York. Surprisingly small, it ranks as the fourth most populous city in California after Los Angeles (3,819,702), San Diego (1,326,179) and San Jose (967,487). The city forms the cultural and financial hub of the San Francisco Bay Area, a nine-county region of 7.15 million people.

San Francisco led the state in population, culture and economic influence

Tai chi, Washington Square
© Mark Downey / SFCVB

Shopping, Union Square

© Jack Hollingsworth / SFCVB

throughout the 19C and early 20C. Within months of the discovery of gold in 1848, the town's population of about 800 doubled, quadrupled and septupled with young men (who outnumbered women by 10 to 1) from every American state and European country, especially England and Ireland, France, the German states and Scandinavia. Great numbers came from China and Mexico, and sizable minorities from Hawaii, Australia, Chile and other Latin American countries. The population rocketed to 34,776 within four years and exploded between 1860 and 1870 from 56,802 to 149,473. Though the rate of growth slowed in the financial depression of the 1870s, by the turn of the 20C San Francisco was still the largest city west of St. Louis, with a population of 342,782. Population peaked at 775,357 in the mid-20C, after which a slow decline mirrored the city's loss of industry and port facilities to Oakland and other Bay Area cities.

The region's population is nothing if not diverse, harboring a rich array of immigrants from Europe, the Americas and Asia. Currently, about 37 percent of San Franciscans are foreign-born.

Latinos

People of Spanish and Mexican ancestry have formed an important segment of the Bay Area's population since the arrival of Europeans in 1776. Politically dominant until the American conquest of 1846, the established Californio families contributed greatly to the founding and development of the village of Yerba Buena, though their political and economic power dwindled considerably with the influx of newcomers from the U.S. Even as generations of Hispanic families acculturate to American society, the continuing arrival of new immigrants, legal and illegal, keeps Latino cultures robust over much of California. People of Hispanic ancestry today comprise about 15 percent of the city's population.

Chinese

Forming about 21 percent of the city's population, the largest of any single ethnic group, the Chinese have constituted a substantial minority since the Gold Rush. Though historically persecuted, the Chinese were instrumental in countless enterprises that developed the West, not least in construction, agriculture and the fishing industry.

The numbers of Chinese in San Francisco dwindled after passage of the Chinese Exclusion Act of 1882, reaching a low of 1.5 percent, or 7,744 people, in the 1920 census. Repeal of the act during World War II heralded a second wave of immigrants, greatly diversifying the Chinese community with wealthy families from Hong Kong and Taiwan, poorer families from China, refugees from Southeast Asia, and students.

33

Although Chinatown has prospered from this influx, most Chinese Americans dwell in widely scattered and well-integrated neighborhoods of San Francisco (especially North Beach, Nob Hill, Russian Hill, the Richmond District and the Sunset District) and the Bay Area.

Italians

After the Chinese were expelled from the fishing wharves in the 1870s, Fisherman's Wharf became known as a Genoese harbor, although Sicilians would later hold it. By the early 20C the heart of North Beach was referred to as Little Italy. Although the nickname has since disappeared, the neighborhood still houses Italian cafes, restaurants, and bakeries. With declining immigration rates, rapid acculturation and movement to the suburbs, the numbers of immigrants have retrenched, but the influence of Italian Americans is still felt in many aspects of city life.

Others

Many of the city's most prominent movers and shakers of the 19C and early 20C were of English, German and Scandinavian stock. Large numbers of working-class Irish families settled in the Mission District from the 1870s, becoming more than 23 percent of the population by 1910. Other ethnic enclaves around the turn of the 20C included the Maltese and the Japanese, who settled after the 1906 earthquake in the present neighborhood of Japantown.

The African American population burgeoned during World War II, when thousands of Southern blacks came to work in Bay Area shipyards. Many settled along Fillmore Street (vacated by the incarcerated Japanese) in the Western Addition. Thousands of Filipinos have settled in the Bay Area since World War II, particularly in Daly City on San Francisco's southern border, and in the East Bay. The old Russian community in the Richmond District, which burgeoned after the 1917 Revolution, then dwindled through acculturation, is once again thriving under a new wave of immigrants.

FOOD AND DRINK

San Franciscans are curious and demanding diners. Their adventurous willingness to experiment with new cuisines and with innovative interpretations of traditional favorites has earned the city a well-deserved reputation for fine dining. Fueled and sated by a dedicated legion of celebrity chefs, this passion has elevated Bay Area dining to the level of high art. The region's multiethnic heritage has created an environment in which international gourmet specialties happily coexist.

LOCALLY GROWN

Thanks to California's mild climate and fertile soil, a year-round abundance of locally grown fruits, vegetables, meats and dairy products flows into the city daily. This produce stocks not only grocery stores and restaurant kitchens but also farmers' markets at locations throughout the Bay Area. A stroll through one of these markets enables food-loving visitors to behold, taste or purchase exotic seasonal delights such as juicy white peaches, sweet fresh apricots, fragrant herbs, young garlic and many varieties of tomatoes. Much of this produce is organically grown. Shoppers will also find fresh eggs, local cheeses, and nuts from the Central Valley agricultural region.

Local waters no longer provide most of the city's seafood, but an enormous variety is flown or trucked in daily. Diners can select from a wide array—salmon and oysters from Washington state, sea bass from Chile, mussels from New Zealand, halibut from Canada—all absolutely fresh thanks to modern shipping techniques. From November through April, **Dungeness crab** appears on menus and in fish markets; this famed San Francisco treat is best consumed with sourdough bread and a glass of crisp white wine.

San Francisco's renowned **sourdough bread** remains a beloved local treasure. True devotees swear it cannot be produced anywhere but in the city. Dating from the 19C gold-mining days, the recipe for this tangy loaf calls for a yeast-like starter, no sugar, and microbes that apparently float only in San Francisco air. California's phenomenally successful **wine** industry produces an array of vintages to suit any palate or budget, from good, hearty table wines to world-class award-winners. Most San Francisco wine lists prominently feature vintages from the Wine Country of the Napa and Sonoma valleys to the northeast, though fine wines also come from Mendocino County, to the north, and from Monterey and the Central Coast, to the south. Many restaurants also stock high-quality selections from Europe.

Locally brewed beers experienced a popular resurgence in the late 20C. Well worth sampling are brews from the San Francisco-based Anchor Brewing Company, whose Steam Beer traces its recipe from the Gold Rush era, and such respected microbreweries as Sierra Nevada, Mendocino Brewing and Anderson Valley Brewing Company, whose Boont Amber is a rich, creamy ale.

INTERNATIONAL FLAVORS

As in many port cities, San Francisco's abundant restaurants proffer cuisine from around the globe. In North Beach, a fragrant array of bakeries, trattorias, delicatessens and cafes dish up glorious **Italian** treats. Besides espresso, cannoli, pasta, pizza and other Italian fare, look for the local specialty *cioppino,* a tomato-based seafood stew. **Chinese** restaurants are so plentiful, there seems to be one on every street corner, especially in Chinatown and the Richmond District. A Cantonese specialty, favored at lunch or brunch, is *dim sum,* a selection of sweet or savory dumplings filled with meat, seafood or vegetables. Lovers of other Asian cuisines (includig Japanese, Vietnamese, Thai and Cambodian) can as easily sample sushi, coconut-milk curries, peanut noodles or teriyaki dishes.

Mexican food may be found all over the city but particularly in the Mission District, where abundant Latino restaurants serve up large portions of tacos, burritos, enchiladas, tamales and *carne asada.* Other Central and South Ameri-

Molinari Delicatessen

© Brigitta L. House / Michelin

can specialties include *seviche,* a citrusy seafood soup.

CALIFORNIA CUISINE

Drawing on California's polyglot heritage, and taking advantage of high-quality, readily available ingredients, a new approach to eating was introduced in 1971 when Alice Waters opened her Chez Panisse restaurant in Berkeley. Reacting to the prepackaged, mass-marketed food that had come to dominate American menus, and drawing on her experiences in France's Provence region, Waters developed a method of cooking based on fresh, seasonally varying, wild and locally grown produce. Presented in a visually appealing manner, **California Cuisine,** as it was called, transformed American gastronomy and reawakened the American palate.

Despite its popularity, California Cuisine also gained a reputation for small portions at high prices. In the late 1980s, a "New American" spin-off took San Francisco by storm. Featuring hearty platefuls of traditional foods, prepared with the California Cuisine emphasis on fresh, locally grown produce, restaurants like the Fog City Diner drew packed houses for their deliciously unpretentious food and lighthearted, retro-Americana ambience. More recently, Bay Area chefs have pioneered a New American

© Brigitta L. House / MICHELIN

approach to Asian cooking, resulting in what is often called Asian fusion cuisine.

RESTAURANTS WITH ATTITUDE

San Francisco's restaurant culture thrives on residents' fascination with the experience of dining out. Local newspapers and web sites exhaustively cover the restaurant scene. Chefs of trendy, successful eateries are feted as celebrities, their comings and goings altering the fates of their establishments almost overnight. In keeping with this heightened sense of importance, restaurateurs pay close attention to style and design. Interiors, table settings, waitstaff attire and music are carefully choreographed to complement cuisine. Some restaurants feature "open kitchens" deliberately exposed to the dining rooms so that customers can keep an eye on proceedings. Bold colors and soaring spaces are the order of the day. Diners generally dress the part, though dress codes are rare and casual clothing is welcomed in many places.

ECONOMY

San Francisco's early economy was shaped by its location. Isolated on the western edge of the continent, without easy access to other U.S. cities until the transcontinental railroad was completed in 1869, mid-19C San Franciscans built their own economy from scratch. The discovery of gold on the American River in 1848 transformed the settlement from the sleepy center of an active trade in cattle hides and tallow to a boomtown of commerce and manufacturing. Guarding the mouth of its great bay, San Francisco also became the premier West Coast shipping hub, a bustling outpost that benefited greatly from the millions of dollars worth of gold, silver and grain ("green gold") that flowed down two inland rivers and out through the Golden Gate.

In more than 150 years that have passed since the Gold Rush, San Francisco has made the slow, sometimes painful transition from small working-class boomtown to large international business center. In recent decades Oakland has assumed most of San Francisco's port activity, and heavy industry and factories have relocated to the East Bay's Alameda and Contra Costa Counties, while San Francisco has fashioned itself as a business and finance headquarters. The mid-90s were a giddy time for the Bay Area, with the economy swelling 24 percent over the period, almost twice as fast as the rest of the nation. The technology sector accounted for nearly a third of that growth. At the top of the market, in December 2000, San Francisco was rated "the No. 2 Best City for Business in the U.S." (after New York) by *Fortune* magazine. The bubble burst shortly thereafter, resulting in the loss of some 350,000 jobs during the period of 2001–2003. A gradual recovery took place, with a greater emphasis on building a diversified economy: while technology—particularly Web 2.0, the second era of internet innovation—is still important, retailing, banking, tourism, biomedical research, legal services and real estate are also high on the list of local industries.

BUSINESS AND FINANCE

San Francisco's Financial District has been called the "Wall Street of the West" since the mid-19C. Although its ability to generate capital remains as dynamic as ever, the city's ranking as the nation's third-largest financial market was challenged in the late 1990s as mergers and acquisitions forced three of its largest banks (Bank of America, Montgomery Securities and Robertson Stephens) to move their headquarters to other cities. The Pacific Exchange, founded here in 1882, was the nation's fastest growing stock exchangeand a key player in the booming U.S.–Asia tradeuntil it merged with the Chicago Board Options Exchange in 1998.

Today San Francisco has the headquarters of Wells Fargo, a bank with deep roots in the American West; Charles Schwab & Co., the nation's largest discount brokerage firm; Bechtel engineering, Visa, Twitter, and apparel makers such as The Gap and Levi Strauss & Co. South of the city, Silicon Valley is home to tech heavyweights such as Adobe Systems, Apple, Cisco, eBay, Facebook, Google, Hewlett-Packard, Intel, and Oracle. The area continues to be a major source of venture capital for new start-ups.

CONVENTIONS AND TOURISM

Tourism is San Francisco's number-one industry. In 2011, the city attracted 16.35 million tourists, business travelers and conventioneers, who together spent $8.46 billion on goods and services. Those dollars sustain more than 71,000 local jobs. San Francisco hosts several hundred conventions, meetings and trade shows each year. The largest local facility, the Moscone Center contains over 990,000 square feet of exhibit space and over 100 meeting rooms, plus over 150,000 square feet of prefunction lobbies.

RETAIL AND RESTAURANTS

More than 7,000 retail establishments, employing upward of 95,000 workers, vie for San Franciscans' and visitors' dollars. Shoppers spend some $8 billion a year here, both in neighborhood shops and in Union Square Area department stores. San Francisco's world-renowned restaurant industry, which employs 32,000 workers in more than 3,500 establishments, caters to foodies of every stripe.

COMPUTERS AND ELECTRONICS

Silicon Valley, situated near the Bay Area city of San Jose, represents the epicenter of U.S. high-tech growth. Some of the biggest names in computers, such as Apple, Hewlett-Packard, Intel and Sun Microsystems, got their starts here, while Bay Area start-ups such as Oracle, Adobe and Autodesk have become big players on the international software scene. Companies continue to proliferate here, driving the region's economic revival.

In San Francisco, the South of Market area has grown into a technology start-up hot spot in recent years. In 2011, the city became even more startup-friendly by approving a 6-year tax break on stock options for companies that go public.

SHIPPING AND TRANSPORTATION

Most of the shipping that goes on in San Francisco today consists of bits and bytes flowing over fiber-optic cables, but from the Gold Rush until well into the 20C, San Francisco's waterfront thrived. In its 1880s heyday, the San Francisco port, which employed thousands of longshoremen and sailors, handled 99 percent of all West Coast imports and 83 percent of all exports. Through the 19C the city was the whaling headquarters of the Pacific coast, but shipping declined with completion of the transcontinental railroad. Although the shipyards came alive briefly during World War II, in the 1960s San Francisco quietly ceded the bulk of its industrial shipping business to Oakland, which had made a sizable investment in up-to-date loading equipment and dredged its harbor to accommodate the latest generation of deep-draft ships.

Today San Francisco Bay maintains three major international ports: San Francisco, Oakland, and Richmond, located north of Oakland in the East Bay. Asia accounts for two-thirds of the Bay Area's shipping trade, with the remainder split between Latin America, New Zealand, and the South Pacific, British Columbia (Canada), and Europe. The Port of Oakland, the fifth-busiest container port in the country, handles 90 percent of the containerized cargo that passes through the Golden Gate. Owned by the city and county of San Francisco, San Francisco International Airport (SFO) contributes $30 million per year to the city's General Fund. It hosted more than 41 million passengers in 2011, making it among the busiest nationwide. SFO also handles over 90 percent of the Bay Area's international air-cargo trade. SFO is a major trade hub with Pacific Rim countries like South Korea, Japan, and Taiwan.

BIOTECHNOLOGY

Employing one third of the global workforce in this sector, the Bay Area is the world capital of biotech, a growing industry that concerns itself with finding marketplace applications for scientific innovations—from genetically engineering plants to provide higher crop yields, to manufacturing human insulin for diabetics. Beginning in 1976, when Genentech was founded just south of the city, biotech companies began flooding the region, complemented by some of the top health education and medical research facilities in the nation at UC San Francisco, UC Berkeley and Stanford University.

SERVICES

As in most densely populated cities, the service industry accounts for the lion's share of jobs in San Francisco. Government agencies employ more than 28,000 workers (125,000 in the three west Bay Area counties). Some 8,200 are employed at area colleges and universities, and there are nearly 32,000 health-care workers in the city. Real-estate, finance, and insurance firms provide 68,000 San Francisco jobs, and development projects such as Mission Bay promise to swell the ranks of local construction companies, which now support 16,000 workers.

LOCAL GOVERNMENT

The City and County of San Francisco are administered jointly as a consolidated unit. While such arrangements are not uncommon elsewhere in the U.S., San Francisco is the only city-county consolidation in the state of California.

The executive branch of government is headed by the **mayor**, who is elected every four years and may serve a maximum of two consecutive terms. The mayor's office oversees more than 50 offices and agencies including the police and fire departments, the civil service, the office of economic development and the office of public works. **Edwin Lee**, San Francisco's current mayor, will complete his first term of office in 2016. The 11-member **Board of Supervisors** constitutes the legislative branch of city and county government. The Board considers legislation, confirms mayoral appointments and approves the city budget (more than $6 billion in 2011). Supervisors are elected every four years (if a Supervisor leaves office before his or her term expires, a successor is appointed by the mayor), and must live in the districts they represent. In the event of the death or resignation of the mayor, the Board President assumes the mayor's duties for the remainder of the term, as happened when Dianne Feinstein served as mayor following the assassination of George Moscone in 1978, and when Edwin Lee served in 2011 after mayor Gavin Newsom resigned to become California's Lieutenant Governor.

San Francisco is a major center of U.S. government activity. Federal agencies maintaining offices here include the Army Corps of Engineers, the Federal Reserve Bank, the Federal Bureau of Investigation (FBI) and the U.S. Mint. In addition, more than 30 foreign countries operate consular offices in the city.

San Franciscans regularly participate in California's legislative process through **ballot initiatives**, a form of direct democracy by which legislation is introduced for consideration through petition of registered voters. Recent initiatives have addressed the issues of same-sex marriage, handgun ownership, the minimum wage and bilingual education.

History

Although it is a young city even by American standards, few places on the globe have changed as dramatically as San Francisco has in the past 250 years. Containing just two permanent structures at the time of the Declaration of Independence, it exploded with gold-seeking dreamers in 1849, only to be decimated by the 1906 earthquake. In the ensuing century it has steadily grown into one of the country's most desirable cities.

TIME LINE

c. 10,000 BC Native Americans first settle in the Bay Area.

1579 Explorer Francis Drake anchors near Point Reyes to repair his ship and claims Alta California for England.

1769 Expedition led by **Gaspar de Portolá** and **Junípero Serra** sets out from Mexico to establish the mission chain in Alta California. Sgt. **José Ortega** first sights San Francisco Bay.

1775 **Lt. Juan Manuel de Ayala** and his crew are the first Europeans to explore and map the bay.

1776 First mass is celebrated near the site of Mission Dolores. The first building on The Presidio is completed on September 17.

1791 Mission San Francisco de Asís (Mission Dolores) is completed.

1833 Following Mexican independence from Spain (1821), the mission chain is secularized.

1834 First town council is organized near Mission Dolores, with **Francisco de Haro** appointed as *alcalde,* or mayor.

1835 William Richardson and his wife build the first structure in Yerba Buena.

1846 American settlers in Sonoma declare the **Bear Flag Republic;** less than a month later, the U.S. flag is raised in San Francisco.

1847 California's first newspaper, *The California Star,* is published by **Sam Brannan**. Yerba Buena is renamed San Francisco.

1848 First commercial bank and first American public school open in San Francisco.

1849 California **Gold Rush** begins.

1852 **Wells Fargo** begins stagecoach service for passengers and freight.

1857 California's first commercial winery, Buena Vista, is founded in Sonoma by Hungarian **Agoston Haraszthy**.

1859 The **Comstock Lode** silver deposits are discovered in Nevada.

1865 Charles and Michael de Young found the *San Francisco Dramatic Chronicle,* later dropping the word dramatic.

1868 The College of California in Oakland is taken over by the state, chartered and renamed the **University of California**. The campus is moved to Berkeley in 1873.

1869 The Central Pacific and Union Pacific railroads are joined at Promontory Point, Utah, creating the first **transcontinental railway** link between San Francisco and the East Coast.

1873 Andrew Hallidie successfully tests the first **cable car** on Clay Street. **Levi Strauss** patents riveted blue jeans. Pacific Coast Stock Exchange is founded.

1882 Enactment of the federal **Chinese Exclusion Act** restricts immigration of Asians to the U.S. It is not repealed until 1943.

1891 **Stanford University** is established in Palo Alto.

1892 **Sierra Club** is founded, with **John Muir** as president.

1904 Produce wholesaler A.P. Giannini founds the Bank of Italy, later renamed **Bank of America**, pioneering branch banking in the state.

1906 **Great Earthquake and Fire** devastate San Francisco; the quake is estimated at 8.3 on the Richter Scale.

1915 **Panama-Pacific International Exposition** in San Francisco celebrates the city's recovery from the 1906 earthquake.

1917 Architect Willis Polk completes **Hallidie Building**, the world's first skyscraper clad in a glass curtain wall.

1919 **Ina Coolbrith** is California's first Poet Laureate.

1936–37 The **San Francisco-Oakland Bay Bridge** and the **Golden Gate Bridge** link San Francisco to the East Bay and Marin County.

1945 **United Nations** charter is drafted at the Fairmont Hotel and signed at the Civic Center.

1958 The New York **Giants** move to San Francisco, becoming the Bay Area's first major-league baseball team.

1964 **Free Speech Movement** sit-ins at the University of California, Berkeley, lead to mass arrests of student protesters.

1965 Promoter **Bill Graham** opens Fillmore Auditorium, staging legendary rock-and-roll concerts.

1967 Haight-Ashbury's "**Summer of Love**" establishes San Francisco as the hippie capital of the world.

1971 Alice Waters opens Chez Panisse restaurant in Berkeley, beginning the rage for **California cuisine.**

1973 First **BART** train travels through the transbay tube from the East Bay to the Montgomery Street station.

1978 San Francisco Mayor **George Moscone** and gay supervisor **Harvey Milk** are assassinated by ex-supervisor Dan White. His sentence of just five years' imprisonment starts riots.

1989 **Loma Prieta earthquake**, measuring 7.1 on the Richter Scale, rocks the entire Bay Area from an epicenter near Santa Cruz.

1993 When Bay Area politicians **Dianne Feinstein** and **Barbara Boxer** are elected to the U.S. Senate, California is the first state to have two women senators simultaneously in office.

1995 San Francisco 49ers win an unprecedented fifth **Super Bowl**.

1998 State law bans smoking from public areas, including restaurants and bars.

2001 After five years of spiraling technology stock prices, the bubble bursts; 30,000 San Franciscans leave the city to find work elsewhere.

2004 Nearly 4,000 **same-sex marriages** are performed at San Francisco City Hall. The California Supreme Court declares the marriages void in August.

2006 Study finds San Francisco to be the second-most-expensive city in the U.S.

2007 San Francisco Giants' **Barry Bonds** slams his 756th career home run, breaking the record set in 1974.

2008 California Supreme Court overturns ban on **same-sex marriages**. Voters then

2009	pass Prop 8, overturning the court ruling.
	San Francisco buys former naval base **Treasure Island** from the U.S. government for $55 million, with plans to develop a cutting-edge green community.
2014	Scheduled completion of new **Transbay Transit Center**, accommodating nine transit systems.

PEOPLE AND EVENTS
BEGINNINGS

Native Americans began settling the Bay Area around the 11C BC, building small villages of brush and tule bulrush. They enjoyed a rich and varied diet of seeds, ground acorn meal, shellfish, deer and other game. Although regional residents spoke various dialects and distinguished themselves by different tribal names, historians group them into three distinct peoples. The **Coast Miwok** dwelt north of the city, in present-day Marin and western Sonoma counties. The **Wintun** lived north of the Carquinez Straits in modern Solano, Napa and eastern Sonoma counties. The **Ohlone**, or Costanoans, inhabited areas east of the bay, on the San Francisco Peninsula and south to Big Sur. Though discussion of death was taboo among the Ohlone, they believed their dead souls transmigrated westward across the sea to the Farallon Islands, which they called the Islands of the Dead.

Despite small-scale but merciless feuds between some villages, trade and inter-marriage promoted a generally peaceful and prosperous existence, as did the region's remoteness from the more bellicose cultures of Mexico and the Great Plains, and from the sea lanes of Europe and Asia. By the time the Spanish arrived in the 18C, the Bay Area supported between 7,000 and 10,000 people, and was North America's most densely populated region north of Mexico.

After conquering Mexico in 1521, the Spanish Crown was eager to expand its influence in the New World, especially over territories that could supply gold and other transportable treasure to subsidize the costs of colonization and war. In 1542 Spain dispatched a sea expedition, commanded by **Juan Rodríguez Cabrillo**, up the coast of Alta California in search of a passage connecting the Pacific Ocean to the Atlantic. Although he made the first documented visit by a European to California, Cabrillo failed to find either the fabled Northwest Passage or the very real passage into San Francisco Bay that John C. Frémont—almost three centuries later—would christen the Golden Gate.

In 1579 English privateer **Francis Drake** put in for repairs at a sheltered bay in northern California—possibly present-day Drakes Bay, in the lee of Point Reyes.

View of Mission Dolores (1856)

San Francisco History Center, San Francisco Public Library

41

He claimed the land for Queen Elizabeth I as Nova Albion, but the English did not follow up on their claims, leaving California to gradual conquest by Spain.

In 1602 **Sebastián Vizcaíno** dropped anchor in Monterey Bay, 85 miles south of the Golden Gate. Although he traveled no farther north, his glowing but inaccurate description of the cove inspired the Sacred Expedition and the first European sighting of San Francisco Bay 167 years later.

HISPANIC ENCLAVE

Mexico dispatched stalwart soldier **Gaspar de Portolá** in 1769 with orders to plant colonies in Alta California, with a provincial capital at the acclaimed Monterey Bay. He was accompanied by a religious contingent, headed by Franciscan friar **Junípero Serra**, charged with founding a chain of coastal missions. While searching for Monterey Bay, but having overshot their mark, a scouting party led by **Sgt. José Ortega** stumbled upon San Francisco Bay in November of that year. Mistaking it for Drakes Bay, which the Spanish had renamed for St. Francis, the great inlet was incorrectly—but permanently—called San Francisco.

Commissioned by the colonial government in Mexico, an expedition led by **Juan Bautista de Anza** arrived at San Francisco Bay in 1776 and formally established the Presidio on a hill overlooking the entrance to the bay. De Anza also selected a site for a mission church near a small lagoon in the sheltered valley to the south, naming the lagoon for Our Lady of Sorrows (*Nuestra Señora de los Dolores* in Spanish). On October 9, 1776, Padre Serra officially dedicated the new mission to St. Francis of Assisi, although it wasn't completed until 1791. Today it is known as Mission Dolores.

The Spanish mandate was to colonize the land and the natives, converting them to Catholicism and teaching agriculture. Overawed by Spanish bravado and firepower, and initially believing the newcomers to be ancestors returned from the Islands of the Dead, the native Ohlone and Wintun allowed themselves to be pressed into mission society. They labored in the fields, lived in barracks segregated by sex, and received religious instruction. Resisters fled to the hills and the marshes of the Solano Delta, from where they mounted raids and were in turn hunted by Spanish and native soldiery. The old ways of life quickly disappeared as the Church seized land around the bay for grazing, eventually establishing three missions in Ohlone territory, and one each in the Miwok (at San Rafael) and Wintun (at Sonoma) homelands. Thousands of natives died of European diseases, especially after smallpox was contracted from a trading expedition to the Russian settlement at Fort Ross in 1837.

After Mexico declared independence from Spain in 1821, the missions were secularized. The government decreed that half of their lands go to indigenous peoples, the remainder to be sold or doled out to soldiers and civilians as private land grants in lieu of pensions or payments. The demoralized and undercapitalized natives, however, failed to work their lands, which were readily absorbed by the private landholders; the natives either went to work for them or drifted into vagabondage.

Among the largest landholders around the bay were the ranching families of **Noe**, **De Haro** and **Bernal** on the tip of the San Francisco Peninsula; **Peralta** and **Martinez** in the East Bay and—most powerful of all—**Mariano Vallejo** to the north of the bay. Another ambitious settler was **John Sutter**, a Swiss adventurer who built extensive workshops and a fort on his land grant in the Sacramento Valley. With little interference from the Mexican government, the Californios, as they called themselves, lived self-sufficient lives. Served by small armies of cheap, native labor, they prospered by selling hides and tallow to visiting ships, many of them Yankee traders who carried glowing reports of the harbor's size and excellence to U.S. East Coast.

YANKEE VILLAGE

Until 1835, most of the San Francisco Peninsula's residents lived near the mission. In June of that year, an English sailor named **William Richardson,** who had married the daughter of the Presidio *comandante,* erected a tent dwelling and trading post on a hill overlooking Yerba Buena Cove. This inlet on the northeastern shore of the peninsula had long been an anchorage for visiting ships, for it provided both sheltering hills and deep-water mooring close to shore.

The Richardsons improved their homestead with adobe buildings and drew up simple plans for a village called **Yerba Buena** (Spanish for "good herb"). Attracted by the prospect of trade with U.S. whalers and other vessels, more American settlers set up trading posts, hotels, shops and other services. Hides and tallow were the biggest commodities, but the Yankees also began stocking a wider supply of ships' provisions, including sailors' grog. Among the most prominent settlers were Ohio trapper-turned-shopkeeper Jacob Leese; Hawaiian traders Nathan Spear and William Heath; **Sam Brannan**, a business leader and renegade agent of Brigham Young's Church of Latter-day Saints; and **William Leidesdorff**, a mulatto entrepreneur from the West Indies, who served as the first U.S. vice consul and was the town's largest landowner at the time of his death in 1848. The focus of the settlement was the sleepy town plaza, where goats were tethered and sailors and vaqueros from the neighboring ranches slept off their hangovers.

Goaded by impending war with Mexico, politicians in Washington sent adventurer **John C. Frémont**, guided by Kit Carson, to assess (and encourage) local interest in joining the Union. Frémont's efforts bore fruit in 1846 when a party of Yankees in Sonoma declared California's independence from Mexico, establishing it as the **Bear Flag Republic**. Less than one month later, Commodore John Sloat claimed California as American territory at Monterey. On July 9, 1846, 70 U.S. marines and sailors, commanded by Captain John Montgomery, raised the Stars and Stripes above Yerba Buena plaza, renaming it Portsmouth Square. As real-estate speculation boomed, other amenities followed, including the town's first school and newspaper. **Washington A. Bartlett**, the town's first American *alcalde* (mayor), changed Yerba Buena's name to San Francisco in 1847, a decision he rightly believed would associate the little town with the growing fame of this huge port. Bartlett also hired Irish engineer **Jasper O'Farrell** to draw up a new town plan. O'Farrell laid out rectangular street grids, cut diagonally by the broad thoroughfare of Market Street.

GOLD RUSH BOOMTOWN

Boosters celebrated San Francisco's promising future, but none could have predicted the extraordinary kismet that was shortly to befall it. This fate was unwittingly set in motion by

"We sailed down the magnificent bay with a light wind, the tide, which was running out, carrying us at the rate of four or five knots… We passed directly under the high cliff on which the Presidio is built, and stood into the middle of the bay, from whence we could see small bays, making up into the interior, on every side; large and beautifully wooded islands; and the mouths of several small rivers. If California ever becomes a prosperous country, this bay will be the centre of its prosperity. The abundance of wood and water, the extreme fertility of its shores, the excellence of its climate, which is as near to being perfect as any in the world, and its facilities for navigation, affording the best anchoring-grounds in the whole west coast of America, all fit it for a place of great importance… "

Richard Henry Dana, *Two Years Before the Mast* (1835)

good-natured John Sutter, whose prospering empire in the Sacramento Valley required timber. Dispatched to build a sawmill on the American River in the Sierra Nevada foothills, Sutter's foreman, James Marshall, noticed a glitter of metal in the mill's tailrace on January 24, 1848: it was gold! Sutter tried to keep a tight lid on the discovery, fearful that a rush of prospectors might overwhelm his enterprise. Rumors did leak out, but San Franciscans remained skeptical until May, when Sam Brannan displayed a bottle full of gold dust and nuggets in Portsmouth Square. "Gold!" he cried. "Gold from the American River!" Much of the city emptied as gold-seekers headed for the mines, and in 1849, the first wave of gold-seekers from the outside world—the **Forty-niners**—hit San Francisco.

As thousands of treasure-hungry prospectors stormed ashore, the town exploded within months from a population of 800 into a boomtown serving 90,000 anxious transients. New American shopkeepers and old-time Californios rubbed shoulders with a floating population of men from Mexico, Hawaii, Australia, China, Chile and all the countries of Europe. Tents crowded the slopes of Telegraph and Rincon Hills, and abandoned ships were winched ashore to serve as hotels and warehouses. New buildings rose daily and burned down with alarming frequency: the city center was virtually destroyed by fire six times in four years. After the May 1851 San Francisco Fire (the most destructive before 1906), the business district was rebuilt of masonry.

By 1852 San Francisco had 30,000 residents, a library, restaurants, hotels, churches and hundreds of saloons and gambling halls, and was the fourth-largest harbor city in the U.S. Enthusiastic audiences filled new theaters to cheer stage companies from thousands of miles away. New piers extending into the bay rapidly became obsolete as Yerba Buena Cove was filled to create a new business district. A few speculators, Brannan among them, became millionaires by selling provisions to miners.

Crime bred furiously in the manic society as gangs robbed and extorted from the general public. Brannan mobilized vigilante action, prodding frustrated citizens to dole out exile and even lynching to brazen criminals. From their makeshift stronghold popularly known as Fort Gunnybags, a Committee of Vigilance lynched corrupt city councilman James Casey and seized control of the city, staging torchlight parades, secret trials and summary executions.

Though the crime rate declined, the governor, mayor, legislature, responsible citizens and newspapers spoke out against the militia tactics, and the committee disbanded after two months.

SILVER METROPOLIS

Just as the Gold Rush seemed to be ending, the 1859 discovery of the **Comstock Lode**, a fabulously rich vein of silver at what would soon become Virginia City, Nevada, brought a new boom. As investors' profits flooded San Francisco, ostentatious new millionaires vied to build spectacular mansions on Nob Hill. To provide service to the precipitous slopes, engineer **Andrew Hallidie** developed the **cable car**, which took the city by storm, opening new tracts of steep or remote land for development. By 1890 San Francisco had 21 cable car lines and more than 100 miles of track.

Foremost among city boosters was **William Ralston**, founder and president of the Bank of California. Ralston had resurrected the profitability of the Comstock mines at a point when their fortunes seemed to be failing. With the help of his ambitious agent in Virginia City, William Sharon, Ralston earned millions and used his boundless capital to elevate San Francisco into a world-class city of economic dynamism and cultural refinement. Among the projects that Ralston helped capitalize were Golden Gate Park; the Spring Valley Water Company; the Palace Hotel, largest in the world in its day; and **Adolph Sutro**'s famous tunnel in the Comstock.

San Francisco investors were almost universally convinced that a plan to link the city to the Eastern seaboard by a

Leland Stanford

San Francisco History Center, San Francisco Public Library

Mark Hopkins

San Francisco History Center, San Francisco Public Library

Collis P. Huntington

San Francisco History Center, San Francisco Public Library

Charles Crocker

San Francisco History Center, San Francisco Public Library

transcontinental railway would enrich California. So in 1861 an ambitious route was plotted across the treacherous Sierra Nevada by engineer **Theodore Judah**.

An army of laborers, including thousands of Chinese men, laid tracks. Driving eastward to meet the Union Pacific Railway at Promontory Point, Utah, the Central Pacific Railway was financed by a quartet of ambitious and cunning small businessmen in Sacramento: **Leland Stanford**, **Mark Hopkins**, **Collis P. Huntington** and **Charles Crocker**. Known as "the Big Four," they leveraged federal railroad right-of-way grants into a vast empire of real-estate holdings under the auspices of the Southern Pacific Corporation. Reaping vast personal fortunes, the Big Four turned the Southern Pacific into the most powerful political and economic force in the West.

Their power and reach, likened to the inescapable tentacles of an octopus, excited popular, passionate hatred and inspired the well-known proletarian novel by Frank Norris, *The Octopus*.

ON THE WRONG TRACK

But rather than a boon to the state, the transcontinental railway, completed in 1869, proved a bust. Cheap goods from eastern factories flooded California, causing factory closures, unemployment and widespread financial ruin in the 1870s. Overextended by $5 million, William Ralston was forced to close the Bank of California; he was found dead the same day, a probable suicide.

Factory owners cut production costs by hiring Chinese workers at reduced wages, bestowing upon them resentment from the unemployed. As militant labor grew stronger, strikes became common. Anti-Chinese riots spread across the West, bringing violence to San Francisco's Chinatown. Political pressure resulted in the federal Chinese Exclusion Act of 1882, which severely limited Chinese immigration until the act was repealed in 1943. Closed off

45

from protection by the broader society, Chinatown fell prey to the **Tong Wars**, violent power struggles between gangs. Despite an undercurrent of unrest, San Francisco's restaurants, hotels and mansions set the style to which other Western towns of the Victorian period aspired, and fed its reputation as the Paris of the West. Ostentation gilded the lives of the wealthy and infiltrated the flamboyant character of a city that cultivated notoriety as well as distinction. Arts and entertainment flourished in this prosperous and stimulating climate. While the **Barbary Coast**, a rough and licentious neighborhood of gambling clubs, saloons and brothels, thrived at the southern foot of Telegraph Hill, great European opera companies and world-famous stage performers routinely played in the glittering footlights of downtown theaters.

Distinguished writers like Mark Twain, Rudyard Kipling, Robert Louis Stevenson and Oscar Wilde celebrated its unique and rambunctious character in novel and essay. A fledgling bohemian movement, nurtured by Ina Coolbrith, Charles Stoddard, Gellet Burgess and Joaquin Miller, cultivated artistic tastes from ramshackle cottages on Telegraph and Russian hills, and at Miller's retreat in the Oakland hills. Architects A. Page Brown, Bernard Maybeck and Willis Polk cut their teeth on Bay Area projects. Photographer Arnold Genthe set up his studio in the city and began taking pictures of old Chinatown. Home from the mountains, John Muir scribbled the essays that would spark the early American conservation movement.

As in many American cities of the era, corruption crept into San Francisco politics, climaxing under Mayor **Eugene Schmitz**, who was elected to office in 1901. Under the pernicious influence of his adviser **"Boss" Abe Ruef**, Schmitz exchanged favors for bribes, leading to his conviction on 27 charges of graft and bribery in 1906. He was ousted from office the following year.

EARTHQUAKE AND FIRE

On the morning of April 18, 1906, San Franciscans were jolted awake by a massive earthquake on the San Andreas Fault. Residents of most neighborhoods were relieved and even bemused to find the most extensive damage to be fallen chimneys, broken water and gas mains, shattered windows, cracked plaster and smashed crockery. Downtown, however, and in the shoddily built neighborhood south of Market Street, the devastation was frightening. Although the modern skyscrapers had withstood the tremor with flying colors, fissures gaped in the streets and wooden tenement row houses listed dangerously, or lay in ruins. The colonnaded walls of City Hall had fallen away, leaving its magnificent dome hovering on a weakened steel frame, the most prominent victim of Abe Ruef's reckless fund-siphoning. The Central Emergency Hospital had collapsed, crushing medical staff and patients. Scores of people were hurt or killed by falling bricks.

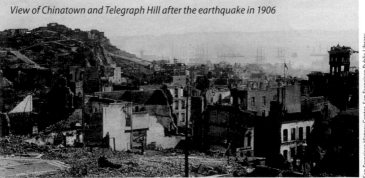

View of Chinatown and Telegraph Hill after the earthquake in 1906

San Francisco History Center, San Francisco Public Library

By noon, 52 fires were burning with impunity around the city. Unable to restore the water supply, firefighters watched helplessly as the conflagration spread alarmingly through the tenements south of Market Street. Hundreds evacuated by ferry to Oakland, which had survived relatively unscathed. By night, the flames of the burning city lit up the skies around the Bay Area.

Mayor Schmitz hastened to the newly finished Fairmont Hotel atop Nob Hill to form disaster plans. Coordinating with Brigadier General **Frederick Funston**, army troops from the Presidio began patrolling for looters (seven of whom were indeed shot) and dynamiting broad fire lines along Van Ness Avenue. By dawn on April 19, the fire crested Nob Hill, destroying the "hill of palaces" and gutting the Fairmont. Prisoners were moved to Alcatraz, and thousands of refugees streamed westward to makeshift tent camps on the Presidio grounds and in Golden Gate Park.

By the third day, the fire had burned south into the Mission District and clear to the northern wharves. Then the wind changed, pushing the flames back onto themselves. The fire was stopped at Van Ness Avenue, sparing the western half of the city. Some 250,000 people were left homeless and 674 were dead or missing. The city center was destroyed, some 514 blocks of offices, homes, warehouses, factories, saloons, churches, and public buildings. Yet a plucky atmosphere prevailed in the refugee camps.

A PHOENIX FROM THE ASHES

Relief funds poured in from around the world and reconstruction proceeded with phenomenal speed. By 1915, the city was ready to celebrate its recovery. Building an enchanting "city" lit by electrical lights on newly filled land in the Marina District, San Francisco hosted the **Panama-Pacific International Exposition**, the most highly regarded of the city's world's fairs.

The momentum of reconstruction culminated in an era of epic civil-engineering projects. The Civic Center was rebuilt on a grand scale in the Beaux-Arts style. Mayor **James "Sunny Jim" Rolph** cleared the way for residential development of the Richmond District by ordering the city's many cemeteries closed and all human remains removed to Colma, south of the city limits. The electric streetcar began replacing the cable car as the premier form of public transport. San Francisco's financial institutions—particularly A.P. Giannini's Bank of Italy (later the Bank of America)—regained the central role in a new California "rush" that outstripped the gold and silver bonanzas of the previous century by capitalizing new farms and agricultural towns and building the state's role as the nation's fruit and vegetable garden.

To secure a dependable source of good water, the city dammed the Tuolumne River at Hetch Hetchy Canyon, 150 miles east in Yosemite National Park, carrying the river water by aqueduct to the Crystal Springs reservoirs on the peninsula. Most spectacularly, in spite of the Great Depression, the city simultaneously built two of the largest bridges in the world—the Bay Bridge, connecting the long-isolated peninsula eastward across the bay to Oakland, and the Golden Gate Bridge north across the Golden Gate to Marin County. To again celebrate its vigor in flamboyant San Francisco style, the city threw another world's fair, the **Golden Gate International Exposition**, which rose on newly completed Treasure Island, the largest artificial island in the world.

Labor problems plagued the city throughout these decades. Springing from resentment against the "robber barons" of the 19C, the 20C labor movement reorganized into an effective, if sometimes corrupt, political force, winning an eight-hour workday and turning San Francisco into a "union town." Labor strikes became a fixture in local politics. Longshoremen staged the largest strike in American history in 1930, eventually winning better pay after strikebreakers stormed their lines, sparking riots that injured scores and left two dead. The century's most notorious unionist court case was the **Mooney Trial**. A rabble-rousing socialist named Tom Mooney was railroaded through court for a bombing that left ten dead at a parade on the eve of World War I. Found guilty, Mooney was pardoned in 1939 after witnesses admitted they lied under oath.

WAR AND UNEASY PEACE

World War II brought another boom to the Bay Area as shipyards at Hunters Point and Sausalito tooled up for wartime production. Thousands of Japanese-American citizens were rounded up from Bay Area cities and expelled to internment camps.

While the army built bunkers and batteries in the Marin Headlands to fend off a Japanese invasion that never came, 1.5 million soldiers, sailors, and marines embarked for the Pacific theater from San Francisco.

The population continued to grow after the war, but with most of the new residents settling in Bay Area suburbs, the city began to lose its luster as a commercial hub. As Los Angeles grew to become the premier manufacturing center of the West Coast, tourism became San Francisco's most important business. North Beach became the national focus of a bohemian movement, the Beat Generation, during the 1950s, when nonconformist writers like Jack Kerouac, Allen Ginsberg and Lawrence Ferlinghetti, encouraged by a society tolerant of unconventional behavior, frequented the Italian coffee houses, wrote poetry and "dug the scene." Curious tourists eventually drove the Beats from North Beach but the city generated another bohemian movement in the 1960s, this time in the Haight-Ashbury: Thousands of young people—hippies and "flower children"—gathered to experiment with drugs, music and libertine society. By the 1970s, that neighborhood was a haven of drug pushers. (It has rebounded as a middle-class enclave today.)

Partly because of these widely renowned social movements, the Bay Area acquired a national reputation for what some might call political and social idealism, others left-wing radicalism. Huey Newton founded the Black Panther Party in Oakland, as neighboring Berkeley, home of the University of California, became a national center of student protest against the Vietnam War and other issues. When thousands of gay men and women moved to San Francisco, the Castro District became the capital of the American gay community. Relaxed immigration laws permitted an influx of larger numbers of Asian and Hispanic immigrants, greatly changing the ethnic makeup of the city.

Urban problems like homelessness, crime and blight compounded in San Francisco during the 1980s, yet single-issue politics and a lack of strong leadership constricted the government's ability to deal with them. The 1990s witnessed a welcome renaissance in many city institutions, most spectacularly in the building of the new San Francisco Museum of Modern Art and a new main library, the birth and growth of an arts center at Yerba Buena Gardens, and the refurbishment of City Hall, the War Memorial Opera House, the Geary Theater and the California Palace of the Legion of Honor. The economy soared, with thousands of entrepreneurs and investors finding ways to exploit the newly formed Internet for financial gain. Many of these dot-commers became millionaires before the inevitable crash of 2001, which led to the exodus of some 30,000 people from the city.

The 2003 election (and 2007 re-election) of Gavin Newsom showed that San Franciscans remained committed to their progressive politics despite the downturn. A champion of small business and environment, Newsom authorized the marriage of nearly 4,000 same-sex partners in 2004 (which were later voided by the California Supreme Court).

Large-scale projects continue: the Asian Art Museum opened in 2003; the de Young Museum in 2005; and the California Academy of Sciences in 2008. Which all goes to show that ups and downs appear to be as much a part of the urban fabric as the city's hills. Like tourists thronging its cable cars, San Franciscans just hold on and enjoy the ride.

Architecture

San Franciscans are well known for their warm embrace of new cultures, attitudes and ideas, and that goes for art and architecture too. While there is a bedrock of tradition, San Francisco artists are eager to innovate. And judging by the number of performances and exhibits on any given night, audiences are equally eager to devour the outcome.

The oldest major U.S. city west of the Rockies, San Francisco revels in examples of many eras and styles of buildings. The city's built environment has been shaped by various entrepreneurial, artistic and political forces, all of which have contributed to its distinctive architectural legacy. San Francisco's role as a commercial and financial nexus continues to attract new and innovative forms of architecture.

NATIVE AMERICANS AND THE MISSION PERIOD

Before the arrival of Europeans, many small Ohlone and Miwok communities dotted the shores of San Francisco Bay. The natives lived in cone-shaped structures made of reeds and trees lashed together. As these natural building materials had a limited life span, no constructions remain from this era, although archeologists have recorded scores of shell mounds marking village sites around the bay shore, as well as acorn-grinding rocks in oak woodlands where the native peoples made seasonal camps comprising many dwellings.

The earliest extant structures in the Bay Area date from the mission period. The center of each mission community was a simple church and monastery, built of thick walls of whitewashed adobe capped by gabled red-tile roofs, supported upon heavy rough-hewn timbers. Spanish friars designed the missions along classical lines, using elements such as pilasters, niches and arcades to embellish the exteriors, and ornate reredos, tiled floors and colorful frescoes to ornament the interior spaces. Much of the interest in mission decoration comes from the folk-art flavors imparted by the Native American laborers who did the construction work. San Francisco's oldest building, the chapel at Mission Dolores, remains the finest example of the architecture of this period, while the surrounding Bay Area holds a variety of others, most notably the well-preserved mission and town plaza of Sonoma.

THE VICTORIAN ERA

From 1860 to 1900, as wealth poured into the city from the gold mines and the silver deposits of Nevada's Comstock Lode, San Francisco's downtown commercial district grew in stature. Grand hotels were constructed to house visitors to the burgeoning metropolis, the most opulent of which was the Palace Hotel, completed in 1875. The U.S. Mint, now called the Old Mint, was built nearby around the same time. By the 1890s, Chicago School office towers such as the Mills Building and the Chronicle Building had begun to rise along the bustling streets. The landmark Ferry Building was begun in 1894, and the Victorian era also saw the construction of elaborate resorts, most notably the second Cliff House and the now-ruined Sutro Baths complex near Seal Rocks on the city's Pacific shoreline.

The best-known and most enduring legacies of the Victorian era remain the many blocks of homes erected in the distinctive sub-styles of this romantic period. Throughout Pacific Heights, Haight-Ashbury, the Castro District and other residential neighborhoods, streets are lined with abundantly decorated wooden houses, most of them built between 1870 and 1906. Using redwood, fir, and pine lumber from the dense forests of the northern California coast, contractors could produce homes quickly and inexpensively for San Francisco's burgeoning middle class. Closely crowded on narrow lots and built to standardized floor plans, these houses were adorned with an almost endless catalog of decorative sidings, elaborately milled

Italianate Style

Queen Anne

moldings and bay windows with carved frames. Some were accented with fanciful turrets, false gables and intricate art-glass windows.

Most Victorian homes were designed not by architects but by home owners, builders and property developers. They often followed general principles laid down by "pattern books" that outlined design precepts of each of the main Victorian "styles." Most prevalent in San Francisco were **Italianate** (1860–80), marked by Neoclassical ornament and pedimented false gables; **Stick** or Eastlake (1870–90), epitomized by comparatively flat wall surfaces and more angular, geometric forms; and **Queen Anne** (1870–1906), the most free-form and asymmetrical of the Victorian styles, often incorporating corner towers, turrets and a sometimes-frenzied variety of wall sidings, all on the same facade. The free spirit of these "painted ladies"— so called because, though once mainly gray, they had flamboyant color schemes

applied—has captured the fancy of visitors and locals alike. Thousands of Victorian homes march up and down San Francisco's streets, imposing a distinctive and colorful stamp on the city's architectural signature. One of them has been preserved for public viewing: the imposing Queen Anne-style Haas-Lilienthal House in eastern Pacific Heights.

The latter part of the Victorian era saw the emergence of the **Arts and Crafts** movement, which in San Francisco brought together a loose grouping of artists and architects interested in the bohemian, "back-to-nature" teachings of local preacher Joseph Worcester. The Swedenborgian Church epitomizes the movement's rustic approach to architecture, adapted by such diverse and prolific architects as A. Page Brown, Willis Polk, Ernest Coxhead and Bernard Maybeck, all of whom built numerous residences around the Bay Area. Using dark-stained shingles of redwood lumber and creating innovative spatial arrangements that took advantage of the picturesque topography and mild climate, these architects satisfied a Bay Area taste for cultivated rusticity.

THE CITY BEAUTIFUL

At the turn of the 20C, San Francisco's civic government considered altering the city's layout along the lines of an ambitious plan proposed by Chicago architect Daniel Burnham. **The Burnham Plan** called for wide boulevards and Baroque public spaces like those of Paris or Washington DC, ideals

Stick Style

at the forefront of the Beaux-Arts-inspired "City Beautiful" movement. The earthquake and fire of 1906 left a clean canvas upon which to implement Burnham's ideas, but urgency propelled the rebuilding of the city according to its previous layout. The only aspect of the Burnham Plan to be constructed after the earthquake was the new Civic Center. This monumental rectangle of libraries, theaters and other public buildings, centered upon the landmark Baroque-style dome of City Hall, forms a grand, dignified public space.

Some of San Francisco's most impressive commercial buildings, including the Bank of California and the grand Fairmont Hotel, date from the post-earthquake period, as do many of the mansions of Pacific Heights. The city's main architectural gesture of recovery was the **Panama-Pacific International Exposition of 1915**, which filled the reclaimed lands of the modern Marina District with a celebratory fairground of eclectic architecture. The sole survivor is Bernard Maybeck's stately Palace of Fine Arts. Across the bay, the Neoclassical campus buildings of the University of California, Berkeley, were erected by John Galen Howard and others, including Julia Morgan.

The growing economy of the 1920s supported another building boom in the Financial District. The city's first skyscrapers sprouted at the end of that decade, including Timothy Pflueger's Art-Deco PacBell Building, the Mayan-style tower at Four Fifty Sutter, and George Kelham's 31-story, Gothic-style Russ Building, then the tallest on the West Coast.

DEPRESSION AND POSTWAR ERA

Commercial construction slowed considerably during the Great Depression. Following World War II, San Francisco underwent a long period of suburbanization, with freeways constructed to reach new tract-housing suburbs of the outlying Bay Area. Through the late 1950s and early 60s, urban renewal

caused the demolition of vast tracts of older buildings, in turn inspiring a movement to preserve the city's architecture. At the same time, a rash of new construction in the Financial District transformed the city's skyline. The first distinctive new project was the 1959 Crown Zellerbach Building, now One Bush Street, an International-style glass box supported on piers above a paved plaza. More skyscrapers continued to be built, culminating in the city's two tallest—Skidmore, Owings & Merrill's monolithic Bank of America, in 1971, and William Pereira's unique Transamerica Pyramid, in 1972.

Public outcry against the pace of growth, which critics claimed had "Manhattanized" the attractive city skyline, resulted in stringent planning controls encoded in the **Downtown Plan** of 1985. This put a cap on the amount of square footage of new construction permitted in the Financial District and effectively shifted future growth to the less densely developed area South of Market.

CONTEMPORARY ARCHITECTURE

Recent years have brought a number of internationally renowned architects to design projects in San Francisco and the Bay Area, among them Philip Johnson, Mario Botta, Daniel Libeskind, James Ingo Freed and Michael Graves, whose signature contemporary take on the Classical style may be seen at Clos Pegase Winery in the Napa Valley. San Francisco has witnessed a renaissance in public architecture through major projects like the expanded Moscone Convention Center and the adjacent Yerba Buena Gardens. In 1995, Botta's new home for the San Francisco Museum of Modern Art opened, followed in 1996 by Freed's striking new San Francisco Public Library at Civic Center. Herzog & de Meuron's copper-clad de Young Museum, unveiled in 2005, is one of the most daring buildings in decades, rivaled by Renzo Piano's California Academy of Sciences, opened in 2008 with a "Green Roof" of 1.7 million native plants.

Visual Arts

The visual arts of San Francisco reflect the history, diversity and excitement of the entire Bay Area, making it one of the art capitals of the American West.

EARLY ARTISTIC LANDSCAPE

San Francisco's rich, multilayered art history began with the Ohlone, Wintun and Coast Miwok Indians, who maintained a beautiful ceremonial culture. Today, baskets produced by native Californians are treasured for their geometric designs and precise weaving; many are on view at the Oakland Museum of California and other collections.

Mission Dolores stands as the primary reminder of the city's Mexican period: Walls and ceilings of the old chapel reveal replicas of beautiful geometric patterns designed by native artisans. The population explosion during and after the Gold Rush introduced European values and aesthetics. Important pioneer artists began visiting San Francisco, including landscape painters Albert Bierstadt and William Keith. Early photographers Carleton Watkins and Eadweard Muybridge (who helped settle a bet about horse racing with his groundbreaking photographic studies of animal locomotion) paved the way for one of the area's most endur-

ing obsessions. The San Francisco Art Association, precursor of today's San Francisco Museum of Modern Art, was founded in 1871 by members Bierstadt, Keith, Muybridge and others to display art publicly and offer classes. Railroad magnates Leland Stanford and Mark Hopkins assembled major collections of European art in the late 19C.

In the early 20C, important developments in the arts took root in San Francisco, including the California **Arts and Crafts** movement in painting, furniture and decorative arts, led by Arthur and Lucia Matthews. **Tonalist** painting, incorporating the colors of the city's distinctive foggy palette, was exemplified by Gottardo Piazonni and Xavier Martinez. Following the influential Panama-Pacific International Exhibition of 1915, where works by European and New York modernists were displayed at the Palace of Fine Arts, an explosion of color appeared in the work of Bay Area painters Clayton S. Price and Selden Gile. The latter was a member of the **Society of Six**, an informal association of artists who practiced a painterly, figurative style during the 1920s. In the 20s and 30s, several artists of Japanese and Chinese ancestry blended aspects of Asian art traditions with Western practices to create innovative Asian-American styles.

Photographers Ansel Adams, Edward Weston, Imogen Cunningham and others founded the **Group f.64** in 1932 and exhibited together the following year. Reacting against the blurred-focus work of their "pictorialist" contemporaries, they embraced a sharp-focus, "precisionist" depiction of forms and textures. Social themes characteristic of the Great Depression are movingly rendered in the works of painter Maynard Dixon and his wife, photographer Dorothea Lange, as well as in pieces by African-American sculptor Sargent Johnson.

Diego Rivera made repeated visits to the city with his wife, Frida Kahlo, during the 1930s; the Mexican muralist executed several works here, engendering mural projects by other artists in public locations across the city.

Diego Rivera painting a mural, Golden Gate International Exposition, November 28 1940

Gabriel Moulin / San Francisco History Center, San Francisco Public Library

ABSTRACT AND FIGURATIVE

After World War II, visiting faculty Clyfford Still and Mark Rothko of the San Francisco Art Institute inspired an explosion of abstract expressionist painting by their students, including Sam Francis and Robert Motherwell. Painters Elmer Bischoff, Richard Diebenkorn and David Park responded with a representational movement known as **Bay Area Figurative**, a motif that Berkeley-based painter Joan Brown and sculptor Manuel Neri later personalized. Beat culture and Zen philosophy helped inspire the work of individualists like Bruce Conner, William Wiley and Jay de Feo. Popular culture of the 1960s is recorded in the work of painters Wayne Thiebaud and Robert Bechtle. The latter counterculture movement also saw unique developments in poster art around Haight-Ashbury, as the cartoon art of R. Crumb and others gained worldwide exposure.

Artists working in craft media have continued to challenge the boundaries of their materials—ceramists Robert Arneson, Viola Frey and Peter Voulkos are known internationally, and textile-based sculptors Kay Sekimachi and Ruth Asawa have helped redefine their medium. Asawa is also the creator of some of San Francisco's most popular public works, including fountains at Ghirardelli Square and at the Grand Hyatt Hotel near Union Square. Sculptor Beniamino Bufano created a menagerie of rounded and evocative animal forms and symbolic human figures that continue to populate city parks and public squares.

THE CONTEMPORARY SCENE

Today, the San Francisco Museum of Modern Art, at home in its new South of Market building, honors its commitment to displaying pieces by Bay Area artists along with cutting-edge works by international artists. Opposite, the Yerba Buena Center for the Arts maintains an ambitious program of exhibitions that keep a continual flow of new art before the public eye. San Francisco's public and private galleries increase visitors' opportunities to see all kinds of visual art, most conveniently during the thrice-yearly Open Studios days when galleries and artists' studios across the city hold open houses. College galleries at San Francisco State University and the San Francisco Art Institute mount exhibitions of national and international work. The city remains the capital of the nation's alternative art centers with its concentration of nonprofit spaces and artist cooperatives, including S.F. Camerawork, Hunters Point Studios, Galeria de la Raza and the Headlands Center for the Arts in Marin County. Commercial galleries, many of them clustered in near Union Square, present a range of exciting contemporary and historical art. Well worth looking into are Gallery Paule Anglim, Hang, and John Berggruen, located within a few blocks of one another. The work of performance and conceptual artists such as Guillermo Gomez-Pena; painters Enrique Chagoya and Oliver Jackson; muralists Juana Alicia and Daniel Galvez; and photographers Richard Misrach and Linda Connor, continue to infuse San Francisco arts with new ideas and vitality.

CINEMA

San Francisco's quirky film history began in 1872 when Eadweard Muybridge, a Bay Area photographer, put together a rapid succession of still photographs to prove that a running horse at one period of his stride has all four feet off the ground. Through the 20C the film industry flourished here as directors from Erich von Stroheim to John Huston to Alfred Hitchcock to Francis Ford Coppola used San Francisco's glorious cityscapes as the backdrop for numerous productions. Fisherman's Wharf, Lombard Street, the Presidio and Pacific Heights have all served as film sets at one time or another. The San Francisco Film Commission is charged with developing policies and incentives to keep the city attractive to production companies; since 2005, 30 films or television series were partially or completely shot here, including *Memoirs of a Geisha* (2005), *Rent* (2005), *Pursuit of Happyness* (2006), *Milk* (2008) and *Contagion* (2011).

Performing Arts

Famed for its cultural diversity, San Francisco has always been a hotbed for the performing arts. A city of immigrants, it has nurtured the European traditions of opera, symphony and ballet while making room for Chinese opera, Latin jazz and ethnic dance. A haven for nonconformists, it has been the birthplace of new strains of rock-and-roll music and postmodern dance.

OPERA

Of all the musical arts, opera is the one that has most enduringly won a place in San Francisco's heart. Even when the city was but a small, gritty mining outpost, luxuriant operas were staged on a regular basis in some of the most sumptuous theaters in the nation. Beginning with Bellini's La Somnabula in 1851, some 5,000 operatic performances were given by more than 20 companies prior to the 1906 earthquake.

In 1923 pianist-producer Gaetano Merola founded the **San Francisco Opera** with a production of La Bohème, but not until 1934 did the company christen the War Memorial Opera House, its permanent home, with a performance of Puccini's Tosca. Widely recognized as the pre-eminent operatic institution in the western U.S., the company has presented

Davies Symphony Hall

© San Francisco Symphony

such greats as Luciano Pavarotti, Angela Gheorghiu and Birgit Nilsson. Smaller companies such as the Lamplighters, a Gilbert and Sullivan company formed in 1952, and Pocket Opera, a troupe that has performed classic works in English since 1968, illustrate opera's mass appeal with their inventive, accessible productions.

CLASSICAL MUSIC

San Francisco's taste for orchestral music is well established. Founded in 1911, the **San Francisco Symphony Orchestra** hosted the adolescent debuts of violinists Yehudi Menuhin (1926) and Isaac Stern (1936) and developed a repertory rooted in the classical and romantic traditions. However, with the 1995 installation of Leonard Bernstein protégé Michael Tilson Thomas as its director, the symphony has undergone a renaissance. Tilson Thomas has challenged his musicians and his audiences with an array of difficult, under-recognized 20C masterpieces by Copland, Debussy, Varese and onetime Bay Area composers Lou Harrison and Darius Milhaud.

Among chamber-music groups, the **Kronos Quartet**, founded in San Francisco in 1977, stands out for crystallizing the city's ethos of experimentation and fun with its original, often-playful arrangements of contemporary works. The male choir **Chanticleer**, a full-time classical a cappella group, has performed an eclectic array of new and ancient music since its inception in 1978, including rare Renaissance choral pieces, vocal jazz and gospel. In 2008 they were named "Ensemble of the Year" by Musical America and inducted into the American Classical Music Hall of Fame.

JAZZ AND ROCK

San Francisco and Oakland enjoyed a brief flowering as jazz hubs in the 1940s and 50s. Breaking from the Dixieland tradition parlayed locally by Crescent City musicians, Bay Area native Dave Brubeck pioneered a new sound, characterized by syncopated rhythms, percussive piano and classical song structures. Brubeck's runaway success with his albums for Fantasy, a local label, made San Francisco one of the world centers for jazz recording. Today a "new jazz" style, grounded in bebop but inflected by rock and funk, has been developed by younger San Franciscans, most notably guitarist Charlie Hunter.

San Francisco's place in the rock-and-roll canon was clinched in the 60s when local bands the Grateful Dead, Jefferson Airplane and Big Brother and the Holding Company (featuring Janis Joplin) wrote the soundtrack for a decade of political protest and cultural revolution. Free concerts in Golden Gate Park and all-night jam sessions at the Family Dog, Fillmore and Avalon ballrooms drew thousands to hear what became known as the **San Francisco Sound**. In the 1970s political folk singers like Joan Baez (from Carmel) and bands like Country Joe and the Fish emerged. Crooner Chris Isaak, whose stylish music has been described as rhythm-and-blues with roots in country and folk, burst onto the scene in the late 1980s. Around the same time, a hardcore punk scene coalesced around Jello Biafra's Dead Kennedys, preparing the way for a punk-pop explosion in the East Bay that hurtled the band **Green Day** from obscurity to platinum status in the 90s. Other popular Bay Area bands at the end of the 20C included **Counting Crows** and **Boyz II Men**.

THEATER

Demonstrating its flair for the dramatic, San Francisco has always supported the theater. In the 1850s, 22 of Shakespeare's 38 plays were staged, but circus acts and minstrel shows were equally popular. In the 1860s some of the most sumptuous playhouses in the nation were built here—just as Barbary Coast melodeons were gaining a toehold. Audacious local stars like Lola Montez, Adah Isaacs Menken and Lotta Crabtree achieved near-mythic status.

Once the transcontinental railroad was completed in 1869, San Francisco became a must-stop on the national touring circuit. It was not until the mid-20C, however, that the city regained a strong local theater community. In 1951 San Francisco State University professors Jules Irving and Herbert Blau founded the **Actors' Workshop,** introducing the work of Harold Pinter, Samuel Beckett and Edward Albee to local audiences. The **San Francisco Mime Troupe**, founded in 1959, today travels the world with its self-styled political satires. In 1967 actor and director William Ball established the **American Conservatory Theater** (ACT), today considered one of the best regional theaters and drama schools in the U.S. In addition, more than 100 professional companies mount everything from the local camp classic *Beach Blanket Babylon* to masterpieces by Shakespeare and Chekhov.

DANCE

Second only to New York in the diversity, innovation and quality of its troupes, San Francisco is at the forefront of classical and modern dance in the U.S. Founded in 1933, the **San Francisco Ballet** is the oldest resident classical ballet company in the U.S. The ballet presented the first full-length American productions of such 19C classics as Tchaikovsky's *Swan Lake* and *The Nutcracker,* in addition to a repertoire of 20C works by George Balanchine, Jerome Robbins and resident choreographers like Lew Christensen and Michael Smuin. In the East Bay, the small, energetic Oakland Ballet has made its name reviving classic 20C ballets by Vaslav Nijinsky and others. Modern dance of every type is also well established in San Francisco. One of its foremothers, Isadora Duncan, was born here in 1877, though she spent most of her life abroad and performed in the city only twice. Anna Halprin emerged in the late 1950s as an influential choreographer; her explorations of ritual, physicality and the creative process sparked groundbreaking postmodern work in New York in the 1960s. Today, the Joe Goode Performance Group has achieved stunning results by combining dance with theater and live music, and a wide array of ethnic dance companies explore everything from butoh and belly dancing to flamenco and capoeira.

Literature

Born in the wake of the Gold Rush, San Francisco's literary tradition began as a torrent of local magazines and newspapers that has since broadened and expanded. Today a host of renowned and up-and-coming journalists, novelists and poets make the city their home and source of inspiration.

THE GOLDEN FIFTIES AND SILVER SIXTIES

Legendary Mormon entrepreneur Sam Brannan founded San Francisco's first major newspaper, the *California Star,* in 1847. By the mid-1850s San Francisco boasted a dozen dailies and nearly 40 weeklies—more publications than in London at the time. While most of these were political organs or advertisers, they also encouraged some of the city's literary voices. Nearly every paper carved out room for a "poet's corner" on the front page, thereby nurturing the talents of miner-bards such as Alonzo Delano and John Rollin Ridge, who wrote under the noms-de-plume Old Block and Yellow Bird, respectively.

Through the 1860s, literary journals such as *The Pioneer,* the *Golden Era, The Californian* and the *Overland Monthly* flourished, as did the unconventional culture that aided and abetted them. Bret Harte and Joaquin Miller drew from their experiences working in mining towns for their early essays, short stories and poems. Others, like Ina Coolbrith and Charles Stoddard, found inspiration in nature and the emotions. Ambrose Bierce and Mark Twain made their reputations writing irreverent satires and burlesques. As the decade wore on, Bierce grew increasingly misanthropic and cynical, earning himself the nickname "Bitter Bierce" by becoming a vociferous champion of suicide and attacking progressive issues such as women's suffrage and the eight-hour workday. Twain, on the other hand, sharpened his skills and applied them to the picaresque fiction that would later assure his place in the American literary canon.

During the financial depression of the 1870s, many publications foundered and talents such as Harte, Miller, Twain, Bierce and Stoddard relocated elsewhere. A steady stream of writers came through the city in the next couple of decades, however. Poet Robert Frost was born in 1874 near the Embarcadero and lived there 11 years; Robert Louis Stevenson wrote in a flat near Union Square in 1879 and 1880; and in the late 1880s British Indian writer Rudyard Kipling tried, unsuccessfully, to publish his stories in the city's major journals. Across the bay Gertrude Stein lived in Oakland from 1880 to 1891 before going east to Radcliffe College and subsequently founding her salon in Paris. Of the 1860s bohemians, only Ina Coolbrith remained in San Francisco, hosting literary salons and encouraging the next generation of writers in their pursuits.

SOCIAL REALISM

One of Coolbrith's many acolytes, Jack London wrote in the tradition of Twain and Harte, using his adventures to fuel his fiction. And like many writers of his time, London addressed larger social and philosophical issues in his work. His story "South of the Slot" contains a sharp critique of class differences in San Francisco (the title refers to Market Street, which once sharply divided the rich from the poor). London's contemporary, Frank

Jack London

San Francisco History Center, San Francisco Public Library

Norris, also saw contradictions in San Francisco society; his acclaimed naturalistic novel *McTeague* (1899), set in the Polk Gulch neighborhood, explores such themes as greed and social Darwinism from the point of view of a beleaguered dentist.

Taking a different tack, poet George Sterling wrote torrid romantic poems and famously described the city as a "cool, grey city of love." Other writers and artists of the era belonged to the fun-loving group Les Jeunes (the Young Ones), which published its work in *The Lark* (1895–97), "a magazine of humorous anarchy." Most members of Les Jeunes did their best-known work after the group's breakup, although founder Gellett Burgess remains famous for his frivolous poem "The Purple Cow," which appeared in *The Lark*.

From 1920 to 1929 crime writer Dashiell Hammett made San Francisco his home; the fog-cloaked slopes of Nob Hill provided a noir backdrop for the nighttime ramblings of Sam Spade, Hammett's hard-boiled detective hero of *The Maltese Falcon*. John Steinbeck also lived in the city in the late 1920s, although he drew from the environs of nearby Salinas and Monterey for his acclaimed novels *East of Eden* and *Cannery Row*.

BEAT HAPPENING

In the 1950s San Francisco underwent a literary renaissance as the Beat Generation came of age in North Beach. From the early to mid-1950s, Jack Kerouac churned out more than a dozen books about wanderlust, love and longing. Kerouac typed *On the Road* as one very long paragraph in 20 days of April 1951; upon publication in 1957, the book catapulted him and his Beat Generation cohorts to fame. According to poet and City Lights bookstore founder Lawrence Ferlinghetti: "The emergence of the Beat Generation made North Beach *the* literary center of SF—and it nurtured a new vision that would spread far beyond its bounds." Poet Allen Ginsberg, one of that vision's most articulate proponents, gave birth to the San Francisco poetry renaissance in 1955 when he read his

Herb Caen

Photo by Mason Weymouth / San Francisco History Center, San Francisco Public Library

poem "Howl" (first published by City Lights) to a standing-room-only audience in the Marina District.

In 1960 and 1961 Ken Kesey wrote *One Flew Over the Cuckoo's Nest,* his best-selling novel about a mental institution, from his home in Palo Alto. Journalist Tom Wolfe vividly captured the psychedelic counterculture in his 1969 book *The Electric Kool-Aid Acid Test*. In the 1970s Armistead Maupin followed the lives of young drifters in his long-running *San Francisco Chronicle* column, later published as the book *Tales of the City*. Before he died of AIDS in 1994, *Chronicle* journalist Randy Shilts *(And the Band Played On)* gained renown in writing about city politics, gay liberation and the AIDS epidemic. For six decades until his death in 1997, Pulitzer Prize-winning *Chronicle* columnist Herb Caen entertained a huge and faithful following of avid readers with his witty blend of gossip and news about the city he loved. Today the San Francisco Bay Area boasts a wide range of resident writers, including novelists Amy Tan *(The Joy Luck Club)*, Alice Walker *(The Color Purple)* and Dave Eggers *(A Heartbreaking Work of Staggering Genius)*—and a lively calendar of public readings by local novelists, essayists and poets.

Nature

San Francisco boasts an incomparable setting of mountains, hills and water at the tip of a long peninsula forming the western boundary of a 496-square-mile bay. Its dramatic topography, its agreeable climate and the pervasive presence of the sea have invited exploration and provided enjoyment for centuries. San Francisco Bay itself was immensely important in the city's early development as the commercial and cultural hub of the western United States.

LANDSCAPE

The hills and valleys that characterize San Francisco and the Bay Area form part of the **Coast Ranges**, a low but rugged belt of mountains extending from Santa Barbara County north to Oregon. Prominent Bay Area summits include **Mt. Tamalpais** (2,571ft), which looms over Marin County to the north; **Mt. Diablo** (3,849ft), which backdrops the hills of Oakland to the east; and **Mt. Hamilton** (4,213ft), which lies southeast of the city near San Jose. Peaks within the city include Mt. Davidson (929ft), Twin Peaks (922ft and 904ft) and Mt. Sutro (908ft).

San Francisco's owes its famed steep streets to surveyor Jasper O'Farrell, who in 1847 laid out a perpendicular street grid in keeping with the standards of the day. The result: byways that abruptly ascend a hill, crest, then plummet vertiginously down the other side. Several commanding hilltops remained squatter settlements until the invention of the cable car made it possible for the well-to-do to get up and down. Later development in the region took topography into account, so that in Berkeley, Oakland and other Bay Area towns, most streets sensibly follow the natural contours of the land.

The great **San Francisco Bay** bisects the Coast Ranges, serving not only as a coastal inlet but as an estuary through which the rivers draining the western slope of the Sierra Nevada and the plains of the Central Valley join and pass to the sea. The bay itself submerges a large, northwest/southeast-running valley that would have been visible 20,000 years ago when a vast amount of water was frozen in continental glaciers.

AN UNSTABLE FOUNDATION

The Bay Area lies atop a complex system of tectonic faults created by the motion of the Pacific and North American plates, giant solidified sections of the earth's crust that move about atop the molten material of the earth's mantle. The two plates slide past each other at an average speed of two inches per year. Movements along faults occur frequently and, under normal conditions, imperceptibly. Occasionally, however, the slide is impeded by rigid material, and pressure increases as the plates strain to move. When the obstruction gives way, the pent-up pressure is released in a sudden lurch, accompanied by shuddering and trembling known as an **earthquake**.

The most notorious fault is the **San Andreas Rift Zone**, extending from the Imperial Valley in southeastern California to Cape Mendocino on the north coast, passing en route beneath the seabed west of San Francisco. Along the San Francisco Peninsula, the long valley of the Crystal Springs reservoirs just west of Interstate 280, marks the zone, as does the valley that separates Point Reyes from the rest of Marin County. In the famous 1906 earthquake, more than 16ft of movement occurred along this fault in a few seconds. Another major quake, with its epicenter in the Santa Cruz Mountains near San Jose, occurred on this fault in 1989.

The San Andreas Fault is the best known in this shear zone. Most ominous is the Hayward Fault, which runs along the base of the Oakland and Berkeley hills, an area that has become densely populated since its last major earthquake.

CLIMATE

San Francisco's cool, dry summers and mild, wet winters are characteristic of a Mediterranean climate—accentuated by the peculiarities of the city's location.

The Sierra Nevada mountains to the east block frigid air masses that sweep across the rest of the United States.

The Pacific Ocean has a regulating effect on temperature extremes: San Francisco registers the lowest mean summer temperature of any city in the U.S. outside of Alaska, and rarely sees a winter frost. Snow has accumulated in the downtown area only twice in the city's recorded history.

Although seasonal temperature variation is remarkably slight, weather within the city—and throughout the Bay Area—is greatly affected by microclimates that result from the hilly topography. The dip of a mountain ridge or change in proximity to the ocean can create pronounced variations in weather between neighborhoods; temperatures may vary as much as 35°F between coast and inland areas. The staggered ridges of the Coast Ranges confine the chilling effect of the Pacific to a rather narrow frontage along the coast.

One of the principal factors in San Francisco's cool summers is the city's renowned **fog**, created when westerly winds, laden with moisture from the Pacific, cross the cold California Current. The moisture condenses, creating dramatic rivers and banks of fog that invade the city from the west, turning a brilliant day into a gloomy one within minutes. This "advection fog" often forms a dense layer that hugs the ground and leaves higher elevations clear. In summer, fog typically builds during the day over the coast, then pours over the hills and through the Golden Gate, shrouding the Sunset District and other coastal areas in a dense gray mist while leaving other neighborhoods with blue skies.

Most rain falls between November and April. In summer, atmospheric circulation creates a cell of high pressure that deflects fronts and storms into the Pacific Northwest. In winter, this high-pressure cell moves south and allows storms in, bringing rain, sometimes for days on end.

FLORA AND FAUNA

As with the human population, much of the Bay Area's plant life originated elsewhere. The grasses that shroud the "golden hills" are mostly European wild oats, seeds of which stowed away in bags of wheat sent to Spanish missions. The eucalyptus trees that perfume many a park, campus and backyard were imported from Australia in the 1860s. Most palms in the Bay Area come from the Canary Islands and other places.

Indigenous features of the plant landscape include stately **live oaks**, which grow widely spaced on grassy hillsides. Coast redwoods, which live more than 2,000 years and grow to heights above 300ft, thrive near the ocean.

Also typical of Bay Area landscapes are dense thickets of **chaparral**, formed not of a single plant but of an association of native species. The shrubby plants grow during wet winters then dry out in late summer, a perfect fuel for brush fires that periodically sweep over the hills. The plants then grow back quickly from burls below ground level.

The Bay Area's salt marshes, mud flats, beaches, tidepools and baywaters are home to a vast array of native **wildlife** species. The rocky coastal areas harbor sea lions, seals and sea otters while dolphins and porpoises frolic offshore. Humpback, gray and blue whales and orcas swim by on annual migrations, and the region lies on the Pacific Flyway, a north–south route for migratory birds. The demise of wildlife habitats, thanks to urban development and a number of disastrous oil spills by passing tankers, has given rise to public and private organizations dedicated to preserving species at risk. The **San Francisco Bay National Wildlife Refuge Complex** administers seven refuges, including the 30,000-acre Don Edwards Refuge in South San Francisco Bay. **Año Nuevo State Reserve** in San Mateo County protects a rookery of northern elephant seals. Rescue organizations such as the Marin Headlands' **Marine Mammal Center** concentrate efforts on rehabilitating injured animals and returning them to the wild.

Legion of Honor

DOWNTOWN

Contrary to its laidback image, San Francisco has a bustling downtown area. The Financial District ranks among the largest business centers in the nation, and the city's retail heartbeat, Union Square, is packed with department stores and high-end boutiques. The elegant, Beaux Arts-style Civic Center draws city government workers by day and chicly clad concertgoers by evening. Other downtown neighborhoods offer their own distinct character and history. Chinatown teems with tiny temples, outdoor markets and dim sum restaurants; higher up the hill, Nob Hill retains its Old World charm and upper class cachet. To the north, lively North Beach boasts a history littered with Italian heritage and literary greats.

Highlights

1 Stroll down lively Chinatown's **Grant Avenue** (p65)

2 Explore the fine **Asian Art Museum** with an audio tour (p74)

3 Sip a cocktail with a view atop Nob Hill at **Top of the Mark** (p90)

4 Browse **City Lights Books** and lounge in a **North Beach cafe** (p95, p101)

5 Climb parrot-filled **Filbert Steps** to mural-adorned **Coit Tower** (p98, p100)

The Changing Face of Downtown

In 1846 Captain John Montgomery officially claimed the small settlement of Yerba Buena for the U.S., raising an American flag at Yerba Buena's central plaza. This plaza, later renamed Portsmouth Square after Montgomery's ship, now rests in the heart of San Francisco's downtown, on the border of Chinatown, the Financial District and North Beach. During the 19C California Gold Rush, these neighborhoods boomed, drawing thousands of treasure hunters who ventured up toward Sutter's Mill in search of gold.

The face of downtown changed drastically in 1906, when a massive earthquake and fire razed the district. By 1909, the area was largely reconstructed, with many of the new buildings showing off the Classical style. Today, Chinatown teems with ethnic eateries, old world pharmacies and outdoor produce markets. In North Beach, the flavors and fragrances of the neighborhood's Italian roots still predominate, as evidenced by dozens of well-patronized trattorias, cafes and delicatessens.

West of the Financial District and Chinatown, Nob Hill also changed after the 1906 disaster, with decimated mansions of San Francisco's elite replaced by posh hotels. Today, residential Nob Hill is peppered with upscale restaurants, apartment buildings, and several of the city's most historic hotels.

Retail and Civic Centers

The first place any self-respecting shopper heads in San Francisco is Union Square, the area bordering the formal park of the same name. Named on the eve of the Civil War, Union Square lies at the center of the city's ritziest retail district. The Westin St. Francis Hotel presides over its western edge, with upscale department stores Saks, Macy's and Neiman Marcus completing the square.

Up Market Street from Union Square, San Francisco's Civic Center remains the sole remnant of a 1905 plan to remake San Francisco according to the principles of the City Beautiful movement— replete with wide boulevards and grand monuments that borrowed heavily from the aesthetics of the then—contemporary Beaux Arts movement. Among the movement's crowning achievements, San Francisco's magnificent City Hall stands out with its sparkling gold-leaf dome. This area is also home to several of the city's grandest performance spaces and cultural institutions, including the San Francisco War Memorial and Performing Arts Center, the gleaming granite San Francisco Public Library, and the stellar Asian Art Museum.

Chinatown★★★

A teeming, colorful fusion of Cantonese market town and American Main Street, San Francisco's Chinatown spreads along the lower slope of Nob Hill overlooking the Financial District. One of the four largest Chinese settlements outside Asia (the others are in New York City, Toronto, and Vancouver), Chinatown ranks among North America's most densely populated neighborhoods. Over 100,000 people live in the 24-block core bounded by Broadway and Montgomery, California and Powell Streets. Most residents are immigrants who maintain their native culture. Chinatown is unique in that it also absorbs and refashions diverse American influences.

A BIT OF HISTORY

Among the thousands who flocked to California during the 1849 Gold Rush were Cantonese men intent on striking bonanzas and returning to China. Few bothered to learn English or assimilate Western culture. As China's ruling Manchu dynasty decayed through the 19C, however, and conditions worsened, ever-greater numbers of Chinese chose to settle in the American West.

By 1870 more than 63,000 Chinese, mostly men, were living in the U.S. In demand as laborers for construction projects, they built much of the western half of the first transcontinental railroad, pioneered the fishing industry on San Francisco Bay, and farmed California's farmlands. In many Western towns, Chinese entrepreneurs opened small businesses such as laundries, retail shops, and grocery stores.

As the premier point of entry for Asian immigrants, San Francisco harbored North America's oldest and largest Chinese community. Settlements formed around the city, but by the 1860s, most Chinese immigrants had established themselves along Sacramento Street a block south of Portsmouth Square. **Surviving Troubled Times** – Waves of

🚋 Powell-Hyde or Powell-Mason. 🚎 Bus 30–Stockton.

📖 **Info:** www.sanfrancisco chinatown.com.

▶ **Location:** Chinatown is bounded by Broadway, Montgomery, California and Powell Streets. To fully experience Chinatown's vibrant, intense character, explore on foot. Steep hills may be a challenge, but Grant Avenue and Stockton Street, the main thoroughfares, are largely flat. To explore in more depth, take a guided tour (℘415-982-8839; www. allaboutchinatown.com).

👥 **Kids:** The dragons, colorful floats, and firecrackers of the **Chinese New Year Festival and Parade** in late January–mid-February (☽see Calendar of Events).

🕐 **Timing:** Temples and businesses typically open after 10am, but Chinatown can be interesting any time of day. Visit Portsmouth Square before 8am to see locals practicing t'ai chi. Saturday morning is particularly busy, especially along Stockton Street.

🅿 **Parking:** Parking garages are at St. Mary's Square (433 Kearny St.; ℘415-434-4400; ✑$2.50-4/hr Mon–Fri, $1-2.50/hr Sat-Sun) and Portsmouth Square (733 Kearny St.; ℘415-982-6353; ✑$3/hr), yet because of Chinatown's proximity to buses and cable cars, we recommend public transportation.

☺ **Don't Miss:** A meal at one of Chinatown's restaurants.

Chinatown Temples

© Brigitta L. House / MICHELIN

Chinatown Temples

Among the most illuminating and evocative manifestations of Chinatown life are its many religious temples. Conventional Western scholarship may categorize Chinese religion as Confucianism, Taoism or Buddhism, but the truth is complex. Most Chinese adhere to elements of all three philosophies:

Confucianism is more an ancient state doctrine than a religion. Its prescribed rites constitute a symbolic pact upholding an ideal of harmonious social order and stability. Its hierarchy traditionally was headed by the emperor, with each member of society happily ensconced in his or her appropriate niche.

Taoism, a mystical religion, might be characterized as a way of organizing the enormous array of Chinese gods and natural forces into a formal system. Among the most popular Taoist deities worshipped in Chinatown temples are Guan Di, the god of warriors and poets, and Tin How (also known as Ma-Tsu), the Queen of Heaven.

Buddhism, carried into China from India more than 1,700 years ago, has been shaped over the centuries into a distinctively Chinese belief system, markedly different from traditional south Asian Buddhism. In China, a pantheon of different Buddhas and faithful disciples is worshiped. A less materialistic form of Chinese Buddhism is Ch'an, better known in the West by its Japanese name of Zen.

Since ancient times, the Chinese have paid reverence to their ancestors and propitiated the forces of nature through sacrifice and prayer. In every temple, worshipers can be seen offering sacrifices of fruit, rice wine, roast meats and flowers, burning incense to resident deities or to tablets inscribed with names of recently deceased relatives. After the spirits are thought to have consumed the essence of the sacrifice, the worshiper will remove the now-sanctified offering and freely partake of it at mealtime. Symbolic offerings of paper cars and houses, "cash" and even paper servants are sometimes burned in a temple furnace, by which means they are sent to deceased loved ones believed to be residing in the spirit world. The person sending the offering will often hit a drum announcing his or her sacrifice to the spirit.

Although Buddhist temples normally house only Buddha images, many Taoist temples freely mix Buddhist statues among figures of several deities. As long as beliefs do not interfere with social harmony—as long as the Confucian doctrine is upheld—the Chinese are very tolerant in matters of religion.

Visitors are welcome in most temples, though it may be necessary to ring a doorbell to gain admittance. Courtesy is expected; photography is not permitted. Contributions left in marked donation boxes are appreciated.

anti-Chinese sentiment swept the West after the economic depression of 1872. As bankruptcies erased jobs, tycoons bolstered profits by hiring Chinese workers at low wages. Mobs of unemployed men stormed Chinese communities, including San Francisco's Chinatown in 1877, beating (and sometimes killing) people and destroying property. Labor organizers pushed passage of the Chinese Exclusion Act of 1882, barring Chinese laborers from entering the U.S. The act prevented thousands of men already in the United States from sending for brides, thus preserving Chinatown's male-dominated society well into the 20C.

Chinese immigrants sought security in *tongs* ("associations" or "companies") whose memberships were usually based upon clan name or members' province of origin. These organizations often paid new arrivals' passage to San Francisco, assuming the roles of labor guild, insurance company, social club, legal advisor, protection agent and undertaker, in return for dues. A few tongs were little more than criminal gangs. By the late 19C, Chinatown had a villainous reputation as a haven for opium dens, gambling halls, and brothels. Violent tong wars erupted between fractions seeking to control profits. In an effort to restore order and to represent Chinese interests, men from the six most powerful tongs in 1882 agreed to form a confederation. Known as the **Chinese Six Companies**, the organization remains an active, if diminishing, force in modern Chinatown.

The repeal in 1943 of the Chinese Exclusion Act and a further relaxation of immigration laws in the 1960s heralded a new influx of immigrants from Hong Kong, China, and Southeast Asia. Families moved to other areas of the city. So many have settled in adjacent North Beach since the 1960s that sections of that neighborhood long known as "Little Italy," are now culturally an extension of Chinatown. Parts of the Richmond and Sunset Districts have also been transformed into "new" Chinatowns inhabited by wealthier, younger, and better-educated Chinese. Old Chinatown, however, remains the heart and soul of the far-flung Chinese community. Chinese from around the Bay Area flock here to shop, eat, and socialize in the lively markets, restaurants, bookstores, and cultural centers. Tourists come by the thousands to wander Grant Avenue, Stockton Street, and the warren of side streets between them, visiting temples and herb shops, dining in the many restaurants, and shopping for Chinese groceries, embroidered linens, artwork, jewelry and souvenirs.

WALKING TOUR
.7mi.

▶ Begin at the intersection of Bush St. & Grant Ave. and walk north.

Grant Avenue★★
The eight blocks of Grant Avenue between Bush Street and Broadway comprise Chinatown's principal thoroughfare for visitors. The street abounds in architectural chinoiserie—painted balconies, curved tile rooflines and predominantly red, green and yellow color schemes—applied during the 1920s and 30s to give the neighborhood an exotic cachet. Ceramic carp and dragons on the roof of the **Chinatown Gate** (*Grant*

Grant Avenue, Chinatown

© Peter Wrenn / Michelin

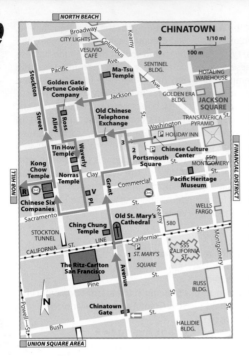

cathedral for Archdiocese of San Francisco.

The Gothic Revival structure was redesignated a church following construction of a new St. Mary's Cathedral on Van Ness Avenue in 1891. Made of brick and iron, the church was gutted by the great conflagration of 1906, but its stout walls survived. The somber inscription from Ecclesiastes on the exterior bell tower, "Son, observe the time and fly from evil," was reputedly aimed at the brothels that once flourished in the neighborhood. Historic photographs displayed in the vestibule offer fascinating views of 19C Chinatown. The church serves as the venue for popular noontime concerts of classical music *(year-round Tue 12.30pm;* ☞ *$5; for schedule* ℘*415-777-3211; www.noontimeconcerts.org).*

Across California Street from the cathedral lies St. Mary's Square, a small, serene park anchored by a steel and granite statue of **Sun Yat-sen (1)** (1938) by sculptor Beniamino Bufano. Sun visited San Francisco's Chinese community several times around the turn of the 19C to raise support to overthrow China's Manchu Dynasty and establish the Republic of China. The successful revolution took place in 1911.

◗ Return to Grant Ave. and continue north, turning right on Clay St.

Portsmouth Square★

Formerly the central plaza of the Anglo-Mexican settlement of Yerba Buena, this broad square is today Chinatown's most important outdoor gathering point. In 1846 Captain John Montgomery officially claimed Yerba Buena for the U.S. by raising the American flag above the plaza, later renamed for his ship. California's first public school opened here in April 1848, and the square was the site of Sam Brannan's announcement

Ave. at Bush St.) symbolize auspicious fortunes. Taiwan's government donated materials for the gateway, which was designed in 1970 by Clayton Lee. North of the gate, shops selling curios, souvenirs, jewelry, furniture, cameras and electronics draw visitors in droves, while hardware stores, banks, markets and small cafes cater to a local clientele. Numerous authentic Taoist, Buddhist and Confucianist temples are tucked away on upper floors behind unassuming doors throughout the neighborhood. Visitors are welcomed at the **Ching Chung Temple★** *(615 Grant Ave., 4th floor;* ◷*open daily;* ℘*415-433-2623),* where portraits of the founders of three Taoist sects distinguish the main altar.

Old St. Mary's Cathedral★

660 California St., at Grant Ave. ◷*Open Mon–Fri 7am–4.30pm, Sat 10am–6pm, Sun 8am–3.30pm.* ♿ ℘*415-288-3800. www.oldsaintmarys.org.*

The largest building in the state at the time of its dedication in 1854, this handsome Catholic church served as the

Chinatown Herb Shops

Along Stockton Street and the side streets leading down to Grant, visitors can find many traditional Chinese herb shops. These shops are recognizable for the collections prominently displayed in the front windows: bottled snakes, preserved ginseng roots that parody an almost human shape, medical charts of the human body, pieces of tree bark, elk horn, dried seahorse and other sundries. These are the stuff of an ancient Chinese system of pharmacology, a lore gathered by early Taoist monks and herbalists, chronicled, tested, and refined over thousands of years.

Entering any shop, visitors will find a counter backed by wooden cabinets with drawers containing hundreds of dried herbs and other medicinals. Most by far are vegetable in origin: ginkgo for tuberculosis, mulberry leaves for colds and headaches, sumac for laryngitis, loquat leaf for coughs, climbing dogbane for rheumatoid arthritis, winter cherry leaf for diabetes, Job's tears for lobar pneumonia. Among the items most exotic to Western medicine might be dried centipedes, a remedy for infantile convulsions, spasms, cramps, and lockjaw; dead silkworm for sore throats and headaches; snakeskin for abscesses; and decoction of silkworm cocoon to relieve exhaustion.

The herb most familiar to Westerners is ginseng, a root sliced and steeped to make a tea celebrated for its curative virtues. The finest examples of ginseng root grow wild in the mountains of north China and Korea, but these can be quite expensive and probably will not be casually displayed in the herbalist's shop. Less expensive grades of ginseng powders and teas, including a variety of American ginseng from Wisconsin, make popular gifts.

that gold had been discovered some 100 miles east of San Francisco. During the Gold Rush, Portsmouth Square served as center of the boomtown. As commercial activity shifted, Portsmouth Square was left on the periphery.

Today elderly men congregate in the square to socialize and play cards or Chinese chess. In the center of the square stands a **statue (2)** of the Goddess of Democracy, a somber memorial to the 1989 Tiananmen Square massacre in Beijing. On the north side stands a sailing-ship **monument (3)** to Robert Louis Stevenson, who enjoyed the square during his extended visit of 1879–80.

To the east, a pedestrian bridge leads across Kearny Street to the **Chinese Culture Center** (Hilton Hotel, 750 Kearny St., 3rd floor; ◷ open Tue–Fri 9am–6pm, Sat 10am–4pm; ☎415-986-1822; www.c-c-c. org), featuring temporary exhibitions of Chinese and Chinese-American art, programs on Chinese culture and heritage and musical performances.

▷ Leave the square and walk uphill on Washington St.

Old Chinese Telephone Exchange
743 Washington St.

The neighborhood's most exuberant example of chinoiserie rises in three graceful pagoda-like tiers above a glossy, red-pillared pediment. Now a branch of East West Bank, the one-story building was opened as the Chinatown Telephone Exchange in 1909 to serve the community's 800 telephones. Operators working the switchboards had to know how to speak Cantonese, Sze Yup and three other Chinese dialects, as well as English.

▶ Turn right on Grant Ave., walk one block and turn right on Jackson St. Walk half a block down the hill and turn left on Beckett street.

Ma-Tsu Temple of USA★

30 Beckett St. ⏱*Open daily 9am–5pm.* ✉*Donation requested.* ♿ ✆*415-986-8818.*

This bright, attractive temple honors the Queen of Heaven using her title as known in Guangdong and Taiwan. The central statue is guarded by figures of two ferocious warriors—the blue-faced Shun Feng Er ("Ear of Favorable Wind") on the left and the red-faced Chien Li Yen ("Eye of 1,000 Li") on the right—noted respectively for their prodigious powers of hearing and sight (a *li* is a unit of distance; hence the guards can detect evil from 1,000 *li.*). Giant puppets of the pair can be seen striding the streets, arms swinging widely and rhythmically, in the annual Chinese New Year Parade.

▶ Return to Jackson St. Turn right up the hill, across Grant Ave., to Ross Alley; turn left and continue to Washington St.

Jackson Street, Ross Alley and Washington Street between Grant Avenue and Stockton Street traverse a densely populated enclave of herbalists, jewelers, restaurants, small groceries and fragrant bakeries. These side streets retain the dark, intriguing ambience of old Chinatown. Many turn-of-late-19C tong war clashes occurred here, and **Ross Alley** is still known among old residents as "Lu Song Hang" or "Spanish Lane," a reference to Hispanic prostitutes in the alley's 19C brothels. Today you'll find a shop purveying shrines, lanterns and religious statuary; several clothing factories hum behind closed doors. Step inside the ever-popular **Golden Gate Fortune Cookie Company★** *(56 Ross Alley;* ⏱*open daily 9am–8pm;* ✆*415-781-3956),* where you'll see cookies being baked and stuffed with "fortunes" by workers seated at rotating griddle-ovens. You can pick up a bag of 40 cookies for $3 or, for 50 cents, snap a picture.

▶ Cross Washington St., walk a few steps downhill; turn right on Waverly Pl.

Waverly Place★

This two-block alley is dubbed "the Street of Painted Balconies" for the handsome chinoiserie gracing the buildings. The colors are symbolic—red stands for happiness, green for longevity, black for money, yellow for good fortune. Among older Chinatown residents, Waverly Place is known as "Tin How Miu Gai" or "Queen of Heaven Temple Street." From the street, pedestrians may hear drums booming from upper floors as youth groups practice lion-dance drills and other festival activities.

Tin How Temple

125 Waverly Pl., 4th floor. ⏱*Open daily.*
The present building of Chinatown's oldest temple dates from 1911. It is devoted to Tin How, a Chinese woman of Fujian Province (AD 960–987) now revered as the Queen of Heaven and protector of seafarers. Credited with the miraculous rescues of sailors, Tin How inspired a cult following her death. The worship came to the U.S. with immigrants who, of course, fell under her care when they crossed the Pacific Ocean. Red paper lanterns cover the ceiling in the incense-filled interior, above a wooden statue of Tin How.

Norras Temple★

109 Waverly Pl., 3rd floor. ⏱*Open daily 10am–4pm.* ✆*415-362-1993.*
A large, gilded statue of the Buddha surrounded by smaller, similar figures dominates this friendly hall of worship, the first purely Buddhist temple in the mainland U.S. when it opened in 1960. As in most Chinese temples, visitors can cast their fortunes by shaking a tube of bamboo slips until one jogs loose, falling to the floor. Take the slip to a temple attendant, who will either interpret your fortune according to the number or hand you a printed interpretation to have translated.

▷ Turn right on Sacramento St., walk uphill to Stockton St. and turn right.

Chinese Six Companies

843 Stockton St.

⚷ *Interior not open to the public.*
The Chinese Six Companies still wields influence among Chinatown's businesses. The building's colorful facade is one of Chinatown's most elaborate.

Kong Chow Temple★

855 Stockton St., 4th floor (elevator entrance to left of post office).
🕐*Open Mon–Sat 9am–4pm.*
The Kong Chow temple first opened on Pine St. in 1857. Among the original furnishings transferred to the present building (1977) are excellent examples of Chinese wood carving. At the main altar, the swarthy-faced statue with a black beard represents Guan Di, A figure seen all over Chinatown in shrines an shop windows. A general in the Three Kingdoms period (AD 220–280), Guan Di fought ferociously and loyally for his lord, a contender for the imperial throne. Killed by treachery, he was elevated into the Taoist pantheon, becoming patron saint of a host of disparate professions, including soldiers, poets, prostitutes, police and gangsters. The figure of Guan Di is flanked by his bearded warrior "brother" Zhang Fei and his gentler son, together symbolizing Guan Di's balanced devotion to both the civil government and the military.

▷ Turn left on Clay St. for one block.

Chinese Historical Society of America Museum (R)

965 Clay St., between Stockton and Powell Sts. 🕐*Open Tue–Fri noon–5pm, Sat 11am–5pm.* 🚫*Closed Jan 1, July 4, Dec 25 and Lunar New Year.* ⊜*$5.* ✆*415-391-1188. www.chsa.org.*
The Chinese Historical Society of America occupies a 1932 red-brick YWCA building designed by famed architect Julia Morgan. A pair of pagoda-like towers rise above a roofline crenellated with imported Chinese tiles, and a cast-stone arch with leaded glazing surmounts the entrance doors.
The main gallery tells the story of the Chinese in America with photographs and artifacts. Two other rooms have rotating art and history exhibits.

▷ Return to Stockton St. and continue north to Broadway.

Stockton Street★

The four blocks of Stockton Street between Clay Street and Broadway feature Chinatown's greatest concentration of markets. The street draws crowds of shoppers from all over the city, especially on weekend mornings. Savory Chinese specialties like pressed or roast duck or barbecued pork and soy-sauce chickens hang in the windows. Mounds of vegetables and fruits (including the aromatic durian), displayed on sidewalk stands, vie for space with vendors peddling live poultry or fresh produce. Market cries and vigorous bargaining contribute to the colorful but amiable havoc.

ADDRESSES

SHOPPING

Ten Ren Tea Co. – *949 Grant Ave.* 🕐*Open daily 9am–9pm.* ✆*415-362-0656. www. tenren.com.* The oldest and largest U.S. outlet of a Taiwan-based tea empire, this purveyor sells loose tea in metal canisters and painted boxes; hot, steaming cups; and cold, sweet "bubble tea." Loose tea costs up to $200 a pound (for high-quality ginseng root)—pricey, but it takes 70,000 young leaves to make a pound of top-grade leaf tea.

Clarion Music Center – *816 Sacramento St. at Waverly Pl. Open Mon–Fri 11am–6pm, Sat 9am–5pm.* ✆*415-391-1317. www.clarion music.com.* A mecca for world-music lovers, this living museum displays and sells such folk instruments as the Chinese *yangqin* and *gu zheng,* Australian didgeridoo, Japanese koto, Bolivian panpipes, thumb drums, and singing bowls. For inspiration and instruction, choose from an array of CDs and books, or take a class.

Civic Center★

San Francisco's center of government occupies one of the finest groups of Beaux-Arts-style buildings in the U.S.. The grandly designed complex still reflects the tenets of the turn-of-the-century "City Beautiful" urban planning movement, updated with sympathetic contemporary constructions.

A BIT OF HISTORY

San Francisco's present-day Civic Center did not materialize until the early 20C, fairly late in the city's life. In order to provide a proper home for the city's government, which through the mid-19C had occupied a series of buildings around Portsmouth Square, a new city hall was planned in the vicinity of Civic Center in 1872. Endemic corruption, within both the construction industry and the city government, delayed completion for more than 25 years and vastly inflated the cost of the structure. When the great 1906 earthquake struck, the building was damaged beyond repair.

In the aftermath of the fire an idealistic group of businessmen and politicians embarked upon an ambitious scheme to create a suitable new center for the city's political and cultural life. The group of buildings that now forms the core of Civic Center was erected over the course of 20 years, beginning in 1913. First completed was the Civic Auditorium for the Panama-Pacific International Exposition of 1915. The new City Hall opened at the end of 1915, while a stately main library and federal office buildings followed soon after. The historic portion of the complex was completed with the opening of the Veterans Building and the War Memorial Opera House in 1932.

United Nations Birthplace – In 1945, the United Nations Conference on International Organization convened in the War Memorial Opera House. The United Nations Charter was signed in the Veterans Building's Herbst Theatre on June 26. Throughout subsequent decades, the Civic Center remained a

Bus 5–Fulton, 19–Polk or 47–Van Ness; all streetcars Civic Center station.
Civic Center station.
Info: 415-391-2000. www.sanfrancisco.travel.
Location: Civic Center is located within the triangle of Market Street, Franklin Street, and Golden Gate Avenue.
Kids: The interactive, all-ages AsiaAlive program at the Asian Art Museum lets participants try their hand Asian crafts like Afghan rug weaving and Chinese calligraphy.
Timing: Civic Center can be seen in half a day; allow an additional half-day for the Asian Art Museum. Morning is a good time to visit, followed by lunch or shopping in Hayes Valley.
Parking: The Civic Center Plaza Garage is located between Polk, Larkin, Grove and McAllister Sts; enter on McAllister (*$2.50/hr; 415-863-1537).
Don't Miss: The Asian Art Museum and the City Hall rotunda.

locus of administration, as well as home to such cultural institutions as the Louise M. Davies Symphony Hall and the War Memorial Opera House.

Although the San Francisco Museum of Modern Art moved to Yerba Buena Gardens in 1995, the area was boosted by the opening of the new Main Library-the SMOMA Research Libraryin 1996, the renovation of City Hall in 1995–99, and the opening of the Asian Art Museum in the Old Main Library in 2003. A new, architecturally distinctive and energy-efficient federal building at Seventh and Mission Streets is expected to foster development along the Market Street corridor.

The City Beautiful

Around the turn of the 19C, civic leaders across the country joined forces to improve the quality of life in American cities. This concerted effort, known as the City Beautiful movement, brought together business leaders, politicians and architects who worked to make urban areas better places to live and work. Their efforts included such seemingly mundane projects as widening streets, installing street lights and building sewer systems, but also encompassed more singularly aesthetic goals.

The most prominent designer associated with the City Beautiful movement was Chicago architect **Daniel Burnham**, who was hired by a group of San Francisco businessmen to develop a plan that would improve the image and efficiency of the city. Over the course of two years Burnham made many trips to the city, spending untold hours in a cabin on the slope of Twin Peaks, sketching and studying the topography and character of the city below. With help from local architect Willis Polk, in 1905 he presented what became known as the **Burnham Plan**, an ambitious proposal for wide boulevards, traffic circles with streets radiating outward, and public monuments much like those of Washington DC or Paris.

The Burnham Plan was adopted with strong support, and the leveling of the city by the great earthquake and fire of 1906 seemed to offer a clean slate on which to implement it. However, concerns for private property rights and the urgency of rebuilding homes and businesses outweighed civic altruism, and reconstruction of the city in the aftermath of the disaster occurred along the old street grid. Construction of Civic Center proceeded more slowly, and today the ensemble stands as San Francisco's only realization of Burnham's grand plan.

WALKING TOUR

.8mi.

◗ Begin at the intersection of Market, Jones and McAllister Sts.

Hibernia Bank★

1 Jones St.

⚯ *Interior not open to the public.*

This long-neglected Beaux-Arts bank (1892, Albert Pissis) ranks among the city's most significant small buildings. The stately main entrance turns the corner of Jones and McAllister Streets with an ornate copper-domed vestibule.

◗ Walk southwest along Market St.

United Nations Plaza★

Linking Market Street with Civic Center, this plaza (1980, Lawrence Halprin) commemorates the 1945 founding of the United Nations. Leading west from Market Street along the Fulton Street pedestrian mall, the plaza is bordered by parallel rows of square columns bearing names of United Nations member countries and the years in which each joined. Brass inlays in the pavement mark the site's longitude and latitude; a large fountain forms a striking centerpiece. A **sculpture (1)** of Simón Bolívar on a horse dominates the west end.

◗ Walk south on Hyde St. to Market St.

Orpheum Theatre★

1192 Market St. (at Hyde & Eighth Sts.)
♿ ☎*415-551-2000. www.shnsf.com.*
Originally designed (1926, B. Marcus Priteca) to showcase vaudeville acts, this theater evokes a glorified, pre-Reformation Spain. The intricate facade is patterned after a 13C Léon cathedral, the high vaulted lobby ceiling is reminiscent of the Alhambras. The 2,200-seat theater housed the 1970 production of *Hair*. Meticulously restored in 1997–98, it continues to stage such Broadway hits as *Hairspray* and *Wicked*.

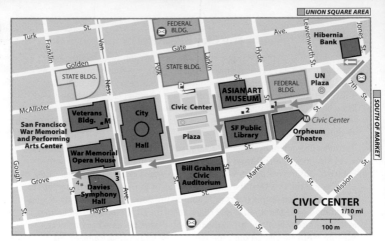

▶ Walk back to the Fulton St. Mall and turn left.

James Lick Memorial (2)

A gift of the James Lick Trust, established by an eccentric mid-19C developer, the work (1894, Frank Happersberger) depicts Eureka standing atop a 30ft central column.

▶ Turn right on Larkin St.

Asian Art Museum★★★

see p 74

▶ Turn left on Larkin St.

San Francisco Public Library★

100 Larkin St. Open Mon 10am–6pm, Tue–Thu 9am–8pm, Fri noon–6pm, Sat 10am–6pm and Sun noon–5pm. Closed major holidays. ✕♿🅿 ☎415-557-4400. http://sfpl.org.
San Francisco's $137 million Main Library (1996, James Ingo Freed and Cathy Simon) blends a contemporary take on Civic Center architecture with high technology. The gleaming granite exterior is from the same quarry that provided stone for early Civic Center structures. The main facade reveals an updated version of Beaux-Arts classicism, while the Hyde Street elevation has an angular, contemporary face. The seven-story interior, replete with catwalk bridges, artworks and an asymmetrical skylit atrium, boasts multimedia computers,

access to electronic databases, as well as books and magazines. Changing displays of art and literature are found in the Jewett Exhibition Gallery.

▶ Cross Larkin & Grove Sts.

Bill Graham Civic Auditorium

99 Grove St. www.billgrahamcivic.com.
Originally completed for the 1915 Panama-Pacific International Exposition, the Civic Auditorium (Arthur Brown, Jr.) has undergone many remodelings and name changes, most recently in memory of popular music promoter Bill Graham, who died in 1992. Banners and flags frequently bedeck the arcade of stone arches that form the Grove Street facade overlooking Civic Center Plaza. The 7,000-seat, four-story Beaux-Arts auditorium has long been one of the city's prime performance and event venues.

▶ Cross Grove and Polk Sts. to City Hall.

City Hall★★

1 Dr. Carlton B. Goodlett Pl. (bounded by Grove, McAllister & Polk Sts. and Van Ness Ave.). Open Mon–Fri 8am–8pm. Closed major holidays. ✍Guided tours Mon–Fri 10am, noon and 2pm. ♿🅿 ☎415-554-6139. www.sfgsa.org.
Testament to San Francisco's civic pride, this monumental Beaux-Arts edifice, crowned by a magnificent dome, is often considered San Francisco's most beauti-

ful building. Designed by Arthur Brown, Jr., a graduate of the École des Beaux Arts in Paris, the building was completed in 1915 under the stewardship of populist mayor James Rolph, who vowed to stamp out the corruption that contributed to the first City Hall's demise.

The massive four-story building covers two city blocks. Its splendid dome, trimmed with gold leaf, rises to a height of 307ft, about 13ft taller than the U.S. Capitol Building in Washington DC. On the Van Ness Avenue facade, handsome Atlas-like telamones support the entrance. Doric pillars and colonnades along the porticoes, facades and dome reinforce the Classical idiom.

Damaged in the Loma Prieta earthquake of 1989, the grand edifice closed in 1995 for $300 million of seismic retrofitting and historic restoration. It reopened in 1999 floating upon 600 "base isolators" (rubber and steel discs) beneath the building that dissipate motion.

Inside, a grand ceremonial marble staircase ascends to a 181ft open rotunda, its east-facing section flanked by city government offices. The mayor's office is beneath the central pediment on the Polk Street facade, with a balcony facing east onto Civic Center Plaza. Two grand public courts with marble walls extend from the rotunda.

To the east of City Hall lies **Civic Center Plaza**, once the site of rallies, demonstrations and fiery speeches. The broad, beautifully proportioned space has been restored to its original 1912 design.

▷ Continue west on Grove St. Cross Van Ness Ave. and walk north.

San Francisco War Memorial and Performing Arts Center★★

Visit by guided tour only (see Louise M. Davies Symphony Hall). Closed major holidays. ✕ ᕦ ℰ415-552-8338 (see Entertainment).

Flanking a formal courtyard designed by Thomas Church, these twin structures erected in memory of San Francisco's war dead served for decades as the city's center for the performing arts.

War Memorial Opera House
301 Van Ness Ave.

The first city-owned opera house in the U (1932, Arthur Brown, Jr.) hosted the plenary sessions that led to the establishment of the UN in 1945. The San Francisco Opera and San Francisco Ballet perform here in an elegantly appointed 3,176-seat auditorium. The proscenium, graced by Edgar Walter's gilded relief sculptures of two Amazons astride horses, is backed by a golden brocatelle curtain.

Veterans Building
401 Van Ness Ave.

This structure is home to city government offices and the intimate 928-seat **Herbst Theatre**. The **San Francisco Arts Commission Gallery** (*open Wed–Sat noon–5pm; ℰ415-554-6080; www.sfartscommission.org*) showcases work by local artists.

Beneath fourth-story skylights is the **Museum of Performance and Design (M)** (*open Wed–Sat 1–5pm; library open only Wed and last Sat of month; ᕦ ℰ415-255-4800; www.muse-sf.org*). This nonprofit gallery and library presents exhibits on the city's arts heritage, from Barbary Coast bawdy houses to the present. A permanent research collection preserves news clippings, playbills and other items documenting the diverse history of Bay Area theater with

City Hall

© Brigitta L. House / MICHELIN

a focus on influential local artists such as Lew Christensen and Isadora Duncan.

▶ Return to Grove St.

Louise M. Davies Symphony Hall

Van Ness Ave. and Grove St. ☜Visit by guided tour only, Mon 10am–2pm. ☜$5 (includes tour of War Memorial Opera House and Herbst Theatre). ♿🅿️☎415-552-8338 (tours); ☎415-864-6000 (tickets). www.sfsymphony.org.

In contrast to the Beaux-Arts buildings of Civic Center, this modern structure (1980, Edward Bassett) features a curving glass facade that reveals the lobby areas of the 2,743 seat hall. It is home to the San Francisco Symphony. The elegant bronze sculpture *Large Four Piece Reclining Figure* (3) (1973) at the entrance is by Henry Moore. Fletcher Benton's *Balanced Unbalanced T* (4) (1981) faces Franklin Street from Goldman terrace.

ASIAN ART MUSEUM★★★

200 Larkin St. between McAllister & Fulton Sts. ◷Open Tue–Sun 10am–5pm (Feb–Sept Thu until 9pm). ◷Closed Jan 1, Thanksgiving Day, Dec 25. ☜$12 (free 1st Sun of the month). ☜Free guided and self-guided audio tours available. ✕♿ ☎415-581-3500. www.asianart.org.

The Asian Art Museum owns the country's finest collection of Asian art. The 18,000 works spanning 6,000 years include art from China, Japan, Korea, India, Southeast Asia and the Himalayas.

A BIT OF HISTORY

The museum's founder, **Avery Brundage** (1887–1975), represented the U.S. in the decathlon during the 1912 Olympics in Stockholm, Sweden, and enjoyed a prosperous engineering career before being appointed to the International Olympic Committee in the 1920s.

During his travels he became fascinated by East Asian cultures, adopted a Taoist philosophy, and collected Japanese woodblock prints and netsuke—carved bone toggles used to fasten kimono sashes. In the 1930s his collections expanded to 3,000-year-old Chinese bronzes, Chinese ceramics and objects from Korea, Southeast Asia, India and the Middle East.

In the 1950s Brundage began to search for a permanent museum for his collection of 5,000 pieces. Believing his museum would be a "bridge of international knowledge and respect," he selected San Francisco as a location and presented the city part of his collection in 1959. The Asian Art Museum opened in the de Young Museum in Golden Gate Park in 1966 (☜*see Golden Gate Park*).

Glazed earthenware camel with Tang-era coloring (690-750), Asian Art Museum

© Daniella Nowitz / Apa Publications

Highlights of the Chinese Dynasties

Neolithic Period (c. 5000–16C BC): Regional cultures emerge, with distinct craft traditions in clay, stone, bone, basketry and textiles.

Shang Dynasty (1122–1028 BC): Transition to Bronze Age is marked by the rise of cities and rival clans. Remarkable piece-mold technique is invented for casting shapely bronze vessels.

Zhou Dynasty (1122–256 BC): Prosperity during unsettled era of state-making creates a market for objects of extreme technical refinement and splendor.

Qin Dynasty (221–206 BC): Short-lived dynasty marks beginnings of imperial China; the Great Wall is unified and a common script is established.

Han Dynasty (206 BC–AD 220): Major dynasty forges a single Chinese nation and imposes a long period of peace marked by expansion and the coming of Buddhism. Prosperity encourages trade along the Silk Road, bringing in foreign influences. The decorative dragon becomes prominent, along with layered and inlaid bronzework.

Six Dynasties (AD 317–589): Empire splits into rival states.

Sui Dynasty (AD 581–618): Empire is reunited; Grand Canal is built. Potters improve glazing techniques.

Tang Dynasty (AD 618–907): Expansive dynasty blossoms into powerful nation, open to foreign trade and spreading Chinese influence, especially to Japan. Aristocratic burial rites are increasingly elaborate; tomb furnishings proliferate in quality and quantity. Buddhism flourishes. AD 907–1125: Empire breaks down into individual states, including the northern **Liao dynasty** (937–1125).

Song Dynasty (AD 960–1279): Humanistic age of extreme aesthetic richness is renowned for fine and varied ceramics and painting. Nomads establish **Jin dynasty** (1115–1234) in the north, but the court moves south to Hangzhou and continues to govern as a sub-dynasty known as the **Southern Song** (1217–1279).

Yuan Dynasty (AD 1279–1368): Mongol dynasty favors blue-and-white porcelains to trade with Islamic nations.

Ming Dynasty (AD 1368–1644): Return to native rule is a classic age of blue-and-white wares.

Qing Dynasty (AD 1644–1911): Period of foreign rule under Manchus features ceramics of brilliant color and eggshell translucency. Contact with West increases.

Following Brundage's death in 1975, it continued to acquire Asian artwork.

A New Home – The museum quickly outgrew its home. After the 1989 Loma Prieta earthquake inflicted structural damage on the building, the museum board decided to move to the Beaux-Arts-style former main library (1916) at Civic Center. Italian architect Gae Aulenti, known for Paris' stunning Musée d'Orsay, designed the $160 million renovation, preserving the original marble staircase, columned loggia and great hall, while adding modern elements.

VISIT

The 2,500 works on display are arranged geographically, broadly tracing Buddhism's spread through Asia. Begin in the third-floor South Asia galleries and proceed through the exhibits down to the second-floor Japanese collection. An authentic Japanese tea room hosts occasional traditional tea ceremonies (check website for upcoming events). Tours depart from the Information Desk; check at the desk for the day's schedule. *Works are regularly rotated; not all pieces discussed here will be on view.*

South Asian Art★★
3rd floor

The collection of art from India, Pakistan, Bangladesh and Sri Lanka boasts a wealth of religious statuary, carved 0artists' prints of British India (c. 1780–1910). The Gandhara style developed in what is now southern Afghanistan and northern Pakistan. At the crossroads between East and West, its sculpture reflects a Hellenistic and Roman style of carving, illustrated by a splendid rendition of a 2C–3C Bodhisattva.

Outstanding are eight fragments of **friezes** depicting the life of Shakyamuni, the Indian prince who became the Buddha. Another prize holding is the **silver elephant throne★★** made in India c. 1870–1920.

Art of the Persian World and West Asia
3rd floor

This small gallery displays objects from present-day Iran, Iraq, Afghanistan, Turkmenistan and Uzbekistan. The works span 6,000 years from prehistoric through Islamic medieval periods. Particularly fine are the Luristani bronzes (c. 1000–650 BC) and ceramics from the 15C Timurid dynasty of Tamerlane.

Southeast Asian Art★
3rd floor

The collection comprises more than 500 pieces from Thailand, Burma, Laos, Cambodia, Indonesia, Vietnam, Malaysia and the Philippines). Sculptures constitute much of the collection. Also included are Thai ceramics, textiles (especially Thai and Lao silks), weaponry (highlighted by sinuous gilt *krises*, Malay-Indonesian daggers) jewelry and manuscripts. The vivid set of nearly 200 Indonesian rod **puppets★★** is rare and beautiful.

Tibetan and Himalayan Art★
3rd floor

This fascinating gallery contains about 300 items from Nepal, Tibet, Mongolia and Bhutan, largely religious art including scriptures and gilt bronze sculptures of Hindu and Buddhist gods. The collection of brilliantly painted *thangkas* (Nepalese and Tibetan scroll paintings) is one of the country's largest.

Hindu and Buddhist subjects coexist peacefully in vivid Nepalese paintings. Spectacular metalwork shrines produced by Newar artisans from the 8C–19C are inlaid with semiprecious stones.

Tibetan artworks, with terrifying and beautiful imagery, are unique expressions of Buddhism. Ritual implements are made of metal, gems, and human bone. Most common are the bell *(drilbu)* and thunderbolt *(dorje)*, respectively representing the feminine feature of wisdom and male feature of skillful means. Bhutan is renowned for textiles woven in cotton, wool and silk. Striped patterns differ between households.

Chinese Art★★★
3rd and 2nd floors

Comprising over half the museum's holdings, the Chinese collection embraces bronzes, sculptures, paintings, textiles and decorative artworks. The museum's oldest pot, a small earthenware **bottle** from the Yangshou culture, dates from 4800–3600 BC. **Oracle bones**, created by priests to divine the future, the first evidence of written language in China. Neolithic artisans produced **jades** in a doughnut shape called *bi*, still a popular finished shape for jade. Harder than steel, jade was thought to have a life-preserving property.

Shang dynasty bronzes, made for tomb offerings, include three-legged pots called *ding,* decorated with spirals and monster heads. A highlight is a rhinoceros-shaped **ritual vessel★★** (12C BC). Depleting bronze resources caused the Han dynasty government to widely ban the ritual bronzes in tombs, resulting in use of pottery. Stoneware and lacquerware developed during this era; look for China's oldest-known (AD 1) **lacquer vessel** with a maker's mark.

Indian influences permeate early works of Chinese Buddhist art. Among them is the earliest known Chinese **Buddha image★★★** (AD 338), a gilt bronze representation of the Indian prince who became the Buddha. The worldly

History of Japan

Prehistoric Age (c. 12,000 BC–AD 552): Contact with China and Korea after c. 300 BC brings new technologies to pottery; metal tools and bronze bells (dotaku) develop. In **Kofun Period** (AD 250–552), imperial Japan takes form.

Asuka to Nara Periods (552–710): Buddhism enters Japan from China via Korea. Along with religious influences, Japan imports Chinese writing, tea and styles of architecture, sculpture and painting.

Heian Period (794–1185): Capital moves from Nara to Heian-kyo (now Kyoto).

Kamakura Period (1185–1333): Rise of the warrior class of samurai. Zen (a Buddhist sect encouraging intellectual spiritualism based on meditation) arrives from southern China. The arts and the tea ceremony become secularized.

Muromachi Period (1333–1573): Under strong shogunate rule, a flourishing of Zen—and reaction against it—infuses the arts, particularly painting and the tea ceremony.

Momoyama Period (1573–1615): Warlords battle for control of Japan while Western traders and missionaries make their first landings on the Japanese coast.

Edo Period (1615–1868): The shogun Tokugawa Ieyasu moves the capital to Tokyo and seals the country from foreign arrivals; a strict class structure (samurai, farmers, craftsmen and merchants) is established. Ensuing prosperity allows the diffusion of art through a broad swath of society.

Meiji Period (1868–1912): Following the 1853–54 visit of U.S. Commodore Matthew Perry, Japan is compelled to abandon isolationist policies and open trade with the U.S. and Europe. Modernization becomes paramount after a new imperial government overthrows the weakening Tokugawa shogunate.

confidence of the Tang dynasty encouraged an appreciation of simplicity, exemplified by the draperies on Buddhist images. Their cultural dynamism also shows in secular works such as the **sancai tomb figures**—three-color ceramic statues depicting horses, Bactrian camels and foreign traders. They also developed true porcelain (a hard, white ceramic of kaolin clay) and cobalt-blue glazes.

Ceramics peaked during the Song dynasty with the development of green celadon glazes, light-blue Jun ware and the opaque, glassy, blue-green glaze of Longquan ware. During this dynasty, a rougher form of pottery was introduced to Japan, carried from southern Chinese monasteries by Japanese monks.

In the Yuan dynasty, potters made glazes thicker and more opaque by adding kaolin clay. The Ming dynasty is noted for the proliferation of glazing and decorating techniques, and five-color ware. Western tastes were profoundly influenced by blue-and-white ware exported from the late Ming dynasty onward.

Unlike post-Renaissance art from the West, which relies on a fixed perspective, Chinese (and Japanese) **landscape painting** traditionally employs a "floating" perspective that invites the eye to enter the painting and to move from feature to feature, promoting meditation. The museum's broad collection focuses on Ming and Qing masters and includes monumental landscapes and still-life scrolls from the 13C onward.

Korean Art★
2nd floor

The 500 objects of the Korean collection include hanging scrolls, stone-ware ceramics from the Three Kingdoms and United Silla periods (57 BC–AD 935), gold jewelry, ash-glazed funerary pottery and celadon-glazed vessels from the Koryo period (AD 918–1392). Korean potters produced many unique ceramic forms, including gourd-shaped bottles with red-pigment celadon glaze. Two slate **daggers** (c. 500–600 BC) are the museum's oldest Korean artifacts. Important Buddhist objects include sculptures,

Seated Buddha, Asian Art Museum

© Daniella Nowitz / Apa Publications

bronze vessels, paintings, lacquerware and furniture. A gilt bronze sculpture of *Amitabha Buddha* (8C) is the largest of such quality in a Western collection. Exceptional portraits include *Buddha Amitabha and Eight Great Bodhisattvas* (14C) and *A King of Hell* (16C).

Japanese Art★★
2nd floor

With more than 4,200 objects, the museum's Japanese holdings make up the most comprehensive collection of Japanese art in the U.S. Highlights are screens and scrolls, ceramics, bronzes, religious sculptures, swords and decorative arts. The museum also has splendid collections of *netsuke* miniatures in horn and ivory, and Japanese calligraphy representing different styles and formats from the 12C to the 20C.

Among prehistoric treasures are earthenware pottery, bronze *dotaku* (bells), mirrors and weapons, and a wealth of *haniwa* (retaining posts for burial mounds) in the shapes of animals, houses, boats and people. Sculptures of the Nara to Meiji periods were made of wood, bronze and dry-lacquer.

Buddhist sculpture and painting reached their zenith during the Kamakura period, as the arrival of Zen inspired artistic expression characterized in painting by monotone landscapes. The demand for **samurai swords** pushed the manufacture of Japanese steel to a high art. Nearly 200 screens (only a handful on display at any time) represent major schools and styles of painting. Among them are the colorful Yamato-e style, monochrome Kanga landscapes, and the abstract, minimalist Haboku (splashed ink) style, a technique expressive of Zen spontaneity. By the middle of the Muromachi period, nonreligious painters of the Kano school—which rejected the narrative traditions of painting to emphasize poetic simplicity of image and line—plied their arts on large screens that were used for blocking drafts and brightening dark castles. A traditional **Japanese tea ceremony exhibit** displays roughly formed Temmoku teaware—a reflection of the secular Japanese appreciation for *wabi* (poverty) and *sabi* (rusticity).

Many painting schools flourished during the Edo period, as did lacquerware, ceramics and stage drama. Highly decorated items from this era include *inro* (small cases for personal effects), a fine *koto* (13-stringed zither), an exquisitely lacquered palanquin, and woodblock prints. The Meiji period enriched contact between Japanese artists and the outside world, reaffirming traditional arts and introducing new themes, styles and techniques.

ADDRESSES

SHOPPING

Hayes Valley – *Hayes St. between Franklin and Laguna Sts. www.hayesvalley online.com.* A few blocks west of Civic Center, artsy Hayes Valley is a great place to eat and shop, with a number of upscale clothing and furniture boutiques and acclaimed restaurants serving everything from sushi to schnitzel. Reservations may be necessary on nights when the symphony or opera performs.

Heart of the City Farmers' Market – *UN Plaza (Market St. between Seventh and Eighth Sts.). Open Sun 7am–5pm, Wed 7am–5.30pm and Fri 7am–2.30pm.* ☏*415-558-9455.* Fresh produce, cut flowers, potted plants, organic meats, candied nuts, kettlecorn, mushrooms and baked goods. You can also buy a lunch of Indian takeout, waffles or Middle Eastern cuisine.

Financial District★★

This cacophonous forest of skyscraping steel, glass, and stone represents the heart of the city's financial community. Though modern in appearance, the district stands on the city's historic core and includes some of San Francisco's oldest and most architecturally significant buildings.

A BIT OF HISTORY

While San Francisco was born in 1776 at Mission Dolores and The Presidio, the roots of the modern downtown lie beneath the Financial District, where the village of Yerba Buena grew up in the early 1840s along what was then a sheltered bayfront. In 1846 U.S. forces occupied the town at the outbreak of the Mexican-American War, and the following year Yerba Buena's name was changed to San Francisco. Irish surveyor Jasper O'Farrell laid out a street grid, designating the muddy path along the waterfront as **Montgomery Street** in honor of the commander of the U.S. forces who took the village. O'Farrell traced Market Street at a diagonal to the already established downtown grid, then laid another grid at a competing angle south of Market Street.

Until 1848, the sleepy community served as a supply center for oceangoing vessels that periodically sailed into the bay. By late 1849, with the discovery of gold in the Sierra Nevada foothills, San Francisco boomed as the principal communication and supply conduit between the mining camps and the rest of the world. Dozens of vessels that sailed into the bay were abandoned by crews who jumped ship for the gold fields. Empty boats served as impromptu warehouses and hotels. Wharves extended east of Montgomery Street to deep-water anchorage; the intervening mud flats were filled in with sand, dredgings and ship carcasses until the waterfront reached the line of the modern Embar-

🚋 California Street. 🚎 Bus 1–California, 2–Clement, 3–Jackson, 4–Sutter, 5-Fulton, 6-Parnassus, 7-Haight,12–Folsom, 41–Union; all streetcars Embarcadero or Montgomery St. stations. 🚇 Embarcadero or Montgomery St. stations.

🛈 **Info:** www.sanfrancisco.travel.

▶ **Location:** The Financial District is concentrated in a roughly triangular area bounded by Kearny, Washington, and Market Sts.

👪 **Kids:** Children can hear the story of the Gold Rush from the seat of a stagecoach at the Wells Fargo History Museum.

🕐 **Timing:** The district is practically deserted at night and on weekends. Visit on a weekday to see it in full swing.

🅿 **Parking:** Garage parking, though plentiful, is expensive; it's best to use the many buses, streetcars or cable cars that serve the area, or try the parking garages in nearby Chinatown. If you do drive, be alert to parking signs, as street parking is prohibited along certain thoroughfares during rush hours.

☺ **Don't Miss:** The Transamerica Pyramid.

cadero. Today very little remains of the Gold Rush city.

Wall Street of the West – San Francisco's role as financial center of the West Coast was cemented by silver. The immense fortunes engendered by Nevada's Comstock Lode during the 1860s brought financial and commercial

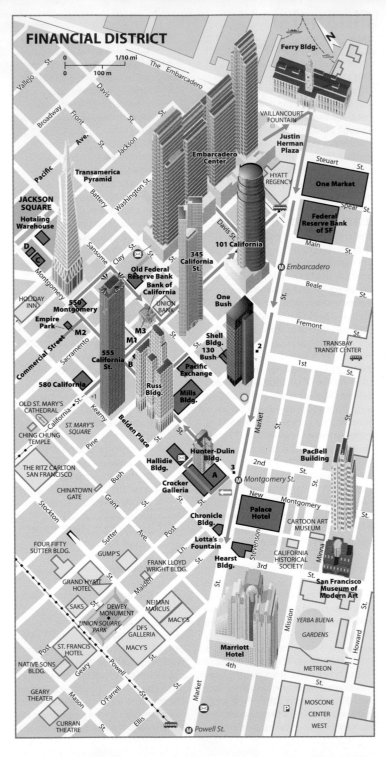

FINANCIAL DISTRICT

0   1/10 mi
0   100 m

The Embarcadero

Ferry Bldg.

N

Vallejo   St.

Davis

Broadway   Front   St.

Pacific   Ave.   St.   Jackson   St.

JACKSON SQUARE

Transamerica Pyramid

Embarcadero Center

VAILLANCOURT FOUNTAIN

Justin Herman Plaza

Hotaling Warehouse

Battery   Washington St.

HYATT REGENCY

Steuart   St.

One Market

Sansome   Clay   St.   St.

101 California

Davis St.

Main   St.

Federal Reserve Bank of SF

HOLIDAY INN

550 Montgomery

Old Federal Reserve Bank
Bank of California

Beale   St.

M Embarcadero

Empire Park

M2

Commercial   Street

M3
M1

Sacramento

555 California St.

UNION BANK

345 California St.

One Bush

Shell Bldg.
130 Bush

Fremont   St.

TRANSBAY TRANSIT CENTER

580 California

B

Russ Bldg.

Pacific Exchange

Mills Bldg.

2

1st   St.

M   Market   St.

OLD ST. MARY'S CATHEDRAL

*1

California   St.

Kearny   St.

Belden Place   St.

ST. MARY'S SQUARE

CHING CHUNG TEMPLE

Pine

THE RITZ CARLTON SAN FRANCISCO

Hallidie Bldg.

Hunter-Dulin Bldg.

A

3

PacBell Building

CHINATOWN GATE

Bush   St.

Crocker Galleria

M Montgomery St.

2nd   St.

Stockton

Grant

Sutter   Ave.   St.

Chronicle Bldg.

New   Montgomery

Palace Hotel

CARTOON ART MUSEUM

FOUR FIFTY SUTTER BLDG.

GUMP'S

FRANK LLOYD WRIGHT BLDG.

Post   Ln.

Lotta's Fountain

Stevenson

Hearst Bldg.

3rd

CALIFORNIA HISTORICAL SOCIETY

Minna   St.

GRAND HYATT HOTEL

SAKS   St.

Maiden   Ln.

NEIMAN MARCUS

San Francisco Museum of Modern Art

Mission   St.

DEWEY MONUMENT

UNION SQUARE PARK

DFS GALLERIA

MACY'S

YERBA BUENA GARDENS

Howard   St.

ST. FRANCIS HOTEL

MACY'S

NATIVE SONS BLDG.

Post   Geary   St.

Powell   St.

Marriott Hotel

4th

METREON

GEARY THEATER

Mason   O'Farrell   St.

Ellis   St.

P

MOSCONE CENTER WEST

CURRAN THEATRE

Market   St.

M Powell St.

80

enterprises and the new transcontinental railroad to the port city. The Financial District quickly emerged as the commercial nexus of the West.

The great earthquake and fire of 1906 razed the district, but within three years it had been largely rebuilt. Many new buildings, such as the Bank of California, epitomized "City Beautiful" ideals, employing Classical motifs to imply order and substance. Another burst of construction occurred in the late 1920s, when three office towers—the Hunter-Dulin, Russ and Shell Buildings—were completed, each with features common to the early Art Deco period, such as ornamental tops and setbacks on the upper stories. The Great Depression and World War II put a temporary halt to growth, but beginning in 1959 with the Crown Zellerbach building, dozens of skyscrapers rose. The construction wave culminated in the early 1970s with the city's two signature towers, the Bank of America Center (now 555 California Street) and the Transamerica Pyramid. The swift pace of wholesale change led preservationists to lobby for protection of many older buildings, and for strict limitations on the height and bulk of new ones. This movement resulted in the **Downtown Plan** of 1985, whose mandatory guidelines put a cap on the square footage of new construction allowed annually in the Financial District. As a result, most development now has shifted south of Market Street. Nonetheless, the hallowed crossing of Montgomery and California Streets remains the heart of financial San Francisco.

WALKING TOUR

2.1mi

◖ Begin at the intersection of Post, Montgomery & Market Sts.

One Montgomery Street (A)

This grand banking hall rose after the 1906 quake as the headquarters of First National Bank (later merged with Crocker Bank). The original section along Post Street, once a 14-story office tower,

was designed by Willis Polk; above that entrance an ornate cast-iron canopy is graced with figures that flank a shield, inscribed with the words "Systematic Saving is the Key to Success." The ornate interior **banking hall★**, now a Wells Fargo branch bank was completed by Charles Gottschalk in 1921. In the 1980s the building was incorporated into the Crocker Galleria.

From the corner, walk west on Post Street and enter the **Crocker Galleria★** (1983, Skidmore, Owings & Merrill), an small, elegant retail center that cuts through the middle of the block, with three tiers of commercial spaces topped by a barrel-vaulted glass roof (◷ *open Mon–Fri 10am–6pm, Sat 10am –5pm;* ✕ ⅌ ▣ ☏*415-393-1505; www. thecrockergalleria.com).*

Chocolatiers, bakeries, clothing boutiques and small eateries attract workers from adjacent office towers. From the upper level of the Galleria, a stairway leads to a tranquil **rooftop terrace** atop One Montgomery, a good place to enjoy a takeout lunch.

◖ Exit Crocker Galleria on Sutter St.

Hallidie Building★★
130–150 Sutter St.

One of San Francisco's most noteworthy works of architecture, the seven-story office block was designed by Willis Polk (1917) and named for Andrew Hallidie, inventor of the cable car. Because the facade is formed by a modular grid of glass panes hanging from a concrete frame, the building is considered the world's first glass-curtain-walled structure.

◖ Walk east on Sutter St.

Hunter-Dulin Building★
111 Sutter St.

This richly detailed building—completed in 1927 by the New York firm of Schultze and Weaver, designers of the Waldorf-Astoria Hotel—combines historical styles in a freewheeling manner. The main shaft incorporates Romanesque arches and cast-iron spandrels

Belden Place

A delightful surprise is this one-block-long alley, extending from Pine to Bush Streets just east of Kearny Street. A piece of Old World Europe transplanted to San Francisco, it is lined with small restaurants—French, Italian, Catalan, American—whose servers attend umbrella-covered tables, packed back-to-back, from one end of the lane to the other.

embellished with medallions of mythical figures. Near the top, a central tower rises four floors to a mansard roof. The elevator lobby boasts a painted, beamed ceiling and inlaid marble floor. Writer Dashiell Hammett set the office of his fictional hero, detective Sam Spade, here.

▷ Walk to corner of Sutter and Montgomery Sts. and turn left.

Mills Building
220 Montgomery St.
One of the few downtown structures to survive the earthquake and fire, this stately office building (1891) reflects the Chicago-school tenets of its designer, Daniel Burnham. The first in the city to be clad in decorative terra-cotta, the building was reconstructed after the quake by Willis Polk. A richly ornamented Romanesque archway forms the main entrance. The 22-story tower along the Bush Street facade was added in 1931 by Lewis Hobart. The environmental conservation group Sierra Club was established here in 1892.

Russ Building★
235 Montgomery St.
This 31-story Gothic Revival landmark (1927, George Kelham) fills an entire block of Montgomery Street. A two-story archway entrance leads to a striking **lobby**★ that features stone vaulting over cloister-like corridors, inlaid mosaic floors and elaborate elevator panels. Glass cases in the lobby display historic

model ships from building owner Walter Shorenstein's collection.

▷ Turn right at Pine St.

Pacific Exchange Building★
301 Pine St. at Sansome St.
⚬━*Interior not open to the public.*
Built in 1915 to house a U.S. Treasury office, this proud structure was enlarged with a tower in 1930. Ralph Stackpole, later a Coit Tower muralist, was commissioned to sculpt the remarkable pair of Social Realist–style monumental statues flanking the entrance.

▷ Backtrack to Montgomery St. and turn right.

555 California Street★★
555 California St. (enter via Montgomery St. plaza). ♿
The city's largest building, with 2 million square feet of office space, this 52-story, dark-red behemoth (1969, Skidmore, Owings & Merrill) competes with the Transamerica Pyramid. Its color comes from slabs of carnelian granite that wrap the central shaft rising 780ft from street level. The broad, open plaza along California Street is anchored by *Transcendence* **(1)** (1969, Masayuki Nagare), a dark, polished sculpture dubbed "The Banker's Heart." From the plaza, glance north at the post-Modern design of **580 California Street** (1987, Johnson and Burgee) with its 12 faceless, hooded human figures encircling the 20th floor.

▷ Cross Montgomery St. and walk east on California St.

Merchant's Exchange Building★ (B)
465 California St.
This 14-story office building (1903, Willis Polk) was the focal point of commerce in c. 1900 San Francisco. Signals from its rooftop belvedere announced the arrival of ships through the Golden Gate. Badly damaged in the 1906 Fire, it was quickly restored. Prolific architect Julia Morgan maintained an office on the 11th floor for most of her 46-year career.

From the Ionic columns at the entrance, walk though the barrel-vaulted elevator lobby to the commodious **Grain Exchange Hall★★**. On the walls are five murals by marine artist William Coulter. (⊶ *Closed to the public, but the hall may be included on some historical tours.*)

▷ Return to Montgomery St. and turn right.

♟♟ Wells Fargo History Museum★ (M1)

420 Montgomery St. ◷*Open Mon–Fri 9am–5pm.* ◷*Closed major holidays.* ♿ ☏*415-396-2619. www.wellsfargo history.com.*

Concord coaches of Wells Fargo & Co. began carrying freight and passengers in 1852. In this modern two-level gallery, Wells Fargo's inherent links to California history are told via photographs, documents, gold nuggets, bank notes and coins. Displays explore such topics as gold assaying, stagecoach robbery and telegraphing. Visitors can view a restored original coach and climb aboard a reconstructed one.

▷ Continue north on Montgomery St. and turn left onto Commercial St.

Commercial Street

Between Montgomery & Kearny Sts.
This narrow alley offers intriguing glimpses of early commercial San Francisco. Before landfill extended the waterfront to the Embarcadero, this block formed the foot of Long Wharf, which ran across the mud flats along the line of present-day Commercial Street to deep-water anchorage.

Look east to see the towers of Embarcadero Center framing a fine view of the top of the historic Ferry Building, which stands at what once was the end of the wharf.

Tiny **Empire Park** was renamed in 1999 to honor "Emperor" Joshua Norton, an eccentric bankrupted businessman who held court on Commercial Street for 20 years in the 1860s and 70s.

Pacific Heritage Museum (M2)

608 Commercial St. ◷*Open Tue–Sat 10am–4pm.* ◷*Closed major holidays and between major exhibitions.* ♿ ☏*415-399-1124.*

This small museum in a bank annex displays changing exhibits on artistic, cultural and economic themes related to peoples of the Pacific Rim. The building (1984, Skidmore, Owings & Merrill) incorporates the exterior walls and basement vaults of its 1877 predecessor, a U.S. Subtreasury building, itself erected on the site of San Francisco's first mint. Interior windows reveal original basement coin vaults from different perspectives.

▷ Backtrack to Montgomery St. and turn left. Cross Montgomery at Clay St.

The Barbary Coast Trail

Through downtown San Francisco, large bronze medallions embedded in sidewalks at street corners indicate the course of the Barbary Coast Trail. Extending 3.8mi from the Old Mint at Fifth and Mission Streets to Aquatic Park at the foot of Van Ness Avenue, this urban stroll cuts through Chinatown, Commercial Street, Jackson Square, North Beach and Fisherman's Wharf, en route linking dozens of historic sites and a handful of museums. It is a fine introduction to the Gold Rush heritage of San Francisco.

The brainchild of writer-historian Daniel Bacon, the privately sponsored trail officially opened in 1997 with implantation of the markers. (The city offered its assistance to the tourism-friendly venture by charging a $10,000 permit fee.) Walking-tour brochures, and Bacon's book, may be purchased at the **San Francisco Museum and Historical Society** (*☏415-775-1111; www.sfhistory.org*) and bookstores throughout the city.

550 Montgomery

550 Montgomery St. ○*Open Mon–Fri 9am–5pm.* ○*Closed major holidays.* ⬥ Within this building is a gem of a **banking hall★** clad in white marble. Egg-shaped semiprecious stones are embedded between window arches. Originally the main San Francisco office of the Bank of Italy, the building was declared a National Historic Landmark in 1982 as the birthplace of branch banking.

▶ Cross Clay St.

Transamerica Pyramid★★

600 Montgomery St. ⚫⚓Not open to the public. *www.transamerica.com.* In the years since its 1972 completion, this bold pyramid has come to symbolize San Francisco, a role similar to New York City's Empire State Building or Chicago's Willis (formerly Sears) Tower. Designed by William Pereira to house the headquarters of the Transamerica Corporation, a leasing and financial institution, the elegant 48-story spire is San Francisco's tallest building, rising 853ft from street level to the tip of its 212ft hollow lantern. Slanted sides reduce the extent of its shadow on surrounding structures. To the east, a peaceful grove with some 40 redwood trees forms a tranquil oasis.

▶ Walk east on Clay St. and turn right onto Sansome St.

Old Federal Reserve Bank★

400 Sansome St. This classical Beaux-Arts gem (1924, George Kelham) makes a dramatic first impression with its eight 25ft Ionic columns and the row of federal eagles perched above its portico. The building exemplifies San Francisco's banking-temple tradition. Artist Jules Guerin, chief muralist for the Panama-Pacific International Exposition of 1915, painted the impressive "Traders of the Adriatic" mural. In 1984 the Fed moved its district headquarters to Market Street.

▶ Cross Sacramento St. and continue south on Sansome St.

Bank of California★★

400 California St. Now Union Bank, this exquisite, classically proportioned bank (1907, Bliss and Faville) displays the resources put into rebuilding San Francisco after the 1906 Fire. A regal ceiling tops the magnificent banking hall, embellished with Corinthian pilasters. Stairs lead down to the tiny **Museum of Money of the American West (M3)** ▪▪ (○*open Mon–Fri 9am–4.30pm;* ○*closed major holidays*), displaying currency circulated during the 19C Gold Rush.

▶ Walk east on California St.

345 California Center★★

345 California St. Two angular towers linked by a glass-enclosed "sky bridge" cap this futuristic skyscraper (1987, Skidmore, Owings and Merrill). The building incorporated the facades of earlier historic structures, including the J. Harold Dollar Building (1920) and the Robert Dollar Building (1919), former steamship-line headquarters. The top 11 stories house the luxurious Mandarin Oriental Hotel *(main entrance at 222 Sansome St.).*

Transamerica Pyramid

© Phillip H. Coblentz / SFCVB

◯ Continue east on California St.

101 California Street★
101 California St.
This stepped-back glass silo (1982, Johnson and Burgee) has a three-story glass atrium that slices into the building's basement and acts as the main entrance. A triangular plaza runs south to Market Street.

◯ Turn left on Davis St. Cross Sacramento St.

Embarcadero Center★
Bounded by The Embarcadero and Clay, Sacramento & Battery Sts. ◷*Open daily 10am–5pm.* ✕♿🅿 ✆*415-772-0700. www.embarcaderocenter.com.*
The city's largest office and commercial complex, this series of four slab-like office towers (1982, John Portman and Assoc.) and the adjoining Hyatt Regency Hotel cover nearly 10 acres. A shopping center occupies its lower floors, running along historic Commercial Street; pedestrian bridges traverse cross streets to link the four structures. More than a dozen sculptures dot public spaces, among them works by Jean Dubuffet and Louise Nevelson.
Linked to the east tower (Four Embarcadero Center) by a pedestrian bridge, the Hyatt Regency (1973) boasts an asymmetrical 17-story **atrium★**. At the east end of the complex is brick-paved **Justin Herman Plaza** ♟♟, where the angular forms of Vaillancourt Fountain (1971) invite exploration.

◯ Cross The Embarcadero to the Ferry Building.

Ferry Building★★ –
♿*See THE EMBARCADERO.*

◯ Cross The Embarcadero to the south side of Market St.

One Market★
1 Market St.
Erected in stages, this office complex weds the facade of the original Southern Pacific Railroad headquarters (1916, Bliss and Faville) to a futuristically redesigned interior (1995, Cesar Pelli and Assoc.). The red brick fortress' belvedere is a focal point for California Street; the view along Market Street extends to Twin Peaks.

◯ Walk southwest on Market St. and cross Spear St.

♟♟ Federal Reserve Bank of San Francisco
101 Market St. 📷*Visit by guided tour (90 min) only; group tours Mon–Thu 9.30am and 1.30pm, reservation required.* ◷*Closed major holidays.* ♿ ✆*415-974-4133. www.frbsf.org.*
A vaulted loggia covers the bank's Market Street frontage, from which the bulk of the building (1982, Skidmore, Owings & Merrill) steps back in a series of terraces. In the lobby, the **The Fed Center★** exhibit offers entertaining lessons in basic economics. Using computer simulators, visitors adjust the rate of money growth, set interest rates or taxes, and gauge the effect on economy. A currency exhibit explores paper money from colonial to modern times.

◯ Continue southwest on Market St. to Battery St.

One of the city's most energetic pieces of public sculpture, the **Mechanics Monument (2)** *(median at Market and Battery Sts.)* vividly memorializes the craftsmen who built San Francisco. Created by Douglas Tilden in 1894, the sculpture was dedicated to Peter Donahue, owner of the city's first iron foundry.

◯ Cross Bush St., then Battery St. to its south side.

Shell Building★
100 Bush St., at Battery St.
Clad in light brown terra-cotta, this graceful Art Deco tower (1929, George Kelham) has a plain, 20-story central shaft that steps back to form a slender, richly ornamented top. Decorative motifs, including a large gilt shell over the entrance and shell forms covering

the parapets, represent the Shell Oil Corporation, which developed the property as its Western headquarters.

Next door, at **130 Bush Street** (1910, McDonald and Applegarth), stands one of the city's narrowest office buildings. Gothic-style ornamentation covers the 10-story, bow-fronted tower that measures just 20ft wide.

▷ Continue west on Bush St. one block and cross.

One Bush Plaza★

Originally the Crown Zellerbach Building, this distinctive tower is San Francisco's best example of International style architecture. Designed by Hertzka and Knowles/Skidmore, Owings and Merrill in 1959, modeled after the latter firm's influential Lever House in New York City, the pale green glass box stands on concrete stilts above a broad plaza. At its base is a sunken plaza anchored by a small, freestanding circular structure that houses a financial firm.

▷ Cross Sutter St., turn right on Market St. Walk southwest to Montgomery St.

An angelic female perched atop a stone shaft, above a miner waving an American flag, is the most prominent element of the **Native Sons of the Golden West Monument (3)**, which honors the establishment of California statehood in 1850. Sculpted by Douglas Tilden in 1897, the statue was originally erected farther down Market Street, then moved to Golden Gate Park before being placed at its present location, at a prominent intersection, in 1977.

▷ Cross Market St.

Palace Hotel★★

2 New Montgomery St. ✕♿🅿
☎*415-512-1111. www.sfpalace.com.*
This elegant hostelry figures prominently in San Francisco history. Constructed in 1875 by financier William Ralston as part of his plan to lure development south of Market Street, the Palace Hotel gained a reputation as the most opulent hotel in the West until it was gutted in the 1906 Fire. It reopened in 1909 with great fanfare. Rivaling the Fairmont Hotel in sophistication and luxury, the new Palace quickly became the focal point of high society. The hotel has hosted many luminaries (Warren G. Harding died here in 1923), and was restored in 1989–91.

Enter at 639 Market Street and stroll the main corridor to the glorious **Garden Court★★**, capped by a canopy of intricatel art glass. The corridor boasts display cases with fascinating mementoes. Also worth seeing is the **Pied Piper Bar** *(off corridor near Market St. entrance)* and its famous allegorical mural of the Pied Piper of Hamelin by Maxfield Parrish.

▷ Cross Market St., turn left and continue to Kearny St.

A cast-iron column rising from a small fountain, beloved **Lotta's Fountain** *(northeast corner of Market and Kearny Sts.)* was given to the people of San Francisco by entertainer Lotta Crabtree in 1875. Every April 18 around 5am, San Franciscans congregate here to commemorate the anniversary of the great earthquake and fire of 1906.

Lotta's Fountain

The intersection hosting Lotta's Fountain once was the heart of the city's newspaper industry. The former **Chronicle Building** (690 Market St.), erected in 1889 by Burnham and Root, is the city's oldest office tower. Across Market Street lies the terra-cotta-clad **Hearst Building** (691 Third St.), an exuberant, Spanish Revival–style structure that was the longtime home of the San Francisco Examiner.

ADDITIONAL SIGHT
Jackson Square★★
Bounded by Washington, Montgomery & Sansome Sts. and Pacific Ave.
Contrary to its name, San Francisco's oldest surviving commercial neighborhood is not a "square," but five square blocks of well-preserved mid-19C structures between North Beach and the Financial District. This former waterfront neighborhood was once the heart of the notorious **Barbary Coast**, the bawdy, Gold Rush-era district of saloons, theaters and burlesque houses that lined Pacific Avenue between Sansome Street and Columbus Avenue. The brick structures outlasted the great earthquake and fire of 1906; since the 1960s, many have been converted to upscale art galleries, design firms, and antique stores.
Today the two- and three-story buildings, with brick, cast-iron or stucco facades, create a cozily uniform departure from the neighboring towers of the Financial District. The oldest buildings lie along Montgomery Street a block north of the Transamerica Pyramid. The **Belli Building (C)** (no. 722) was constructed in 1851 on a foundation of redwood that literally floats upon former tidelands. First a tobacco warehouse, later a raucous nightclub where Lotta Crabtree got her start, it served as the law offices of famed attorney Melvin Belli from the 1960s until it was damaged in the 1989 earthquake and has long been neglected. The attached **Belli Annex** (no. 726), a three-story brick Italianate built in 1852, marks the site of the first meeting (in 1849) of the California Freemasons. Next door, the two-story **Golden Era Building (D)** (no. 730) was built in 1852 as the home of the West's premier literary magazine, the Golden Era, whose contributors included Mark Twain, Bret Harte and Joaquin Miller. Around the corner, the Italianate-style **Hotaling Warehouse** (451–455 Jackson St.) was constructed for whiskey distilling and storage in 1866. The building was rescued from the 1906 conflagration thanks to the valiant efforts of sailors, who strung a water hose over Telegraph Hill from their ships, and local firefighters. If the liquor had exploded, Jackson Square would have gone up with it.

Pacific Avenue, the northern boundary of Jackson Square, was for years (before and after the earthquake) the rowdiest street in San Francisco.
Many of its buildings were at one time saloons, dance halls, gambling parlors, brothels or boarding houses catering to transient sailors. Painted white pilasters and naked, dancing nymphs, sculpted in bas-relief on the exterior walls of the 1907 **Hippodrome** (no. 555), are a vivid reminder of its post-earthquake heyday. Early 20C dances such as the turkey trot were popularized here, to the sounds of ragtime and Dixieland jazz bands, before spreading across the country.

ADDRESSES

SHOPPING
William Stout Architectural Books – 804 Montgomery St. ✆415-391-6757. www.stoutbooks.com. When books and magazines overflowed his apartment, architect Stout went into business as a bookseller. A huge selection of architectural titles, as well as art, photography, and landscaping themes now overflow this charming shop.

ⵙ/EAT
$$ Tadich Grill – 240 California St. ✆415-391-1849. **Seafood.** Fresh fish is the fare of choice at this San Francisco institution, which began during the Gold Rush as a coffee stand. Go for the charcoal-grilled sole, the cold seafood salads, and the no-nonsense service by white-jacketed waiters in long aprons.

Nob Hill★★

Nob Hill, which witnessed one of San Francisco's first infusions of wealth, today remains a vivid example of the city's diverse urban community. Cable cars trundle up and down the steep slopes, passing restored Edwardian homes and 1920s high-rise apartment buildings. Cozy bistros, corner grocery stores, and boutiques nestle together along the serene, tree-lined side streets. Sloping down to the southwest, Lower Nob Hill, bordered by Geary and Polk Streets, has a grittier feel.

🚋 All lines.

ℹ **Info:** www.sanfrancisco. travel/neighborhood/ nob-hill.

▶ **Location:** West of Chinatown, north of Union Square, and uphill from everywhere.

👫 **Kids:** The Cable Car Museum, next-best thing to a cable car ride.

🕐 **Timing:** Plan about two hours to visit Nob Hill.

🅿 **Parking:** Be sure to check signs for scheduled street-cleaning days before sliding into a spot on the street.

☺ **Don't Miss:** A swooping cable-car ride up and down Nob Hill's steep flanks!

A BIT OF HISTORY

Nob Hill acquired its reputation as home to San Francisco's elite during the city's earliest years. In 1856 Dr. Arthur Hayne, a well-to-do dentist, became the first to settle on the craggy hill, erecting a modest home on the 376ft summit where the Fairmont Hotel stands today. Soon after, merchant William Walton built a grander residence at the present-day corner of Washington and Taylor Streets. By the late 1860s, a handful of millionaires had built homes near the summit, establishing it as a choice residential locale.

The exclusive cachet was ensured after cable-car lines were installed on its steep flanks in 1873, opening the door to development of formerly inaccessible summits, and construction on the crest of Nob Hill boomed. As the rest of the city battled the Panic of 1893, an economic depression affecting all industrial cities in the U.S., Nob Hill became what author Robert Louis Stevenson called "the hill of palaces," thanks in good part to a group of newly minted millionaires.

The Big Four – In 1859 four middle-class Sacramento merchants—**Leland Stanford**, **Charles Crocker**, **Mark Hopkins**, and **Collis Huntington**—together purchased a modest number of shares in what seemed at the time an impossible venture: a railway across the western U.S. A decade later the railroad was complete and their investments yielded millions of dollars. The four promptly moved to San Francisco, purchased lots on the summit of Nob Hill and built sprawling mansions ("Nob" is a contraction of "nabob," a term for European adventurers who made fortunes the Far East).

In the 1880s the Big Four were joined on the hill by two "Bonanza Kings," who had extracted huge fortunes from Nevada's Comstock silver lode in 1873. **James Fair**, a former miner, bought Dr. Hayne's property, and **James Flood** erected his Italianate brownstone mansion, today the Pacific-Union Club.

Through the late 19C, large Victorian houses appeared on the flanks of the hill, near cable-car routes established along California and Powell Streets. After its destruction by the great quake and fire of 1906, the area was rebuilt with tall, narrow Edwardian homes and high-rise apartments. Today Nob Hill maintains turn-of-the-20C charm, although many wealthier San Franciscans now live in neighborhoods to the northwest, where larger plots accommodate palatial mansions. Asian families populate the northeast slopes near Chinatown, and a large singles population occupies studios and small apartments to the southwest.

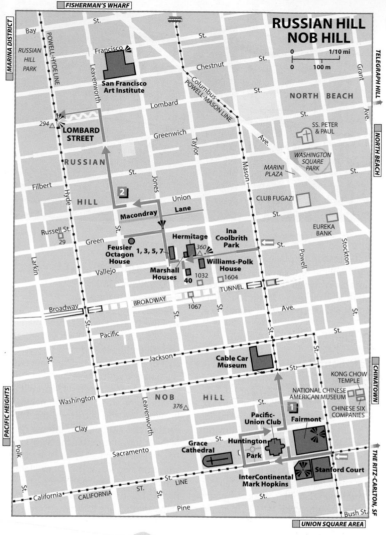

RUSSIAN HILL
NOB HILL

WALKING TOUR

▷ Begin at the southwest corner of Powell and California Sts.

.6mi. The first of the Big Four to build his mansion atop Nob Hill, Leland Stanford constructed an immense Italianate villa on this corner lot in 1876. Today it is the site of the **Stanford Court Hotel**, remodeled in 1972 from an elegant apartment building. The gray stone retaining wall was built in the 1870s and was the only part to survive the 1906 Fire.

▷ Walk west up California St.

InterContinental Mark Hopkins San Francisco

One Nob Hill (999 California St. at Mason St.). ✕ ⚹ 🅿 ✆*415-392-3434. www.intercontinentalmarkhopkins.com.* In 1877 Mark Hopkins began construction of a sprawling Victorian mansion to rival Stanford's in elegance and ostentation. Hopkins died in 1878 before it was completed; in 1893 his widow donated the residence to the California School of Design. The 1906 Fire razed the struc-

Pacific-Union Club

© Brigitta L. House / MICHELIN

ture, and in 1926 the Mark Hopkins Hotel rose in its place. It underwent a $51 million renovation in 2000. The hotel is crowned by the **Top of the Mark**, a swank restaurant and bar (☞see Addresses) with panoramic **views★★★**.

◐ Cross California St.

Fairmont Hotel★★
Bounded by California, Mason, Powell and Sacramento Sts. ✕☖🅿 ℰ415-772-5000. www.fairmont.com/sanfrancisco.
With its opulent lobby, dignified facade and illustrious history, the Fairmont offers a glimpse of early 20C Nob Hill. Designed by James and Merritt Reid, its construction began in 1902 under the stewardship of Tessie Fair Oelrichs, James Fair's daughter. Work was nearly complete when the 1906 Earthquake struck and fire swept the hill, leaving only the granite outer walls intact. Architect Julia Morgan oversaw the restoration and completion of the building in its original Italian Renaissance style. On April 18, 1907, exactly a year after the earthquake, the Fairmont reopened, quickly becoming the city's premier hotel. In 1945, the United Nations Charter was drafted in the elegant Garden Room; commemorated by the UN-member flags above the hotel's main entrance. A modern tower was added in 1961. In the ornate main lobby, massive marble pillars and wrought-iron balconies remain from Morgan's 1906 design.

◐ Walk west on California St.

Pacific-Union Club★
1000 California St.
☞ Not open to the public.
The only structure on Nob Hill to survive the 1906 blaze, silver baron James Flood's mansion was built in 1885 by English architect Augustus Laver at a cost of $1.5 million. Unlike other Nob Hill palaces, which were made of California redwood, Flood's 42-room Italianate home was built of Connecticut brownstone and withstood the 1906 earthquake, although the intense heat of the ensuing fire gutted the lavish interior. In 1908 architect Willis Polk added wings on two sides. The bronze fence surrounding it was patterned after a piece of lace favored by Flood's wife. Today the building is home to the exclusive Pacific-Union Club, which traces its origins to 1852.

◐ Continue west on California St. and cross Taylor St.

Grace Cathedral★
1100 California St. at Taylor St. ◷Open Mon–Fri 7am–6pm, Sat 8am–6pm, Sun 8am–7pm. ☞Guided tours (1hr) Mon–Fri 1pm–3pm, Sat 11.30am–1.30pm, Sun 12.30pm–2pm, or by appointment. ☖🅿 ℰ415-749-6300. www.gracecathedral.org.
The third-largest Episcopal cathedral in the U.S. crowns the crest of Nob Hill, its

French Gothic spires soaring over the city. Consecrated in 1964, the edifice occupies the lot formerly owned by Charles Crocker, whose Second Empire-style mansion stood next to his son's Victorian villa. After both homes were destroyed in the 1906 Fire, the family donated the land to the Episcopal diocese. Grace's cornerstone was laid in 1910 and construction began in 1928. Work was halted by the Great Depression and again by World War II. The Notre Dame-inspired design by Lewis P. Hobart was executed in steel-reinforced concrete to withstand seismic tremors. Set between the main entrance doors in the Gothic eastern portal, the bronze **Gates of Paradise** are the cathedral's most prized architectural feature. Duplicates of a set cast by Florentine sculptor Lorenzo Ghiberti, the 16ft doors are divided into ten richly ornamented panels illustrating scenes from the Old Testament. Inside the cathedral, dozens of stained-glass windows and murals depict a diversity of figures, including Robert Frost, Franklin D. Roosevelt and Albert Einstein. The alterpiece, painter Keith Haring's *A Life of Christ,* was dedicated in 1995. A magnificent Aeolian-Skinner organ resounds with 7,286 pipes. Two labyrinths invite exploration: an outdoor terrazo stone path to the right of the east entrance, and a second limestone labyrinth inside.

▷ Exit cathedral on Taylor St. and cross to the park.

Huntington Park

Banked slightly above street level, Huntington Park gracefully crowns Nob Hill. John McLaren, who designed Golden Gate Park and other Bay Area public gardens, oversaw the design and cultivation of this 1.75-acre plot, donated to the city after Collis Huntington's opulent mansion on the adjacent lot was destroyed in the 1906 Fire. Blackwood acacias and sycamores thrive here, framing the 20C replica of Rome's Tartarughe ("Tortoise") Fountain, purchased in Italy by William Crocker's wife, which forms the park's centerpiece.

▷ Walk east on Sacramento St. and turn left on Mason St.

Cable Car Museum★★

1201 Mason St. at Washington St.
Open Apr–Sept daily 10am–6pm. Rest of the year daily 10am–5pm. Closed Jan 1, Easter Sunday, Thanksgiving Day, Dec 25. ℰ415-474-1887. www.cablecarmuseum.com.
This weathered brick building on the steep north slope of Nob Hill offers an up-close look at the nerve center of San Francisco's renowned cable-car system, the only one of its kind in the world. Besides serving as a powerhouse and car-storage barn, the structure houses a unique history museum.

On the upper level, a balcony overlooks the cable-car mechanism. Motors hum and giant wheels called "sheaves" rotate, powering continuous loops of cable for the system's three lines. Instructive panels and a video presentation explain how the system works. Historical displays tell the story of the cable cars from their invention, to the present. Other exhibits include historic photos, rudimentary hand tools, and public transportation memorabilia. Among the treasured pieces is **Car No. 8**, only survivor of the Clay Street Hill Railroad, San Francisco's first cable-car line, which began operation in 1873.

On the lower level, a small viewing area offers a glimpse of the room where the thick steel cables enter the building.

ADDITIONAL SIGHT
The Ritz-Carlton, San Francisco

600 Stockton St. (between California and Pine Sts.) ℰ415-296-7465. www.ritzcarlton.com.
Built on the Chinatown flank of Nob Hill (1909, Napoleon Le Brun & Sons) as the West Coast headquarters of the Metropolitan Life Insurance Co., the original 80ft cube was expanded in 1914 and 1920 with two symmetrical wings. A facade of 18 Ionic columns supports an entablature that features hourglasses and lions' heads; an allegorical figure ("Insurance") spreads its wings over

© PhotoDisc, Inc.

Getting A Grip: San Francisco's Cable Cars

More than 8 million visitors and San Franciscans annually ride the city's signature cable cars, a public transportation system invented and developed by Scotsman Andrew Smith Hallidie in 1873. Inspired by the work of his father, who had been awarded the world's first patent on iron-wire rope in 1835, 16-year-old Hallidie came to California in 1852, at the height of the Gold Rush, to build wire-rope transport systems for the mines. In his 20s he moved to San Francisco, where he established a wire-rope manufacturing company and developed suspension bridges and cable tramways for Nevada Comstock Lode's silver mines. In 1869 Hallidie first conceived of a similar system for public transportation. Four years and $85,000 later, the idea that had been dubbed "Hallidie's Folly" took form as a primitive cable car line that ascended Clay Street between Kearny and Leavenworth Streets at 6mph.

A testament to the quality of Hallidie's design, today's cable cars work in much the same way as those of 1873. Huge loops of steel cable run at a continuous 9.5mph beneath Powell, Hyde, Mason and California Streets, powered by electric motors. To start the car moving, the "gripman"—in the middle of the car—operates a lever that extends down through a slot in the street. At the underground end of the lever, a "grip" closes and opens like a jaw on the moving cable. The tighter the grip closes, the faster the car goes. To reduce speed, the gripman opens the grip to release the cable; brakes are applied to stop. A conductor at the rear of the car helps with braking when necessary.

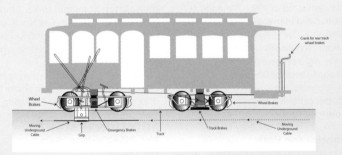

Crank for rear track wheel brakes

Wheel Brakes

Wheel Brakes

Moving Underground Cable

Grip

Emergency Brakes

Track

Track Brakes

Moving Underground Cable

Because the soft metal dies, inside the jaws of the grip, are the only contact between the cables and the cars (which can weigh up to ten tons), they must be replaced every four days. The cables, constructed of six strands of 19 wires twisted around a core of sisal rope, must be replaced every few months through a labor-intensive process of cutting and splicing each individual strand. The track is inspected daily for imperfections, as are each car's three sets of brakes: wheel brakes, track brakes and emergency brakes. This is essential, considering the harrowing 18–21 percent grades the cars negotiate.

Designated a National Historic Landmark in 1964, the system today has 40 cars operating on three lines (Powell-Mason, Powell-Hyde and California Street). The entire system, including the powerhouse, was rehabilitated in 1982–1984, preserving this unique, characteristic part of San Francisco's past and present.

anarchic assortment of poor and disillusioned—"beaten"—writers and artists bent on rejecting established societal and artistic norms. Calling themselves the **Beat Generation** and dubbed "beatniks" (by columnist Herb Caen), they adopted nonconformist bohemian lifestyles, smoked marijuana, drank red wine and espresso, listened to jazz and be-bop, and read poetry at favorite haunts like the Co-Existence Bagel Shop and The Place (both long since vanished). Of their principal gathering places, few remain; City Lights Bookstore, Vesuvio Café, Tosca Cafe and Caffé Trieste are rare survivors.

The movement inspired an outpouring of creative activity by its leading lights: poets Lawrence Ferlinghetti, Kenneth Rexroth, Gregory Corso and Allen Ginsberg; novelist Jack Kerouac; and visual artists Jay DeFeo and Robert LaVigne. The 1955 reading of Ginsberg's raw, apocalyptic poem "Howl" gave birth to the San Francisco Poetry Renaissance and an enduring cultural legend. "I saw the best minds of my generation destroyed by madness," Ginsberg intoned, "starving, hysterical, naked, draggin themselves through negro streets at dawn lookin for an angry fix..."

Within a decade, the movement was over, ruined in part by busloads of "square" tourists who overran North Beach in their search for "cool." By the mid-60s, the best minds of the Beat Generation had either passed away or moved on.

North Beach Today – Few in the counterculture could now afford the high rents of North Beach's surprisingly uniform, three- to four-story flats and apartment houses, built in a nine-year flurry of reconstruction after the 1906 Earthquake and Fire. The northward flow of families and businesses from Chinatown, begun in the 1960s as immigration restrictions on Asians eased, continues the district's long tradition of multiethnic coexistence. Many nonresident Italian Americans still consider North Beach home, returning often to shop, dine or gather at one of the venerable institutions still operated by descendants of the original owners. Around and on Washington Square are some of North Beach's best (and best-loved) restaurants.

▶️ WALKING TOUR

1.6mi

▶ Begin at the corner of Columbus Ave. & Broadway.

City Lights Bookstore★

261 Columbus Ave. 🕐*Open daily 10am–midnight.* 🕐*Closed Thanksgiving Day and Dec 25.* 📞*415-362-8193. www.citylights.com.*

Founded in 1953 by poet Lawrence Ferlinghetti, this former beatnik hangout was the first all-paperback bookstore in America. It remains one of the best-known independent shops in the U.S., as much for its history as for its meandering layout, ambience and unique titles—many released by City Lights Publishers. In the upstairs poetry and Beat literature room, comfortable chairs encourage browsers to linger with their selections. Enlarged over the years, the store maintains its alternative reputation despite the presence on its shelves of clothbound books and other inevitable marks of changing times.

Across Jack Kerouac Alley from City Lights Bookstore lies **Vesuvio Café**

City Lights Bookstore

© Brigitta L. House / MICHELIN

(255 Columbus Ave.; ✕ ♿ ☏ 415-362-3370; www.vesuvio.com), another popular landmark of North Beach's Beat heyday. It was here that a black-clad crowd of beatniks gathered on October 13, 1955, before attending Ginsberg's now-legendary reading of "Howl" at the Six Gallery (long gone from its former Marina District location). Vivid paintings and leaded glass enliven the cafe's wood-trimmed walls, which are crammed with photos and memorabilia from the Beat era.

Just steps southeast on Columbus Avenue is the **San Francisco Brewing Company** *(155 Columbus Ave.; ✕ ♿ ☏ 415-434-3344; www.sfbrewing.com)*, one of the first brew pubs in the U.S. when it began producing its own beer in 1985. Established at the edge of the Barbary Coast in 1907 as the Andromeda Saloon, it attracted such diverse personalities as Jack Dempsey, a 1913 bouncer who became world heavyweight boxing champion, and Baby Face Nelson, public enemy no. 1, captured at the Andromeda by the FBI in 1939. Modern decor is characterized by historic photos and antiques, including the 1916 "Pukka Walla" fan of brass and palm fronds that rotates above the bar.

▶ Walk north to Broadway, turn right and cross Columbus Ave.

As you cross, glance to your right for an impressive view of the Transamerica Pyramid. The **Sentinel Building** *(916 Kearny St.)*, a green, copper-trimmed, flatiron-shaped office building (1905, Salfield and Kohlberg), rises in the foreground. Filmmaker Francis Ford Coppola purchased and restored the tower in the 1970s; on the ground floor, Café Zoetrope *(☏ 415-291-1700)* maintains a light menu with vintages from the Italy and California, including the Napa Valley's Niebaum-Coppola Estate.

Broadway

Broadway between Columbus Ave. and Montgomery St.

Though its reputation for danger, vice and sin has gentled in recent decades,

the strip of sex shops and topless clubs along Broadway and Kearny Street harks back to San Francisco's less-than-savory past. Broadway's notoriety originated in the waterfront dives of Sydney Town in the 1850s, when a zone of dance halls, brothels, gambling dens and outlaw nests known as the **Barbary Coast** arose along lower Pacific Avenue, extending to present-day Jackson Square and parts of Chinatown. Sailors on shore leave enjoyed the strip's diversions at great peril: "Shanghaiing" was an all-too-common practice (the word, meaning "recruiting someone forcefully for maritime service," is said to have originated here). Civic pressure led to the cleanup of the Barbary Coast after the 1906 earthquake and fire, and bars offering exotic entertainment were restricted to Broadway, where they have persisted, mostly undisturbed, for years. Several risqué venues opened in the 1960s and early 1970s, among them the Condor Club at the intersection of Broadway, Columbus and Grant Avenues. For several decades a neon figure of **Carol Doda**, the "queen of topless dancing," hung provocatively above the street, drawing scores of visitors. The cartoonish landmark was removed (and auctioned off piecemeal) in 1991, but several all-nude venues remain.

▶ Continue up Columbus Ave.

Columbus Avenue

Designed in 1872 as a direct path from the Financial District to the industrial zone growing along the northern waterfront, this broad, busy avenue traces the valley between Russian and Telegraph Hills, indiscriminately cutting across the city's square grid and creating several confusing six-way intersections. Called Montgomery Avenue at its construction, it was later renamed for Christopher Columbus to honor North Beach's Italian community. Today anchored by the Transamerica Pyramid, the thoroughfare extends through North Beach to The Cannery on Fisherman's Wharf. The blocks between Broadway and Filbert Street, lined with fragrant bakeries, gar-

T'ai Chi

Early-rising visitors enjoying a morning trek through North Beach, Russian Hill, Nob Hill or other residential areas are likely to spy individuals or groups of people dressed in everyday clothes performing what appears to be a slow-motion outdoor ballet. *T'ai chi ch'uan,* an ancient, noncompetitive martial art, is practiced by many citizens as a form of exercise. The slow, meditative transitions between specified stances and positions is said to condition the body and relax the mind by harmonizing of the passive and active principles of yin and yang. Almost any serene plot can be a good place to perform this ritual, but groups tend to gather at Ina Coolbrith Park, Huntington Park, St. Mary's Square, and especially Washington Square Park.

licky trattorias, pungent delicatessens and aromatic cafes, preserve the soul of Italian North Beach.

⊙ Continue to Stockton St. and turn left.

The melding of cultures that distinguishes present-day North Beach is clearly visible in the block of Stockton Street between Vallejo and Green Streets. Asian markets and Chinese street signs rub shoulders with old-fashioned Italian shops advertising fresh tagliarini and imported olive oil.

⊙ Return to Columbus Ave. and continue northwest.

Washington Square Park★

With a broad, sunny lawn and clusters of willow, cypress and sycamore trees, this pentagonal park occupies the heart of North Beach. The popular neighborhood gathering spot was donated to the city by its first mayor, John W. Geary, and set aside as a public park in 1847 by Jasper O'Farrell, surveyor of San Francisco's downtown street grid. After Columbus Avenue sliced off its southwest corner (now called Marini Plaza) in 1873, the park was landscaped to Victorian taste with shade trees and a broad, curving path for promenading. Hundreds of refugees camped here during the year following the 1906 earthquake and fire. Today, elderly Asians gather each morning to practice *t'ai chi,* a graceful form of martial arts (⊙*see above*), and Italian retirees spend hours on the benches fac-

ing Union Street. Visitors and locals alike often picnic on the grassy lawn.

Saints Peter and Paul Church★

666 Filbert St., north side of Washington Sq. ⊙*Open Mon–Fri 7am–4pm, Sat–Sun 6.30am–7pm.* ♿ ✆*415-421-0809. www.sspeterpaulsf.org/church.*
Built in Gothic Revival style with Italianate details, this handsome, twin-spired church (1924) is fondly known as the Italian Cathedral. Lawrence Ferlinghetti dubbed it "the marzipan church on the plaza," a description particularly true at night when floodlights bathe its cream-colored exterior. The imposing facade bears the opening line of Dante's *Paradiso:* "The glory of Him who moves all things penetrates and glows throughout the universe." The interior is warm and inviting, enclosed by an unusual flat ceiling of dark wood and illuminated by banks of votive candles and richly colored stained-glass windows. A spectacular, 40ft-high altar, made of Mediterranean marble and onyx, features a sculpted reproduction of da Vinci's *Last Supper.*
Screen legend Marilyn Monroe and baseball great Joe DiMaggio took wedding photos on the front steps of SS. Peter and Paul, contributing to the myth that they were married inside. (Both were in fact married in the church, though not to each other.) DiMaggio grew up in North Beach, and as a youth in the 1930s was a member of the church's boys' club—along with New York Yankees teammates Tony Lazzeri and Frankie Crossetti.

View of North Beach area with Saints Peter and Paul Church and Coit Tower

© Can Balcioglu / iStockphoto.com

The church reflects North Beach's multiethnic character, offering Mass in English, Italian, Latin and Cantonese.

▶ From the church, walk east up Filbert St. and climb the hill, following the "Stairs to Coit Tower" signs. To avoid the steep climb, take the 39–Coit bus from Washington Square.

Telegraph Hill★

The abrupt rise that punctuates the eastern edge of North Beach was named for a long-vanished semaphore erected atop its summit in 1849. A precursor to modern telegraph systems, the semaphore signaled the arrival of ships through the Golden Gate by vari-colored flags hoisted along its two arms, positioned according to the type and nationality of the vessel. Gold Rush-era shacks and tent cities that dotted the steep, rocky flanks developed into working-class neighborhoods that persisted until the early 20C, when the auto-

mobile opened the way for wealthier citizens. Most of the structures on the hill (and in surrounding North Beach) burned to the ground during the 1906 Fire, but houses on the east slope were saved by determined Italian Americans, who beat back the flames with blankets soaked in red wine.

The tree-filled expanse at the hill's 274ft summit, today known as **Pioneer Park**, was donated to the city in 1876 by a group of businessmen intent on preserving the open space for future generations. The bronze statue of **Christopher Columbus (3)** at the center of the Coit Tower parking area was erected by the local Italian-American community. Panoramic **views★★** from the summit encompass major landmarks including Twin Peaks, Lombard Street, the Golden Gate Bridge, Alcatraz and the Bay Bridge. On clear days, the East Bay hills come into view. As you gaze, listen for the sounds of barking sea lions drifting up from Pier 39.

Jungle City

The relative warmth of Telegraph Hill and Washington Square attracts colonies of colorful parrots, believed to be descendants of escaped household pets. The parrots now form a curious and vocal part of North Beach's landscape, their loud screeches and brilliant colors enlivening Telegraph Hill's verdant flanks and the leafy canopies of Washington Square.

🏛 Coit Tower★★★

Summit of Telegraph Hill. ⏰*Open daily 10am–6pm.* 🅿 ☎*415-362-0808. sfrecpark.org/coittower.aspx.*
Towering 180ft above a 32ft rectangular base, this fluted, concrete column (1934, Arthur Brown, Jr.) was an enduring gift to San Francisco's citizens from an unusual woman who wished to add "to the beauty of the city which I have always loved." Initially infamous for the heated social controversy incited by its lobby murals, Coit Tower ranks today among the city's best-known landmarks.

"Firebelle" Lillie

When **Lillie Hitchcock Coit** (1843–1929) was a child in San Francisco, daring teams of volunteers battled the many fires that regularly ravaged the city. It is said that one afternoon in the 1860s young Lillie, who had been saved from a fire during her childhood, came upon Knickerbocker Engine Company No. 5 struggling up Telegraph Hill en route to a blaze. Throwing down her school-books, she rallied onlookers to help the firemen. In return, the company made her an honorary member. For the rest of her life, even as a wealthy widow in Paris, Coit wore a gold, diamond-studded fireman's badge everywhere she went; it was pinned to her clothing when her remains were cremated in 1929. In her will, she bequeathed $125,000 to the city, part of which paid for the statue of her beloved volunteer firemen in Washington Square Park. The bulk of the gift provided funds for Coit Tower, which, despite persistent local lore, was not designed to resemble a firehose nozzle.

The Murals

The first major commission of the Depression-era Public Works of Art Project (PWAP), a New Deal initiative that engaged artists to decorate public buildings, the 19 fresco **murals★★** in the lobby of Coit Tower were created in 1934. Working for an average of $31.22 a week, 26 local painters and numerous assistants labored for five months

to produce a series of frescoes depicting contemporary life in California. While celebrating the state's abundance and diversity, the works contained powerful images that bluntly criticized the economic inequities of life during the Great Depression. The murals' left-wing content raised the hackles of San Francisco's conservative elite. Fueling the controversy, a tense labor conflict smoldered along the waterfront at the base of Telegraph Hill, erupting into the longshoremen's Pacific Maritime Strike just as work on the murals drew to a close. The sometimes-violent strike crippled the entire West Coast and caused some to view any form of social criticism as radical agitation. Responding to civic pressure, the San Francisco Art Commission delayed the opening of Coit Tower and considered destroying the murals.

Murals, Coit Tower

© Brigitta L. House / MICHELIN

After vigorous debate on both sides of the issue, only the most blatant (hammer-and-sickle) symbols of left-wing sympathy in Clifford Wight's mural (no. 4) were effaced, and the building was finally opened to the public in October 1934.

Visit

The murals display remarkable uniformity in both theme and style despite the fact that so many different artists created them. **California Industrial Scenes** (John Langley Howard) depicts the despair of the era through an image of a migrant family posing beside their disabled Model-T, while a group of well-to-do day-trippers gazes on them as if they were a tourist attraction. **The Library** (Bernard Zakheim) inspired controversy for its suggestion that the works of Karl Marx might offer a viable form of government. In **City Life** (Victor Arnautoff), perhaps the best-known mural, a bustling street scene none-too-subtly criticizes the indifference of urban dwellers to one another. A brief elevator ascent (⟋$7; purchase tickets in gift shop) and a short flight of stairs take visitors to the observation deck. From here, panoramic **views★★★** sweep Angel Island and Marin County to the north, the Bay Bridge and Treasure Island to the east, downtown San Francisco to the south, and Russian Hill and the Golden Gate Bridge to the west.

▷ From Coit Tower, descend the curving sidewalk along Telegraph Hill Ave. to the first corner and turn left at Filbert St.

Filbert Steps★★

Coit Tower to Sansome St.
Concrete and wooden stairs, descending this steep section of Filbert Street, comprise one of the city's most charming and surprising pathways. At **1360 Montgomery Street** (1937), the stairs pass a gleaming, Streamline Moderne apartment house that appeared in the 1947 film *Dark Passage* as the place where Lauren Bacall's character hid an escaped convict (Humphrey Bogart).

Below Montgomery Street, the wooden staircase follows lushly landscaped garden terraces named for Grace Marchant, their original designer and a longtime neighborhood resident.

Those who live along the steps today cultivate her verdant legacy, and the gardens flourish year-round. Inhabitants of the treehouse-like precincts along the pedestrian streets of **Darrell Place** and **Napier Lane** occupy handsome, mid-19C wooden cottages in styles typical of the vernacular architecture of the post-Gold Rush period. Note the simple facade at **no. 228** (1869), a delicately restored example of the Carpenter Gothic style, and the cottage at **no. 224** (1859).

▷ At the bottom of the steps, cross Sansome St.

Levi's Plaza

Filbert St., between Sansome and Battery Sts.
Completed in 1982, this award-winning group of buildings (Hellmuth, Obata & Kassabaum) was designed to harmonize with the varying architectural styles of the surrounding neighborhood. Look west from the intersection of Battery and Filbert Streets to appreciate how its stacked-box profile mimics the houses marching steeply down Telegraph Hill. Administrative headquarters of Levi Strauss & Co., the complex boasts beautifully landscaped open spaces that serve as a placid haven amid the bustle of the nearby Embarcadero.

▷ Walk north on Sansome St. to Greenwich St. and turn up the steps.

The **Greenwich Steps**, while not as lushly picturesque as the Filbert Street staircase, these steps scale nasturtium-covered rocks and patches of fragrant anise along the ascent to the top of Telegraph Hill.

ADDRESSES

CAFES

NORTH BEACH CAFES

For decades, North Beach denizens have stopped at the neighborhood's famed Italian coffeehouses to get their morning jolt.

At **Caffé Trieste** *(601 Vallejo St.; ☏415-392-6739; www.caffetrieste.com; cash only)* and **Mario's Bohemian Cigar Store** *(566 Columbus Ave.; ☏415-362-0536)*, a cup buys you a table for hours to work on your novel; the latter serves up the best focaccia sandwich going.

Big windows at **Caffé Puccini** *(411 Columbus Ave.; ☏415-989-7033)* and **Caffè Greco** *(423 Columbus Ave.; ☏415-397-6261; www.caffegreco.com)* offer glimpses of daily life in North Beach.

The coffee at **Caffè Roma** *(526 Columbus Ave.; ☏415-296-7942; www.cafferoma.com)* comes fresh from a brass-trimmed roaster sitting in the window.

NORTH BEACH DELICATESSENS

Molinari Delicatessen *– 373 Columbus Ave. ☏415-421-2337. Open Mon–Fri 9am–5.30pm, Sat 7.30am–5.30pm.* Heady whiffs of parmesan, basil, salami and olives waft from this century-old North Beach institution. Neighborhood denizens pop in early to pick up handmade ravioli, tortellini, cheeses, olive oils, and vinegars from Italy. Later in the morning, meats and cheese appear on the chopping block for the sandwich-at-the-desk and picnic-in-Washington Square crowds.

NORTH BEACH BAKERIES

Liguria Bakery *– 1700 Stockton St., ☏415-421-3786. Open Mon–Fri 8am–2pm, Sun 7am–noon.* This is one for early birds only. Available in just a few flavors (including raisin, garlic, rosemary and black olive), the melt-in-your-mouth focaccia drips with olive oil and sells out quickly. Cash only.

Stella Pastry and Cafe *– 446 Columbus Ave. Open Mon 7.30am–8pm, Tue–Thu & Sun 7.30am–10pm, Fri–Sat 7.30am–midnight. ☏415-986-2914. www.stellapastry.com.* Opened in 1942, this tiny bakery is famed for its traditional Italian pastries, particularly its light, creamy sacripantini cake. Also on the menu are éclairs, napoleons, cannolis and all manner of cakes and tarts.

© Doug Olson / Fotolia.com

Coffee in North Beach

Black as night, strong as sin...

Long before every shopping mall and fast-food joint in America installed a coffee bar, before the Beats of the 50s were bolting shots of espresso in smoky cafes, the Italian-American residents of North Beach were drinking fine coffee. Today, with more than a dozen cafes and two traditional roasteries, North Beach is still a prime spot to enjoy some form of the bitter black liquid.

THEATER

BEACH BLANKET BABYLON

Club Fugazi *– 678 Beach Blanket Babylon Blvd. (formerly Green St.). ☏415-421-4222. www.beachblanketbabylon.com.* Where else could you find Paris Hilton and Donald Trump, Brad Pitt and Mr. Peanut—plus some of the most ludicrous hats ever created—together on the same stage? This outrageous spoof of current events and pop culture has played before packed houses at the same location since 1974, and is acclaimed as the longest-running musical revue in theater history.

Russian Hill★

Russian Hill rises abruptly from the landfill flats of Fisherman's Wharf and North Beach. Its precipitous flanks harbor a number of pre-1906 architectural gems and a rich history of literary activity. Topping 360ft at Vallejo Street between Taylor and Jones, and 294ft at Lombard and Hyde, the hill's two summits offer splendid views of Coit Tower, the Financial District, Alcatraz and the bay. Several secluded pedestrian stairways and paths negotiate the dips between the two peaks, making for beautiful, if vigorous, walks. Pleasant sidewalk cafes, restaurants, bars and shops on nearby Hyde and Polk Streets provide welcome places to eat, relax or browse.

A BIT OF HISTORY

According to San Francisco lore, Russian Hill was named in the mid-19C when the graves of Russian seal hunters were discovered atop the crest of present-day Vallejo Street. After thousands of people turned out to see the city's first public hanging here in 1852, Joseph Atkinson built the first house on the south side of Russian Hill. Others followed, mainly working-class families who built simple wooden residences and climbed the steep slopes on foot. By the 1880s, cable-car lines had crept up Russian Hill's flanks. Small Victorian flats were built side-by-side with simple shingled cottages. A community of writers and artists moved in, securing Russian Hill's reputation as a bohemian enclave before upscale development took root. From 1856 through the 1890s, Catherine Atkinson kept her home (at 1032 Broadway) open to such literary lights as Mark Twain, Ambrose Bierce and Robert Louis Stevenson. From the late 1860s until 1906, local literary maven Ina Coolbrith also hosted literary salons, inviting Twain, Bierce, Bret Harte, Charles Stoddard, George Sterling and others to her house at 1604 Taylor Street. For more than two decades after the 1906 quake and fire, the California Literary

🚋 Powell-Hyde or Powell-Mason.

ⓘ **Michelin Map:** *See RUSSIAN HILL, NOB HILL* p89

🛈 **Info:** ☎415-391-2000. www.sanfrancisco.travel.

▶ **Location:** Russian Hill is bounded by Francisco, Taylor, Pacific, and Polk Streets.

👫 **Kids:** Lombard Street, for the fun and the great view.

🕐 **Timing:** Plan a couple of hours to visit Russian Hill, a bit more if hill-climbing isn't your forte.

🅿 **Parking:** Street parking is available, but it's more fun to take the cable car.

☺ **Don't Miss:** Stair-streets: Vallejo Street and Macondray Lane.

Society met in Coolbrith's upstairs flat at 1067 Broadway. In the 1940s Russian Hill provided the setting for several mystery novels, and in 1952 Beat writer Jack Kerouac spent six months on the hill, staying with friends Neal and Carolyn Cassady at 29 Russell Street and working on several novels, including *On the Road*. Unlike elite Nob Hill, Russian Hill continued to develop as a middle-class neighborhood, with small homes set relatively far apart and separated by gardens and wells. Although a few residential enclaves survived the 1906 Fire, many homes were destroyed, and the ensuing architectural ferment of 1906–20 continues to define Russian Hill's aesthetic. Two- to four-story Edwardian buildings flourished, as did a number of pueblo-style stuccoes and Spanish and Art Deco apartment towers. Several less attractive high-rises were erected in the 1960s and 70s, blocking views; a 40ft height limit was imposed in 1974. Russian Hill today is a living testament to the city's architectural diversity. Its lofty heights, well-tended homes and tranquil parks and gardens make it one of San Francisco's most picturesque neighborhoods.

WALKING TOUR

.1mi.

▶ Begin at Mason & Vallejo Sts. and walk west, climbing the left staircase.

Ina Coolbrith Park

A narrow plot of steep hillside bursting with Monterey pines, agave plants and hydrangea bushes along the Vallejo Street stairs, Ina Coolbrith Park was dedicated in 1931 as a memorial to the acclaimed poet and avatar of San Francisco's turn-of-the-20C literary community. The niece of Mormon prophet Joseph Smith, **Ina Donna Coolbrith** (1841-1928) moved west with her family as a child. During the 1860s Coolbrith wrote poetry for and helped edit *The Californian* and the *Overland Monthly*, both highly esteemed literary journals, while spearheading the vibrant local salon scene. Later, Coolbrith encouraged writer Jack London and dancer Isadora Duncan in their artistic pursuits. The state legislature named her California's poet laureate in 1919.

From the Taylor Street stairhead, Coit Tower, the Bay Bridge and Yerba Buena Island are visible to the east through the trees. Begonias, zinnias and other blooming flowers garnish the paths that zigzag across the tiny park, and benches provide a peaceful place to rest.

▶ Cross Taylor St. and continue up the Vallejo St. stairs to the summit.

Charming historic residences and outstanding eastward bay **views★★** mark the summit of **Vallejo Street**. Tucked behind tall shrubbery and a redwood fence, the **Williams-Polk House★** *(1013–1019 Vallejo St.)* was designed in 1892 by Willis Polk. The house is seven stories high on the side facing Broadway *(not visible)*. Inspired by the Arts and Crafts aesthetic, Polk embellished his creation with indigenous materials. So pleased was he with his design and with the view from the house that the architect waived his fee in exchange for quarters in the eastern third of the building.

Steepest Streets of San Francisco

♦ Filbert between Hyde and Leavenworth – **31.5%** grade

♦ Jones between Union and Filbert – **29%** grade

♦ Duboce between Buena Vista and Alpine – **27.9%** grade

♦ Jones between Green and Union – **26%** grade

♦ Webster between Vallejo and Broadway – **26%** grade

♦ Duboce between Alpine and Castro – **25%** grade

♦ Jones between Pine and California – **24.8%** grade

♦ Fillmore between Vallejo and Broadway – **24%** grade

The large, shingled structure at 1020 Vallejo Street contains the **Hermitage Condominiums** (1982, Esherick, Homsey, Dodge & Davis). The building occupies the former site of a one-story cottage that was home to the Rev. Joseph Worcester, an early proponent of the Arts and Crafts movement in the West. (Worcester had a hand in designing the Swedenborgian Church.) Many small cottages were demolished in the mid-20C to make way for large-scale building projects. Two of Worcester's original designs, the three-story, gable-roofed **Marshall Houses** *(1034 and 1036 Vallejo St.)*, both built in 1889, have survived the century largely unaltered.

▶ Continue walking west to Florence Ln. on the left.

Screened by a charming, rose-covered fence, the shingled mansion at **40 Florence Lane** (1857) was remodeled by Willis Polk in 1891, and expanded nearly a century later by architect Robert A.M. Stern.

▶ Cross the street to Russian Hill Pl.

View of Lombard Street

© Kevin Connors / Dreamstime.com

Polk in 1916 built the houses at **1**, **3**, **5 and 7 Russian Hill Place**, which appear from the front as tiny Mediterranean-style cottages.

▷ Turn right on Jones St. and walk north to Green St.

From the corner of Jones and Green Streets, fine **views**★★ extend to the north over Alcatraz. The 1000 block of Green, known as the "Paris Block" due to its elegance, features 12 beautifully restored Victorian-era earthquake survivors, all of which are on the National Register of Historic Places. The 1857 **Feusier Octagon House** at no. 1067 was sold in 1870 to Louis Feusier; the handsome mansard roof was added several years later.

▷ Return to Jones St. Turn left, continuing to Macondray Ln. Turn right and stroll to the wooden staircase.

Macondray Lane★

This enchanting little walking street, overhung by lush greenery, was one of Ina Coolbrith's favorite places to roam; it also appeared as "Barbary Lane" in author Armistead Maupin's serialized 1970s epic, *Tales of the City*.
The quintessential hidden garden of flowering plants and trees, turn-of-the-20C clapboard houses and modern glass condominiums share the cozily private, cobbled lane.

▷ Return to Jones St. and continue north, turning left on Union St. Turn right on Leavenworth St. and continue to Lombard St.

👥 Lombard Street★★★

Among San Francisco's most photographed attractions, the 1000 block of Lombard Street boasts eight switchbacks in its one-block descent from Hyde to Leavenworth. The block's natural 27 percent grade was gentled to 16 percent in 1922, when cobblestones were used to pave the street. Today, roughly three-quarters of a million cars negotiate the hairpin turns each year, descending through banks of hydrangeas.
Climb the stairs flanking the curves to Hyde Street, where **views**★★ extend north and east. From here, cable cars coast down to Ghirardelli Square and the Hyde Street Pier against a backdrop of Alcatraz and Angel Island.

ADDITIONAL SIGHT
San Francisco Art Institute★

800 Chestnut St. ◷*Open Mon–Fri 9am–5pm.* ✕&. ℘*415-771-7020. www.sfai.edu.*
Founded in 1871, this prestigious fine-arts college occupies a Spanish Colonial Revival-style building (1926, Arthur Brown, Jr.), expanded in the béton brut style by English-born architect Paffard Keatinge Clay in 1969. A cultural center as well as a college, the institute wel-

comes the public to exhibits, galleries and screenings of avant-garde films. Displays of student work change regularly in its open-air courtyard; temporary exhibits are mounted in the **Walter and McBean Galleries** (◷open Tue 11am–7pm, Wed–Sat 11am–6pm). The chapel-like **Diego Rivera Gallery** (◷open daily 9am–5pm; closed major holidays) features The Making of a Fresco Showing the Building of a City (1931), a two-story mural by the famed Mexican artist, one of four Rivera murals in the Bay Area. Rivera himself appears in the work along with his wife, Frida Kahlo and the English sculptor Clifford Wright. From the rooftop deck, grand **views**★★ extend over Telegraph Hill and the northern waterfront.

ADDRESSES

♀/EAT

San Francisco Art Institute Cafe – Open during semesters Mon–Fri 8.30am–4.30pm. ☎415-749-4567. Wind your way up to the Institute's broad back deck. Grab a sandwich or daily entree and sit back. The stunning backdrop of city, bay and sky may inspire you to bring out your brushes.

Swensen's Ice Cream – Union St. at Hyde St. ☎415-775-6818. When his troop ship sailed into the South Pacific, San Francisco Earle Swensen, looking for the coldest place aboard, volunteered to make ice cream. Upon the war's conclusion, he opened shop here. The flagship in Swensen's fleet of 200 ice cream parlors holds only about a dozen customers, so most eat their cones out front while waiting for the cable car.

Union Square★

The Union Square area bustles as San Francisco's most vibrant and prestigious urban shopping district. Dominating the square itself, major department stores stand shoulder-to-shoulder with upscale boutiques and a turn-of-the-20C hotel. To the east, designer shops crowd in beside art galleries and specialty stores, and chichi cafes set up umbrella-shaded tables along secluded pedestrian lanes. To the west extends the city's theater district, where large and small venues mix with art galleries, hotels, and all-night diners.

A BIT OF HISTORY

In 1850, San Francisco mayor John White Geary (1819–1873) presented the city with Union Square Park, a precious gift during the height of the Gold Rush when land was at a premium. For the next two decades the neighborhood remained largely residential, with staid Victorian homes and churches flanking the open square.

Through the 1880s and 90s, the area grew increasingly commercial as mer-

🚋 Powell-Hyde or Powell-Mason. 🚍 Bus 2–Clement, 3–Jackson, 4–Sutter, 30–Stockton, 38–Geary or 45–Union-Stockton; all streetcars Powell St. station. 🚉 Powell St. station.

🛈 **Info:** ☎415-391-2000. www.sanfrancisco.travel.

◖ **Location:** Bounded by Sutter, Taylor, Kearny and O'Farrell Streets.

👫 **Kids:** Ruth Asawa Fountain

🕐 **Timing:** Midday is a great time for people-watching as shoppers and office workers break in the park.

🅿 **Parking:** Below the square; 🛢$3.50/hr).

☺ **Don't Miss:** A ride up the Westin St. Francis Hotel's exterior elevators.

chants, attracted to the upscale, picturesque central square, rented the homes of wealthy residents who had relocated west to the more spacious environs of Pacific Heights. Sutter Street became

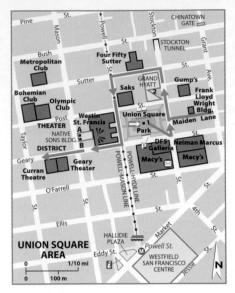

UNION SQUARE AREA

facades. In the following decades, several exclusive and prestigious social clubs were founded in the area, among them the Romanesque Revival-style **Olympic Club** (524 Post St.), the Moderne-influenced **Bohemian Club** (624 Taylor St.) and the **Metropolitan Club** (640 Sutter St.) for women only. Today this preponderance of theaters and shopping destinations, along with numerous hotels, makes Union Square one of the city's liveliest districts. During the day, shoppers mob the stores around the square, especially **Saks Fifth Avenue**, **Neiman Marcus**, and **Macy's**, while flower vendors, buskers and panhandlers cram the sidewalks and traffic chokes the streets. At night, crowds shift west toward the theater district.

the area's first fashionable shopping artery, followed by the streets flanking the square itself.

Large retail establishments began appearing in 1896 when the **City of Paris** department store took up residence at the corner of Geary and Stockton Streets. Across the park at Geary and Powell, white-gloved porters opened the doors of the St. Francis Hotel for the first time in 1904. With its grand lobby, luxurious guest rooms and fine restaurants, the St. Francis, along with City of Paris and **Gump's** (135 Post St.), an esteemed interior-design gallery, ensured Union Square's elite cachet.

The 1906 earthquake and fire nearly razed the district, but determined entrepreneurs lost no time in rebuilding. In 1908 the City of Paris rose anew; architects Bakewell & Brown preserved much of its original design and added a stained-glass rotunda reminiscent of one in Paris' Galeries Lafayette. The St. Francis was reconstructed and expanded that same year in its original Renaissance Revival style. In the blocks east of the square, Gump's was rebuilt, and new boutiques appeared along Maiden Lane.

To the west, numerous theaters took root, many sporting Neoclassical

WALKING TOUR

.5mi.

▶ Begin at the center of Union Square Park.

Union Square Park★

Bounded by Post, Stockton, Geary, and Powell Sts.

One of the few designated parks in Jasper O'Farrell's rigid street plan, this 2.6-acre parcel was landscaped in the early 1850s and was named on the eve of the Civil War, when it hosted numerous rallies in support of the Union. In 1901 the **Dewey Monument (1)**, commemorating Admiral George Dewey's 1898 defeat of Spanish naval forces in the Bay of Manila, was erected at the center of the square. Newton Tharp designed the slender, 97ft granite Corinthian column and Robert Aitken cast the bronze figure of Victory—armed with wreath and trident—surmounting it. A five-story parking garage was built beneath the square in 1942, raising the park slightly above street level. The park fell into decline in the 1980s, but a $25 million-dollar restoration completed in 2002 spiffed up the

Box Office

If you're interested in seeing a play or performance while you're in San Francisco, be sure to visit the **TIX Bay Area** box office in Union Square Park *(Powell St. between Post and Geary Sts.;* ⏰*open daily 7am-6pm; closed Jan 1, Thanksgiving Day, Dec 25;* ✆*415-430-1140; www.theatrebayarea.org).* Here you can buy both advance tickets and same-day, half-price tickets—many for well under $30—to many live shows around the city. Half-price tickets go on sale at 11am every day and are available on a first-come, first-served basis. You may also order half-price tickets in advance online through Tix in Advance (✆*415-433-1235; www. tixbayarea.com).*

square with new granite surfaces, steel benches and public art installations, regenerating the economic vitality of the surrounding area.

Union Square Park has hosted many heated demonstrations over the decades, but today its palm trees and green lawns create a peaceful respite for workers, shoppers and passersby. Music and dance performances occur regularly on the stage along the park's north side. Street musicians avail themselves of the open spaces during the day.

▷ Cross the square to the corner of Geary and Stockton Sts.

Neiman Marcus

150 Stockton St. (at Geary St.). ⏰*Open Mon–Sat 10am–7pm (Thu 8pm), Sun noon–6pm.* ⏰*Closed Thanksgiving Day, Dec 25.* ✕⚓ ✆*415-362-3900. www.neimanmarcus.com.*

With its rose-colored, harlequin-patterned granite exterior and rounded glass-and-aluminum entrance corner, this post-Modern department store (1982, Johnson & Burgee) marks a sharp architectural departure from the Renaissance-style, Baroque-ornamented City of Paris store that once stood here. The beloved City of Paris landmark was demolished in 1981, but its exuberant stained-glass **rotunda★** was preserved and today soars above the entrance foyer, framed by enameled, wrought-iron balconies. As befits its original surroundings, the rotunda depicts Paris' emblem, a sailing ship, and its motto, *Fluctuat nec Mergitur* ("He Floats but Does Not Sink").

▷ Walk north up Stockton St. to Maiden Lane.

Maiden Lane

Once flanked with low-rent brothels, Maiden Lane was reincarnated after the 1906 Fire as a quaint pedestrian street lined with maple trees, cafes, boutiques, salons and galleries. At no. 140 stands the **Frank Lloyd Wright Building★** (1949), the only structure in San Francisco designed by Wright and a forerunner to the famed architect's Guggenheim Museum in New York City. Now home to the fine collection of Folk Art International, the skylit gallery boasts a curvaceous interior with many circular and spiral motifs, including small round porticoes used as display cases, cutout porthole-like windows, a huge hanging planter and a ramp spiraling up to the second floor.

▷ Return to Stockton St. and continue north.

👥 Ruth Asawa Fountain (2)

Stockton St. deck (corner of Post St.), Grand Hyatt hotel.

This playful fountain (1972) by San Francisco sculptor Ruth Asawa represents a triumph of collective creativity. Asawa asked 250 city residents, ages 3 to 90, to sculpt city landmarks out of baker's dough. She cast the flour-and-water bas-reliefs in metal and arranged them around the fountain's cylindrical base in a map-like fashion. Look for whimsical depictions of the Transamerica Pyramid and Sutro Baths, juxtaposed with fantastic elements such as Superman in flight above Montgomery Street.

▶ Continue north to Sutter St. and turn left.

Four Fifty Sutter★

450 Sutter St. ◷Open Mon–Fri 8am–7pm, Sat–Sun & holidays 9am–2pm. ✕♿🅿 ✆*415-421-7221.*
This 26-story tower (1929, Timothy Pflueger), housing medical and dental offices, is one of San Francisco's finest Art Deco skyscrapers. Mayan motifs cover the spectacular gold-painted elevator lobby, adorn the plaster ceiling and decorate the undulating terra-cotta exterior all the way up to the top floor.

▶ Continue west to Powell St. and turn left.

Westin St. Francis Hotel★★

335 Powell St. ☛*Self-guided walking tour maps available at concierge desk.* ✕♿🅿 ✆*415-397-7000.* *www.westinstfrancis.com.*
Internationally renowned, this elegant Renaissance and Baroque Revival structure fronts the entire west side of Union Square. Commissioned by millionaire Charles Crocker, it opened in 1904 as the Hotel St. Francis. After the 1906 Fire, Bliss & Faville rebuilt and enlarged the hotel, which had previously occupied only half the block; it resumed business in 1907. In the decades since, celebrities and dignitaries have favored the St. Francis for its sumptuous interior, its central location and its emphasis on service.

Today the hotel's early 20C grandeur is most evident in the beautiful entrance hall, where coffered ceilings, marble-sheathed Corinthian columns and ornate balconies create a luxurious ambience. The "Magneta" grandfather clock is a favorite rendezvous point for San Francisco socialites. A 32-story tower (William L. Pereira Assoc.) was added to the rear of the hotel in 1972. Visitors who brave the vertiginous ride up in its glass exterior **elevators** 👤👤 are rewarded with expansive **views★★** of Union Square, the Financial District and the Bay Bridge.

▶ Continue south on Powell St. to Geary St. Turn right.

Theater District

Bounded by Sutter, Powell, Geary & Taylor Sts.
San Francisco's theater district contains about 10 venues ranging from spare, intimate houses to enormous, ornate, multi-balconied palaces.

Westin St. Francis Hotel

© Brigitta L. House / MICHELIN

Grandest among the latter are the **Geary Theater**★ *(415 Geary St.)*, designed by Bliss & Faville in 1909, and the adjacent **Curran Theatre**★ *(445 Geary St.)*, by Alfred Henry Jacobs in 1922. Registered National Historic Landmarks, the Geary and the Curran were constructed of reinforced concrete in the Neoclassical style. The Geary's fancifully embellished terracotta columns and stolid exterior set off the Curran's Romanesque arches and mansard roof. Home to the celebrated American Conservatory Theater since 1967, the Geary was closed in 1989-96 for renovation and seismic retrofitting after suffering structural damage in the Loma Prieta earthquake. The Curran Theatre has staged long-running Broadway shows since it opened.

Nearby are the **Cable Car Theater (A)** *(430 Mason St.)* and the **Stage Door Theatre (B)** *(420 Mason St.)*, housed in the Native Sons Building; look for the medallion portraits of prominent Californians embedded in the building's facade. The Stage Door is now the home of the Ruby Skye nightclub (℘*415-693-0777*).

Geary Theater

© Marco Lorenzetti / American Conservatory Theater

♿Consult Your Stay in the City for more San Francisco and Bay Area theater listings and ticket information.

ADDRESSES

BARS

The Redwood Room – *Geary St. at Taylor St. in the Clift Hotel.* ℘*415-929-2372.* A single redwood tree (felled by lightning) provided the 22ft columns and all the wood paneling for this posh hotel bar. Sip a cocktail beneath the gilded artworks that adorn the walls (don't let the moving paintings spook you), and let the streamlined Art Deco fixtures soothe your senses.

SHOPPING

Art Galleries and Rare Book Shops – *49 Geary St., between Grant & Kearny Sts.* Collectors of art and rare books know they have to penetrate the bland facade here to find the treasure trove within. The second floor contains antiquarian and rare book shops, and on the floors above, cavernous spaces designed to house Western Union machinery have been converted into galleries. Several art dealers specialize in photography.

Hang Art – *567 Sutter St. Open Mon–Sat 10am–6pm, Sun noon–5pm.* ℘*415-434-4264. www.hangart.com.* This spacious, relaxed showcase for emerging Bay Area painters and sculptors aims at luring new collectors by pricing most work under $2,000. Inspired by an engaging and knowledgeable young staff, rave reviews have showered Hang since its opening in mid-1998. Events, artist panel discussions and talks offer the opportunity to learn about the work on display.

BAYSHORE

The Bayshore region of San Francisco includes some of the city's most popular attractions Fisherman's Wharf, Alcatraz and the Golden Gate Bridge—as well as the peaceful, sprawling Presidio, an 1,480-acre park with coastal trails, golf courses, and a fine arts museum. At Fisherman's Wharf, along the Northern Waterfront between Telegraph Hill and the Marina District, relics of San Francisco's maritime past occupy the city's shoreline. Farther west, the waterfront includes Crissy Fields, beloved by joggers and bikers. Views from the waterfront's splendid setting take in passing freighters, the Golden Gate Bridge, Alcatraz, and the rugged shoreline of Marin County.

Highlights

1. Explore **Alcatraz** by night (p111)
2. Take a stroll through the **Ferry Building Farmers' Market** (p115)
3. Tour historic ships at **Fisherman's Wharf**, eat a sundae at **Ghirardelli Square** (p121, p126)
4. Bike the **Golden Gate Bridge** (p128)
5. Visit the **Exploratorium's Tactile Dome**, then picnic at **Crissy Field** (p139, p145)

On the Waterfront

Once an industrial zone, Fisherman's Wharf is San Francisco's most popular tourist destination. Its piers offer everything from carousel rides to sea lions on Pier 39, to maritime history on Hyde Street Pier. Fisherman's Wharf also serves as the departing point for ferries to Alcatraz. This infamous 12-acre island served variously as a fortress, military prison and U.S. Federal Penitentiary until its 1972 conversion to a national park.

To the east of Fisherman's Wharf, the Embarcadero lines the waterfront along the bay. The Embarcadero was once the hub of San Francisco's shipping and transportation. Revitalization began after the 1989 Loma Prieta earthquake damaged the Embarcadero Freeway. Once the freeway was razed, massive redevelopment began, creating the palm-line boulevard, airy plazas, and green spaces that define the area today. The farmers' market at the Ferry Building has become one of the best in the country, selling local and organic produce and drawing some 20,000 visitors each week.

East of Fisherman's Wharf is the Marina District, running between the wharf and the Presidio, and from the northern waterfront to Pacific Heights. The Marina is a popular neighborhood for young, wealthy professionals. Visit on a sunny weekend and you'll see why—Union Street and Chestnut Street are both chock-full with chi-chi boutiques, bars, and wonderful restaurants.

Outdoorsy types love to bike or jog along Marina Green past Crissy Field to the Golden Gate Bridge and beyond. The Golden Gate Bridge is a major attraction. Opened in 1937 and painted bright orange, it spans the Golden Gate Strait and is the ninth-largest suspension bridge in the world. On the Golden Gate's southern side is the Presidio. Maintained by the National Park Service, the Presidio lures visitors with its lushly forested expanse as well as its rich history as a military installation.

Sea Lions, Pier 39

© Trish Foxwell / SFCVB

Alcatraz★★★

Alcatraz cruises depart from Fisherman's Wharf

A mere 1.5mi from the comforts of San Francisco, this infamous 12-acre island, now inhabited by scores of seabirds who nest among its crumbling ruins, once held scores of prisoners incarcerated atop its sheer cliffs. Aptly nicknamed "the Rock" and isolated from shore by the cold, treacherous currents that swirl through the bay, Alcatraz served variously as a fortress, military prison, and U.S. Federal Penitentiary until its conversion to a national park and museum in 1972. A visit to Alcatraz provides a haunting journey into one of the harshest chapters of American judicial history.

A BIT OF HISTORY

For thousands of years before Spanish and Portuguese explorers first set sights on Northern California, some 10,000 indigenous people lived on the coastal area between the San Francisco Bay and Point Sur.

According to Native American oral history, the Alcatraz island was originally used to ostracize members of the tribe. It was also used for food gathering.

The first Europeans to sight the barren island were Spanish explorers José de Cañizares and Juan Manuel de Ayala in 1775. Noticing the large number of gannet-like cormorants nesting on the cliffs, they named the rocky spot *Isla de los alcatraces,* or "island of gannets."

With no freshwater and little natural vegetation, the island remained uninhabited until President Millard Fillmore designated it a military reservation in 1850. Alcatraz' location at the mouth of the bay made it a natural choice for a fortress, and Army engineers planned to make the island one of three forts in a "Triangle of Defense" to guard the entrance of San Francisco Bay. The other two points of the triangle would be the forts at Fort Point and Lime

Info: www.nps.gov/alcatraz. Tickets ☎415-981-7625 or www.alcatrazcruises.com. Ticket booth located at Pier 33, Fisherman's Wharf.

Location: Ferry service to Alcatraz is provided by Alcatraz Cruises (♿see p111). Ticket prices include ferry transport, interpretive talks and ranger-led hikes by National Park Service rangers, and the cellhouse audio tour.

Timing: During peak tourist season (July and August), tours to Alcatraz are often booked weeks in advance, so reserve as early as possible or purchase tickets online. The Alcatraz day tour takes 2–2.5hrs; the evening tour takes 3hrs.

Don't Miss: The excellent cellhouse audio tour; the price is included in the ticket price.

ALCATRAZ CRUISES

Ferries depart from Pier 33 at Fisherman's Wharf ◷*Open mid-Mar–late Oct daily 9am–3.55pm every 30–45min (evening tours Thur-Mon 6.10 and 6.45pm); rest of the year daily 9.30am–1.55pm every 30–45min (evening tours 4.20pm). Closed Jan 1, Thanksgiving Day, Dec 25.* ✆*$28 ($35 for evening tour); children and family discounts available.*
Alcatraz Cruises, LLC – Pier 33, Hornblower Alcatraz Landing. ☎415-981-ROCK (7625). www.alcatrazcruises.com

Point, although the fort at latter was never built.

Construction on a garrison began in 1853, and was completed by December 1859. Captain Joseph Stewart took com-

Alcatraz

© P. Fuszard / SFCVB

mand of Alcatraz Island with 86 men of Company H, Third U.S. Artillery. Though cannons were mounted on the island, advancing military technology soon rende-red them obsolete; not one was ever fired in defense.

In 1861 Confederate sympathizers and renegade U.S. soldiers were incarcerated at the garrison. In the 1870s its walls held Native American prisoners from various Indian wars in California and the West. The largest group of Native Americans held at Alcatraz was a group of 19 Hopis held from January 3 to August 7, 1895, who were incarcerated for refusing to send their children to government-run boarding schools and for refusing to farm on individual plots away from the mesasthe isolated flat-topped, steep-sided hills on which they lived.

In 1901 the last cannons were dismantled, and six years later regular troops abandoned the island, to be replaced by members of the U.S. Military Guard. **"Super Prison"** – Mounting costs and increasing protest over conditions led to the 1933 transfer of the property to the U.S. Department of Justice, which established a federal penitentiary on the island. Banishment to the maximum-security facility on Alcatraz was reserved for the most "desperate and irredeemable criminals" in the federal system, including those designated "public enemies" and deemed a danger to society, even behind bars. The ratio

of one guard to every three prisoners, a strict "no talking" rule, brutal isolation cells, and a near-impenetrable security system quickly established Alcatraz's reputation as America's bleakest prison. Some 1,545 prisoners were held at Alcatraz over 28 years. Notorious inhabitants of "the Rock" included mobster Al "Scarface" Capone, bank robber George "Machine Gun" Kelly, Alvin "Creepy" Karpis, and Robert "Birdman" Stroud (who, contrary to popular lore, never kept birds here).

Over the years, 36 men tried to escape from Alcatraz in 14 attempts, all of them apparently unsuccessful. Some of the escapees were captured, some were shot, and some disappeared forever in the bay. The most notorious attempt in 1962, in which three inmates disappeared, raised serious questions about the prison's deteriorated condition. That, combined with the high cost and the complaints of San Franciscans worried about the prison in their bay, led to the decision to close Alcatraz. The prison officially closed on March 21, 1963.

After the last inmates were transferred in 1963, the island fell vacant until 1969, when a group of Native Americans occupied it. They cited an 1868 treaty granting them the right to claim uninhabited federal land. The occupation ended 19 months later, its goals unrealized. The occupation did, however, kickstart the Pan-Indian Movement.

On October 12, 1972, Alcatraz was designated part of the Golden Gate National Recreation Area, and was opened to the public the following year. The following year the site was opened to the public. Today, it is one of the most visited sites in the National Park Service.

VISIT

The ferry trip *(15min)* to the dock at Alcatraz offers stunning **views★★** of the city skyline, the Golden Gate Bridge and the cliffs of the island. Graffiti from the Indian occupation can be spotted on the bluffs and dock buildings. At the ferry wharf, rangers provide an information near the landing, after which visitors are free to inspect the exhibit area on the lower floor of the Barracks Building (1867), view an **orientation video** *(15min)* in the theater, or climb the steep switchback road past the ruins of the Post Exchange and Officers' Quarters to the cellhouse.

The award-winning Alcatraz **Cellhouse Audio Tour** is recommended. It covers the inside of the cellhouse (at the top of the island) during the penitentiary era (1934–1963), and is included in the ticket price. Ranger-led talks and guided strolls in otherwise inaccessible parts of the island are occasionally offered; a list of the day's topics is available at the landing dock. Evening tours offer a more guided exploration of the cellhouse, and a darker view of prison life. A haunting view of the city skyline, sometimes as it becomes obscured by fog, contributes to the sense of isolation.

Once on the island, visitors can stay as long as they like; ferries depart for San Francisco about every 30min, and visitors can return on any ferry.

Cellhouse★★

While most of the island's buildings have been reduced to ruins and turned over to raucous flocks of seabirds, the forbidding cellhouse is intact enough to provide a chilling glimpse into the bleak life of the federal prisoners who were sentenced here. Built by convicts in 1911, it was, for a time, the largest reinforced concrete structure in the world.

Visitors enter the building near the bunker-like control center, formerly an arsenal of arms and tear gas. Beyond the control center lies the Visitation Area, where prisoners were separated from visitors by thick plate glass and spoke over a monitored telephone.

Once inside the cavernous main room, visitors can stroll down "Broadway," the wide central passage between B and C Blocks leading to "Times Square," and step into a cramped, cold cell furnished with a regulation army cot, a folding table and chair, and a squat, open toilet. Prisoners who violated the strict rules of Alcatraz were subjected to solitary confinement in the dank isolation rooms, or "dark holes," of D Block. Robert "Birdman" Stroud was one of the Alcatraz prisoners kept in isolation. Indeed, he spent more time in isolation than any other federal prisoner in history. Stroud was incarcerated for 54 years; 43 of them were spent in solitary confinement.

Access to the recreation yard and library, now open for exploration, was a privilege awarded for good behavior. Several concrete paths lead around the perimeter of the island. Most of the land is not accessible to the public. The main road to the cellhouse and the western road from the cellhouse to the base of the recreation yard exit remain open year-round.

Bird-watching enthusiasts will be pleased to find a wide variety of birds on Alcatraz. The island is now a sanctuary for seabirds and waterbirds, including cormorants, pigeon guillemots, snowy egrets and black-crowned night herons. The first half of the year offers the greatest chance for spotting them.

The Embarcadero★

A waterfront promenade stretching three miles from Fisherman's Wharf to China Basin, The Embarcadero ("boarding place" in Spanish) combines expansive views of the bay with public artworks and attractions.

A BIT OF HISTORY

The vibrant hub of San Francisco's shipping and transportation industries from the Gold Rush until the 1950s, the Embarcadero took shape in the 1850s when landfill extended the shore from its natural line along present-day Montgomery Street. As San Francisco boomed through the late 19C, sailors, longshoremen and warehouse workers frequented the growing number of gambling dens and union halls.

Ferries from points across the bay began docking here before the turn of the 20C, and the waterfront swarmed with daily commuters until 1936, when rail service and auto lanes over the new San Francisco–Oakland Bay Bridge siphoned away ferry traffic. Through the mid-20C, the Embarcadero fell into disuse as shippers gradually transferred their activities across the bay to the better-equipped Port of Oakland.

The construction of the elevated **Embarcadero Freeway**, planned as a link between the Bay Bridge and the Golden Gate Bridge, in the 1950s further diminished the waterfront's appeal by interposing a dirty concrete roadbed between the city and the bay. Construction had reached north to Broadway before massive protest halted progress in 1959. The freeway was razed after being damaged in the 1989 Loma Prieta earthquake, to many San Franciscans' glee.

A New Beginning – Ongoing redevelopment projects have revitalized this historic area. Extending 3.2mi from Fisherman's Wharf to China Basin is **Herb Caen Way**, a promenade named for the popular late *San Francisco Chronicle* columnist whose trademark ellipses punctuated many a morn-

🚌 Bus 7–Haight, 14–Mission, 21–Hayes, 31–Balboa, or 71–Haight-Noriega; all streetcars Embarcadero station. 🚊 Embarcadero station.

📍 **Michelin Map:** *See YERBA BUENA GARDENS.*

📋 **Info:** ✆415-391-2000. www.onlyinsanfrancisco.com.

▶ **Location:** The main Embarcadero attractions are Fisherman's Wharf, the Ferry Building, and AT&T Park. While the distances between them can be long for walkers, the Embarcadero is ideal for jogging.

👥 **Kids:** A baseball game at AT&T Park (or a tour, if you're not here on a game day).

🕐 **Timing:** You may not want to visit the Embarcadero sights together. The sights are linked to adjacent neighborhoods: Fisherman's Wharf to North Beach, the Ferry Building to the Financial District, and AT&T Park to SoMa.

🅿 **Parking:** Very little public parking is available on the Embarcadero; drivers might try the lot at the Embarcadero Center (*see FINANCIAL DISTRICT*) or Fisherman's Wharf (the garage is across from Pier 39). We highly recommend the F-Market & Wharves historic streetcar, running between Fisherman's Wharf and the Castro District.

👁 **Don't Miss:** The Ferry Building—its gourmet indoor marketplace and outdoor farmer's market have become a magnet for chefs and food lovers across the Bay Area.

ing read from 1938 to 1996. This long ribbon of sidewalk draws visitors and residents to enjoy glorious views of the bay, the Bay Bridge and the towers of the Financial District. The road itself is brightened by Canary Island palms and by the F-Market streetcars that rattle along its length. Fishermen gather at the end of **Pier 7** *(near Broadway)* with its old-fashioned wrought-iron railings and park benches and their expansive views of the bay.

South of the Ferry Building, brick warehouses and factories of the onetime waterfront industrial belt are reborn as residential and office spaces, some with trendy eateries. **Hills Plaza**, with its distinctive brick tower, is a noteworthy example; erected in 1924, it originally housed the headquarters for Hills Brothers Coffee Company.

New commercial and residential complexes enliven the west side of the Embarcadero from the Bay Bridge to AT&T Park at China Basin. En route, the thoroughfare passes attractive **South Beach Park**, anchored by Mark diSuvero's towering abstract sculpture *Sea Change* **(1)**.

SIGHTS
Ferry Building★★
Embarcadero at Market St. ○*Open Mon–Fri 10am–6pm, Sat 9am–6pm, Sun 11am–5pm.* ○*Closed Jan 1, Thanksgiving Day, Dec 25.* ✕ ⴓ

Ferry Building

© Brigitta L. House / MICHELIN

☏*415-983-8030. www.ferrybuilding marketplace.com.*
A hugely successful renovation, completed in 2003, has brought this landmark back into the spotlight as an airy gourmet retail and restaurant complex. Designed by A. Page Brown of Colusa sandstone and anchored on 111 steel-framed concrete piers, the building was hailed at its dedication in 1898 as the most solidly constructed edifice in California, a claim that was proved when it survived the great earthquake of 1906. The Ferry Building's 240ft clock tower, designed by Willis Polk, was inspired by the Giralda of Seville and boasts four huge (and accurate) clock faces.

The Historic Streetcars of the F-Market Line

San Francisco's cable cars are not the city's only rolling history: Since September 1995, a colorful fleet of historic streetcars has glided up and down Market Street, a historical grace note amid the throngs of pedestrians, cars, buses, and streetcars that swarm the bustling thoroughfare. Since 2000, these beloved antiques have traversed the shoreline along the Embarcadero from China Basin to Fisherman's Wharf, south and north of Market Street. Elegantly streamlined and colorfully painted, PCC cars were manufactured in the U.S. from 1936 to 1952 and put into service throughout North America and Europe. The rehabilitated cars today reflect not only the Muni green-and-cream colors, but also more than two dozen color schemes of other cities where these streetcars were used, including Boston (orange, cream, and silver), Baltimore (yellow and gray), Los Angeles (red, orange, and gray), and Kansas City (cream, black, and silver). Also on the tracks are retired streetcars from cities around the world, such as England, Zürich, Melbourne, Milan, and Hiroshima.

Outdoor market, Ferry Building

© Peter Wrenn / Michelin

Until completion of the Golden Gate and Bay Bridges in the late 1930s, the Ferry Building served as San Francisco's main transportation hub. An estimated 50 million people passed through it annually, Marin County and East Bay commuters. In 1956, after ferry traffic declined, the northern half of the structure was converted into office space, and in 1962 the southern half was remodeled as well.

The recent $100 million renovation created 65,000 sq ft of marketplace space along the first floor's central nave, with shop space for area food producers and eclectic shops. There are also a number of popular restaurants. Stroll behind the building to the wooden sundeck, where commuter ferries still depart for Sausalito and Larkspur in Marin County. Just north, another ferry offers services to Alameda, Oakland, Tiburon and Vallejo. The tranquil monument to Mohandas K. Gandhi **(2)** was donated to the city in 1988.

Nearby, the new two-acre Rincon Park (along the waterfront at the foot of Folsom St.) was dedicated in early 2003. Marked by a bayfront promenade with **views**★★ of the sparkling bay, Bay Bridge and Treasure Island, Rincon Park showcases Cupid's Span, a 60ft-tall bow and arrow made of fiberglass and steel by sculptors Claes Oldenburg and Coosje van Bruggen.

Rincon Center★

101 Spear St. at Mission St. ○*Open daily.* ╳⛄🅿 ✆*415-777-4100.*
This complex (1989), a block south and west of the Ferry Building, boasts a panoply of stores and cafes. The former Rincon Annex Post Office (1940, Gilbert S. Underwood), which now functions as the center's **lobby,** remains its most gripping feature. Especially worthy of note are Russian-born artist Anton Refregier's **murals**★ depicting Northern California's rough-and-tumble history, from the arrival of Sir Francis Drake in 1579 until World War II.

Completed in 1948 and rendered in broad, muscular strokes and bold colors that underscore Refregier's thematic emphasis on labor, struggle, and war, these 27 panels provide an unsparing view of the wild West. Adjacent display cases present artifacts and photographs. In the lofty atrium off the lobby, an 85ft **Rain Column** (1988, Doug Hollis) forms the eye-catching centerpiece of a spacious food court.

🚻 AT&T Park★★

24 Willie Mays Plaza, at 3rd & King Sts. ➤➤*Tours ($17.50) daily 10.30am and 12.30pm except when game conflicts. Coca-Cola Fan Lot (free) open 2hrs before scheduled first pitch on days of home games, and on non-game days Sept–May Sat–Sun 10am–4pm, Apr–*

Aug daily 10am–4pm. ⊜*Game tickets $20–$225.* ✕&🅿*℘415-972-2000. http://sanfrancisco.giants.mlb.com.*

Many baseball insiders consider San Francisco's new $319 million major-league stadium to be the finest in the world. Opened in 2000, it couples the mood of an early 20C urban ballpark, such as Boston's Fenway Park or Chicago's Wrigley Field, with modern amenities. HOK Sport designed the 40,800-seat stadium to shield players and spectators from wind and fog. Upper-level tiers offer spectacular views of the city skyline, Bay Bridge and Oakland.

The park's main entrance is at **24 Willie Mays Plaza,** where a red-brick facade rises behind William Behrends' 9ft bronze statue of the Hall of Fame outfielder, who wore the number 24 throughout his playing career (1951–73). The **Coca-Cola Fan Lot** features pop-bottle slides, a wiffleball field, speed-pitching, baserunning areas, and "the world's largest baseball glove," a sculpture of a three-finger mitt. Behind the right-field wall, 335ft from home plate, rare home runs may splash into **McCovey Cove** (named for Giants' first baseman Willie McCovey), a part of the Bay known as China Basin.

Ambitious fans watch games from boats in the cove, hoping to fish out home run balls.

ADDITIONAL SIGHTS
San Francisco–Oakland Bay Bridge★★

🕐*Open daily.* ⊜*$6 toll westbound only from Oakland. Nonvehicular crossing of the bridge prohibited. ℘510-286-4444. www.dot.ca.gov.*

Though often overshadowed by the celebrity of the Golden Gate Bridge, this double-deck engineering marvel is a distinctive and beloved landmark in its own right. Begun in 1933, the project was financed by a $77 million federal loan during the nadir of the Great Depression. Engineers Charles H. Purcell, Charles E. Andrew and Glenn B. Woodruff joined forces with architect Timothy Pflueger to design the bridge, which had to cross 8.4mi of water—including approaches, its span is nearly eight times that of the Golden Gate.

To traverse the distance, the bridge was conceived as two structures meeting at Yerba Buena Island, a rocky promontory midway across the bay. The western section, comprising two 2,310ft suspension bridges, joins San Francisco and the island. The roadway hangs suspended from steel cables draped between four distinctive X-braced towers; a concrete pier rises 48 stories from the floor of the bay to anchor the two suspension bridges in the center. The eastern section, joining Yerba Buena Island and

Bay Bridge

© Phil Coblentz / SFCVB

Oakland, is a cantilever-truss design—the roadway rests on steel-and-concrete piers joined by a network of steel beams. Between the two sections, a tunnel pierces Yerba Buena Island; 76ft wide and 58ft high, its diameter may be the largest of any vehicular tunnel in the world. Completed in November 1936, the bridge carried trains on its lower level and cars on its upper level for two decades. Today each deck bears five lanes of automobile traffic. Travelers on the westbound upper deck enjoy **views★** of the Financial District and the Embarcadero as they approach the city. Next to the bridge, a new bridge is being built with an estimated completion date of 2013 and a $6 billion price tag.

Treasure Island★

◯ *Take I-80 across the Bay Bridge; exit at Treasure Island/Yerba Buena Island.* 🚌 *Bus 108–Treasure Island.* 📞*415-274-0660. www.sftreasureisland.org.*
Lying in San Francisco Bay midway between San Francisco and Oakland, this 400-acre man-made isle was constructed in 1938 from the rubble of the Bay Bridge tunnel to host a world fair. Today it offers stupendous panoramic views as well as charming insights into a sometimes-overlooked chapter of San Francisco history.

Opened on February 18, 1939, the **Golden Gate International Exposition of 1939–1940** drew more than 17 million visitors during its two-year run. In all, 36 nations and 31 states participated in the fair, themed "The Pageant of the Pacific" to prompt awareness of trade potential with Pacific Basin nations. World War II brought an abrupt end to the jubilant celebration of Pacific relations. Naval Station Treasure Island operated on the island from World War II until it closed in September 1997.

Today, the island is mainly residential, with a few restaurants. Building 1, holding administrative offices, also contains art exhibits. The causeway at the gated entry area affords a sweeping **view★★★** over the city, encompassing, from south to north, the suspension portion of the Bay Bridge, the San Francisco skyline

and backdrop hills, the Golden Gate, Alcatraz, Mount Tamalpais, Angel Island and the North Bay, with the Richmond-San Rafael Bridge.

ADDRESSES

ORGANIC TREASURES

San Franciscans are well known for paying close attention to the food they eat and where it comes from. They fervently support local farmers and artisan food producers, particularly those using certified organic or eco-friendly techniques. The crème de la crème of artisan food producers maintain outlets in the Ferry Building's grand central hall, making it a mecca for foodies. **Cowgirl Creamery**'s (no. 17) delectable artisan cheeses, many of them made locally, can be sampled on site or shipped home. **Prather Ranch Meat Company**'s (no. 32) methods are certified humane and organic; the staff cheerfully educates customers about sustainable husbandry. If you're needing bread for a picnic or a roll for a snack, pop into the **Acme Bread Company** (no. 15), famed for artisan loaves made from organic flours. For dessert, try a fresh galette or pastry at **Frog Hollow Farms** (no. 46); their jellies and conserves are also very popular.

SHOPPING / CAFES

Ferry Plaza Farmers' Market – *Market St. at The Embarcadero. Open Tue and Thu 10am–2pm, Sat 8am–2pm.* 📞*415-291-3276. www.cuesa.org.* The city's most prestigious farmers' market brings together Bay Area farmers and artisanal food producers three days a week. Live music and cooking demos are regular fixtures on the scene. Crafts are sold across the street at Justin Herman Plaza.

Java House – *The Embarcadero at Townsend St. Open daily 7am–5pm.* 📞*415-495-7260. www.javahousesf.com.* Pick up a tasty, cheap cheeseburger or tuna sandwich, settle down on a stool and get a taste of colorful, workaday San Francisco from this shack on Pier 40 beside the South Beach yacht harbor.

Fisherman's Wharf★★★

San Francisco's colorful maritime legacy survives in this bustling district on the northeastern tip of the peninsula. A carnival atmosphere prevails on the rowdier east end of the wharf, especially at the Pier 39 marketplace, where there's a pod of vociferous and amusing sea lions, and souvenir shops. Street performers and sidewalk seafood stands add to the chaos. The western end of the wharf has historic sailing ships, a maritime museum, some art galleries, a relaxing park, and two shopping centers housed in historic factories.

A BIT OF HISTORY

In 1853, **Henry "Honest Harry" Meiggs**, councilman, entrepreneur, and later the most notorious embezzler of public funds in the city's early history, constructed a wharf extending 1,600ft from Francisco and Powell Streets across North Point Cove into the bay. From its inception, Meigg's Wharf was an important center of industry. The ferry terminal to Sausalito was located at its far end, and a sawmill, a pipe works, and a junk shop crowded its length. Shipbuilding flourished and visitors came down to the wharf to enjoy bay views and the cheap beer, cracked crab and hot chowder.

In the 1860s, North Point Cove from Bay Street to the current shoreline was filled with rock, creating a flat stretch of land that became a manufacturing and industrial zone. After anti-Chinese legislation in the 1870s restricted commercial opportunities for the Asians, who previously had dominated the fishing industry, Genoese immigrants took to the seas. Over time, the fishermen (*pescatori* in Italian) were outnumbered by their compatriots from Naples, Calabria and Sicily.

Today descendants of Sicilians dominate, from the fishing boats that continue to depart from here to the wildly popular restaurants and sidewalk seafood stands that bear the names of their prominent Italian-American founders.

🚃 Powell-Hyde or Powell-Mason. 🚊 Streetcar F-Market. Bus 19–Polk, 30–Stockton, 39–Coit, or 47–Van Ness.

🛈 **Info:** www.fishermans wharf.org.

▶ **Location:** Fisherman's Wharf is centered on Jefferson St. between Grant and Hyde Sts.

👥 **Kids:** The carousel on Pier 39 is great fun for little ones, as is the Aquarium of the Bay. They'll also love trying to tackle the Earthquake sundae at the Ghirardelli Soda Fountain and Chocolate Shop.

🕐 **Timing:** In summer and on most weekends, crowds make movement difficult, especially along Jefferson Street. In winter, when crab fishing is in swing, the wharf is at its most interesting and least congested.

🅿 **Parking:** Public transportation is the best way to get here—try the F-Market streetcars and Powell Street cable cars. For drivers, there are large garages across from Pier 39 *(Beach St. between Stockton & Powell Sts.)* and underneath Ghirardelli Square *(Beach St. at Larkin St.)*, but they are expensive and often full.

😋 **Don't Miss:** Clam chowder in a bread bowl or a crab sandwich, plus a glimpse at the sea lions at Pier 39 and the historic vessels at Hyde Street Pier and Pier 45.

Fisherman's Wharf

© Lewis Sommer / SFCVB

Through the first half of the 20C, fishing remained a major industry. As maritime technology became more efficient, however, the bay and surrounding waters were overfished, forcing the boats to move farther and farther beyond the Golden Gate or to relocate altogether. By the 1950s the fleet's numbers had been severely reduced, and large sections of the old industrial zone had become run-down or abandoned.

Tidal Wave of Tourism – The opening of the National Maritime Museum in 1951 marked the beginning of the waterfront's rebirth as a tourist destination. The area boomed in the 1960s when developers began purchasing properties such as the California Fruit Canners Association building and the old Ghirardelli Chocolate Factory, converting them into showpieces.

In years since, burgeoning tourism has sparked an explosion of related businesses, few of them linked to the maritime legacy that makes the wharf such an interesting place to visit.

Brightly lit T-shirt shops and souvenir stands line the south side of Jefferson Street along with several novelty museums, including the **Wax Museum at Fisherman's Wharf** (*145 Jefferson St.; open daily 10am–9pm; $16; 415-202-0416; www.waxmuseum.com*) and the nearby **Ripley's Believe It or Not! Museum** (*175 Jefferson St.; open mid-Jun–Labor Day Sun–Thu 9am–11pm, Fri–Sat 9am–midnight; rest of the year Sun–Thu 10am–10pm, Fri–Sat 10am–midnight; $18.99; 415-202-9850; http://sanfrancisco.ripleys.com*.

Yet underneath the honky-tonk veneer, much of the area retains its salty character of old. Visitors who step off the main path will discover a series of working piers, fabulous views of the bay, and several evocative monuments to the city's maritime past.

Fisherman's Wharf

© Jerry Lee Hayes / SFCVB

SIGHTS
Sights below are listed from east to west.

👥 Pier 39★

Embarcadero at Beach St. 🕐*Open Sun–Thu 10am–8pm, Fri–Sat 10am–9pm (later hours apply in spring and summer).* ✕♿🅿 *℘415-981-7437. www.pier39.com.*

Built over a dilapidated c.1900 pier, this festive, bilevel marketplace ranks among the top tourist destinations in the state. After the Port of San Francisco lost its shipping supremacy to Oakland in the 1970s, Pier 39 was nearly demolished, but a redevelopment (1978) attracted retailers from video arcades to confectioneries, boutiques and restaurants. A brightly painted carousel anchors the far end of the complex.

At the base of the pier lies the **Aquarium of the Bay★** *(👥🕐open Memorial Day–Labor Day daily 9am–8pm; rest of the year Mon–Thu 10am–6pm, Fri–Sat 10am–7pm;* 🕐 *closed Dec 25;* ✏$18; ♿ *℘888-732-3483 or 415-623-5300; www.aquariumofthebay.com).*

Visitors here may enter and view the undersea world up close with a stroll through two clear 300ft-long tunnels that burrow through tanks containing 23,000 aquatic creatures, including Pacific octopus, eels, and sharks. There's also a series of touch pools that allow you to touch live bat rays and leopard sharks. Adding to Pier 39's carnival atmosphere, a group of wild California **sea lions★** occupies the docks off its west side. The reason for the blubbery creatures' arrival here in 1990 is a mystery, but it is thought that they are members of the same colony that inhabits Seal Rocks, near Cliff House; their raucous barking can be heard from as far away as Telegraph Hill. Informal interpretive talks on the sea lions are offered on weekends (weather permitting) by volunteers from the **Marine Mammal Center** *(℘415-289-7373; www.marinemammalcenter.org),* which maintains a kiosk near the docks and a gift shop on the mall's second level.

Adventurous types should visit City Kayak *(℘800-725-0790; www.citykayak.com),* which rents boats to kayakers of all abilities. Beginners can paddle along the waterfront and experts can venture all the way to the Golden Gate Bridge or around Alcatraz Island. For those who'd rather experience thrills from dry land, there's 7D-Experience *(✏$15; ℘415-445-0120),* a simulation theater whose chairs pitch and yaw as you use lasers to shoot the robot cowboys or zombies projected on a screen.

👥 Bay Cruises★

A scenic cruise on San Francisco Bay offers visitors a new perspective of the city, from a peek at the underside of the Golden Gate Bridge to wide **views★** of steep hills and the skyline. From the vantage point of the bay, visitors can learn about San Francisco and get a glimpse of the waterfront as a working port. The Blue and Gold Fleet's **Bay Cruise Adventure** *(🕐departs Pier 39 May–Sept Mon–Fri 10am–6pm, Sat–Sun 10am–7pm; rest of the year Mon–Fri 10am–4pm, Sat–Sun 10am–6pm;* 🕐 *closed Dec 25; round-trip 1hr; English-language commentary;* ✏$26; ✕♿ *℘415-705-8200; www.blueandgoldfleet.com)* travels west along the shoreline, circles beneath the Golden Gate Bridge and passes close to Angel Island, Alcatraz, and Pier 39's sea lions. The Red and White Fleet's **Golden Gate Bay Cruise** *(🕐depart from Pier 43½ May–Sept daily 10am–6.15pm; rest of the year daily 10am–4.15pm; round-trip 1hr; commentary;* ✏$26; ✕♿ *℘415-673-2900; www.redandwhite.com)* follows a similar route; individual headsets broadcast a well-produced narrative (available in twelve languages).

👥 Boudin at the Wharf★★

160 Jefferson St., between Mason & Taylor Sts. 🕐*Baker's Hall open daily 8am–9pm; museum and bakery tour (*✏$3*) open Wed–Mon 11.30am–9pm; restaurant and bar hours vary.* ✕♿. *℘415-928-1849. www.boudinbakery.com.*

Opened in spring 2005, this airy, 26,000sq ft shrine to sourdough bread adds a note of elegance to Fisherman's Wharf. Sporting a 30-ft-long observation window along Jefferson Street so that passersby can watch the bakers at work, the structure contains a cafe, restaurant, demonstration bakery, and museum. The Boudin family began making sourdough bread more than 150 years ago for fortune-seekers headed to the Nevada hills during the Gold Rush. The same recipe for the tart, chewy bread—unbleached flour, water, a pinch of salt, and a portion of so-called mother dough—has been used ever since. Try it Fisherman's Wharf style—hollowed out and filled with clam chowder.

▲▲ Musée Mécanique

Pier 45, Shed A (Embarcadero at Taylor St.). ⏱Open Mon–Fri 10am–7pm, Sat–Sun 10am–8pm. ♿ ☎415-346-2000. www.museemecaniquesf.com.
Formerly housed in a small gallery at the Cliff House (ⓒ*see SUTRO HEIGHTS*), this curious collection of antique mechanical amusements includes coin-operated player pianos, mobile dioramas made entirely of toothpicks, and penny-arcade picture machines. Many of the mechanisms were collected from Playland, most notably "Laughing Sal," whose rambunctious guffaws—audible from a considerable distance—recall the days when small change could buy a laugh.

▲▲ USS Pampanito★★

Pier 45, Fisherman's Wharf. ⏱Open daily from 9am. Call for closing times. 👓$12. ☎415-775-1943. www.maritime.org.
A World War II, Balao-class submarine built in the Portsmouth naval shipyard in 1943, this deep-diving, 311ft vessel made a half-dozen patrols during her two years of service in the Pacific, sinking six Japanese ships and damaging four others. In September 1944, the *Pampanito* and two other submarines jointly attacked a convoy of Japanese ships in the South China Sea carrying oil, raw rubber and other war supplies. After sinking several ships, the three subs pursued the surviving vessels out of the area. When the *Pampanito* returned a few days later, the crew spotted men clinging to pieces of wreckage; the 73 rescued were British and Australian pris-

oners of war who had been aboard the sunken vessels. That number—73—is commemorated on the *Pampanito's* flag, displayed on the pier. Other informative panels describe the workings of a submarine and tell the story of the *Pampanito*.

Visit

ⓘ*Some physical agility is required to slip through the submarine's narrow corridors and small hatches.*
The haunting, self-guided audio tour begins on the upper deck and moves from the rear (aft) torpedo room through the maneuvering room, engine rooms, galley, control room and officers' quarters to the cramped forward torpedo room, where members of the crew slept beside the massive weapons. A former commander of the sub narrates the audio tour, his matter-of-fact voice and understated descriptions effectively conveying the claustrophobia, fear and boredom that faced those who signed

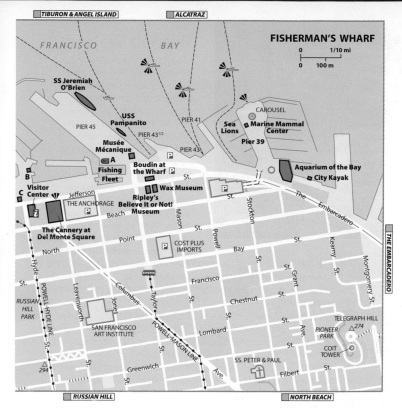

on for submarine duty. Pampanito veterans have added their personal accounts, complemented by sound effects and other historic recordings.

👥 S.S. Jeremiah O'Brien★

Pier 45. 🕐 Open daily 9am–4pm. 🕐 Closed Jan 1, Thanksgiving Day, Dec 25. 🎫 $12. ✆ 415-544-0100. www.ssjeremiahobrien.org.

This noble gray vessel formed part of the 5,000-ship armada that stormed Normandy Beach on D-Day in 1944. Launched on June 19, 1943, she was one of a fleet of 2,751 Liberty Ships that served as the backbone of the supply line to U.S. Armed Forces during World War II. Lovingly restored and maintained by volunteers, the ship remains fully operational. Self-guided tours cover all areas, including the wheelhouse, engine room, crew's quarters, deckside guns and ship's store. On "steaming weekends" *(3rd weekend Jan–Apr, Jun–Sept & Nov)*, the crew fires up her triple-

expansion steam engines, used in the blockbuster movie *Titanic* to replicate the engines of that ill-fated luxury liner.

Fishing Fleet★

North side of Jefferson St. between Jones and Taylor Sts.

The small, colorful fishing boats tied up at the docks just off Jefferson Street are remnants of an active and successful fleet that once numbered more than 450 vessels. Today the fishermen take out their vessels very early in the morning to fish for rex and petrale sole, sea bass, mackerel, sand dab, rock cod, ling cod and herring in the waters outside the Golden Gate, then return to unload their catches along this and other piers behind the Jefferson Street Lagoon. Although most of the fish sold in the city is now flown and trucked in, 20 million pounds of seafood still come into this port annually.

Visitors may take a self-guided tour of this active wharf area by following 30

Sidewalk Seafood

Dungeness crabs being cooked and cracked at Fisherman's Wharf

© Rick Gerharter / SFCVB

A stroll along the north side of Jefferson Street between Jones and Taylor Streets leads through a symphony of smells and tastes whose overriding note is fresh seafood. The tradition of eating outdoors on the wharf dates from the early 20C, when Italian fishermen returning from early-morning runs grabbed bowls of chowder from sidewalk stands before hurrying off to sell the day's catch. In 1916, Tomaso Castagnola began offering walkaway crab cocktails to tourists who came down to see the colorful fishing fleet. His success led Italian fishing families to set up their own steaming pots along the wharf from which they sold freshly cooked Dungeness crab. Even the opening of large, full-service restaurants in the 1930s could not diminish the popularity of the sidewalk stands.

Today, a ladle of creamy clam chowder in a hollowed-out loaf of sourdough bread has become a mandatory part of the San Francisco experience. Another quintessentially San Franicsco food available at the wharf is Dungeness crab, a symbol of the local fishing industry. The season typically begins in November, when it's sold fresh from daily trapping by street vendors, many of whom make a rhythmic show of cracking the sweet crustacean's ten legs. You can either buy them cooked and steamed, or take it home raw to work your own magic.

Out of season, fresh crab is flown in, and remains a fixture on the wharf's restaurant menus.

Although nontraditional items such as pizza have recently appeared, the best fare on the wharf still comes from the sea—including shrimp or crab salad sandwiches on crusty sourdough rolls, freshly steamed Pacific rock lobster, prawn and crab cocktails, oysters, crab cakes, and an assortment of fried squid, fish, and clams.

Fisherman's Wharf seafood

© Richard Nowitz / Apa Publications

Kids playing on the C.A. Thayer, Hyde Street Pier
© Brigitta L. House / MICHELIN

interpretive signs describing the history and operation of the fishing industry. A small building of brown wood with a stained-glass ship's wheel over its door rests at the western foot of **Pier 45**. Erected in 1980, this **Fisherman's and Seamen's Memorial Chapel (A)** remains truly ecumenical, hosting christenings, bar mitzvahs, Latin masses, Buddhist memorials, and weddings of all sorts.

The Cannery at Del Monte Square★★

2801 Leavenworth St. at Jefferson St. Shops open Mon–Sat 10am–6pm, Sun from 11am (summer until 8pm). Restaurant hours vary. ✕ ⚐ ℘415-771-3112. www.delmontesquare.com.
Anchoring the west end of Jefferson Street, this airy shopping complex belies its industrial origins. Constructed in 1907 as a packing plant for the California Fruit Canners Association, the building housed the most productive peach-canning operation in the world from 1916 to 1937. Rough economic times during the Great Depression forced the owner, Del Monte, to close the plant. The building was used mainly as a warehouse until a developer bought it in 1963 and renovated it. Four external brick walls are all that remain of the original structure. The interior, completed in 1967, reveals a seamless modern design of open stairwells, bridges, and spacious

courtyards lined with 30 boutiques, restaurants and gourmet shops. On sunny days, the courtyard on the west side is a pleasant spot to relax with a cold drink and listen to street musicians.

♣♣ Hyde Street Pier★★

Open Jun–Aug daily 9.30am–5.30pm; rest of the year daily 9.30am–5pm. Guided pier walks and boat tours daily; call for schedule. Closed Jan 1, Thanksgiving Day, Dec 25. $5. ℘415-447-5000. www.nps.gov/safr.
The historic ships and maritime artifacts on display at this long wooden pier evoke the era when San Francisco was an active and bustling port. Built as a ferry terminal in the years before construction of the Golden Gate and Bay Bridges, the Hyde Street Pier eventually became the mooring for six historic ships purchased and restored by the San Francisco Maritime Museum. The pier is now part of the **San Francisco Maritime National Historical Park,** which maintains the fleet. In addition to its six ships—three of which may be boarded and explored—the pier houses a turn-of-the-20C "ark" (a flat-bottomed houseboat that served as a summer retreat on the bay), the 1850s-era office of Tubbs Cordage, several old tug boats and a **small boat shop (B)** that offers lessons in boat building and restoration. At the corner of Jefferson

and Hyde Streets, the visitor center has maps, seafaring exhibits and a schedule of the day's events. The **Maritime Store** (**C**) at the entrance provides information and offers a vast array of books.

Eureka★

Right side of pier.

This enormous sidewheel ferry, built in 1890 and still the world's largest wooden floating structure, could carry up to 2,300 commuters at a time. Originally named the *Ukiah,* the ship served as a railroad-car ferry until 1922, when she was rebuilt as the *Eureka* and launched as a passenger and auto ferry between Sausalito and San Francisco. After 1941 the *Eureka* plied the waters on the Oak-land-San Francisco run until her giant walking-beam engine snapped in 1957. Today, visitors can wander the massive decks or operate a model walking-beam that stands beside the actual four-story, steam-powered engine.

C.A. Thayer★

Across from the Eureka.

Built in 1895 to haul logs of heavy Douglas fir between Washington and California, this venerable, three-masted wooden sailing schooner is one of only two such ships in the country (the other, the *Wawona,* is berthed in Seattle). Her single deck, open hold, shallow draft, and relatively wide beam enabled her small crew to hold the 156ft craft steady in shallow, turbulent coves called "dog-holes" as timber was loaded from the bluffs above. Visitors who now descend into the ship's hold find themselves in a dark cave, its walls worn smooth by many loads of rubbing logs. Just above are the handsome captain's quarters and adjacent formal dining room. In the fore-castle, a video *(11min)* recounts the story of the ship's last voyage. Deckhands in period costume often introduce the boat to groups of schoolchildren.

Balclutha★★

End of pier on the left.

Looming over the pier, this three-masted, steel-hulled square-rigger was launched in Glasgow in 1886, rounding Cape Horn 17 times on voyages between Europe and California. A deep-sea cargo vessel measuring 301ft, the *Balclutha* carried wine, spirits, hardware and coal from European ports to San Francisco, returning to the continent loaded with California wheat. In 1904 her owners based her in San Francisco and she began a long career in the salmon industry, running cannery supplies and workers between Alaska and California. A promoter bought the ship in 1933, renamed her the *Pacific Queen,* and dis-played her in various ports as a "pirate" ship. Following this ignominious stage of her career, she came to rest on the Marin mudflats, a near wreck. In 1954 the National Maritime Museum pur-chased and refurbished her, restoring her original name.

Today visitors admire the vast decks, inspect the bird's-eye maple cabinets and elegant Victorian furnishings of the captain's quarters. In the *Balclutha's* cavernous hold are displays of various anchors, mast riggings and rudders, bal-last tubs and a model salmon cannery.

Aquatic Park Beach

This small beach fronting a grassy lawn was created in the 1930s as part of a WPA recreational complex. The beach is protected from the open water by the Municipal Pier. While most people consider the waters of San Francisco Bay too cold for swimming, intrepid mem-bers of the century-plus-old Dolphin Club and the South End Rowing Club still take daily dips here. Line fisher-men frequent the 1,850ft **Municipal Pier** (1934), along with others seeking a quiet place to stroll.

♠♣ Ghirardelli Square★

900 North Point St. between Polk, Larkin & Beach Sts. ◐*Hours for shops and restaurants vary.* ◑*Closed Jan 1, Thanksgiving Day, Dec 25.* ✕♿▣ ✆*415-775-5500.* *www.ghirardellisq.com.*

One of the finest examples of San Francisco's dedication to preserving its historic buildings, this redbrick shop-ping and dining complex was once the

Ghiradelli Square

© Richard Nowitz / Apa Publications

home of the Ghirardelli Chocolate Factory. Stop by the popular **Ghirardelli Soda Fountain and Chocolate Shop★**, home of the Earthquake sundae—eight scoops, eight toppings—and many other types of chocolate confections (**👥👥**1st floor of Clock Tower Building; 🕐open Sun–Thu 9am–11pm, Fri–Sat 9am–midnight; ☎415-474-3938).

National Maritime Museum★
Beach St. at Polk St. ☛Closed for renovation; 🕐lobby & veranda open daily 10am–4pm. ☎415-447-5000. www.nps.gov/safr/.

Resembling an ocean liner at berth on the edge of Aquatic Park, this unusual Streamline Moderne building (1939) houses a fine collection of maritime artifacts and historical displays. Its upper floors are recessed from a flat roof to create the impression of a ship's decks, a nautical effect enhanced by railings, porthole windows and cowl ventilators that look like smokestacks. It was built as the Aquatic Park Casino, centerpiece of the WPA's never-fully-realized recreational complex.

Unusual slate intaglio reliefs by Sargent Johnson adorn its recessed doorway, while the interior boasts undulating undersea murals by Hilaire Hiler and a terrazzo floor designed by Richard Ayer, based on a shoal chart of the bay.

The museum forms part of the San Francisco Maritime National Historical Park (www.maritime.org). In the entrance hall you'll find a large anchor, the hull of a scow schooner and three fine models (including one of the Preussen, a unique, five-masted square-rigger). One collection is devoted to steam-powered ocean travel from post-Civil War to the 1980s; the first floor also hosts temporary exhibits. A larger exhibition hall (2nd floor) focuses on the 1850s–60s—the city's early years as a sea and inland port. Fisheries, whaling, and shipbuilding are portrayed through unusual artifacts. Displays on the traditional arts of the sailor include knotting, modeling, whittling and scrimshaw carving. Large windows to the north, as well as an open observation deck (3rd floor), offer grand views of the historic sailing ships at Hyde Street Pier.

ADDRESSES

🍽/**EAT**

Buena Vista Cafe – 2765 Hyde St. ☎415-474-5044. Known as the first bar in the U.S. to serve Irish coffee (a concoction of Irish whiskey, coffee and whipped cream), the Buena Vista remains a local institution. Breakfast is served all day by aproned waiters who willingly direct visitors to local attractions.

Golden Gate Bridge★★★

Stretching across the narrow strait of the Golden Gate above the swirling union of the Pacific Ocean and San Francisco Bay, this elegant Art Deco suspension bridge remains one of San Francisco's most beloved symbols.

A BIT OF HISTORY

Imagined by a madman in 1869 and proposed intermittently over the next four decades by saner visionaries, the bridge across the treacherous strait between the San Francisco Peninsula and Marin County elicited passionate emotions and aggressive resistance at every stage of its conception. Few took the idea seriously until 1916, when auto transportation was fast becoming a way of life, and San Francisco's Board of Supervisor's commissioned the first feasibility study in 1918.

Initial cost estimates for the structure ran as high as $100 million, but Joseph Strauss, a tireless and innovative engineer who already had built more than 400 bridges around the world, claimed that he could span the "unspannable" passage for a mere $27 million. Excited by Strauss' plan, citizens of counties from San Francisco to the Oregon border offered financial and political support. Two major foes, however, stood in the way—the powerful Southern Pacific Railroad (sole owner of all transbay ferry operations), which stood only to lose from Strauss' railless design, and the U.S. War Department, which feared that the bridge would hinder navigation and provide a target for enemy bombs in the event of war. Some naysayers claimed that the deep and turbulent waters of the bay were too treacherous for such an undertaking, and still others decried Strauss' estimate as being nearly $75 million too low.

For years parties on both sides wrangled. When the War Department withdrew its opposition in 1924, the Southern Pacific filed a battery of law-

ᴍᴜᴍ Bus 28–19th Ave., 29–Sunset or 76-Marin Headlands

ᴗ **Michelin Map:** *See THE PRESIDIO* pp142-143

🖪 **Info:** ☎415-921-5858. www.goldengate bridge.org.

▶ **Location:** The Golden Gate Bridge spans the mouth of San Francisco Bay, joining the northwestern tip of the San Francisco Peninsula with the Marin Headlands. Car access from US-101/ Hwy. 1 or from Lincoln Blvd. ⊜$6 toll (southbound only). Pedestrian access to the bridge (east sidewalk only) Apr–Oct 5am–9pm, rest of the year 5am–6.30pm. Bicycle access 24hrs/day; press the button to open the remote-activated security gate during night-time hours. You can get to the pedestrian path from Fort Point National Historic Site (ᴗ*see THE PRESIDIO*), though you'll have to make a steep climb.

🕐 **Timing:** Beautiful any time, the bridge is particularly so at sunset.

🅿 **Parking:** There are two parking lots on the San Francisco side of the bridge, one on either side of the roadbed; the east lot is metered parking and the west lot costs $5 per day at weekends; the lot is reserved for employees only on weekdays. Keep in mind that, with only 150 spots between them, the lots fill up quickly on nice days.

🎴 **Don't Miss:** The walk across the span on the east sidewalk; dress warmly!

Golden Gate Bridge

© MICHELIN

suits designed to keep the project in litigation for decades. During the same period, several of the counties that had originally joined the Golden Gate Bridge and Highway District pulled out, citing danger and expense. Since no federal or state funding was to be allocated, the remaining counties faced shouldering even more of the financial burden to achieve their goal of a link to the city across the bay.

By the time the last obstacles were removed—the railroad finally dropped its lawsuits under public pressure—the Great Depression had crushed the economy and citizens couldn't afford the bonds issued for public support. Then A.P. Giannini, visionary founder of the Bank of Italy, stepped forward and announced that his bank would finance the bridge. In January 1933, nearly 12 years after Joseph Strauss first submitted his proposal, groundbreaking ceremonies finally took place.

Spanning the Gate – Unemployed laborers turned out in droves to compete for plum jobs on the bridge despite the widely held belief that one life would be lost for every $1 million spent. Fortunately Strauss and his principal assistant engineer, Clifford Paine, addressed that grim prospect by enforcing unprecedented safety procedures, including safety belts, nets and filter glasses to block the blinding sun. Their stringency paid off. Over the course of the bridge's construction, the safety nets saved the lives 19 men, who became known as the "Half-Way-to-Hell Club." The first fatal accident, the toppling of a derrick onto a young steel worker, did not occur until the fourth year of construction. Then, only three months before the bridge opened, a scaffold suspended below the roadway tore loose and plummeted into the safety net, carrying a dozen men with it. The net held for an instant, then ripped open, dropping the victims into the deepest part of the channel. Two survived the plunge, but the rest were lost in the vicious currents.

Despite this tragedy, the Golden Gate Bridge was hailed as a model of safety, economy and grace at its inauguration on May 27, 1937, with the *San Francisco Chronicle* referring to its a $35 million steel harp.

A holiday atmosphere prevailed in the city on opening day. Schools, offices and stores either closed or operated on a reduced schedule. By 6am, 18,000 people were waiting to cross the bridge from both sides. The first to cross the full span was Donald Bryan, a sprinter from San Francisco Junior College. Others rollerskated, walked on stilts, played musical instruments, walked backwards or walked their pets, all setting first-time records.

In total, a crowd of more than 200,000 surged across the span on foot on opening day. Automobiles followed

Joseph Strauss statue

©Richard Nowitz/Apa Publications

The Golden Gate Bridge

Measuring 1.7 miles from end to end (with a suspension span of 1.22 miles), the Golden Gate Bridge stood for many years as the world's longest suspension bridge until it was superseded by the Verrazano-Narrows Bridge, connecting the Staten Island and Brooklyn boroughs in New York, in 1964. Unlike more rigid types of bridges, a suspension bridge relies on gravity for its stability: the massive weight of the roadway, suspended from cables anchored on land, keeps the structure from falling. The cables provide enough flexibility for the mid-span of the bridge to deflect transversely up to 27ft in high winds without jeopardizing the structure's integrity. There are **five** main components to a suspension bridge: piers, anchorages, towers, cables and a roadway, constructed in that order.

- The Golden Gate Bridge's two **piers** form the bases of the towers. The Marin pier stands close to shore, but the San Francisco pier had to be poured a quarter-mile offshore in 100ft of water because the nearer bedrock was deemed unstable. An oval concrete fender, 27.5ft thick at its top and as long as a football field, surrounds this southern pier, protecting it from battering waves and collisions.

- The two **anchorages**, each a collection of massive concrete blocks able to withstand 63 million pounds of pull from the cables, were sunk into pits deep enough to hold a 12-story building.

- The twin steel **towers** rise 746ft (65 stories) above the piers, each supporting a total load of 123 million pounds from the two main cables.

- The massive **cables**, spun out of 80,000 miles of wire, rest in saddles at the tops of the towers and are embedded into the anchorages on land. Under normal conditions (70°F and no load on the span), the cables bend the towers toward the shore by 6in.

- The steel-reinforced **roadway** hangs from ropes attached to the cables at 50ft intervals.

Since the Golden Gate Bridge's inauguration, weather conditions have forced it to close only three times. The bridge is continually maintained by a team of electricians, ironworkers and painters. Since 1937, the bridge has been repainted repeatedly to prevent corrosion from salt air, fog, winds and auto exhaust. Its trademark shade, dubbed "International Orange," was selected for aesthetic reasons, and in part because of its visibility in fog.

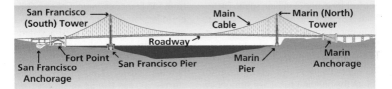

next, continuing a week-long round of festivities celebrating the conquest of the "unbridgeable" Golden Gate. The final cost of construction was around $35 million.

The Golden Gate Bridge has only been closed a handful of times. In addition to brief closures for visiting dignitaries President Franklin D. Roosevelt and French President Charles de Gaulle, there have been three closures due to extremely high winds. On December 1, 1951, wind gusts of up to 60mph resulted in a 3hr closure. On December 23, 1982, 70mph winds closed the bridge for 2hrs. Winds of up to 75mph on December 3, 1983 resulted in the bridge's longest closure, of 3hrs 27min. None of the winds caused structural damage.

Today, over 100,000 vehicles traverse the Golden Gate Bridge daily, while pedestrians and cyclists take to its sidewalks to admire its soaring towers, graceful cables and wondrous views. The busiest traffic day to date was October 27, 1989, ten days after the massive Loma Prieta earthquake, when 162,414 vehicles crossed the bridge.

The Golden Gate Bridge ranks as the world's tenth-longest suspension bridge, surpassed by spans in Japan, England, Denmark, China, South Korea and New York. The bridge makes its presence known from afar at many points in San Francisco and Marin County, especially from Land's End, the Presidio, Marin Headlands, the Marina District and Fisherman's Wharf.

VISIT

On the south side of the bridge, a cross-section of a cable, a dignified statue of Joseph Strauss, and panel displays lead from the parking area through nearly five acres of manicured gardens of annuals and perennials. Just beyond, from a series of viewing platforms, you can drink in the sight of the bridge's massive towers and cables.

Three plaques commemorate distinctions awarded by the American Society of Civil Engineers. The bridge was named a California Historic Civil Engineering Landmark in 1976 and a National Historic Civil Engineering Landmark in 1984. It was also awarded a special citation for infrastructure rehabilitation in 1986.

The historic **Round House** (1938), was originally built as a restaurant for passing motorists. It now houses a popular gift shop (*open daily 9am–6pm*), offering a variety of historical information as well as books, photographs, videos, posters and other souvenirs. Nearby, the Bridge Café offers light refreshments.

For closeup inspections, a stroll across the bridge on the east sidewalk is a must, but be sure to wear a jacket to ward off stiff winds. Pedestrians and bicyclists share the busy east sidewalk on weekdays. A pedestrian fee for crossing the bridge was imposed from 1937–1970, collected by a coin turnstile, but today pedestrians cross free of charge.

At the southern entrance to the west sidewalk, note the memorial plaque at dedicated to the eleven men killed while building the bridge. Then walk to the center of the 1.7mi span for **views★★** of Alcatraz, the Marin Headlands and the Pacific Ocean. From here, you can get a sense of Strauss' magnificent accomplishment by gazing up the sleek, looping cables that rise in a smooth arc to the top of the towers. At mid-span the bridge is 220ft above the waters of the bay. Continue across the bridge to reach the **Vista Point** on the Marin County side. Here are lovely **views★★** of the bridge from the north, backdropped by the forested hills of the Presidio. The sweeping perspective encompasses the entire northern waterfront of the city, as well as the San Francisco–Oakland Bay Bridge. Also on the Marin side's viewing station is the Lone Sailor Memorial, dedicated on April 14, 2002 to all of the American sea services, including the Navy, Marine Corps, Coast Guard and Merchant Marine. The memorial represents sea service members' last glimpse of America's West Coast before heading out for their service at sea.

Marina District★

Ensconced on the northern waterfront between the Presidio and Fisherman's Wharf, the Marina District is a desirable residential neighborhood, especially among young professionals. Many blocks of pale, stucco facades are enlivened by an abundance of Mediterranean Revival–style architectural details, including columns, tile roofs, and arched windows and doors. The most expensive homes border the broad swath of Marina Green and overlook San Francisco Bay.

A BIT OF HISTORY

Early Spanish settlers were not attracted by the muddy, marshy inlet, although the high ground hemming it on either side greatly interested military commanders charged with guarding the Golden Gate. Soldiers established the Presidio on the rise to the west in 1776 and in 1797 emplaced a battery of five bronze cannons atop the knoll now known as Black Point, to the east. The guns were never used, but in 1850 the site caught the eye of American military strategists, who established an army reservation there. To stave off Confederate attack during the Civil War, the Union Army terraced Black Point and installed a new battery of 12 cannons. Like its predecessor, this battery never saw battle. Development came slowly to the mud flats, sand dunes, and marshes between Black Point and the Presidio. At the beginning of the 19C, dairy farms covered the hills and valleys to the south (present-day Cow Hollow) and a roadhouse stood on the site of the Palace of Fine Arts, an area then called Harbor View. In 1911, city boosters seeking a location for a world's fair—to promote the rebirth of the city after the 1906 earthquake and fire, and to celebrate the opening of the Panama Canal—decided upon this largely empty tract. The Army Corps of Engineers erected a seawall along the muddy waterfront and by 1913 had filled the 600 acres inside it with tons of sand and earthquake

🚌 Bus 22–Fillmore, 28–19th Ave., 30–Stockton, 41–Union, 45–Union-Stockton, or 47–Van Ness.

ℹ **Info:** www.sanfrancisco.travel.

◐ **Location:** The Marina is bounded by San Francisco Bay, Van Ness Avenue, the Presidio, and Lombard Street.

👥 **Kids:** Playing and exploring at the Exploratorium.

🕐 **Timing:** Marina Green, Chestnut Street, and Union Street are pleasant for strolling by day or evening. Union Street is especially festive at Christmas time, when its Victorian houses ("Victorians") are bedecked with white lights. An Easter Parade and summer art festival are also held here (☾see Calendar of Events). Fort Mason Center's galleries are open by day, but most theater performances are held at night; call the Fort Mason box office at ☎415-345-7575 or visit www.fortmason.org for information about events and cultural offerings.

🅿 **Parking:** Street parking is usually available in the Marina District's residential areas, though time limits (usually 2hrs) are strictly enforced. Limited free parking is available in the Marina Yacht Harbor, along Marina Green, and at the Exploratorium. There is a paid lot for visitors to Fort Mason Center, but spaces often fill up early on weekends.

⊙ **Don't Miss:** The Palace of Fine Arts.

View of Marina District from Pacific Heights

© Brigitta L. House / MICHELIN

debris, creating a flat, attractive site for the buildings of the Panama-Pacific International Exposition of 1915.

At the fair's close, its structures were all razed except the Palace of Fine Arts. Developers took over, building choice homes for sale. The Marina District, as it became known, gained a reputation as a desirable middle-class address.

Ironically, the same uncompacted landfill laid down for a fair that advertised San Francisco's recovery from the 1906 earthquake proved disastrous during the Loma Prieta quake of 1989. The unstable ground beneath the Marina District liquefied during the tremor, causing several homes to collapse and heavily damaging dozens of buildings. Today, however, the marks of Loma Prieta are largely erased and the Marina District remains an affluent residential neighborhood distinguished by its architectural harmony, its glorious views of the Golden Gate, and its tourist attractions at Fort Mason, the Palace of Fine Arts, and the Exploratorium.

FORT MASON★
Upper Fort Mason★

The gentle slope and broad crown of a low hill overlooking the bay was a logical place for a military reservation. The Army failed to occupy the attractive site for more than a decade after 1850, however, and several well-to-do civilian families, in the interim, erected homes on Black Point before Union forces repossessed the property in 1863 during the Civil War. Named in 1881 for Col. Richard Mason, California's first military governor (1847–49), the outpost formed the western command center for the U.S. Army during the Indian Wars of the late 19C. Gen. Frederick Funston's interim government established headquarters here in the anxious hours immediately following the 1906 quake, and tents were set up on the fort's broad meadow to house refugees from the devastated areas of the city.

Upper Fort Mason maintains the orderly feel of a 19C Army command post.

GGNRA Headquarters

Bldg. 201, MacArthur St. (entrance at Franklin & Bay Sts.). ◷*Open Mon–Fri 8.30am–4.30pm.* ⓖ🅿 ℘*415-561-4700. www.nps.gov/goga.*

Built in 1901, this three-story structure served briefly as an army hospital before its conversion to administrative offices after 1906. Inside, visitors may obtain abundant maps and information on GGNRA activities, and limited material on other national parks of the West.

Behind the headquarters building lies the charming **Fort Mason Community Garden**, a public plot where local residents may register for space to grow vegetables, flowers and root crops (dozens of such gardens exist in the city). Stroll along Pope Street to see examples

Golden Gate National Recreation Area

Embracing San Francisco's northern and western boundaries as well as Angel Island, Alcatraz, and a large portion of coastal Marin County, the Golden Gate National Recreation Area was established by act of Congress in 1972. The 26,000-acre system of national parks, encompassing historic landmarks, military sites, redwood forests, beaches, and undeveloped coastal lands, came about largely through the efforts of U.S. Congressman Phillip Burton, who championed the movement to preserve the area's unused military lands as parks for nature conservation and recreation. Today the GGNRA attracts more than 13 million visitors annually.

GGNRA sites described in this guide include: Alcatraz, Baker Beach, Crissy Field, China Beach, Cliff House, Fort Funston, Fort Mason, Fort Point NHS, Land's End, Marina Green, Marin Headlands, Muir Beach, Muir Woods NM, Ocean Beach, The Presidio, San Francisco Maritime NHP, Stinson Beach, Tennessee Valley

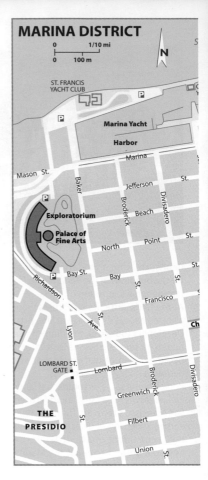

of early military construction, including a wooden base chapel (1942). Originally a barracks, the American Youth Hostel at the head of the street dates from the Civil War period.

Black Point Battery
North end of Franklin St.
In 1797, Spanish soldiers installed five-gun Batéria San José atop this serene bluff overlooking San Francisco Bay. The homes erected—without permission—by civilians in 1855 were confiscated by the army in 1863; several remain today along the east side of Franklin Street, used as officers' quarters. Most prominent of the civilian "squatters" was explorer-politician John C. Frémont, whose house was demolished

when Black Point was terraced for gun emplacements. Although the guns have been removed, Black Point Battery still offers lovely **views** east to tall-masted ships and small boats anchored off Aquatic Park, with the downtown towers and East Bay hils beyond.

The Great Meadow
Near Bay and Laguna Sts.
Site of a tent city erected to shelter thousands of refugees from the 1906 quake, this broad, undulating lawn today draws picnickers and sunbathers. In the meadow stand a statue of the Madonna (1) by Italian-American sculptor Beniamino Bufano and a bronze figure of Bay Area Congressman Phillip Burton (2), whose efforts spearheaded creation of the GGNRA.

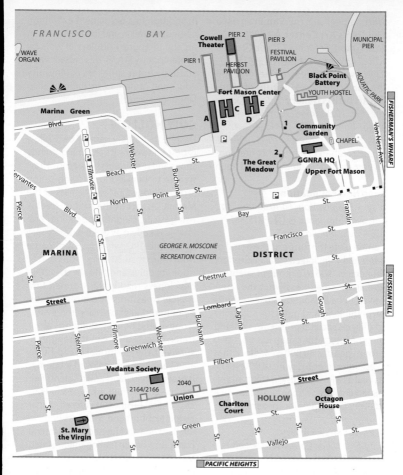

Fort Mason Center★

🛈 *Info:* ☎415-345-7500 or 415-345-7575 (box office). www.fortmason.org.

Built on landfill during the early 20C, this bayside complex of barracks, warehouses, and docks served as the official embarkation point for Americans serving in Pacific theaters of war from 1910 through the Korean War.

More than 1.5 million GIs and 23 million tons of cargo shipped out from its three sturdy docks during World War II, making Fort Mason the second largest Army port in the U.S. at that time.

This lower, bayside section of Fort Mason was decommissioned for civilian use in 1962 and was completely transformed as a cultural and community complex by 1977. Today its renovated military structures (dubbed "Landmark Buildings A-E") house theaters, small museums, galleries, Greens restaurant and philanthropic organizations.

Evenings draw theatergoers to any of several stages, including the **Cowell Theater**, built over the water on the middle pier, which also houses the Herbst Pavilion. The **Magic Theatre** (Bldg. D, 3rd floor; ☎415-441-8822; www.magictheatre.org) produces innovative plays from established and emerging writers; the **Young Performers Theatre** (Bldg. C, 3rd floor; ☎415-346-5550; www.ypt.org) specializes in dramatics for children; and the **Bayfront Theater** (Bldg. B, 3rd floor; ☎415-474-6776; www.improv.org) is home to improvisational "theatersports."

Worth a peek are the **San Francisco Children's Art Center** 👥👤 *(Bldg. C, 1st floor;* ⏰*Mon–Sat 9am–5.30pm;* ⏰*closed school holiday weeks;* ♿📶 📞*415-771-0292; www.childrensartcenter.org)* and the **San Francisco Museum of Modern Art Artists Gallery** *(Bldg. A;* ⏰*open Tue–Sat 10.30am–5.30pm;* ⏰*closed major holidays;* 📶 📞*415-441-4777; www.sfmoma.org/visit/artists_gallery),* where rotating exhibits of contemporary art are shown on the ground floor.

Long Now Foundation

Bldg. A. ⏰*Open Mon–Fri 10.30am–5pm, Sat–Sun 11am–6pm.* ♿📶 📞*415-561-6582. www.longnow.org.*
Contemplate the future at the home of a forward-thinking cultural institution, founded in 1996 by a group of scientists and artists to address what they perceived to be a dangerous rise in short-term thinking and quick-fix solutions to difficult societal problems. Looking into the future, the group has built two prototypes of a 10,000-year clock that is accurate to one day in 20,000 years, as well as a Rosetta disk, a small nickel-plated disk that will contain a sentence of every language ever spoken.

J. Porter Shaw Library

Bldg. E, 3rd floor. ⏰*Open 3rd Sat of the month 10am–5pm and by appt. only Mon–Fri 1–4pm.* ⏰*Closed major holidays.* ♿📶 📞*415-561-7030. www.nps.gov/safr.*
Operated by the San Francisco Maritime National Historical Park, this library of maritime history maintains a collection of about 32,000 books plus oral history archives, sea chanteys, recorded interviews, vessel registers, photographs, and other nautical items centering on West Coast shipping and whaling.
The Oceanic Society maintains offices here and launches **whale-watching cruises** (👁*see p 146)* from the harbor.

Museo ItaloAmericano

Bldg. C, 1st floor. ⏰*Open Tue–Sun noon –4pm and by appt. Mon.* ⏰*Closed major holidays.* ♿📶 📞*415-673-2200. www.museoitaloamericano.org.*

In addition to a permanent exhibition of modern Italian and Italian-American art and temporary displays of work by contemporary artists, this museum and cultural center sponsors community education programs, including Italian language classes.

COW HOLLOW

Despite its homely name, Cow Hollow is best known for its charming, trendy shops and restaurants housed in attractive Victorians along bustling Union Street. Wedged below the flats of the Marina District at the foot of steeply rising Pacific Heights, the rolling "hollow" was known as Golden Gate Valley in the mid-19C, when herds of cattle from more than 30 dairy farms grazed upon its dales and hills. In the 1890s developers readily transformed Cow Hollow's pastures into a respectable neighborhood of two- and three-story wood-frame houses. Buildings along Union Street, the main thoroughfare, survived the earthquake and fire of 1906, and the area enjoyed a boom as it greeted merchants and residents fleeing the burned-out areas of San Francisco. Local businesses catered primarily to neighborhood shoppers until the 1950s, when antique shops and interior decorators began renting Union Street's Victorian storefronts. Other fashionable shops and restaurants followed suit. Much of Cow Hollow's genteel, early 20C architecture survives, along with several evocative reminders of its rural past.

Union Street★

www.unionstreetsf.com.
Lined with refurbished Victorians, Union Street's eight-block retail district between Van Ness Avenue and Steiner Street invites leisurely exploration. Old houses have been converted to boutiques, galleries, arts-and-crafts shops, and small, urbane restaurants. Particularly attractive is **Charlton Court** *(south side of Union St. between Laguna & Buchanan Sts.),* a quiet lane thought to have once served as a depot for milk wagons. The house and barn (c. 1870) of James W. Cudworth, Cow Hollow's

The Panama-Pacific International Exposition of 1915

As stewards of the West Coast's busiest port in the early 20C, San Francisco residents took keen interest in the construction of the Panama Canal. The resurrection of the city from the 1906 earthquake and fire, and increasing competition from the port at Los Angeles, heightened San Franciscans' resolve to celebrate the canal's completion in a way that would unequivocally announce that the city was rebuilt, rejuvenated and ready to resume its place as the economic and cultural center of the American Pacific coast.

On a 635-acre tract of reclaimed land, an esteemed group of architects, including Louis C. Mullgardt, Bernard Maybeck, Willis Polk, and William B. Faville, set about designing a fabulous complex of pavilions representing 25 countries and 29 states. From its opening day in February 1915, the fair dazzled the public with its attractions and architecture. Indirect lighting, an innovation of the era, accented a fantasy city of Renaissance palazzos, Spanish missions, Classical temples, and Byzantine domes. The Great Palace of Machinery was vast enough for an airplane to fly through it.

The Oregon State pavilion resembled the Parthenon, only using redwood trunks instead of marble pillars. Visitors were awed by a working scale model of the Panama Canal. At the center of the fairgrounds rose the Tower of Jewels, covered with more than 100,000 cut-glass jewels backed by tiny mirrors and suspended on wires, so that the tower appeared to shimmer in the breeze. Most beloved by San Franciscans was the Palace of Fine Arts *(www. palaceoffinearts.org)*. The fair was acclaimed far and wide as the most ambitious event ever hosted by the city, attracting nearly 20 million visitors in its ten months of operation and earning a substantial profit—but ultimately failing to lure back the shipping business lost to Los Angeles' growing port.

Constructed primarily of wood and plaster, most fair buildings were demolished at the exposition's close in December 1915. Only the Marina Yacht Harbor and the reconstructed Palace of Fine Arts remain today.

first dairyman, still stand behind a palm tree at no. 2040. A roofed passage at no. 2164/2166 leads to an old barn and leafy carriage yard, where plants and garden ornaments are displayed for sale.

Cow Hollow's most unusual building, visible to the north from the corner of Union and Webster, is the former temple of the **Vedanta Society of Northern California** (1905) *(2963 Webster St.)*. Built by Joseph Leonard after a design by Swami Trigunatita, the three-story wooden building sports an ecumenical medley of ornamentation representing diverse religions and cultures.

St. Mary the Virgin Episcopal Church

2325 Union St. at Steiner St. ⊙Open Mon –Fri 9am–5pm, Sun during services. ⊙Closed major holidays and Christmas week. ♿ ☎415-921-3665. www.smvsf.org.

Partially hidden behind its fence and lych-gate, this charming church (1891) evokes the feel of an English country parsonage, though its wooden frame and redwood-shingle cladding herald the Arts and Crafts style characteristic of northern California architecture. Peace and tranquillity pervade the quiet, A-frame sanctuary and grounds. The gushing spring in the entry courtyard was used to water dairy herds, and is one of Cow Hollow's most beguiling reminders of its bucolic past.

Octagon House★

2645 Gough St. at Union St. ⊙Open 2nd & 4th Thu, & 2nd Sun of the month, noon–3pm. ⊙Closed major holidays. ⊛Donation requested. ☞Guided tours (30min) available. ☎415-441-7512.

Built in 1861 by William C. McElroy, this small house was moved from a nearby lot to its present site in 1953 by the National Society of Colonial Dames of America in California, which uses it as a museum for its collection of decorative arts from the Colonial and Federal periods. The two-story structure took its curious shape from Orson Squire Fowler's popular 1848 book, *A Home for All,* which theorized that octagonal houses provided more light, space and ventilation than conventional square-cornered houses, and were consequently healthier. The interior floor plan was substantially altered when the central stairwell was moved to the west wall by its present owners. Most of the rooms on the second floor, which is naturally lit by a central octagonal cupola that protrudes above the main roof, retain their original dimensions.

The museum displays many fine pieces of early American furniture, portraits, samplers, looking glasses, pewter and silverware, as well as examples of ceramics and other decorative items from the lively import trade during the Colonial era and early Republic. One room houses a collection of signatures and handwritten documents by all but two of the signatories to the Declaration of Independence, including Thomas Jefferson, John Hancock, Benjamin Franklin and John Adams.

ADDITIONAL SIGHTS
Chestnut Street

The four blocks of Chestnut Street between Divisadero Street and Fillmore Street, about halfway between Union Street and Marina Green, comprise the Marina District's main commercial avenue. A pleasant thoroughfare for shopping, dining and strolling, Chestnut Street projects a comfortable, friendly and relaxing atmosphere reminiscent of a small-town main street.

Marina Green

Encompassing an expansive stretch of Marina District waterfront between Webster and Scott Streets, this broad, 10-acre greensward is popular with locals for its stiff breezes—ideal for kite-flying—and for its stupendous **views**★★

of San Francisco Bay, the Golden Gate Bridge, and yachts anchored offshore. A favored spot of sunbathers, volleyball players, and joggers, the lawn is bordered by handsome dwellings in a diverse array of architectural styles. Most were built in the 1920s and incorporate Spanish and Italian Baroque details inspired by the 1915 Panama-Pacific International Exposition.

Enclosed by a 1,500ft jetty extending parallel to Marina Green, the **Marina Yacht Harbor** encloses a flotilla of boats, many of them belonging to members of the private St. Francis Yacht Club, which occupies an attractive, tile-roofed structure (1928, Willis Polk). Visitors who walk to the end of the jetty can see the "wave organ," a sculpted jumble of concrete and stone embedded with pipes, each with one end in the water. One hears the gurgling "music" of the sea—theoretically—by putting an ear to an exposed pipe end.

Palace of Fine Arts★★

3301 Lyon Street. 🖉*415- 567-6642. www.palaceoffinearts.org*

This grand rotunda and peristyle were replicated from structures designed by renowned architect Bernard Maybeck to house art exhibits for the 1915 Panama-Pacific International Exposition. The original building, designed to be impermanent, was framed in lath and chicken wire and covered with a plaster and burlap-fiber mixture called "staff," its surface sprayed to resemble travertine. When the buildings of the fair were torn down, aesthetically minded citizens lobbied to spare the Palace of Fine Arts. No efforts were made to strengthen the building, however, and it slowly disintegrated until a plan for restoration was made in 1962. Workers made casts of the columns, statuary and artistic details, and the building was entirely reconstructed in concrete and steel in 1964–1967.

Maybeck's design was purely romantic in concept, inspired largely by the work of 18C engraver Giovanni Piranesi and *The Isle of the Dead,* a 19C painting depicting a royal tomb. Maybeck himself

Palace of Fine Arts

© PhotoDisc, Inc.

described the building as "an old Roman ruin" and stated his intent to project sadness. Reinforcing the sense of mystery and melancholy, the female figures sculpted by Ulric Ellerhusen along the top of the peristyle face inward, their faces buried in their arms.

The rotunda, 110ft high and 135ft across, is decorated with eight large panels carved in low relief. Angels look down from the interior of the dome; two of the original 14ft angels are preserved inside the Exploratorium. On clear, calm days, the lagoon spreading from the foot of the rotunda reflects mirror images.

♟♟ Exploratorium★★

3601 Lyon St.(moving to Pier 15/17 in Spring 2013) ⏰*Open Tue–Sun 10am–5pm.* ⏰*Closed Mon (except holidays) Luther King Jr. Day, Presidents Day, Memorial Day, & Labor Day), Thanksgiving Day, Dec 25.* ⊜*$25; free 1st Wed of month.* ✗♿🅿 ☏*415-561-0360. www.exploratorium.edu.*

Located in the semicircular structure behind the Palace of Fine Arts, this museum has served as a model for similar science museums since its opening in 1969. The Exploratorium's creator, physicist Frank Oppenheimer, maintained a novel philosophy that a museum can best teach science through "hands-on" participation.

The museum boasts more than 1,000 exhibits (400 on display) in physics, electricity, life sciences, thermodynamics, weather, light, psychology, linguistics, sense perception and a host of other subjects. By pushing buttons, rotating wheels, peering through prisms, activating motors, engineering arches, arranging chimes, shouting into tubes, and performing a wide variety of other actions, visitors set experiments in motion, observe the results and speculate on the causes. Instructions and explanations accompany each exhibit, and staff members are available to answer questions.

Among the most popular exhibits are the miniature **tornado demonstration**; the photosensitive **Shadow Box**, where people's shadows are recorded on a wall; and the **distorted room**, where visitors can enter an optical illusion. Do not miss the pitch-black **Tactile Dome★** *(*⏰*entry Tue–Sun 10.15am, noon, 1.45pm, 3.30pm, 5pm, Fri–Sat after-hours at 6.45pm;* ⊜*$12; reservations advised;* ☏*415-561-0362)*, a multilevel crawl chamber through which visitors feel their way.

ADDRESSES

♀/EAT

Greens – *Fort Mason Center, Bldg. A. ✆415 -771-6222. www.greensrestaurant.com.* Opened in 1979 by disciples of the San Francisco Zen Center, this gourmet vegetarian restaurant (its wine list is a national award winner) gets much of its produce from the center's Green Gulch Farm in Marin County. Reserve ahead for lunch or dinner, or stop in for coffee and a home-made scone while drinking in the lovely view of the bay and the Golden Gate Bridge.

Rose's Cafe – *2298 Union St. ✆415-775- 2200. www.rosescafesf.com.* You can get breakfast, lunch and dinner—or just a cappuccino or glass of wine at this stylish Marina bistro-cafe, a neighborhood institution for its ample sidewalk seating, friendly service, and tasty house-made breads, pastries, soups and pastas.

Liverpool LiL's – *2942 Lyon St. ✆415- 921-6664.* Fans of cuisine from across the pond will enjoy this traditional English pub at the western edge of the Marina District. The menu cannily blends local treats like Dungeness crab ravioli with pub fare and continental comfort food like fish & chips, shepherd's pie, and braised beef dishes.

BARS

California Wine Merchant – *2113 Chestnut St., between Steiner & Pierce Sts. ✆415-567-0646. www.californiawine merchant.com.* For more than three decades, owner Greg and Deborah O'Flynn have tracked the astonishing growth and variety of California wines. You won't see the big names here: their no-gimmicks shop and wine bar specializes in vintages from top-of-the-line, small-production wineries in California and the Pacific Northwest.

The Presidio★★

For more than two centuries, the Presidio's privileged setting on 1,480 acres overlooking the Golden Gate earned it a reputation as the most beautiful military installation in North America. Residents and visitors are drawn to the lushly forested expanse to enjoy its handsome and eclectic mix of architectural styles, its traces of San Francisco's military history, its recreational opportunities, and the spectacular views extending from its miles of wooded trails. Closed as an army base in 1994, the Presidio is now administered by a federal trust agency in partnership with the National Park Service.

A BIT OF HISTORY

Selected as the site of the northernmost military installation of the far-reaching Spanish colonial empire, the Presidio (the word means "military garrison") was dedicated on September 17, 1776,

🚍 Bus 28–19th Avenue, 29–Sunset, 41–Union, 43–Masonic or 45–Union-Stockton.

ℹ **Info:** ✆415-561-4323. www.nps.gov/prsf or www.presidio.gov.

▶ **Location:** The Presidio occupies a large, roughly square area in the city's north-west corner. Pick up a guide at the **Presidio Visitor Center,** in the Presidio Officers' Club at the Main Post *(50 Moraga Ave.).*

👥 **Kids:** Cannon drills at Fort Point; Pet Cemetery; live tidepool tank and interactive displays at the Marine Sanctuary Visitor Center.

🕐 **Timing:** Outdoorsy types could easily spend a day exploring trails around here. History buffs can

by Lt. José Joaquin Moraga. Originally an adobe quadrangle about 300yds on each side located approximately where the Main Post now stands, the Presidio was San Francisco's first European settlement, predating Mission Dolores by a month. The Spanish never considered the outpost to be of primary importance despite its strategic location. Official disinterest, combined with decades of rain, earthquakes, wind and salt air, kept the fortress in a perpetual state of disrepair, even after Mexico acquired it (along with independence from Spain) in 1821.

The Presidio's outlook changed in 1846 when John C. Frémont and a group of civilians staged the capture of the crumbling, largely defenseless fort from the Mexican government. The American flag was raised over the decaying garrison following cession of California to the U.S. in 1848. San Francisco's growth as a commercial hub during the Gold Rush caused President Millard Fillmore to issue an executive order in 1850 reserving the property for military use. Over

spend a few hours in the Main Post area.

P **Parking:** Follow signs for ample free parking. Enter by **Lincoln Boulevard** (which skirts the Coastal Defense Batteries, offering stunning bridge **views★★**) or by historic gates. The **Lombard Street Gate** *(Lombard St. at Lyon St.)* and **Marina Gate** *(Marina Blvd. at Lyon St.)* are close to the Marina District; the latter brings you by the Crissy Field Center. **The Presidio Boulevard Gate** *(Presidio Blvd. at Pacific St.)* and **Arguello Boulevard Gate** *(Arguello Blvd. at Pacific St.)* enter from the south.

⊘ **Don't Miss:** Environmental programs at Crissy Field Center, dramatic ocean views from Baker Beach.

PresidiGo

A free shuttle-bus service makes nearly 40 stops in the park and departs the Presidio Transit Center Mon–Fri 6.30am–7.30pm every 30min and Sat–Sun 11am–6.30pm every hour (☎415-561-5300; www.presidio.gov/shuttle).

the next decade the fort was restored and enlarged, while other installations were erected around the bay, including Fort Point and Alcatraz.

Bulwark of National Defense – The timing of this military construction was fortuitous. Following the outbreak of the Civil War, defense of San Francisco Bay moved to top priority from the Union's point of view. Gold and silver from California and Nevada mines were at stake. The Presidio undertook a major military buildup to guard against invasion by Confederate forces.

Following the Civil War, the Presidio housed U.S. troops engaged in conflicts with the Modoc, Apache, and other Native American tribes across the West. Between 1886 and 1976, the magnificent eucalyptus, cypress, and pine forests—in all, 100,000 trees of 200 species—were planted in military rows on the rolling lands of the base, both to beautify it and to protect its terrain from erosion. The coastal defense batteries along the bayfront also were constructed. After 1898 the Presidio served as the launching pad for American expansion into the Pacific.

The presence of a large, standing army proved vital at the time of the 1906 earthquake and fire. Presidio troops helped maintain order as martial law was proclaimed, and more than 16,000 refugees camped on the fort's open lands. When the United States entered World War I, troops trained here for combat in France. During World War II, the Presidio became headquarters for the Western Defense Command, as nearly 2 million troops shipped out from San Francisco. In the 1950s the base was named the command center

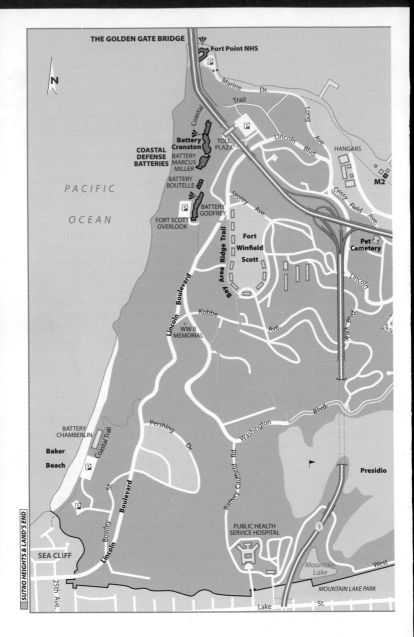

for Nike missile defense of the bay and served as headquarters for the Sixth U.S. Army until 1994.

Swords to Plowshares – In 1962 the site was named a National Historic Landmark District. When the Golden Gate National Recreation Area (GGNRA) was created a decade later, Congress tagged the Presidio, whose military importance had waned, for future inclusion in the park. In 1989 the Presidio was designated for closure as part of a general defense reduction and consolidation, and on October 1, 1994, the Sixth Army marched off the grounds for the last time as the Presidio came under the

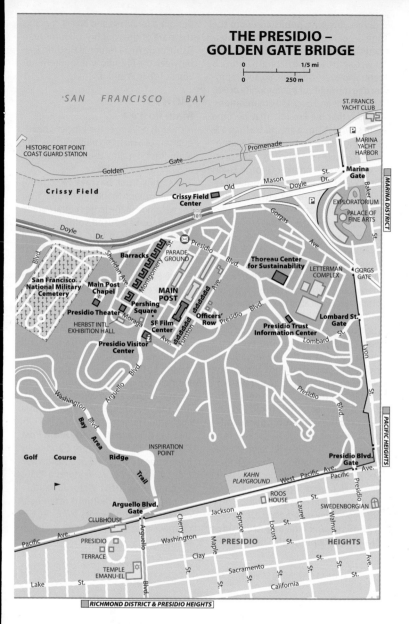

THE PRESIDIO – GOLDEN GATE BRIDGE

0   1/5 mi
0   250 m

SAN   FRANCISCO   BAY

ST. FRANCIS YACHT CLUB

HISTORIC FORT POINT COAST GUARD STATION

MARINA YACHT HARBOR

Promenade

Golden   Gate

Crissy Field

Marina Gate

Old   Mason   Doyle   St. Dr.

Crissy Field Center

EXPLORATORIUM

PALACE OF FINE ARTS

Doyle   Dr.

Gorgas

Presidio

MARINA DISTRICT

Baker St.

Barracks

PARADE GROUND

Blvd.

Thoreau Center for Sustainability

LETTERMAN COMPLEX

GORGS GATE

San Francisco National Military Cemetery

Main Post Chapel

MAIN POST

Sheridan Ave.

Montgomery St.

Ave.

Lombard St. Gate

Presidio Theater

Pershing Square

Moraga

SF Film Center

Officers' Row

Presidio Blvd.

Presidio Trust Information Center

Lombard

Lyon St.

PACIFIC HEIGHTS

HERBST INTL. EXHIBITION HALL

Funston Ave.

Presidio Visitor Center

Arguello Blvd.

Presidio Blvd.

Washington Blvd.

Bay Area Ridge Trail

INSPIRATION POINT

Golf   Course

Presidio Blvd. Gate

KAHN PLAYGROUND

West Pacific Ave. Pacific

Presidio

Arguello Blvd. Gate

ROOS HOUSE

SWEDENBORGIAN

CLUBHOUSE

Pacific   Ave.

Jackson   St.

Laurel St.

Walnut St.

PRESIDIO TERRACE

Arguello Blvd.

Washington

Cherry St.

Maple St.

Spruce St.

Locust St.

PRESIDIO   HEIGHTS

TEMPLE EMANU-EL

Clay   St.

Sacramento St.

St.

St.

Ave.

Lake   St.

California

supervision of the National Park Service. The remnants of the earliest 18C structures were discovered beneath the Main Post parking lot in 1996, shedding new light on what was believed to be the size of the original Presidio.

Today an official unit of the GGNRA, the property is managed by **The Presidio Trust**, a presidentially appointed, non-profit board charged with maintaining the Presidio's aesthetic, ecological and historic integrity while weaning it from federal dollars by 2013. About 80 percent of Presidio lands are under the direct aegis of the trust, while coastal areas are managed by the National Park

Service. Ensuring public access to the fine Greek, Colonial, Mission, Mediterranean Revival and Victorian buildings, as well as to trails and natural habitats, is central to every decision. So, too, is protecting the rights of a community of 800 households and over 150 organizations. In order that the Presidio may become self-supporting, administrators are allowing some commercial development. Despite resistance by some preservationists, filmmaker George Lucas (Star Wars) developed the former Letterman Army Medical Center complex (1899), on the east side of the Presidio, as a campus for the digital arts, incorporating a seven-acre "Great Meadow." Already occupying 12 buildings of the complex is the **Thoreau Center for Sustainability** (1016 Lincoln Blvd.; www.thoreau.org), whose 60 member organizations are dedicated to environmental and social-justice issues.

Their often-eclectic causes range from waste management and women's empowerment to the preservation of indigenous ancestral lands and the use of tree-free fiber in paper and textiles. Formerly a private club reserved for Presidio officers, the Arnold Palmer-designed **Presidio Golf Course** today welcomes all golfers to tackle its 18 scenic holes (300 Finley Rd. near Arguello Gate; ⏱open daily 6am–dusk; ⊘closed Dec 25; ✕🅿️⬚$39–$145 per nonresident person; club rental $50; reservations may be made up to 30 days in advance; ℘415-561-4667; www.presidiogolf.com).

A 2.5mi stretch of the **Bay Area Ridge Trail** extends through The Presidio; designed for hikers and bikers, it marks the start of the roughly 1,000mi Juan Bautista de Anza National Historic Trail between the Presidio and southern Arizona's Tubac Presidio.

SIGHTS
Main Post★★

Although no longer the efficient headquarters of a bustling military base, the Main Post remains the focal point of activity at The Presidio.

The stately brick **barracks★** (c.1890) stretching along Montgomery Street, on the west side of the large central Parade Ground, once housed soldiers of the Spanish-American War. The dignified row today contains The Presidio's main visitor center and offices of the GGNRA. At the Parade Ground's southern end stands **Pershing Square**, site of the home of Gen. John "Black Jack" Pershing, later commander of the American Expeditionary Forces in Europe during World War I. Pershing's wife and daughters perished in a 1915 blaze that destroyed the house (a son survived); a flagpole signifies its location. A nearby monument marks the corner of the original adobe and thatched-roof Presidio compound built by the Spanish in 1776. Just west, on a low rise, the **Main Post Chapel** (130 Fisher Loop; ⏱open by appointment only; ℘415-561-3930; www.interfaith-presidio.org) features a 1930s WPA mural by artist Victor Arnautoff. Diverse spiritual traditions often hold ceremonies and events here. At the chapel's east end is a small Vietnam memorial.

Barracks on Montgomery Street

© Anne Marie Scott / MICHELIN

The **San Francisco Film Center** *(39 Mesa St.;* 📞*415-561-3456; www.sffilm centre.com)* has revamped one Mission-style barracks building on the east side of the Parade Ground as a home for numerous small movie-makers and publishers, with production facilities and a screening room.

Tree-lined Funston Avenue, one street farther east of the Parade Ground, was once reserved for officers. The Neoclassical and Italianate cottages (1862–63) at the southern corner, known as **Officers' Row★**, originally faced west but were turned towards the east in 1878 to present a more pleasant aspect to visitors. An ongoing dig by University of California archeology students has turned up 150,000 artifacts from this era. Farther along Funston Avenue, more elaborate residences representing several Victorian substyles were reserved for higher-ranking officers.

San Francisco National Military Cemetery★

Entrance off Sheridan St. at Lincoln Blvd.
In 1884 The Presidio's 28-acre burial ground was designated a National Military Cemetery, allowing any U.S. veteran the privilege of being buried here. Graves date from as far back as the Civil War. Well-known persons laid to rest here include Gen. Frederick Funston, acting Presidio commander during the 1906 earthquake and fire, and U.S. Rep. Phillip Burton, sponsor and champion of the GGNRA. Eucalyptus and pine woods surround the cemetery.

A short distance away, beneath the Crissy Field Avenue overpass leading to the Golden Gate Bridge, lies a small **Pet Cemetery** 👤👤, with whimsical, and often poignant headstones marking the graves of generations of Presidio pets.

Crissy Field

Crissy Field Ave. off Lincoln Blvd.
Gazing over this broad, flat marsh, visitors may not understand why it is widely hailed as San Francisco's most impressive environmental restoration in recent years. Yet the work done to bring it back to its natural state was

tremendous. Once a soggy marsh, the field was drained and filled for the 1915 Panama-Pacific International Exposition, then covered with 70 acres of asphalt as an Army aircraft test site from 1919 to 1936. (Many original buildings still stand, including hangars that once housed cloth biplanes.) The National Park Service undertook a three-year, $32-million project to restore the original tidal marsh, beach and dunes, anchoring them with native grasses and other plants. Today the 100 acres of wild, windswept shoreline is a favorite place for walkers, joggers, bicyclists, windsurfers, and birds.

The project is detailed at the interim **Crissy Field Center** (👤👤 *1199 E. Beach;* 🕐*open Mon–Sat 10am–5pm;* 🕐*closed major holidays;* 🅿️ ♿ ✕ 📞*415-561-7690; www.crissyfield.org),* whose exhibits and programs focus on the convergence of urban and natural environments. The eco-friendly interim center opened in late 2009 as result of the Doyle Drive replacement project nearby. After the project's completion, expected in 2015, the center plans to return to its permanent location at 603 Mason Street.

👤👤 Gulf of the Farallones National Marine Sanctuary Visitor Center (M2)

Bldg. 991 at the Crissy Field Beach.
🕐*Open Wed–Sun 10am–4pm.*
🕐*Closed Jan 1, Thanksgiving Day, Dec 25.* 🅿️ 📞*415-561-6625. www.farallones.org.*
Exhibits describe research and conservation efforts in the 1,200sq mi sanctuary, whose boundaries embrace Marin County coastlines to the mean high-tide mark and the rocky Farallon Islands (26mi west of the Golden Gate), home to the largest concentration of breeding seabirds in the continental U.S. The sanctuary also harbors more than two dozen species of marine mammals. In the visitor center are a live tidepool tank; interactive computer displays outlining such sanctuary activities as whalewatching, bird watching, fishing and kayaking; and murals depicting life

A Whale of a Time

Few experiences may be more thrilling, and perhaps more unsettling, than tossing in salty swells on a small boat beyond the sight of land, surrounded by a good dozen of the largest creatures ever to inhabit the earth.

Such may be the predicament of those who venture into the Gulf of the Farallones National Marine Sanctuary. This stretch of sea is extraordinarily rich in krill, tiny shrimp-like crustaceans that are the favorite food of baleen whales. Blue whales, who may consume four tons in a single day, grow to 100ft long and 200 tons in weight; in summer and fall, these gargantuan creatures converge near the Farallon Islands, spouting and raising their fins and tails as they roll in the waves. Agile humpback whales may approach boats at closer proximity. In winter, gray whales, migrating between Alaska and Baja California, pass through these seas; they may be accompanied by newborn calves as they travel north in spring.

Unless you own your own boat, the only practical way to visit the sanctuary is aboard a marine research vessel. The Oceanic Society's naturalist-led *Wacky Jacky,* a 50ft motorboat with an observation deck and indoor salon, accommodates 50 passengers and crew (☞*$99–$125; ☎415-474-3385; www. oceanic-society.org*); it departs San Francisco Yacht Harbor bordering Marina Green weekend days rain or shine (except late May and December) year-round; call or check website for schedule. Keep in mind that the boat, though bound for the Farallon Islands, may turn back short of the avian-rich rocks, depending upon what marine life or inclement weather it encounters en route.

in the Gulf of the Farallones and adjacent Cordell Bank sanctuaries.

Fort Winfield Scott
Entrance on Kobbe Ave. near Park Blvd.
A horseshoe-shaped group of white, Mission Revival-style barracks, Fort Winfield Scott was built in 1910 to house the Coast Artillery Corps. The only complex in the Presidio of uniform architectural style, Fort Scott provides a quiet, attractive setting from which to view the piers of the Golden Gate Bridge.

Coastal Defense Batteries★
Scattered along the cliffs that border Lincoln Avenue between Fort Point and Baker Beach, these crumbling concrete bunkers offer spectacular **views★★★** of the sea, the Marin Headlands and the Golden Gate Bridge.
Linked by the Coastal Trail, the batteries were constructed between 1853 (at Fort Point) and 1910 to protect San Francisco Bay from invasion by sea. As with most of the fortifications around the bay, however, their guns were never fired in defense.

The best way to enjoy the view is to stroll along the Coastal Trail south from the Golden Gate Bridge toll plaza through **Battery Cranston** (1897), Battery Marcus Miller (1891), Battery Boutelle (1900), and Battery Godfrey (1895) to the Fort Scott Overlook. At Battery Chamberlin (1902), overlooking Baker Beach farther down the Coastal Trail, the public may assist in cleaning, loading and firing a 50-ton "disappearing" gun the first full weekend of each month (◷*open Sat–Sun 11am–3pm*).

Baker Beach★
Bowley St. off Lincoln Ave., southwest corner of the Presidio.
Popular as much for its smooth sand as for the high dunes that protect it from all but the coldest winds, Baker Beach attracts two types of beachgoer. The southern end draws families and adolescents; the northern end, with its more dramatic view of the Golden Gate Bridge and the sage-covered cliffs, is popular with devotees of nude sunbathing—an activity tolerated (though not officially permitted) on federal land.

ADDITIONAL SIGHT
♠♦ Fort Point National Historic Site★

Long Ave. and Marine Dr. ◷*Open Fri –Sun 10am–5pm.* ◷*Closed Jan 1, Thanksgiving Day, Dec 25.* ☞*Guided tours (30min) available; candlelight tours held Nov–Mar (reservations suggested).* 🅿 ✆*415-556-1693. www.nps.gov/fopo.*

Tucked beneath a steel arch at the southern anchorage of the Golden Gate Bridge, this impressive, multi-storied brick-and-granite fort stands as a fine example of Civil War-era masonry and military architecture.

Designed as the first of three enormous fortifications to guard the entrance to San Francisco Bay (the other two were to be built on Alcatraz Island and at Lime Point, now the northern anchorage of the bridge), Fort Point was erected in 1861 atop the site of Castillo de San Joaquín (1794), an abandoned Spanish gun battery.

The original design, calling for a rectangular structure of granite blocks, was modified (after construction began) to a brick fortress with defensive towers on the east and west. Master brickmasons were hired to build the structure; their fine craftsmanship remains evident throughout. As the Civil War approached, the U.S. military, anticipating Confederate attacks on San Francisco Bay, ordered the uncompleted and unarmed fort occupied. For months a garrison stood guard over empty gun casements.

Like other military installations around the bay, Fort Point's ordnance was never fired in defense. By 1885 its guns were considered obsolete and were removed for scrap. Long periods of minimal occupation or complete abandonment followed, with the thick walls occasionally serving as a damp, lonely barracks for unlucky companies of soldiers.

Initial plans for the Golden Gate Bridge placed Fort Point on the exact spot where Joseph Strauss, the bridge's designer, intended to sink the southern anchorage. After visiting the fort, Strauss was so impressed by the quality of its masonry that he designed a massive steel arch over the fort to preserve it.

Visit

Restored and rebuilt by the National Park Service in the 1970s, Fort Point provides visitors with an excellent glimpse into military life on the California coast in the late 19C. Information panels throughout the building detail the history of the fort and the lives of the soldiers stationed there. Just inside the "sally port," the only entrance to the structure, lies a Spanish bronze cannon (1684), saved from Castillo de San Joaquín, and a huge 1844 Rodman cannon, typical of those that once guarded the Golden Gate (*cannon drill demonstrations are presented regularly; check at front desk for day's schedule*).

To the right of the sally port, the former sutler's store (post exchange) houses a visitor center, bookstore, and a small theater presenting slide shows and short films about the fort and the Golden Gate Bridge. Handcut granite spiral staircases lead to the upper tiers, with their intricate masonry and arching ceilings. Officers' quarters and privates' barracks are hung with historical photographs, and there are exhibits documenting the experiences of 20C African-American soldiers and the wartime contributions of American women. From the top-level barbettes, visitors can marvel at a unique and stunning **view★★** of the southern pier and underbelly of the Golden Gate Bridge.

ADDRESSES

CAFE

Café Crissy – *In permanent Crissy Field Center.* ✆*415-561-7756.* In keeping with the center's "green" philosophy, utensils and service items here are recyclable, biodegradable or compostable, and the cafe's profits help fund center programs. Pastries, beverages and sandwiches draw rave reviews, from the Mediterranean-style tuna salad panini to the chicken curry, portobello and egg-salad sandwiches.

CENTRAL NEIGHBORHOODS

San Francisco's central neighborhoods encompass a diverse group of districts, including the ritzy Pacific Heights, home to the city's social elite, and its neighbors Japantown and Presidio Heights. To the south, the sprawling Richmond district and the rolling, landscaped Golden Gate Park stretch 52 blocks from Haight-Asbhury to the Pacific Ocean. The Golden Gate Park is often considered part of the Richmond or Sunset Districts, but it is truly a neighborhood in its own right; larger than New York City's Central Park, it is home to lakes, gardens, trails, museums, windmills, a buffalo paddock, and nearly every kind of sport arena, from bocce courts to polo fields to flyfishing ponds.

Highlights

1 Enjoy 360-degree views from the **de Young Museum's observation tower** (p153)

2 Admire 20 million specimens at the **California Academy of Sciences** (p155)

3 Take in stellar views from **Twin Peaks** (p160)

4 Explore **Pacific Heights** on architectural walking tour (p163)

5 Shop **Fillmore St.** and see a movie at Japantown's **Sundance Kabuki Theater** (p166, p161)

From the Park to Pacific Heights

Streching 3 miles inland from Ocean Beach to Stanyan Street, Golden Gate Park is a 1,017-acre rectangle greensward home to a complex of art and science museums and a wealth of recreational opportunities.

An enchantingly natual yet entirely purpose-built urban oasis of meadows, gardens, lakes and woodlands, the park is the result of careful planning by two inspired landscape architects and the labor of an army of gardeners.

Directly to the west of the park sits the Haight-Ashbury neighborhood. Although more than four decades have passed since the "Summer of Love," a 1960s counterculture ethos still clings to the Haight, which borders Haight Street between Central Avenue and Stanyan Street, just west of the Castro.

The stretch of Haight Street between Central Avenue and Stanyan Street, known as the Upper Haight, is packed with vintage boutiques and coffee houses, most of which cater to hip twentysomethings.

Edging the Pacific Ocean and the northern side of the Golden Gate Park is the Richmond District. At the turn of the 20C, Richmond's western reaches were condemned as the Great Sand Waste until the establishment of Geary Boulevard opened the district to settlement. Today, the neighbohood is a residential haven with a middle-class small-town feel. Its population incorporates a cultural mix that is apaparent in the area's myriad restaurants, including Chinese, Thai , Burmese, Vietnamese and Korean eateries. Richmond's main thoroughfare, Clement Street teems with shops and markets hawking everything from bok choy to flip-flops. Where the Richmond meets the ocean sits the Cliff House, the ruins of Sutro Baths, and the California Palace of the Legion of Honor.

To the north and east of the Richmond, Pacific Heights sits along a high east–west ridge between Van Ness Avenue and the Presidio. This tiny residential enclave is synonymous with wealth. It offers great opportunities for strolling, eating and shopping, and holds some of the city's finest houses and loveliest views, as well as some killer steep streets.

At the south end of Pacific Heights, in a part of the city known as the Western Addition, Japantown abounds with Japanese architecture and culture. At the heart of Japantown is the Japan Center, a complex of shops, sushi bars, theaters and hotels. Crowned by a five-tiered pagoda, the center hosts celebrations such as the annual Cherry Blossom Festival in April (nccbf.org).

Golden Gate Park★★★

Encompassing more than 1,017 acres of meadows, gardens and public buildings, verdant Golden Gate Park is the largest cultivated urban park in the US. It has 27 miles of footpaths and 7.5 miles of equestrian trails, all linking an enchantingly natural, yet entirely man-made, landscape of lakes, waterfalls, swales and woods.

A BIT OF HISTORY

As San Francisco prospered in the 1860s, William Ralston and others began laying plans for a city park to rival designs for Central Park in New York City. They selected a tract of the sandy scrublands known as the Outer Lands as an affordable location. When Mayor H.P. Coon consulted Frederick Law Olmsted, designer of Central Park, the famous landscape architect eyed the dunes and advised that large trees would never grow on the site. Undaunted, city planners in 1871 contracted engineer and surveyor William Hammond Hall to build a park on the maligned tract.

Raising a bulwark behind Ocean Beach to deflect ocean winds, Hall graded the inland dunes into gentle hills and valleys, securing them by sowing barley, lupine and ammophila grass. When this natural matting had taken root, he began to plant trees. Starting on the eastern end of the park, Hall laid out roads in a meandering fashion, partly to discourage speeding but also to imitate the leisurely ambience of a rural road. By the late 1870s, the park was a resounding public success.

"Uncle John" – In 1890 Hall appointed **John McLaren** (1846–1943) as the new park superintendent. Fondly known as "Uncle John" by his staff and an admiring public, the cantankerous, Scottish-born McLaren ran Golden Gate Park with a patriarchal hand. Believing that a park should provide a refuge from city life, he fought hard against new buildings, statues and other urban encroachments for 53 years, and personally planted millions

MUNI Bus 5–Fulton, 21–Hayes or 44–O'Shaughnessy. 📞415-673-6864 or www.511.org for more information. A park shuttle ($2) operates on weekends.

Info: 📞415-751-2766 or 415-831-2700. www.sfgate.com/travel/neighborhoods/sf/goldengatepark/.

Location: Golden Gate Park is three miles long and 0.5mi wide, bordered by Ocean Beach, Stanyon Street, Fulton Street and Lincoln Way. The main visitor center 🛈 is at the Beach Chalet in the park's western end (🕐open daily 9am–5pm; 📞415-751-2766). At the east end brochures are available at McLaren Lodge park headquarters (🕐open Mon–Fri 8am–5pm; 📞415-831-2700).

Kids: California Academy of Sciences, Koret Children's Quarter, the buffalo paddock, a boat ride on Stow Lake or renting bicycles and riding through the park.

Timing: Visit popular attractions in the morning to avoid large crowds.

Parking: The Music Concourse Garage (entrance at 10th Ave. & Fulton St.) is open daily 7.30am–10pm. On weekends spots fill up quickly and street parking is difficult. John F. Kennedy Drive between Kezar Drive and 19th Avenue is closed to car traffic on Sundays.

Don't Miss: de Young Museum, Japanese Tea Garden, boating on Stowe Lake, the Conservatory of Flowers and the Dutch Windmill.

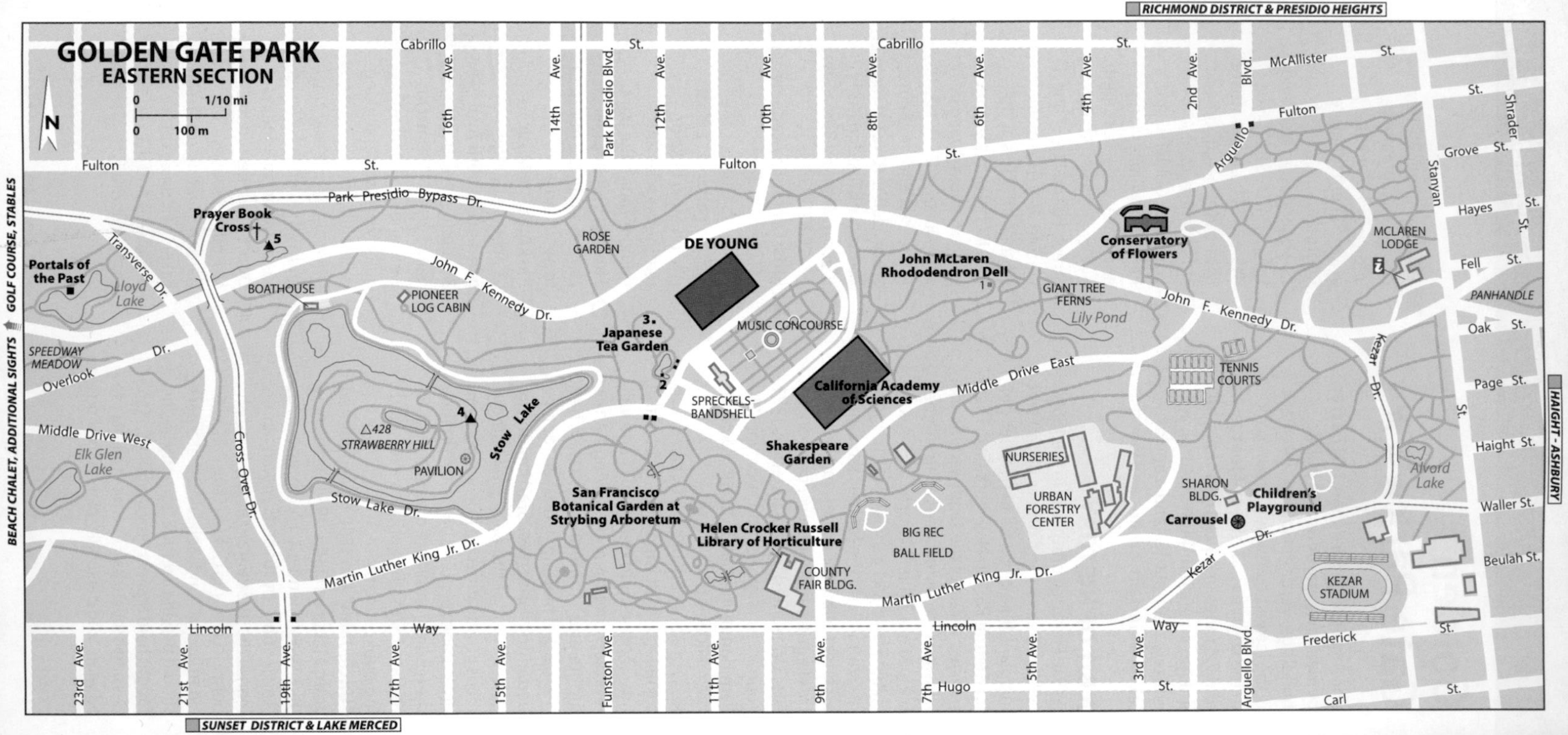

RICHMOND DISTRICT & PRESIDIO HEIGHTS

SUNSET DISTRICT & LAKE MERCED

BEACH CHALET, ADDITIONAL SIGHTS

GOLF COURSE, STABLES

GOLDEN GATE PARK
EASTERN SECTION

N

| 0 | 1/10 mi |
| 0 | 100 m |

Shrader St.
Grove St.
Hayes St.
Fell St.
Oak St.
Page St.
Haight St.
Waller St.
Beulah St.

PANHANDLE

Stanyan St.

McLAREN LODGE

Kezar Dr.

Alvord Lake

Carl St.

Frederick St.

KEZAR STADIUM

Fulton St.

McAllister St.

Arguello Blvd.

2nd Ave.

John F. Kennedy Dr.

Conservatory of Flowers

TENNIS COURTS

Children's Playground

SHARON BLDG.

Carrousel

3rd Ave.

4th Ave.

GIANT TREE FERNS

Lily Pond

Middle Drive East

NURSERIES

URBAN FORESTRY CENTER

5th Ave.

Kezar Dr.

Arguello Blvd.

6th Ave.

John McLaren Rhododendron Dell   1

Martin Luther King Jr. Dr.

Cabrillo St.

8th Ave.

California Academy of Sciences

BIG REC BALL FIELD

Lincoln Way

7th Ave.

Hugo St.

MUSIC CONCOURSE

DE YOUNG

Shakespeare Garden

COUNTY FAIR BLDG.

9th Ave.

10th Ave.

Fulton St.

SPRECKELS BANDSHELL

Helen Crocker Russell Library of Horticulture

11th Ave.

12th Ave.

Park Presidio Blvd.

ROSE GARDEN

3   Japanese Tea Garden

2

San Francisco Botanical Garden at Strybing Arboretum

Funston Ave.

14th Ave.

15th Ave.

Stow Lake

Martin Luther King Jr. Dr.

16th Ave.

John F. Kennedy Dr.

PIONEER LOG CABIN

4

△ 428 STRAWBERRY HILL

PAVILION

Stow Lake Dr.

17th Ave.

Park - Presidio - Bypass - Dr.

Cabrillo St.

BOATHOUSE

Prayer Book Cross   5

Cross Over Dr.

19th Ave.

21st Ave.

Lincoln Way

Portals of the Past

SPEEDWAY MEADOW

Transverse Dr.

Lloyd Lake

Overlook

Middle Drive West

ELK GLEN Lake

23rd Ave.

Fulton St.

Recreation

Recreational opportunities abound in the park. Public sports facilities include baseball/softball diamonds at **Big Rec Ball Field** (*415-831-5510*) and tennis courts (*415-831-6301*) north of the **Children's Playground**. Pedal boats and row boats may be rented at **Stow Lake**, off John F. Kennedy Drive .5mi west of 10th Avenue (*open daily 10am–4pm; 415-752-0347*). The nine-hole **Golden Gate Park Golf Course** is located near 47th Ave. & John F. Kennedy Dr. (*415-751-8987*). Paved biking and skating trails ramble the park; Middle Drive West is a car-free skaters' haven on Saturdays, while a portion of John F. Kennedy Dr. is dedicated to **skaters** and bicyclists on Sundays and holidays (*rentals at several shops along Stanyan St., and behind Stow Lake Boathouse; 415-668-6699*). Extensive **hiking paths** wind through the park, and a variety of free **walking tours** are conducted year-round; call or check the website for schedule (*415-263-0991; www.sfpt.org*).

of flowers, bulbs and trees. By the time of his death at age 97, McLaren had succeeded in cultivating one of the world's most varied gardens.

The Midwinter Fair of 1894 – Four years after McLaren's appointment, journalist Michael H. de Young, inspired by the World's Columbian Exposition of 1893 in Chicago, successfully convinced city officials that San Francisco should mount its own fair at Golden Gate Park to promote the city's splendid winter climate. Five fancifully domed and spired buildings and a 266ft Electric Tower were erected around a quadrangle called the Great Court, and the California Midwinter International Exposition of 1894 (also called the Midwinter Fair) opened on January 27. All of California's counties, four other states and more than 19 foreign countries participated, drawing some 2.5 million visitors during its six months of operation. The complex was adapted and expanded over the years to accommodate the de Young museum and the Asian Art Museum, but after suffering major damage during the 1989 Loma Prieta it was slowly dismantled, with the Asian Art Museum moving to Civic Center in 2003 and the de Young constructing an architecturally daring new home on the site in 2005.

In addition to being a leafy retreat, Golden Gate Park has had many uses during the 20C. Refugees set up temporary homes here after the 1906 earthquake. Thousands flocked here during

the "Summer of Love" in 1967, when hippies hung out and crowds gathered for mass celebrations and concerts at Speedway Meadow.

Today the park continues to host free music concerts at the Music Concourse and Sharon Meadow and to serve as a glorious backyard—a place for family picnics, neighborhood baseball games, outdoor sports and contemplative strolls.

SIGHTS
Conservatory of Flowers★

100 John F. Kennedy Dr. at Conservatory Dr. W. Open Tue–Sun 9am–4.30pm. Closed major holidays except Memorial Day, July 4 and Labor Day. $7. 415-831-2090. www.conservatoryofflowers.org.

Conservatory of Flowers

© Carol Simowitz / SFCVB

This ornate Victorian glass palace shelters more than 1,700 species of rare and exotic plants under an octagonal central dome and two flanking wings. Golden Gate Park's oldest structure, the lacy white wood-frame building was prefabricated in Dublin, Ireland, modeled after the glasshouses of London's Kew Gardens; it was shipped to the San Jose estate of James Lick for installation. Arriving after Lick's death in 1876, the structure was purchased by a consortium of San Francisco businessmen led by Leland Stanford, and donated to Golden Gate Park. Seasonal blooms in formal geometric designs grace the parterres in front.

John McLaren Rhododendron Dell

John F. Kennedy Dr. at 6th Ave.
At the heart of this 20-acre, spring-blooming garden stands a **statue of John McLaren (1)** contemplating a pine-cone. The life-size proportions and quiet pose contrast with the host of heroic bronze figures that surround the nearby **Music Concourse**, an ironic contradiction to McLaren's lifelong campaign to keep statues from cluttering the park's scenery.

♣♣ Koret Children's Quarter

Kezar Dr.
A pioneering concept when it opened in 1888, this municipal playground was centered on the sandstone Sharon Building, which provided refreshments, stored play equipment, and stabled goats for the kids' "barnyard." Today the building houses the **Sharon Art Studio**, a venue for art classes for children and adults (*℘415-753-7004; www.sharonartstudio.org*).
The magnificent Herschell-Spillman **Carrousel in Golden Gate Park★**its princely stable of carved wooden animals under a dome supported by 16 fluted columnswas built in 1912 and restored in 1984 (Ⓝopen daily Memorial Day through Labor Day, 10am–4.30pm; rest of the year Fri–Sun. Ⓝclosed Jan 1, Thanksgiving Day, Dec 25; ⊜$2/adult, $1/ child; ℘415-831-2770).

♣♣ Japanese Tea Garden★★

Hagiwara Tea Garden Dr. ⒪*Open daily Mar–Oct 9am–6pm, Nov–Feb 9am–4.45pm.* ⊜$7. &✕🅿 ℘415-666-3232; japaneseteagardensf.com.
Harboring a delightful maze of winding paths, stone lanterns, ornamental ponds, bonsai, a wooden pagoda, a Zen garden and a teahouse, this tranquil, five-acre garden has been an attraction since it was built for the Midwinter Fair of 1894. The garden continued operating under the direction of master gardener Makoto Hagiwara, who also tended the tea concession and is credited with inventing the fortune cookie here in 1909.
The garden is most colorful around April, when its cherry trees burst into bloom. The exquisitely crafted ceremonial gateway at the front entrance is a traditional feature of Japanese shrines. Inside, the steeply arching wooden **Moon Bridge (2)** takes its name from the orb formed by the bridge and its reflection in the pond below. Near the center of the garden sits a 10.5ft statue of the Buddha, cast in Japan in 1790. Visitors enjoy sipping green tea and nibbling delicate cookies in the open-air **teahouse (3)**.

San Francisco Botanical Garden at Strybing Arboretum★★

Martin Luther King, Jr. Dr. at 9th Ave. ⒪*Open Mon–Fri 8am–4.30pm, Sat–Sun and holidays 10am–5pm.* ☛*Guided tours (1hr) Mon–Fri 1.30pm, Sat–Sun 0.30am, 1.30pm (bookstore); Wed, Fri and Sun 2pm (Friend Gate).* ⊜*Donation requested.* ✕🅿 ℘415-661-1316. www.sfbotanicalgarden.org.
This outstanding botanical collection comprises 8,000 species of plants from all over the world. The arboretum emphasizes regions of Mediterranean climate, with collections from California, the Cape Province of South Africa, southwestern Australia and Chile. Other attractions include a hillside garden of succulents; the Cloud Forests, where mist emitters supplement the fog; the Nature Trail; and the Primitive Plant Garden of moss, cycads, horsetails, gingko trees, ferns, and conifers.

The Garden of Fragrances features a wall built of stones removed from a medieval Spanish monastery purchased by William Randolph Hearst, who had it dismantled and shipped to Golden Gate Park for reassembly. A fire destroyed the crates and identifying markings, leaving a great pile of indistinguishable stones from which the Park Department has drawn over the decades. Housed in the County Fair Building to the west of the Arboretum's main entrance, the **Helen Crocker Russell Library of Horticulture** (Ⓒ open Wed–Mon 10am–4pm; Ⓒ closed major holidays) has more than 27,000 books and 450 plant and garden periodicals and presents quarterly exhibits of botanical prints and other art.

Shakespeare Garden★

Martin Luther King, Jr., Dr. and Middle Dr. E.
Established in 1928, this small English garden nurtures plants mentioned in the works of William Shakespeare. The locked box in the back wall contains a bust of the Bard, a copy from the sculpted image at the poet's tomb carved by Gerard Johnson after Shakespeare's death in 1616.

♣♦ Stow Lake★

Stow Lake Dr.; access from John F. Kennedy Dr. or Martin Luther King, Jr., Dr. Ⓒ *Boathouse open daily 10am–4pm, weather permitting.* ♿ *$19/hr pedal boat; $14/hr rowboat.* ♿✕🅿 ℘415-752-0347. www.parks.sfgov.org.
The park's main irrigation reservoir surrounding Strawberry Hill is the largest of the 15 man-made lakes that dot Golden Gate Park. Swarms of waterfowl share the water with the small boats which may be rented on the northwest shore. The 428ft summit of Strawberry Hill, reached by footpath, is the highest point in the park. Constructed in 1894, a **waterfall (4)** named for industrialist Collis P. Huntington cascades 125ft from the summit to the surface of the lake. Immediately north of Stow Lake, **Prayer Book Cross**, a 57ft Celtic cross carved of sandstone, dominates the hill above **Rainbow Falls (5)**.

DE YOUNG MUSEUM★★★

50 Hagiwara Tea Garden Dr. at John F. Kennedy Dr. Ⓒ *Open Tue–Sun 9.30am –5.15pm (Fri mid-Jan–Nov until 8.45pm).* Ⓒ *Closed Jan 1, Thanksgiving Day and Dec 25.* ♿ *$10 (allows same-day admission to the Legion of Honor* ♿ *see SUTRO HEIGHTS and LAND'S END); $2 discount for bus riders with transfer. Free first Tue of the month.* ♿✕🅿 ℘415-750-3600. www.deyoungmuseum.org.
Survivor of a turbulent past, the de Young is today a major force on the West Coast museum scene. Its collection from the pre-Columbian era to the present traces the history of art in the Americas, complemented by significant holdings in textiles and African and Oceanic art. The collection, along with that of the Legion of Honor, belongs to the city of San Francisco; together these institutions form the **Fine Arts Museums of San Francisco**.

A BIT OF HISTORY

The de Young Museum was established by **Michael H. de Young**, co-founder of the *San Francisco Chronicle* and organizer of the 1894 California Midwinter International Exposition. When the fair closed, he persuaded the city's Park Commission to preserve the Egyptian Revival-style Fine Arts Building as a museum, which he filled with an eclectic assortment of artworks and natural history exhibits.
New wings were added in the 20C, one of them to house the Asian Art Museum, but the entire structure was badly damaged in the 1989 Loma Prieta earthquake. Temporary bracing couldn't solve the building's safety issues, and it was demolished in 2002. In 2003 the Asian Art Museum took up residence in the refurbished former Main Library at Civic Center, and in 2005 the de Young Museum welcomed visitors to its new home in Golden Gate Park.
Funded by $190 million in private donations, the daring three-story building was created by Swiss architects Jacques Herzog and Pierre de Meuron, designers of London's Tate Gallery of Modern Art. A total of 950,000 pounds of copper

sheaths the exterior; over the the next decade it will fade from bright copper to cinnamon, then to a rich green that will blend in with the surrounding trees.

VISIT

The interior is centered on a vast, airy lobby. Throughout, you'll find rich native woods and Italian stone, as well as two gardens with ferns and eucalyptus. Selections from the 25,000-piece permanent collection are displayed on the Concourse and Upper levels. The basement (Lower Level) has a large space for special exhibits and a gift store. On the west side of the building you'll find a courtyard cafe and sculpture park.

Enter the museum on the Concourse Level. If the line for tickets here is long, head to the Lower Level, where there's rarely any line at all. Digital screens on both floors display the day's schedule of docent-led tours and family activities. Audio tours ($7) are available at the main lobby kiosk. Be sure to treat yourself to the 360-degree views from the Observation Deck atop the de Young tower.

American Art★★

Concourse and Upper levels

Eighteen galleries are devoted to the museum's extensive collection of paintings, decorative arts and sculpture. Works are arranged chronologically starting on the Upper Level, where in intimate galleries you'll find artwork from the colonial era through the Arts and Crafts movement of the early 20C. The museum's major works from this period include paintings by John Singleton Copley, Frederic Edwin Church, Mary Cassatt and John Singer Sargent, as well as furniture by the Herter Brothers and Chippendale.

The survey of American art continues on the Concourse level, whose nine light-filled galleries are designed to accommodate large-scale pieces. The collection here ranges from Grant Wood's *Dinner for Threshers* (1934) through postwar paintings by heavy-hitters like Willem de Kooning and Mark Rothko to contemporary works in new media by emerging artists. Selected pieces of sculpture, including works by Isamu Noguchi and Louise Nevelson, are on display in the Sculpture Garden.

Art of the Americas★

Concourse Level

This important collection, comprising works from Mesoamerica, Central and South America and the West Coast of North America, is housed in four large galleries. Indigenous art from the west coast of North America includes fine basketry, storage containers for intertribal "potlatch" gatherings, and rare 19C

de Young Museum

© Michael Layefsky / Fine Arts Museums of San Francisco

totem poles depicting ancestral animal spirits. A special gallery is devoted to ancient objects from Mexico, including the museum's outstanding grouping of Teotihuacan murals. Here you'll also find a five-ton Olmec stone head.

African Art★
Upper Level
The **African art** exhibit—the de Young's charter collection—contains pieces from 80 distinct sub-Saharan cultures, mostly West African from AD 1200 to the present. Note especially the early 20C Shrine Figure of a Seven Headed Bush Spirit, a six-foot-tall sculpture from the Niger River Delta acquired by the museum in 2004.

Oceanic Art★
Upper Level
The museum's holdings of Oceanic art come from Melanesia, Indonesia, Polynesia, the Caroline Islands of Micronesia and the Maori peoples of New Zealand. Wood carvings predominate here. The Jolika Collection of New Guinea art features more than 400 works including several towering figures, masks and ceremonial costumes.

Textile Art★
Upper Level
More than 12,000 textiles and costumes from around the world make up this collection. You'll find everything from Turkish carpets to the latest couture.

♣♦CALIFORNIA ACADEMY OF SCIENCES★★
55 Music Concorse Drive. ◐Open Mon–Sat 9.30am–5pm, Sun 11am–5pm. ◐Closed Thanksgiving Day, Dec 25. ⛟$24.95; $3 discount for bus riders with transfer; free third Wed of the month. ⛭✕🅿 ✆415-379-8000. www.calacademy.org.
The oldest scientific institution in the West, the venerable California Academy of Sciences has since its inception aimed at exploring, explaining and celebrating the natural world. Its three branches— the **Kimball Natural History Museum**, the **Steinhart Aquarium** and the **Mor-**

rison Planetarium—today occupy a groundbreaking new building that showcases institutional philosophy and cutting-edge technology along with the academy's ever-expanding collections.

A BIT OF HISTORY
Founded in 1853 in a surge of post-Gold Rush enthusiasm for knowledge about California's physical environment, the Academy of Sciences began as a clubby group of naturalists who collected specimens, presented scholarly papers, and eventually began to function as a natural-history museum. In 1891 the organization took up residence at 833 Market Street. Charles Crocker and Leland Stanford were among those who donated funds for an exhibit to display birds, mammals, plants and other specimens from the collections.
The Market Street building was destroyed by the earthquake and fire of 1906, but the academy was re-established in Golden Gate Park. Over time the site expanded to 12 connected buildings that by the mid-1980s had begun to show their age. The 1989 Loma Prieta inflicted enough damage to convince directors that a new facility was needed. Pritzker Prize-winning architect Renzo Piano was engaged to design a building integrating all three branches of the Academy under one roof. A hallmark of Piano's 410,000sq ft, $400 million structure is a "living roof" made up of 1.7 million native Caliornia plants and 60,000 photovoltaic cells. This unique lid not only helps the building meld with its surroundings but also absorbs rainwater to decrease runoff and provides natural insulation.

VISIT
The academy's 20 million scientific specimens—including insects, scorpions, reptiles, amphibians and thousands of fish—occupy displays that teach visitors about the incredible variety of earth's environments. Kids especially will love the Africa Hall, with its pod of 20 South African penguins; the swamp exhibit with its underwater viewing panels; and the **Rainforests of the World**,

Rainforests of the World exhibit,
California Academy of Sciences

© Tim Griffith / California Academy of Sciences

a 4-story glass sphere in the central courtyard that transports visitors from understory to canopy to root systems. The aquarium features an extraordinary living coral reef with 4,000 fish.

ADDITIONAL SIGHTS IN THE PARK

The western section of Golden Gate Park, from Stow Lake to the ocean, abounds with great stretches of meadows, woods and sports facilities. Reflected in Lloyd Lake, the portico known as **Portals of the Past** are the remains of a Nob Hill mansion destroyed in the earthquake and fire of 1906. Halfway to the ocean from Stow Lake lies the immense **Polo Field;** football, rugby, soccer and lacrosse games are held here, and runners, bicyclists and equestrians use its tracks. At **Spreckels Lake,** model-boat enthusiasts launch their own radio-controlled vessels. A bit farther west along John F. Kennedy Drive, at the ▲♦ **Bison Paddock** a small herd of the shaggy beasts grazes under eucalyptus trees.

In the park's northwest corner, the small **Queen Wilhelmina Tulip Gardens** (bloom early spring) provide a setting for the **Dutch Windmill**★ ▲♦ (1902), one of the world's largest, which pumped water for park irrigation until 1929. The windmill was restored for decorative purposes in 1981. Its companion, the **Murphy Windmill** (1905), in the park's southwest corner, is undergoing restoration.

Beach Chalet★

🕑Visitor center open daily 9am–5pm.
🕑Closed Dec 25. ✕♿🅿 ℘415-751-2766.
Designed by Willis Polk, this Spanish Colonial-style pavilion (1921) operated for years as a workingman's bar.
The structure is graced with some of the city's finest WPA-funded **murals**★, frescoes executed in 1937 by Lucien Labaudt depicting recreation and diversion. They have been carefully restored and the building's main floor modified to serve as a park **visitor center**. An elegantly sinuous banister, designed by Labaudt in the form of a serpent and carved of honey-hued magnolia wood, leads to the popular Beach Chalet Brewery and Restaurant (℘415-386-8439; www.beachchalet.com), with ocean views.

ADDRESSES

🍴/EAT

Park Chow – 1240 9th. Ave. ℘415-665-9912. www.chowfoodbar.com. A half block from Golden Gate Park, this busy, friendly spot serves up healthy American comfort fare at sidewalk tables, inside by the fireplace, or up on the rooftop deck.

Haight-Ashbury ★

Although more than three decades have passed since the Human Be-In and Summer of Love, a countercultural ethos still clings to Haight-Ashbury, usually called "the Haight." Named for two streets intersecting at its heart, this neighborhood draws hordes of young people to its thrift stores, bars and coffeehouses. With 90 percent of its housing stock predating 1922, the Haight also boasts some of the city's loveliest Victorian homes.

A BIT OF HISTORY

Culture... Before the early 1870s, the neighborhood was a sandy scrubland sparsely populated by farmers. But as San Francisco's population skyrocketed, the city pushed westward and the street grid was extended into what is now the Haight-Ashbury district.

As Golden Gate Park and the panhandle developed, a resort area took shape in the neighborhood surrounding Stanyan Street. Beginning in 1895 **The Chutes**, an amusement park on the south side of Haight Street between Cole and Clayton streets, drew large crowds with its vaudeville theater, zoo, carnival rides and 300ft water slide.

Property values quintupled and new homes proliferated so rapidly that the architectural style of the day, Queen Anne, still characterizes the Haight today.

...and Counterculture – A haven for refugees fleeing the burnt-out parts of the city after the 1906 earthquake and fire, by the 1950s the neighborhood hosted an eclectic mix of students, gays, African Americans and beatniks fleeing tourist-ridden North Beach.

Bus 6–Parnassus, 7–Haight, 33–Stanyan, 37–Corbett, 43–Masonic, or 71–Haight-Noriega; streetcar N–Judah.

Info: ℘415-391-2000. www.onlyinsanfrancisco.com or www.sfgate.com/neighborhoods/sf/haight/.

Location: Haight Street extends from the eastern edge of Golden Gate Park, just south of the panhandle.

Kids: The Randall Museum.

Timing: Hang in the Haight for an hour or so, longer if you want to people watch in a coffee shop or browse through a bookstore.

Parking: Try for a spot on the residential lanes crisscrossing Haight Street.

Don't Miss: Picture-postcard views from Twin Peaks and Alamo Square.

Residential Architecture

Hundreds of unique, eye-catching Victorian period houses, most in the Queen Anne style, adorn Haight-Ashbury. Characterized by asymmetrical massing, a panoply of external surfaces and designs, bay windows and sometimes turrets, the homes date primarily from the building boom of the 1880s and 90s. Because houses in the Haight were so much in demand, Queen Annes were frequently built in rows of four or five similar structures, but a variety of color and detailing options provided ample opportunity for homeowners to distinguish their abodes from their neighbors'. A stroll along Central Avenue or Page, Masonic or Waller streets reveals fanciful examples of Queen Annes, many restored during the gentrification trend that swept the neighborhood in the 1980s and 90s. The rows at **1214–1256 Masonic Avenue** and **1315–1335 Waller Street★** embody the spirit of the style.

© PhotoDisc, Inc.

👥 Postcard Row: Alamo Square Victorians

The row of Victorians located at 710–720 Steiner St., between Hayes and Grove Streets, strikes a familiar chord with most San Francisco visitors. One of the most photographed vantages in the city, "Postcard Row" stands before a remarkable, snapshot-ready backdrop featuring many city landmarks, including 555 California Street and the Transamerica Pyramid. Lush, grassy Alamo Square Park, across the street, conveniently allows photographers ample time to focus. The houses also featured in the opening scenes of the *Full House* TV show.

Distinguished externally by window and door treatments and by color, the three-story, wooden, gable-roofed houses were completed in 1895 and sold for $3,500 apiece by Irish-born carpenter and real-estate developer Matthew Kavanagh, who lived at no. 722 from 1892–1900. All seven homes are private, one- or two-family dwellings. The J. Frank Moroney house at no. 710 is distinguished by its jewel-encrusted stained-glass windows and ornate gable. It sold for $87,500 in 1974. In 2010 no. 722 went on the market for a cool $4 million.

A decade later, the Haight blossomed into a countercultural lodestar, drawing hippies from around the US with promises of mind-altering drugs and free love. An estimated 20,000 people crammed into Golden Gate Park in January 1967 for Timothy Leary and Allen Ginsberg's **Human Be-In,** an anti-establishment celebration featuring poetry readings and rock concerts. Jerry Garcia's Grateful Dead held court at 710 Ashbury Street; neighbors included Janis Joplin and members of Jefferson Airplane. These musicians invented the wandering, melodic "San Francisco Sound" that catapulted them to international fame. Haight-Ashbury reached its peak later that year during what became known as the **Summer of Love,** when some 75,000 young people flocked to the neighborhood, sleeping in Golden Gate Park and attending free concerts and parties.

In 1968, many hippies left the Haight, and heroin replaced LSD and marijuana as the drug of choice. By 1971, more than a third of the shops on Haight Street were boarded up, and violent crime soared. Yet the neighborhood survived; crime dropped as incomes and property values rose. By 1980 the Haight had re-emerged as a middle-class enclave. Today the Haight is more mainstream than it was during its late 60s heyday, with a number of upscale designer-clothing shops and restaurants serving young professionals, but disaffected youths still congregate on street corners and in Golden Gate Park, and graying hippies abound. Even as the Queen Annes are restored to their late-19C beauty, vestiges of the 60s live on.

SIGHTS
Haight Street★

Lined with coffee shops, boutiques, pubs and restaurants, Haight Street from Stanyan Street to Central Avenue is the neighborhood's main drag. The narrow sidewalks are often packed with skateboarders, shoppers and tourists; incense wafts from New Age shops; and rock music pulses from frenetic thrift stores. While the buildings here are not the district's most distinguished, some, like the colorful, curvaceous structure at **no. 1679–81** (1904, James F. Dunn), display a certain charm.

Buena Vista Park

Rising abruptly south of Haight Street, between Central Avenue and Baker Street, this sylvan hill boasts tantalizing glimpses of the city from between the trees that crowd its steep slopes. The 36.5-acre park was reserved for public use in 1867, and John McLaren supervised the planting of cypress, live oak, pine and eucalyptus trees during the early 1900s. Sweeping **views** of San Francisco's residential areas stretch away toward bay and ocean from the summit, reached after a challenging climb.

ADDITIONAL SIGHTS
St. Ignatius Church★

650 Parker Ave. at Fulton St. ◷*Open Mon –Fri 8.30am–5pm, Sun 8.30am–noon.* ℘*415-422-2188. www.stignatiussf.org.* This imposing domed Renaissance Revival church (1914, Charles J. Devlin),

on the campus of Jesuit-affiliated University of San Francisco, features two 213ft towers flanking a facade dominated by Corinthian columns.

A campanile at the northeast corner houses a three-ton bell cast in England in 1859. In the interior, a deeply coffered ceiling and free-standing columns offer a dramatic framework for the sanctuary, whose paintings and stained-glass windows were added between 1938 and 1962.

A polychrome white-oak baldachin stands over an altar of Italian marble with Moroccan onyx inlays, containing relics of St. Ignatius.

♣♦ Randall Museum

199 Museum Way, Corona Heights. ▶ *From Haight St., take Masonic Ave. south to Roosevelt Way; turn left, then right after three blocks on Museum Way.* ◷*Open Tue–Sat 10am–5pm.* ◷*Closed major holidays.* ℘*415-554-9600. www.randallmuseum.org.* This family-oriented science museum sits at the end of a dead-end street with a view over the Mission District. Interactive exhibits address such issues as recycling and earthquakes; there is also a live-animal nursery.

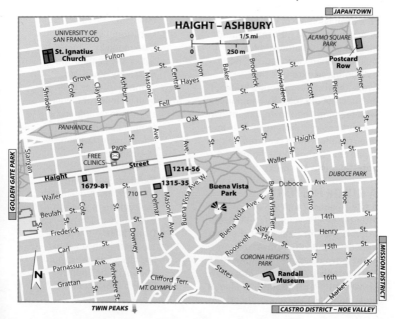

♨♟ Twin Peaks★★★

▶ *From Haight St. drive south on Clayton St. to Carmel St.; cross and continue up Twin Peaks Blvd. to Christmas Tree Point.*

These two high points dominate the horizon west of downtown and are visible from more areas of the city than Mt. Davidson, highest point in San Francisco at 929ft. The two distinct but adjacent peaks reach 904ft (north peak) and 922ft (south peak).

Most visitors content themselves with the grand **panorama★★★** of the north and east sides of the city from the parking lot at Christmas Tree Point, although it is possible to climb up the grassy slopes of either peak for a view to the west as well. On clear days, Mt. Diablo to the east in Contra Costa County, and Mt. Tamalpais, to the north in Marin County, come into view. Architect Bernard Maybeck, who designed the Palace of Fine Arts for the 1915 Panama-Pacific International Exhibition, had grandiose plans for Twin Peaks, including a great monument at the summit with waterfalls cascading to the valley below. The plans never materialized.

Today visitors and locals throng the viewpoint, particularly on weekend afternoons.

ADDRESSES

SHOPPING

Bound Together Anarchist Collective Bookstore – *1369 Haight St. Open daily 11.30am–7.30pm.* ✆*415-431-8355. boundtogetherbooks.wordpress.com.* For decades this volunteer-run outlet has supplied required reading for the counterculture: books, magazines and pamphlets on alternative thinking and the remaking of society.

Japantown

Known as Nihonmachi by local residents, Japantown is a locus of Japanese-American cultural life in the Bay Area. Its tidy, six-block core displays some of the city's finer groupings of well-maintained Victorian houses alongside modern buildings, many with stucco and half-timbered exteriors that evoke the traditional countryside architecture of Japan. By comparison with teeming Chinatown, Japantown is a much more subdued, orderly and open neighborhood centered on the Japan Center shopping, dining and entertainment complex.

A BIT OF HISTORY

A few Japanese came to San Francisco after the Meiji revolution of 1868, but arrivals did not peak until the first decade of the 20C. Anti-Asian sentiment slowed Japanese immigration considerably by the 1920s. Most new arrivals settled in the South of Market area, but when that neighborhood was

ᴍᴜᴍ bus 38–Geary, 2–Clement, 3–Jackson or 4–Sutter.

🚲 **Michelin Map:**
See PACIFIC HEIGHTS p164.

🅸 **Info:** www.sfjapan town.org.

▶ **Location:** Japantown is bounded by Fillmore, Sutter and Laguna Streets and Geary Boulevard.

🕐 **Timing:** Try to arrive in time for lunch or dinner so you can sample sushi, tempura or noodles from one of the restaurants in Japan Center or Nihonmachi Mall.

🅿 **Parking:** Japan Center Garage is located beneath the center (entrance on Geary Blvd.; $2/hr).

😊 **Don't Miss:** A traditional Japanese bath at Kabuki Springs & Spa, the exquisite interior of the Buddist Church of San Francsico.

devastated by the earthquake and fire of 1906, residents took refuge in the Western Addition. The new community, popularly known as Little Osaka, harbored about 7,000 Japanese-American residents within a 20-block rectangle formed by Fillmore, Pine, Octavia and O'Farrell streets.

Little Osaka was abandoned during World War II when anti-Japanese hysteria following the Pearl Harbor attack culminated in Executive Order 9066, forcing the evacuation of 112,000 Japanese-Americans to internment camps. Empty residences soon were inhabited by an influx of civilian workers, many of them black, who came to fill wartime shipyard jobs. Diminished from its pre-war size, Japantown took on its present appearance in the late 1960s and 70s when massive urban-renewal projects cleared blocks of Victorian housing and widened Geary Boulevard. Since then, new construction has generally echoed Japanese architectural themes.

SIGHTS
Japan Center
Between Post, Fillmore & Laguna Sts. and Geary Blvd. ◑*Open daily. Most shops open daily 10am–6pm, restaurants and lounges later.* ◑*Closed Jan 1, Thanksgiving Day, Dec 25.* ✕♿🅿 *www.sfjapantown.org.*
Reminiscent of contemporary Japanese architecture, this five-building complex (1968, Minoru Yamasaki) of shops, restaurants, cinemas and the Kabuki Hotel serves as a focal point for community celebrations. Its most striking Japanese touch is the **Peace Pagoda (1),** inspired by the miniature round pagodas dedicated to eternal peace by Empress Koken more than 1,200 years ago in Nara, Japan. Rising 110ft above the plaza in five copper-roofed concrete tiers, the pagoda is capped by a golden ball atop a copper spire, symbolizing virtue.
From the Peace Plaza, stroll west through the Kintetsu and Kinokuniya buildings, linked by an arching bridge over Webster Street. They are home to a colorful row of Japanese restaurants, music and video stores, electronics

stores, shops, a Japanese bookstore and the Ikenobo Ikebana (flower-arranging) Society. The complex's westernmost building houses the **Sundance Kabuki Theatre**, a popular venue for first-run films and for the annual **San Francisco International Film Festival** in April and May *(www.sundancecinemas.com/kabuki.html).*

Buchanan (Nihonmachi) Mall
Buchanan St., between Sutter & Post Sts. This attractive outdoor pedestrian street (1976) evokes the atmosphere of a Japanese village, with cobbled paving and "half-timbered" buildings. A small police *koban* (kiosk) stands at the Post Street end, while traditional restaurants and shops selling Japanese furniture, stationery, chinaware, gifts, kimonos and publications line its sides.

Konko Church of San Francisco
1909 Bush St., at Laguna St. ◑*Open Mon–Sat 8am–6pm, Sun 8am–3pm.* ✆*415-931-0453.*
With a handsome "half-timbered" exterior surface and timbers jutting from the roof, this steel-frame building (1973, Van Bourg, Nakamura & Associates) blends traditional Japanese aesthetics with modern engineering.
The interior incorporates a natural-wood Shinto altar with Christian influences such as pews. English-language services are held Sundays. Inspired by a Japanese farmer's revelation in 1859, the Konko (Eternal Golden Light) sect of

Shintoism advocates earthly happiness and respect for all life.

Sokoji-Soto Zen Buddhist Temple

1691 Laguna St., at Sutter St.
℘415-346-7540.
Dedicated in 1984, this overseas-mission temple building is handsomely clad with half-timbered stucco facing. Images of Koso-Dogen Zenji and Taiso-Keizan Zenji, celebrated as the founders of the Soto sect of Zen, flank the golden image of Shakyamuni Buddha at the center of the elaborate altar.

Buddhist Church of San Francisco★

1881 Pine St., at Octavia St. ◷Open Mon–Fri 10am–5pm. English-language service Sun 9.30am. ◷Closed major holidays. ☞Guided tours available. ☜Donation requested. ℘415-776-3158. www.bcsfweb.org.
This most exquisite of Japantown temple interiors occupies the second floor of an otherwise unprepossessing building (1938, Gentoko Shimamato). It is capped by a stupa, a bell-shaped pagoda, containing relics of the Buddha presented by the Thai royal court in 1935.
The Jodo Shinshu (True Pure Land) sect of Buddhism has long adopted such American cultural influences as pews, pulpit, and an organ, but the golden altar embodies Japanese tradition. Central is a small standing image of Amida Buddha, raising his right hand in a sign of wisdom and lowering his left in compassion. He is flanked on the right by an image of Shinran Shonin (1173–1262), founder of the Jodo Shinshu sect.

The Cathedral of St. Mary of the Assumption★★

1111 Gough St, at Geary Blvd. ◷Open daily 6.45am–4.30pm. ☞Guided tours Apr–Oct Mon–Sat 9am–noon; Sun after 11am service. Organ recitals Sun 3.30pm. ♿P ℘415-567-2020. www.stmarycathedralsf.org.
Sheathed in white travertine marble and visible from miles around the city, San Francisco's third Catholic cathedral

(1971) resembles a giant washing-machine agitator. It was designed by Pier Luigi Nervi & Pietro Belluschi, with McSweeney, Ryan & Lee. Enter through the main doors facing Geary Boulevard to see the bronze overpanel, an image of Christ rising above human figures to represent the ecumenical search for God throughout civilization. Backed by stained glass, the overpanel is also impressive when viewed from the interior. The building's most daring design attribute is its reinforced concrete **cupola**, formed of hyperbolic paraboloids that join to enclose a soaring atrium. At eye-level, glass panels afford fine city views. All 2,400 seats offer unobstructed views of the massive marble altar. Narrow stained-glass windows rise steeply from the four compass points to meet at the cupola's apex, forming a brilliant cross 190ft above the sanctuary floor. Suspended on wires 75ft above the altar is a contemporary **baldachin**, a shimmering canopy of anodized aluminum rods designed by Richard Lippold to sparkle in the slightest breeze. A magnificent, 4,842-pipe Ruffatti organ perches on a concrete pedestal. Cast-bronze shrines depict events in the lives of Mary and Jesus.

ADDRESSES

TAKING A BREAK
Kabuki Springs & Spa – *1750 Geary Blvd. in Japan Center. ℘415-922-6000. www.kabukisprings.com.* A sojourn in this day spa will revive even the most bone-weary traveler. Opt for a traditional Japanese bath or select from a full range of spa treatments, including ayurvedic rebalancing, seaweed wraps and *shiatsu* massage.

SHOPPING
Soko Hardware – *1698 Post St. at Buchanan St. Open Mon–Sat 9am–5.30pm. ℘415-931-5510.* Nestling up to hammers and screwdrivers, a glorious array of housewares such as tatami mats, mulberry wrapping paper, rice cookers and flower-arranging supplies brings Japan to San Francisco.

Pacific Heights★★

Stretching along a high east-west ridge between Van Ness Avenue and the Presidio, this elegant residential neighborhood holds some of the city's finest houses and loveliest views. The name Pacific Heights connotes San Francisco wealth, and its reputation is fully deserved: no other neighborhood gives a grander vision of the life of affluent San Franciscans.

A BIT OF HISTORY

The area today known as Pacific Heights occupies a favored location equidistant from San Francisco's three main historic centers: Mission Dolores, the Presidio and the commercial area around Yerba Buena Cove (today's Financial District). Trails linking these three centers converged near the highest point of the ridge, called the divisadero, but the neighborhood's precipitous streets were not developed until late in the 19C. Improvements in public transportation, notably the invention of the cable car, brought the area within easy reach of downtown, and at the end of the 1870s Pacific Heights experienced its first of many real-estate booms.

Gingerbread Houses – While the city's most successful merchants constructed huge mansions on the eastern edge of the neighborhood (Van Ness Avenue), speculative developers began building more modest but still impressive homes. Often erecting between five and ten houses at a time, side by side on the narrow lots, contractors followed formulaic floor plans but adorned the exteriors with prefabricated decorative elements that could be ordered from catalogs. The abundance of such "gingerbread"—including fish-scale shingles, ogive-arched window frames and finely carved verge boards—earned these houses the nickname "Gingerbread Victorians," and the many examples are among San Francisco's most cherished treasures.

꘡꘡꘡ Bus 3–Jackson, 22–Fillmore, 24–Divisadero, 41–Union, or 45–Union-Stockton

Info: ℰ415-391-2000. www.onlyinsanfrancisco.com.

Location: Pacific Heights is roughly bounded by Van Ness and Presidio Avenues and Pine and Vallejo Streets. The main shopping corridor is Fillmore Street between Bush and Jackson Streets. Bear the terrain in mind when planning a visit; streets ascend and descend abruptly, sometimes as much as 100ft in one block (☝for a list of San Francisco's steepest streets, see RUSSIAN HILL), so while, for example, Pacific Heights might look close to Cow Hollow on a map, it's actually a tough walk if you're headed south.

Timing: To get a sense of life in Pacific Heights, visit during early evening or a sunny weekend afternoon, when the people who live here jog the streets or walk their dogs. Better yet, arrive for lunch, shop and see the sights in the afternoon, then dine at a Fillmore Street bistro.

Parking: Though the neighborhood is easily accessible by bus, street parking is generally easier to find here than elsewhere in the city. There is a metered lot at California and Steiner Streets.

Don't Miss: A walking tour of the Haas-Lilienthal House, an intact Victorian home open to the public.

Although many of the Van Ness mansions were dynamited by the US Army in order to create a firebreak during the

An Architectural Smorgasbord

Pacific Heights' wealthy denizens spent fortunes ensuring that their residences reflected their financial and social status. As a result, the neighborhood constitutes a showcase of design. A slow meander along its quiet streets reveals examples of almost every architectural style and period that exist in San Francisco. Because elite taste leaned toward refined Classical motifs, many architects looked to the Italian Renaissance palazzo for inspiration and followed the rules and precepts established by the École des Beaux Arts in Paris (which many of them had attended). Stone and brick were a popular building materials, and designs tended to follow one consistent historical style rather than mix aspects from different periods.

For more on Pacific Heights architecture, take the **Pacific Heights Walking Tour** offered by San Francisco Architectural Heritage every Sunday afternoon (*2hrs; meet at the Haas-Lilienthal House at 12.30pm; $8; 415-441-3000).

1906 quake and fire, wealthy San Franciscans who had lost homes on Nob Hill and elsewhere resettled here, attracted by the neighborhood's bay views and peaceful, noncommercial ambience. Most of the district's largest homes date

from 1906–16, a time of great energy in every aspect of San Francisco's civic life. Along Broadway, for example, Comstock mining magnate James Leary Flood, whose Nob Hill residence was gutted by the fire, built a pair of mansions, each of

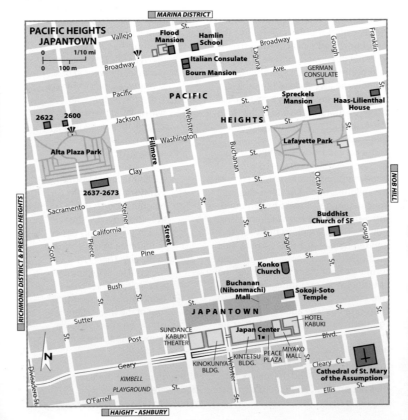

which would cost $25–50 million today. Other bankers, industrialists and civic leaders built stately homes nearby. Only the very rich could afford to maintain such massive residences, and beginning in the 1920s apartment towers were built to lodge the city's elite on a more modest scale—though some of these buildings have come to rank among San Francisco's most desirable addresses, offering splendid views.

Today many Pacific Heights mansions house schools or consulates, such as those of Italy *(2590 Webster St.)* and Germany *(1960 Jackson St.)*.

SIGHTS
Haas-Lilienthal House★★

2007 Franklin St., between Washington & Jackson Sts. ✎Visit by guided tour *(1hr) only Wed and Sat noon–3pm, Sun 11am–4pm.* ⊘ *Closed major holidays and some Saturdays; call ahead.* ⊜$8. ℘415-441-3000. www.sfheritage.org.
One of the city's few Victorian-era residences open to the public, this edifice (1886, Peter R. Schmidt) is among the last survivors of the many ornate single-family houses that once filled this neighborhood. The elegant residence typifies the aspirations of the city's upper-middle class at the end of the 19C—whereas the grandiose mansions atop Nob Hill were for the affluent elite. Constructed for William Haas, a prominent whole-saler, it passed to his daughter and son-in-law, Alice and Samuel Lilienthal, in 1916. After Alice's death in 1972, her family donated the house to the Foundation for San Francisco's Architectural Heritage, which currently maintains it. The exterior embellishments are typical of the Queen Anne style and include a variety of patterned siding, ornately bracketed gables and a deceptive corner tower with windows 10ft above the floor. The basement, once used as a ballroom, now displays photographs showing the house in its pre-1906 neighborhood context. Upper-floor rooms, including two parlors, a dining room and one of the original six bedrooms, are furnished in a range of decorative styles dating from the 1880s to the 1920s.

Spreckels Mansion★★
2080 Washington St.
Of all the many grand mansions in Pacific Heights, none is more ostentatious than the elaborate French Baroque-style palace built in 1913 for sugar magnate Adolph Spreckels and his wife, Alma de Bretteville Spreckels.
The main facade consists of five arched windows separated by pairs of ornate Ionic columns. The house faces onto lushly landscaped **Lafayette Park**. The rear gardens, which drop steeply down to Jackson Street, boast a covered swimming pool.

Spreckels Mansion

Broadway Mansions★

Broadway between Fillmore and Buchanan Sts.

These two elegant blocks of Broadway bear witness to the emergence of Pacific Heights as home to San Francisco's elite after the 1906 earthquake. One of the finest buildings in the city is the former **Flood Mansion★** *(no. 2222)*, designed by local architects Bliss and Faville in 1912 for James Leary Flood. The house is a refined and beautifully crafted version of an Italian Renaissance palazzo, its Tennessee marble hung on an earthquake-resistant steel frame. A pair of brick mansions, both dating from the same period, stand alongside the Flood Mansion; they now house private schools. Just south of Broadway, the **Bourn Mansion** *(2550 Webster St.)* was designed by Willis Polk in 1896 for William Bourn, the mining magnate for whom Polk also created the magnificent Filoli estate south of San Francisco. Designed as a pied-à-terre, the stately home contains only two bedrooms; rough clinker brick softens the Classical formality of the facade. Most unusually, the design plays down the importance of the entrance, which is set back in a deep vestibule beneath the upper-floor balcony.

In the block east of Webster lie two other remarkable mansions, the stately **Italian Consulate** *(no. 2590 Webster St.)*, and the blue-and-gray, Baroque Revival-style **Hamlin School** *(no. 2120)*. James Flood had the latter (1901) constructed on land owned by his sister, then moved to the Flood Mansion after its completion.

Fillmore Street★

Lively and inviting, Pacific Heights' commercial district lies along Fillmore Street between Jackson and Bush Streets. Impeccably turned-out locals fill the cafes, bistros and a welter of boutiques that range from frighteningly haute to more down-to-earth.

South of California Street, Fillmore runs past the Japan Center and across Geary Boulevard through the heart of the Western Addition. To the north, it reaches the edge of Pacific Heights at Broadway, where it offers one of the city's finest bay **views★** before dropping swiftly down into Cow Hollow.

Alta Plaza Park

Bounded by Jackson, Scott, Clay and Steiner Sts.

Set aside as a public park in the mid-1850s, the lush green oasis of Alta Plaza lies at the heart of Pacific Heights. Basketball and tennis courts and a children's playground occupy the center of the park, and the green lawns attract picnickers. Terraces drop down on Alta Plaza's south side, forming a distinctive ziggurat of concrete and shrubbery.

The houses facing the south side are among Pacific Heights' oldest: a series of elaborate Italianate Victorian houses at **2637–2673 Clay St.**, all designed and built by the same contractor in 1875.

On the park's north side, Jackson Street features a pair of houses created by two influential turn-of-the-20C architects whose use of Classical Beaux-Arts models contrasts with the lighthearted playfulness of other Victorian-era designs. The former Music and Arts Institute at **2622 Jackson St.** was the first of architect Willis Polk's many commissions in the city. Built of stone in 1894 and styled like a Renaissance-era Tuscan villa, the house was acclaimed by *The San Francisco Examiner* as "the first Classical residence in San Francisco."

Nearby, the angular brick facade of **2600 Jackson St.** was designed by Ernest Coxhead and built in 1895 by industrialist Irving Scott as a wedding present for his daughter.

ADDRESSES

SHOPPING

Cars Dawydiak – *1450 Franklin St. at Bush St.* ☎415-928-2277.
With its temperate weather and twisty highways, the Bay Area is sports-car heaven. This long-standing dealer with an 8,000sq ft showroom specializes in European sports models from 1955 to the 1990s, with an emphasis on Porsches. The knowledgeable sales staff are happy to answer questions.

Richmond District and Presidio Heights

One of San Francisco's most ethnically diverse neighborhoods and a haven of the middle class, the Richmond District is a relatively flat expanse of undistinguished row houses sandwiched between Masonic Avenue to the east, California Street to the north, Golden Gate Park to the south and the Pacific Ocean to the west. Just to the north, between California Street and the Presidio, lies Presidio Heights, a wealthier residential enclave comprised largely of spacious, single-family homes.

A BIT OF HISTORY

The Richmond District and Presidio Heights both were once part of the Outer Lands, a vast expanse of scrubs and dunes. Cemeteries occupied its Eastern edge. In the final two decades of the 19C, Adolph Sutro purchased vast amounts of the sandy acreage cheaply. He built a steam railway along the present course of California Street to his Cliff House and bathhouse at Land's End. Construction in the Richmond District proceeded quickly after the 1906 earthquake. Two years later, Mayor Jim Rolph ordered all cemeteries moved south of the city to the town of Colma, spurring construction of yet more single-family row houses until the Great Depression struck in 1929. These new tracts drew residents of broad ethnic diversity, including White Russians fleeing the 1917 Russian Revolution, Jews from Eastern Europe and, after World War II, Japanese-Americans returning from internment camps. Chinese-Americans have formed the largest ethnic group since the 1970s, but the 1990s witnessed a resurgence of Russian immigration. Presidio Heights developed more slowly, as wealthy families built unique, often palatial homes. A casual stroll along Pacific Avenue, Jackson Street and Washington Street, reveals a variety of architectural styles. Specially designed door knockers, mailboxes, gates and gardens add to the appeal.

Particularly worth noting is **Roos House** (3500 Jackson St.), a massive, half-timbered residence designed in 1909 by renowned Arts and Crafts architect Bernard Maybeck.

SIGHTS

San Francisco Columbarium

1 Loraine Ct., north of Anza St.
Open Mon–Fri 8.30am–5pm, Sat–Sun 10am–3pm. Guided tours available on request. 800-445-3551. www.neptune-society.com.

Owned by the Neptune Society of Northern California, a cremation organization, this copper-roofed, Neoclassical rotunda recalls the days when cemeteries covered the Richmond's dunes. Erected in 1898 as part of the Oddfellows Cemetery, the columbarium was spared when the graves were removed

---

Richmond District: bus 38–Geary, 1–California, 2–Clement or 4–Sutter. Presidio Heights: bus 3–Jackson or 43–Masonic.

Info: www.sfgate.com/neighborhoods/sf/innerrichmond.

Location: These neighborhoods lie quite near to each other, just south of the Presidio between Presidio Ave. and Park Presidio Blvd.

Kids: The San Francisco Fire Department Museum.

Timing: Plan a morning here, followed by lunch on Sacramento Street.

Parking: Spaces are fairly easy to find along the residential streets.

Don't Miss: Breathtaking views from the Lyon Street steps.

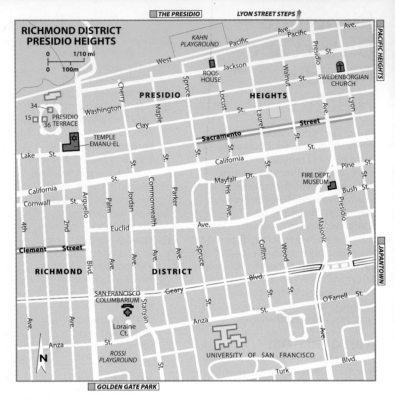

THE PRESIDIO — LYON STREET STEPS

RICHMOND DISTRICT
PRESIDIO HEIGHTS

0   1/10 mi
0   100m

KAHN
PLAYGROUND
Pacific — Pacific — Ave. — Ave.

West — Jackson — Presidio — St.

ROOS
HOUSE

SWEDENBORGIAN
CHURCH

PRESIDIO — HEIGHTS

Washington — Clay — Locust — Walnut — Lyon

34

15   PRESIDIO
36   TERRACE

TEMPLE
EMANU-EL

Sacramento — Street

Lake — St. — Laurel

California

Mayfair — Dr. — Iris — FIRE DEPT.
MUSEUM

California — Pine — St.

Cornwall — St. — Arguelo — Palm — Jordan — Commonwealth — Parker — Bush — St.

4th — 2nd — Euclid — Ave. — Masonic

Clement — Street — Spruce — Collins — Wood

RICHMOND — DISTRICT — Blvd.

SAN FRANCISCO
COLUMBARIUM — Geary — O'Farrell — St.

Loraine
Ct. — Staryan — Anza

Anza

N

ROSSI
PLAYGROUND — UNIVERSITY OF SAN FRANCISCO — Blvd.

Turk

GOLDEN GATE PARK

PACIFIC HEIGHTS — JAPANTOWN

to Colma in 1914. Today it contains more than 4,400 niches, including those of several prominent San Francisco families. The flamboyant interior is adorned with a mosaic-tile floor, stained-glass windows and skylights, and brightly painted plaster filigree.

Clement Street

The more charming of the Richmond's main shopping thoroughfares (the other being highway-like Geary Boulevard), Clement Street is popular for its markets, bookshops, household-goods stores and excellent yet understated restaurants.

The 12-block stretch between Arguello and Park Presidio boulevards is sometimes known as "New Chinatown" because so many of its residents have relocated from downtown's Chinatown. But while Asian restaurants predominate, a culturally diverse community thrives on Clement Street.

Temple Emanu-El★

2 Lake St. Visit by guided tour only, Tue–Thu 1.30pm or by appt. Closed Jewish holidays. 415-751-2535. www.emanuelsf.org.

Rising 150ft from the ground and visible for miles, this synagogue's spectacular, orange-tiled, Byzantine-style dome crowns a massive, architecturally unified complex of offices and meeting halls. Designed by Sylvain Schnaittacher, John Bakewell and Arthur Brown, Jr., the building was dedicated in 1926 as the third synagogue for the venerable Reform Jewish congregation, founded in San Francisco in 1850. Outside the sanctuary doors, a cloistered courtyard is dotted with plants named in the Old Testament as well as a lion-headed fountain. Visitors enter through the vestibule, its ceiling decorated with a brilliant blue and yellow fresco of a star-studded sky. The temple, which seats 1,700, is lit by two stained-glass windows representing fire (west) and water (east). Four massive bronze chandeliers symbolize the tears of the Jews. At the altar, the Ark of the Covenant stands beneath a marble canopy, housed in a gilded bronze tabernacle box inlaid with cloisonné; the box was built in London by Californians Frank Igerson and George Dennison. The synagogue is home to the **Elizabeth S. and Alvin I. Fine Museum**, whose exhibits in the temple foyer integrate Jewish art and history into the congregational mind set. The permanent collection includes many antique ritual objects. Immediately north of the synagogue is **Presidio Terrace**, an exclusive residential enclave since 1905, with many elegant homes by noteworthy architects, including no. 15 (1905, Bakewell & Brown), no. 34 (c. 1910, George Applegarth) and no. 36 (1911, Julia Morgan).

Sacramento Street

The discreet but charming stretch of Sacramento Street between Lyon and Spruce Streets forms the elite shopping district of Presidio Heights. Its upscale boutiques, intimate restaurants and small cinema cater to a mostly local clientele.

Swedenborgian Church★★

2107 Lyon St. at Washington St.
○*Open Mon–Fri 9am–5pm, Sun service 11am.* ℘*415-346-6466. www.sfswedenborgian.org.*
This diminutive, lovingly crafted wood-and-brick chapel is named after Swedish scientist and philosopher Emanuel Swedenborg, who inspires the congregation. A fine example of Arts and Crafts design and construction, the church was conceived in 1895 by the congregation's founder, the Rev. Joseph Worcester. Bruce Porter sketched the design from an Italian original, while A. Page Brown served as chief architect and Bernard Maybeck as draftsman. Willis Polk designed the adjacent Parish House.
The church interior replicates the natural beauty of a California woodland. The ceiling is supported by bark-covered branches of native California madrone. Landscape painter William Keith contributed the pastoral scenes of the California

countryside along the north wall, while Porter designed the windows along the south wall. The solid chairs were built without nails, of maple wood and woven tule rushes from the Sacramento River delta. A giant clam shell near the altar is the baptismal font in which poet Robert Frost, among many others, was sanctified as an infant. Outside brick walkways frame lush gardens planted with trees from around the world.

Lyon Street Steps

Between Broadway and Green St.
Too steep for vehicular traffic, this part of Lyon Street was landscaped c. 1915 and today forms one of the city's most attractive public spaces. Dropping toward the bay from the west end of Broadway along the eastern wall of the Presidio, the steps offer a memorable **view★★** out over the great dome of the Palace of Fine Arts across the bay to Angel Island and Mt. Tamalpais. Flower beds and other plantings soften the Beaux-Arts stairs, landings and balustrades, and benches offer a place to rest while taking in the view. The corner of Broadway and Lyon offers pedestrian access to the Presidio.

▲▲ San Francisco Fire Department Museum

655 Presidio Ave., between Bush and Pine Sts. ○*Open Thu–Sun 1–4pm.*
&. ℘*415-563-4630 or 415-558-3546. www.guardiansofthecity.org.*
This converted firehouse garage houses a wonderful collection of historic fire engines, including the city's first hand-drawn pump cart (1849). Historical displays, photos and memorabilia, including eclectic collections of fire extinguishers, helmets, hydrants and uniforms, tell of the city's several devastating fires and of heroic figures from San Francisco's firefighting past.
Worth noting is the helmet that belonged to Lillie Hitchcock Coit, the eccentric booster of the San Francisco Fire Department; an ornate certificate proclaims her an honorary member of Knickerbocker Engine Co. No. 5. Visitors may also inspect the modern-day fire engines and equipment in adjacent Firehouse no. 10.

San Francisco's southern neighborhoods include the lively Castro and Mission Districts and the sprawling, industrial South of Market region. Epicenter of gay San Francisco, the Castro hums with energy night and day along its central commercial coridor, Castro Street. Its neighbor, the sunny Mission District, is San Francisco at its most bohemian, with artists, dot-commers, and activists coexisting with a vibrant Latino community. San Francisco's hardscrabble history meets its high tech-present in the large heterogeneous region known as SoMa. Within SoMa, the Yerba Buena area has transformed in a major arts and cultural enclave.

Highlights

1 See a movie at the historic **Castro Theatre** (p173)

2 Chill at sunny **Dolores Park** with a burrito from a nearby tacqueria (p179)

3 Tour **Balmy Alley**'s colorful mural (p179)

4 Taste microbrews at the **Anchor Brewing Company** (p181)

5 Explore the **San Francisco Museum of Modern Art** (p185)

Castro, Mission and SoMa

The once quiet suburb of Eureka Valley adopted its present Castro character in the 1970s, when enterprising gay designers began purchasing the 19C Victorians at rock-bottom prices and fixing them up. In 1977, residents succeeded in elecitng one of their own, Harvey Milk, to the Board of Supervisors. Slain by fellow supervisor the following year, Milk remains a revered figure for being the first openly gay elected official in U.S. history. Today, the rainbow flag, a universal symol of gay pride, is everywhere; it flies over the streets and adorns the district's vibrantly painted Victorian houses.

To the east of the Castro is the Mission District, named for Mission Dolores, which anchored a small village in the early 1800s. By the turn of the 20th century, the neighborhood was mainly populated by European immigrants who worked in the warehouses, breweries and factories south of Market. Forced out of their homeland by the revolution,

Mexicans began arriving in the 1920s. Central and South Americans have followed in the decades since. Though gentrification has pushed many Latinos out of the area, the stretch of 24th Street between Mission and Potrero Streets still dances to a salsa beat. Known as *El Corazón de la Misione*, or "the heart of the Mission," it's home to a large collection of Latino-themed murals.

The Mission is also home to dozens of good, cheap (and no-so-cheap) restaurants, and plentiful bars and nightspots that draw young hipsters. Funky art galleries stand shoulder-to-shoulder with thrift shops and used-book stores, while residential blocks are lined with pastel-painted Italianate row houses, some dating as far back as the 1870s.

Northeast of the the Mission is SoMa (South of Market). During the Gold Rush Days, SoMa was home to the town's weathy and elite citizens. When the 1906 earthquake destroyed most of the area, this region bounded by 12th, Market and King Streets, and the Embarcadero then became known as South of the Slot, a reference to its location on the wrong side of the Market Street cable-car track. As manufacturing declined in the mid-20C, architects, graphic designers, software companies and publishers divvied up former industrial building and warhouses into loftlike offices. Then in 2000, the Internet bubble burst, leaving nearly half of the offfices vacant. SoMa is now booming again, eclipsing the Financial District with new construction, and the Yerba Buena area is home to such powerhouses as the San Francisco Museum of Art, Yerba Buena Gardens and the Contemporary Jewish Museum.

Castro District★ and Noe Valley

Bounded roughly by 16th, 22nd, Douglass and Dolores Streets, the lively, 44sq-block Castro District forms the heart of San Francisco's vibrant gay community, as well as the geographical center of the city. Bars, restaurants, trendy clothing stores and boutiques crowd together along Castro, Market and 18th Streets, while residential side streets lined with beautifully refurbished Victorians invite leisurely exploration.

A BIT OF HISTORY

Part of a 4,000-acre land grant given to San Francisco's last Mexican mayor, José de Jésus Noe, the present-day Castro District and neighboring Noe Valley were used primarily for cattle-ranching and sheep-grazing until shortly after the Gold Rush. In 1854, during a citywide wave of land speculation, a wealthy produce merchant named John Meirs Horner bought much of Noe's ranch, plotted a street grid, and began peddling land tracts to working-class Irish and German immigrants. By 1887 the Market Street Cable Railway extended down Castro Street, linking Eureka and Noe valleys and opening the 21st Street summit to development.

As the district sustained only minor damage in the 1906 earthquake and fire, campgrounds for refugees were quickly erected. Many of the temporary residents opted to stay, and a tight-knit working-class community thrived well into the 1920s, when a commercial building boom graced Castro Street with the majestic Castro Theatre and several other fine structures. The Great Depression forced many landowners to divide and rent out single-family homes, and federal housing subsidies in the 1950s further encouraged the working-class families' slow march out of the city.

A New Alternative – In the early 1970s gay San Franciscans began purchasing the neighborhood's neglected Victorians

Bus 24-Divisadero; streetcars F-Market, K-Ingleside, L-Taraval, M-Oceanview or T-third Street to Castro St. station.

Michelin Map: See MISSION DISTRICT.

Info: www.sanfrancisco. travel/neighborhood/ castro-upper-market

Location: The Castro District is roughly bounded by Market, Dolores, 22nd and Douglass Streets. Castro Street between Market and 19th Streets is the liveliest strip in the neighborhood, with bars, restaurants, cafes and shops. Market Street between Castro and Church Streets also has a number of restaurants and shops. In quaint Noe Valley the main drag is 24th Street between Church and Castro Streets.

Timing: During the day, the Castro's cafes and shops do a brisk business. At night, neon signs of bars and the spectacular Castro Theatre light up, dance music is ratcheted up a few notches and the air buzzes with palpable energy.

Parking: Street parking here is difficult. You're better off taking public transport, particularly the F-Market historic streetcar, which will deposit you right in the heart of the district at Castro and Market Streets. To get to Noe Valley from here, take the 24–Divisadero bus on Castro Street south (over a mammoth hill) to 24th Street.

Don't Miss: A performance at the Castro Theatre.

AIDS Memorial Quilt displayed in the National Mall, Washington DC in 1996

© The Names Project Foundation

The AIDS Memorial Quilt

Invoking both an American tradition of quilting and a historic practice of honoring the dead with national monuments, the AIDS Memorial Quilt, sponsored by the NAMES Project Foundation, represents a unique, moving response to the AIDS epidemic. Composed of coffin-sized 3ft-by-6ft panels, each handmade in memory of someone who died of the virus, the quilt tours the world in sections to increase AIDS awareness and to raise funds for North American AIDS-service organizations.

The idea for the quilt originated with Cleve Jones, a San Francisco gay-rights activist. In 1985, after learning that more than 1,000 city residents had died of AIDS-related illnesses, Jones asked participants in the 1985 memorial march for Harvey Milk to carry signs bearing the names of friends and acquaintances who had succumbed to the virus. At the end of the march, the posters were affixed to the facade of the San Francisco Federal Building, and the resulting patchwork resembled a quilt.

In 1986, Jones founded the NAMES Project, and in spring 1987 he made the first cloth panel in memory of his best friend. Soon, handmade panels adorned with such diverse materials as spray paint, leather, sequins and photographs began arriving at the NAMES Project headquarters in San Francisco from all over the United States.

In October 1987, when the quilt was displayed for the first time in Washington DC, it comprised 1,920 panels and covered a space larger than a football field. A 1996 display in the capital was made up of an estimated 41,000 panels, covering roughly 29 football fields. That was the last time the quilt was displayed in its entirety. As of 2012, the quilt had more than 48,000 panels, attesting to both the devastation of the illness and the spirit and joie de vivre of those who have died.

For more information, visit www.aidsquilt.org.

and bringing them back to their former grandeur. The first gay bars appeared on Castro Street in 1972 and thanks to the social liberalization of the period and significant gains in gay civil rights, they operated largely without harassment. It soon gained a reputation for being one of the most vital gay neighborhoods in the world. In 1977 residents of the Castro were instrumental in electing **Harvey Milk,** one of their own, to the city's Board of Supervisors, making him the first openly gay elected official in U.S. history. Milk's life and career were cut short the following year when he and then-Mayor George Moscone were gunned down at City Hall by City Supervisor Dan White. In 1978 San Francisco passed the Gay Bill of Civil Rights, forbidding discrimination in housing and employment on the basis of sexual orientation.

Crisis struck the neighborhood in the 1980s with the onset of the AIDS epidemic. In response, public-education organizations, support groups and health-news clearinghouses took root all over the Castro. Many continue to thrive. Today an upbeat, neighborly attitude pervades the district. On Castro Street dance music pulses in many shops, whose creative, sometimes outrageous window displays are among the most eye-catching in the city. Along the quiet residential streets, rainbow flags, symbolizing gay liberation, brighten the windows of many Victorian homes.

CASTRO DISTRICT
Castro Street

Flanked with bookstores and bars, boutiques and cafes, the bustling shopping strip between Market and 19th Streets has served the neighborhood since the 1850s. Named for Vincent Castro, an early Mexican rancher, the busy thoroughfare overflows day and night with foot and car traffic.

In recent years, **Market Street** between Castro and Church streets has also become a vibrant shopping strip. Full-grown Canary Island palm trees were planted along the median in 1994, adding a welcome touch of green. In 1995,

the refurbished streetcars of the historic F-Market line began clanging through, balancing the trend-setting designer clothing boutiques, funky gift shops and new restaurants with a charming touch of the past.

At the southwest corner of Market and Castro streets is **Harvey Milk Plaza**, dedicated in late 1997 on the 20th anniversary of Milk's election to office. Above a simple memorial flies a huge eight-color rainbow flag, the universal symbol of sexual diversity that was created in the Castro.

Milk lived in a blue Victorian at **575 Castro Street**. His apartment was above his camera store, his campaign headquarters in the rear of the building. Today, a mural of Milk, clad in a T-shirt adorned with a rainbow flag, gazes from an upstairs window. In an eerily prescient letter, Milk wrote one year before his death: "In the event that I am killed by an assassin's bullet, may that same bullet shatter every closet door."

Castro Theatre★

429 Castro St., at Market St. ◷*Open daily, at showtimes. Theater interior also accessible on Cruisin' the Castro tour (*⌖*see below).* ♿ ℘*415-621-6120. www.castrotheatre.com.*

Declared a San Francisco Historic Landmark in 1977, this splendid Spanish Renaissance Revival theater (1922, Timothy Pflueger) represents the city's finest example of early 20C movie-

Castro Theatre

Cruisin' the Castro

🕐 *Open Mon–Sat 10am–noon.*
💰*$30. Reservations required.*
📞*415-255-1821. www.cruisin thecastro.com.*

Get the full scoop on the Castro District's past and present by taking a 2hr Cruisin' the Castro Historical and Cultural Walking Tour. A local will take you past the major landmarks, dip into a number of fetching shops, discuss gay and lesbian history and explain the neighborhood's significance in the lesbian, gay, bisexual, and transgender civil rights movement.

palace architecture. The front exterior facade features Spanish Colonial-style ornamentation above the low-hanging marquee and a huge, pink-neon sign, both added in 1937. The grand, 1,520-seat interior's gently curved green and gold-leaf ceiling, two-story proscenium framed by columns and an ornate lintel, and sumptuous murals combine to create a magical ambience. Attend one of the two nightly screenings to hear resident musicians playing the Mighty Wurlitzer organ, which slowly rises from the orchestra pit for the performance, then sinks back down as the lights dim. Screening Hollywood classics, kitschy favorites, rare foreign films and new independent fare, the Castro Theatre also hosts several annual film festivals, including the San Francisco Jewish Film Festival and the Gay and Lesbian Film Festival.

NOE VALLEY

Cradled in the lowlands south of the Castro District, Noe Valley features wide, Victorian cottage-lined streets intersecting a quaint, bustling shopping strip. Like the Castro, the neighborhood was part of José Noe's huge ranch until well into the 1850s, and harbored a thriving community of working-class immigrants through the mid-20C. In the 1970s the area gained popularity with hippies and

artists, and the enclave was nicknamed "Nowhere Valley" and "Granola Valley" due to its relative isolation and liberal-thinking population.

Today residents can only wish for such anonymity: Noe Valley in recent years has become a desirable neighborhood for young professionals and families. Its colorful commercial thoroughfare, **24th Street** (between Church & Castro Sts.), retains its modest appeal. During the day, the sidewalks fill with denizens walking dogs and pushing strollers; cafes overflow with latte-sipping customers; and designer clothing shops, bookstores, flower stands and wine merchants beckon shoppers. Although there's not much nightlife to speak of, Noe Valley does have several excellent restaurants that are ideal for a romantic dinner, as well as a few local bars.

ADDRESSES

SHOPPING

Isak Lindenauer Antiques – *4143 19th St., between Castro & Collingwood Sts. Open Sat 11am–6pm, Sun noon–5pm and by appointment. 📞415-552-6436.* This small antiques dealer began specializing in Arts and Crafts and Mission-style furniture and fixtures in 1973, long before the styles were widely collected. It's well worth a stop—Lindenauer might have just taken delivery of a new shipment of Gustav Stickley pieces, his specialty.

Global Exchange – *4018 24th St., between Noe & Castro Sts. Open Sun–Mon 11am–6pm, Tue–Fri 11am–7pm, Sat 10am–7pm. 📞415-648-8068. www.globalexchange.org.* A fair return to the craftsperson is the idea behind this nonprofit shop. Handicrafts from 40 countries (many of them developing nations) show up in this small space. Children's overalls from Guatemala, soapstone carvings from Kenya and Indonesian slide whistles are typical of the variety of attractively priced items for sale. Another Global Exchange store is in Berkeley at 2840 College Ave (📞510-548-0370).

Mission District★★

With its freewheeling, festive Latino flavor, the Mission District is one of the city's liveliest neighborhoods. It's also one of its warmest—a high ridge on the scenic western edge of the district protects the area against the chill fogs and ocean winds that afflict many other parts of the city.

A BIT OF HISTORY

In 1776, Spanish explorer Juan Bautista de Anza chose this location for a Catholic mission dedicated to St. Francis of Assisi—the origin of the city's name. A primitive village grew up in the vicinity of the mission, but the surrounding lands remained largely uncultivated. After secularization in 1834, wealthy Californio ranchers used the property for cattle grazing, although Yankee squatters' rights prevailed after the U.S. won the Mexican-American War in 1848. During the post-Gold Rush boom in 1851, a plank road was laid through the marshy South of Market area, providing a connection to the flourishing downtown waterfront and opening the neighborhood to development.

A street grid was platted, with 16th Street serving as the main commercial thoroughfare. The Mission District mostly attracted working-class people, many from Germany and Scandinavia—and, later, Italy and Ireland—who had arrived on trade vessels and stayed on to work in the burgeoning city.

Latino Enclave – Because much of the district survived the earthquake and fire of 1906, many of those left homeless by the conflagration resettled here. Throughout the 1920s, Mexicans fleeing revolution in their homeland swelled the ranks of Latinos in the core of the Mission; in subsequent decades, new waves of Latinos replaced many European-descended families. Social and political unrest in Central and South America since the 1970s has fueled an influx of new immigrants.

囸囸囸 Bus 14–Mission, 22–Fillmore, 26–Valencia or 33–Stanyan. 🚇 16th St. or 24th St. station.

🔲 **Info:** www.sanfrancisco. travel/neighborhood/ mission-district

▶ **Location:** The vast Mission District is roughly bounded by Potrero Avenue and Dolores, 14th and Cesar Chavez Streets. Many Latino restaurants are crowded on 24th Street east of Mission Street. Bookstores, galleries and cafes are on Valencia Street between 16th and 22nd Streets. ⏏Exercise caution at night.

👪 **Kids:** A banana split royale at St. Francis Fountain.

🕐 **Timing:** The Mission is fun both by day and night. To enjoy the best of both worlds, come for lunch, then visit Mission Dolores, shop on Valencia Street, see the murals on 24th Street and stay for dinner. Exuberant celebrations occur regularly, including **Cinco de Mayo** (first Sunday in May) and **Carnaval** (Memorial Day Sunday). ⏏See Calendar of Events.

🅿 **Parking:** The Mission is easily accessible via public transportion; BART is particularly convenient. Street parking is sometimes possible to find (don't leave valuables in the car, though). A parking garage is at 3255 21st Street, at Mission Street.

😊 **Don't Miss:** A visit to the historic Mission Dolores and a Mission-style burrito at a taqueria before strolling down Balmy Alley to admire the vibrant murals.

The area east of Valencia and south of 16th Street today remains predominantly Latino and largely working-class, though artists and entrepreneurs have discovered the Mission, giving rise to a trendy cafe and bar scene. On the western edge of the district, an artistic, politically active cadre has engendered chic new restaurants alongside the taquerias, cafes and used bookstores.

SIGHTS
Mission Dolores (Mission San Francisco de Asís)★★

3321 16th St. at Dolores St. ◷*Open daily 9am–4pm (Good Friday until noon; Easter Sunday 10am–1pm).* ◷*Closed Jan 1, Thanksgiving Day, Dec 25.* ◉*$5 donation requested.* ♿ ☏*415-621-8203. http://missiondolores.org.*

Flanked by a historic cemetery and a lavishly ornamented 20C basilica, San Francisco's oldest extant structure serves as a distinct reminder of the city's Spanish heritage and a repository of early European history.

The sixth mission in the Alta California chain was first established in 1776 near the present-day corner of Camp and Albion Streets, two blocks east of its present site. A nearby lake named for Our Lady of Sorrows (Nuestra Senora de los Dolores) gave the mission its centuries-old nickname, Mission Dolores. The present chapel was completed in 1791. After secularization in 1834, the property was occupied by squatters. The Catholic Church reacquired it in 1860, erecting a series of larger churches alongside the old chapel to accommodate a growing

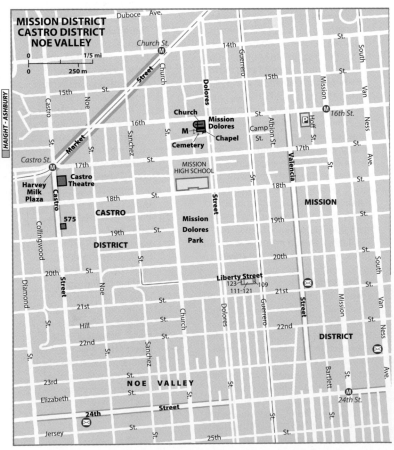

Mission Dolores

© Rick Gerharter / SFCVB

congregation. The present **church★** (1918), with its gloriously ornate Churrigueresque facade, was designated a basilica in 1952.

Visit

A remarkably sturdy structure, the **chapel★★** has survived major earthquakes in 1868, 1906 and 1989 as well as abandonment and neglect. Today it appears much as it did in 1791, thanks to a conscientious restoration program completed in 1995. Cement stucco covers 4ft-thick adobe walls. The ornate, hand-carved reredos and side altars were imported from Mexico in 1780, and bronze bells high in the chapel's front exterior facade were brought as gifts in 1792, 1795 and 1797. The remarkable multicolored motifs painted on the

high, beamed ceiling are patterned after Ohlone basket designs.

A small passage north of the chapel contains a splendid **diorama** of the mission as it appeared in 1799; the model was created for the Golden Gate International Exposition of 1939–40. The mission's small **museum (M)** houses artifacts discovered during restorations, as well as baptismal records and vestments dating from the colonial period.

On the south side extends a tranquil **cemetery★**; here, amid verdant plantings, are buried many of San Francisco's early leaders, including Luis Antonio Arguello (1784–1830), first governor

Mission Dolores cemetery

© Marni Miyata / SFCVB

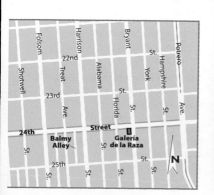

Coit Tower Mural

© Daniella Nowitz / Apa Publications

Speaking Walls: The Murals of San Francisco

San Francisco tallies nearly 600 wall paintings within its 49sq mi. Some record traditional history. Others serve as vibrant pictorial voices for communities without expression in mainstream art institutions—groups united by race, ethnicity, class, gender or politics.

The great Mexican muralist **Diego Rivera** visited the city during the early 1930s, executing important works at the San Francisco Art Institute and the Pacific Exchange. Fresco murals at Coit Tower and the Beach Chalet reflect Rivera's influence during this period.

During the late 1960s, **David Alfaro Siqueiros** improved techniques for outdoor painting, and the Mission District witnessed an explosion of outdoor art the following decade. The fences, walls and garage doors of **Balmy Alley**, off 24th Street, were originally decorated by schoolchildren. Many Mission District artists painted their first murals in the alley, including Patricia Rodríguez, Graciela Carillo and Irene Pérez, who later founded Mujeres Muralistas, a group of women artists who pictured the beauty of their cultures.

Many of those early murals were subsequently replaced in the 1980s by the **PLACA** group—this time with themes of the struggle for peace in Central America. More recent Balmy Alley murals include portraits of Mexican art icons, a relief mural made with plywood cut-outs, and a mural tribute to Mujeres Muralistas. Maradiaga Mini-Park contains murals drawn to teach local kids about their Latin-American heritage.

Following is a brief list of some exceptionally interesting Mission District murals. For more information, drop by or call the **Precita Eyes Mural Arts and Visitors Center** *(2981 24th St. near Harrison St.; ☎415-285-2287; www.precitaeyes.org)* which offers lectures and walking tours of Mission District murals *(Sat–Sun at 11am & 1.30pm; $12–$15; call or check website for details and meeting place)* as well as a useful map pinpointing more than 90 murals in the area if you wish to explore the neighborhood independently.

- *Las Lechugueras* (1983) by Juana Alicia; Taquería San Francisco, 24th and York Streets.

- *Silent Language of the Soul* (1990) by Juana Alicia and Susan Cervantes; Cesar Chavez Elementary School, Shotwell & 22nd Sts.

- *Five Hundred Years of Resistance* (1993) by Isaías Mata; St. Peter's Church, 24th St. at Florida St.

- *Maestrapeace* (1995) by various women artists; Women's Building, 3543 18th St.

Other mural locations described elsewhere in this guide include:
Balmy Alley (☝p179)
San Francisco Art Institute (☝p104)
Beach Chalet (☝p156)
National Maritime Museum (☝p127)
Coit Tower (☝p98)
Rincon Center (☝p116)

of California; and Francisco De Haro (1803–48), first mayor of San Francisco.

Dolores Street

Between 16th and 21st Sts.
Rolling hills, lofty palm trees and an eye-catching assemblage of architectural styles characterize this attractive stretch of Dolores Street. At 18th Street, Mission Dolores' architecture is echoed in the huge, red-tile-roofed Mission High School (1926, John Reid, Jr.). Lush, hilly **Mission Dolores Park** was laid out in 1905 and served as a cemetery for two Jewish temples.

South of the park is **Liberty Street** *(between 20th and 21st Sts.)*, lined with Victorians dating from the 1860s. All major styles are represented, including Italianate *(no. 109)*, Stick *(nos. 111–121)*, and Queen Anne *(no. 123)*.

24th Street★

Between Mission and Potrero Sts.
This lively, tree-lined shopping strip exudes the gritty, exuberant aura of the Mission District. Community residents flock here daily to pick up produce, meats, cheeses and baked goods. Bright awnings shadow fruit stands overflowing with exotic picks; Spanish rolls off the tongues of shopkeepers and shoppers alike; and modest eateries serve up Latin American treats.

Stroll down **Balmy Alley★** *(between Treat & Harrison Sts.)* to admire the colorful murals adorning nearly every garage door and wall surface. Occupying an unassuming corner storefront, **Galería de la Raza** *(2857 24th St. at Bryant St.;* ⏰ *open Wed–Sat noon–6pm;* ✆ *415-826-8009; www.galeriadelaraza.org)* has sustained and nurtured the Chicano art movement since 1970. The gallery showcases new artists along with established ones; exhibits reflect Chicano and Latino social and cultural issues.

Valencia Street★

Between 16th and 23rd Sts.
A profusion of restaurants, thrift stores and bars lines this section of Valencia Street and the cross streets to Guerrero Street, transforming the working-class

Dolores Park
© Daniella Nowitz / Apa Publications

neighborhood into a trendy "new Bohemia." The area is becoming a magnet for the young and the hip. Regulars drift through its coffeehouses, used bookstores and thrift shops by day; at night, its restaurants, bars and clubs are packed.

ADDRESSES

⑂ EAT

👥 $ St. Francis Fountain – *2801 24th St. at York St. Open Mon–Sat 8am–10pm, Sun 8am–9pm.* ✆*415-826-4210. www.stfrancisfountainsf.com.* The city's only surviving soda fountain, built in 1916, was last remodeled in 1948. Take a booth or a stool at the counter and sip a soda or dig into hot fudge ice cream sundaes, banana splits, root beer floats, and old-fashioned milkshakes.

Taqueria Cancun – *2288 Mission St. at 19th St. Open daily 10am–2am.* ✆*415-252-9560.* Many locals consider the big, juicy burritos at this authentic taqueria to be among the best in the city. They come wrapped in grilled tortillas and slathered with fresh avocado and sour cream. Order an agua fresca to wash it all down.

South of Market

San Francisco's hardscrabble history meets its high-tech future in the area known as South of Market. Like New York City's SoHo (which inspired South of Market's sobriquet, "SoMa"), the area is largely dominated by industrial buildings. On and around Third and Fourth Streets, the **Yerba Buena Gardens** development is fast becoming a prime cultural center, and many industrial buildings have been reborn as offices, sleek restaurants, clubs and galleries.

A BIT OF HISTORY

SoMa differs from other San Francisco neighborhoods in two major respects— its streets run at a 45-degree angle to those of the rest of the city, and its blocks are four times as big. Irish engineer and surveyor Jasper O'Farrell planned it that way in 1847 in anticipation of industrial growth, and gasworks, shipyards, refineries, foundries and breweries took root along the waterfront

Despite all this industry, well-to-do San Franciscans built elegant Victorian mansions atop nearby Rincon Hill; and an enclave of Georgian townhouses encircled a private oval common known as South Park. Encroaching development and the advent of the cable car in 1873 whisked most of the rich denizens away to the slopes of Nob Hill.

Neighborhood in Transition – After the earthquake and fire of 1906 razed the sector, SoMa's population remained largely male and working-class. After 1985 when the Downtown Plan limited skyscraper construction in the Financial District, several large office towers rose in the blocks between Mission and Market Streets. Work on Yerba Buena Gardens began in the early 1990s, and architects, performing artists, filmmakers and cyberartists began carving up SoMa's warehouses into live/work spaces. Many dot-com companies were based here, too, prior to the 2001 tech-stock crash,

MUNI Streetcar N–Judah .
MUNI Bus 10–Townsend, 12–Folsom, 30–Stockton, 45–Union-Stockton, 47–Van Ness BART Embarcadero, Montgomery St., Powell St. or Civic Center stations.

& **Michelin Map:** See Yerba Buena Gardens.

Info: 415-391-2000. www.sanfrancisco.travel.

Location: The term SoMa applies mainly to the blocks between Market and Townsend Streets, from 11th Street to the Embarcadero. This is a huge, diverse area, with everything from avant-garde art to baseball. For the purposes of this guide, we've given **Yerba Buena Gardens**, which is part of SoMa, its own chapter since it contains so many closely packed cultural attractions. Keep in mind when visiting SoMa that the blocks here are twice as long and twice as wide as those in other neighborhoods, with about five blocks per mile.

Timing: SoMa is best visited in the daytime with a specific destination in mind. Use caution around Sixth Street. At night, take a taxi.

Parking: There is a parking garage at Fifth and Mission Streets.

Don't Miss: The ever popular tour of the Anchor Brewing Company, mecca for lovers of this tart microbrew.

after which commercial vacancy rates rose as high as 30 percent. Though not as exuberant as it once was, SoMa still has a lively after-dark scene—clustered along 11th Street between Folsom and

Harrison streets, and in the area around Yerba Buena Gardens—offering nightclubs and galleries, microbreweries and bistros in converted industrial buildings.

SIGHTS
Old Mint
88 5th St. at Mission St. ○━ Not open to the public. ℘415-537-1105. www.sfhistory.org.
The Old Mint—fondly known as The Granite Lady—is one of San Francisco's finest Neoclassical buildings. Made of brick with stone facing in 1874, the structure served as a U.S. Mint until 1937, narrowly surviving the fire of 1906 when employees, with the help of soldiers and a tiny firehose, fought the flames to save $200 million in silver and gold. Though the building exudes indomitability with its six great Doric columns and pyramidal granite staircase, it was badly damaged in the 1989 earthquake and forced to close in 1995. It is currently under restoration to become a new history center. *(expected date of completion: 2015).*

South Park
Bounded by 2nd, 3rd, Brannan and Bryant Sts.
Modest apartment houses and charming cafes flank this sedate oval park, bringing a touch of gentility to a warehouse-dominated neighborhood. Designed in the early 1850s to resemble London's Berkeley Square, South Park, like nearby Rincon Hill, was home to high society until the early 1870s. Writer Jack London was born nearby in 1876 (a plaque marks his birth site at 601 3rd St.). Today the eclectic surface treatments of homes and storefronts bear witness to the growing presence of design firms.

Folsom Street
A hive of activity for alternative society, this street—and those adjoining it between 6th and 11th Streets—holds a high concentration of nightclubs. The street hosts the leather-centric Folsom Street Fair the last Sunday of September, but its draw on most nights of the week is much more diverse. Ground zero for hip club goers is the area around 11th and Folsom Streets, where queues form outside SoMa institutions like the **DNA Lounge** *(375 11th St.; ℘415-626-1409; www.dnalounge.com)* as well as newer bars like Butter *(354 11th St.; ℘415-863-5964; www.smoothasbutter.com)* and Wish *(1539 Folsom St.; ℘415-431-1661; www.wishsf.com)*. Nearby, gargantuan dance clubs like **Ten 15** *(1015 Folsom St.; ℘415-431-1200; www.1015.com)* pack in the crowds with world-renowned DJs.

Don't miss **Brain Wash** *(1122 Folsom St.; ℘415-255-4866; www.brainwash.com)*, which combines a bar and cafe with a laundromat. Improvisational comedy and folk-rock are regular features here. Two venerable nearby churches were built by early 20C working-class ethnic communities. The 1906 **Ukrainian Orthodox Church of St. Michael** *(345 7th St. at Harrison St.; ℘415-861-4066)* served a sizable colony of Ukrainian immigrants. A double stairway approaches its twin-towered facade. **St. Joseph's Church** *(1415 Howard St. at 10th St.)*, now closed due to earthquake damage, anchored an Italian community.

ADDITIONAL SIGHTS
Potrero Hill
This eclectic residential neighborhood features windswept streets, lovely views, comfortable commercial strips and historic factories. Many design studios have recently relocated along De Haro Street between 16th and Mariposa streets. **Eighteenth Street** between Connecticut and Texas streets harbors a cozy commercial strip, boasting scenic **views★** of downtown.

Anchor Brewing Company
1705 Mariposa St. at DeHaro St. ☛Brewery visit by guided tour (90min) only Mon–Fri 10am & 1pm. Reservations required (up to 6 months in advance). ℘415-863-8350. www.anchorbrewing.com.
Housed in an attractive Art Deco factory (1937), the Anchor Brewing Company has earned a reputation for its **Anchor Steam Beer**, a tart, amber

lager. The company sparked a 1990s trend in the United States toward beers from microbreweries. Founded in 1896, Anchor was purchased in the mid-1970s by Fritz Maytag, heir to the Maytag appliance fortune. He struggled for more than a decade to perfect its brew, and moved the operation to its present location in 1979. Guided tours include a visit to the factory's main room, where barley, hops and malt begin the long transformation into beer, and to the high-speed bottling room. An optional tasting session follows.

ADDRESSES

SHOPPING

Bonhams and Butterfields – *220 San Bruno Ave., between 15th & 16th Sts. ℘415-861-7500. www.bonhams.com.*

Previews and auctions—all open to the public (though you have to register to bid)—occur two or three weekends a month at the largest U.S. auction house outside New York City. Specialties include California paintings, fine and rare wines, American and European arms and armor and Asian art. The SoMa Auction, held one Sunday a month, draws legions of antiques dealers with high-quality items such as estate silver, jewelry, and furniture.

NIGHTLIFE

Slim's – *333 11th St. ℘415-255-0333. www.slims-sf.com.* Rock, blues, alt-country and cover bands all have a home at this long-standing nightclub, which has hosted the likes of Patti Smith and Pearl Jam. R&B legend Boz Skaggs founded the joint. Clubbers can dine on the balcony or dance on the huge floor beneath.

Yerba Buena Gardens★★

The contemporary heart of the South of Market district, this once-rundown industrial zone has evolved into San Francisco's cultural hub. With six museums (and two more soon to open), the city's principal convention center, a performing-arts center, a children's center, and a high-tech shopping-and-entertainment complex, it pulses with activity from morning until late at night. At the core of one of the biggest urban-renewal projects in the U.S., this 5.5-acre park opened in 1993 between 3rd and 4th, Mission and Howard Streets. Adjacent neighborhoods now bustle with architecture and graphic-design firms, film- and software-production studios, trendy restaurants, and nightclubs. Along the fringe of Market Street, just one block north of the Gardens, new high-rise office towers are sprouting.

◔ **Michelin Map:**
See p80, p184.
⧨ Bus 14–Mission, 30–Stockton or 45–Union-Stockton. ▦ Montgomery St. or Powell St. stations.
▯ **Info:** www.yerbabuena gardens.com.
◔ **Location:** The Yerba Buena Gardens cultural district stretches roughly from Second to Fifth Streets between Mission and Folsom Streets. Its centerpiece is the block enclosed by Mission, Howard, Third and Fourth Streets. Here you'll find the Yerba Buena Center for the Arts galleries and performance spaces, as well as a pleasant park and the Sony–Metreon cinema and shopping complex. A footbridge arches over Howard Street to the family-centered Rooftop

Moscone West

© San Francisco Convention and Visitors Bureau

A BIT OF HISTORY

For more than three decades, beginning in the 1960s, San Francisco's urban redevelopment agency cast its eyes south across Market Street. Residents fought planners and real-estate developers to prevent their declining community from becoming a high-rise ghetto. The first big step took place in 1981 with the completion of **Moscone**

at Yerba Buena Gardens. On surrounding blocks, particularly along Mission Street, lie a number of interesting museums.

- 👥 **Kids:** The Rooftop at Yerba Buena Gardens, with its ice skating and bowling center, carousel, and interactive-media space, the Children's Creativity Museum.
- 🕐 **Timing:** A visit could easily take all day, especially if you dip into adjacent neighborhoods.
- 🅿 **Parking:** There is a parking garage at Fifth and Mission Streets, but Yerba Buena Gardens' proximity to all the Market Street Muni and BART lines makes public transportation easy.
- 🏛 **Don't Miss:** The San Francisco Museum of Modern Art's stunning collection.

Convention Center (Hellmuth, Obata and Kassabaum) on the south side of Howard Street. Later additions came in 1988 and 1991, bringing total exhibition space to 442,000sq ft. Moscone West opened in 2003, giving the center a total of 650,000sq ft. A sports arena originally was scheduled for construction in the block north of the convention center. But citizens' voices won out, and a multicultural focus was agreed upon. Its centerpiece became the Yerba Buena Gardens. Today the district boasts eight museums, a children's entertainment complex, art galleries, a cineplex, an inviting park, live-performance spaces and more.

SIGHTS
Yerba Buena Center for the Arts★ (A)

Third and Mission Sts. 🕐 *Galleries open Thu–Sat noon–8pm, Sun noon–6pm.* 🕐 *Closed major holidays.* 🎟 *$10; free 1st Tue of month (noon–8pm).* ♿ 𝒸 *415-978-2700. www.ybca.org.*

Exploring such issues as race, class, gender, history, technology and art itself, the changing exhibitions in this low-slung, modernistic building (1993, Fumihiko Maki) reflect the cultural diversity and experimental élan of the Bay Area. Designed to resemble an ocean liner—its tall flagpole suggesting a mast and the angled Mission Street facade recalling a stern—the $44 million structure contains a 6,700sq-ft performance space, two cavernous first-floor galleries and a sculpture plaza. Upstairs, a high-tech gallery accommodates film, video

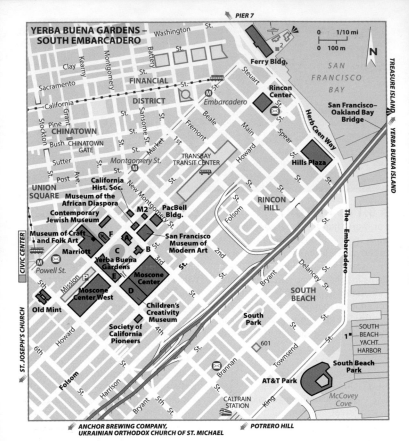

ANCHOR BREWING COMPANY,
UKRAINIAN ORTHODOX CHURCH OF ST. MICHAEL — POTRERO HILL

and multimedia installations, while an open terrace overlooks the large downstairs gallery and spacious lobby. Galleries host temporary exhibitions of work by emerging and established artists.

Immediately south of the galleries stands the 750-seat **Yerba Buena Center for the Arts Theater (B)** (1993, James Stewart Polshek and Partners). Exposed steel cross beams emphasize its boxy, geometrical design, accented by red and yellow flourishes around the lobby and entranceway. The theater hosts performance groups that share the center's goal of promoting multiculturalism.

Esplanade★ (C)

Incorporating gently rolling hills, trees, gardens, eclectic sculptures and an outdoor performance area, the manicured Esplanade is a quiet haven. Paths meander about the ground level, which lies atop an underground extension of Moscone Center.

The south side is dominated by **Revelations★**, a site-specific memorial to Dr. Martin Luther King, Jr. Behind an exhilarating waterfall, 50ft wide and 20ft high, are 12 glass panels engraved with quotations from the civil-rights leader's speeches and writings. It was the joint work of sculptor Howard Conwill, poet Estella Majoza and architect Joseph De Pace.

On a second-story terrace, the Sister City Garden features plants and shrubs from the 14 international cities that nurture cultural and political relations with San Francisco.

Fine sculptures stud the Esplanade, including wild-eyed *Shaking Man* by Terry Allen *(terrace level)* and *Deep Gradient/Suspect Terrain,* a 20ft steel-and-glass sinking "ship" by John Roloff in the east garden.

ROOFTOP AT YERBA BUENA GARDENS★★ (D)

Fourth St. between Howard and Folsom Sts.

This $56 million children's complex, which sits atop the west wing of Moscone Center's South Hall, is one of the city's leading attractions for families. Attractions (the **Children's Creativity Museum** and the **Ice Skating & Bowling Center**) are centered around a 100,000sq ft Children's Garden, where kids can frolic on a giant play structure with tunnel-slides or get lost in a hedge labyrinth.

Children's Creativity Museum

221 4th St. at Howard St. Open Wed– Sun 10am–4pm. For holiday closures, call or consult website. $11 415-820-3320. www.creativity.org.

Housed in a zany round building by architect Adele Naude Santos, this museum is a multimedia arts center for kids. Inside the Main Gallery you'll find a sampling of high- and low-tech tools to make digital music and videos, and to put on digital puppet shows. Creature costumes are provided so kids can be the stars. On other floors children can make a Claymation film with their own clay figures, play on a computer-generated maze and create digital art. Many of the exhibits involve making souvenirs (CDs, DVDs, artwork) to take home. Just outside the entrance, the illuminated, glass-enclosed **Carousel★** (*open 10am–5pm; $3 for two rides*) features a whirling menagerie of hand-carved animals. It was constructed in Rhode Island by craftsman Charles Looff in 1906.

Yerba Buena Ice Skating & Bowling Center

750 Folsom St. at 3rd St. Open daily 10am–10pm; however, public-access hours vary depending on activity, day and season; call or visit website. Varies depending on day and season;

call or visit website. 415-820-3532. www.skatebowl.com.

This 12-lane bowling alley and NHL-regulation indoor ice-skating rink offer hours of diversion. Skating lessons and skate rentals are available at the rink.

SAN FRANCISCO MUSEUM OF MODERN ART★★

151 3rd St. Open Memorial Day– Labor Day Thu–Tue 10am–5.45pm, Thu until 8.45pm. Rest of the year Thu– Tue 11am–5.45pm, Thu until 8.45pm. Closed major holidays. $18 (free 1st Tue of the month, half-price Thu 6pm –8.45pm). Guided tours (30min & 1hr) available; 415-357-4000. www.sfmoma.org.

San Francisco's premier showcase for modern art is housed in a delightful building that seems to gaze benignly out over Yerba Buena Center for the Arts. Together these institutions form the creative heart of the district.

A BIT OF HISTORY

The present-day museum began in 1871 as the San Francisco Art Association, a group of artists and art lovers determined to promote artistic expression and appreciation in the Bay Area. Housed at the Palace of Fine Arts after the Panama-Pacific International Exposition of 1915, the organization, renamed the San Francisco Museum of Art,

San Francisco Museum of Modern Art

© Henrik Kam / San Francisco Museum of Modern Art

moved in 1935 to new quarters in the War Memorial Veterans Building at Civic Center. The museum quickly gained a reputation for bringing new and challenging works before the public eye, organizing the first solo exhibitions of works by then-unknown artists Arshile Gorky, Clyfford Still, Jackson Pollock, Robert Motherwell and Mark Rothko.

As early as 1970, problems inherent in the Veterans Building space—lack of climate control, no ground-floor presence, insufficient gallery space and inadequate storage—inhibited the flow of donations. In 1988, the board of trustees initiated massive fund-raising efforts to begin construction of a new home for the museum on land situated across from Yerba Buena Gardens. Swiss architect Mario Botta, reputed for his humanistic modernism and skillful use of natural light, was selected to design the new space, with Hellmuth, Obata & Kassabaum, Inc. as the architect of record. The commission represented Botta's first building in the U.S.

A Modern Home for Modern Art – Botta's design is a striking composition of symmetrically arranged, stepped-back, brick-clad masses. Though at first glance the building appears simple and blocky, fine brickwork creates a rhythmic play of light and shadow across its exterior.

Piercing the center of the building is a massive shaft, set off from the red-brown brick by stripes of alternating black and white stone. Botta created a huge skylight by slanting the top of the cylinder toward 3rd Street and facing the slanted surface with glass. This great central oculus serves as both beacon and receptor while suffusing the building's upper galleries and atrium with natural light.

Botta, who studied and worked extensively in Italy, envisioned the museum's interior street level as a piazza-like urban space. Paved in alternating bands of polished and unpolished black marble, the stunning central **atrium**★★ leads to a stylish cafe, a bookstore, a 299-seat theater, classrooms and special-events spaces. Its open design reveals the building's spatial arrangement at a glance, giving a clear sense of five levels arrayed around the great, catwalk-crossed tower shaft and accessed by a stairway.

In the galleries, the colors of materials provide a neutral backdrop for artworks. The blacks and grays of stone and the slickness of glass and steel play against the somber warmth of wood tones of Nordic birch sheathing the wainscoting and maple floors.

The Collections – Now numbering more than 27,000 works of art, the permanent collection was initiated in 1935, just six years after the Museum of Modern Art was founded in New York City. The initial gift of 36 works—including Diego Rivera's *The Flower Carrier*—was presented by local insurance magnate Albert M. Bender, one of the institution's founding trustees. Through the 20C the holdings grew steadily in size and scope while staying true to the museum's contemporary bent. Today the painting and sculpture collections represent all major movements of modern art, with significant strengths in early Modernism and works by California and Bay Area artists.

In 1936, the museum began to present photography as a fine-art, and works by Alfred Stieglitz, Ansel Adams, Imogen Cunningham and other members of the Group f.64 augmented the collection. An initial architectural show in 1940 gave rise to the museum's Department of Architecture and Design; further exhibitions of the work of such noted architects as Le Corbusier and American designers Charles and Ray Eames have helped to secure the museum's reputation in this field.

The Department of Media Arts celebrates the Bay Area's position as a hub of activity in video, film, digital and online works.

VISIT

First-time visitors are advised to take the interactive SFMOMA Collection Highlights audio tour (☎ *rental table on 1st floor),* recorded by museum curators and directors. The tour provides excellent insights into the collection. Stop by the **Koret Visitor Education Center** *(2nd floor)* where you can investigate key ideas and issues in modern art and access a multimedia archive of California artists. 👥 There are also art activity bins for kids. In addition to hosting important temporary and traveling shows, the museum mounts thematic exhibitions and retrospectives using works from the permanent collection and offers free screenings of films related to the art on view. Check at the front desk or visit the website for the schedule.

Second floor

Paintings, sculpture and works of architecture and design drawn from the permanent collection occupy galleries here. Though artworks are frequently rotated, visitors are likely to see mainstays of the painting collection. Henri Matisse's landmark *Femme au Chapeau* (1905) created outrage when it was exhibited at the Paris Salon d'Automne of 1905; critical response to the painting, and to similar works exhibited with it, gave rise to the term "Fauvism" to describe the use of vivid, non-naturalistic colors. Georges Braque's *Violin and Candlestick* (1910), created during the height of Cubism, represents objects simultaneously from multiple points of view. A small gallery rotates the museum's Djerassi Collection of works on paper by Paul Klee. Visitors should not miss Mexican muralist Diego

Rivera's sympathetically idealized paean to peons, *The Flower Carrier* (1935), nor self-taught artist Frida Kahlo's insightfully detailed portrait of herself and her husband, *Frieda and Diego Rivera* (1931), which she painted especially for museum trustee Albert Bender, her friend and patron.

Jackson Pollock's immensely influential *Guardians of the Secret* (1943), one of the museum's most important pieces, opened the gateway to American Abstract Expressionism as well as to Pollock's own "drip" period. One gallery is dedicated to selections from the museum's 30 huge, abstract canvases by Clyfford Still.

Berkeley painter Joan Brown's *Noel in the Kitchen* (c. 1964) embodies the Bay Area Figurative movement's return to recognizable subject matter. Other California artists whose work may be on view include Richard Diebenkorn, Elmer Bischoff, David Park, Robert Arneson, Edward Kienholz, Wayne Thiebaud and Bruce Connor. Works by Jasper Johns, Robert Rauschenberg and Pop artists James Rosenquist and Andy Warhol reflect the styles that evolved in the postwar period in reaction to Abstract Expressionism. Other noteworthy works include paintings by Pablo Picasso, Joan Míro, Salvador Dalí, Georgia O'Keeffe, Roy Lichtenstein and Mark Rothko.

The Department of Architecture and Design taps its permanent collection to present frequently changing shows on furniture, graphic arts, and building design.

Third Floor

Lower ceilings here keep scale appropriate to exhibitions of photography and works on paper. The museum's 9,000-piece photography collection is international in scope and rich in both historic and contemporary holdings. Strengths include works by mid-20C American masters Edward Weston, Imogen Cunningham, Ansel Adams, Edward Steichen, Diane Arbus, Margaret Bourke-White, Robert Mapplethorpe and Alfred Stieglitz (including one portrait of his wife, painter Georgia O'Keeffe).

Untitled [Tashman Party, Hollywood 1931] (1931)by Edward Steichen

© Estate of Edward Steichen / San Francisco Museum of Modern Art

Fourth Floor

This floor is dedicated to the exhibition of large-scale, contemporary pieces and installations, often incorporating works from the permanent collection. Film and video art is screened on an ongoing basis in a small theater. A sculpture terrace displays three-dimensional objects.

Fifth Floor

Natural light washes the white surfaces of these high-ceilinged upper galleries, though subtle screens and filters can adjust its quality. Here you'll find a rotating selection of contemporary paintings and sculptures from SFMOMA's permanent collection, as well as a small gallery devoted to the work of emerging artists. Be sure to venture across the fifth floor's dramatic steel **turret bridge★**, which stretches out across the atrium

ADDITIONAL SIGHTS
PacBell Building★

140 New Montgomery St.
o—•*Not open to the public.*
This 30-story building (1925, Timothy Pflueger) was the only skyscraper south of Market Street for decades. Today it still boasts an elegant terra-cotta facade and brass doorways topped by ogee arches. The elegant **lobby★** features black marble walls and columns, an intricate plaster ceiling with Asian motifs.

California Historical Society

678 Mission St., between 3rd and New Montgomery Sts. ◑*Open Tue–Thur noon–5pm.* ⊛*$5.* ♿ ☏*415-357-1848. www.californiahistoricalsociety.org.*
The state's official historical research organization, founded in the late 19C, carries out an active program of collection and exhibition on California's colorful, rambunctious past. In its attractive building (1922), the society maintains a library (◑*Wed–Thur noon–5pm)* of books, original documents, journals, maps, photographs and fine arts covering the great sweep of California's history, with some publications dating from the 17C. A spacious public gallery on the first level houses changing thematic exhibits curated by society staff, as well as traveling exhibits organized by other historical institutions. There also is an specialty bookshop off the lobby.

St. Patrick's Catholic Church (F)

756 Mission St., between 3rd & 4th Sts. ◑*Open daily 6.30am–6pm.* ♿ ☏*415-421-3730. www.stpatricksf.org.*
Founded by Irish immigrants during the golden days of 1851, St. Patrick's first red brick church was erected on this site in 1872, and served working-class families through the late 19C. Destroyed by the quake and fire of 1906, it was rebuilt in 1909 in Gothic Revival style using many of the original bricks. Fire scars still mark some walls. Green-veined Irish marble lines the vestibule; stained-glass windows depict scenes from the life of St. Patrick; even the vestments are embroidered with Celtic patterns. Ironically, the congregation is now largely Filipino in ancestry, and mass is celebrated in the Tagalog language as well as in English.

Marriott San Francisco Hotel

55 4th St. ✕♿🅿 ☏*415-896-1600.*
Although adjacent buildings tend to obscure its futuristic 39-story profile, this Postmodern building (1989, Anthony Lumsden) is a landmark. Its neo-Deco silhouette and fan-shaped windows once led to its being labeled "the Jukebox" by a local columnist.

It is best viewed looking south down Grant Avenue from Chinatown.

👥 Cartoon Art Museum (M2)

655 Mission St. 🕐*Open Tue–Sun 11am–5pm.* 🕐*Closed Jan 1, Easter, July 4, Thanksgiving Day, Dec 25.* 🎟*$7; 1st Tue "pay what you wish."* ♿ ☎*415-227-8666. www.cartoonart.org.*

This friendly museum is the only one of its kind in the western United States. Founded in 1984 to foster appreciation of cartoon art, it was homeless until 1987, when Peanuts creator Charles M. Schulz provided it with an endowment to rent a public space. It has since amassed an 6,000-piece permanent collection, including work dating from the late 18C. Samples are displayed alongside temporary exhibits of international and local cartoonists, many of whom use the medium to critique the status quo.

Society of California Pioneers

300 4th St. at Folsom St. 🕐*Open Wed –Fri & 3rd Thur 10am–4pm.* 🕐*Closed major holidays.* ♿ 🎟*$5.* ☎*415-957-1849. www.californiapioneers.org.*

This showcase for 19C and early 20C treasures, collected by descendants of pre-1850 Californians, opened in September 2000. On the first floor, the Seymour Pioneer Museum presents changing exhibits on California history drawn from the permanent collection of 6,000 artifacts and 50,000 photographs. On the second floor, the Moore Gallery offers early portraits and landscapes by the likes of Thomas Hill and William Keith, as well as prints and lithographs. The third floor holds the Sullivan Library, a research center open by appointment.

Museum of the African Diaspora

685 Mission St. at 3rd St. 🕐*Open Wed–Sat 11am–6pm, Sun noon–5pm.* 🕐*Closed major holidays.* 🎟*$10.* ♿ ☎*415-358-7200. www.moadsf.org.*

The vibrant MoAD occupies an elegant three-story building. Permanent and temporary exhibitions of work by artists of African descent tell the story of the scattering of African culture around the globe, hewing in general to four universal themes: Origins, movement, adaptation and transformation.

Museum of Craft and Folk Art

51 Yerba Buena Lane. 🕐*Open Wed–Sat 11am–6pm.* 🕐*Closed major holidays.* 🎟*$5.* ♿ ☎*415-227-4888. www.mocfa.org.*

The only folk art museum in northern California rotates thematic exhibits in a small gallery. A recent show explored the concept of Mexican identity in California. The store stocks an excellent selection of pottery, glassware, jewelry and other items by local artisans.

Contemporary Jewish Museum

736 Mission St. between 3rd and 4th Sts. 🕐*Open Fri–Tue 11am–5pm, Thu 1–8pm.* 👣*Tours Fri–Tue 11.30am, 1pm and 2pm, Thu 5pm and 6pm.* 🕐*Closed Jewish holidays, Jan 1, July 4, Thanksgiving Day.* ♿🎟*$12, free 1st Tue of month.* ☎*415-655-7800. www.thecjm.org.*

This award-winning museum mounts about three exhibitions per year to promote understanding of Jewish culture through contemporary art. Established in 1984, it maintains strong community ties via ongoing educational programs. The $50 million renovation of its new home (opened in June 2008), the Jessie Street Power Substation (1907, Willis Polk), was overseen by renowned architect Daniel Libeskind.

ADDRESSES

CAFE

$ CAFFÈ MUSEO *– In SFMOMA.* ☎*415-357-4500. www.caffemuseo.com.* Glowing woods and fixtures match the museum's decor at this elegant cafe, where sidewalk tables offer a pleasant place to refresh with an espresso, a focaccia sandwich or other light, Italian fare while viewing the comings and goings at Yerba Buena Gardens across the street.

On the far western edge of the city, the oceanfront's stunning natural setting is its most enduring attraction. Beach-goers sunbathe and surf; hikers weave along wild, windswept bluffs; hang-gliders flock to Fort Funston; and music lovers picnic in Sigmund Stern Memorial Grove during free summer concerts. The Legion of Honor, the city's premier fine arts museum, spreads its collonaded wings towards the Golden Gate from its spectacular perch in Lincoln Park. Adolph Sutro's former estate and Sutro Baths afford a glimpse into the past and sweeping views of the ocean. At the southern edge of the broad Sunset District, which spreads below Golden Gate Park, the 125-acre San Francisco Zoo attracts nearly one million visitors each year.

Highlights

1 A summer picnic at **Stern Grove** with free music (p191)

2 Watching the hang-gliders at **Fort Funston** (p192)

3 A sunset dinner with sweeping ocean views at **Cliff House** (p195)

4 Hiking the breezy **Coastal Trail** (p195)

5 Seeing one of the finest **Rodin collections** outside Paris (p199)

An Oceanfront Transformation

In 1881 "Comstock King" Adolph Sutro returned to San Francisco after making a fortune on the silver of Nevada's Comstock Lode (the first major U.S. discovery of silver and gold ore). Touring San Francisco's oceanfront on a leisurely buggy ride, Sutro chanced upon a commanding site with spectacular views and bought it immediately. While the sharp investor would eventually come to own one twelfth of all property in San Francisco—including hundreds of acres of windswept sand dunes between downtown and the ocean—he chose to make this plot his home, landscaping the grounds with imported, drought-resistant plants, decorating with hundreds of statues, and then opening the grounds to the public.

Sutro transformed San Franciscans' experience with the westernmost part of their city. He bought up the oceanfront Cliff House, which had been spoiled by a fire and an unfavorable reputation, and replaced it with an ornate castle of restaurants, galleries, parlors, private lunch rooms and panoramic views. He also built a railway that, for five cents, transported passengers from downtown to the enormously popular Sutro Baths. Completed in 1894, these baths included seven saltwater swimming pools (each with its own slide), 500 private dressing rooms and bleacher seating for 5,300.

With Sutro's lush estate, railway, baths and Cliff House, the oceanfront became a favorite leisure destination for pleasure-seeking San Franciscans.

At the time of Sutro's shorefront revitalization, the Sunset District was a windswept region of sand dunes. Developer Aurelius Buckingham built the first row of houses on present-day Lincon Way in 1887, but it wasn't until the 1930s, with the completion of the Twin Peaks Tunnel, that a building frenzy was ignited. The 1930s also saw the initial plans designed for the San Francisco Zoo, as well as the 3-acre Sigmund Stern Memorial Grove presented to the city as a park in 1931 by Rosalie Stern in memory of her husband, who had gone on to become mayor of the city.

In the 1970s much of San Francisco's west coast, including Ocean Beach, Sutro Heights and Land's End, were acquired by the National Park Service as part of the Golden Gate National Recreation Area (GGNRA).

Today, San Franciscans still flock to these sites for leisure activities, enjoying dinner with a panoramic view at the restored Cliff House, visiting the enduring Legion of Honor at its stunning Lincoln Park perch, and touring Sutro's former estate and the ruins of the Sutro Baths.

Sunset District and Lake Merced

The Sunset District encompasses a broad, flat grid of regularly spaced residential streets with row after orderly row of tract houses. Most attractions lie along the coast or scattered around natural Lake Merced in San Francisco's southwesternmost corner.

A BIT OF HISTORY

Part of the wind and fog-scoured expanse of sand dunes known as the Outer Lands during the city's early decades, the Sunset is today a wind and fog-scoured expanse of stucco row houses erected after construction of a streetcar tunnel under Twin Peaks, opened the area in the 1930s. During the ensuing building frenzy, contractors raced each other along the newly platted streets to throw up mass-produced row houses. Although derided by architectural critics, the bungalows offered the possibility of home ownership to people of less-than-substantial means. The Sunset's two most interesting neighborhoods, **Forest Hill** (east end of Taraval St.) and **St. Francis Wood** (east end of Sloat Blvd.), predate the Twin Peaks tunnel.

The Sunset District harbors the main campus of San Francisco State University and the medical center of the University of California at San Francisco. On the district's southern border is Lake Merced, a recreation destination for its golf course and biking and running trails. The area's most visible landmark is the city's tallest structure, **Sutro Tower,** a pronged, red-and-white-striped television transmitter atop Mt. Sutro, which rises above the district on the northeast.

SIGHTS
👥 Ocean Beach★

🚌 Bus 18-46th Ave. or 48-Quintara-24th St.; streetcars L–Taraval or N–Judah.

🚌 Bus 18-46th Ave., 23-Monterey, 28-19th Ave., 29-Sunset, or 48-Quintara-24th St.; streetcar L-Taraval, M-19th Ave., or N-Judah.

📄 **Info:** www.sunset district.org.

▶ **Location:** The Sunset District extends south from Golden Gate Park and from the Pacific coast inland to about Stanyan Street.

👥 **Kids:** The San Francisco Zoo, of course, but also the intriguing Cayuga Playground.

🕐 **Timing:** Fog shrouds the area pretty much round-the-clock; try an early-afternoon visit if you wish to avoid it.

🅿 **Parking:** Sights have parking lots, except for Sigmund Stern Grove.

👁 **Don't Miss:** A stop at Fort Funston to see hang-gliders taking off.

This expansive beach creates a broad, sandy seam between the city and the Pacific Ocean. Pounding surf and a dangerous undertow make swimming here unwise, although surfers often paddle out from the beach at the foot of Taraval Street. A paved **promenade**, landscaped with dune-stabilizing grasses and shrubs, extends north 3mi from Sloat Boulevard to just south of Cliff House, making the beach popular with bikers and runners.

Sigmund Stern Memorial Grove
19th Ave. and Sloat Blvd.
There is no public parking lot, and street parking is extremely limited.
🚌*Bus 23-Monterey or 28-19th Av; streetcars K-Ingleside or M-Oceanview.*
🕐*Open daily sunrise–sunset. Concerts: mid-Jun–mid-Aug Sun 2pm.* ✕🅿
📞*415-252-6252. www.sterngrove.org.*
Presented to the city as a park in 1931 by Rosalie Stern in memory of her husband

Sigmund, this 33-acre sylvan "grove" lies at the bottom of an east-west-running ravine. Redwoods and fragrant eucalyptus trees hem the sides of the narrow valley surrounding Stage Meadow, which forms a natural amphitheater. Free musical performances are staged as part of a popular, long-running concert series endowed by Mrs. Stern in 1938. Music lovers of every stripe bring blankets and picnic fare to enjoy concerts in a range of musical styles from jazz to opera. Just east of Stage Meadow sits the dignified, Victorian **Trocadero** (1892), built by earlier landowner George M. Greene and popular as a saloon before Prohibition.

♟♟ San Francisco Zoo★

Sloat Blvd. at 45th Ave. ⅏⅏ ⅏ *Bus 18-46th Ave. or 23-Monterey; streetcar L-Taraval.* ⏱*Open daily 10am–5pm, Nov–Mar to 4pm.* ⬤*$15, children 4–14 $9.* ✖️🅿️ ☎*415-753-7080. www.sfzoo.org.*

Set on 125 acres on the southern fringe of the Sunset District, the San Francisco Zoo attracts some 925,000 visitors each year. Its original plan took shape in the 1930s. By the 1980s, its diminutive concrete enclosures were out of step with the times, as by that time other zoos around the country had adopted the cageless, "natural habitat" displays. In 1993, the city and the nonprofit San Francisco Zoological Society partnered to manage the zoo and raise funds for physical renovation, species conservation and breeding programs.

In 1997, San Franciscans approved a $48 million bond to rebuild two-thirds of the zoo by 2004, focusing on more naturalistic habitats for its 1,000 denizens. In 2002 the Lipman Family Lemur Forest debuted, harboring five species of this primate from Madagascar, and in 2004 the zoo introduced a 3-acre African savanna exhibit with giraffes, zebras, kudus and ostriches; in 2007 a grizzly bear exhibit opened.

Visit

Just past the entrance, the **Children's Zoo** features meerkats and prairie dogs, an insect zoo, terrariums at kids' eye level, and a petting barnyard where

human youngsters can make friends with domestic animals. Admire the graceful inhabitants of **Flamingo Lake**, then continue to the superb **Primate Discovery Center★**, where 15 species of rare and endangered monkeys and prosimians cavort and swing in open atriums. A spur trail leads to **Gorilla World**, a lushly landscaped, one-acre domain home to a six-member society of lowland gorillas.

For a glimpse of animal life below the Equator, stroll left from the main entrance to the **Australian Walkabout**, an outdoor habitat for kangaroos (one of them albino), wallabies and emus. Nearby are the **Billabong**, home to waterfowl from Down Under; **Koala Crossing,** patterned after an Outback station; and **Rainbow Landing**, an aviary aflutter with colorful lorikeets. **Puente al Sur** ("Bridge to the South") features such Latin American creatures as capybaras, tapirs and Andean condors. At **Grizzly Gulch**, watch a pair of grizzly bear sisters swim and fish (⏱*feedings daily 11am*). The **Feline Conservation Center,** near the zoo's South Gate, harbors small and medium-sized cats—including snow leopards, jaguars and panthers—for breeding and study. Visitors to **Penguin Island** can view the world's most successful breeding colony of Magellanic penguins (⏱*feedings daily 10.15am and 3.30pm*). Detour to the **black rhinoceros** enclosure where you'll find Elly, one of the most prolific breeders in the country: she has given birth to 14 calves, many of them moved to other zoos to contribute to the captive gene pool.

Before departing, take a spin around the track on **Little Puffer** (⬤*$4*), a miniature turn-of-the-20C steam train gleamingly restored and brought back from premature retirement.

Fort Funston

Enter from Rte. 35 (Skyline Blvd.) just south of John Muir Dr. ⅏⅏ ⅏ *Bus 18-46th Ave.* ☎*415-561-4323.*

This expansive former military post overlooking the Pacific Ocean was established in 1898 during the Spanish-American War but never tested in combat. The fort was renamed in 1917 in honor of General Frederick Funston, the Presidio co-commandant who organized military forces to maintain order in San Francisco in the aftermath of the 1906 earthquake and fire. With the approach of World War II, heavy cannonry was installed; Battery Richmond Davis, built in 1938, held two 16in guns. In a strategy worthy of Lewis Carroll, destination-less "roads" were created within Funston's grounds at this time to confound any invaders arriving by sea. Today the former military lands (decommissioned in 1963) are managed by the Golden Gate National Recreation Area as a 250-acre park. Ice plants cloak the dunes atop bluffs that rise 200ft above a clean sand beach; these dunes are considered among the finest hanggliding spots in the U.S. Visitors gather on a viewing deck to watch the aerialists in flight. The north end of the park is a stopover for migratory Central and South American bank swallows, which burrow into the bluffs and nest there from April through July. At that time, the habitat is closed to public visitation.

Visit

🏃 The scenic **Sunset Trail** *(.75mi)* meanders atop the windswept dunes and past Battery Davis before looping back to the parking lot. Long-distance hikers may link this trail to other sections of the Coastal Trail for a 4.7mi walk to Cliff House.

San Francisco State University

1600 Holloway Ave. at 19th Ave. 🚍*Bus 18-46th Ave. or 29–Sunset; streetcar M–19th Ave.* ♿ *415-338-1111. www.sfsu.edu.* Founded in 1899 as a teacher-training college, this was the first normal school in the U.S. to require a high-school diploma for admission. The college had a high national profile during the late 1960s, as student protests against racial discrimination, the Vietnam War, the military draft and "irrelevant" college classes culminated in November 1968 in the longest campus strike in history. Acting university president S.I.

Hayakawa refused to give in to the students, and strife finally ended in March 1969 with both sides claiming victory. A lasting legacy was the establishment of the nation's first School of Ethnic Studies and an expanded Black Studies Department. Today the 141-acre campus claims more than 30,000 students.

An emphasis on multiculturalism is evident at the **Art Department Gallery** *(Room 238, upper level of Fine Arts Bldg., between Tapia Dr. & Cesar Chavez Student Center;* 🕐*open during shows (2 per semester) Wed–Sat 11am–4pm;* 🕐*closed major holidays and in summer;* ✆*415-338-6535)*, whose changing exhibits feature contemporary art, historical examinations of diverse California art, and student art. Two Ruth Asawa sculptures flank the lobby. Inquire in the gallery for a map to campus sculptures. **The Poetry Center** and American Poetry Archives *(Humanities Bldg., Tapia Dr. opposite Fine Arts Bldg.;* 🕐*Mon–Thu 10am–5pm;* 🕐*closed major holidays;* ✆*415-338-2227)*, founded in 1954 with a gift from W.H. Auden, harbors the world's largest videotaped collection of poets and authors reading their own works—more than 2,000 in all. The **Sutro Library** *(480 Winston Dr., north campus;* 🕐*open Mon–Fri 10am–5pm;* 🕐*closed major holidays;* ✆*415-731-4477)*, part of the California State Library system, has one of the West's earliest and largest genealogical collections, inherited from the estate of Adolph Sutro.

👤👥Cayuga Playground

Cayuga & Naglee Aves., one block west of Alemany Blvd. 🚍*Bus 29-Sunset.* This urban oasis, the work of gardener Demetrio Braceros, uplifts an otherwise-downtrodden neighborhood. From the stumps of fallen trees, Braceros carved likenesses of the Virgin Mary and Jesus, Michael Jordan, Princess Di and others, including a menagerie of animals. He also wove branches into fences, railings and benches; designed two walking paths, the Garden of Eden Trail and the New Trail of Hope; planted flowers, vegetables and fruit trees, and inscribed rocks with inspirational messages.

Sutro Heights and Land's End★★

The rugged northwest corner of San Francisco, between Ocean Beach and Lincoln Park, has drawn visitors to its rocky cliffs and sheltered coves since Ohlone Indians camped here. Comprising ghostly ruins, a historical roadhouse, trails and breathtaking views, this stretch of the Golden Gate National Recreation Area (GGNRA) provides an impressive natural refuge. Its highlight is the Legion of Honor, San Francisco's preeminent repository for European art, which enjoys a spectacular setting amid the Monterey pines and cypresses of Lincoln Park, overlooking the rugged shores of the Golden Gate.

A BIT OF HISTORY

Settlement came slowly to San Francisco's coastline. In the early days of the gold rush, a few intrepid Europeans tried to homestead here, but it wasn't until the mid-1850s that Seal Rock House, an early precursor to today's Cliff House, was constructed near the shore, drawing city dwellers on Sunday beach outings. In the mid-1860s, prominent San Francisco families adopted the area as their summer playground. However, in the last two decades of the 19C the area lost its upper-class cachet, largely thanks to a populist-minded entrepreneur.

The Comstock King – In 1851, Prussian-born **Adolph Sutro** (1830–98) arrived in San Francisco in search of Gold Rush riches. After establishing himself as a tobacconist, the self-educated engineer relocated in 1860 to Virginia City, Nevada, where fortunes were being made from the Comstock Lode's silver. Mining proved treacherous due to poor ventilation and water in the shafts, so Sutro designed a 4 mile-long passage beneath the silver vein, wrangling for nearly 15 years with banks, mine owners and investors over funds. When the

🚌 Bus 18–46th Ave. or 38–Geary

ℹ️ **Info:** ✆415-561-4323. www.parksconservancy.org.

▷ **Location:** The area occupies the northwestern corner of the city. Paths lace the unspoiled green expanses; a golf course lies in the southeastern corner of Lincoln Park.

👥 **Kids:** The Camera Obscura provides a fun science lesson.

🕐 **Timing:** The Cliff House has a wall of west-facing windows overlooking the ocean. Views are particularly glorious at sunset.

🅿️ **Parking:** Parking spaces just in front of Cliff House tend to fill quickly, but lots may be found above Sutro Baths on Merrie Way; across Point Lobos Avenue from Merrie Way; and at Fort Miley beside the USS *San Francisco* memorial. There is also parking at the Legion of Honor.

👁️ **Don't Miss:** A hike along the Coastal Trail; the walk is bracing but not difficult, and the views are stellar. Wear sturdy shoes.

Sutro Tunnel finally opened, its engineer was dubbed the Comstock King. A shrewd businessman, Sutro sold his shares in the tunnel just prior to the crash of the mine stock in 1880. Returning to San Francisco, he quickly invested his fortune in land, eventually coming to own one twelfth of all the property in the city, including hundreds of acres of windswept sand dunes between downtown and the ocean. His enormously popular Sutro Baths, his lush estate atop Sutro Heights, his five-cent railway and his rebuilt Cliff House ballooned the oceanfront's fame as a favorite leisure destination for pleasure-seeking San Franciscans of every economic stripe.

A Popular Playland – By 1921 a beach-side entertainment zone of dance halls and rides had sprung up between Sutro Heights and Golden Gate Park. Renamed **Playland-at-the-Beach** in 1928, the strip resounded with shrieks of pleasure from the Big Dipper roller coaster and sprightly music from a Looff carousel (*since restored and moved to the Rooftop at YERBA BUENA GARDENS*). Streetcars brought revelers from downtown to whoosh down the Fun House slide and munch on hot dogs and ice-cream cookie sandwiches.

By the mid-20C Playland had fallen into seediness; it succumbed to the wrecking ball in 1972. In the mid-1970s much of San Francisco's west coast, including Ocean Beach, Sutro Heights and Land's End, were acquired by the National Park Service as part of the GGNRA. Today this region's dramatic natural beauty has again become its central attraction.

SUTRO HEIGHTS
Cliff House★★

1090 Point Lobos Ave. ✗ &. 🅿 *415-386-3330. www.cliffhouse.com.*
Renovated in the early 2000s, the historic Cliff House offers both casual and upscale dining, as well as panoramic views, from its perch atop a high bluff overlooking the Pacific Ocean.

The present building is the third incarnation of a roadhouse erected in 1863 by real-estate tycoon Charles Butler, who hoped to spark Coney Island-style development of the adjacent coastal area. By the 1880s it had acquired a reputation as a gambling hall to which "gentlemen" repaired for afternoon trysts. Adolph Sutro, who bought the property in 1881, remade it as a family resort, building the Sutro Railroad to transport the general public to and from the city.

This first Cliff House burned on Christmas Day 1894, but Sutro lost no time in hiring architects Emile Lemme and C.J. Colley to design its replacement: a flamboyant, many-spired confection resembling a French chateau. Critics decried Sutro's extravagance, but the public loved the ornate castle and its restaurants, art galleries, luxurious parlors with panoramic ocean views, private lunch rooms and observation tower 200ft above the sea. Its glory was short-lived, however—the building survived the 1906 earthquake only to succumb to fire the next year.

In 1909 the **Reid Brothers**, architects of the Fairmont Hotel (*see NOB HILL*), designed the third Cliff House. It was abandoned in the mid-20C until the National Park Service acquired it in 1977. For years it housed the Musée Mécanique of antique arcade games, but in the early 2000s the museum moved to Fisherman's Wharf and the Cliff House was expanded and restored.

♟♟ Camera Obscura (A)

🕐*Open daily 11am–5pm.* 🕐*Closed rainy & foggy days.* ☞*$3.* &. 🅿 *415-750-0415. www.giant camera.com.*
Housed in a small building, this curious instrument employs a mirror and two opposing lenses to magnify and project views of the surrounding area onto a 6ft parabolic screen. The motorized contraption completes a 360° rotation every 6min.

Sutro Baths Ruins★

Access by footpath from Louis' Restaurant or steps from the end of the Merrie Way parking lot. www.sutrobaths.com.
The haunting vestiges of the Sutro Baths lie in a cove just north of Cliff House. Lupine and ice plants cover the hills surrounding the concrete foundations that hardly evoke the magnificence of the structure they once supported. A tunnel, which once dumped dirt from the baths, pierces the bluff to the north, leading to a stretch of craggy coastline. Above the tunnel, a path leads to an **overlook** from which the remains of long-grounded ships can be spotted.

Coastal Trail★★

🚶 *3.4mi loop. From the Merrie Way parking lot, follow the sandy path to the wide main trail. www.nps.gov/goga.*
This well-maintained loop provides an invigorating walk along a wild, heavily

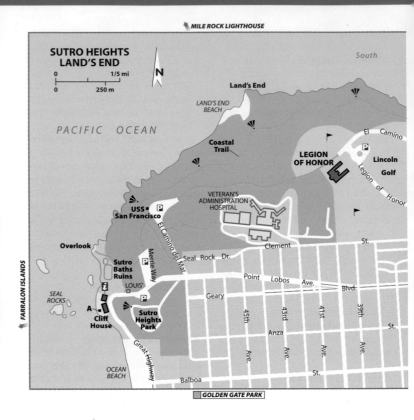

SUTRO HEIGHTS
LAND'S END

MILE ROCK LIGHTHOUSE

PACIFIC OCEAN

FARRALON ISLANDS

SEAL
ROCKS

Land's End

LAND'S END
BEACH

Coastal
Trail

VETERAN'S
ADMINISTRATION
HOSPITAL

LEGION
OF HONOR

South

El Camino

Lincoln
Golf

Legion of Honor

Clement   St.

USS
San Francisco

Overlook

Sutro
Baths
Ruins

LOUIS'

A

Cliff
House

Merrie Way

El Camino del Mar

Seal Rock Dr.

Sutro
Heights
Park

Point Lobos Ave.

Geary

45th

43rd

41st

39th

Blvd.

St.

Anza   Ave.

Great Highway

OCEAN
BEACH

Balboa   St.

GOLDEN GATE PARK

Sutro Baths

Adolph Sutro's most beloved contribution to San Francisco was the fabulous Sutro Baths, an elaborate and luxurious public swimming facility the millionaire erected among the rocks below his Sutro Heights estate. In 1891, construction began on the three-story, glass-domed structure, designed to utilize tidal ebb and flow to fill and empty its pools. After its completion in 1894, citizens paid 5 cents to travel out to the baths on Sutro's own railroad. From the Greek-inspired entrance portal, they descended a grand stairway bounded by palm trees to a cavernous main hall with seven saltwater swimming pools, ranging in temperature from bathwater-warm to ocean-cold. Patrons could change into rented woolen swimming suits in one of 500 private dressing rooms, lounge on bleachers seating 5,300 people, dine in any of three restaurants, or simply wonder at an astounding display of curiosities collected by the Comstock King. There were seven slides, one for each pool, and 30 swinging rings strung above the 1.8 million gallons of water.

Despite their enormous popularity, the baths operated at a financial loss, and in 1934 Sutro's heirs covered part of the swimming pools with a skating rink and basketball courts. After World War II, the deteriorated pools were closed. The skating rink continued to operate until 1966, when plans were made to demolish the structure and build apartments on the site. A fire of unexplained origin hastened the building's demise but the apartments were never built and the National Park Service acquired the property in 1980.

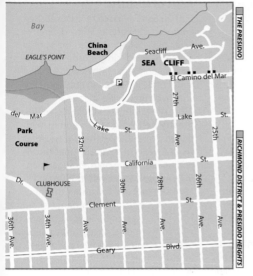

was heavily damaged in the naval Battle of Guadalcanal (1942).

Sutro Heights Park★

Point Lobos Ave. at 48th Ave.
The grounds of Adolph Sutro's former estate occupy a striking promontory overlooking Cliff House and Ocean Beach. Although the residence was demolished in 1939, the property remains a paradise of well-tended lawns and stately groves of distinctive trees. Sutro chanced upon the commanding site in 1881 and purchased it forthwith.

The original small cottage was enlarged to a comfortable, though not opulent, country home. Sutro lavished his attention on the grounds, importing drought-resistant flowers and trees from all over the world, including Norfolk Island pines, Canary Island date palms and Monterey cypresses. He designed a wind-powered watering system, built a glass conservatory for delicate plants, and installed more than 200 statues.

Ever the populist, Sutro placed a sign at the entrance inviting the public "to walk, ride, and drive therein." After his death in 1898, Sutro's daughter Emma continued this open-door policy, bequeathing the estate to the city in 1938. In 1976, the National Park Service acquired Sutro Heights.

Visit

Two stone lions, copies of originals now housed in Park Service archives, flank the park's entrance. To the left of the broad driveway, figures of a stag and the goddess Diana rise among the foliage. Sutro's glass conservatory (now demolished) stood to the east of the circular drive that served as a carriage turnaround. A white Victorian gazebo—originally the property's wellhouse—lies to the west on a grassy lawn where intricate carpets of brightly colored flowers once flourished.

wooded shoreline boasting spectacular **views★★★** of the ocean, the Golden Gate Bridge and the Marin Headlands. For part of its length, the lower trail follows an old railroad bed atop sheer bluffs that plunge abruptly to swirling waters. Eucalyptus trees scent the hills rising to the south, while Monterey pines and firs hold the crumbling cliffs in place. Stairs scale the steeper inclines, and smaller trails lead off the main path, one of them to the secluded Land's End Beach. The main trail, narrow and winding in places, leads to a viewing platform overlooking the posh Sea Cliff neighborhood. Descend the steps to the overlook for a lovely view of rocky Eagle's Point. The return route leads up from the overlook to follow a wide, paved berm along El Camino del Mar through the **Lincoln Park Golf Course★** *(34th Ave. and Clement St.,* 🅿 *℘415-221-9911).* These city-owned public links, landscaped by John McLaren in 1909, boast spectacular views. Pass to the right of the Legion of Honor through a parking lot above the golf course to rejoin the footpath, which leads to the trail's end at the Fort Miley parking lot. Across from here, part of the bullet-torn bridge of the **USS San Francisco** commemorates the commander and crew of this vessel, which

Follow the wide dirt path past the gazebo, veering left off the main driveway to Sutro's now-overgrown viewing parapet to enjoy some of the area's finest ocean **views★★**; on the clearest days, the Farallon Islands can be spied 26mi offshore.

LEGION OF HONOR★★★

100 34th Ave. at El Camino del Mar, Lincoln Park. ⊙*Open Tue–Sun 9.30am –5.15pm.* ⊙*Closed major holidays.* ⊛*$10 (free 1st Tue of the month); includes same-day admission to the de Young Museum; $2 discount for bus riders with transfer.* ☞*Guided tours available daily.* ✕ ♿ 🅿 ✆*415-750-3600. http://legionofhonor.famsf.org.*

A gift to San Francisco from **Alma de Bretteville Spreckels**, this museum houses her personal collection of sculptures by Auguste Rodin, plus a treasury of European, particularly French, art, spanning some 4,000 years.

Together, the Legion of Honor and the de Young museum *(*⊙*see GOLDEN GATE PARK)* form the Fine Arts Museums of San Francisco.

Gallery 3, featuring the ceiling from the Palacio de Altamira in Torrijos, Spain

© Richard Barnes / Fine Arts Museums of San Francisco

A Bit of History

Born in San Francisco to impoverished European immigrants, Alma de Bretteville (1881–1968) inherited the energy of her hardworking mother and the imagination of her father, who instilled in her pride in the faded nobility of the French de Bretteville lineage.

Alma grew into a statuesque, willful, mostly self-educated woman who defied convention in many ways. After several years of a socially unacknowledged liaison, she married sugar magnate **Adolph Spreckels** in 1908, and in 1914 she met and fell under the influence of American-born dancer Löie Fuller, the toast of Belle Epoque Paris, who convinced her to become a patron of the arts with Löie as her chief adviser. In 1915 plans to build the Legion of Honor were set into motion.

The building (1924, George Applegarth) was modeled after the 1915 Panama-Pacific International Exposition's French Pavilion, itself a version of the Hôtel de Salm, a 18C Parisian residence designated by Napoleon in 1804 as the Palais de la Légion d'Honneur. On Armistice Day 1924, the new museum was dedicated to the 3,600 Californians who had perished in World War I.

The Collection – Dance-related art and European decorative arts initially formed the core of the museum's holdings, along with one of the finest collections of works by French sculptor Auguste Rodin (1840–1917) outside the Musée Rodin in Paris. Alma, introduced to Rodin in 1914, acquired many of the pieces during the artist's lifetime, when his sculptures were cast by his favorite *fondeur,* Alexis Rudier. The museum now owns 106 sculptures by Rodin, of which the most famous, *The Thinker* (1880), greets visitors in the Court of Honor.

In 1950, the Legion received the city-owned **Achenbach Foundation for Graphic Arts**.

This immensely important body of works on paper today numbers 80,000 prints, drawings, photographs, and illustrated books, including the 3,000-work archive of Crown Point Press and special collections of theater and dance designs, Asian miniatures and prints, and early photography.

Visit

Arrayed with neoclassical symmetry around the central rotunda, the 19 main-floor galleries present a selective, chronologically organized survey of medieval to modern European art, including paintings, sculptures, textiles and decorative arts. Large galleries on the terrace (lower) level host temporary exhibitions; works from the Achenbach Foundation for Graphic Arts; and Greek, Etruscan, Roman and Egyptian antiquities and porcelain collections.

A bookstore, cafe and theater are also located on the lower level. **Audio tours** (⊚$7) present collection highlights.

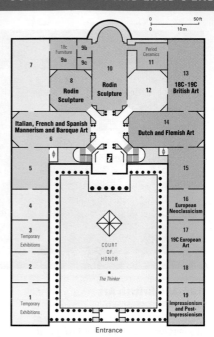

Medieval Art, Mannerism and Baroque Art

Galleries 1–5.

The progressively idealized human form and increasingly secular subject matter of High Renaissance art yielded around 1520 to the figural elongation and harsh coloring associated with Mannerism. El Greco was a master of this style: In his *St. John the Baptist* (c. 1600), a strange play of light, like that of an electrical storm, charges the picture and the elongated central figure.

The Baroque style emerged in Rome around 1600 as a conscious reaction to the artificiality of the Mannerist style, and reflects the period's scientific discoveries, such as the inventions of the telescope and microscope. Representation of movement in space and time, and a fascination with light effects and the emotional state, contribute to the style's vigor and theatricality. Worth note are the Georges de la Tour companion portraits, *Old Man and Old Woman* (c.1618); and *Samson and the Honeycomb* by Il Guercino (c.1657), which exemplifies the Baroque style with rounded forms, individualized faces, blowing trees, and a sumptuous play of light.

The Rococo Style

Galleries 6 and 7.

The Rococo style flourished in mid-18C France. Jean-Antoine Watteau, François Boucher, Jean-Honoré Fragonard and Venetian painter Giovanni Battista Tiepolo all employed a profusion of ornament, asymmetrical motifs, pastel colors and exquisite craftsmanship to create an ambience of pleasure. A **marquetry table** (1680–90) is attributed to French cabinetmaker André-Charles Boulle, who was retained by Louis XIV to create pieces to ornament Versailles.

Rodin Sculpture

Galleries 8, 10 and 12.

Gallery 10 displays large casts of great works by Auguste Rodin, widely considered the "father of modern sculpture." Look for the justly famous *Burghers of Calais* (cast c. 1889), *The Kiss* (cast c. 1887) and *The Three Shades* (cast c. 1880). Rodin's raw, unfinished bases proclaim his struggle to wrest form and meaning from mass—a stylistic trait shared by the sculptor's inspiration, Michelangelo. Sculptures by Rodin contemporaries share gallery 12. Galleries 9 and 11 are period spaces displaying 18C furniture and ormolu-mounted ceramics.

Detail of The Tribute Money (c. 1612) by Peter Paul Rubens

18C–19C British Art

Gallery 13.

Founded in 1768, the Royal Academy of the Arts moved to elevate British painting. Guided by its president, Sir Joshua Reynolds, the academy championed history painting but also encouraged portraiture and landscape. Reynolds' *Anne, Viscountess Townshend* (1779) places the subject against a carved relief suggesting ancient Greece. By the early 19C, landscape painting, thanks in particular to Thomas Gainsborough (*Landscape with Country Carts*, c.1784) and John Constable, emerged as the primary genre. Later artists such as John Martin interpreted the elements in a more dramatic manner. Examples of *chinoiserie* decoration include a scarlet-lacquered bureau-cabinet and a commode by Pierre Langlois.

Dutch and Flemish Art

Galleries 14 and 15.

Protestant Holland and Catholic Flanders split politically in the early 17C, forging divergent artistic styles. In the Netherlands, Rembrandt's school documented the citizenry and their surroundings in portraits, still lifes, landscapes and genre paintings. One fine Rembrandt painting portrays sea captain *Joris de Culerii* (1632). Artists near Flanders continued under the patronage of monarchy and Church, employing richer colors and concentrating on religious subjects. Anthony van Dyck's *Portrait of a Lady* (c.1620) communicates the aristocratic status of its subject, while *The Tribute Money* (c.1612) by Flemish master Peter Paul Rubens employs sumptuous color and drama, expressing a Counter-Reformation mission to attract the faithful. Smaller Dutch pictures, such as Willem van Aelst's remarkable still life *Flowers in a Silver Vase* (1663), detail everyday life in a commercial center, while Flemish works express a connection to aristocracy. Frans Pourbus the Younger's *Portrait of a Lady* (1591), though restrained, depicts rich, fashionable clothing.

European Neoclassicism

Gallery 16.

The excavations of Pompeii and Herculaneum in the mid-18C inspired new enthusiasm for antiquity, expressed in art through the sober elevation of civic virtue and public morality. Jacques-Louis David became a foremost exponent of the new classicism following the exhibition of his *Oath of the Horatii* at the Paris Salon of 1785; two of his paintings are in this gallery. Pierre-Henri de Valenciennes' *A Capriccio of Rome with the Finish of a Marathon* (1788) reflects the classical landscape tradition of the 17C master Poussin. Fine French silver by Martin-Guillaume Biennais and Henri Auguste is also on view here.

19C Painting and Victorian Art
Galleries 17 and 18.

Europe in the 19C witnessed one of the richest and most complex periods in Western art. Reflecting radical changes in social, political and intellectual spheres, a wide variety of artistic styles rapidly evolved. Jean-Baptiste-Camille Corot (*View of Rome: The Bridge and Castel Sant'Angelo with the Cupola of St. Peter's,* c. 1827) pioneered landscapes based on sensations of light and color, influencing the Barbizon School and later the Impressionists. *Equestrian Portrait of Charles V* (c. 1814) by Théodore Géricault displays the restless searching and dash of Romanticism, and Jean-Léon Gérôme's *The Bath* (c. 1880–85) reveals a new exoticism. Tapestries by William Morris, founder of the Arts and Crafts movement in England, hang in Gallery 18.

Impressionism and Post-Impressionism
Gallery 19.

In the late 19C, painters began developing a new visual vocabulary to record their scrutiny of nature and contemporary life. Depicting the transient moment with spontaneous brushwork, blurred outlines and colors in vibrant interrelation, the Impressionists were rejected by the Paris Salon of 1873; in response, they mounted their own, immensely influential exhibition. Realism and themes of modern urban life absorbed artists such as Edgar Degas (*Musicians in the Orchestra,* 1870) and Edouard Manet (*At the Milliner's,* 1881). Works by Pierre-August Renoir, such as *Landscape at Beaulieu* (1893), show the dissolution of outline into warm color. *Eiffel Tower* (1889) reveals Georges Seurat's experimentation with pointillism. Paul Cézanne's *Forest Interior* (c. 1898) anticipates Cubism, rendering a scene from more than one viewpoint.

A great wave of artistic experimentation broke over Europe soon after the beginning of the 20C, inaugurating movements such as Cubism, Futurism, German Expressionism and Surrealism.

Anchored by a late Claude Monet *Water Lilies* (c. 1914–17), the gallery showcases two of Pablo Picasso's stylistic transformations; two paintings demonstrating Henri Matisse's mastery of abstract design and color; and works by other innovative 20C artists such as Georges Braque and Salvador Dalí. A black lacquer and straw table and chairs by Armand-Albert Rateau are also on view.

ADDITIONAL SIGHTS
Sea Cliff★
Entrance from El Camino del Mar at 27th Ave.

Curving, gently sloping streets accommodate this secluded residential enclave's rolling terrain, winding among luxurious Mediterranean-style homes sheathed in brick or pale stucco. Most buildings here date from the 1920s. An early local example of planned residential development, the quiet, elegant neighborhood is one of the city's most desirable addresses.

♣♣ China Beach
End of Seacliff Ave. off El Camino del Mar at 27th Ave. P*Parking available at beach entrance or on El Camino del Mar.*

Fringing a gentle cove, this pleasant strip of sand is one of the few places in the city where swimming is safe, though its cold ocean waters tempt few. Sheltered from the Golden Gate's incessant winds by a jutting headland, the beach was nicknamed for Chinese fishermen who camped here in the 19C. Shower rooms, a broad deck and a small area with tables and barbecue grills make China Beach a favored place for sunning and recreation.

ADDRESSES

CAFE

$ Legion of Honor Café – ✆*415-750-7639. Rest your art-filled senses at this attractive spot on the Legion's terrace level. Lunch on sandwiches, salads, and soups, or nibble on artisan cheeses and delicious desserts.*

Vineyard in Napa Valley
©Peter Wrenn/Michelin

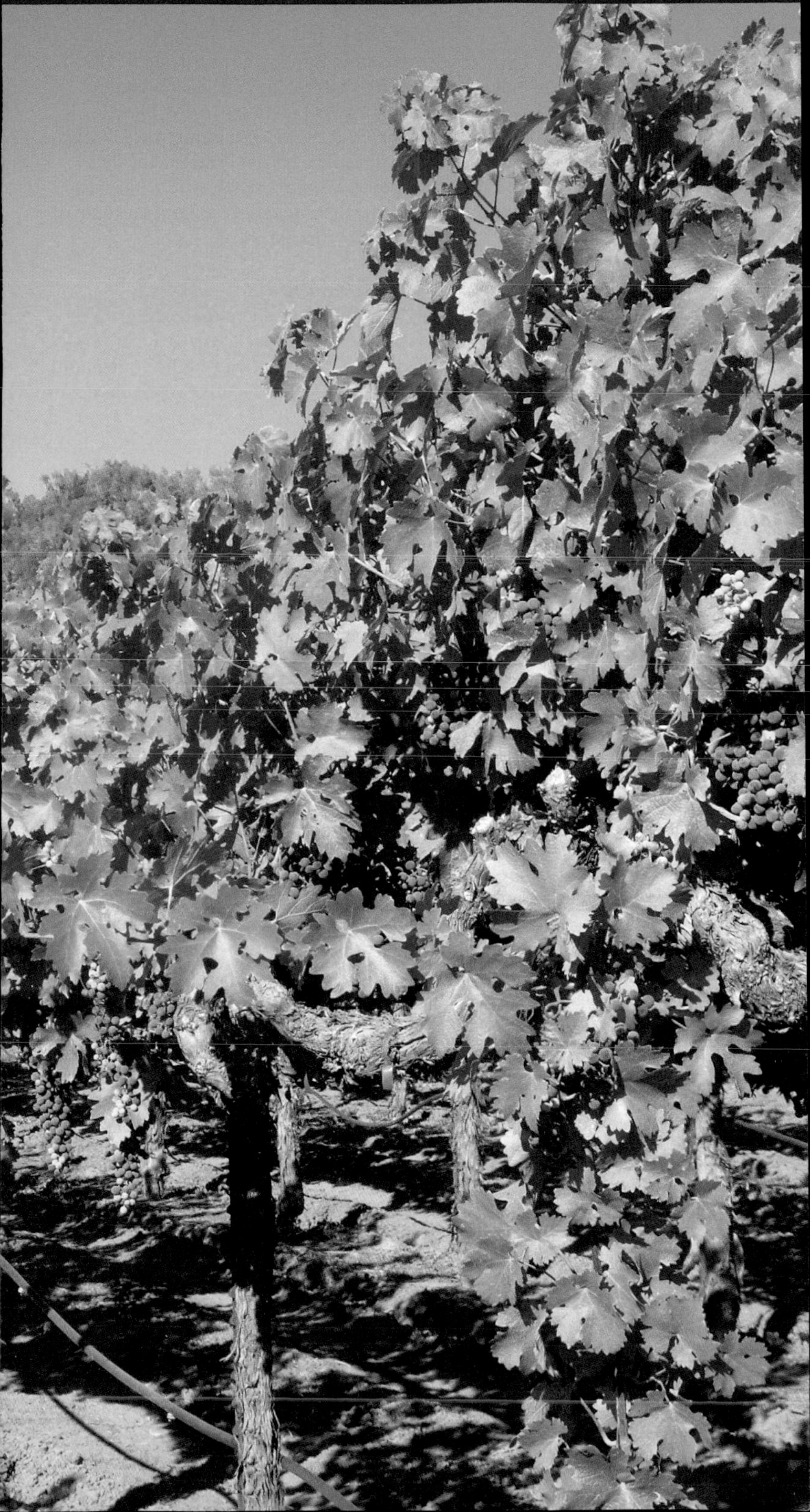

A short hop across the San Francisco–Oakand Bay Bridge or ride on the BART from San Francisco, the neighboring cities of Berkeley and Oakland have their own individual charms. Each is worth a visit in its own right. Berkeley is home to the storied University of California at Berkeley campus, Alice Waters' Chez Panisse restaurant, an impressive botanical garden, and the lovely Tilden Park. Oakland, currently undergoing a major revitalization, boasts a downtown with historic theaters, the recently renovated Oakland Museum of California, as well as an attractive waterfront district.

Highlights

1 Climb the **Campanile** for sweeping views (p211)

2 Stroll through **Sproul Plaza** to the heart of **UC Berkeley** (p214, p208)

3 Explore the **Berkeley Botanical Garden** (p214)

4 Take in a jazz show at **Yoshi's** in **Jack London Square** (p221, p226)

5 Tour the **Oakland Museum of California** (p222)

Berkeley

Synonymous with the renowned University of California at Berkeley, this bohemian college town is Oakland's erudite little sister—a small city with a big reputation for political activism. Things have calmed down here since the Free Speech Movement was launched on Berkeley's campus in the 1960s, but political protests are still not uncommon and the concepts of green and sustainable are taken very seriously. Cruise Telegraph Avenue to experience student life, great bookstores and music shops.

Berkeley has long enjoyed a reputation for attracting intellectuals, idealists, and eccentrics whose diverse tastes have left their mark on the city's history, architecture, and ambience. Alice Waters, a New Jersey native who graduated from UC Berkeley in 1967, changed America's food scene for ever in 1971 when she opened Chez Panisse and gave rise to California cuisine. Today, Waters' restaurant occupies the same Arts and Crafts–style bungalow on a bustling restaurant row on upper Shattuck Avenue known as the Gourmet Ghetto.

Oakland

Named for its expansive growth of oak trees, Oakland was incorporated in 1852 as a quiet bedroom community for the woollier metropolis across the bay. Today, this workaday city is experiencing a renaissance. Businesses have replaced vacant warehouses on downtown blocks, and new office towers and condominium communities have sprung up—with more development on the way. The thanks go in part to former Mayor Jerry Brown, whose 10K Initiative catalyzed retail interest downtown. Here, a vitual gumbo of ethnic restaurants, cafes, and fine-dining establishments caters to taste buds as diverse as the city's population. Meanwhile, despite some persistent problems with crime, new nightclubs and bars, and revitalized shopping districts lure residents and visitors to the downtown core. Local famers' markets eliminate the need for Oakland residents to cross the bay to buy fresh organic produce. Another downtown draw is Jack London Square, a sparkling, pedestrian-friendly complex of shops, restaurants, and entertainment and cultural attractions that nestles along the Oakland Estuary at the site of the once-gritty dock area. The square is named for author Jack London, who spent his early years in Oakland. One of London's favorite watering holes, Heinold's First and Last Chance Saloon, still operates as a bar, though it now ranks on the National Register of Historic Places.

Upscale Rockridge has emerged between Berkeley and Oakland to unite these two metropolitan areas: blocks of restaurants, bars, locally owned boutiques and spas are found on the streets radiating from College Ave.

ADDRESSES

🏠 STAY

$ The French Hotel – *1538 Shattuck Ave., Berkeley.* ☎*510-548-9930. www.french-hotel-berkeley.com. 18 rooms.* Clean, cozy rooms here attract international travelers. Eat at the in-house cafe or wander Berkeley's "Gourmet Ghetto."

All Organic Farmer's Market, North Berkeley's Gourmet Ghetto

$$ Hotel Durant – *2600 Durant Ave., Berkeley.* ☎*510-845-8981. www.hotel durant.com. 144 rooms.* You can almost hear ghosts of students past charge through this renovated six-story 1928 hotel, next to the University of California campus. Historic late-19C and early 20C photos line corridor walls.

$$$ Lafayette Park Hotel – *3287 Mount Diablo Blvd., Lafayette.* ☎*877-283-8787. www.lafayetteparkhotel.com. 138 rooms.* A French provincial-style oasis west of Walnut Creek, this gracious hotel extends its elegance to antique-furnished guestrooms, which surround a trio of courtyards.

$$$ Waterfront Plaza Hotel – *10 Washington St., Oakland.* ☎*510-836-3800. www.waterfrontplaza.com. 143 rooms.* In the heart of Jack London Square, right on the Oakland waterfront, this fine hotel is centrally located for ferry, BART or auto access to attractions throughout the Bay Area.

$$$$ Claremont Hotel, Club & Spa – *41 Tunnel Rd., Berkeley.* ☎*510-843-3000. www.claremontresort.com. 279 rooms.* A mere 20-minute drive from downtown San Francisco, the castle-like Claremont Resort and Spa was considered a country getaway when it opened in 1915. Today,

between the fitness center, full-service spa, tennis club, pools and day camp for kids, there's no excuse to be bored here. Ask for a room in the new wing with its spacious marble baths.

🍽 EAT

$ Bette's Ocean View Diner – *1807 Fourth St. at Delaware St., Berkeley.* ☎*510-644-3230. www.bettesdiner.com. Breakfast and lunch only.* **American**. There's no ocean view, but this classic diner—with its chrome jukebox and model train circling overhead—is a good stop for classic and unusual (soufflé pancakes with chocolate) breakfasts.

$ Picante – *1328 Sixth St., between Gilman & Camelia Sts., Berkeley.* ☎*510-525-3121. www.picanteberkeley.com* **Mexican**. This upscale West Berkeley taqueria gets rave reviews from locals for its fresh ingredients, homemade chorizo tacos, and *tamales* of braised pork, butternut squash, and mild *poblano* chiles.

$$ Bay Wolf – *3853 Piedmont Ave., Oakland.* ☎*510-655-6004. www.bay wolf.com.* **Californian**. Established in 1975, Bay Wolf reigns as a longtime favorite of East Bay residents. The full gamut of Cal-Med dishes contributes to a changing menu, served in a romantic setting in a refurbished Victorian home.

$$$ Oliveto – *5655 College Ave., Oakland.* ☎*510-547-5356. www.oliveto.com.* **Italian**. With an upstairs view on the bustling Rockridge neighborhood, Oliveto offers seasonal Italian cuisine in a country trattoria setting.

$$$$ Chez Panisse – *1517 Shattuck Ave., Berkeley.* ☎*510-548-5525. www.chez panisse.com. Closed Sun.* **Californian**. California cuisine was born in this Craftsman-style restaurant in 1971, under the watchful eye of culinary doyenne Alice Waters. Just-picked organic greens and baby vegetables pair up with free-range meat and fish fresh from the sea to create stellar prix-fixe menus. Upstairs, the more casual Café at Chez Panisse serves simpler—and less expensive—fare for both lunch and dinner.

Berkeley★★

The ultimate college town, Berkeley is remarkable for its academic prowess, political awareness and vibrant artistic and culinary communities. Hub of most of the action is the University of California—locally known as "Cal" or UC Berkeley—which has a student body of 36,000. But other forces are at work too: Though their student days are long past, a good number of hippies and activists from the 1960s have stayed on, giving the area around Telegraph Avenue a laid-back feel. A recent tide of sophisticated San Franciscans have fueled the growth of a "Gourmet Ghetto" on Shattuck Avenue, centered on Alice Waters' legendary Chez Panisse restaurant.
For those who like to stroll or bicycle, the beautiful, tree-filled neighborhoods of Claremont, Elmwood and the North Berkeley hills are well worth exploring.

A BIT OF HISTORY

Like Oakland, the lands of present-day Berkeley pastured cattle before becoming part of Luis María Peralta's Rancho San Antonio in 1820. The land was eventually overtaken by squatters. In 1852, Francis Kittredge Shattuck subdivided lands along the middle course of Strawberry Creek into farms. The nearest town, Ocean View, sprang up more than a mile away along the bay shore. Not until the 1860s, when a site on the upper forks of Strawberry Creek was selected for an institution of higher learning, did shops and hotels begin to sprout along Shattuck's farm road, today's **Shattuck Avenue**.
In 1866 the fledgling community at the edge of the undeveloped campus was named after the Irish bishop and philosopher George Berkeley (1685–1753), author of the oft-quoted line, "Westward the course of empire takes its way." For the next four decades, after it merged with Ocean View, the town grew up steadily around "Cal," as the

Berkeley station.
▶ **Population:** 113,905
Info: Berkeley Visitor Information Center (2030 Addison St., Ste.102; open Mon–Fri 9am–5pm; closed major holidays; ♿ 510-549-7040 or 800-847-4823; www.visitberkeley.com), or **UC Berkeley Visitor Center** (101 Sproul Hall, near Bancroft Way & Telegraph Ave.; open Mon–Fri 8.30am–4.30pm; closed Dec 25–Jan 1; ♿ 510-642-5215; visitors.berkeley.edu).
Location: University Ave. leads from the bayshore east to the UC campus; Shattuck Ave. runs north-south at the campus' western edge. The campus lies between the flatlands, where streets are on a grid, and the foothills, where they follow the contours of the hills. A view from UC Berkeley's Campanile is an excellent way to get the lay of the land.
Kids: Tilden Park hosts a petting zoo and miniature train rides.
Timing: Berkeley's restaurants and cafes hum from morning to night. Check the Berkeley Repertory Theater's schedule to coordinate your visit with a play.
Parking: Paid garages are on the south and east sides of campus; most street parking is metered. We recommend taking BART to the Berkeley Station, then walk or take the campus shuttle.
Don't Miss: The campanile and a stroll in the botanic gardens.

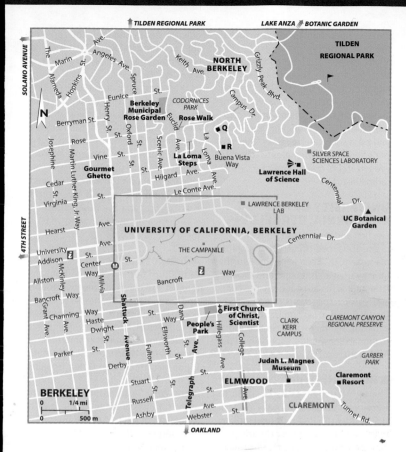

university is called. In the aftermath of San Francisco's great earthquake and fire of 1906, a tidal wave of new settlers flooded Berkeley.

Cultural Ferment – Berkeley has long enjoyed a reputation for attracting intellectuals, idealists and eccentrics whose diverse and often highly cultivated tastes have left their mark on the city's history, architecture and ambience. While Beaux-Arts aesthetics and pockets of greenery became the hallmark of campus architecture in the early 20C, builders beyond the university property integrated leafy yards and landscaped footpaths with neighborhoods of highly original and imaginative architecture. A gastronomic version of this passion for art and nature swept Berkeley in 1971 when Alice Waters opened her famed Chez Panisse restaurant, giving rise to California Cuisine and lending the moniker **Gourmet Ghetto** to upper Shattuck Avenue *(between Rose and Virginia Sts.)*. Today Berkeley revels in its numerous fine restaurants—including a rich array of ethnic eateries—located on Shattuck and in the neighborhoods along **Solano Avenue★** in north Berkeley, **Telegraph Avenue★** just south of the UC campus, and behind the early 20C storefronts of the **Elmwood** shopping district *(along College Ave. at the intersection of Ashby Ave.)*. Bookstores, cinemas, coffee houses and craft shops also thrive in these areas.

In particular, the erstwhile industrial sector along **4th Street** *(north of University Ave.)* has become a popular shopping area with an upscale edge.

Just off this strip, Takara Sake U.S.A. *(708 Addison St.; ☎510-540-8250)* offers sips of Sho Chiku Bai in the tasting room of the largest sake brewery in the U.S.

Berkeley's penchant for idealism fueled the student protest movements of the 1960s, spreading its reputation as a hotbed of radicalism. Though now considerably mellowed from the late 70s and early 80s—when the city government cultivated its own foreign policy, promoted itself as a model for socialism, and was widely referred to as "the People's Republic of Berkeley"—the city today retains many reminders of its radical heyday.

UNIVERSITY OF CALIFORNIA, BERKELEY★★

The first and most prestigious campus of the acclaimed University of California system, UC Berkeley is noteworthy for its varied architecture and profuse landscaping, its outstanding museums and research collections, its notoriety in the 1960s and 70s as a hotbed of student activism, and its myriad contributions to human knowledge, especially in the field of nuclear physics.

A BIT OF HISTORY

The university owes its creation to clergymen scholars from the eastern U.S., led by the Rev. Samuel Hopkins Willey and the Rev. Henry Durant, who chartered the College of California in Oakland in 1854. Seeking to expand two years later, the trustees acquired lands on the twin forks of Strawberry Creek, officially dedicating their enterprise in 1861 at **Founders' Rock (1)**, still visible on campus today *(corner of Hearst Ave. & Gayley Rd.)*.

In 1864, landscape architect Frederick Law Olmsted was commissioned to plan the college grounds and an adjacent residential neighborhood. Olmsted aligned the campus on an east-west axis, but a shortage of funds curtailed construction of this initial plan. In 1867, the college merged with the state-sponsored Agricultural, Mining and Mechanical Arts College, and the new institution was dedicated the following year as the University of California.

Athens of the West

At the turn of the 19C, noted philanthropist and university regent **Phoebe Apperson Hearst** financed a competition to expand construction of the main campus "with landscape gardening and architecture forming one composition." Supported by Hearst's money and state funds, architect John Galen Howard set out to make Berkeley the "Athens of the West," establishing Beaux-Arts as the hallmark architectural style with a phalanx of white granite buildings sporting red-tile roofs and Neoclassical ornamentation. In the course of expansions during the first half of the 20C, campus architecture diversified with the addition of buildings by such

The Campanile of UC Berkeley with a view to San Francisco Bay

© Rafael Ramirez / Fotolia.com

UC Berkeley campus, looking southwest from the Campanile

© Steve McConnell / UC Berkeley

noteworthy architects as Bernard Maybeck, Julia Morgan, George Kelham and Arthur Brown, Jr.

In addition to its 178-acre main campus, the university embraces 1,054 acres in the steep Berkeley Hills, including lands occupied by the Lawrence Berkeley Lab (*⚲ not open to the public*). Founded by Ernest O. Lawrence (1901–1958) as the Radiation Laboratory in 1936, the laboratory housed several progressively more powerful cyclotrons that fueled profound breakthroughs in 20C physics, including Glenn Seaborg's 1941 discovery of plutonium, an event that heralded the Atomic Age.

Today, with 14 separate colleges and schools, 1,582 fulltime faculty members and an ethnically diverse student body that numbers some 36,000, UC Berkeley ranks among the nation's leading universities. Many of its graduate programs are annually rated at or near the top of national standings, and Berkeley graduates earn more PhDs than those of any other American university. Nine Nobel laureates are among the current faculty: Five physicists, one chemist, and three economists. The campus is an active center of culture and sport; the year's biggest sporting event is the November football game against cross-bay

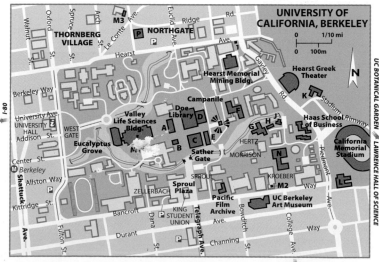

UNIVERSITY OF CALIFORNIA, BERKELEY

archrival Stanford University—called, simply, The Big Game.

VISIT

Most of UC Berkeley's buildings lie within the rectangle described by Oxford Street, Hearst Avenue, Gayley Road and Bancroft Way. Near the intersection of Bancroft Way and Telegraph Avenue is Sproul Hall, home to the campus **Visitor Center**, which offers offers daily **guided tours** (*Mon–Fri 10am, meet at the visitor center; Sat 10am & Sun 1pm, meet at the Campanile; reservations required*) of the campus.

There are parking garages at Oxford and Kittridge Streets and at Telegraph Street and Channing Ave. *(www.ci.berkeley. ca.us)*, but public transport is also an option: the Berkeley BART station is only one block from campus, and the university runs shuttle buses around the perimeter of campus and from the Mining Circle up to the Lawrence Hall of Science and the Botanical Garden (*operates Mon–Fri 7.30am–7pm; $1; 510-643-7701*).

👣 WALKING TOUR

▷ Begin at West Gate (Oxford St. between University Ave. and Center St.).

Planted in 1877, the **Eucalyptus Grove** on the south side of University Drive contains the tallest hardwood trees in North America. Some measure nearly 200ft high.

Valley Life Sciences Building★

The largest academic building in the nation when it was completed (1930, George Kelham), this massive pseudo-Egyptian "temple" to science supports dense rows of immense pilasters; it is intriguingly decorated with bas-relief tableaux, American bison skulls, sabertooth tiger heads, griffins and other designs. The interior houses laboratories and world-class natural-history specimen collections, including the **Museum of Paleontology★ (M1)** 👥♿ (*open

during academic session Mon–Thu 8am–10pm, Fri 8am–5pm, Sat 10am–5pm, Sun 1–10pm; call for hours in summer; ♿ 510-642-1821; www.ucmp.berkeley. edu*). Though only a small portion is on public display, this is one of the oldest (1921), largest and most important research collections in the country, with more than five million invertebrates and 135,000 catalogued vertebrate specimens, including the largest triceratops skull ever found, an ichthyosaur skeleton and the assembled skeleton of a *Tyrannosaurus rex*. Specimens are on view in the Wallace Atrium and on the second floor; consult the museum's website for more extensive online exhibits.

▷ Walk east of the building on the pedestrian walkway, past the flagpole. Beyond California Hall, turn uphill toward the Campanile.

Campanile Way passes among a quartet of monumental Neoclassical structures, all designed by John Galen Howard, including **California Hall (A)** (1905), **Durant Hall (B)** (1912) and **Wheeler Hall (C)** (1918), headquarters of the English department. The grandest of the four structures, **Doe Library★** (1911; additions in 1917 and 1995) recalls a Roman temple with a Corinthian colonnade on its northern facade.

On the ground floor, the wood-paneled **Morrison Library** provides a cozy haven for casual readers. Upstairs, note

Heyns Reading Room, Doe Library

© Steve McConnell / UC Berkeley

The Free Speech Movement

As early as the 1930s, UC students had railed against social injustice. But political events of the 50s and 60s stirred a stronger reaction and fueled Berkeley's reputation for radical behavior.

The first rumblings of the Free Speech Movement began with opposition to the House Un-American Activities Committee hearings of Sen. Joseph McCarthy and the would-be invasion of Cuba's Bay of Pigs during the Kennedy Administration. Soon civil-rights marches and Vietnam War protests catapulted the city to the forefront of national attention. On Sept. 30, 1964, the university's Board of Regents called in police to break up a peaceful sit-in demonstration by students of Sproul Plaza. Subsequent years were marked by a campaign of harsh reprisals against students who dared to declare their right to self-expression. Governor Ronald Reagan sent riot police and the National Guard to squelch demonstrations with tear-gas assaults, mass arrests and even a 17-day campus occupation.

Conflict reached its apex in spring 1969, when Berkeley residents attempted to turn an abandoned piece of university land, three blocks south of the campus, into "Power to the People Park." Trees and flowers were planted in April, but a month later, the Regents re-staked their claim by having fences built around the park. Rioting predictably ensued, with hundreds injured and one man killed by a stray bullet. The fence was not removed until 1972. People's Park is today an unstated and unspectacular memorial to that epoch.

the barrel-vaulted Reference Room and the old circulation hall with its magnificent coffered bronze ceiling and suspended lamps.

Bancroft Library(D)

🕐*Open during academic session Mon–Fri 10am–5pm, between sessions Mon–Fri 1–5pm.* ♿ 📞*510-642-3781. http://bancroft.berkeley.edu.*

This annex (1948, Arthur Brown, Jr.) on the east side of the Doe Library stores rare books, manuscripts, archival materials and special collections, including the country's largest assemblage of manuscripts, notebooks and papers belonging to author Mark Twain. The Bancroft is famed for its holdings of Western Americana. Treasures periodically rotated through the library anteroom include paintings of the old West, first editions and printed posters.

South of the Bancroft Library stands the oldest building on campus, the red-brick **South Hall (E)** (1873, David Farquharson), built in the French Second Empire style. Once the university president's office, the building now houses the School of Information.

▷ Ascend the stairs to the Campanile.

👥 The Campanile (Sather Tower)★★

🕐*Open Mon–Fri 10am–3.45pm, Sat 10am–4.45pm, Sun 10am–1.30pm, 3–4.45pm.* 🕐*Closed Dec 25–Jan 1.* 💰*$2.*

Modeled on the bell tower in Venice's St. Marks Square, this 307ft, steel-framed, granite-clad shaft (1914, John Galen Howard) is crowned by a quartet of obelisks surmounted with bronze urns, and a soaring central spire capped by a bronze lantern. A memorial to university benefactor Jane K. Sather, the Campanile houses a carillon of 61 bells. From its open-air observation platform, arched windows frame panoramic **views★★** of the Berkeley hills, downtown Oakland, San Francisco Bay and the intriguing geometry of the campus. When school is in session, carillonists at a keyboard play the bells from an enclosure at the platform's center in a fascinating, if deafening, performance (🕐*concerts daily 7.50am, noon and 6pm; longer concert Sun 2pm*).

▷ Walk north from the Campanile, turning right at the first corner.

Hearst Memorial Mining Building

This granite-clad Beaux-Arts building (1907, John Galen Howard and Julia Morgan) was named for Sen. George Hearst, who made his fortune in mining. The facade bears three archways and a row of corbels carved to resemble men and women straining to support the massive wooden cornices. It houses offices, laboratories and classrooms.

▷ Walk south across Mining Circle and cross University Dr.

The route passes the back of **Le Conte Hall (F)**, the physics building where J. Robert Oppenheimer (1904–67), Edward Teller and other physicists drafted a blueprint of the first atomic bomb in the summer of 1942.

▷ Turn right, then left, crossing Strawberry Creek under an arch with a Latin inscription, and over a concrete footbridge.

At the lush green known as Faculty Glade, a path beside Strawberry Creek leads east behind the partially wood-shingled **Faculty Club (G)** (1902, Bernard Maybeck), which blends beautifully with the surrounding oaks, laurels and redwoods. After crossing and recrossing the creek on adjacent bridges, pass behind the redwood log **Senior Hall (H)** (1906, John Galen Howard) and turn left onto a path that leads past the cabin to the brown-shingled **Women's Faculty Club (J)** (1923, John Galen Howard), ensconced in a pretty English garden.

▷ Pass along the front of the club, climb steps and cross to ascend a broad stairway on the north side of Cheit Hall.

The assemblage of buildings constituting the **Haas School of Business★** (1995, Moore/Ruble/Yudell/VBN) projects the atmosphere of a prosperous quar-

ter in a north German city, complete with street lamps, gabled roofline, multi-paned windows and an enclosed parapet walk above its arching western gateway. Pass under the eastern portal arch to Piedmont Avenue, and look left to the concrete, Tudor Revival "castle" of **Bowles Hall (K)** (1929, George Kelham), rising magnificently on a hillside and surmounted by chimneys, gables and steep red-tiled roofs.

Hidden by trees a little farther to the north, the 8,500-seat outdoor **Hearst Greek Theater** (1903, John Galen Howard and Julia Morgan) was modeled after the ancient amphitheater at Epidarus. Directly across the street stands **California Memorial Stadium** (1923, John Galen Howard), home field for the Cal Bears football team.

▷ Turn right and walk to Bancroft Ave.

International House (L)

2299 Piedmont Ave. ╳ ⴵ ☏ *510-642-9490. http://ihouse.berkeley.edu.*
Iberian flourishes highlight this residential and cultural center (1930, George Kelham), the Berkeley branch of a movement to encourage cultural exchange between Americans and foreigners. A Moorish domed tower and balconies dominate the exterior. Many of the large public rooms reveal traditional Spanish decorative elements such as red-tile floors, carved-wood doors and iron chandeliers.

▷ Walk down the south side of Bancroft Way.

UC Berkeley Art Museum and Pacific Film Archive★

2626 Bancroft Way. ⏰ *Open Wed–Sun 11am–5pm, some Fri until 9pm.* ⏰ *Closed university holidays.* ⴹ *$10; $7 some Fri after 5pm (free first Thu of the month).* ╳ ⴵ ☏ *510-642-0808. www.bampfa.berkeley.edu.*
Housing one of the largest university art collections in the U.S., the UC Berkeley Art Museum was born in 1963 when Abstract Expressionist painter Hans

© Steve McConnell / UC Berkeley

Hearst Greek Theater

Hofmann (1880–1966), having left Nazi Germany with the aid of two UC professors, donated 45 paintings and $250,000 to the university.

After a 1997 inspection showed that its distinctive home (1970, Mario Ciampi, Richard Jorasch, and Ronald Wagner) did not meet seismic standards, the museum announced plans for a new museum *(projected completion late 2014)* at Oxford and Center Streets near the university's western entrance.

In addition to Hofmann's work, the 16,000-piece permanent collection is strong in 20C art, pre-20C European painting, Asian ceramics and painting, and a mix of contemporary art and sculpture. The museum also hosts special exhibitions.

Associated with the museum, the renowned **Pacific Film Archive★** preserves 14,000 films, videos and rare prints of classic films emphasizing Japanese, Soviet and American art cinema. In 2009 the archive was selected to house the Film Arts Foundation's media archive, posters, and publications. Screenings are held year-round nightly at its theater across the street at 2575 Bancroft Way (*☏510-642-1124; ⊙$9.50).

▶ Backtrack up Bancroft Ave. to College Ave. Cross the street to Kroeber Hall.

Phoebe A. Hearst Museum of Anthropology (M2)

102 Kroeber Hall. ⊘*Temporarily closed for renovation until 2014.* ♿ ☏*510-643-7648. http://hearstmuseum. berkeleyedu.*

Among the country's most significant anthropological research museums, the Hearst was established around a core collection obtained in a series of expeditions funded by Phoebe Apperson Hearst, starting in 1899. Today the **collections★** have grown to contain nearly four million artifacts from around the world, with emphasis on California archaeology, ancient Peru, Classical Greece and Italy, ancient Egypt, Central American textiles and ethnological artifacts from West Africa, Oceania and the Arctic and sub-Arctic regions. Selections from the permanent collection are displayed in two exhibits. "From the Maker's Hand" contains objects and artifacts from antiquity to the present, many from China and Africa. "Native Californian Cultures" displays 500 indigenous objects in large glass cases.

Rising across the courtyard northeast of Kroeber Hall, the 10-story concrete **Wurster Hall (N)** (1964, DeMars, Escherick, Olsen) is a striking example of the Brutalist style.

▶ Passing between Morrison and Hertz Halls, turn left at Faculty Glade and follow the creek downstream.

Pause at the wall of the old brick powerhouse to admire Byzantine-inspired mosaics created in 1936 by WPA-sponsored artists Helen Bruton and Florence Swift.

▶ Continue west to Sproul Plaza.

Sather Gate

Spanning the broad pedestrian entrance to the main campus, this monumental, filigreed bronze gateway (1910, John Galen Howard) arches between four granite pillars capped by banded glass globes.

Telegraph Avenue once met the campus at Sather Gate, but the commercial zone was cleared to Bancroft Avenue in the 1950s and replaced in 1960 by **Sproul Plaza★**. Best known as the site of student protests in the 1960s and 70s, the plaza draws students, musicians and other entertainers, protesters, political campaigners, street preachers and eccentrics of every stripe. Commemorating its revolutionary birthright, a 6in circle at the center of the plaza is ceremonially declared an extraterritorial zone "not subject to any entity's jurisdiction." On the plaza's east side stands Sproul Hall, which houses university administrative offices.

The Martin Luther King, Jr. Student Union complex on the west side contains food services, bookstores, sundry shops. To the west is Zellerbach Auditorium, the university's largest enclosed performance venue.

ADDITIONAL SIGHTS ON CAMPUS
UC Botanical Garden★

200 Centennial Dr. ◷ *Open daily 9am–5pm.* ◷ *Closed 1st Tue of each month, Jan 1, Martin Luther King Jr. Day, Thanksgiving Day, Dec 24, 25 & 31.* ⊜ *$10 (free 1st Thu of the month).* ⌁ *Guided tours (1hr) available Thu, Sat and Sun 1.30pm.* ♿ ℗ ℘ *510-643-2755. http://botanicalgarden. berkeley.edu.*

Some 19,000 plants of more than 9,600 species grace the slopes of Strawberry Canyon in a sylvan setting above the main campus, overlooking the bay. Most of the garden is organized geographically, representing flora of Asia, Africa, the Mediterranean and Europe, New Zealand, Australia, Meso-America, North America and California.

Thematic gardens nurture palms and cycads, old roses and Chinese medicinal herbs. A sequoia forest and redwood grove are located across Centennial Drive.

♟♟ Lawrence Hall of Science

1 Centennial Dr. ◷ *Open daily 10am–5pm.* ◷ *Closed Thanksgiving Day, Dec 25.* ⊜ *$12; children ages 7–18 $9; ages 3–6 $6.* ✕ ℗ ℘ *510-642-5132. www. lawrencehallofscience.org.*

Sather Gate

© Richard Nowitz / Apa Publications

Dramatically situated high in the Berkeley hills, this futuristic museum (1968, Anshen and Allen) is dedicated to teaching children about physics, biology, chemistry, navigation, mathematics, computers and lasers through interactive exhibits, laboratories and a comprehensive program of classes. The planetarium complements an active Saturday-night astronomy program. Frequently changing temporary exhibits explore a variety of science topics ranging from prehistoric life to space travel, recent exhibits have explored the physics of roller coasters and the geologic forces that shape the San Francisco Bay. The **view**★★ from the front patio overlooks much of the northern Bay Area.

UC Botanical Garden

© www.VisitBerkeley.com

SIGHTS IN BERKELEY
Telegraph Avenue★

Between Bancroft and Dwight Ways.
From morning through late evening this compelling thoroughfare flows with students, bibliophiles, crafts sellers, street people and tourists, all of whom frequent its many coffeehouses, bookstores, eateries and shops.

East of the avenue, sandwiched between Dwight Way and Haste Street, **People's Park** remains a potent symbol of Berkeley radicalism. Seized from the university by students and political activists in 1969, the park sparked a series of riots between police and protesters before a sort of truce was reached, in which the city of Berkeley manages the property in partnership with the university. Some space today has been turned into community gardens. Many of the city's homelesss camp out in the park.

First Church of Christ, Scientist★★

2619 Dwight Way at Dana St. •◦Visit *by guided tour (45min) only 1st Sun of each month 12.15pm. Public services Sun 11am.* ♿ 🅿 ☏ 510-845-7199. *www.friendsoffirstchurch.org.*
Bernard Maybeck's masterwork (1910) harmonized a wealth of styles, yet copied none, in a unique Arts and Crafts structure of unsurpassing beauty and serenity. The church fuses multiple roof-lines with Spanish tiles and rectangular, fluted columns. In the shape of a Greek cross, the sunken auditorium is naturally lit by side windows and diagonally spanned with arching beams, imparting a feeling of great spaciousness. The milled woodwork in the ceiling beams and the interior furnishings, all of which Maybeck himself designed, show exquisite craftsmanship.

The Magnes Collection of Jewish Art and Life★

2121 Allston Way 🕐 *Tue–Fri 11am–4pm.* 🕐*Closed major & Jewish holidays.* 💰*$6 suggested donation.* •◦*Guided tours available.* ☏*510-643-2526. www.magnes.org.*
Recently relocated near the university campus, the Magnus Collection of Jewish Art and Life is the nation's third-largest museum of Jewish history and art. Named for a prominent San Francisco rabbi, the museum sponsors changing exhibits *(main level)* highlighting Jewish history and the works of 19C and 20C Jewish artists and photographers. Galleries on the upper level are reserved for rotating exhibits of ceremonial and cultural items from the museum collections, including Hanukkah lamps, Torah pointers, wedding robes, Torah cases and arks, and Sephardic artifacts from around the world.

Claremont Hotel, Club & Spa

© Claremont Hotel, Club & Spa

Claremont Resort★

41 Tunnel Rd., end of Ashby Ave.
🕐Open daily. ✕&🅿 ☎510-843-3000.
www.claremontresort.com.

Looming like a white castle in the hills between Berkeley and Oakland, this stately old hotel (1915, Charles Dickey) forms the centerpiece of an upscale resort. A reputation for dullness dogged the hotel for many years, largely because laws forbade the sale of liquor within a mile of the UC Berkeley campus. An enterprising student actually measured the distance in 1936 and discovered that the southern end of the hotel lay beyond the mile radius; the following year, the Terrace Lounge opened on the "wet" side of the invisible line. (The Claremont rewarded the student with free drinks for the rest of her life.) International tournaments have been played on the hotel's 10 tennis courts, and its full-service spa draws a devoted following.

▲▲ Tilden Regional Park

▶ *From Berkeley take Spruce St. north to Grizzly Peak Blvd., cross and make a sharp left on Cañon Dr. Follow signs to the Nature Area. 🕐Open daily dawn–dusk. ▲✕&🅿 ☎510-544-2747.*
www.ebparks.org.

Sprawling over 2,079 acres on the eastern side of the ridge above Berkeley, this predominantly undeveloped preserve offers varied attractions to people of all ages, including swimming and fishing in **Lake Anza,** golf, picnicking, group camping, hiking trails, a petting zoo, a carousel and miniature train rides. Also here are the walking paths of the 740-acre **Tilden Nature Area** (🕐open daily 5am–10pm; &🅿 ☎510-544-2233), whose Environmental Education Center hosts a wide variety of naturalist programs. Next door stands the Little Farm (🕐open daily 8.30am–3.30pm), which delights kids with its live animals.

Also within the park, the 10-acre **Botanic Garden** (🕐open daily June–Sept 8.30am–5.30pm, Oct–May 8.30am–5pm; ☎510-544-3169) cultivates the world's largest collection of California native plants. Landscaped on picturesque terraces along the banks of Wildcat Creek, the garden's more-than-1,500 species are divided into 11 separate sections that correspond with geographical regions of the state.

Northgate

This neighborhood was named for its location immediately outside the north entrance to the University of California campus. Above the first block of Euclid Avenue, lined with pleasant shops and restaurants, the rise where Ridge Road intersects with Le Conte Avenue has been dubbed "Holy Hill" for its uncanny concentration of theological schools. Paramount among the venerable institutions is the Graduate Theological Union *(2465 Le Conte Ave.),* a Georgian

Revival mansion built of red clinker-brick in the 1920s. The GTU administers a union of nine schools and 1,300 students as well as the **Flora Lamson Hewlett Library (P)** *(2400 Ridge Rd.; ℘510-649-2500)*, one of the country's largest theological collections.

Walter J. Ratcliff's Holbrook Building *(1798 Scenic Ave.)*, an impressive Tudor Revival structure, is part of the Pacific School of Religion, oldest seminary in the western U.S. Its **Badè Museum of Biblical Archaeology (M3)** displays a fine collection of Old Testament (1000–800 BC) antiquities. They were excavated in the early 20C by Dr. William Badè at Tell en-Nasbeh (thought to have been the biblical Mizpah of Benjamin) in Israel *(○open Tue, Thu and Fri 10am–3pm ○closed major holidays, last week in Dec; guided tours by reservation at least 2 weeks in advance; ♿ ℘510-849-8286; http://bade.psr.edu)*.

The museum also features a collection of 300 historic Bibles from the 15C–18C, a gallery of contemporary theological art and a table that once belonged to naturalist John Muir.

Thornberg Village★, better known locally as Normandy Village *(1817–1839 & 1781–1783 Spruce St.)*, lies two blocks west of Holy Hill. Erected in 1927–28 in "Hansel and Gretel" style by William R. Yelland, the residential complex is a storybook fantasy of Gothic arches and towers, eccentrically peaked rooflines, carved-wood gargoyles, cobbled drives and meandering stairways.

North Berkeley Hills

Long a magnet for well-educated residents, the steep hills north of the UC Berkeley campus earned their reputation for high aestheticism after the turn of the 20C. Encouraged by the Hillside Club, a social organization with strong interests in preserving the natural beauty of the hills, developers introduced landscaped footpaths to complement the Arts and Crafts and brown-shingled houses that dominated the neighborhood. When a wild-fire destroyed between 500 and 600 neighborhood homes in 1923, many

residents rebuilt in an eclectic array of period revival styles inspired by Norman castles, Swiss chalets, Spanish missions, Italian villas, and Japanese and classic Greek temples.

Today the area offers pleasant if strenuous strolls along its streets and paths, including **Rose Walk** *(linking Euclid & LeRoy Aves.)* and **La Loma Steps** *(between LeRoy Ave. & Buena Vista Way)*. At the heart of the neighborhood, the four-acre **Berkeley Municipal Rose Garden★** *(Euclid Ave. north of Bayview Pl.)* flourishes on terraces that descend down the canyon of Codornices Creek. The garden was completed in 1937, and today contains more than 3,000 rose bushes of 250 species. One spectacularly eccentric house, the **Hume Cloister (Q)** *(2900 Buena Vista Way)*, replicates a 13C French monastery. An even more unusual structure, the **Temple of the Wings (R)** *(2800 Buena Vista Way)* with a pair of Corinthian colonnades joined to a central dance stage, was designed by Bernard Maybeck and completed in 1914.

ADDRESSES

TAKING A BREAK

Peet's Coffee & Tea – *2124 Vine St. at Walnut St. ℘510-841-0564. www.peets. com.* Berkeley-born Peet's places nearly as much value upon educating customers about coffee as it does to making a sale. Bean up at this three-decade-old anchor store of the popular chain while perusing the wide variety of coffee fixings and paraphernalia for sale.

SHOPPING

BOOKSTORES ON TELEGRAPH

Great bookstores can be found between Haste Street and Dwight Way: **Moe's** *(no. 2476; ℘510-849-2087; www.moesbooks.com)* sells used books on four floors; an antiquarian section occupies the top floor. Down the block, **Shakespeare & Co.** *(no. 2499; ℘510-841-8916)* stocks its tall shelves and narrow aisles with used books and discounted review copies.

Oakland★

Directly across the bay from San Francisco, linked to it by the San Francisco-Oakland Bay Bridge, bustling Oakland boasts a large and busy port, gleaming waterfront, and civic-center districts. Also found here is an exceptional museum and a profusion of ambitiously restored mid-19C–20C residential and commercial buildings.

A BIT OF HISTORY

Part of a 44,800-acre ranch from 1820 to the Gold Rush, Oakland was incorporated on May 4, 1852. The arrival of the **transcontinental railroad** in 1869 established the city as a regional transportation hub, and businesses sprang up along 8th, 9th and Washington Streets—the area today known as Old Oakland. When the 1906 earthquake and fire devastated San Francisco, Oakland sheltered more than 150,000 refugees, many of whom elected to remain. Skyscrapers grew up along Broadway through the early 20C, and in 1936 the city was joined to San Francisco by the Bay Bridge, the largest civil engineering project of the time. Oakland's population grew by a third during the years of World War II when the Kaiser Shipyards attracted thousands of workers. With the end of the war, however, came economic decline and social unrest. In the 1960s Oakland suffered through race riots and rising rates of urban poverty and violent crime. Natural disasters also took their toll—the Loma Prieta earthquake of 1989 collapsed the "Cypress Structure" section of the double-deck I-880 freeway through West Oakland, while a devastating hill fire in 1991 razed substantial residential areas.

A Gradual Rebuilding – Although vacant storefronts continue to haunt Broadway, major civil-engineering programs have brought a measure of recovery to downtown. The expanded, modernized **Port of Oakland** now ranks among the top 20 in the world. In addition, the opening of eight BART stations in Oakland in 1974, the re-establishment of passenger ferry

12th Street/City Center or Lake Merritt station. Alameda/Oakland ferry to Jack London Square.

▶ **Population:** 395,817

Info: ✆510-839-9000. www.oaklandcvb.com, www.oaklandnet.com.

Location: Most Oakland sights are located along the waterfront and within the square formed by I-880 and I-980 and Lake Merritt. All are within (lengthy) walking distances of each other. You'll need a car or public transporation to get to the Additional Sights.

Kids: The Chabot Space & Science Center and the Oakland Zoo are geared toward families. Children's Fairyland is fun for very young visitors.

Timing: Downtown Oakland bustles only during weekday business hours, the best time to visit the area. The waterfront area is a pleasure to explore on foot throughout the day, though the Oakland Produce Market is best seen in the early morning. Visit the Old Oakland Farmers' Market on Friday mornings.

Parking: Parking is available in downtown Oakland garages. BART's 12th Street/City Center station is convenient to downtown, Chinatown, and Old Oakland. The Lake Merritt station accesses the Oakland Museum of California and the south side of Lake Merritt. Jack London Square offers abundant garage parking.

Don't Miss: The Oakland Museum of California.

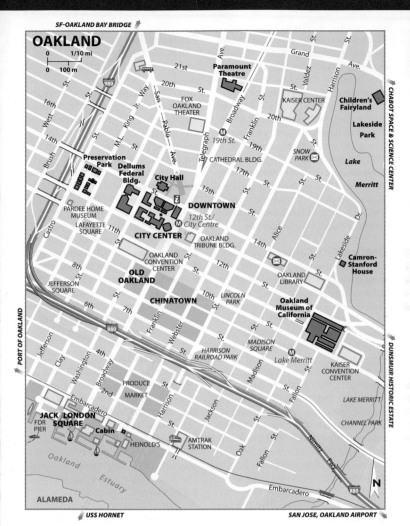

service to San Francisco in 1989, and the completion of a new Amtrak passenger station in 1995 renewed Oakland's traditional role as a Bay Area transportation center. The City Center and Jack London Square areas underwent massive redevelopment in the 1980s. Meanwhile, the city has aggressively preserved its rich architectural heritage, buying and refurbishing scores of Victorian and 20C houses and commercial buildings in Old Oakland and Preservation Park. Gentrified neighborhood shopping precincts, including **Piedmont Avenue** (between MacArthur Blvd. and Pleasant Valley Ave.) and **College Avenue** in the Rockridge district, attract shoppers and diners by day and evening.

DOWNTOWN

🚇 12th St./City Center station.
🚶 Free 90min guided walking tours of downtown Oakland are offered May–Oct Wed & Sat at 10am; reservations recommended but not required. ☎510-238-3234. www.oaklandnet.com/walkingtours.

City Hall

1 Frank Ogawa Plaza. 🕑Open Mon–Fri 9am–5pm. 🕑Closed major holidays. ♿ ☎510-444-2489.

The present-day center of downtown Oakland was ordained by city planners to be the dynamic intersection where Broadway, San Pablo Avenue and 14th Street converged. Since the opening of City Center in the 1980s, the focus of business has shifted one block south. A vaulting symbol of the city's progressive spirit, when it was completed in 1914 (Palmer, Hornbostel & Jones), City Hall's 18-story shaft rises from a three-story Beaux Arts podium, capped by a Baroque-style clock tower. Inside, an elegant staircase leads from the lobby to a third-floor Council Chamber.

Oakland City Center★

Between Broadway and 12th, 14th, and Clay Sts. ✕&◨ *℘510-628-9170. www.oaklandcitycenter.com.*
The pleasantly landscaped John B. Williams Plaza conducts pedestrians via escalators upward from the sunken BART station to this open-air mall. At its center stands a brightly painted metal **sculpture (1)** by Roslyn Mazzilli entitled *There* (1988). The title is a jocular allusion to Gertrude Stein's famous (and usually misinterpreted as spiteful) observation—"There is no there there"—following a visit to her childhood hometown. To the west, three-story rows of modern commercial buildings frame a view of the Federal Building's twin towers.
East from the plaza, sight lines converge on the 21-story **Oakland Tribune Building** *(13th and Franklin Sts.).* The jaunty landmark (1923, Edward Foulkes), housed the offices of *The Oakland Tribune* until the newspaper moved to Jack London Square in 1992.

Ronald Y. Dellums Federal Building★

Between 12th, 14th, Clay & Jefferson Sts.
This monumental, twin-towered structure is the largest building in Alameda County. Completed in 1993, the limestone-clad towers are linked by a 75ft glass rotunda that serves as a lobby. A marble-and-granite map of the Bay Area spreads across the rotunda floor.

Preservation Park

13th St. and Martin Luther King, Jr. Way. ℘510-874-7580. www.preservation park.com.
These 16 splendidly landscaped Victorian homes were relocated from their original sites and restored as a charming office park. Labels recount the history of each of the houses, which span the decades from about 1870 to 1910. Worth a special visit is the Italianate **Pardee Home Museum★** *(672 11th St. at Castro St.; visit by guided tour (1hr) only, Wed, 2nd Sat of month & 2nd Sun of month 2pm (call ahead);* ◷*closed major holidays;* ⊜*$5; ℘510-444-2187; www.pardeehome.org),* family mansion of two Oakland mayors: Enoch Pardee and, later, his son George. Built in 1868, the mansion is maintained as it was in 1981 at the death of George Pardee's daughter. Tours reveal a hodgepodge of furnishings and thousands of objets d'art.

Old Oakland★

Bounded by Broadway and 7th, 10th, and Washington Sts. ◷*Farmers' market held Fri 8am–2pm on 9th St. between Broadway and Clay St.*
This restored historic district formed the heart of downtown Oakland during the 1870s. Today it remains an extraordinary grouping of 19C commercial buildings. The shops, hotels and restaurants were built between 1868 and 1880 for the throngs of travelers passing through the Central Pacific passenger depot at 7th and Broadway (terminus of the first transcontinental railroad). The sturdy, two- and three-story structures were restored in the 1980s and are splendid showcases of Victorian craftsmanship. Exotic culinary items abound at the commodious **Housewives' Market** *(9th and Washington Sts.;* ◷*open Mon–Sat 9am–6pm),* which shelters an ethnically diverse emporium of food counters, produce and fish markets, butcher shops and other stalls.

Oakland Chinatown

Bounded by Broadway and 7th, 10th & Harrison Sts.
Although the first Chinese immigrants

arrived in Oakland in the early 1850s, they gathered in the present nine-square-block quarter during the 1870s. Unlike its San Francisco counterpart, Oakland's Chinatown does not court tourists, although many visitors enjoy exploring the bustling array of shops and restaurants. If you happen to be in town during the last weekend in August, be sure to drop by the Oakland Chinatown StreetFest *(www.oaklandchinatownstreetfest.com)*, when hundreds of vendors draw thousands of visitors with calligraphy and origami demonstrations, face painting, barbecue, music and other attractions.

Paramount Theatre★★

2025 Broadway. 🚇 *19th St.* 🚶*Visit by guided tour (2hrs), held 1st & 3rd Sat of month 10am.* 👝 *$5.* 🕐 *Closed major holidays.* 📞 *510-893-2300. www.paramounttheatre.com.*

This monumental movie palace (1931, Timothy Pflueger) is one of the nation's finest examples of Moderne design. The building's resplendent Art Deco detailing describes flowers, foliage, birds and people in addition to the more abstract designs typical of the style. Authentically restored in 1973, it is now owned by the city as a performing-arts facility. The exterior boasts two majestic tile mosaics of puppeteers, divided by the towering Paramount sign. The amber-colored *Fountain of Light* dominates the lobby; the glass sculpture appears to be rising in spectacular billows toward a green-lit grillwork ceiling. With seating for nearly 3,000 people, the lavish auditorium features a gold-lit filigreed ceiling, and paneled side walls sculpted in bas-relief scenes of maidens and warriors. Ralph Stackpole sculpted the horsemen on the orchestral panel above the stage. A Wurlitzer organ mounted on a hydraulic lift rises to stage level for performances. Also worth a gaze are the splendidly decorated men's and women's restrooms and the curving foyers. Nearly as fantastic is the nearby **Fox Oakland Theater** *(1815 Telegraph Ave., www.thefoxoakland.com)*. Built in 1928 (Diggs, Weeks & Day), this exotic, Moor-

ish-style movie palace conjures visions of Arabian Nights. In its day, it was said to have been grander than anything on Hollywood Boulevard.

The theatre was restored and reopened in late 2008 as a live-performance venue; the structure also houses the Oakland School for the Arts *(📞510-869-3519; www.foxoakland.org).*

WATERFRONT

Southwest of downtown.

👥 Jack London Square★

Along the Embarcadero from Clay to Alice St. 🕐*Farmers' market Sun 9am–2pm.* 🅿❌♿ 📞*510-645-9292. www.jacklondonsquare.com.*

Stretching along the busy Inner Harbor of the Oakland Estuary southeast of Broadway, this once-gritty dock area has been developed as an attractive, pedestrian-friendly complex. In addition to shops, restaurants, hotels, cinemas, a farmers' market and a yacht harbor, it has become the East Bay's hippest night-life district. Oakland's passenger lines, Oakland Estuary water-taxi service, and ferries from San Francisco converge near the marina.

The square was named for writer Jack London, who lived in Oakland as a boy and young man. His adventurous spirit is recalled in the historic **Jack London Cabin**, a reconstruction from original timbers of the rustic, single-room log cabin that London occupied during the winter of 1897–98 while prospecting for gold in the Yukon Territory.

Near the cabin stands one of London's favorite watering holes, **Heinold's First and Last Chance Saloon** *(48 Webster St.; 📞510-839-6761; www.heinoldsfirstandlastchance.com)*, built in 1883 from the timbers of a whaling ship. Heinold's was also patronized by authors Ambrose Bierce, Joaquin Miller and, for a short time, Robert Louis Stevenson. Still operating as a bar, it was declared a National Literary Monument in 1997.

A floor contorted by the 1906 earthquake (and never repaired) holds three small tables and a half-dozen bar-stools; wonderful historical photos cover the walls.

USS Potomac

FDR Pier, end of Clay St. (Visitor center opposite at 540 Water St.) ◷*Dockside tours (45min) Wed, Fri and Sun 11am–3pm.* ◷*Closed mid-Dec–mid-Jan.* ⊜*$10. History cruises (2hrs) May–Nov alternating Thu and Sat by reservation.* ⊜*$45.* ✆*510-627-1215. www.usspotomac.org.*

Franklin Delano Roosevelt's presidential yacht is berthed at Jack London Square. The 165ft former Coast Guard cutter was built in 1934 and officially recommissioned as a U.S. Navy vessel for the use of the Commander in Chief two years later. Today the *Potomac* has been renovated to match its appearance when it served as a presidential retreat on the Potomac River and along the Atlantic seaboard. Points of interest include the Presidential Cabin, the engine room and a radio room from which Roosevelt made a national broadcast on March 29, 1941.

Corrugated metal awnings roof the sidewalks of the **Oakland Produce Market** *(2 blocks east of Jack London Square).* From early morning to early afternoon, workers on forklifts shuttle crates of fresh fruits and vegetables between waiting trucks and warehouse buildings, some of which have been brokering wholesale produce since 1917. Some warehouse bays have been converted to restaurants.

LAKE MERRITT AREA

East of downtown.
🚃*Lake Merritt station.*

Lake Merritt

Bounded by Lakeside Dr. and Grand and Lakeshore Aves.

The shores of this 155-acre saltwater tidal lake offer a haven of green serenity near the bustling heart of the city. The shimmering expanse of water was a marshy tidal slough until 1869, when Dr. Samuel Merritt, an ex-mayor who owned land on its shores, dammed the outlet at 12th Street to create the lake. In 1870, he successfully lobbied the California legislature to declare it an official wildlife refuge. Although many private landowners built mansions at its edge, the city eventually secured the properties and turned them into public parkland. A pleasant esplanade winds around the lake's 3.5mi shoreline, broadening on the northern side into **Lakeside Park** *(Bellevue & Grand Aves.)* This lush oasis of 122 oak-shaded acres includes a bandstand, show gardens, and ♣♦**Children's Fairyland** *(699 Bellevue Ave.;* ◷*open 10am–4pm daily Jun–Aug, Wed–Sun Apr–May & Sept–Oct, Fri–Sun Nov–Apr;* ◷*Dec 22–Jan 1 and during inclement weather;* ⊜*$8;* ✕♿🅿✆*510-238-6876; www.fairyland.org)*, an amusement park for the very young.

Camron-Stanford House

1418 Lakeside Dr. ☞*Visit by guided tour only, 3rd Sun of the month 1–4pm and by appt.* ◷*Closed Jan 1 & Dec 25.* ⊜*$5.* 🅿 ✆*510-874-7802. www.cshouse.org.*

This sedate Italianate residence (1876) on the southwest shore of Lake Merritt was home to a succession of prominent figures, including Josiah Stanford, brother of railroad magnate Leland Stanford. The mansion served as the first Oakland Public Museum from 1910 until 1967, when most of the exhibits were removed for storage pending completion of the new Oakland Museum building. The interior was painstakingly restored to its 19C appearance and reopened for public tours in 1978. The lower floor still exhibits some of the original museum's Oakland history collections, while the main floor showcases Victorian-era interior decoration and furnishings.

♣♦Oakland Museum of California★★

1000 Oak St. ◷*Open Wed–Sun 11am–5pm.* ◷*Closed Jan 1, Jul 4, Thanksgiving Day, Dec 25.* ⊜*$12 (free 1st Sun of month).* ✕♿🅿✆*510-318-8400. http://museumca.org.*

A city showpiece, this 7.7-acre cultural complex celebrates California's natural and human history and its art. A setting for public art and celebration, the museum's innovative gardens—a geometric weave of landscaped passages, courtyards, terraces and stairways—encour-

Gallery of California History, Oakland Museum of California

age visitors to explore the building from its sunken central lawn court to its scenic rooftops.

In the early 1960s, city officials and private individuals launched a massive public campaign to build a grand new museum complex that would help revive inner-city Oakland. The facility consolidated three existing collections—the Snow Museum, which focused on natural history; the Oakland Public Museum, devoted to Native Californian ethnology and the state's pioneer history; and the Oakland Art Museum.

Internationally acclaimed architect Eero Saarinen was the leading candidate to design the museum when he died unexpectedly in 1961. His colleague Kevin Roche was then chosen to undertake the project. With assistance from architectural technologist John Dinkeloo, Roche created a series of tiered horizontal galleries around a central courtyard, overhung with terraced roof gardens. Composed solely of reinforced concrete, plate glass and wood, the building's strongly angular lines are graced by statuary and softened with flowers, shrubs and trees—including orchard varieties like olive and pear that recall the state's important agricultural roots. The museum opened in 1969 to rave reviews, with *New York Times* critic Ada Louise Huxtable calling it "one of the most thoughtful revolutionary structures in the world."

The three main departments—natural sciences, history and art—occupy the principal halls on three separate levels of the building. In 2010, the Art and History Galleries reopened after an expansion and renovation designed by Kevin Roche which showcases new acquisitions. The **Great Hall** features major traveling exhibitions, art shows and temporary presentations drawn from the museum's own collections.

Natural Sciences Gallery★
1st level.

Inspired by Elna Bakker's book *An Island Called California,* this hall (also known as the Hall of California Ecology) is arranged to guide visitors on a walk eastward through central California to experience the astounding breadth and richness of the state's geography and biodiversity. Detailed dioramas of native flora and fauna re-create eight distinct biotic zones that stretch across the middle of the state: the Coastline, the foggy Coastal Mountains, the dry Inner Coast Ranges, the Central Valley, the Sierra Slope, the High Sierra, the sagebrush deserts of the Great Basin, and the rocky Mojave Desert. Located off the main hall is the Aquatic California Gallery, where realistic displays in resin illustrate life in the state's coastal and delta waters, salt marshes and freshwater streams.

Gallery of California History★
2nd level.

The new hall displays some 3,000 artifacts and artworks arranged chronologically to explore the theme of "Coming to California." Exhibits explore the story of California, from the incredible diversity of early Native American culture, to the Gold Rush and growth of San Francisco, through the rise of Los Angeles and Hollywood, to the tumultuous decades of the 1960s and 70s. It concludes with a frequently updated and rotating gallery space that addresses current issues and contemporary perspectives. The gallery also features multimedia viewing and listening stations, and offers visitors chances to share their own stories.

Gallery of California Art★★
3rd level.

Installed thematically with a focus on "California's Land, People, and Creativity," this light-infused gallery is devoted to works by artists who have lived, worked or studied in California. The collection contains paintings, sculptures, drawings, prints, photographs and mixed-media works from the early 19C to the present. Of special note are the 19C California landscapes, including paintings of the Sierra Nevada by Thomas Moran, Albert Bierstadt, Thomas Hill and William Keith. The museum holds the largest collection of work from California Arts and Crafts practitioners Arthur and Lucia Kleinhans Mathews. California Impressionist works are represented by Guy Rose, Joseph Raphael and E. Charlton Fortune, and by the Oakland-based "Society of Six" landscapists: William Clapp, August Gay, Selden Gile, Maurice Logan, Louis Siegriest and Bernard von Eichman.

The collection includes works by Richard Diebenkorn, Elmer Bischoff, David Park and other adherents to the Bay Area Figurative movement, as well as by Abstract Expressionists Clyfford Still, Mark Rothko, Sam Francis, Frank Lobdell and Hassel Smith. Later 20C works by Wayne Thiebaud, Robert Bechtle, David Hockney and Bruce Conner share space with contemporary sculptures by Deborah Butterfield, Manuel Neri and ceramist Robert Arneson.

The museum owns the world's largest collection of Dorothea Lange's photographs and negatives, and photography by Eadweard Muybridge (an early San Francisco panorama) and such group f.64 members as Edward Weston, Ansel Adams and Imogen Cunningham.

ADDITIONAL SIGHTS
♟♟ Chabot Space & Science Center★

10000 Skyline Blvd. ▶ *Exit I-580 at Park Blvd.; continue east across Rte. 13, then right on Mountain Blvd., which becomes Ascot Blvd. Climb to ridgetop, then right on Skyline Blvd.* ◷*Open Wed–Thu 10am–5pm (early Jul–early Aug Tue–Thu), Fri–Sat 10am–10pm; Sun 10am–5pm, federal holidays 10am–5pm.* ◷*Closed Thanksgiving Day, Dec 25. Museum (includes two planetarium shows)* ⊜*$15.95; children ages 3–12, $11.95.* ✕♿🅿 ✆*510-336-7300. www.chabotspace.org.*

Thirteen years in the making, this impressive 86,000sq ft hilltop center occupies 13 acres of parkland. Within are an acclaimed planetarium and theater, hands-on exhibits and science labs, and powerful telescopes that invite public access. The surrounding site has an amphitheater and a natural garden. To the right of the main entrance, in the East Building, the 241-seat **Ask Jeeves Planetarium** can project up to 9,000 stars with fiber-optic technology and its Zeiss projector. To the left, the 205-seat **Tien Megadome Theater** (⊜*$16 for two shows; $12 children 3–12)* presents such 70mm films as *To Be an Astronaut* and *SolarMax.* Among the center's hands-on exhibits is *"Destination Universe,"* which lets kids crawl into a black hole and see what happens when galaxies collide. **"Astronomy in California: 1850–1950"** charts the state's rich astronomical history with displays of antique telescopes and descriptions of those who brought some of the best ones to California.

A sky bridge leads to the West Building. Solar and meridian-transit **telescopes**★ are attached to this building; beyond is an historic 8in refractor telescope, moved from the original 1883 Oakland Observatory. Weekend viewing *(free)* is offered at a 20in refractor nicknamed "Rachel." A 36in telescope, Nellie, is located in a rolling-roof observatory that offers 180-degree views of the heavens.

⚉Oakland Zoo

9777 Golf Links Rd., just east of I-580. ⏱Open daily 10am–4pm. ⏱Closed Thanksgiving & Dec 25. ☜*$13.75; $9.75 children ages 2–14.* ✗♿▣ ☎*510-632-9525. www.oaklandzoo.org.*

This small but friendly zoo boasts more than 600 native and exotic animals. Among the most popular are chimpanzees, elephants and lions, as well as sun bears in Rain Forest Canyon. A 2/3-size replica of a **Civil War-era train** *(⏱open daily 11am–4pm;* ☜*$3)* pulled by a steam locomotive, winds through the southern part of the zoo. The 15min **Sky Ride** *(⏱open Sat–Sun 11am–4pm;* ☜*$3)* overlooks American bison and tule elk.

Dunsmuir Historic Estate★

2960 Peralta Oaks Ct., off 106th Ave. south of Knowland Park. ⚑**Mansion** *visit by guided tour only Apr–Sept Wed 11am;* ♿▣ ☎*510-615-5555. www.dunsmuir-hellman.com.*

Built by Alexander Dunsmuir, son of a wealthy British Columbia coal baron, this historic 50-acre estate is one of Oakland's unsung highlights. Dunsmuir had the house built in 1899 as a wedding gift for his wife, Josephine; but on the couple's honeymoon in New York, Alexander took ill and died. Josephine lived in the house for fewer than two years before her own death. The estate was purchased by the City of Oakland in the early 1960s.

Visit

House tours begin at the quaint **Dinkelspiel House,** built for the Hellmans' daughter Florence in the early 1930s. The long driveway to the mansion leads through a meadow landscaped in part by John McLaren, best known for his work in Golden Gate Park. A new pavilion above the meadow is a venue for concerts and other special events. The centerpiece of the estate is 37-room **Dunsmuir House**, built in Neoclassical Revival style with symmetrical facades, hipped or gabled roofs and Palladian windows. Measuring more than 16,000sq ft in three stories, the house has a Tiffany-style dome, 10 fireplaces and inlaid parquet floors.

Roads lead south to a historic farm area. Of note is the **Carriage House,** with mahogany-paneled walls and wrought-iron horse feeders.

Oakland Aviation Museum

8252 Earhart Rd, Building 621, North Field, Oakland Airport. ⏱*Open Wed–Sun 10am–4pm.* ☜*$10.* ♿▣ ☎*510-638-7100. www.oaklandaviation museum.org.*

This vintage (1940) hangar, built as a training facility for World War II aircraft mechanics, is home to this surprising museum. On display are Naval fighters and a sister craft to the L-10 piloted by Amelia Earhart. The impressive Ahrens Collection offers 1/72 scale-model U.S. military aircraft; other exhibits feature women and African American aviators, aerial photography, air racing, and Col. Jimmy Doolittle's 8th Air Force.

Outdoors is the Short Solent four-engine Flying Boat *(tours* ☜*$7)*, built in 1946. Almost 90ft long, with the tip of its tail 37ft above the ground, the plane was designed to take off and land exclusively in water. Converted to luxury passenger service in 1949, it became the property of reclusive billionaire Howard Hughes in 1959. It was restored after his death.

USS Hornet★★

Pier 3, Alameda. ▷ *Take Atlantic Ave. north off Webster St. (Rte. 61) and follow signs.* ⏱*Open daily 10am–5pm (last entry 4pm).* ⏱*Closed Jan 1, Thanksgiving Day, Dec 25.* ☜*$16.* ✗▣ ☎*510-521-8448. www.uss-hornet.org.*

Commissioned in November 1943, this Essex-class aircraft carrier was the eighth in a line of U.S. naval vessels to be named *Hornet*. With a length of 894ft, the 41,200-ton ship was designed to carry up to 3,400 servicemen and an attack force of F6F Hellcat fighters, TBM Avenger torpedo bombers and SB2C Helldiver dive bombers.

Steaming from Pearl Harbor in March 1944, the USS *Hornet* moved quickly to the forefront of the Pacific war. In action at Iwo Jima in June 1944, air crews shot down 67 Japanese aircraft, commencing an extraordinary string of victories that earned the ship seven battle stars, and her pilots Navy records for the number of planes shot down in one month (255) and in a single day (72).

At the invasion of Okinawa in April 1945, the *Hornet* scored the first crippling hits on the largest battleship of its day, the 72,000-ton *Yamato,* which was sunk in the battle. The *Hornet* ended the war with a combat record of 1,420 aircraft, 42 cargo ships, 10 destroyers, a carrier, a cruiser and a battleship destroyed.

in 1969 the Hornet retrieved the crew of Apollo 11 upon their return from the first manned moon mission.

The splashdown in the Pacific was witnessed live by President Richard Nixon from the *Hornet's* bridge. Later that year, the *Hornet* also retrieved the returned astronauts of *Apollo 12*. The ship was decommissioned in June 1970 and declared a National Historic Landmark in 1991.

Visit

Boarding the ship on its vast **Hangar Deck**, where aircraft were stored between sorties, you may view a short orientation program and peruse a gallery of historic photographs before commencing self-guided tours.

At mid-ship, a set of painted footprints marks the first steps of Apollo 11's lunar astronauts back on "earth," when they walked from the retrieval helicopter to quarantine in a customized trailer; an adjacent exhibit highlights that event. A 5min **flight simulator** (∞*$6),* equipped with computer-generated film and hydraulic lifts, lets you experience the sensation of launching and landing an aircraft on a carrier deck.

Steep, narrow ship ladders climb to the sprawling **Flight Deck,** above which rises the massive "Island" or control tower. You may climb to the Navigation Bridge, where the captain and officers piloted the ship, and the Flag Bridge, where the fleet admiral commanded a task force of support ships. From the Primary Flight Control Bridge overlooking the runways in the aft of the control tower, the "Air Boss" monitored the take-offs and landings of aircraft.

Descending to the **Second Deck**, below the Hangar Deck, you may tour the refurbished officers' quarters, lounge and dining hall, the Marine Detachment quarters, the enlisted men's mess and the engine room.

ADDRESSES

⊮/**EAT**

$ G.B. Ratto & Co. – *821 Washington St. at 9th St.* ☏*510-832-6503. www.rattos.com.* An Oakland institution, this venerable specialty-food emporium has catered to the particularities of East Bay tastes for 100 years. Linger over the lengthy cheese counter beneath hanging salamis, then wend your way to the cafe in back.

$ Oakland Grill – *301 Franklin St. at 3rd St.* ☏*510-835-1176. www.oakland grill.net.* Get to this produce district eatery around 8am to down a hearty breakfast against a backdrop of fruits and vegetables being unloaded and readied for sale. All four buildings on this nostalgic corner sport corrugated metal awnings.

$$$ Yoshi's – *510 Embarcadero West.* ☏*510-238-9200. www.yoshis.com.* One of the top venues for jazz in the San Francisco Bay Area is in a Japanese restaurant just off Jack London Square. The cabaret-style theater, open nightly, presents many of the biggest names in contemporary jazz music. A San Francisco outpost opened in late 2007.

East Bay Area

East of the ridge line backdropping Berkeley and Oakland lies a series of hills and valleys overshadowed by regal Mt. Diablo. Martinez, Concord, Walnut Creek, Alamo, Danville and other pleasant suburban communities spread over the valley floors, while exclusive developments extend higher into the grassy hills. The historic Solano County towns of Vallejo and Benicia guard either end of narrow Carquinez Straits in the northeast part of San Francisco Bay.

SIGHTS
♣♣ Mount Diablo State Park★

North Gate Rd., 35mi from San Francisco. ▶ *From Oakland, take Rte. 24 east through Caldecott Tunnel to Walnut Creek. Continue east on Ygnacio Valley Rd. for 2.5mi; take a right on Walnut Ave., which turns into North Gate Rd. after 1.5mi and leads another 12mi to the summit.* ◷*Park open daily 8am–dusk.* ◷*Closed during very high fire-risk days; call in advance for information.* ⊚*$10/car.* △⌖🅿 ✆*925-837-2525. www.mdia.org.*

The sweeping panoramic **view★★★** from the 3,849ft summit of Mt. Diablo is said to encompass more than 40,000sq mi. That would make it the second most extensive view over land from any point on earth, after Africa's Mt. Kilimanjaro.

On clear days, the naked eye can easily pick out such far-flung landmarks as San Francisco (27mi west), the Farallon Islands (62mi west), Mt. Lassen (165mi northeast), the Sacramento River Delta to the north, and the long wall of the Sierra Nevada range to the east. A good pair of binoculars can bring Yosemite National Park's El Capitan (130mi east) into focus. From this remarkable vantage point, Colonel Leander Ransom in 1851 established the Mt. Diablo Base and Meridian, used to make the first surveyed maps of Northern California and Nevada. A year later, R.D. Cutts mapped the state's northern waterways for the Coast Survey from here.

Info: www.sfgate.com/neighborhoods/eb.

▶ **Location:** Sights in this section are located north and east of Berkeley and Oakland; all lie within 40mi from San Francisco.

♣♣ **Kids:** Six Flags Discovery Kingdom, the perfect combination of sea creatures, wildlife and thrill rides.

◷ **Timing:** Rush-hour traffic into San Francisco in the morning and back out in the evening will slow your transit time to these sights, so plan accordingly and avoid peak traffic hours if you can.

☻ **Don't Miss:** The Blackhawk Museum, a must for auto and design buffs.

Both survey marks still can be seen upon the rock now enclosed by the small **Summit Museum Visitor Center** (◷*open daily 10am–4pm;* ✆*925-837-6119*), built of locally quarried sandstone by the Civilian Conservation Corps in 1940.

Exhibits within the museum focus on Mt. Diablo's geology and its natural and human history; telescopes mounted on an observation deck assist viewing of distant sites. ☻*Note: summer fogs often obscure views.*

Summit of Mt. Diablo

© Jim Mitchell / Mount Diablo State Park

On the mountain's flanks are extensive outcrops of fossilized seashells and prehistoric mammal bones. The park is also home to some 400 plant species, as well as deer, cougar, coyote, bobcat and about 200 species of birds, including bald eagles. Mt. Diablo offers camping, picnicking, hiking on more than 150mi of trails, and climbing in the weird sandstone formations known as **Rock City**. The Mitchell Canyon section of the park also has a visitor center (*open Sat–Sun and some holidays spring and summer 8am–4pm, fall and winter 9am–3pm*).

▲▲ Lindsay Wildlife Museum

1931 First Ave., Walnut Creek, 45mi from San Francisco. ▶ *From Oakland, take Rte. 24 east, turning north on I-680. Turn left at the Treat/Geary Exit onto Geary Rd.; left again on Buena Vista Ave.; then right on First Ave.* *Hours vary seasonally; call or visit website.* *Closed Mon, Tue, week following Labor Day.* *$7, children 2–17 $5.* ⬥🅿️ *925-935-1978. www.wildlife-museum.org.*

This small community-oriented natural-history museum is both an educational center and the largest wildlife-rehabilitation hospital in the U.S. More than 50 species of native injured animals that cannot be returned to the wild live out their days here, under conditions carefully designed to satisfy both their physical and psychological needs. Eagles, hawks and other raptors roost on perches, while squirrels, coyotes and other mammals cavort below eye level. Live reptiles and amphibians, as well as mounted insect collections, introduce yet more local fauna.

Eugene O'Neill National Historic Site★★

Kuss Rd., Danville, 28mi from San Francisco. ▶ *From I-680 east of Oakland (between Rte. 24 & I-580), exit at Sycamore Valley Rd.; National Park Service van picks up visitors at Museum of San Ramon Valley in Danville for drive to Tao House.* *Visit by guided tour (2.5hrs) only, Wed–Fri and Sun 10am and 2pm (shuttle pickup times), reservations required. Also open Sat without reservation (check website).* *Closed Jan 1, Thanksgiving Day, Dec 25.* ⬥ *925-838-0249. www.nps.gov/euon.*

Situated on a scenic knoll in the shadow of the Las Trampas wilderness, this modest yet comfortable dwelling was home for more than six years to playwright **Eugene O'Neill** (1888–1953). Author of nearly 60 plays, winner of four Pulitzer Prizes for drama, and the only American playwright to win the Nobel Prize for Literature (in 1936), O'Neill is one of the nation's most influential dramatists.

Tragedy and Triumph

The son of a successful traveling actor, O'Neill was born in a New York City hotel and raised largely "on the road" by a loving but troubled family. O'Neill's personal life was filled with difficulties. His mother was addicted to morphine and his brother to alcohol. Both of his sons, Eugene Jr. (1910–50) and Shane (1919–77), committed suicide and he was bitterly estranged from his daughter, Oona (1925–91), following her 1943 marriage to much-older comic actor Charlie Chaplin.

Suffering from tuberculosis, alcoholism and severe depression himself, O'Neill overcame his afflictions to find fulfillment first as a seaman and ultimately as a playwright. His heavily autobiographical tragedies helped transform American theater from an arena of pure entertain-

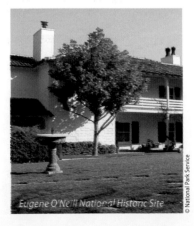

Eugene O'Neill National Historic Site

© National Park Service

ment into a high art form. O'Neill's six years at **Tao House**, a then-remote home he built with his third wife—Carlotta (née Hazel Tharzing, 1888–1965), an actress and a former Miss California—were among the happiest and most productive of his life.

In 1936, the intensely private O'Neills bought 158 acres of almond and walnut orchards on the flank of Las Trampas Ridge, attracted by the site's remoteness and its handsome views of Mt. Diablo and the San Ramon Valley.

Designed by architect Frederick Confer, their white, two-story Monterey-style house was built of concrete blocks intended to resemble adobe brick, with a black-tile roof and verandas on the second floor. The couple christened their home Tao House after Carlotta's taste for chinoiserie and Eugene's interest in the Taoist philosophy. Here O'Neill wrote six plays, including four of his greatest: *The Iceman Cometh, Hughie, A Moon for the Misbegotten* (whose intended setting is thought to be the old barn on this property) and his masterpiece, *A Long Day's Journey into Night.*

O'Neill's degenerative illness and an inability to hire local assistance during World War II forced the couple to sell the house in February 1944 and return to the East Coast, where the playwright died in 1953. After the property became a National Historic Site in 1980, the National Park Service began efforts to restore the home and furnishings.

Visit

On the downstairs floor, guided tours lead through the kitchen, living room, guest room (which hosted Bennett Cerf, Somerset Maugham and John Ford), and "Rosie's Room," named for O'Neill's cherished player piano. Upstairs are O'Neill's writing den, which he furnished in a style fitting for a shipboard cabin, and the couple's bedrooms—the writer's still containing his original bed, an antique Chinese opium couch from Gump's. The 13-acre site also preserves the pool built for the playwright, an avid swimmer, and the grave of the O'Neills' beloved Dalmatian dog, Blemie.

Blackhawk Museum★★

3700 Blackhawk Plaza Cir., Danville, 33mi from San Francisco.
▷ *Exit I-680 at Sycamore Valley Blvd. (which becomes Camino Tassajara) and continue 5mi to Blackhawk Plaza.*
Open Wed–Sun 10am–5pm.
Closed Jan 1, Thanksgiving Day, Dec 25. $10. Guided tours (1hr) available Sat–Sun 2pm. ⼵ℙ 925-736-2280. www.blackhawkmuseum.org.

At the eastern end of Blackhawk Plaza —a beautiful, Mediterranean-style luxury shopping complex landscaped with a cascading artificial creek—rises the rose-granite and glass facade of this museum. It displays a stunning collection of some 90 beautifully restored vintage automobiles spanning the 1890s through the 1960s. Informatively labeled and attractively arranged through two levels, the rare and historic vehicles are presented as works of art. From the ground floor, an interior hall leads to the Moving Inspirations Art Galleries, comprising nearly 4,000 pieces of automotive art and memorabilia.

John Muir National Historic Site★

4202 Alhambra Ave., Martinez, 30mi from San Francisco. ▷ *Take I-80 northeast from Oakland to Rte. 4 East; exit at Alhambra Ave. and turn left.*
Open daily 10am–5pm. Guided tours daily 2pm. Closed Jan 1, Thanksgiving Day, Dec 25. ✕⼵ℙ 925-228-8860. www.nps.gov/jomu.

This comfortable home surrounded by orchards formed part of the 2,600-acre fruit ranch owned by **John Muir** (1838–1914). The legendary conservationist resided here during the final decades of his life, tending orchards and writing works that have since become landmarks of the environmental movement. Born near Dunbar, Scotland, Muir arrived in Wisconsin with his family at the age of 11. Detesting the drudgery of farm work, he eventually departed to pursue the life of a wandering botanist, walking first to the Gulf of Mexico in 1867, where he took ship passage for San Francisco. His many visits to the Sierra Nevada invoked a lifelong love for rugged wilderness. A fine scientist and gifted writer, Muir published observations of nature that attracted a following among East Coast readers and opened minds to the then-novel idea of conserving wilderness lands.

Muir helped found and served as the first president of the Sierra Club, and eventually prevailed upon the U.S. Congress to bolster the young National Parks movement with new or expanded parklands in the Sierra Nevada and elsewhere.

Visit

Built in 1882 by Muir's father-in-law, Dr. John Strentzel, this two-story, Italianate frame residence was John Muir's home from 1890 until his death. The house reflects the Victorian proclivities of the Strentzel family more than Muir's own simple tastes. The conservationist wrote many of his influential books in the second-floor "scribble den," which retains his original desk and objects collected on his trips throughout the U.S.

Muir himself planted the large *Sequoia gigantea* (giant sequoia) that grows sturdily near the northwest corner of the house. The park also preserves a number of grape vines and fruit trees, and beyond, 326 acres of land on Mt. Wanda. Beyond the orchard stands the **Martinez Adobe** (1849), received by Vicente Martínez as part of an early 19C land grant of 17,750 acres.

A film on Muir's life is shown in the visitor center. Muir and his family are interred in a nearby private graveyard.

Benicia

34mi from San Francisco.
❍ *Take I-80 northeast from Oakland across the Carquinez Bridge, then east on I-780 to 2nd St. exit in Benicia.* ✆*707-745-2120. www.beniciachamber.com.*

Established on part of General Mariano Vallejo's vast land holdings, this small, friendly community on the north shore of the Carquinez Straits was named for Vallejo's wife. The town—second to be incorporated in the state—grew up along 10 blocks of First Street north of the waterfront, today a pleasant boulevard of cafes and shops. From February 11, 1853, to February 25, 1854, Benicia served as the California state capital.

Benicia Capitol State Historic Park *(115 West G St.;* ❍*open Sat–Sun 10am–5pm;* ❍*closed Jan 1, Thanksgiving Day, Dec 25;* ⊜*$6 parking;* 🅿 ✆*707-745-3385; www.parks.ca.gov)* preserves the old brick statehouse, furnished as it may have been during its one-year tenure.

Benicia Arsenal

❍ *From 1st St. drive east on Military East, pass through the old army gate. Follow signs to the Camel Barn and Clocktower.*

The U.S. Army founded a military reservation in Benicia in 1849, establishing the Benicia Arsenal the following year. One of four U.S. arsenals at the time, it served until it was deactivated in 1964, after which it was converted to the Benicia Industrial Park. Many of the old military buildings today house offices and artists' studios, some of which are open to the public.

Among historic reminders of the army's presence are the oldest military cemetery in the Pacific states (1849), the turreted arsenal storehouse known as the Clocktower (1859), the commandant's house, and the **Benicia Historical Museum** *(2060 Camel Rd.;* ❍*open Wed–Sun 1–4pm;* ⊜*$5 (free 1st Wed of month);* ♿🅿 ✆*707-745-5435; www.beniciahistoricalmuseum.org)*, where the army auctioned camels in 1864 after experimenting with them as pack animals in the North American deserts.

Port Chicago Naval Magazine National Memorial

Concord Naval Weapons Station, 38mi from San Francisco.
❍ *Take I-80 northeast from Oakland to Rte. 4 East; exit at Port Chicago Hwy. and proceed to main gate.*
🐪*Visit by guided tour (1hr) only Thur–Sat 1.30pm (2wk advance reservation required).* ❍*Closed Jan 1, Thanksgiving Day, Dec 25, during Concord Naval Station operations.* ♿🅿 ✆*925-228-8860. www.nps.gov/poch.*

This somber memorial was dedicated on July 17, 1994, on the 50th anniversary of a World War II munitions explosion that killed 320 mostly African-American military and civilian workers. Wayside exhibits line a brick walkway that leads to the Suisun Bay tidal basin, where the memorial stands. Names of all victims are etched into its polished black granite. Inland, a chapel and visitor center contains further exhibits.

Vallejo Naval & Historical Museum

734 Marin St., Vallejo. ○*Open Tue–Sat noon–4pm.* ⬭*$5.* ♿🅿️☎️*707-643-0077. www.vallejomuseum.org.*
Located in the former Vallejo City Hall (1927), this fine small museum has five galleries that recount regional history. It highlights the naval presence with a submarine periscope installed through the roof for a 360-degree view.
Walking tours of the **Mare Island Naval Shipyard**, in adjacent San Pablo Bay, are arranged through the museum. The U.S. Navy purchased Mare Island in 1852 and assigned David Farragut ("Damn the torpedoes, full speed ahead") as its first commandant. The base grew to become the largest ship construction and repair site in the world. Tours take in 19C–20C housing of many styles, a hospital complex, dry docks and other facilities.

👥 Six Flags Discovery Kingdom★

1001 Fairgrounds Dr., Vallejo, 30mi from San Francisco.
◗ *Take I-80 northeast from Oakland and exit at Rte. 37. Or take Blue & Gold Fleet ferry from Pier 41 (San Francisco) to Vallejo with shuttle service to the park.*
○**Park** *open daily mid-May–Labor Day; Sat–Sun early Sept–Dec and Mar–mid-May.* ○*Closed Jan–mid-May except school holidays. Hours vary seasonally; check website.* ⬭*$57.99; children under 4ft $37.99.* ✕♿🅿️ *($18).* ☎️*707-643-6722. www.sixflags.com/discoverykingdom.*
This 160-acre landscaped park combines three distinct elements—a zoo,

an oceanarium and an amusement park—while entertaining and educating visitors about conservation issues with various shows and exhibits. Begun as a modest theme park in 1968 in Redwood City, 25mi south of San Francisco, it was renamed Marine World Africa USA in 1972 and relocated in 1986 to its present site in Vallejo. The Six Flags chain of theme parks acquired the park in 1999.

Visit

A visit to the Discovery Kingdom is best structured around live animal performances in various outdoor amphitheaters *(shows last 2–30min; map and schedule available at entrance).* Prominent are the bottle-nosed acrobats of **Dolphin Harbor**; the **Shouka Celebration**, in which an orca dives, cavorts and splashes the audience; and the **Wildlife Theater**, where the presentation of exotic animals from around the world furthers appreciation for endangered species.
There also are seal, sea-lion and tropical-bird displays. Visitors pass through a transparent viewing tunnel as sharks swim overhead in **Shark Experience★**; hand-feed giraffes at the **Giraffe Dock**; team up in a game of tug-of-war with pachyderms at **Elephant Encounter**; watch frisky walruses through a glass-walled tank at the **Walrus Experience★**; and explore the steamy jungle setting of the **Butterfly Habitat★**. The **Odin's Temple of the Tiger★** provides an underwater viewing window on 400-pound Bengals. Also worth visiting are a saltwater aquarium, the **Marine Research Center** and an animal nursery. **Looney Tunes Seaport** is a children's ride and amusement area.
Among the most popular rides are the **V2: Vertical Velocity**, which spirals riders to speeds of up to 70mph in less than 4 seconds; and **Monsoon Falls**, in which rafters plunge over a 55ft rapid. The half-dozen roller-coasters are even better known; they include **Medusa**, which travels at 65mph through seven inversions; and **Roar,** a classic wooden coaster that drops more than ten stories at speeds above 50mph.

Introduced by the windswept ridges, sheltered valleys, and sandy coves of the Marin Headlands, Marin County lies just over the Golden Gate Bridge from San Francisco. Here, surrounded on three sides by water, you'll find uparalleled natural sites such as the wave-lashed sands of Point Reyes National Seashore, the lofty peak (2,571ft) of Mount Tamalpais, and the majestic stands of redwoods (one of only two stands of virgin growth in the National Park Service) at Muir Woods National Monument. Western Marin County in particular remains a favorite desination for day and weekend trippers from San Francisco, especially Sausalito, Point Reyes and Muir Woods.

Highlights

1 Admire classic views of San Francisco from **East Fort Baker** (p235)

2 Drive the amazingly scenic **Conzelman Road** (p237)

3 Walk beneath awe-inspiring redwoods at **Muir Woods** (p241)

4 Wild, windswept views at **Point Reyes Lighthouse** (p246)

5 Stroll along stylish Bridgeway Boulevard in **Sausalito** (p251)

History

The uplift of the coast ranges some 25 million years ago established a new coastline for California. Today's many marine terraces, marking the shoreline of millenia past, are a visible legacy of this dramatic uplift that continues to raise the mountains. The ruggedness of these shores ensured their isolation for centuries after initial European exploration in the 16C. Despite the claims of Sir Frances Drake for England in 1579, the coast Miwok, Pomo, Yuki, and other tribes lived virtually untouched by the outside world until 1812, when the Russians established a colony at Fort Ross. Though Russian efforts were short-lived, they provoked greater interest in northern California from Mexican authorities. Mexicans grazed cattle here after they threw off the Spanish yoke in 1821. Meanwhile, Americans logged the redwood forests to near depletion into the early 20C. During World War II, defenses were built along the Marin Headlands, and the Marinship naval shipyard employed thousands of workers. By the latter half of the 20C, Marin County had become synonymous with the California lifestyle.

Visiting Today

Marin County's natural beauty, coupled with the laid-back atmosphere of the rural towns, provide a welcome break

Homes line the Sausalito slopes

© Geoffrey Kuchera / iStockphoto.com

from the dynamism of San Francisco city life. Not to mention the fact that this area makes a great launching point for exploring the wineries of the Sonoma Valley. Sausalito is a favorite excursion for both residents and visitors, lying just a short drive or ferry ride across the bay from San Francisco. Indeed, the most appealing way to get here—on a nice day—is to hop aboard a ferry from the city. Once you disembark, it's an easy stroll along Bridgeway Boulevard, the community's commercial spine. Here you'll find upscale shops, gorgeous views, and eateries galore. Restaurants on the water offer vistas that stretch across the blue bay to Tiburon and Angel Island. On the land side, tiers of pricey private residences climb down the steep slopes to the bay.

Keep traveling north on Highway 101 to discover charming towns like Mill Valley and Larkspur, whereas a detour along the coast will bring you to tiny Inverness and bohemian Tomales Bay. Also in Marin Country is the Muir Woods National Monument. The 560-acre plot of Coast Redwoods was named for Scottish immigrant, John Muir, the revered naturalist and pioneer in the U.S. forest conservation movement—which celebrated its 100th anniversary in 2008.

ADDRESSES

🛏 STAY

$ Point Reyes Hostel – *Point Reyes National Seashore, 8mi from Bear Valley Visitor Center in Point Reyes Station. ℘415-663-8811. www.norcalhostels.org. 44 beds (10-bed dorms, one private room, private group rooms).* Situated off Limantour Road, 2mi from the Pacific and 25mi from the Lighthouse, this simple hostel offers a common kitchen and other shared facilities.

$$$ Mill Valley Inn – *165 Throckmorton Ave., Mill Valley. ℘415-389-6608. www.marinhotels.com. 25 rooms.* French doors open onto private decks or balconies overlooking a redwood grove or the streets of charming Mill Valley. Breakfast, included in the room rate, is served on an outdoor terrace.

$$$ Mountain Home Inn – *810 Panoramic Hwy., Mill Valley. ℘415-381-9000. www.mtnhomeinn.com. 10 rooms.* High on the slopes of Mt. Tamalpais, this B&B sits at a popular trailhead for hikers and mountain bikers.

$$$ Waters Edge – *25 Main St., Tiburon. ℘415-789-5999. www.marinhotels.com. 23 rooms.* Located on the downtown Tiburon waterfront, this stylish new luxury boutique hotel offers stunning views and modern comfort. Most rooms have private bay-view balconies; all have fireplaces.

$$$$$ The Harbor House Inn - *5600 S. Hwy. 1, Elk. ℘800-720-7474. www.theharborhouseinn.com. 10 rooms and cottages.* Though north of Marin County along the southern Mendocino coast, this luxurious rural inn—built by lumber-company execs in 1916 atop challenging ocean cliffs—is a worthy place to rest one's head and dine during a northbound excursion from Point Reyes.

🍴 EAT

$$ Buckeye Roadhouse – *15 Shoreline Hwy., Mill Valley. ♿🅿 ℘415-331-2600. www.buckeyeroadhouse.com.* **American**. Hearty home cooking is given a gourmet touch in this charming 1937 lodge. You can't go wrong with the "smoky barbecue" or roast chicken.

$$ Guaymas – *5 Main St., Tiburon. ♿ ℘415-435-6300. www.guaymas restaurant.com.* **Mexican**. Diners sip margaritas and dine on Jaliscan-style tacos, tamales and mesquite-grilled dishes, while enjoying a panoramic view of Angel Island and the San Francisco skyline from a pierside location.

$$$ Murray Circle – *601 Murray Circle (at Fort Baker), Sausalito. ℘415-339-4750. www.cavallopoint.com.* **Californian**. A romantic sense of history flows through this charming restaurant, housed in a white Colonial-style wood building at Fort Baker. The farm-to-table Californian cuisine marries local ingredients to herbs, spices, infusions, and emulsions.

Marin Headlands★★

Rising north of the Golden Gate, these 15 square miles of pristine coastal lands encompass windswept ridges, sheltered valleys, sandy coves and scattered vestiges of the area's military history. Protected since 1972 as part of the Golden Gate National Recreation Area (and by the U.S. Army before that), the Marin Headlands offer unequaled views of the city-fringed bay, the Golden Gate Bridge elegantly overlapping San Francisco's skyline, and the vast Pacific Ocean stretching away to the western horizon. Hiking, biking, fishing, and camping opportunities abound.

A BIT OF HISTORY

The headlands' strategic importance became evident to U.S. Forces soon after their takeover of California in 1846. A fort was planned at Lime Point (today the north pier of the Golden Gate Bridge) to complement Fort Point and Alcatraz in guarding the mouth of the strait. The fort was never built, but other defenses—batteries, bunkers and gun emplacements—appeared along the bluffs. Many installations rapidly grew obsolete, to be replaced by newer armaments at Forts Baker, Barry and Cronkhite. No gun was ever fired in defense, and today the grounds of the forts harbor a multitude of abandoned coastal defense installations ranging from post-Civil War earthen bunkers to Cold War-era Nike missile sites.

Thickly covered with coastal grasses, sagebrush, coyote brush and oak woodlands, the headlands are a wilderness providing habitat for lizards and snakes, elusive bobcats and foxes, and blacktailed deer. In spring, lupine, Indian paintbrush and other colorful wildflowers decorate the hillsides, and in fall, various species of raptors pass by on their annual migration to winter nesting grounds in the south—sometimes up to as many as 100 hawks fly overhead each

Bus 76-Headlands (Sundays and holidays only)

Info: ☎415-331-1540; www.nps.gov/goga/marin-headlands.htm.

Location: By car, follow US-101 north across the Golden Gate Bridge and exit at Alexander Ave. (2mi); follow Marin Headlands signs. For visitors without cars, bus 76-Headlands offers hourly transit on Sundays and holidays.

Kids: Geared especially for kids under 10 years old, the popular Bay Area Discovery Museum has imaginative exhibits on the local environment.

Timing: In summer, ocean-born fogs pour over these hills, freshening the air but obscuring the stunning views of the bridge, bay and city. In fall and spring—the best seasons to visit—the hills bask in sunshine. If possible, avoid crowds by going mid-week; Sundays are especially popular.

Parking: There are free parking lots at nearly all the sights in the Marin Headlands.

Don't Miss: The classic views south overlooking the Golden Gate Bridge from Conzelman Road and the bluffs of East Fort Baker.

hour. Lagoons and coves attract stately egrets and herons, while fleets of brown pelicans patrol the coastal waters. The seas cliffs are renowned by geologists for their pillow bassalt exposures; offshore rocks provide haven for seals, sea lions and nesting shorebirds.

Marin Headlands

SIGHTS
Fort Baker

▶ *From San Francisco, follow US-101 north across the Golden Gate Bridge to the Alexander Ave. exit, just past Vista Pt. At Bunker Rd., turn left and follow signs to the Bay Area Discovery Museum.*

Named in honor of Col. Edward Dickinson Baker, a Civil War hero and friend of Abraham Lincoln, this attractive group of buildings and batteries was the first military post on the north side of the Golden Gate. Eight small batteries were

constructed between 1873 and 1943, including the still-visible Battery Yates (1905) near Cavallo Point—the easternmost tip of Horseshoe Cove.

Today, the section east of the bridge, called **East Fort Baker**, is home to the Army's 91st Division Reserve, a U.S. Coast Guard station, the Presidio Yacht Club and the Bay Area Discovery Museum (below). Stroll the bluffs overlooking Horseshoe Cove for dramatic **views**★★ of the Golden Gate Bridge.

🚶 The **Bay Trail** *(.25mi)* along the shore east of Cavallo Point offers views of the

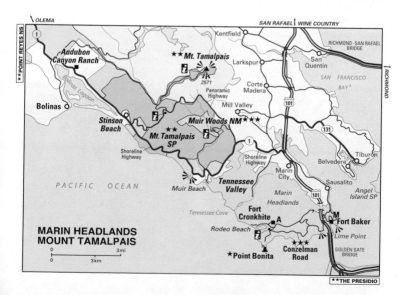

Father of the National Parks

United State Mint image

When William Kent donated land for Muir Woods National Park in 1908, he insisted that the park be named after California's most famous and beloved naturalist, John Muir. Born in Dunbar, Scotland in 1838, Muir emigrated to America with his family in 1849. In the fields and woods of Wisconsin's countryside, Muir cultivated a deep love of the natural world.

In 1867, following a recovery from an eye injury, Muir set out to explore the natural world. After traveling throughout the US and Central America, he entered Yosemite's high country in 1868 and fell in love. He would go on to write, "Then it seemed to me the Sierra should be called not the Nevada, or Snowy Range, but the Range of Light...the most divinely beautiful of all the mountain chains I have ever seen."

Muir became the valley's most devoted champion. In 1875 he wrote an article proposing that Yosemite be declared a national park, and in 1890 Congress passed the Yosemite National Park bill, setting aside the wilderness around Yosemite Valley and Mariposa Grove. In 1905, after lobbying by Muir and others, California ceded the valley and Mariposa Grove to the federal government to be incorporated in the park.

In addition to Yosemite, Muir helped create the Sequoia, Mount Rainier, Petrified Forest and Grand Canyon national parks. He is also credited with the 1892 founding of the Sierra Club, a preeminent organization dedicated to preservation and expansion of wildlife and wilderness areas. In 2005, California honored Muir by commemorating him on California's State Quarter.

Muir's prolific writings about his travels and naturalist philosophy continue to inspire readers to explore the country's wilderness.

Upper Yosemite falls, Yosemite National Park

© Martyn Goddard / Apa Publications

Conzelman Road leading to Point Bonita

© Peter Dean / iStockphoto.com

East Bay, Angel Island and Alcatraz while skirting the habitat of the endangered Mission Blue butterfly.

👥 Bay Area Discovery Museum★ (M)

East Fort Baker, 557 McReynolds Rd., Sausalito. 🕐*Open Tue–Sun 9am–5pm.* 🕐*Closed major holidays and the last 2 wks of Sept.* 🎟*$11 (free 1st Wed of month).* ✕♿🅿 ✆*415-339-3900. www.baykidsmuseum.org.*

One of the Bay Area's excellent children's museums, this newly expanded complex of learning-oriented halls delights children ages one through ten. In the **Entrance Pavilion**, young computer whizzes head for the multimedia computer center to check out the latest educational CD-ROM programs before heading off to the science room or maze of illusions.

The **San Francisco Bay Hall★** highlights some of the activities and animals of the bay. Kids can pretend to go crabbing off Fisherman's Wharf, explore an undersea tunnel, or fish for salmon on the Discovery Boat. **Tot Spot**'s whimsical, multicolored rooms and outdoor areas safely occupy kiddies three-and-under, and the **Art Studios** offer a variety of drop-in art activities.

New features of the museum include Lookout Cove—a 2.5-acre outdoor exhibit with real tidal pools, a sea cave

to explore, and native animal homes to build—and the 180-seat **Discovery Theater**, where kids can watch performances (dance, puppets, theater) put on by members of some of the best troupes in the Bay Area.

Conzelman Road★★★

▶ *From Fort Baker, return to Alexander Ave., turn right toward US-101, pass under the freeway and continue to Conzelman Rd., following signs for Marin Headlands.*

This gloriously scenic route snakes along the Headlands' rugged bluffs past abandoned military batteries. Turnouts provide opportunities to drink in outstanding **views★★★** of San Francisco Bay, the Golden Gate Bridge and the Pacific.

Stop at **Battery Spencer** (.25mi), a massive concrete casement built in 1896 to house three cannons, for a formidable city view framed by the looming north pier of the bridge. The curious can crawl into a command station overlooking a gun mount.

Battery Construction 129 (1.75mi), the highest gun battery in the U.S., was begun in 1942 to house a 16in gun capable of firing shells over 20mi; construction halted in 1944 and the battery was left unarmed.

From mid-August to mid-December, **Hawk Hill★**, just above Battery 129, draws legions of birders to witness

237

Ohlones and Coast Miwoks

When the Spanish explorers arrived in the 18C, the Bay Area supported some 7,000–10,000 people, and was North America's most densely populated region north of Mexico. The **Coast Miwok** dwelt north of the city, in present-day Marin and western Sonoma counties. Their rich cultural heritage included basket-making, dances, ceremonies, and a complex and intricate language. Their diet included large game, seafood, buckeye nuts, clover, honey, and dried kelp. The **Ohlone**, or Costanoans, inhabited areas on the San Francisco Peninsula, east of the bay and south to Big Sur. The semi-nomadic people lived in light and portable structures built of tule, and moved according to ancient seasonal patterns of hunting and gathering for foods such as acorns, berries and salmon. Their deep connection to the natural world was expressed in creation myths enacted in songs, dances, and games.

the southward migration of raptors—eagles, hawks and falcons—plying the only such flyway on the West Coast. Beyond Battery 129 the road crests and becomes a winding one-way passage that curves down along the precipitous edge of a high sea cliff. Entering decommissioned Fort Barry, it heads past Battery Rathbone-McIndoe (1905) to Batteries Alexander (1905), Wallace (1918) and Mendell (c. 1905). From the latter, views extend west and north over the coastal headlands, guano-covered Bird Rock, Rodeo Valley and the stark barracks and buildings of Fort Cronkhite. Point Bonita can be seen due south of Battery Mendell.

Point Bonita Lighthouse★

From the end of Conzelman Rd., follow lighthouse signs to trailhead for a hike (.5mi) to Point Bonita (sturdy shoes advised). Open Sat–Mon 12.30–3.30pm. Guided tours (45min) weekends 12.30pm. 415-331-1540. www.nps.gov/goga/pobo.htm.

Perched on the rocky tip of Point Bonita, this lighthouse has helped guide mariners through the Golden Gate since 1855. Though automated in 1981, the it still employs its original Fresnel lens, through which beacons of light were beamed to 19C passenger ships, lumber schooners and naval fleets of both world wars. Extensive restorations to the lighthouse were completed in 1996.

Marin Headlands Visitor Center★

From Conzelman Rd. take Field Rd. to the corner of Bunker Rd. Open daily 9.30am–4.30pm. Closed Thanksgiving, Dec 25. Call ahead for schedule of guided tours (1–2hrs). 415-331-1540. www.nps.gov/goga/marin-headlands.htm.

Located in Fort Barry's former post chapel (1941), this ranger station/visitor center mounts excellent, hands-on natural history displays and exhibits on the human inhabitants of the headlands—Coast Miwok, 19C vaqueros (Mexican and Native American cattle ranchers), Portuguese dairy ranchers, lighthouse keepers, and soldiers. Browse the well-stocked bookstore for books, field guides and maps.

Near the visitor center lies Missile Site SF 88L, a former **Nike missile site**, one of several around the bay. Its original but unarmed Nike missiles are open to the public for viewing (*open Wed–Fri and 1st Sat of each month 12.30–3.30pm; call in advance to confirm; 415-331-1543*).

Fort Cronkhite

Follow Bunker Rd. to Mitchell Rd. and continue along Rodeo Lagoon to beach parking lot.

Named for a World War I commander, the fort houses gun batteries and a Nike missile. It is one of the best examples of these mobilization posts in the country. Visitors can walk around the barracks, mess halls and supply buildings.

Mount Tamalpais★★

The geographic focal point of southern Marin County, kingly Mt. Tamalpais *(tam-ul-PIE-us)*—known locally as Mt. Tam—towers majestically over San Francisco from the north. Its rocky, 2,571ft summit affords some of the Bay Area's finest views, while its flanks harbor an extraordinary abundance of trails, meadows, forests and other enticements to delight lovers of natural beauty and outdoor sports. Largely undeveloped, its terrain protected as state and national parklands or county watershed, it has been a treasured recreation resource for Bay Area urbanites for more than a century.

A BIT OF HISTORY

Coast Miwok tribes made their home on the bay and ocean fringes of Mt. Tamalpais for at least 3,000 years prior to European exploration and settlement of the area. The mountain itself was considered sacred. In 1772, Spanish explorers Don Pedro Fages and Padre Juan Crespí named the mountain La Sierra de Nuestro Padre de San Francisco ("The Mountain of Our Father of San Francisco"). Its present name is thought to have been derived from the Coast Miwok words *tamal*, meaning "bay," and *pa* (later corrupted by the Spanish to *pais*), meaning "mountain."

Trail, Rail and Carriage – In the decades following the Gold Rush, residents and visitors looked to the mountain for leisure and recreation. Hiking trails were established, and in 1884 a wagon road to the west peak was built. By 1896 tourists could ascend from the foothill town of Mill Valley to the summit aboard the steam-powered Mill Valley and Mt. Tamalpais Scenic Railway (later known as the Mt. Tamalpais and Muir Woods Railway). Dubbed the "Crookedest Railroad in the World," the train chugged along a steep 8.2mi route, negotiating 281 curves. In 1907, a "gravity car" line to

⌖ **Michelin Map:** See p235.

ℹ **Info:** ✆415-258-2410. www.mttam.net.

▶ **Location:** To get to Mt. Tam from San Francisco, take US-101 north over the Golden Gate Bridge to the Mill Valley/Stinson Beach exit and turn left onto shore-hugging Rte. 1 (Shoreline Hwy.). Turn right on Panoramic Highway and follow the signs to Mt. Tamalpais. The **Muir Woods Road** branches off the Panoramic Highway.

▲▲ **Kids:** A walk under the mighty redwoods at Muir Woods National Monument.

🕓 **Timing:** The mountain is a favored recreation destination, and each season has advantages. In spring, myriad small creeks run full, grassy ridges wear a lush green coat, and wildflowers festoon the slopes. In summer, thick fogs can blanket the mountain's lower slopes; yet the summit is often sunny and can afford extraordinary views of fog-wrapped San Francisco Bay. Fall and winter tend to be cool. While possible to visit all sights described on Mt. Tamalpais in one day, visitors may wish to plan more leisurely visits to individual sights.

🅿 **Parking:** The five parking lots on the mountain ($8/ car) are East Peak, Rock Spring, Pantoll Ranger Station, Bootjack Picnic Area and Mountain Theater.

🙂 **Don't Miss:** The awe-inspiring Muir Woods redwoods.

Muir Woods was installed, wherein passengers glided silently down from the summit to the Muir Woods Inn before hiking or riding horse-drawn carriages to the redwood forest. The railway ceased operation in 1930.

The work of preserving Mt. Tamalpais' unspoiled beauty was initiated by **William Kent,** an ardent and wealthy Marin County conservationist and state representative. Kent's donations and political lobbying helped create Muir Woods National Monument and Mount Tamalpais State Park.

A nature lover's paradise, Mt. Tamalpais is blessed with abundant wildlife and a tremendous variety of vegetation. Some 300 species of birds have been spotted here, including red-tailed hawks, turkey vultures, black ravens, Stellar's jays, quail, wrens and pileated woodpeckers. Black-tailed deer, Western gray squirrels, Sonoma chipmunks and brush rabbits all make their homes here. Nocturnal bobcats are present but rarely seen, and sightings of mountain lions and coyotes have been reported, though most were hunted out in the early 1800s.

SIGHTS
Mount Tamalpais
State Park★★

801 Panoramic Hwy, Mill Valley, 18mi from San Francisco. ◐Park open daily 7am–sunset. ◐Closed during high fire-risk days. Maps and recreation information available at Pantoll ranger station (◐open summer daily 8am–dusk, rest of the year weekends; hours vary) and Mt. Tamalpais Interpretive Association's East Peak Visitor Center (◐open Fri–Sun; hours

vary seasonally). ☎*$8/car.* ⚠ *☎415-388-2070. http://parks.ca.gov.*

The park began as a 200-acre gift from William Kent and was later enlarged through the efforts of local hiking clubs. Today it completely surrounds Muir Woods National Monument. Nature lovers flock to Mt. Tam's trails year-round, and summer brings theatergoers to the Mountain Theatre, a woodsy amphitheater with terraced stone seats, which mounts popular musicals on weekends in May and June *(E. Ridgecrest Blvd., just east of intersection with Pantoll Rd.; ☎415-383-1100; www.mountainplay.org).*

East Peak

▶ *From the Pantoll ranger station, take Pantoll Rd. to Ridgecrest Blvd. and continue toward the summit.*

Numerous turnouts, picnic spots, trailheads and scenic overlooks mark the long ascent to a parking area a quarter-mile below the top of Mt. Tamalpais. From here, cities, towns and majestic bay appear as if on a giant raised relief map, backdropped to the east by Mt. Diablo, 35mi away. The 360-degree panorama is one of the finest **views★★★** in the Bay Area. On exceptionally clear winter days, the snow-capped Sierra Nevada mountains are visible 140mi to the east, as are Mt. St. Helena to the north and the Farallon Islands to the west.

Vegetation at this elevation consists mostly of the brushy mix of scrub oak and red-barked manzanita known as chaparral. From the East Peak parking lot, a short but rocky and strenuous path *(.3mi)* leads to the summit fire lookout, rebuilt in 1937 by the Civilian Conservation Corps *(•⊷closed to the public).* The

A Cradle for Mountain Biking

In the early 1970s, a group of local bicycle enthusiasts began modifying and equipping their traditional balloon-tired "cruiser" bikes to withstand travel across Mt. Tamalpais' rugged trails and fire roads. Riding and racing such bikes became a local passion, and the ensuing years brought increasing technological innovations that resulted in today's sophisticated "mountain bikes." Mt. Tamalpais continues to attract a steady stream of bicycling enthusiasts, many of whom make the strenuous ascent to the summit on the unpaved Old Railroad and Eldridge grades.

🚶 **Verna Dunshee Trail** *(.7mi)* makes a level, paved loop around the summit. Many trails guide hikers and cyclists to East Peak and other points around the park. One of the more popular mountain-bike routes starts from a trailhead at **Mountain Home Inn,** a bed-and-breakfast lodge built on the site of a historic railroad inn *(810 Panoramic Hwy.; park in public lot across from the inn)*. The path ascends on unpaved fire roads that follow, in part, the old railway grade. Hikers may prefer to start higher on the mountain, at Pantoll, where several possible routes lead to the summit. Another popular destination is the **West Point Inn** (1904), a rustic wooden structure situated on a ridge just below the summit. Hikers, equestrians and bicyclists congregate here to relax on the shady veranda and take in panoramic **views**. From the inn, the Old Railroad Grade continues to East Peak.

👥 MUIR WOODS NATIONAL MONUMENT★★★

17mi from San Francisco.
▶ *Take US-101 north to Rte. 1 (Shoreline Hwy.); continue to Panoramic Hwy. and turn right, then left on Muir Woods Rd.* 🕐*Open daily 8am–sunset. Ranger talks and tours available; call for information.* 👁$7. ✕👶♿️🅿️ 🕿*415-388-2596. www.nps.gov/muwo.*
Situated on the slope of Mt. Tamalpais along Redwood Creek, Muir Woods harbors one of the largest stands of ancient coast redwoods in the Bay Area. The tranquil grove of majestic red-barked trees, some 1,100 years in age, attracts more than 1.5 million visitors annually.

A Tree-Lover's Monument

The world's tallest trees, coast redwoods *(Sequoia sempervirens),* can attain heights equal to that of a 36-story building. They are among the few conifers that can sprout from knotty outgrowths, called burls, as well as reproduce by seeds. The absence of resin in the trees' 6in- to 12in-thick bark, coupled with the high tannin content of the wood, renders them resistant to fire, insect damage and disease, enabling them to live

Muir Woods National Monument

© Damien Michelin

for hundreds of years. Muir Woods is a relatively young grove; its oldest trees are more than a millennium old. California's tallest, oldest redwoods thrive north of here in the Redwood Empire. Prior to the arrival of Europeans on the west coast, millions of acres of primeval redwood forest blanketed the coastal reaches of California and southern Oregon; aggressive logging has since wiped out all but 150,000 acres. Much of Mt. Tamalpais' virgin redwood forest was logged in the years following the Gold Rush, but the trees in present-day Muir Woods escaped the lumbermen's saws and axes, owing to their relative inaccessibility. The forest became a national monument in 1908 after William Kent donated 295 acres of land in Redwood Canyon to the federal government in 1907, insisting that the park be named for conservationist John Muir. In a letter of thanks to Kent, Muir wrote, "This is the best tree-lover's monument that could possibly be found in all the forests of the world."

Visit

Begin at the visitor center and adjacent bookstore, which stock trail maps and information about local natural history. From the visitor center, six miles of trails (some paved) wind about the forest floor, following the paths of Redwood Creek and Fern Creek. The **Main Trail** [hiker](*1mi*) crosses over a series of wooden bridges, looping under a dense canopy of mature redwoods that rise like spires toward the heavens. Amid groves of living trees, trunks of fallen giants lie in various states of decay in a lush undergrowth of sword ferns, azaleas and horsetail, a primitive plant whose ancestry dates back 300 million years. Muir Woods' most impressive trees stand in **Cathedral Grove** and **Bohemian Grove,** site of the park's tallest tree (unmarked), measuring 253ft.

The Main Trail connects to the Hillside Trail (*1.9mi loop*) or to the Ocean View, Lost and Fern Creek trails (*3.1mi loop*). Trails also connect with unpaved hiking trails in Mount Tamalpais State Park.

ADDITIONAL SIGHTS
Muir Beach Overlook
17mi from San Francisco.
▷ *Take US-101 to Rte. 1 (Shoreline Hwy.); from Muir Woods, take Frank Valley Rd. 2.5mi and turn right on Rte. 1.*
Steps lead down to a railed promontory that affords sweeping **views**★★ of the coast to the north and south. Hooded concrete burrows on the bluff behind the promontory were installed during World War II; signs illustrate how they were designed to target enemy vessels.

South of the overlook, Shoreline Highway passes **Muir Beach,** a small, scenic stretch of sand situated at the mouth of Redwood Creek. Tables and grills make this an excellent spot to relax, though dangerous tides and currents make swimming inadvisable.

Stinson Beach
Rte. 1, 5mi north of Muir Beach Overlook.
Called Willow Camp in the late 19C, this charming beach town is a popular stop for coastal travelers, with its assortment of restaurants and art galleries, bookstore, surf shop and outdoor theater. The excellent **beach**★★, one of the few in the area safe for swimming (when it's not being patrolled by sharks), is the town's principal attraction. In addition to swimmers, the 3.5mi sandy crescent draws surfers, sunbathers and kayakers.

Stinson Beach is the finishing point for the annual Dipsea Race in which runners traverse Mt. Tamalpais from Mill Valley.

♣♣ Audubon Canyon Ranch
4900 Shoreline Hwy. (Rte. 1), 3.5mi north of Stinson Beach. ◔*Open mid-Mar–mid-Jul, call for hours.* ♒*$15 donation suggested.* [P] ℘*415-868-9244. www.egret.org.*
This 1,000-acre bird sanctuary is located in a woodsy canyon adjacent to Bolinas Lagoon. In spring, the center's grounds and trails are open for observing great blue herons and white egrets nesting in the trees. A small museum mounts exhibits on local geology and natural history.

Bolinas
5mi north of Stinson Beach. Take first left turn off Rte. 1 north of Bolinas Lagoon.
In a captivating setting on an off-the-beaten-path peninsula between the Pacific Ocean and Bolinas Lagoon, this picturesque community has in recent decades developed a reputation as an insular outpost of counterculture. Settled in 1835 on the Baulenes Rancho land grant, the town boomed during the Gold Rush when schooners came here to load timber destined for building sites in San Francisco.

Today, the quaint downtown features a charming bar, a health-food store, several cafes and the small **Bolinas Museum** (*48 Wharf Rd.;* ◔ *open Fri 1–5pm, Sat–Sun noon–5pm;* ◔*closed Jan 1, Dec 25;* ♿[P] ℘*415-868-0300. www.bolinasmuseum.org).* The pleasant beach near downtown attracts swimmers, surfers and sunbathers.

ADDRESSES

Point Reyes National Seashore★★

Windy, wave-swept and often cloaked in fog, the Point Reyes Peninsula is an enchantingly varied expanse of wilderness. Jutting from the west Marin County pasturelands into the Pacific Ocean, this 30-mile coastal wedge harbors long sandy beaches, lush forests, rugged sea cliffs and vast wetlands, all populated by diverse animal, bird and marine life. Laced by 140 miles of trails, the 102 square-mile peninsula was designated a National Seashore in 1962.

A BIT OF HISTORY

Formed by the San Andreas Fault, the Point Reyes Peninsula rides on the eastern edge of the Pacific tectonic plate, creeping northwesterly at about 2in per year, while the adjacent North American plate travels westward at a slower rate. The two plates meet in a rift zone that runs south through the Olema Valley and northwest beneath narrow Tomales Bay, which separates the peninsula from the rest of Marin County. The jut of land was thrust more than 16ft northwest of the mainland by the great earthquake of 1906. A legacy of the peninsula's ancient journey along the San Andreas Fault is its granite backbone, **Inverness Ridge**, which has geologic origins in the Tehachapi Mountains 300mi to the south. Five million years ago, the peninsula occupied the site of present-day Monterey Bay; someday it will be an island sliding toward the Gulf of Alaska.

"White Bancks and Cliffes" – For thousands of years, Point Reyes was home to Coast Miwok Indians. The peaceable Miwoks harvested acorns and berries, fished for shellfish and salmon, and hunted deer and elk. In summer 1579, Francis Drake, an English explorer sponsored by Queen Elizabeth I, turned south from his search for a Northwest Passage

Info: ℰ415-464-5100. www.nps.gov/pore.

Location: The Point Reyes Peninsula lies some 40mi north of San Francisco. From the city take US-101 north to Mill Valley/Stinson Beach exit (Rte. 1); continue on Shoreline Hwy. (Rte. 1) to Bear Valley Rd. (27mi). For a quicker if less dramatic route, continue north on US-101 to the Greenbrae exit (10mi) to Sir Francis Drake Blvd. west, turn right on Rte. 1 and take the first left onto Bear Valley Rd.

Kids: Kule Loklo, a re-created Miwok village.

Timing: Weather conditions can change dramatically from one area to the next on the peninsula; visitors should always be prepared for cool winds and damp conditions. The autumn months are usually mildest. Winter, the rainiest season, is the best time to see migrating gray whales.

Don't Miss: Point Reyes Lighthouse for its wild, windswept views. Also, the Earthquake Trail, for intriguing glimpses of terrain disrupted by the 1906 earthquake.

and anchored his ship, the *Golden Hind,* for repairs in the vicinity of Point Reyes. The "faire and good baye" he described is thought to be the protected bay now known as Drakes Bay. Drake claimed his landfall for England, calling it "Nova Albion" after "the white bancks and cliffes" (resembling the blanched palisades of England's Dover coast) that rise over Drakes Beach.

In the next decades the area was visited by Spanish explorers, including Sebastián Vizcaíno, who in 1603 named

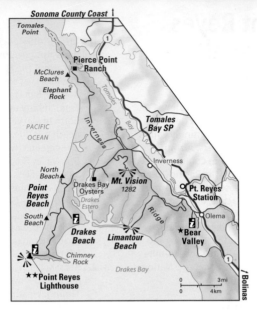

Sonoma County Coast

it La Punta de Los Reyes or "Point of the Kings." In 1792, British Captain George Vancouver gave Drakes Bay its name. But Francis Drake's claim to Nova Albion was never upheld by Vancouver or other English visitors. The area became a distant colony of Spain. After Mexican independence in 1821, Point Reyes became a center for cattle ranching, remaining so after the U.S. takeover of California. In the 1950s, development threatened to change the peninsula forever, but fierce preservation efforts led to the creation of the Point Reyes National Seashore in 1962.

Numerous historic cattle ranches, dating from the 1850s to 1870s, continue to operate within the park's boundaries, and drivers must be ready to pause for herds crossing the roads.

SIGHTS
BEAR VALLEY AREA
Bear Valley Visitor Center★

🕐Open Mon–Fri 9am–5pm, weekends & holidays 8am–5pm. 🕐Closed Dec 25.
♿🅿️ 🕿415-464-5100.
www.nps.gov/pore.
Rangers on duty at this attractive, barn-like park headquarters provide information, answer questions and post times and meeting places for guided hikes and

other interpretive programs. Spend time in the center's fine **exhibit hall,** where displays on coastal wetlands, birdwatching hot spots, marine mammals and cultural history provide an introduction to the peninsula.

From the Visitor Center parking lot, the pleasant, easy **Earthquake Trail★** (.6mi) invites strollers to see the dramatic effects of ground-shifting that took place during the 1906 quake, whose epicenter was in this rift zone. One spot on the trail shows how a wooden fence split and separated as it rode with the moving ground.

Also leading from the parking lot, the **Woodpecker Nature Trail** (.7mi) offers a quick introduction to the natural wonders of Point Reyes.

Morgan Horse Ranch

🕐Open daily 10am–4.30pm. 🅿️
Situated just behind the Visitor Center, this 100-acre ranch maintains a herd of more than a dozen compact, muscular Morgans used by park rangers for backcountry patrol. A self-guided tour of the ranch (including a blacksmith's shop, pole barn and stables) trots visitors through two centuries of history about the Morgan, the first American breed of horse.

👥 Kule Loklo

A short walk *(.5mi)* from the Visitor Center, this re-created Coast Miwok village offers a glimpse into the lifestyle and culture of the peninsula's native inhabitants. The village's structures, built according to authentic Miwok techniques, include redwood-bark shelters, an underground sweat lodge and a ceremonial dance house. At the time of Francis Drake's visit, some 100 Miwok villages similar to this one were scattered across present-day Marin and south Sonoma Counties.

Bear Valley Trail★

8.2mi round-trip. Trailhead near Visitor Center.

Hikers, bikers, joggers and equestrians range this wide, easygoing path along Coast Creek. Traversing redwood forests and picnic-perfect Divide Meadow, the trail ends at the Arch Rock **viewpoint** overlooking the ocean. Several more-strenuous trails branch off the Bear Valley Trail, including the Sky, Glen and Old Pine trails; the Coast Trail intersects it near Arch Rock.

Limantour Beach

▶ *From the Visitor Center, drive 1.5mi north on Bear Valley Rd. Turn left on Limantour Rd. and continue 6mi.*

This splendid curve of land along Drakes Bay is famous for its fine **views** of the white cliffs of Point Reyes. At the northern end, the shoreline narrows to form Limantour Spit, which separates the wildlife-rich waters of Limantour Estero (*estero* is Spanish for "estuary") from the deeper waters of Drakes Bay. From September through May, Limantour Estero and nearby Drakes Estero are major wintering and migratory grounds for shorebirds and seabirds.

POINT REYES PENINSULA AREA

The tip of Point Reyes, protruding some 15mi into the Pacific Ocean, has for centuries constituted a severe hazard for mariners. Numerous ships have met their demise here, lost in the dense fogs and stormy weather that frequently drape the exposed jut of land. High winds and heavy surf rake the northwest-facing bluffs; beaches and estuaries on the southeast side enjoy sheltered conditions.

Mount Vision

▶ *From Bear Valley Rd., veer left onto Sir Francis Drake Blvd. and turn left on Mt. Vision Rd.*

From the overlook enroute to **Mt. Vision**'s 1,282-ft summit, sweeping **views★★** extend over Point Reyes, Drakes Estero and the rolling Pacific Ocean. The narrow, winding road continues to the peak, where hikers can connect to several different trails scaling the flanks of Inverness Ridge.

West of Mt. Vision Road, take Drakes Estero exit off Sir Francis Drake Boulevard to **Drakes Bay Oysters** *(17171 Sir Francis Drake Blvd., Inverness;* 🕐 *open daily 8.30am–4.30pm;* ♿🅿 *℘415-669-1149; www.drakesbayoyster.com)*, a purveyor of sustainably grown, freshly harvested shellfish.

Drakes Beach

▶ *Follow signs from Sir Francis Drake Blvd.*

Here, visitors enjoy one of the peninsula's most serene stretches of sand, sheltered from pounding surf and stiff ocean winds. Gentle waves lap the shore, and the adjacent estuary attracts birds (and birdwatchers) year-round. The small **Kenneth C. Patrick Visitor Center** here provides information and exhibits on the marine ecosystem of Drakes Bay *(*🕐*open Sat–Sun and holidays only 10am–5pm;* 🕐*closed Dec 25;* ✕♿🅿 *℘415-669-1250)*.

Point Reyes Beach

▶ *Follow Sir Francis Drake Blvd. southwest 4.7mi from Mt. Vision Rd.; turn right at sign to North Beach.*

The wide, splendid, 12-mi strip comprising **North Beach** and **South Beach** faces northwest—directly into the strongest winds and roughest surf of the open ocean. The beaches offer glorious walks, but strong currents make them unsafe for swimming, surfing or wading.

Point Reyes Lighthouse

© MICHELIN

🏛🚶 Point Reyes Lighthouse★★

End of Sir Francis Drake Blvd.
🕐*Open Thu–Mon 10am–4.30pm, weather permitting.* 🕐*Closed Dec 25.*
🅿 *Parking area is 22mi from Bear Valley Visitor Center. 5mi walk to visitor center & lighthouse.* 📞*415-669-1534. www.nps.gov/pore.*

Perched halfway down the sheer south face of precipitous Point Reyes headland—considered perhaps the foggiest and windiest point in the continental U.S.—this beacon guided countless mariners for more than a century, from 1870 to 1975. A steep staircase of 308 steps *(closed when winds exceed 40mph)* descends to the station, where visitors can admire the three-ton Fresnel lens cast in 1867 *(🕐lens room is open as staffing permits).* The brass-mounted light, still fully operational, is visible for more than 24 nautical miles.

On clear days, the headlands offer excellent **views★★★** of the coast, the Farallon Islands to the southwest and distant San Francisco. The spot is popular with birders and whale-watchers, who congregate here to spy gray whales as they pass close to shore during their annual migration season *(Dec–Apr).*

Sea lions and seals perch on rocky abodes just east of the point. Chimney Rock is one of the best places to spot elephant seals in the Bay Area.

TOMALES POINT AREA

Dairy and cattle ranches blanket the peninsula's northern point, set between the Pacific Ocean to the west and Tomales Bay to the east.

🏛🚶 Pierce Point Ranch

▶ *From Bear Valley Visitor Center, take Sir Francis Drake Blvd. north 7.5mi. Turn right on Pierce Point Rd. and continue to its end.* 🕐*Open dawn–dusk.* ♿🅿.

Established in 1858 by Vermont dairy farmer Solomon Pierce, this pastoral spread of farm buildings remains the only one of the park's 26 historic dairy and cattle ranches open to the public. A self-guided tour leads among the ranch buildings, while exhibits describe such farm activities as butter churning and hay collecting.

The wide, mile-long stretch of **McClures Beach** *(turn left at end of Pierce Point Rd.; follow steep .5mi dirt path to beach)* is bounded by granite outcrops. At the south end, a narrow passageway through the rocks *(accessible only at low tide)* opens onto a pocket beach where cormorants nest on Elephant Rock.

The lands surrounding the beach and the ranch today form a 2,600-acre reserve for a flourishing herd of some 440 **tule elk**, reintroduced in 1978; these animals once roamed the entire peninsula before being hunted out in the late 19C. More than 150 white-spotted **axis deer** graze on the moors between Marshall Beach Trail and Estero Trail; a similar number of **fallow deer** (many with pure white coats) range over the peninsula.

Tomales Bay State Park

1208 Pierce Point Rd., 4mi north of Inverness. 🕐*Open Fri–Mon 8am–sunset.* 🚗*$8/car.* ⛺♿🅿 📞*415-669-1140. http://parks.ca.gov.*

Tiny **Heart's Desire Beach** and Shell Beach offer excellent opportunities for swimming and wading in sheltered Tomales Bay. Follow interpretive signs along the **Nature Trail** *(.5mi)* to Indian Beach, where a traditional native shelter can be visited.

ADDITIONAL SIGHT
Point Reyes Station
2mi north of Olema by Rte. 1.
This small town grew up as a dairy center and stop along the North Pacific Coast Railroad. Although bakeries, restaurants, art galleries and antique shops now occupy some of its late-19C structures, dairy ranchers still swap stories at the local diner and load up supplies at the feed barn, preserving the community's bucolic atmosphere.

EXCURSION
SONOMA COUNTY COAST
North of Point Reyes Station, Highway 1 snakes along the precipitous Pacific coastline for 74mi before entering Mendocino County (*see The Green Guide California*). Spectacular views abound of steep, rocky cliffs pummeled by roiling surf. Sleepy seaside towns and state parks punctuate the wild shoreline, which nurtures a variety of birds and marine animals.

Bodega Bay
34mi north of Point Reyes Station.
The second-largest salmon port on the Pacific coast bears the name of Spanish explorer Juan Francisco de la Bodega y Cuadra, who reached its sheltered anchorage in October 1775. Commercial fishing took off in the 1940s; today, the waterfront bustles with the comings and goings of some 300 boats. From the bluffs atop **Bodega Head** *(3mi off Hwy. 1 on Eastshore Rd., north of Bodega Bay)*, on the far side of the bay, stretch splendid **views★** of the coast from Point Reyes to Fort Ross. Between January and May, the bluffs are popular with whale-watchers. Six miles east in **Bodega** is the building *(17110 Bodega Lane)* that served as the schoolhouse in Alfred Hitchcock's classic film *The Birds* (1962). Originally the Potter School (1873), the Italianate structure is now a private residence.

Sonoma Coast State Beaches★
Extending 18mi, Bodega Head to Meyers Gulch, just north of Jenner. ◐*Open daily.* ∞*$8/car.* △ & ▯ ☎*707-875-3483. http://parks.ca.gov.*

This spectacular strip of coast affords striking seascapes and numerous opportunities for fishing, hiking, camping, sunbathing and beachcombing. Rocky outcrops separate the 15 small, sandy crescents that punctuate the shoreline. Some of the most dramatic **views★** are from **Duncan's Landing** *(5mi north of Bodega Dunes)*.
One of the most accessible of the Sonoma Coast beaches is **Goat Rock Beach★** *(8mi north of Bodega Dunes)*, at the mouth of the Russian River, where visitors enjoy a unique **view** of river and ocean, barely separated by a narrow spit of sand. From November to March, throngs of resident harbor seals vie with fishermen to catch schools of salmon that return each year to spawn.
Turnouts abound on this stretch of highway. North of Jenner, the road is a series of switchbacks above the ocean *(average speed 25mph)*. Several miles south of Fort Ross, the road flattens out and marine terraces appear on the left.

Fort Ross State Historic Park★★
19005 Coast Hwy 1, Jenner, 22mi north of Bodega Bay. ◐*Grounds open Fri–Sun dawn–dusk. Visitor center open Fri–Sun 10am–4.30pm.* ◐*Closed Thanksgiving Day, Dec 25.* ∞*$8/car.* & ▯ ☎*707-847-3286. http://parks.ca.gov.*
Built high on a desolate promontory above an azure cove and flanked by mountains to the east, Fort Ross provided a base from which Russian colonists hunted sea otters for their valuable pelts and supplied food to Russia's more remote outposts in Alaska.
Settlement Rossiia (Russia), as the colony was christened, was established in 1812 by members of the Russian-American Company. The first colonists, a group of 25 Russians and 80 Alaskan Aleuts (recruited for their skill in hunting sea otters), negotiated with the resident Kashaya Pomo Indians for land before constructing the garrison. Several hundred people subsequently led a peaceful existence cultivating the land and its resources, but by the mid-1830s, California's sea otter population was

Fort Ross State Historic Park

©honestmike/iStockphoto.com

decimated and the colony abandoned. The present fort has been partially restored to its early appearance. A short, paved loop trail *(.5mi)* leads from a **visitor center**—offering displays on the history of the fort and earlier Pomo tribes—through a cypress grove to the fort. Constructed of redwood and modeled after traditional edifices in Siberia, the stockade contains six structures of clean, simple lines. Most buildings are replicas; only the **Rotchev House** *(north wall)* is partially original. The **officials' quarters** *(southwest wall)* display artifacts evoking the fort's early days.

The small **chapel**—first Russian Orthodox church in North America outside Alaska—boasts a distinctive, hexagonal tower and round cupola. This building is the third incarnation of the original structure that was erected in 1825 but collapsed during the 1906 earthquake.

Salt Point State Park

9mi north of Fort Ross. ○*Open daily dawn–dusk. Visitor Center open Apr–Oct weekends 10am–3pm.* ⊗*$8/car.* ○*Closed during inclement weather.* ⚠ 🅿 *℘707-847-3221. http://parks.ca.gov.* Named for the substance that Native Americans once collected from submarine crevices for preserving seafood, this 6,000-acre park runs along 4mi of coastline. Divers favor the site for its underwater **Gerstle Cove Marine Reserve**. Off the shores of the cove, seals sun themselves on glistening rocks.

The adjacent **Kruse Rhododendron State Reserve** *(entrance 3mi north of Salt Point)* protects 317 acres studded with thickets of coast rhododendron that succeeded vegetation razed years ago by a forest fire. This site is best visited from April to June, when the towering rhododendrons burst into bloom.

ADDRESSES

🛏 STAY

Bed-and-breakfast inns and **cabins** are available in Inverness, Olema and Point Reyes Station. A hostel is located at Point Reyes (*℘415-663-8811)*. The penisula's camping areas range from primitive to modern; for reservations call Bear Valley Visitor Center (four campgrounds, all for hikers and bikers; *℘415-663-8054)*; Tomales Bay State Park (boat-in camping; *℘415-663-8054)*; or private Olema Ranch (one campground, cars welcomed; *℘415-663-8106)*.

RECREATION

Hiking: easy and strenuous trails; stop at Bear Valley Visitor Center for maps and information. **Biking:** on roads and designated trails; rentals in Olema and Point Reyes Station. Guided **horseback** trail rides: Five Brooks Stables (*℘415-663-1570)*. **Bird-watching:** Point Reyes Bird Observatory (west of Bolinas); Estero de Limantour (east of Drakes Estero). **Whale-watching:** Point Reyes Lighthouse.

Sausalito★

Nestled into the bay side of the Marin Headlands, just a few miles north of the Golden Gate Bridge, this upscale residential community draws throngs of visitors on sunny days and weekends. Sausalito's winding streets, quaint boutiques and lush hillsides dotted with attractive homes and gardens create a relaxed yet cultured ambience, and its privileged setting affords some of the finest views of San Francisco and the bay islands.

A BIT OF HISTORY

On the afternoon of August 5, 1775, the Spanish supply ship *San Carlos,* under the command of Lt. Juan Manuel de Ayala, dropped anchor just outside the Golden Gate. Ayala's first mate and six crew members, sent ashore to explore potential anchorage sites, became the first Europeans to enter the bay from the sea. Ayala named their chosen anchorage after the trees they found growing along freshwater streams (the Spanish word *sauces* means "willows").

Sausalito's first Anglo settler, **William Richardson,** arrived in San Francisco Bay in 1822 at age 27, while serving as first mate on a British whaler. In 1825, having acquired Mexican citizenship, Richardson married the daughter of the *comandante* of the Presidio. Through family connections, he later acquired title to the 19,572-acre Rancho del Saucelito, which stretched from the Marin Headlands to Stinson Beach on the west side of the peninsula. In 1849, after the U.S. takeover of California, his property came under dispute and he was forced to sell the southern portion of the land.

Railroad and Shipping Hub – In 1875, the North Pacific Coast Railroad extended its tracks from San Rafael to Sausalito. Trains carrying lumber from the northern redwood forests halted here to unload their cargoes onto a fleet of ferryboats that carried travelers and commerce between rural Marin County and booming San Francisco.

▶ **Population:** 7,136

Info: ✆415-332-0505. www.sausalito.org.

Location: Sausalito lies just north of Golden Gate Bridge, along the eastern side of the Marin County peninsula. Driving from San Francisco, take US-101 over the Golden Gate Bridge to the Alexander Ave. exit, just past Vista Point; continue 2mi to Bridgeway Blvd. The ferry (see Addresses) is an excellent option for a visit to Sausalito; the trip takes about 30min and the Sausalito ferry landing is conveniently located downtown within walking distance of shops and restaurants.

Kids: Budding dam-builders will love the Bay Model Visitors Center of the U.S. Army Corps of Engineers.

Timing: Sausalito's scenery, shops and eateries make it a great day trip from San Francisco. For a stroll in the residential neighborhoods along Bulkley Avenue, come in the morning; afternoon is best for leisurely exploration of Bridgeway's shops and boutiques.

Parking: Street parking and public lots fill to capacity on weekends, forcing drivers to park on residential streets high on the hillsides. Consider visiting during the week if you're behind the wheel.

Don't Miss: A walk on Bulkley Avenue, for a sense of the Sausalito lifestyle.

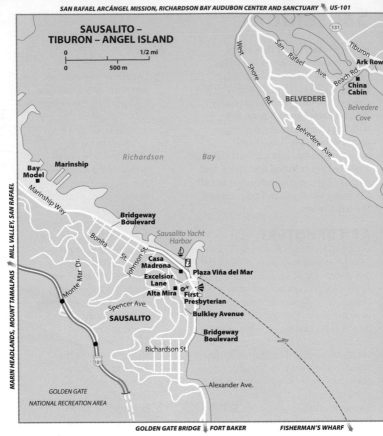

SAN RAFAEL ARCÁNGEL MISSION, RICHARDSON BAY AUDUBON CENTER AND SANCTUARY — US-101

SAUSALITO – TIBURON – ANGEL ISLAND

0 — 1/2 mi
0 — 500 m

131

Tiburon
Ark Row
China Cabin
BELVEDERE
Belvedere Cove

West Shore Rd
San Rafael Ave.
Beach Rd.
Belvedere Ave.

Richardson Bay

Bay Model
Marinship
Marinship Way

Bridgeway Boulevard
Sausalito Yacht Harbor

Bonita St.
Johnson St.

Casa Madrona
Plaza Viña del Mar
Excelsior Lane
Alta Mira
First Presbyterian
Bulkley Avenue
Bridgeway Boulevard

Monte Mar Dr.
Spencer Ave.
SAUSALITO
Richardson St.

MARIN HEADLANDS, MOUNT TAMALPAIS — MILL VALLEY, SAN RAFAEL

101

GOLDEN GATE NATIONAL RECREATION AREA

Alexander Ave.

GOLDEN GATE BRIDGE — FORT BAKER — FISHERMAN'S WHARF

In 1942, three months after the U.S. entered World War II, the U.S. Maritime Commission hired the W.A. Bechtel Company to construct a new West Coast shipyard capable of quickly building standard **Liberty Ships** and oil tankers. Bechtel selected 210 acres of undeveloped Sausalito waterfront as the site of the new facility, known as Marinship; in 1942–43, 75,000 men and women poured into the town to build vessels for the American war effort. Beginning just before the war—in the years following the 1937 completion of the Golden Gate Bridge—Sausalito also experienced an influx of writers, artists, poets and other free-spirited souls. They found inexpensive refuge in the hulks of retired ferryboats and in houseboats made from the hulls of old military landing craft. The close-knit community of "floating home"

dwellers persists today, continuing the 1890s tradition of houseboating on Richardson Bay.

SIGHTS
Bridgeway Boulevard★

This attractive thoroughfare skirting Sausalito's waterfront was originally called Water Street. The name was changed to Bridgeway in 1937, as highway engineers had planned to route Golden Gate Bridge automobile traffic directly through Sausalito. An alternate route above the village was ultimately selected and Bridgeway instead became the anchor of a charming district of restaurants, cafes, galleries, shops and inns like the **Casa Madrona Hotel and Spa** (801 Bridgeway; ℘415-332-0502; www.casamadrona.com), a restored Victorian villa (1885) nestled on the wooded hillside overlooking the yacht harbor.

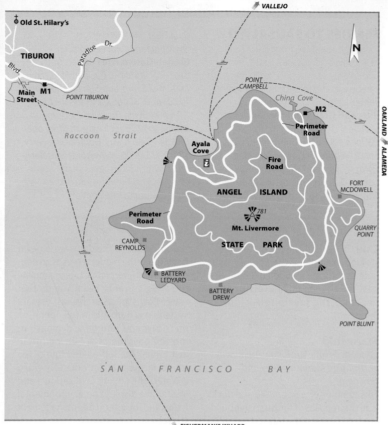

Near the ferry landing, across from the Mission-style Sausalito Hotel and The Inn Above Tide, is tiny **Plaza Viña del Mar**. The plaza honors the city of Viña del Mar, Chile, one of Sausalito's two sister cities (the other is Sakaide, Japan). South of the ferry landing, Bridgeway's wide sidewalks offer delightful **views★★**.

Sausalito Visitor Center & Historical Exhibit

780 Bridgeway. ○*Open Mon–Sat 11.30am–4pm.* ○*Closed major holidays.* ♿ 🅿 ✆ *415-332-0505. www.sausalito.org.*

Occupying a former ice house, this small museum's displays trace the history of Sausalito from the days of the Coast Miwok to the present. Look out for photographs of the Golden Gate Bridge under construction, and portraits of

such famous residents as actor Sterling Hayden; Sally Stanford, a San Francisco madam who became mayor of Sausalito; and infamous rum-runner and bank robber "Baby Face" Nelson.

Bulkley Avenue

▷ *From Bridgeway, follow Princess St. (first street south of Plaza Viña del Mar) to Bulkley Ave. and turn right.*

A walk up shady Bulkley Avenue, through the hills that backdrop Sausalito's waterfront, brings visitors to elegant homes and contemporary compounds embellished by elaborate gardens and forests of pine, oak, acacia and eucalyptus trees. The **Alta Mira**, a sprawling, Spanish-style hotel built in 1927, commands spectacular bay **views★★** from its terrace of Alcatraz, Angel Island, San Francisco and the bay. Opposite, the **First Presbyterian**

FERRIES TO SAUSALITO

Although the drive from San Francisco to Sausalito is fairly quick and undeniably scenic, parking in Sausalito can be expensive and difficult to find. Ferries are a good alternative.

Blue and Gold Fleet ferries depart from Pier 41 at Fisherman's Wharf *Open daily year round; times vary. Check website for current schedule. No service Jan 1, Thanksgiving Day, Dec 25. Duration 30min. $10.50 each way, children, $6.25 each way. Blue &*

Gold Fleet 415-705-8200. www.blueandgoldfleet.com.

Golden Gate ferries depart from the Ferry Building. *Open Mon–Fri 7.40am–7.55pm, Sat–Sun and holidays 10.40am–6.30pm. No service Jan 1, Thanksgiving Day, Dec 25. Duration 30min. $9.75 each way, children ages 6-18 $4.75 each way. Golden Gate Ferry 415-455-2000. www.goldengateferry. org.* A visitor information kiosk at the ferry landing provides brochures and other Sausalito information.

Church (1909, Ernest Coxhead) is a striking example of the Shingle style; note its intricate wooden exterior. Just past the church, tiny **Excelsior Lane** descends the precipitous slope to Bridgeway.

Marinship

From downtown, follow Bridgeway north 1mi to Marinship Way and turn right.

This complex of warehouses and docks is all that remains of the huge shipbuilding facility that transformed Sausalito during World War II. In 1942 and 1943, more than 90 vessels were constructed here, including 15 Liberty Ships, 62 T-2 oil tankers and 16 Navy oilers, all in record time.

When the American fleet gathered in Tokyo Bay on August 14, 1945, to accept Japanese surrender, eight Marinship-built tankers were sent, including the yard's flagship, the USS *Tamalpais*.

Bay Model Visitor Center of the U.S. Army Corps of Engineers★
2100 Bridgeway. Open summer Tue–Fri 9am–4pm, Sat–Sun 10am–5pm; rest of the year Tue–Sat 9am–4pm. 415-332-3871. www.spn.usace.army. mil/bmvc.

Located in a former Marinship warehouse, this 1.5-acre scale model of the San Francisco Bay and Sacramento-San Joaquin Delta was originally conceived to test the effect on the shallow bay of

proposed dams. The dams were never built. Today the model serves as an educational and interpretive tool to simulate the tides, currents, salinity and other water-flow aspects of the vast estuary system; it is normally in full operation on Fridays and Saturdays, demonstrating the passage of a 24hr period in just 15min. The self-guided tour of the model includes an introductory video ("Water: The Link to Civilization") and interactive displays on environmental issues and long-term bay management strategy.

Visitors walk above and beside the sprawling miniature representation of 343sq mi of bay, delta and Pacific coastline. Near the lobby is a fascinating **display★** on Marinship and Sausalito's World War II shipbuilding years.

ADDRESSES

STAY

$$$$ The Inn Above Tide – *30 El Portal, Sausalito; 415-332-9535, www.innabove tide.com.* Guests at this charming luxury inn—the first Bay Area lodging to be built over the water—can be excused for thinking they're afloat. All 30 rooms, most with fireplaces, face onto the water. Seals and pelicans glide past private balconies as sailboats materialize from the bay's haunting fog. At night, the San Francisco skyline is startlingly bright.

Tiburon★
Angel
Island★★

A breezy maritime ambience, a historic Main Street, a bustling waterfront promenade and popular restaurants lure visitors to this charming bayside village at the southern tip of the Tiburon peninsula.

A BIT OF HISTORY

Lt. Juan Manuel de Ayala, the first European to visit the area, named Punta de Tiburon (Shark Point) during his 1775 voyage to explore and chart San Francisco Bay. Tiburon formed part of an 1834 Mexican land grant, and in 1884 became a busy railroad town when a branch line of the San Francisco and North Pacific Railroad was built along the peninsula, making it possible to travel from San Rafael and the Redwood Empire to San Francisco via train and ferry. Today, roads and a bike path along Richardson Bay mark the route of the long-defunct railroad.

SIGHTS
Main Street

False-fronted buildings on charming Main Street evoke the atmosphere of the late 19C. Walkways skirt the shore, and ferryboats docking from San Francisco and Angel Island add to the hubbub. West of downtown, Main Street turns sharply north to become pleasant **Ark Row**, where trees shade a charming collection of grounded houseboats, or "arks," that once floated on the bay as summer residences.

Tiburon Railroad-Ferry Depot Museum (M1)

1920 Paradise Dr., 3 blocks east of ferry landing. ○Open Apr–Oct Wed, Fri–Sun 1–4pm; rest of the year by appointment only. ◎Donations requested. ℘415-435-1853. www.landmarks-society.org. The only dual-use rail-and-ferry station west of New York's Hudson River,

  Michelin Map: See SAUSALITO pp250-251.

  Info: Tiburon: ℘415-435-5633; www.tiburonchamber.org. Angel Island: ℘415-435-5390; www.parks.ca.gov.

  Location: The easiest and most scenic route to Tiburon is by ferry. Blue and Gold Fleet ferries depart from San Francisco's Ferry Building and Pier 41 at Fisherman's Wharf daily (◎$10.50 each way; ℘415-705-8200; www.blueandgoldfleet.com). The journey takes about 30min and offers splendid views of the city and Alcatraz. If you are driving from San Francisco, take US-101 north 6mi to the Tiburon Blvd. (Rte. 131) exit; continue 4mi to the town center.

  Timing: Weekends bring throngs of visitors to Main Street; in the evening relax on the outdoor deck of a waterside restaurant.

  Parking: Parking lots are located on Tiburon Blvd. next to the Boardwalk Market; on Main St. next to the Tiburon Playhouse theater; and at Point Tiburon.

Donahue Depot (1884) was once the key link between San Francisco and the Redwood Empire. It was not retired from active use until 1968. Now on the National Register of Historic Places, it contains a c.1900 model of Point Tiburon and walls of historic photos.

The China Cabin★

52 Beach Rd. Turn west from Tiburon Blvd. ○Open Apr–Oct Sat–Sun 1–4pm; rest of the year by appointment only.

Arks Around the Bay

Through the late 19C and early 20C, numerous San Franciscans spent their summers aboard floating homes known as "arks," moored off the shores of Sausalito and other southern Marin County towns such as Tiburon. Popular summer retreats, these quaint structures enhanced the good life on San Francisco Bay and Richardson Bay. Some of them have been preserved on land as shops and homes on Bridgeway (north end of Sausalito Yacht Harbor) and "Ark Row" (downtown Tiburon). A refurbished ark is displayed at the Hyde Street Pier in San Francisco.

⊕Donations requested. ✆415-435-1853. www.landmarks-society.org.
Resting atop pilings in Belvedere Cove, this beautiful, Victorian-era social salon was salvaged from the *SS China* (1866), a sidewheel steamer that once traversed the Pacific Ocean from San Francisco to Hong Kong and Yokohama for the Pacific Mail Steamship Company.

The interior, restored to its full, gilded grandeur, offers a tantalizing glimpse of the elegance and luxury of 19C social salons.

Old St. Hilary's

201 Esperanza St. ▶ *From Tiburon Blvd. turn east on Beach Rd. and follow signs across Mar West St. (.7mi).* ⊙*Open Apr–Oct Sun 1–4pm; rest of the year by appointment only.* ⊕*Donations requested.* ♿🅿 ✆*415-435-1853. www.landmarks-society.org.*
Perched on a hillside above town, this former Roman Catholic church (1888) represents an excellent example of the Carpenter Gothic style. The historic landmark is surrounded by **St. Hilary's Preserve**, which protects 217 species of wildflowers, two-thirds of them native to the Tiburon Peninsula. Scenic paths lead through the preserve, where the wildflowers bloom for much of the year.

Richardson Bay Audubon Center and Sanctuary

376 Greenwood Beach Rd., 3.2mi west of downtown off Tiburon Blvd. ⊙*Open Mon–Sat 9am–5pm.* ✆*415-388-2524. www.tiburonaudubon.org.*
Administered since 1961 by the National Audubon Society, this bayside refuge comprises 11 acres of land and 900 acres of San Francisco Bay, and is used by the society to educate people about natural history, particularly waterfowl. Grounds include a .5mi mountain trail, a redwood grove, a hummingbird garden and four bird watching platforms with scopes. The centerpiece of the property is the 1876 **Lyford House** (↠*tours by appointment only*), an 1876 Victorian built by a prominent 19C doctor.

ANGEL ISLAND STATE PARK★★

Access from San Francisco's Pier 41 on Fisherman's Wharf via Blue and Gold Fleet ferry only (20min each way; ⊕*$17 round-trip;* ✆*415-705-5555; www.blueandgoldfleet.com); a ferry also connects the island to Tiburon (10min each way;* ⊕*$13.50 round-trip; includes park admission fee;* ✆*415-435-2131; www.angelislandferry.com).* ⊙*Open daily 8am–sunset.* ⚠✗♿ ✆*415-435-5390. www.angelisland.org or www.parks.ca.gov.*
This hilly, forested island, separated from Tiburon by tide-swept Raccoon Strait, is a peaceful oasis amid busy San Francisco Bay. Over its long history of human habitation, the 750-acre island—the largest in the bay—has served as a Coast Miwok haven, a Spanish land-grant cattle ranch, a U.S. military base, a quarantine station and an immigration facility.

The island was christened Isla de Los Angeles (Angels Island) by Lt. Juan Manuel de Ayala in 1775. After years of military use and a period (1910–40) as an immigration station, the island was declared surplus property by the federal government in 1948. In 1963 the entire island (except a Coast Guard installation at Point Blunt) became part of California's state park system. Today it draws tourists to its myriad trails, campsites and tranquil picnic spots.

VISIT
Ayala Cove
Ferries dock at this cozy little cove named for Lt. Juan Manuel de Ayala, who anchored his ship here for a month in 1775. The cove's broad sweep of lawn is a popular picnic spot. Stop at the state park **visitor center** (○*open daily; 415-435-5390*) for information and exhibits on the island's history.

Perimeter Road
5mi loop. Trailhead to left of Ayala Cove. This mostly paved road rings the island's forested flanks and offers an easy, scenic stroll past military installations and garrisons recalling the island's human history. From various points along the road, **views★★★** take in the jagged San Francisco skyline, shiplike Alcatraz and the Golden Gate Bridge spanning the mouth of San Francisco Bay. From the main path, spur roads and trails lead to several fine beaches and enclaves of historic buildings. At China Cove (North Garrison), a barracks that formerly housed Chinese, Russian, Japanese and South American immigrants today houses a small **museum★ (M2)** (*visit by 45min guided tour only; call for schedule 415-435-5390*). The **Fire Road** (3mi loop) circumscribes the island at a higher elevation, providing bikers and hikers a more challenging route.

Mt. Livermore
The 781ft summit of the island's central peak, accessible from Ayala Cove by the moderately strenuous Northridge *(2mi)* and Sunset *(2.5mi)* trails, offers an unobstructed **panorama★★★** sweeping over San Francisco, the bay and the communities surrounding it. The mountain was named for Caroline Livermore, leader of the movement to preserve Angel Island.

ADDITIONAL SIGHT
San Rafael Arcángel Mission
10mi north of Tiburon at 5th Ave. & A St. in San Rafael. ▶ *Take Rte. 131 to US-101 north and continue to Central*

San Rafael exit. ○*Chapel open daily 6.30am–6.30pm.* ○*Closed major holidays.* *Guided tours available on request; call ahead.* *Donations requested.* *415-454-8141.*
The 20th and penultimate mission of the California chain was founded in 1817 as an *asistencia* to Mission Dolores in San Francisco. The branch mission was used as a sanitarium for San Francisco parishioners in failing health, and was named for the patron saint of bodily healing. The buildings were razed in 1870; the current replica on the site dates from 1949. Fragments from the original church are displayed in the gift shop.

ADDRESSES

RECREATION

Angel Island State Park is open daily 8am–dusk, beckoning recreation enthusiasts with its scenic trails, secluded coves and rustic campsites. Summer is by far the busiest season; the island is peaceful at other times of year, but you should call ahead if you want to rent a bike, kayak or eat at the Cove Cafe, as hours are limited. Concessionaires operate with limited days and hours Nov–Mar.

Open-air motorized tours *(1 hr; audio commentary; $15)* and **mountain bike** rentals *($12.50/hr or $40/day)* are available through **Angel Island Tram Tours** *(hours vary seasonally; call for current schedule; 415-435-3544; www.angelisland.com).* You may also bring your own bike on the ferry.

Sea Trek offers **sea kayak** tours *(open May–Oct; guided tour from Sausalito $85, half-day tour $75; reservations required; 415-332-8494; www.seatrek.com).*

The **Angel Island Association** offers information on **hiking** and **biking** trails *(415-435-3972; www.angelisland.org).* Limited overnight **camping** is available by advance reservations only *(800-444-7275; http://parks.ca.gov).*

The **Cove Cafe** offers light lunch fare and outdoor dining *(open Mar–Nov 10am until last ferry leaves).*

WINE COUNTRY

Lying inland within a two-hour drive of San Francisco, the Napa Valley and Sonoma County thrive on the abundant sunshine and fertile soil that produce grapes for some of North America's finest wines. Though vineyards flourish along many of California's inland coastal areas from Eureka to San Diego County, and even as far east as the foothills of the Sierra Nevada, these areas just north of San Francisco have garnered a reputation as the state's preeminent winemaking regions. Visitors and locals flock here, drawn by the temperate climate, varied natural beauty and acclaimed wineries that make the Wine Country one of California's foremost tourist destinations.

Highlights

1. Sonoma **farmers' markets** (p259)
2. Pair wine with art at the **Hess Collection Winery** (p264)
3. Cooking demonstration at the **Culinary Institute of America** (p269)
4. Sterling's **aerial tramway** (p270)
5. Tour the lush **Luther Burbank Home and Gardens** (p278)

From Criollas Cuttings to a Gastronomic Center

Cuttings of Criollas grapevines first traveled to Alta California with missionary Franciscan padres during the late 17C. Wines made from these "mission" grapes were used mostly for trade or sacramental purposes. In the early 1830s, Frenchman Jean-Louis Vignes established a vineyard near Los Angeles using European grapevines *(Vitis vinifera)*, and by the mid-19C winemaking had become an important California industry.

After various ups and downs over the past 150 years, wine country seems to be on firmer ground. In recent decades the Napa and Sonoma Valleys have experienced tremendous development. The late 20C witnessed an explosion of small-scale operations, some housed in old wineries updated with state-of-the-art equipment.

Researchers at the University of California at Davis' renowned Department of Viticulture and Enology develop new methods of grape cultivation and winemaking, while trade associations work to promote California wines throughout the world.

Today the Wine Country has become a center for fine art and gastronomy. Trendy restaurants shine like stars in the culinary firmament, and in 1995 the renowned Culinary Institute of America installed a campus in the former Christian Brothers/Greystone Cellars winery. Recent years have seen the rise of showplace operations—among them Opus One, Clos Pegase, Artesa and the Hess Collection Winery—that combine wine production with the display of fine art and innovative architecture.

Downtown Sonoma

© Peter Wrenn / MICHELIN

A Bit of History

In 1857 **Agoston Haraszthy** (1812–69), a Hungarian immigrant, purchased a 400-acre estate in Sonoma County, named it Buena Vista, and cultivated Tokay vine cuttings imported from his homeland. The grapes flourished, inspiring Haraszthy to redouble his efforts at producing premium wines in northern California, experimenting with assorted varieties of *vinifera* cuttings and trained area grape growers. The quality of California wines steadily improved.

Boom and Bust – Haraszthy's discoveries created a boom in the wine industry throughout the Napa and Sonoma Valleys in the last decades of the 19C. Among the wineries established during this period were **Gundlach-Bundschu (1)** (1858), **Charles Krug (2)** (1861), and **Schramsberg Vineyards** (1862), first of the region's hillside wineries to hew storage caves out of rock. **Beringer**, **Beaulieu** and **Inglenook**, renowned names of the present-day wine industry, were also established during this period. As the 19C drew to a close, northern California grapevines fell prey to the root louse phylloxera; entire vineyards were decimated. Researchers discovered they could combat phylloxera by replanting vineyards with disease-resistant rootstocks from the midwestern U.S., onto which *vinifera* cuttings had been grafted. The wine industry achieved a modicum of recovery by the early 20C only to be faced with another setback: on January 29, 1919, the U.S. Congress ratified the 18th Amendment prohibiting the manufacture, sale, importation and transportation of intoxicating liquors.

Prohibition – Prohibition brought California's winemaking industry to a near-standstill. Licenses were granted to only seven California wineries to produce wines for sacramental and medicinal use. Home production of "non-intoxicating" grape juice for private consumption was also permitted. In 1933, when Prohibition was repealed, wine growers began rebuilding their industry. The Great Depression slowed the recovery, and it was not until the early 1970s that the demand for fine table wines rose and California's wine industry was fully re-established.

The Art of Winemaking

The Wine Country is organized into **Approved Viticultural Areas**, each suitable for the cultivation of certain types of grapes. Growing conditions vary depending on soil type and climate. Volcanic activity in the region has produced porous soils in which wine grapes thrive, but minerals, soil depth and moisture vary from region to region. **Weather** is considered the most important factor affecting the cultivation of wine grapes, which require a long growing season of hot days and cool nights. In the Wine Country, grapes ripen slowly from April to October, giving flavors and acids plenty of time to develop. The average annual rainfall of 33in occurs mostly in winter. Differences in elevation, proximity to the sea and exposure to sun, fog and wind create numerous microclimates.

The Wine Country's current production is based primarily on descendants of European *vinifera* cuttings. Best adapted to Wine Country growing conditions is the **Cabernet Sauvignon**, a small, blue-black grape from the Médoc district of France's Bordeaux region that produces a rich, full red wine. Burgundy's **Pinot Noir** grape is used for both table wine and California sparkling wine. Other red wine grapes from Europe include **Cabernet Franc**, **Petite Sirah**, **Napa Gamay** (derived from France's Gamay Beaujolais) and **Zinfandel**.

Some of California's finest white wines are made from **Chardonnay**, the premier white grape of France's Chablis and Burgundy regions. Chardonnay produces a dry, richly flavored wine. The **Sauvignon Blanc**, used in the making of French Sauternes and Pouilly-Fumé, grows well in Wine Country's cooler areas. **Pinot Blanc** is an important ingredient in many sparkling wines. Other white European varieties include **Riesling** and **Chenin Blanc**.

From Vine to Barrel to Bottle – Once grapes have achieved desired levels of sugar and acid, they are picked by hand or machine and placed into a stemmer-crusher, where paddles remove the stems and break the skins to produce a soupy mixture of seeds, skins and juice called **must**. In the making of white wines, the must is pressed immediately, usually in a device known as a **bladder press**. The pressed juice is clarified, inoculated with yeast, transferred to tanks, and left to ferment. During **fermentation**, which can last three days to six weeks, the yeast organisms consume the sugar in the grapes, creating ethyl alcohol, carbon dioxide and heat. If left unchecked, this heat can speed the fermentation process, completing it before desired flavors have had time to develop, so modern fermentation tanks are equipped with cooling sheaths to

---

Area Code: 707

GETTING THERE

BY CAR – Consult individual entries for directions to the **Napa Valley, Sonoma Valley** and the **Upper Sonoma-Russian River Region.**
BY BUS – **Golden Gate Transit** buses run between San Francisco and many cities in Sonoma County (*℘415-455-2000; www.goldengate.org*).

GENERAL INFORMATION

WHEN TO GO – The best times to visit the Wine Country are in the spring, when yellow mustard plants blossom in the vineyards before the summer's heat sets in; and in the fall, when temperatures are comfortable, the sun shines without fail, and winemakers begin the harvest and crush (pressing of grapes). Advance reservations are recommended for lodging and attractions in summer and fall.

VISITOR INFORMATION – Contact the following agencies to obtain maps and information on recreation, accommodations and seasonal events: **Napa Valley Destination Council** (*600 Main St., Napa; ℘251-9188; www.visitnapavalley.com*);
Napa Valley Vintners Association (*P.O. Box 141, St. Helena; ℘963-3388; www.napavintners.com*); **Sonoma Valley Visitors Bureau** (*453 1st St. E., Sonoma; ℘866-996-1090; www.sonomavalley.com*); **Sonoma County Tourism Bureau** (*3637 Westwind Blvd., Santa Rosa; ℘522-5800; www.sonomacounty.com*); **Sonoma County**

Vitners (*3637 Westwind Blvd., Santa Rosa; ℘522-5840; www.sonomawine.com*); **Santa Rosa Convention & Visitors Bureau** (*9 Fourth St., Santa Rosa; ℘577-8674; www.visitsantarosa.com*); **Russian River Wine Roads** (*PO Box 46, Healdsburg; ℘433-4335; www.wineroad.com*).
For a copy of the **Napa Valley Guide** (*$5.95*) or the **Sonoma County Guide** (*$5.95*), which include complete information on accommodation, dining and shopping, call ℘800-651-8953 or visit www.napavalley guidebook.com (free pdf at www.visitnapavalley.com).

ACCOMMODATIONS – Charming **bed-and-breakfast inns** can be found in towns along Rte. 29 (Napa Valley), Rte. 12 (Sonoma Valley) and US-101 (Russian River Valley). Larger **hotels** are located in Napa, Sonoma and Santa Rosa. Bed-and-breakfast and hotel reservation services include: **Napa Valley Welcome Center** (*℘251-9188 or ℘855-333-6272*), **Napa Valley Reservations Unlimited** (*℘252-1985; www.napavalleyreservations.com*), and **Bed and Breakfast Association of Sonoma Valley** (*℘800-969-4667; www.sonomabb.com*). It is wise to reserve well in advance as the best accommodations fill up during peak tourist season. Year-round **camping** is available at Bothe-Napa Valley State Park (*℘942-4575*), Sugarloaf Ridge State Park (*℘833-5712*), and at Lake Sonoma (*℘433-9483*).

control temperature. In making red wines, fermentation occurs before pressing so that the skins and seeds impart rich, dark colors and tannins to the fluid.

After fermentation, impurities are removed by filtration, centrifuging or **racking** (in which wine is transferred from tank to tank, leaving settled sediments behind). In the last clarification, called **fining**, substances such as clay, gelatin or egg whites may be introduced; sediments and impurities adhere to these materials, which are then easily removed. Many wines are **barrel-aged** in white-oak barrels; aging can last months or several years. Certain varieties require a blending stage in which wines are mixed to achieve desired flavors. Some wines are bottled before the final aging period.

ADDRESSES

RECREATION

Ballooning – Balloon tours *(3–5hrs)* depart at sunrise and fly year-round. Prices range from $195 to $295/person and may include a champagne brunch after the flight. Advance reservations required. Prices can vary with the number of passengers carried; inquire when booking.
Napa Valley companies include **Napa Valley Aloft** (*℘944-4400; www.nvaloft.com*), **Calistoga Balloons** (*℘942-5758; www.calistogaballoons.com*) and **Napa Valley Balloons Inc.** (*℘800-253-2224; http://napavalleyballoons.com*).
Sonoma County companies include **Above the Wine Country Balloons and Tours** (*℘538-7359; www.balloontours.com*).

Biking – A good way to enjoy the gentle, rolling terrain of the Wine Country is by bicycle. Rental shops offering trail information are in Napa, Sonoma and Calistoga. **Get-Away Adventures** leads weekend and day **bicycle tours** of the area *(equipment provided; day trip $149; longer trips offered; ℘568-3040; www.getawayadventures.com)* as well as hiking, cycling and kayaking trips of 1–6 days, $99–$2,499 all-inclusive.

Farmers' markets – These bustling markets offer local produce, poultry and other farm products (arrive early for the best selection):
Napa Downtown Farmers' market *(500 1st St.; May–Oct Tue and Sat 7.30am–noon; ℘501-3087; www.napafarmersmarket.com)*, **Santa Rosa Downtown Market** *(4th St. between Mendocino Ave. and E St., Santa Rosa; mid-May–Aug Wed 5pm–8.30pm; www.srdowntownmarket.com)*, **Sonoma Farmers' market** *(Plaza; early Apr–Oct Tue 5.30pm–dusk ℘694-3611; Depot Park; Fri 9am–12.30pm; ℘538-7023)*, **Healdsburg Farmers' market** *(1 block west of plaza, May–Nov Sat 9am–noon; North and Vine Sts., Jun–Oct Wed 4pm–6.30pm; ℘431-1956; www.healdsburgfarmersmarket.org)*.

Sightseeing – **California Wine Country Tours** take passengers by motor coach through Marin County to the Sonoma Valley *(8hrs; depart San Francisco Fisherman's Wharf Pier 43 1/2; daily 9.15am; $67; Gray Line Tours; ℘888-428-6937*. The **Napa Valley Wine Train** leaves from downtown Napa and offers dining and wine tasting on a 3hr excursion *(℘800-427-4124; www.winetrain.com)*.

🕮 STAY

$$$ Beazley House – *1910 First St., Napa. ℘707-257-1649. www.beazleyhouse.com. 11 rooms.* Napa's first bed-and-breakfast when it opened in 1981, this antique-filled 1902 Colonial Revival mansion still ranks among the valley's best. Five of the rooms are in a replicated carriage house; all are within walking distance of downtown.

$$$ Camellia Inn – *211 North St., Healdsburg. ℘707-433-8182. www.camelliainn.com. 9 rooms.* A home-like hideaway in the charming Russian River Valley, this Italianate-style Victorian offers nightly wine tastings and eclectic antique decor.

$$$ Sonoma Hotel – *110 W. Spain St., Sonoma. ℘800-468-6016. www.sonomahotel.com. 16 rooms.* From the stone fireplace in the lobby to the claw-foot tubs in the guest rooms, the hotel exudes country charm. Formerly a dry-goods store on Sonoma's plaza, the beautifully restored hotel offers cozy rooms equipped with rustic iron headboards and twig nightstands.

$$$$ La Résidence – *4066 Howard Ln., Napa.* ℰ*707-253-0337. www.laresidence. com. 26 rooms.* A gracious bed-and-breakfast complex in a rural setting near Napa, La Residence sprawls across two acres of gardens framed by oaks and pines. Antique decor and personalized hospitality make this a good Wine Country choice.

$$$$ Villagio Inn & Spa – *6481 Washington St., Yountville.* ℰ*707-944-8877. www.villagio.com. 112 rooms.* Reminiscent of a Tuscan village—with two-story villas surrounding lush gardens and vineyards, fountains and waterways—the Villagio combines its resort atmosphere with a health spa. Rates include a welcome bottle of wine, afternoon tea and a champagne continental breakfast.

$$$$$ Auberge du Soleil – *180 Rutherford Hill Rd., off the Silverado Trail.* ℰ*707-963-1211. www.aubergedu soleil.com. 50 rooms.* The breezy terrace of this elegant country inn offers unparalleled view across the Napa Valley. Silvery acres of olive grove surround the inn.

$$$$$ Meadowood – *900 Meadowood Lane, St. Helena.* ℰ*707-963-3646. www. meadowood.com. 85 rooms.* A private estate built in the early 1960s, this elite and secluded resort lies just off the Silverado Trail, a perfect perch for Wine Country adventures. Rustic cottages dot a cool wooded grove; golf, tennis, a full spa, and the excellent Restaurant at Meadowood round out the amenities.

♈/EAT

$$ Dempsey's Restaurant & Brewery – *50 E. Washington St., Petaluma.* ℰ*707-765-9694. www.dempseys.com.* **American**. Organic vegetables and fruits dominate the seasonal menu at this eatery beside the Petaluma River.

$$ Tuscany – *1005 First St., Napa.* ℰ*707-258-1000. www.tuscanynapa.com. Closed Sun and Tue.* **Italian**. This place serves dishes like fresh salmon-and-mussel stew with artichokes followed by a memorable tiramisu.

$$$ Bouchon – *6534 Washington St., Yountville.* ℰ*707-944-8037. www. bouchonbistro.com.* **French** This adorable, lively little bistro oozes charm. The menu is a goldmine of rustic French offerings.

$$$ John Ash & Co. – *4330 Barnes Rd., Santa Rosa.* ℰ*707-527-7687. www.vintners inn.com. Lunch Wed-Fri, Dinner daily.* **Californian**. In a secluded restaurant surrounded by vineyards at the Vintners Inn, chef Thomas Schmidt blends fresh seasonal ingredients in dishes like roast chicken with baby artichokes, dried tomatoes and Princess Laratte potatoes.

$$$ Mustards Grill – *7399 St. Helena Hwy., Yountville.* ℰ*707-944-2424. www. mustardsgrill.com.* **Contemporary**. A long-standing favorite, this ranch-style restaurant draws winemakers and industry VIPs for its fresh cuisine and top-notch wine list. The menu ranges across American regional dishes with nods to continental and Asian touches.

$$$$ French Laundry – *6640 Washington St., Yountville.* ℰ*707-944-2380. www. frenchlaundry.com.* Some food writers say the French Laundry—lodged in a century-old stone laundry building—is the best restaurant in the U.S. Chef Thomas Keller, masterful in the preparation of sophisticated and creative French cuisine, offers a nine-course tasting menu ($270) nightly. A sommelier matches wines on request. Reserve two months ahead.

$$$$ La Toque – *1314 McKinstry St., in the Westin Verasa Napa, Napa.* ℰ*707-257-5157. www.latoque.com. Dinner only.* **Contemporary French**. Designed to be a "progression of flavors"—the nightly changing five-course prix-fixe menu often features Sonoma foie gras, diver scallops, and Niman Ranch meats.

$$$ Tra Vigne –*1050 Charter Oak Ave., St. Helena.* ℰ*707-963-4444. www.travigne restaurant.com.* **Italian**. Italian for "among the vines," Tra Vigne represents chef Michael Chiarello's success in bringing southern Italian fare to northern California. He has since moved on, but the kitchen continues his ways with traditional housemade pastas and slow-cooked meats.

Reading a Wine Label

Who made the wine and where was it bottled? Where and when were the grapes grown? How much alcohol is contained therein? The label on a bottle of wine says all of this and more. Labeling information is regulated by the U.S. Treasury Department's Bureau of Alcohol, Tobacco and Firearms, and certain elements are required by law.

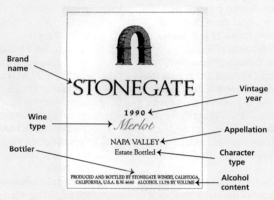

Required elements

Brand name – May be the name of the producer, or a secondary or special brand name of the producer.

Wine type – If 75 percent of the grapes used in the wine are of one type, such as Chardonnay, Zinfandel or Pinot Noir, that name must appear on the label as the name of the wine. Otherwise the wine may be called "table wine" or take a generic name such as Burgundy or Chablis.

Appellation – This is the geographic origin of the grapes used in making the wine. In order for the name of an Approved Viticultural Area, such as Napa Valley, to appear on the label, 85 percent of the grapes used must come from that particular area. If the appellation is a county such as Napa or Sonoma, the grape content from that appellation must be 75 percent. If the appellation is the state of California, the wine must be produced entirely from California-grown grapes.

Bottler – The name of the bottling winery may be different from that of the brand name. "Produced and Bottled by" indicates that at least 75 percent of the wine was fermented by the bottler. "Made and Bottled by" indicates that at least 10 percent of the wine was fermented by the bottler.

Alcohol content – Table wines may contain 7–14 percent alcohol by volume; aperitif wines 15–24 percent; dessert wines 14–24 percent or greater. There is no requirement for sparkling wines.

Optional elements

Vintage year – The year in which the grapes were grown may only appear on a label if 95 percent of the grapes used in the wine were harvested that year.

Character type – Additional information such as "Estate Bottled" indicates that the vineyard is managed by the winery, and that the vineyard and the winery are located within the stated appellation.

Vineyard – If the label indicates a specific vineyard, 95 percent of the grapes used must come from that vineyard.

Napa Valley★★

Cradled between two elongated mountain ranges, this world-renowned valley extends roughly 35 miles in a northerly direction from San Pablo Bay to Mt. St. Helena. The Napa Valley is home to some of California's most prestigious wineries, many of them clustered thickly along Route 29 as it passes through the towns of Napa, Yountville, Oakville, Rutherford, St. Helena and Calistoga. Others dot the more tranquil Silverado Trail to the east and the intervening crossroads.

SIGHTS
Described from south to north.

Napa
Originally settled in 1832, this small city on the banks of the Napa River experienced its first significant population boom as a resort town during the post-Gold Rush period. Riverboat captains and bankers established businesses and elegant Victorian residences through the late 19C, transforming Napa into an active shipping and administrative center. Now Napa County's largest city, with nearly 78,000 residents, it still serves as a gateway for the abundance of wines and agricultural goods produced in the verdant Napa Valley. The name is derived from a Native American word meaning "plenty."

Downtown
1st and 2nd Sts. between Main and Randolph Sts.
At the friendly heart of downtown Napa, the venerable **Goodman Building** (1901), with its gray stone facade *(1219 1st St.)*, is now home to the research library and museum of the Napa County Historical Society. Just across the street and one block north, an enormous contemporary **Clock Tower** overlooks the site where the first Magnavox speaker was invented in 1915 (a bronze sculpture of a vintage speaker commemorates the achievement). Other noteworthy buildings include the stately, ornate

⚅ **Michelin Map:** See p264.

▯ **Info:** ✆707-251-5895. www.visitnapavalley.com.

▷ **Location:** From San Francisco (55mi), drive north on US-101; exit at Rte. 37 and drive east to Rte. 121. Turn left (north) on Rte. 121 and continue to Rte. 29 north. For a quicker if less scenic route, drive north on I-80 to Rte. 37 west and continue to Rte. 29 north. Auto traffic, especially during peak seasons, can be heavy.

♟ **Kids:** A ride on the aerial tramway at Sterling Vineyards.

◷ **Timing:** To fully experience the region's relaxed pace and easygoing character, it's best to select no more than four wineries per day for tasting, and to limit guided tours to one or two per day. Travelers on tight schedules should bear in mind that although the Wine Country is blessed with lots of lush vegetation, inspiring vistas and an enviable climate, tourist attractions other than wineries are few. Visitors for whom wines and winemaking hold limited appeal should plan less time to visit the region.

⊙ **Don't Miss:** At least one winery tour and tasting.

Winship-Smernes Building *(948 Main St.)* and the **Italianate Napa Opera House** *(1030 Main St.; ✆707-226-7372; www.nvoh.org)*.
Constructed in 1879 and closed in 1914, the Opera House was reopened in 2003 after massive renovation and is now used as a multidisciplinary performance space.

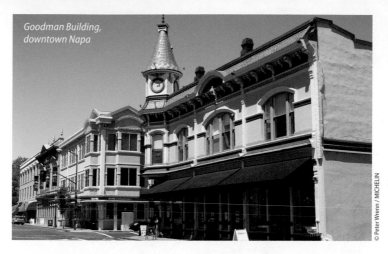

Goodman Building, downtown Napa

© Peter Wrenn / MICHELIN

Victorian Neighborhoods

South and west of downtown.
Residential neighborhoods hold a wealth of elegant houses from the late 19C and early 20C. A stroll or slow drive in the vicinity of **Jefferson, First, Third** or **Randolph Streets** reveals numerous well-restored homes built in the Italianate, Queen Anne, Eastlake and Shingle styles characteristic of Victorian architecture at the turn of the 19C.

di Rosa Preserve— Art and Nature★★

5200 Sonoma Hwy. (Rte. 121), Napa (2.5mi west of Rte. 12). Gatehouse Gallery ⏱*Open Wed–Fri 10am–4pm, May–Oct until 6pm;* ⊛*Suggested donation $5.* ⏱*Grounds may be visited by guided tour only Wed–Sun 10am, 11am and 1pm, May–Oct also 4pm Sat–Sun; reservations recommended.* ⊛*$12–15.* ⏱*Closed most federal holidays and Dec 24–Jan 1.* ℙ ℰ*707-226-5991. www.dirosaart.org.*
This 217-acre former winery in the Carneros region of the Napa Valley has been turned into an art and nature preserve to showcase the land's natural beauty and its owner's formidable art collection. Son of a U.S. ambassador to Italy, René di Rosa began acquiring works by undiscovered artists in the 1950s. In 1960, he bought an abandoned 460-acre vineyard here, converting the 1886 stone winery into his home.

Di Rosa and his wife eventually amassed a personal collection of more than 1,500 works by 650-plus Bay Area artists, including Robert Arneson, Joan Brown, Bruce Conner, Manuel Neri and William T. Wiley. Styles, media and subject matter vary widely; much of the collection is avant-garde.
Visitors have access to the historic residence, galleries, and *(guided walking tour only)* seasonal hikes and meadow walks in the grounds.

Artesa Vineyards and Winery

1345 Henry Rd. From downtown Napa take Rte. 29 south to Rte. 121. ▶ *Turn right and drive west 4mi, turning right on Old Sonoma Rd. Turn left on Dealy Ln. then veer left on Henry Rd. Continue .3mi to driveway entrance.* ⏱*Open daily 10am–5pm.* ⏱*Guided tours (30min) available 11am and 2pm.* ⏱*Closed Jan 1, Thanksgiving Day, Dec 24–25.* ⊛*$10 tasting fee.* ♿ ℙ ℰ*707-224-1668. www.artesawinery.com.*

Wineries described in this section have been selected and rated on their historic, architectural and cultural merits.
For a comprehensive, updated listing of wineries throughout California, consult the websites *www.californiawineinfo.com* or *www.cawinemall.com.*

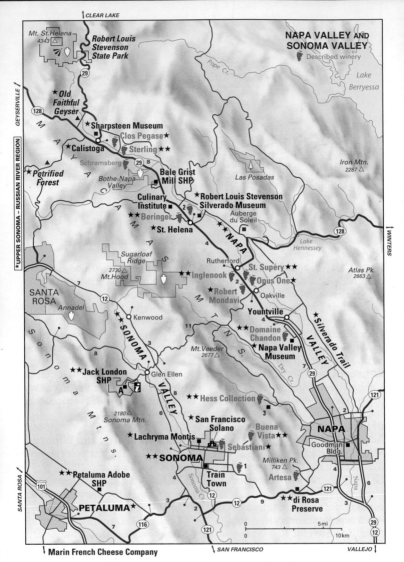

NAPA VALLEY AND SONOMA VALLEY

🍇 Described winery

CLEAR LAKE

Mt. St. Helena 4343 △

Robert Louis Stevenson State Park

29

Pope Cr.

Lake Berryessa

GEYSERVILLE

128

★ Old Faithful Geyser

UPPER SONOMA – RUSSIAN RIVER REGION

■ Sharpsteen Museum

Clos Pegase ★

★ Calistoga

Sterling ★★

Iron Mtn. 2287 △

Schramsberg ★

29 8

Bale Grist Mill SHP

★ Petrified Forest

Bothe-Napa Valley

Las Posadas

Culinary Institute

2

Robert Louis Stevenson Silverado Museum

★★ Beringer

Auberge du Soleil

★ St. Helena

NAPA

4

Lake Hennessey

128

WINTERS

Sugarloaf Ridge

2730 △ Mt. Hood

Rutherford

St. Supéry ★★

Atlas Pk. 2663 △

★★ Inglenook

2

Opus One ★

SANTA ROSA

★ Robert Mondavi

Oakville

12

Annadel

Kenwood

Yountville

11

4

Silverado Trail

SILVERADO VALLEY

Mt.Veeder 2677 △

★★ Domaine Chandon

★ Napa Valley Museum

29

121

★★ Jack London SHP

Glen Ellen

8

SONOMA VALLEY

2180 △ Sonoma Mtn.

★★ Hess Collection

3

San Francisco Solano

Buena Vista ★★

NAPA

Goodman Bldg.

★ Lachryma Montis

Sebastiani ★

★★ SONOMA

Milliken Pk. 743 △

Artesa ★

SANTA ROSA

101

★★ Petaluma Adobe SHP

Train Town

1

121

PETALUMA ★

12

9

★★ di Rosa Preserve

121

Napa

6

116

121

12

0   5mi
0   10km

29

12

Marin French Cheese Company

SAN FRANCISCO

VALLEJO

In 1872 the Codorniu family of Barcelona became Spain's first producers of sparkling wine made in the méthode champenoise tradition. Their Napa Valley operation, which shifted its focus to still wines in 1997 and changed its name to Artesa (meaning "craftsman") in 1997, occupies an innovative contemporary structure (1991, Domingo Triay) at the foot of Milliken Peak. Sloping, grass-covered earth berms bury the winery's walls, maintaining consistently cool temperatures in storage and production areas within. From the entrance plaza a view extends eastward over the lower Napa Valley. Galleries around a serene courtyard hold 16C–17C European winemaking equipment and changing displays of works by local artists.

The Hess Collection Winery★★

4411 Redwood Rd. From Rte. 29 in Napa take the Redwood Rd./Trancas exit and drive west on Redwood Rd. 6mi to winery entrance. ⏱*Open daily 10am–5.30pm (galleries close*

Méthode Champenoise

Most sparkling wines produced in the Wine Country are made by the méthode champenoise developed in 17C France by Dom Perignon, a Benedictine monk. In this process, a still wine traditionally blended from Pinot Noir and Chardonnay grapes is inoculated with yeast and sugar, bottled, capped and allowed to ferment a second time. The carbon dioxide gas retained in the bottle infuses the wine with bubbles, creating pressures of up to 110 pounds per square inch inside the bottle. The bottle is then stored on its side for as many as six years to let the wine age. Following aging, the wine is clarified by "riddling," a painstaking process of turning and lifting the bottles daily, bit by bit, until they are nearly upside down, so that yeast and sediments gather in the neck. The wine must then be "disgorged": The neck of the bottle is immersed in a brine solution so that the sediments within it freeze; when the bottle is then uncapped, pressure from within forces out the plug of frozen sediment. A *dosage* of sugar and brandy or other wine is added to the bottle before final corking and labeling.

5pm). 🕐*Closed Jan 1, Easter Sunday, Thanksgiving Day, Dec 24–25.* 👁*$10 tasting fee.* ♿🅿 ✆*707-255-1144. www.hesscollection.com.*

Nestled in a remote southwestern corner of the Napa Valley on the slope of Mt. Veeder, this beautifully renovated structure contains one of the nation's largest and finest private art collections open to the public, as well as a state-of-the-art winemaking facility.

The original stone structure (1903) was acquired by the Christian Brothers in the early 1930s to house the Mont LaSalle winery. In 1983, Swiss entrepreneur Donald Hess leased the property, transforming the upper floors into galleries to exhibit his outstanding collection of works by contemporary American and European artists. Francis Bacon, Robert Rauschenberg, Robert Motherwell and Frank Stella are among those represented in the collection.

Through wide windows in the stairwells, visitors strolling through the sweeping galleries glimpse the steel tanks and ultra-modern bottling room of the winery. A graceful audiovisual presentation (12min) focuses on the seasonal beauty of the vineyards and highlights the unique process of making wine in a mountain region.

The property adjacent to The Hess Collection Winery is graced by the **Christian Brothers Retreat and Conference Center (3)** *(4401 Redwood Rd.;* ✆*707-*

252-3810; www.christianbrosretreat.com), a Mission Revival-style complex (1932) interspersed with serene courtyards.

Yountville

This small community of 3,000, ranging along the east side of Route 29, was named for George C. Yount (1794–1865), a North Carolina frontiersman who established vineyards here in 1836 on a portion of the 11,814 acres granted him by the Mexican government.

Today Yountville's charming inns, trendy boutiques and excellent eateries make it a popular base for visitors to the southern Napa Valley.

Of particular note is the historic brick Groezinger winery (1870), now restored as **V Marketplace** *(* ✆*707-944-2451; www.vmarketplace.com),* a festival marketplace for specialty shops, restaurants and winetasting.

Napa Valley Museum★

55 Presidents Cir. ▷ *From Rte. 29/ Yountville exit, drive west .3mi toward Veterans Home. Museum is on right.* 🕐*Open Tue–Sun 10am–4pm.* 🕐*Closed major holidays.* 👁*$5.* ♿🅿 ✆*707-944-0500. www.napavalleymuseum.org.*

The highlight of this innovative museum (1998, Fernau and Hartman) is an impressive multimedia display entitled **California Wine: The Science of an Art★★**. An interactive audiovisual program allows visitors to experience a full year in Napa

Domaine Chandon winery

© M. Linda Lee / MICHELIN

winemaking, exploring soils, climates and microclimates, grape growth, rootstocks, pests, cloning, varietal characteristics, harvest, crushing, fermentation, racking, storage, blending and bottling. An upper gallery features **The Land and People of the Napa Valley**, with exhibits that describe the artistic, cultural and environmental heritage of the region. Additional temporary exhibits range from history to art.

Domaine Chandon★★

1 California Dr. ◗ *From Rte. 29/ Yountville exit, drive west .2mi toward Veterans Home. Entrance is on right.* ◷*Open daily 10am–5pm.* ☛*Guided tours (35min) available 11am, 1pm, 3pm and 5pm.* ◷*Closed Jan 1, Thanksgiving Day, Dec 24–25.* ≋*$18–25 tasting fee, $12–32 tour (some include tastings).* ✕♿🄿 ☏*707-944-2280. www.chandon.com.*

Visitors to this innovative winery complex (1973) are introduced to French winemaking tradition with a dash of California visual style and appeal. Commissioned by Moët-Hennessy, owners of France's famed Moët et Chandon, the modern structures of gray concrete harmonize with the sweeps and curves of the surrounding terrain; the arched ceilings are reminiscent of traditional wine caves in France's Champagne region. In the entrance hall, an attractive gallery

highlights skills and trades related to winemaking; an informative guided tour explains the principal stages of sparkling wine production according to the méthode champenoise. Guided tours cover the principal stages involved.

An upscale restaurant is located within the visitor center; its outdoor terrace allows picturesque glimpses of the beautifully landscaped winery grounds, old oak trees and vineyards.

Inglenook★★

1991 St. Helena Hwy. (Rte. 29), Rutherford. ◷*Open daily 10am–5pm.* ◷*Closed Jan 1, Easter Sunday, Thanksgiving Day, Dec 25.* ≋*$50 (including tour).* ♿🄿 ☏*707-968-1100. www.inglenook.com.*

The imposing stone winery (1882) at the center of the Inglenook—formerly Rubicon and Niebaum-Coppola—Estate was built by Gustave Niebaum, a Finnish sea captain and enterprising founder of Inglenook Wines (1879). Most of Niebaum's property, including his Victorian home and 1,600 acres of adjacent land, was purchased in 1975 by filmmaker Francis Ford Coppola (The Godfather trilogy) and his wife, Eleanor. The estate was renamed in 2002 after its flagship wine, and later after the original estate. A tree-lined courtyard surrounds a reflecting pool in front of the **Inglenook Chateau**, which is thought to have been the first gravity-flow winery in the valley. Upon entering the building, visitors can peek into the **Captain's Room** (1889) on the right, a replica of Niebaum's ship's quarters that includes 17C stained-glass windows, 16C Flemish wine cups and a 400-year-old lamp. The **Centennial Museum**, an intriguing monument to film and winemaking, reflects the careers of both of the winery's charismatic owners, Niebaum and Coppola.

Opus One★

7900 St. Helena Hwy (Rte. 29).
Open daily by appointment 10am–4pm. Guided tour (90min) available 1.30pm or 2.30pm; reservations required. Closed major holidays. $60 tour (tasting included), $40 tasting fee. 707-944-9442. www.opusonewinery.com.
Every detail of this innovative structure (1991, Johnson Fain & Partners)—from the French-style limestone walls to the California redwood pergola crowning the building—testifies to the unique international collaboration that created Opus One, the first ultra-premium winery in the U.S. In 1970, Baron Philippe de Rothschild of Pauillac, France, approached Napa Valley vintner Robert Mondavi to discuss a joint winemaking venture based in California. The team produced its first vintage in 1979. Visitors pass through an olive tree-studded courtyard before entering the reception hall. Works by well-known artists grace the walls and open spaces of the comfortable Salon, where Continental antiques blend seamlessly with luxurious contemporary furnishings. Descending a grand staircase shaped like the inside of a barrel, visitors enter an elegant tasting room and walk into the semicircular Grand Chai, or cellar.

Robert Mondavi Winery★

7801 St. Helena Hwy. (Rte. 29), Oakville.
Open 10am–5pm. Closed Jan 1, Easter Sunday, Thanksgiving Day, Dec 25. Guided tours (30min–2hrs; $15–$55); reserve. 888-766-6328. www.robertmondaviwinery.com.
Constructed in 1966, this striking building anticipated a new generation of modern wineries designed to showcase art, architecture and wine. Sculptor Beniamino Bufano's figure of St. Francis with outstretched arms greets visitors beneath the monumental arched entry to the complex, and temporary exhibits of works by local artists are regular features at the winery. A popular Summer Music Festival and a winter concert series are held here annually.

St. Supéry★★

8440 St. Helena Hwy. (Rte. 29), Rutherford. Open daily 10am–5pm. Closed Jan 1, Thanksgiving Day, Dec 25. $15–$25 tasting fee. 707-963-4507. www.stsupery.com.

Opus One Winery

© Craig Cozart / iStockphoto

267

The modern winery structure houses a comprehensive **Wine Discovery Center**★, featuring in-depth displays on seasonal viticulture, the winemaking process, soil types and appellations. Especially interesting is the **Smella Vision** exhibit, a "nose-on" display where visitors can sniff eight characteristic aromas associated with Cabernet Sauvignon or Sauvignon Blanc varietals, and examine the color variations for each type of wine.

Adjacent to the winery is a model vineyard with detailed panels and exhibits explaining how vines are trained, trellised and pruned according to the variety of grape. Also on the property is the charming Victorian home built by Joseph Atkinson, the first vintner to own the property. The house has been restored with period pieces to reflect the life and times of an 1880s winemaker.

St. Helena★

Rte. 29, 12mi north of Napa.

A picturesque main street graces this charming town of 5,800 at the heart of the Napa Valley. Plentiful and widely varied accommodations, intriguing and innovative restaurants, and a central location close to a number of popular wineries make St. Helena an excellent base for exploring the entire valley.

Robert Louis Stevenson Silverado Museum★

1490 Library Ln. ◗ *From Main St. northbound, turn right on Adams St., cross the railroad tracks and turn left.* ◷*Open Tue–Sat noon–4pm.* ◷*Closed major holidays.* ◠*Donation suggested.* ♿🅿 ☏*707-963-3757. www.silveradomuseum.org.*

Housed in a pleasant gallery within the town library building, this small, memorabilia-packed museum is devoted to the life and works of Robert Louis Stevenson (1850–94), renowned and beloved author of such popular 19C stories as Treasure Island, Kidnapped and A Child's Garden of Verses. Stevenson honeymooned in a cabin on the slopes of Mt. St. Helena in summer 1880 and immortalized this Napa experience in his book The Silverado Squatters.

The museum's holdings—comprising photographs, books, manuscripts and the author's personal artifacts—are considered second in importance only to the Stevenson collections at Yale University's Beinecke Library.

The Silverado Quaffer

When Robert Louis Stevenson honeymooned in the Napa Valley in 1880, he expressed his affection for the region's fledgling wine industry in word and taste. "I was interested in California wine," he wrote in *The Silverado Squatters.* "Indeed, I am interested in all wines, and have been all my life, from the raisin wine that a schoolfellow kept secreted in his play-box up to my last discovery…

"Wine in California is still in the experimental stage; and when you taste a vintage, grave economical questions are involved… Meanwhile, the wine is merely a good wine; the best that I have tasted better than a Beaujolais, and not unlike."

Stevenson was particularly fond of the **Schramsberg Vineyards** *(1400 Schramsberg Lane off Petersen Lane west of Rte. 29;* ☏*707-942-4558; www. schramsberg.com).* "Mr. Schram's place… is the picture of prosperity," the author scribed. "I was tasting wines in the cellar. To Mr. Schram this was a solemn office; his serious gusto warmed my heart; prosperity had not yet wholly banished a certain neophite and girlish trepidation, and he followed every sip and read my face with proud anxiety. I tasted all, I tasted every variety of Schramberger, red and white Schramberger, Burgundy Schramberger, Schramberger Hock, Schramberger Golden Chasselas, the latter with a notable bouquet, and I fear to think how many more."

Beringer Vineyards★★

2000 Main St. (Rte. 29), north of downtown St. Helena. ◐Open June–late Oct daily 10am–6pm; rest of the year daily 10am–5pm. ⊶Guided tours available (30min–1hr; ⊜$25–$40, tasting included). ◐Closed Jan 1, Thanksgiving Day, Dec 25. ⊜$20–$40 tasting fee. ✧🄿 ℘707-963-8989. www.beringer.com.

The Napa Valley's oldest continuously operating winery was established in 1876 by Jacob and Frederick Beringer, German immigrants who arrived in the U.S. in the 1860s. The brothers' winery escaped the worst of the legislative strictures of Prohibition because they acquired a license to produce wine for religious and medicinal purposes. Extending into the sloping hillside behind the complex are over 1,000ft of tunnels where the temperature remains a constant 58°F, an ideal environment for aging wine.

The centerpiece of the property is the stately **Rhine House** (1883), constructed by Frederick Beringer as his residence. Modeled after the Beringer ancestral home in Germany, the 17-room mansion features elegant woodwork, inlaid floors and exceptional **stained-glass windows★**. The regal oleander trees about the property were planted at the turn of the 19C by Jacob Beringer.

The Culinary Institute of America at Greystone

2555 Main St. (Rte. 29), north of downtown St. Helena. ◐Open daily 10am–6pm. Cooking demonstrations Sat–Sun 1.30pm; reservations recommended (⊜$20; ℘707-967-2320). ⊶Guided tours available daily 11.45am, 2.45pm, and 5pm (30min, ⊜$10. ◐Closed Thanksgiving and Dec 25. ✕✧🄿. www.ciachef.edu.

The massive stone **building★** looming over Rte. 29 was erected in 1889 by William Bourn as Greystone Cellars, a cooperative effort by Napa Valley wine-growers in need of aging and storage facilities. The largest freestanding stone building in California when it was built, the winery changed hands several times

before being purchased in the 1950s by the Christian Brothers, a Catholic teaching order.

Today the building houses the West Coast campus of the renowned Culinary Institute of America, which offers continuing education for professionals in the food, wine, health and hospitality fields. Visitors are welcome to explore the delightful herb gardens or browse through the Spice Islands Marketplace *(open daily 10.30am–6pm)*, a lively culinary retail outlet with a pastry cafe.

In the **Wine Spectator Greystone Restaurant** *(◐open Sun–Thu 11.30am–9pm; Fri–Sat 11.30am–10pm; ◐closed Thanksgiving, Dec 24–25; reservations ℘707-967-1010)*, professional chefs expertly prepare meals in an open kitchen.

The Institute also houses a whimsical **corkscrew collection** of more than 1,800 wine openers, some dating from the 18C. The collection was assembled over a period of 40 years by Brother Timothy, cellarmaster of the Christian Brothers.

♦♦ Bale Grist Mill State Historic Park

3369 St. Helena Hwy. (Rte. 29), 3mi north of downtown St. Helena. ◐Park open Sat–Sun 10am–5pm. ◐Closed major holidays. ⊜$3. ✧🄿 ℘707-942-4575. www.parks.ca.gov.

From the parking area, a pleasant, sylvan path leads to this charming historic **grist mill★**, powered by a 36ft waterwheel. Established in 1846 by Edward T. Bale, an Englishman who married a niece of Gen. Mariano Vallejo, the mill ground into flour the grain harvested by Napa Valley farmers. The wooden mill and waterwheel, which ceased operation about 1905, are partially restored. Docent tours and an audiovisual presentation provide a good introduction to the milling process, and demonstrations allow a look at the mill in action (call for demonstration schedule). Interpretive displays focus attention on the milling process and on local pioneer history. Visitors can purchase flour and cornmeal milled on site.

Sterling Vineyards★★

1111 Dunaweal Ln., 6.8mi north of St. Helena via Rte. 29 (entrance on right). Open Mon–Fri 10.30am–4.30pm, Sat–Sun 10am–5pm. Closed Jan 1, Easter Sunday, Thanksgiving Day, Dec 25. $25 includes tramway, wine tasting and self-guided tour; 707-942-3344. www.sterling vineyards.com.

Perched like a secluded Greek monastery on a 300ft knoll rising abruptly from the valley floor, this complex of pristine white buildings (1969, Martin J. Waterfield) is one of the Napa Valley's architectural grace notes.

Visitors ascend to the winery from the parking area by a hushed ride on the vineyard's **aerial tramway**, from which tranquil views extend over the surrounding area. At the summit, follow informative panels on a self-guided tour through the winery, across terraces with **views★** of the northern Napa Valley, and under campaniles representing a contemporary take on traditional mission-style bell towers.

The collection of eight bells dating from the early 18C was acquired for Sterling Vineyards in 1972 from London's church of St.-Dunstan-in-the-East.

Clos Pegase★

1060 Dunaweal Ln., 6.8mi north of St. Helena via Rte. 29 (entrance on left). Open daily 10.30am–5pm. Guided tours (30min) daily 11.30am and 2pm. Closed Jan 1, Easter Sunday, Thanksgiving Day, Dec 25. nominal tasting fee. 707-942-4981. www.clospegase.com.

Housed in a harmonious sprawl of terra-cotta and earth-toned structures at the base of a small volcanic knoll, Clos Pegase (1987, Michael Graves) is a striking example of the Napa Valley's variety of architectural styles.

The winery is named for Pegasus, the famed winged horse of Greek mythology, who is said to have first created wine when he struck his hooves to the ground of Mt. Helicon, unleashing the Spring of the Muses and irrigating a vineyard below.

The monumental winery complex reveals architect Graves' signature view of themes from classical antiquity, reflected in oversized columns, triangular pediments and an open central atrium. Selections from owner Jan Shrem's private art collection appear throughout the winery, even in the 20,000sq ft of storage caves hewn into the knoll of volcanic tufa. Shrem's residence, also designed by Graves, crowns the knoll (not open to the public).

Calistoga★

Rte. 29, 6mi north of St. Helena.

Founded in 1859 in the shadow of Mt. St. Helena and at the very top of the Napa Valley, this residential and resort town of 5,200 unites the flavor of the late-19C frontier era with 20C modernity. Thermal activity in the area, manifested in numerous geysers and hot springs, fueled Calistoga's development as a resort where tourists flocked to "take the waters"; local Native Americans had long sworn by their medicinal properties.

According to legend, Calistoga founder **Sam Brannan** (1819–88) stumbled upon the town's name by confusedly (some say drunkenly) declaring it "The Calistoga of Sarafornia" (Saratoga of California) after upstate New York's famed Saratoga Hot Springs.

Today, hot-spring spas and bottled mineral water continue to fuel the town's popularity.

False-front facades along **Lincoln Avenue**, the town's main thoroughfare, provide a charming frontier flavor, as does the historic **Railroad Depot** *(1458 Lincoln Ave.).* Erected in 1868 to serve the long-defunct Napa Valley Railroad Company, the structure now houses shops, a restaurant and the visitor center.

Sharpsteen Museum★

1311 Washington St., 2 blocks north of Lincoln Ave, Calistoga. Open daily 11am–4pm. Closed Thanksgiving Day, Dec 25. $3 donation requested. 707-942-5911. www.sharpsteen-museum.org.

The highlight of this small museum is an intriguing assemblage of miniature

dioramas re-creating scenes of Calistoga's colorful past.

Founded in 1979 by Ben Sharpsteen—one of Walt Disney's original 11 animators and later an Oscar-winning producer—the museum also features a collection of early 19C photos, a restored stagecoach and assorted artifacts pertaining to the town's history.

Adjoining the museum building is a **cottage** from Sam Brannan's resort, relocated from its original site and fully refurbished to appear as it would have during Calistoga's resort heyday.

♣♦ Old Faithful Geyser★

◗ *From Calistoga drive east on Lincoln Ave.; bear left on Grant St. and continue 1mi. Turn left on Tubbs Ln. Entrance on the right.* ◷*Open Apr–Oct daily 9am–6pm; rest of the year daily 9am–5pm.* ◌*$10.* ✕♿⸿₽ ✆*707-942-6463. www.oldfaithfulgeyser.com.*

Located at the foot of Mt. St. Helena, this privately owned geyser is one of the world's three known "faithful" geysers, so named for their regular eruptions (the others are located at Yellowstone National Park and in New Zealand). Approximately every 40 minutes, the geyser spews a column of superheated water some 60ft into the air in a splendid shower of droplets and steam. There is also a small petting zoo on site.

♣♦ Petrified Forest★

4100 Petrified Forest Rd., 6mi west of Calistoga. ◗ *Drive north on Rte. 128; turn left on Petrified Forest Rd, continue .5 miles to the entrance.* ◷*Open Jun–Sept daily 9am–7pm; rest of the year daily 9am–5pm.* ◷*Closed Thanksgiving Day, Dec 25.* ◌*$10.* ♿₽ ✆*707-942-6667. www.petrifiedforest.org.*

A circuit trail through this small, privately owned forest winds past the stone remnants of giant redwoods that were petrified more than three million years ago when Mt. St. Helena erupted, covering the surrounding area with ash and molten lava. Among the highlights is The Giant, an ancient redwood 60ft long and 6ft in diameter.

Old Faithful Geyser, Calistoga
© Stephan Hoerold / iStockphoto.com

Robert Louis Stevenson State Park

7mi north of Calistoga. ◗ *Take Lincoln Ave. east; turn left at the Silverado Trail and right at Rte. 29.* ◷*Open daily dawn–dusk.* ₽ ✆*707-942-4575. www.parks.ca.gov.*

This largely undeveloped park provides an excellent opportunity for hikers and bikers to explore the rugged, picturesque slopes of Mt. St. Helena (4,343ft). On its ascent to the summit, a trail passes the site (near an abandoned silver mine) where Robert Louis Stevenson and his wife, Fanny Osborne Stevenson, spent their honeymoon in 1880.

After one mile, the trail emerges from the forest to join an unpaved fire road up to the summit; from the road, sweeping **views★★** extend over the northern Napa Valley and beyond. Another trail winds six miles east below cliffs of volcanic origin.

Silverado Trail★

Running parallel to Route 29 along the eastern edge of the Napa Valley between Napa and Calistoga, this scenic road offers a tranquil alternative to the often traffic-choked main highway. Its many dips and curves accommodate the rolling terrain at the base of the ridges bordering the valley, and acres of serene vineyards are punctuated by numerous wineries. Several crossroads link the pastoral Silverado Trail with Route 29.

Sonoma Valley★★

The Sonoma Valley is agriculturally and topographically more diverse than the Napa Valley. Anchored by the historic town of Sonoma, the valley dominates the southern portion of Sonoma County, where vineyards and wineries abut orchards and fields. The region enjoys a reputation for excellent produce and other farm products, as well as for wines. Approved Viticultural Areas here include Los Carneros, Sonoma Valley and Sonoma Mountain.

SIGHTS
Sonoma★★

Site of the California mission chain's northernmost and final outpost, this charming community of about 10,000, set amid the sun-soaked orchards and vineyards of the Sonoma Valley, is the Wine Country's most historically significant town. Sonoma was born in 1823 with the founding of the San Francisco Solano Mission. Nearby, the Mexican government established a military outpost to guard against the threat of Russian encroachment from Fort Ross, 30mi north. After missions were secularized in 1834, Gen. Mariano Vallejo was assigned to oversee distribution of the mission lands and to establish a pueblo at Sonoma.

The town's central plaza was the scene on June 14, 1846 of the **Bear Flag Revolt**, an uprising of American settlers disgruntled with Mexican control of California. Hoisting a white flag with a brown bear and a star, the group proclaimed California an independent republic.

A month later, U.S. Forces captured Monterey, declared California a U.S. possession, ending the short-lived republic. Formally incorporated in 1850, Sonoma flourished as a supply and trade center for the area's farms and nascent winemaking industry. The town retains the charming flavor of that period. Several noteworthy examples of 19C

- ⚅ **Michelin Map:** See p264, p272.
- 🗎 **Info:** ℘707-996-1090; www.sonomavalley.com.
- ▷ **Location:** From San Francisco (49mi), take US-101 north; exit at Rte. 37, continue to Rte. 121 and turn left (north). Continue to Rte. 12. Most wineries lie in the vicinity of Sonoma and along or near Rte. 12 as it leads through the town of Sonoma to Santa Rosa and to the Upper Sonoma-Russian River Region.
- 🧍 **Kids:** Train Town: a giant model train that you can ride on.
- 🕐 **Timing:** For a perfect day in Sonoma, try to see the historic sights early, then have a picnic lunch, followed by a leisurely afternoon in the wineries.
- 🙂 **Don't Miss:** Farmers' markets abound in this area, revealing the local passion for the gourmet, the organic and the homegrown. The ones on the plazas in Sonoma and Healdsburg are particularly enticing.

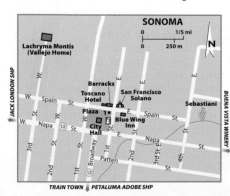

SONOMA

Lachryma Montis (Vallejo Home) · Barracks · Toscano Hotel · San Francisco Solano · Plaza · City Hall · Blue Wing Inn · Sebastiani · BUENA VISTA WINERY · JACK LONDON SHP · TRAIN TOWN · PETALUMA ADOBE SHP

residential architecture grace the streets south and west of the plaza, displaying elements of the Mission, Bungalow and Monterey Colonial styles.

Sonoma State Historic Park★★

All sights open Fri–Wed 10am–5pm. Closed Jan 1, Thanksgiving Day, Dec 25. Guided tours available weekends 11am–2pm. $3 ticket includes same-day admission to all sights (purchase at any sight or at Petaluma State Historic Park, below). ℘707-938-9560. www.parks.ca.gov; www.parks.sonoma.net.

Headquartered near the Toscano Hotel, the park maintains and operates the town's key historic sites, including the San Francisco Solano Mission, the Sonoma Barracks, the Toscano Hotel, the Vallejo Home and Petaluma Adobe.

Plaza★

Bounded by Spain St., 1st St. W., Napa St., and 1st St. E.

Laid out by Mariano Vallejo in 1835, Sonoma's eight-acre plaza is the largest of its kind in California. Anchored at its center by the **City Hall** (1908), an eye-catching Mission Revival structure of roughly hewn basalt, the plaza today is attractively landscaped, laced with walkways and dotted with duck ponds, benches and play areas.

On the east side of the Plaza, the **Sonoma Valley Visitor Center** *(453 1st St. E., ℘707-996-1090; www.sonomavalley. com)* is lodged in a restored Carnegie Library building (1913). A dramatic bronze **statue (1)** near the northeast corner depicts a soldier raising the Bear Flag, commemorating the 1846 revolt. Shady yews, sycamores and plane trees create a peaceful atmosphere amid the bustle of surrounding streets.

San Francisco Solano Mission★

E. Spain St. and 1st St. E. Guided tours Fri–Sun 11am, noon, 1pm and 2pm. ℘707-938-9560.

Founded in 1823 by Father José Altamíra, California's final mission was part of a Mexican government effort to strengthen its holdings against

San Francisco Solano Mission

© Megan Clouse / SonomaValley.com

potential Russian invasion. The original wooden church and other structures, destroyed during an uprising in 1826, were replaced by adobe buildings. The mission operated until secularization in 1834, when Mariano Vallejo dismantled the property and erected a parish chapel on the site of the original church.

About half of the original mission complex remains standing. It includes the chapel and part of the priests' quarters, restored around 1912. Displays of period furnishings and artifacts retell mission history. They precede an impressive collection of watercolor **paintings** depicting the California missions, executed by Norwegian artist Chris Jorgensen (1859–1935). In the restored chapel, the Stations of the Cross and framed paintings are authentic to the mission period. Across Spain Street *(no. 217)* stands the **Blue Wing Inn** (1840), an attractive, symmetrical adobe structure that formerly served as a saloon and hotel.

Sonoma Barracks★

Spain St. and 1st St. E. ℘707-939-9420.

This spacious, two-story adobe structure (1841), its wide balcony overlooking the plaza, housed Mexican troops stationed here to guard Sonoma. Following U.S. occupation of California, the barracks served various American regiments during the Mexican-American War. Now a museum of the historic park, the barracks contains displays illustrating aspects of Sonoma's history, including artifacts from the various periods of Mexican and American settlement.

Adjacent to the barracks lies the historic **Toscano Hotel** *(guided tours Sat–Mon 1pm–4pm)*, built as a general store in the 1850s and converted to a boardinghouse in the 1880s for Italian immigrants working in nearby quarries. Today the wood-frame building's fancy Victorian furnishings belie its rough-and-tumble origins. Visitors can peek into cramped upstairs sleeping rooms, examine an intricate hair sculpture fashionable in the mid-19C, or explore the restored kitchen and dining room behind the main building during park visiting hours.

Lachryma Montis (Vallejo Home)★

North end of 3rd St. W., .5mi from the plaza. ◗ *Leave the plaza by W. Spain St. and turn right on 3rd St. W.* ☛*Guided tours weekends 1pm, 2pm and 3pm.* ✆*707-938-9559.*

The elegant Gothic Victorian home (1852), set amid attractive landscaped grounds, was named "tear of the mountain" in Latin for the mountain spring on the property. The lovely residence served as the final home of Mariano Vallejo (1807–90), one of Mexican California's most powerful and colorful figures.

The airy, spacious interior of the four-bedroom house is furnished to reflect the period when Vallejo lived there. A brick storehouse containing a small interpretive center and collection of artifacts from the 19C, among them a graceful French phaeton used by Vallejo and his family for excursions into town.

Buena Vista Winery★★

18000 Old Winery Rd. ◗ *From downtown Sonoma drive east on Napa St., turn left on 7th St. and right on Lovall Valley Rd., then left on eucalyptus-lined Old Winery Rd. for .5mi to the winery.* ◕*Open daily 10am–5pm.* ◕*Closed Jan 1, Thanksgiving Day, Dec 25.* ⊛*$10–50 tasting fee; self-guided tour free.* P ✆*800-926-1266. www.buenavistacarneros.com.*

Sonoma County's first premium winery occupies a pleasantly rolling site amid eucalyptus, oak and bay laurel trees. It was founded in 1857 by Agoston Haraszthy.

Visitors may peer through an iron gate into Haraszthy's renowned **wine cellars**,

dug into the limestone hill behind the winery by Chinese laborers in 1863. The stone **Press House** (1862), reputed to be California's oldest remaining winery building, today boasts a handsomely refurbished interior; the wooden beams are original. The second-floor gallery hosts an artist-in-residence program featuring works by local artists.

Sebastiani Vineyards★

389 4th St. E. ◗ *From downtown Sonoma drive east on Spain St. and turn left on 4th St. E.* ◕*Open daily 11am–5pm.* ☛*Guided tour (90min) 11am, 1pm and 3pm, reservations recommended.* ◕*Closed major holidays.* ⊛*$10–20 tasting fee.* ♿P ✆*707-933-3230. www.sebastiani.com.*

This sprawling winery incorporates sections of a livery stable purchased by Italian immigrant Samuele Sebastiani in 1904. Sebastiani transformed the stone structure into a wine cellar; construction of additional buildings progressed throughout the first half of the 20C. The winery's reception room displays rudimentary casks, crushers and other equipment from the early part of the century. On the guided tour, visitors see Sebastiani's two 60,000gal oak fermentation tanks, reputed to be the largest in the world outside of Heidelberg, Germany. Scattered throughout the winery are more than 300 wooden cask heads and doors embellished with whimsical **carvings** executed from 1967 to 1984 by local artist Earle Brown.

👥 Train Town

20264 Broadway, 1mi south of the Plaza on Rte. 12. ◕*Open Jun–early Sep daily 10am–5pm; rest of the year Fri–Sun and holidays 10am–5pm.* ◕*Closed Thanksgiving Day, Dec 25 and during heavy rain.* ⊛*Free general admission, rides $5.75 ages 12 and up.* ♿P ✆*707-938-3912. www.traintown.com.*

An old-fashioned carousel and a working scale-model railroad make Train-Town a fine destination for families with small children. Passengers sit on benches in low, open-top train cars for a 20min ride through ten acres of landscaped countryside with bridges, tunnels, waterfalls and miniature buildings. The train stops midway at a petting zoo. Fairground snacks add to the old-time carnival atmosphere.

Jack London State Historic Park★★

10mi from Sonoma. 2400 London Ranch Rd., in Glen Ellen.
▶ *From Sonoma, drive 5mi north on Rte. 12, turn left on Madrone Rd. and right on Arnold Dr. Continue into Glen Ellen and turn left on London Ranch Rd.*
🕐*Open Thu–Mon 9.30am–5pm; cottage noon–4pm.* ⊚*$10/car.*
☞*Guided tours (1–2hrs) available.*
🄿 ℘*707-938-5216. www.parks.ca.gov or www.jacklondonpark.com.*

Sprawling among peaceful hills in the shadow of Sonoma Mountain is the 800-acre "Beauty Ranch," home of writer Jack London (1876–1916) during the last years of his life. Today a state park, the ranch commemorates this beloved American author of such adventure stories as *The Call of the Wild* (1903) and *The Sea Wolf* (1904).

Sailor on Horseback

Born illegitimately in San Francisco in 1876, Jack London was raised in Oakland, where as a boy he labored in the city's canneries and mills. His huge capacity for hard work and his love of adventure were united with a voracious appetite for books. He joined a sealing expedition to Siberia and joined the Klondike Gold Rush in 1897. Forced by scurvy to return to Oakland the following year, London directed his energies to writing stories of his adventures in the far north. His first short story, published in the *Overland Monthly,* earned him only $5 but launched a hugely successful career as a novelist, foreign correspondent, short-story writer and lecturer.

In 1905 London, by then renowned as an author and advocate of socialism, purchased a run-down ranch in the hills near Glen Ellen and settled there with his second wife, Charmian. In 1911 the Londons began construction of

Wolf House, a massive four-story mansion of hand-hewn lava boulders and redwood logs. Its 26 rooms and nine fireplaces occupied 15,000sq ft. On the night of August 22, 1913, a month before the couple was to move in, a fire roared through the house, leaving only stone walls. Crushed, the Londons never rebuilt Wolf House, but continued to live in a small cottage on the ranch. Jack London died there in 1916 at the age of 40 of uremic poisoning.

Visit

Erected by Charmian London in 1919 as her residence, with the intention of making it a museum to honor her husband, the rustic stone **House of Happy Walls★ (A)** today serves as the park visitor center. The massive building contains memorabilia of both Londons, including artifacts from the author's life and work, letters, photographs, clothing and objects amassed during the couple's world travels, notably Pacific meanderings aboard their boat, the *Snark.*

A trail (🄺*1.2mi round-trip; trailhead at House of Happy Walls)* winds through rolling meadows and forests to the ghostly ruins of **Wolf House★**, in the heart of a glade overlooking a peaceful valley. A short detour leads to the Londons' gravesite atop a peaceful hill. The **Beauty Ranch Trail★** (🄺*.5mi loop; accessible from the upper parking lot)* wanders about the property past stables, silos, a piggery and the Londons' modest cottage (⊚*$4).*

More extensive hiking trails lead throughout the park and up the steep slope of Sonoma Mountain *(summit on private property).*

Petaluma Adobe State Historic Park★★

3325 Adobe Rd., Petaluma, 10mi from Sonoma. ▶ *Leave Sonoma by Rte. 12 south; turn right on Leveroni Rd., left on Arnold Dr. and right on Rte. 116; continue 3mi and bear right on Adobe Rd. Continue 3.25mi to fork in road; turn sharply right and proceed .25mi to park entrance on right.*🕐*Open Thu–Sun 10am–5pm.* 🕐*Closed Jan 1,*

Thanksgiving Day, Dec 25. ⌨$3.
🅿 *☎707-762-4871. www.parks.ca.gov.*
In 1834, Mariano Vallejo established a 100sq mi ranch headquarters on this hilltop site overlooking the rolling Sonoma County countryside. Rancho Petaluma thrived, producing cattle, horses, sheep and crops of grain until Vallejo leased out the property in September 1850.

Today the restored two-story dwelling, one-half its original size, re-creates the atmosphere of a prosperous 19C ranch with interpretive displays and period furniture. In the courtyard stand hive-shaped ovens once used to prepare meals for the adobe's residents.

Petaluma★

12mi west of Sonoma via Rte. 116 west from Rte. 12. Tourist information ☎877-273-8258. www.visitpetaluma.com.
Set astride the Petaluma River in a fertile valley 40mi north of San Francisco, this agricultural town of nearly 60,000 grew from a hunters' camp to a grain-shipping port in 1852. The **Great Petaluma Mill** *(Petaluma Blvd. N. and B St.; restored as a shopping complex)*, once the region's largest feed mill, survives as a testimony to the city's early industry. Dubbed the "World's Egg Basket," Petaluma shipped as many as 600 million eggs per year until high labor and feed costs caused the decline of the poultry industry after World War II. The city today remains a dairy center; its wholesome appearance has led it to become a shooting location for such movies as *American Graffiti*.

The **Old Petaluma** historic district *(north of B St. along Petaluma Blvd. N. and Kentucky St.)* reflects the town's Victorian heritage with its cast-iron architecture. Petaluma's finest row of ironfront architecture *(Western Ave. between Kentucky St. and Petaluma Blvd.)* is bounded on the north corner by the Italianate **Mutual Relief Building** (1885) and on the south by the **Masonic Hall** (1882), topped by a landmark clock tower. Nearby, the **McNear Building** *(15–23 Petaluma Blvd. N.)*, with its elegant row of second-story arches, actually incorporates two structures; the

original (1886) and the addition (1911) were owned by one of Petaluma's first families. Garlands, wreaths and marbled columns constitute some of the rich detail that distinguishes the facade of the Old Opera Housea *(149 Kentucky St.)*, built in 1870 to host minstrel shows and theater productions.

Free walking tours of the historic downtown, led by costumed docents *(Guided tours May–Oct Sat 10.30am)*, depart from the **Petaluma Historical Library and Museum** *(20 4th St.;* open Thu–Sun 10am–4pm; closed major holidays; ☎707-778-4398; www.petalumamuseum.com).*
The 1906 Classical Revival building's free-standing, stained-glass dome is the largest in California. The **Heritage Wall** (1998, Steve della Maggiora) muralizes Petaluma history on a wall of a building *(Petaluma Blvd. N. and Washington St.)* that once housed the world's only pharmacy for chickens.

Marin French Cheese Company

7500 Red Hill Rd.; 9mi south of Petaluma via D St. Extension. Open daily 8.30am–5pm. Guided tours daily 10am, 11am, noon and 3pm. Closed Jan 1, Thanksgiving Day, Dec 25. ✕ 🅿 ☎707-762-6001. www.marinfrenchcheese.com.*
Among tranquil hills next to a tree-shaded pond, the factory offers a behind-the-scenes glimpse of the cheese-making process, from separating the curd to aging the cheese and packaging the final product. A salesroom carries a full line of the company's products.

ADDRESSES

⑂/EAT

Sonoma Cheese Factory – *2 Spain St.* ☎707-996-1931. www.sonomacheesefactory.com.* Step off the plaza to taste Jack cheese made at this diminutive "factory," one of the area's largest cheese producers. A gourmet deli offers many local delicacies, perfect for picnicing or sampling on the side terrace.

Upper Sonoma-Russian River Region★

This region of northern Sonoma County comprises three principal wine areas: the **Russian River Valley,** the Dry Creek Valley and the Alexander Valley. Smaller areas include Knight's Valley, Green Valley, Northern Sonoma and Chalk Hill. The Russian River Valley follows the curving path of the Russian River as it meanders south through Healdsburg and veers west toward the coast, passing picturesque wineries, vineyards and brooding stands of redwood trees. Swimming and kayaking are popular sports on the river where it passes through the resort communities of Forestville, Guerneville, Monte Rio and Duncans Mills, and the surrounding forests offer ample opportunities for hiking and camping. Hemmed by majestic mountain ridges, the **Alexander Valley** extends along the Russian River east and north of Healdsburg. Small, rustic wineries dot the curves and corners of Route 128 as it wanders across a pastoral landscape of vineyard-covered foothills. The 20 mile-long valley was named for Cyrus Alexander, a Pennsylvania trapper who settled here in the 1840s. The delightful **Dry Creek Valley★** extends from the Warm Springs Dam on Lake Sonoma to just south of Healdsburg. Approximately 12 miles long, the narrow valley is laced with small, winding roads that meander among vineyards, beneath canopies of trees and across the valley floor. Zinfandel grapes have been grown here, and in the Alexander Valley, for more than a century.

SIGHTS
Santa Rosa
26.5mi southeast of Sonoma.
The sprawling city of 169,000 is the commercial hub and seat of Sonoma County.

🕭 **Michelin Map:** See p278.

🈂 **Info:** ☏ 707-869-9000. www.russianriver.com.

◖ **Location:** The region lies northwest of the Napa and Sonoma Valleys, linked to San Francisco by US-101. From San Francisco take US-101 north to Santa Rosa (49mi) or to Healdsburg (64mi).

👪 **Kids:** The Charles M. Schulz Museum, mecca for fans of the beloved *Peanuts* comic strip.

🕐 **Timing:** If you're in Healdsburg around lunchtime, the town's main plaza is an excellent spot for an alfresco picnic.

☺ **Don't Miss:** Luther Burbank Home and Gardens, birthplace of the Santa Rosa plum, among other fruits and vegetables.

Incorporated in 1858, it boomed after the opening of the Golden Gate Bridge in 1937. Native sons include botanist Luther Burbank (1849–1926) and cartoonist Charles Schulz (1922–2000), as well as collector Robert Ripley (1893–1949) of *Believe It or Not!* fame.

US-101 bisects the old and new sections of town. Santa Rosa's historic district, known as **Railroad Square** *(bounded by 3rd, Davis and 6th Sts. and the railroad tracks)*, is west of the freeway; it comprises a charming cluster of restored brick and stone buildings constructed in 1870 to serve the Santa Rosa and North Pacific Railroad.

Today the square is an attractive group of offices, specialty shops, boutiques, restaurants and inns; a visitor center occupies the former train depot *(☏707-577-8674; www.visitsantarosa.com).*

East of US-101 and the Santa Rosa Plaza mall is the downtown area, centered on **Courthouse Square** *(Mendocino and*

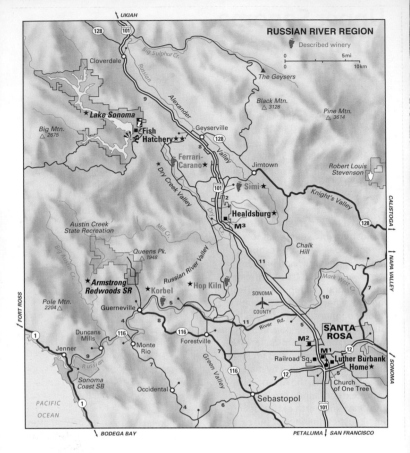

RUSSIAN RIVER REGION

🍇 Described winery

Santa Rosa Aves. at 3rd and 4th Sts.).
Framed by fountains, the grassy swath
is a popular site for outdoor concerts.
Northeast of downtown are lovely residential streets lined with well-preserved
late-19C Victorian homes.

Luther Burbank Home & Gardens★

Sonoma and Santa Rosa Aves.,
Santa Rosa. ⏱*Open Apr–Oct Tue–Sun*
10am–4pm (🏠home visit by guided
tour only, 💲*$7). Gardens open daily*
8am–dusk. ♿ 📞*707-524-5445.*
www.lutherburbank.org.
Visitors can tour the modest home of the
renowned botanist, who moved to Santa
Rosa from Massachusetts in 1875, or
stroll among lush gardens, which today
feature many of Burbank's experimental
hybrids, including some 100 varieties of
roses. Burbank's extensive experiments

in plant hybridization—resulting in such
now-commonplace strains as the Russet
Burbank potato, the Shasta daisy and
the Santa Rosa plum—produced more
than 800 new varieties of fruits, nuts and
vegetables and earned him a reputation
as magician of the botanical world.
In the renovated carriage house, displays tell the story of Burbank's life
and work. The simple furnishings of
his charming Greek Revival home bear
witness to the horticulturalist's simple
lifestyle, although he clearly had many
high-powered friends: photos show him
with the likes of Henry Ford, Thomas Edi-
son, Jack London and Helen Keller.

Church of One Tree

Juilliard Park, across Santa Rosa Ave.
from Burbank Home, Santa Rosa.
🔒*Closed to the public.*

Constructed of boards from a single 275ft redwood tree, this now-dilapidated Gothic Revival church formerly housed a small museum dedicated to the life and discoveries of native-son Ripley, creator of *Believe It or Not!*

Sonoma County Museum★ (M1)

425 7th St., Santa Rosa. ◷*Open Tue–Sun 11am–5pm.* ◷*Closed major holidays.* ☜*$7.* ♿🅿 ℘*707-579-1500. www.sonomacountymuseum.org.*
Santa Rosa's former post office (1909), designed in the Classical Revival style, showcases the art, history and culture of Sonoma County. Historical exhibits cover the period from the early 18C, when Miwok, Pomo and Wapo peoples occupied the area, through the growth of the wine industry and recent population growth. Landscapes by William Keith and Thomas Hill are among works presented in the California Gallery of 19C painting. The museum also boasts the largest private collection of works (more than 100 drawings, sculpture, collages and photographs) by site-specific artists Christo and Jeanne-Claude.

♨♟ Charles M. Schulz Museum and Research Center (M2)

1 Snoopy Pl., off W. Steele Ln. and Hardies Ln, Santa Rosa. ▷ *Exit US-101 north at Steele Ln. and turn left.* ◷*Open Memorial Day–Labor Day Mon–Fri 11am–5pm, Sat–Sun 10am–5pm; rest of the year closed Tue.* ◷*Closed major holidays.* ☜*$10, children 4–18 $5.* ♿🅿 ℘*707-579-4452. www.schulzmuseum.org.*
For nearly 50 years, until his death in early 2000, Santa Rosa resident Charles Schulz wrote and illustrated the popular comic strip, Peanuts. The often funny, often poignant, always memorable saga of underachiever Charlie Brown and his overachieving dog, Snoopy, appeared in 3,000 newspapers in 75 countries and 40 languages, and was read by hundreds of millions of people.
Opened in 2002, the museum aims at building an understanding of cartoonists and cartoon art while telling the story of Schulz's life and career, integrating artists who influenced Schulz and whom he in turn influenced. The museum also celebrates the Peanuts characters through rotating exhibits of 6,000 original comic strips and examples of 50 years of product items. A 100-seat auditorium presents daily screenings of the Peanuts animated shows.

♨♟ Snoopy's Gallery and Gift Shop

1665 W. Steele Ln., Santa Rosa. ◷*Open daily 10am–6pm.* ◷*Closed major holidays.* ♿🅿 ℘*707-546-3385 or 800-959-3385. www.snoopygift.com.*
Lovers of *Peanuts* enjoy a visit to this gallery, where memorabilia, cartoons, and original drawings are displayed on the mezzanine level.

♨♟ Redwood Empire Ice Arena

1667 W. Steele Ln., Santa Rosa. ◷*Open daily 9am–9pm.* ◷*Closed major holidays.* ✗♿🅿 ℘*707-546-7147. www.snoopyshomeice.com.*
Schulz himself directed the construction of this Swiss chalet-style arena in 1969. It hosts concerts, hockey games and ice shows, and is open for public skating *(rentals available;* ◷*call or visit website for schedule).* The facility includes the **Warm Puppy Café**, where Schulz had a Snoopy-like breakfast of jelly donuts every morning.

Healdsburg★

15mi northwest of Santa Rosa.
Founded in 1857 by Harmon Heald, a migrant farmer-turned-merchant, tranquil Healdsburg (HEELDS-burg) sits at the confluence of the Alexander, Dry Creek and Russian River valleys. Several excellent restaurants and inns make it an ideal starting point for forays into these areas. At the heart of this town of 11,300 is picturesque, one-acre **Plaza Park** *(Healdsburg Ave. and Plaza, Center and Matheson Sts.).* Dozens of different species of trees grow in and around the plaza; request a walking-tour brochure, "Tree Walk of Healdsburg," from the Healdsburg Area Chamber of Commerce *(217 Healdsburg Ave.;* ℘*707-433-6935; www.healdsburg.com).*

Healdsburg Museum (M3)

221 Matheson St., 2 blocks east of the plaza. ⊙*Open Wed–Sun 11am–4pm.* ⊙*Closed major holidays.* ♿🅿 ✆707-431-3325. www.healdsburgmuseum.org.
Housed in a beautifully preserved former Carnegie Library, this small museum contains a collection of artifacts from indigenous peoples and from California's Mexican period. Highlights include photographs, Pomo Indian baskets, grinding rocks and weapons, bringing to life upper Sonoma's colorful history.

Lake Sonoma★

11mi north of Healdsburg by Dry Creek Rd. 🏃⚠ (⊜*$10–$40; reservations* ✆877-444-6777). 🅿 ✆707-431-4553. www.parks.sonoma.net.
Nestled in the coastal foothills of northern Sonoma County, this elongated lake was created in 1983 when the Warm Springs Dam was constructed at the confluence of Warm Springs and Dry creeks. Now a popular recreation area, Lake Sonoma offers a plethora of activities including boating, swimming, fishing, picnicking, hiking and camping in and around its sapphire waters.

👪 Visitor Center and Fish Hatchery★★

3333 Skaggs Springs Rd., Geyserville. ⊙*Visitor center open daily.* ✆707-431-4533. www.spn.usace.army.mil/lake_sonoma/vcandfh.htm.
Displays of craftwork and artifacts in the Visitor Center exemplify the traditions and beliefs of the indigenous Pomo people. Panels illustrate local geological formations and thermal activity. The state-of-the-art hatchery building, created by the U.S. Army Corps of Engineers to mitigate environmental disruption of Dry Creek caused by the Warm Springs Dam, offers a rare opportunity to observe the spawning and hatching of steelhead trout and coho (silver) and chinook salmon. Fish climb a "ladder" into the hatchery where they are held, sorted and spawned—activities visible from a mezzanine-level interpretive center.

Lake Sonoma Overlook

2.5mi from Visitor Center via Stewarts Point Rd.; follow signs.
Designed in harmony with its natural surroundings, the wood-timbered overlook offers soaring **views★★** of the lake, dam and surrounding mountains, including Mt. St. Helena in neighboring Napa Valley.

👪 Armstrong Redwoods State Reserve★

2mi north of Guerneville on Armstrong Woods Rd. ⊙*Open daily 8am–one hour past sunset; visitor center open daily 11am–3pm.* ✆707-869-2958. ⊜*$8/car.* 🅿 ✆707-869-2015. www.parks.sonoma.net.
Lush, dense forests of varied species of trees surround a 500-acre grove of ancient redwoods that survived 19C logging operations thanks to conservationist efforts of Col. James Armstrong. Today the grove forms the heart of an 800-acre state park with some of Sonoma County's finest surviving redwood trees. A self-guided nature trail (.5mi) passes through fern-laced glades.

WINERIES
Simi Winery★

16275 Healdsburg Ave., Healdsburg. ⊙*Open daily 10am–5pm.* ⊜*$10 tasting fee.* 🍷*Tour daily 11am and 2pm.* ⊙*Closed Jan 1, Easter Sunday, Thanksgiving Day, Dec 25.* ✕♿🅿 ✆707-473-3236. www.simiwinery.com.
Founded in 1883 by Italian immigrants Giuseppe and Pietro Simi, this winery today boasts some of the oldest vines and stone cellars in California alongside an ultra-modern winemaking facility. The massive stone cellars were built in two phases, visible in the building's two types of stonework. In the mid-1880s, Chinese workers constructed the original south side, as well as railroad tracks that still run through the middle of the property. (They were once used to ship bottles directly from the cellars.). The north side was constructed in 1904 by Italian masons under the direction of Isabel Simi, Giuseppe's daughter, who

(according to local lore) took over management of the winery at age 14. Legend has it that after Prohibition, with the winery all but bankrupt, Isabel rolled a barrel onto the old highway and offered free sips of wine, thereby establishing California's first tasting room.

A guided tour takes visitors through the historic stone cellars and into a high-tech fermentation center.

Ferrari-Carano Winery★

9mi north of Healdsburg at 8761 Dry Creek Rd. ⓒ*Open daily 10am–5pm.* *$5 tasting fee.* *Guided tours Mon –Sat 10am by reservation.* *707-433-6700. www.ferrari-carano.com.*

Five acres of stunning parterre gardens surround a spectacular Italianate villa on this fine estate. Visitors enter through wrought-iron gates, meandering along garden paths, past a rippling stream. An Italian courtyard provides the formal entrance to the Renaissance-style Villa Fiore (1997), its stone columns and arches rising above the Dry Creek Valley. From the tasting room and wine shop, a curving stone staircase descends to a vaulted, cobblestone-floored viewing area, revealing more than 1,100 French oak barrels aging fine red wines.

Hop Kiln Winery★

6050 Westside Rd., 6mi southwest of Healdsburg. ⓒ*Open daily 10am–5pm.* ⓒ*Closed major holidays.* 🅿 *707-433-6491. www.hopkilnwinery.com.*

This historic hop barn (1905), one of the finest examples of its type, functioned as part of northern California's hop-growing industry. Hops were dried in three wooden kilns, resembling giant inverted funnels, before being pressed and baled for shipment to breweries. The kiln was renovated as a winery in 1975.

Korbel Champagne Cellars★

13250 River Rd., 2.5mi northeast of Guerneville. ⓒ*Open 10am–5pm.* *Winery tour daily 11am–5pm.* ⓒ*Closed major holidays.* ✕👤🅿 *707-824-7000. www.korbel.com.*

Korbel dates from the late 1870s, when Czech immigrants Anton, Francis and

Ferrari-Carano Winery vineyards

© M. Linda Lee / MICHELIN

Joseph Korbel planted grapevines on the site. In 1886 they built a large, handmade-brick building for the production of brandy and sparkling wine. The highlight of a visit to Korbel is an informative guided tour covering both historic and contemporary processes of méthode champenoise sparkling-wine production. Enjoy a wander through the 250-variety antique rose garden (*guided tours mid-Apr–Oct Tue–Sun 11am, 1pm and 3pm*) on the slope below the Korbel family summer home.

Stroll through the old train depot, formerly the terminus of the Fulton-Guerneville branch of the Northwest Pacific Railroad. After dining in the restaurant or picking up picnic food in the deli, you can take a tour of the Russian River Brewing Company—Korbel's response to visitors with champagne tastes but beer pockets.

ADDRESSES

🏨 STAY

$$$ Hotel La Rose – *308 Wilson St.; Santa Rosa.* *707-579-3200. www.hotel larose.com. 47 rooms.* A charming historic hotel, the La Rose was built in 1907 of locally quarried sandstone. Fully renovated, it offers modern rooms with Victorian touches, both in the main building and in contemporary suites across 5th Street.

SOUTH BAY AND PENINSULA

The Bay Area bedroom communities south of San Francisco range down the east side of the Santa Cruz Mountains sandwiched between US-101 and I-280. From north to south, Millbrae, Burlingame, San Mateo, Redwood City, Palo Alto, Mountain View, Los Altos and Santa Clara stretch down toward San Jose, California's third-largest city, located in the Santa Clara Valley along Coyote Creek and the Guadalupe River. Cutting-edge technology is one of the reasons to visit the valley, but by no means the only one. San Jose offers a wealth of cultural attractions, from the downtown historic district—which dates back to 1777—to the 132,000sq ft Tech Museum of Innovation.

Highlights

1 Visit Stanford campus' **Rodin collection** (p285)
2 Wander the 16-acre **botanical gardens** at **Filoli** (p287)
3 Play with interactive exhibits at the **Tech Museum of Innovation** (p288)
4 Learn about semiconductors at the **Intel Museum** (p293)
5 Observe sea elephants at the **Año Nuevo State Reserve** (p299)

Silicon Valley

The self-proclaimed capital of Silicon Valley, San Jose was founded in 1777 as El Pueblo San Jose de Guadalupe, by Lieutenant Jose Joaquin Moraga on order of the Viceroy of New Spain, as the first civilian settlement in Nueva California (later Alta California). Then, it served as an agricultural community providing fruit, vegetables, wheat and beef during the Spanish conlonial and Mexican periods to the military personnel at the nearby Presidio of San Francisco and Presidio of Monterey.

Agriculture remained the city's chief industry from the 1850s until the mid-20C. After World War II, a population explosion in the area spurred rapid development and urbanization. By the 1950s, electronics industries began to supplant the orchards and ranches. Beginning with the development of the semiconductor industry in the mid-20C, innovative new enterprises arose in the Bay Area to fill the growing demand for electronic products. By the 1970s, Silicon Valley, which included such com-

puter giants as Hewlett-Packard, Apple Computer, Intel and a host of semiconductor laboratories, had moved well beyond their humble garage beginnings to become the dominant industry in San Jose and the neighboring communities.

In the late 1990s, a new breed of technology-based companies came to town. Known as dot-coms, these Internet companies and their stock prices rocketed in the short term, making millionaires of many investors as well as many stock option-holding employees, until the bubble burst in March 2000.

Today, IT professionals in the Silicon Valley—home to giants like Yahoo!, NetFlix, eBay, Oracle, Google, and Facebook, to name just a few—rank among the highest paid in the country.

The local braintrust includes Stanford University in Palo Alto, with its lovely Richardsonian Romanesque–style buildings roofed with tiles and surrounded by eucalyptus, bay and palm trees. Established by railroad magnate Leland Stanford in 1891, Stanford University boasts a distinguished tenure-line faculty that includes Nobel laureates, Pulitzer Prize winners and recipients of the National Medal of Science.

San Mateo County Coast

From the San Francisco city limits, Hwy. 1 stretches beside the Pacific Ocean through the rural and almost totally undeveloped coastline of San Mateo County, 70 percent of which is dedicated open space.

The beaches here sprawl—from wide-open sandy strips, to hidden rocky coves—and each is wildly different from the next. Small towns and lush, green farms dot the countryside.

ADDRESSES

🛏 STAY

$$$ Costanoa – *2001 Rossi Rd., Pescadero, 1hr drive south of San Franscisco on Hwy. 1.* 📞*650-879-1100. www.costanoa.com. 52 units.* A "base camp for coastal adventures" near the Año Nuevo State Reserve, Costanoa offers three types of accommodation—a stylish 40-room lodge, a set of cabins favored by families and couples, and a handful of tent bungalows. A general store and spa complete the complex.

$$$ The Fairmont San Jose – *170 S. Market St., San Jose.* 📞*408-998-1900. www.fairmont.com. 808 rooms.* Catering primarily to business travelers, this 20-story grand hotel offers elegant and sophisticated guest rooms.

$$$ Hotel De Anza – *233 W. Santa Clara St., San Jose.* 📞*408-286-1000 or 800-843-3700. www.hoteldeanza.com. 100 rooms.* Built in 1931 and fully renovated six decades later, the historic De Anza retains an Art Deco-era appeal. Rooms are spacious and contemporary; guests get a morning paper with their coffee and are invited to "raid the pantry" for late-night deli snacks!

$$$$ Stanford Park Hotel – *100 El Camino Real, Menlo Park.* 📞*650-322-1234. www.woodsidehotels.com. 163 rooms.* Near Stanford University, this handsome inn boasts rooms with vaulted ceilings, granite fireplaces, English yew-wood armoires and writing desks, and courtyard views. Its warm decor and guest library contribute to a high-brow academic flavor.

🍴 EAT

$ Palo Alto Creamery – *566 Emerson St., Palo Alto.* 📞*650-323-3131. www.paloalto creamery.com.* **American.** This 1923 soda fountain keeps its menu and prices as authentic as its atmosphere. Cheeseburgers, milkshakes, meatloaf and fried chicken.

$$ Blue Mango – *635 Coleman Ave., San Jose.* 📞*408-885-9222. www.bluemango cuisine.com.* **Thai.** A striking painting of Thailand's Temple of Dawn dominates the inviting dining room. On the menu you'll find standbys like pad Thai alongside updated versions of traditional fare. There's also an extensive vegetarian menu.

$$ Evvia Estiatorio – *420 Emerson St., Palo Alto.* 📞*650-326-0983. www.evvia.net.* **Greek.** No stodgy Balkan eatery, Evvia's open kitchen focuses on Californian approaches to Aegean classics. You'll get spanakopita (spinach pie) and moussaka (lamb-eggplant casserole), to be sure, but also octopus with roasted bell peppers and salmon with a tomato-ouzo sauce.

$$ Moss Beach Distillery – *140 Beach Way, off Hwy. 1, Moss Beach.* 📞*650-728-5595. www.mossbeachdistillery.com.* **American.** Built in the 1920s as a Hollywood retreat, this historic building became a Prohibition-era hideout for bootleggers. It's now a steak-and-seafood eatery (the Sunday Brunch draws raves) where diners can take in beautiful sunsets while whale-watching from an outdoor patio.

Manresa

© Mark Holthusen / Manresa

$$$$ Manresa – *320 Village Ln., Los Gatos.* 📞*408-354-4330. www.manresa restaurant.com. Wed–Sun dinner only.* **Contemporary.** Hidden down a narrow side street, Manresa is full of fresh ranch house charm, from exposed wood beams to silk drapes and a curvy fireplace. Influenced by French and modern Catalan cooking, chef David Kinch offers an ever-changing four-course meal built around biodynamic vegetables from nearby Love Apple Farm. Dishes might include spiced Maine lobster with shallots, baby turnips and cherry vinaigrette; or beef bavette with spring alliums and toasted quinoa.

Palo Alto★

An affluent college town of about 65,000, Palo Alto derives its name from the twin-trunked coast redwood under which Gaspar de Portolá camped on his 1769 expedition. Now single-trunked and timeworn, **El Palo Alto,** "the tall tree," still stands in a small park by the railroad tracks off Alma Avenue. It remains the official symbol of Stanford University.

STANFORD UNIVERSITY★★

Circled by Campus Dr. E. & W., west of El Camino Real (Rte. 82) via Palm Dr.
◐ *From San Francisco drive south on US-101 and exit west at Embarcadero Rd., which becomes Galvez St. as it enters campus. Visitor information center at 295 Galvez St. (◐open Mon–Fri 8.30am–5pm, Sat–Sun 10am–5pm; ◐closed Dec 19–Jan 3). ◐Student-led campus tours (1hr) depart from visitor center early Jan–late Dec 11am and 3.15pm. ✕&🅿 ☎650-723-2560. www.stanford.edu.*

Established by railroad magnate Leland Stanford, this renowned institution sprawls across 8,180 acres. Its gracious, Spanish-flavored Richardsonian Romanesque buildings are shaded by eucalyptus, bay and palm trees.

Born in New York state, the university's founder, **Leland Stanford** (1824–93), moved to California during the Gold Rush, became state governor, then president of the Central Pacific Railroad, a risky venture that earned him a fortune. In 1884 Stanford and his wife, Jane, lost their only child, 15-year-old Leland, Jr., to typhoid fever. The bereft couple, declaring that "the children of California shall be our children," set out to establish a university on the grounds of their Palo Alto ranch. Architect Charles Allerton Coolidge and landscape architect Frederick Law Olmsted jointly conceived the campus plan and the low, arcaded buildings of the university, which opened in 1891. Two years later, Stanford died at age 69 and the 1890s financial depression threatened the existence

Info: ☎650-324-3121. www.paloaltochamber.com.
◐ **Location:** Palo Alto is located about 33mi south of San Francisco via US-101, between the marshlands of southern San Francisco Bay and the Santa Cruz Mountains.
◐ **Timing:** Plan about a day to enjoy the sights in Palo Alto.
🅿 **Parking:** There are metered spaces for visitors at various locations throughout the Stanford campus, and a visitor lot behind Memorial Auditorium. Other Palo Alto sights offer free parking.
◐ **Don't Miss:** The Cantor Center for Visual Arts, with its impressive collection of Rodin scuptures.

of the university. By the early 20C, with the economic crisis resolved, Stanford University was on its way to becoming a celebrated academic institution. The campus has remained a leading academic and research center, with more than 10,000 students. Among its 1,910 faculty members are 19 Nobel laureates, four Pulitzer Prize winners, and 18 recipients of the National Medal of Science. The northwest corner of that campus still holds the **Red Barn** *(Fremont and Electioneer Rds.)*, original Victorian stables built by Leland Stanford more than a century ago. Extending beside it is the **Stanford Golf Course** *(Junipero Serra Blvd. & Campus Dr. W.)*, where the world's most famous golfer, Eldrick "Tiger" Woods, first achieved teenage fame.

Main Quadrangle★

The main entrance road from downtown Palo Alto leads up Palm Drive to the historic heart of campus. The expansive, tiled courtyard is bordered by the university's 12 original colonnaded buildings and anchored by magnificent **Memorial Church**★★ *(◷open Mon–Fri 8am–5pm, Sun 11.30am–3.30pm; ⬝⬝guided tours Fri 2pm & last Sun of the month 11.15am; ◷ closed major holidays; ✆650-723-1762)*. Built in 1903 by Jane Stanford to commemorate her husband, the church features elaborate Byzantine-style mosaics, stained glass and three renowned organs equipped to play Renaissance and Baroque music.

Hoover Tower★

◷Observation deck open daily 10am–4pm.◷Closed between academic quarters. ⬝⬝$2. ♿ ✆650-723-2053.
The landmark 285ft campanile houses part of the Hoover Institution on War, Revolution and Peace, a public-policy research center inspired by university alumnus Herbert Hoover. Two museum galleries *(both sides of entrance hall)* are devoted to the considerable accomplishments of Hoover and his wife, Lou Henry Hoover. The top of the tower features a 48-bell carillon and an observation deck offering panoramic views of the campus and of San Francisco and the Bay Area to the north.

Iris & B. Gerald Cantor Center for Visual Arts★

Lomita Dr. and Museum Way. ◷Open Wed–Sun 11am–5pm, Thu 11am–8pm. ◷Closed major holidays. ✕♿🅿✆650-723-4177. www.museum.stanford.edu.
This university museum houses a dazzling, eclectic collection of 20,000 pieces of ancient to contemporary sculpture, paintings, crafts and ceremonial artworks from Africa, Oceania, Asia, Europe and the Americas. Noted for its cultivated eclecticism, it is renowned for its ambitious collection of Rodin sculptures, the world's largest outside Paris. The Cantor's precursor was founded by Leland and Jane Stanford as a memorial to their son, an amateur collector of eclectic tastes. Leland, Jr.'s well-rounded collections formed the nucleus of the museum (1894, Percy and Hamilton), designed after the National Archaeological Museum of Athens and built of reinforced concrete.

Although Jane Stanford bolstered the collection by donating 15,000 additional objects before her death in 1905, the early museum closed after suffering heavy damage in the earthquake of 1906. The museum was revived in the 1950s, but severe structural damage during the Loma Prieta earthquake of 1989 again forced its closure. The university responded with an ambitious campaign to retrofit the original 72,000sq ft building, while architect James Polshek & Partners designed a rectangular, 42,000sq ft addition of steel, glass and stucco. It reopened in 1999.
It is now a premier university teaching museum that illustrates comparative objets d'art from a broad spectrum of cultures and eras.

Visit

Designed by Venetian artist Antonio Paoletti, the 13 mosaics across the front facade of the original building illustrate the progress of civilization through learning and arts. Three pairs of massive entry doors, each weighing 600 pounds, are encased in bronze panels depicting examples of ancient architecture. The two-story entry hall, clad in marble with floors of terrazzo, is presided over by a statue of Athena. Flanking the entrance, the two original wings exhibit the Classical, historical and international collections, while the new addition—behind the entry hall—houses contemporary art and rotating exhibits. Two courtyards are devoted to sculpture.
A central gallery behind the entrance lobbies acknowledges the museum's origin in the **Stanford Family Collection**. It includes family portraits, curios from young Leland's collections, the boy's death mask, and the **Golden Spike** from the ceremonial completion of the first transcontinental railroad.

Rodin Sculpture Garden★

Located on the southwest side of the Cantor Center, this one-acre garden displays 20 large-scale bronze casts by French sculptor Auguste Rodin, including his famed *The Gates of Hell* (1880–1900). A half-dozen casts from Rodin's

Herbert Hoover

One of Stanford University's most illustrious alumni was Herbert Hoover (1874–1964), a member of the institution's first class in 1891 and a graduate in geology. Hoover traveled the globe as a mining engineer for nearly two decades—managing mines in Russia, China, Burma and Australia—before entering public life in 1914, when he established a humanitarian relief organization in Europe. His role as an adviser to President Woodrow Wilson led to his appointment as secretary of commerce in the Harding and Coolidge administrations of the 1920s. Hoover subsequently was elected U.S. President in 1928 and served one term.

In 1945, Hoover was called back to public service by President Harry Truman to coordinate dispersal of food to 28 nations during a postwar famine. He served as an adviser to President Dwight Eisenhower in the 1950s.

Before he died at age 90, Hoover wrote more than 30 books and expanded a world-renowned library that he had established at Stanford in 1919. He maintained an office on the 11th floor of the Hoover Tower, built in 1941.

series *The Burghers of Calais* are also displayed in a courtyard on the Serra Street side of the Main Quad.

Elsewhere on campus are sculptures by such prominent artists as Joan Miró, Alexander Calder and Henry Moore. A free *Guide to Outdoor Sculpture* is available at the art museum and the campus visitor information booth.

Stanford Linear Accelerator Center

2575 Sand Hill Rd., just east of I-280, Menlo Park. ⏱*Visitor center open Mon–Fri 9am–4pm.* ☞*Guided tours (1.5hrs) available 1st and 3rd Fri of month 1.30pm and 3.30pm.* ✕❤️🅿️ 𝒫*650-926-2204. www.slac.stanford.edu.*

Operated by the university for the U.S. Department of Energy, SLAC opened in 1961 as a research facility in particle physics. Within this 480-acre facility, which includes a 2mi-long linear accelerator, scientists probe the structure of matter on atomic and subatomic levels with x-rays and particle beams.In the small visitor center, exhibits describe such discoveries as quarks, and explore successes in biomedical and environmental research. Also displayed is a skeletal cast of an ancient walrus-like mammal, **Paleoparadoxia**, found during excavation at SLAC.

EXCURSIONS
NASA Ames Research Center

Moffett Field, Mountain View.
▶ *From US-101, take Moffett Field exit; turn right to main gate, then left .4mi on R.T. Jones Rd. to Gate 17C.* ⏱*Visitor center open Tue–Fri 10am–4pm; Sat–Sun noon–4pm.* ⏱*Closed major holidays.* 𝒫*650-604-6274. www.arc.nasa.gov.*

Founded in 1939 at a former naval air field as an aircraft research laboratory, this 430-acre facility has been a part of the National Aeronautics and Space Administration since 1958. Now the hub of NASA information technologies, Ames is also the lead NASA agency in the study of gravity, astrobiology and Mars exploration, to name but a few. The center harbors the world's largest wind tunnel and several advanced flight simulators. The visitor center boasts the west coast's largest immersive theater. Displays showcase planetary exploration, spacesuit technology and artifacts from past missions.

Filoli★★

13mi north of Palo Alto at Woodside and 30mi south of San Francisco.
▶ *Take I-280 to Edgewood Rd.; exit west, turn right on Cañada Rd. and continue 1.3mi to gate.* ⏱*Open Tue–Sat 10am–3.30pm and Sun 11am–3.30pm (last admission 2.30pm). Guided tour (2hrs) available Tue–Sat 10am and 1pm,*

additional tour at 11.30am Apr–May; reservations required. Additional Camelia tours, orchard tours and guided nature hikes offered, call or consult website for times. ⊘*Closed major holidays.* ⊶*$15.* ✕*(Tea Room)* ♿🅿 ℘*650-364-8300, ext. 507. www.filoli.org.*

Nestled into the inland side of the Coast Range's heavily wooded foothills, this 654-acre estate is precariously situated astride the San Andreas Fault. Yet its elegance exemplifies the gracious lifestyle made possible at the turn of the 20C by fortunes derived from several of California's great economic forces: mining, real-estate speculation, water development and agriculture.

The formal Italian Renaissance gardens and U-shaped, "Modified" Georgian Revival mansion (1915–17, Willis Polk) were commissioned by William Bourn II (1857–1936), owner of the Empire Mine in Grass Valley; at the time, the Empire was California's most productive hard-rock gold mine. Bourn was also president of the Spring Valley Water Company, consisting of Crystal Springs Lake and its adjacent lands, and it was here that he sited his 43-room country estate. Filoli (named for a favorite Bourn credo, *Fight for a just cause; Love your fellow man; Live a good life*), with its large, mature trees spreading shadows over acres of well-kept lawns, still expresses the confidence of settled rural wealth. After the deaths of Bourn and his wife in 1936, Filoli was acquired by its only other owner, William P. Roth. Roth died in 1963. His widow donated Filoli to the National Trust for Historic Preservation in 1975.

Mansion★★

The ground floor features furniture and art from both the Bourn and Roth families; an extensive collection of 17C–18C Irish and English furnishings and decorative arts bequeathed by Melville Martin in 1998; and pieces on loan from the Fine Arts Museums of San Francisco.

House tours commence in the Reception Room, where a 17ft by 33ft Persian car-

Sunken garden, Filoli

© Filoli

pet (19C), woven over three generations, covers the floor. The kitchen features an impressive ship's stove acquired in 1942 from the Matson Navigation Company, owned by Lurline Roth's father. The grand ballroom, with its 22ft ceilings, is adorned with Ernest Peixotto murals (1925) depicting Ireland's Lakes of Killarney and Muckross House, an 11,000-acre estate given by the Bourns to their daughter on her marriage in 1910.

Gardens★★★

Designed by Bruce Porter with continuing assistance from Isabella Worn, this 16-acre botanical wonder (1917–20) successfully combines the formal with the natural. Planned as a sequence of outdoor "rooms," each with its own horticultural and seasonal delights, the gardens are aligned along the same north-south axis as the house, extending the lines of the mansion's hallway.

Some of the most interesting plants were gifts or purchases from foreign governments, disposing of display specimens after the 1915 Panama-Pacific International Exposition.

Many of the column-shaped Irish yews, used as pillars in Filoli's garden "architecture," started as cuttings from the yews at Muckross.

San Jose★

Now California's third largest city with some one million residents, the self-proclaimed "capital of Silicon Valley" bustles with high-tech prosperity. In San Jose's revitalized downtown, stately old buildings sit alongside modern high-rises amid palm-lined plazas and avenues. The city boasts a number of unusual museums, from innovative new ones to "mysterious" older ones.

A BIT OF HISTORY

Spanish administrators chose this site in the fertile Santa Clara Valley in 1777 for the founding of the first civilian settlement in Alta California. The new farming community on the banks of the Guadalupe River supplied food to soldiers in San Francisco and Monterey. Twenty years later, the San José Mission was founded 13mi to the north. In 1849, three years after the American takeover of California, members of the state's Constitutional Convention chose San Jose as the state capital, an honor it held for several months before the seat of government was moved to Vallejo.

From the mid-19C to mid-20C, agriculture remained San Jose's chief industry. Abundant flowering orchards attracted weekend tourists who came from throughout the Bay Area to enjoy "the Garden City in the Valley of Heart's Delight."

In the postwar period, the character of Santa Clara County changed dramatically as structures housing electronics industries began to sprout in place of the orchards, and by the late 1960s "Silicon Valley" had encompassed San Jose. Such computer giants as IBM, Hewlett-Packard, Apple, Novell and Adobe Systems developed facilities in the city and in neighboring communities.

SIGHTS
👥 Tech Museum of Innovation★★

201 S. Market St. at Park Ave. ◗ *From US-101 exit at Guadalupe Pkwy for 2.5mi; exit at Park Ave/San Carlos St.*

🚉 Fremont Station
ⓒ **Michelin Map:** *See* inside back cover.
🔢 **Info:** ☎408-295-9600. www.sanjose.org.
◗ **Location:** The downtown heart of San Jose, focused around **Plaza de Cesar Chavez** *(Market St. & Park Ave.)*, site of frequent civic festivals, bustles seven days a week.
👥 **Kids:** There's lots for kids to do in San Jose, including the Children's Discovery Museum, the Tech Museum of Innovation, the Winchester Mystery House with its confounding twists, turns and stairways, and the quaint Happy Hollow Park and Zoo.
🕐 **Timing:** San Jose swarms during the week; try to plan a weekend visit, when traffic is light and parking lots are less crowded.
🅿 **Parking:** Parking is available at many downtown garages. The **Valley Transportation Authority (VTA)** light-rail system *(☎408-321-2300; www.vta.org)* runs 24 hours daily, linking most hotels and attractions at a nominal cost.
👁 **Don't Miss:** The Tech Museum of Innovation, a fitting introduction to the sights of Silicon Valley.

🕐*Open daily 10am–8pm.* 🕐*Closed Dec 25.* ✍*$20 museum and IMAX show.* ✕ ♿ ☎*408-294-8324. www.thetech.org.* This state-of-the-art, interactive exhibit hall (popularly known as "The Tech") is designed to encourage the spirit of innovative curiosity characteristic of the original techno-tinkerers of Silicon Valley. Housed in a domed, mango-colored building with azure highlighting, The Tech is entertaining for all ages, but specifically courts the youthful "information generation" with playful, participatory exhibits in such fields as communications, microelectronics, space exploration, robotics and biotechnology.

Established in 1990, the museum increased its size six-fold (to 132,000sq ft) when it moved to its present site in 1998. A fascinating mobile sculpture, George Rhoads' *Science on a Roll,* enlivens the side-entrance sidewalk on Park Avenue, where crowds gather outside to watch a continuous sequence of clanging and clattering billiard balls travel by ramps and elevator through a precisely synchronized mechanical maze.

Visit

The main entrance is on the middle floor of a three-story atrium. Escalators lead up and down to exhibit floors. On the Upper Level, exhibits in **Life Tech** invite adults and children to ride a virtual Olympic bobsled ride; design a human-powered bicycle, boat or airplane; and tour a virtual operating room that depends on non-invasive technologies for diagnosis and treatment.

Innovation provides a glimpse of robotics and computer-generated design, encouraging visitors to try their hands at inventing a roller coaster or high-tech bicycle, or in creating a three-dimensional self-portrait with a laser scanner. One display relates how companies design and manufacture silicon microchips in a "cleanroom," an industrial innovation that sparked Silicon Valley's heady propulsion to the forefront of the technology revolution.

Changing exhibits in **The Spirit of American Innovation** portray state-of-the-art technology now under development. In **Exploration,** budding explorers may pilot a robotic submarine, test-drive a remote-control planetary rover, design an earthquake-proof building, or test hand-eye coordination with a laser affixed to a space-age chair.

In Idea House you can use technology to design a "snack contraption" for a person with a broken leg and the munchies. Adjacent to the ground-floor street entrance, the 295-seat **Hackworth IMAX Dome Theater** screens documentary films on a hemispherical screen that covers 80 percent of the dome, engulfing the audience with images and sound.

San Jose Museum of Art

110 S. Market St. ❯ *Exit I-280 at Guadalupe Pkwy North; exit and turn right on Santa Clara St. for 5 blocks to Market St. and turn right.* ◷*Open Tue–Sun 11am–5pm.* ◷*Closed Jan 1, Thanksgiving, Dec 25.* ﹩$8. ✕♿ ✆*408-271-6840. www.sjmusart.org.*

Established in 1933 in an old sandstone Richardsonian Romanesque post office (1892) and expanded in 1991 with a modern wing of glass, aluminum and concrete, the museum faces Fairmont Plaza. At any one time, four major exhibits are presented; rotated quarterly on a staggered schedule, they may feature cutting-edge paintings, sculpture, photographs and installation art by California artists, as well as nationally significant traveling shows. Three Dale Chihuly glass chandeliers above the main entrance are among the 1,400 works of 20C and 21C art in the museum's permanent collection. Wall text is in Vietnamese and Tagalog as well as Spanish and English, an indication of the great ethnic variety in the South Bay area.

Cathedral Basilica of Saint Joseph

80 S. Market St. ❯ *Exit I-280 at Guadalupe Pkwy North; exit and turn right on Santa Clara St. for 5 blocks to Market St. and turn right.* ◷*Open daily.* ✆*408-283-8100. www.stjosephcathedral.org.*

Founded in 1803 as a small adobe church, hub of the first Catholic parish in California, this beautiful building was constructed in 1877 by Brian Clinch— a devout architect who read the New Testament in Greek. The cathedral was dedicated as a minor basilica in 1997. The impressive interior is worth a visit.

San Jose Museum of Quilts & Textiles

520 S. 1st St. ▶ *Exit I-280 at Virginia St.; turn right, then right again on S. 1st St.* ⏱*Open Wed–Sun 10am–5pm (1st Fri of month 7–11pm).* ⏱*Closed major holidays and between shows.* ⊛*$8 (pay what you can 1st Fri).* ♿ ☏*408-971-0323. www.sjquiltmuseum.org.*

The oldest quilt museum in the United States offers regularly changing exhibits of works by traditional and contemporary quilt and woven tapestry artists. Costumes and dolls from various ethnic communities suggest the diversity of design and craft traditions.

♟ Children's Discovery Museum of San Jose★

180 Woz Way, off W. San Carlos St. at Rte. 87. ▶ *Exit I-280 at Bird Ave. and turn north; turn right on W. San Carlos St. and right on Woz Way.* ⏱*Open mid-Jun–Labor Day Mon–Sat 10am–5pm, Sun noon–5pm; rest of the year closed Mon.* ⏱*Closed Jan 1, Dec 25.* ⊛*$12.* ✗♿ ☏*408-298-5437. www.cdm.org.*

Housed in a whimsical purple structure (1991, Ricardo Legorreta) that resembles building blocks, this bilingual (English-Spanish) museum dominates Guadalupe River Park. Hands-on exhibits and programs are geared to families and school-age children. Highlights include **Streets**, an intersecting corridor demonstrating the workings of urban infrastructure; **Current Connections**, an introduction to electricity; interactive arts and nature exhibits; and activity areas designed to teach cultural diversity. A theater features a variety of performers.

Peralta Adobe and Fallon House★

175 W. St. John St. at San Pedro St. ☙*Visit by guided tour (90min) only, by appointment.* ♿ ☏*408-918-1055 (tours) or 408-287-2290. www.historysanjose.org.*

Ensconced amid the modern structures of downtown, an early 19C adobe and a luxurious Italianate mansion recall San Jose's Spanish Colonial beginnings and its early 19C growth.

Erected for Thomas Fallon, a flamboyant former guide with the Frémont party who had married a Californio land-grant heiress, Fallon House was the grandest residence in San Jose when it was completed in 1855. Among other luxurious accoutrements, the mansion boasted marble fireplaces, elaborately decorated ceilings and woodwork carefully painted to look like oak. After serving as a hotel and a restaurant through the early 20C, it was acquired by the city and painstakingly restored. The lower level contains an excellent small museum detailing San Jose's development from Spanish Colonial pueblo through the American period.

Across the street, the modest Peralta Adobe was the residence of Luís María Peralta, a high-ranking pueblo official and wealthy landowner. The bedroom of the structure appears as it would have around 1800 (note the intriguing, suspended cradle), while the living room, or *sala*, is more elaborately furnished as it would have been around 1840.

♟ Kelley Park

1300 Senter Rd. at Story Rd., 3mi southeast of downtown via S. 1st St. and Keyes St. ⏱*Open daily 8am until 30min after sunset.* ✗♿◻ ☏*408-794-7275.*

The former orchard estate of Judge Lawrence Archer, a San Jose mayor, and his daughter and son-in-law, Louise and Frank Kelley, this 156-acre park on Coyote Creek contains a variety of attractions. **Happy Hollow Park and Zoo** (♟ ⏱ *open daily 10am–5pm, until 6pm Sat–Sun Jun–Aug, until 4pm weekdays Sept–Oct, until 3pm weekdays Apr–May, check website for winter hours,* ⏱*closed major holidays;* ⊛*$12.95;* ☏*408-794-6400; www.hhpz.org)* harbors more than 150 animals, including a jaguar and a pygmy hippo; children's rides, and a puppet theater. Broad shaded lawns attract throngs for weekend picnics. There's also a Greek-style amphitheater and a miniature train linking the zoo and the historical museum.

History Park at Kelley Park★

1650 Senter Rd. at Phelan Ave. ○*Open Tue–Sun 11am–4pm.* ○*Closed Jan 1, Thanksgiving Day, Dec 25.* ⊘*$8 May– Oct, free Nov–Apr* ✕🅿 *408-287- 2290. www.historysanjose.org.*

This 14-acre complex, with paved streets and a running trolley, evokes life in San Jose around the turn of the 20C. The park comprises some two dozen historic homes and shops, a third of which are re-creations; the rest were relocated from their original sites. Two or three shops are open each day on a rotating schedule and staffed by docents.

It's hard to miss the 115ft reproduction of the **San Jose Electric Tower**, a fanciful metal-beamed pyramid of street lights; and the **H.H. Warburton Doctor's Office**, with its medical and dental paraphernalia. Other highlights include the **Print Shop**, where traditional typesetting and printing techniques are demonstrated, and a brick reproduction of the city's **Chinese Temple**, featuring an elaborately carved Cantonese wooden altar from the original 1880s temple. Exhibition galleries are in the Pacific Hotel.

Japanese Friendship Garden★

○*Open daily 10am–sunset.* &🅿 *408-277-5254.*

The meticulously landscaped 6.5 acres, built in the early 1960s, are modeled after Korakuen Garden in Okayama, Japan, San Jose's sister city. Paths wind past stone lanterns, a small pagoda and a variety of flora, including flowering cherry trees and carefully placed conifers. On the upper level, a large pool—populated by brightly colored koi, turtles, ducks and blue herons—is spanned by a lovely Moon Bridge.

A waterfall pours over ornamental rocks into a lower pool, site of a teahouse. The shapes of the two ponds resemble the Japanese characters for *kokoro*, a word designating heart and soul.

Overfelt Gardens

Educational Park Dr., .25mi north of McKee Rd. ▷ *Exit US-101 at McKee Rd. and drive east; follow signs to the park.* ○*Open daily 10am–dusk.* &🅿 *408-251-3323.*

This 33-acre park was the lifelong home of Mildred Overfelt (1873–1967), whose father established a prosperous grain and dairy farm here in the 1850s. The original ranch house still stands. Highlight of the park is the Chinese Cultural Garden; its monuments include a 30ft statue of ancient philosopher Confucius overlooking a reflecting pond, and pavilions dedicated to nationalist statesmen Sun Yat-sen and Chiang Kai-shek. Three lakes attract abundant waterfowl and aquatic life.

▲▲ Winchester Mystery House

525 S. Winchester Blvd. ▷ *Exit I-280 S at Winchester Blvd. and turn left, then left onto Winchester Blvd.* ↝*Visit by guided tour only, daily 9am–5pm (7pm Sat–Sun late Apr–Sept); call or consult website for schedules. Three tours are offered: Mansion (1hr, ⊘$30); Labyrinth & Garden (⊘$10); combination Grand Tour (2hrs, ⊘$40).* ✕&🅿 *408-247-2101. www.winchester mysteryhouse.com.*

This strange, rambling 160-room Victorian hodgepodge is the creation of Sarah Winchester, widow of rifle magnate William Wirt Winchester. After purchasing an eight-room San Jose farmhouse in 1884, she added to it compulsively until her death in 1922. Local legend avers that Mrs. Winchester was guided in her architectural excesses by the ghosts of those who had lost their lives to Winchester firearms. Now largely unfurnished, the house is notable for its collection of Tiffany and European **art glass**. The **Winchester Firearms Museum** on the grounds displays an international collection of pistols and rifles.

Rosicrucian Egyptian Museum★

1660 Park Ave at Naglee Ave. ▷ *From I-280 take I-800 N, exit at Alameda and turn left, then right onto Naglee Ave.* ○*Open Wed–Fri 9am– 5pm, Sat–Sun 10am–6pm.* ○*Closed Mon–Tue & major holidays.* ⊘*$9.*

&P 𝒞408-947-3635.
www.egyptianmuseum.org.
Modeled after the Temple of Amon at Karnak, the exterior is dominated by a columned entryway and gold-paneled doors incised with hieroglyphs. The interior features one of the most extensive displays of Egyptian and Mesopotamian artifacts on the West Coast, numbering some 5,000 pieces. Note in particular the display on mummification *(gallery A)*, with painted coffins; **sarcophagi**; human and animal remains, including an unsheathed, mummified body; and a full-scale reproduction of a Middle Kingdom **Rock Tomb** *(visit by guided tour only)*.

Displays of Egyptian pottery, jewelry, glass, funerary objects, writing implements and statues of deities *(galleries B, C & D)* range from the pre-Dynastic period (4800 BC) to the Coptic period (late 2C–mid-7C AD) and include Babylonian, Sumerian and Assyrian cylinder seals and cuneiform tablets.

The museum is located on the edge of **Rosicrucian Park**, a five-acre city block filled with statues, gardens and Egyptian- and Moorish-style buildings that serve as headquarters for the English Grand Lodge of the nonsectarian Rosicrucian Order, AMORC (Ancient and Mystical Order Rosae Crucis). The grounds now house research and administrative buildings, an auditorium, a **planetarium** and the museum.

EXCURSIONS
Santa Clara
2.5mi northwest of downtown San Jose.
The city of Santa Clara was founded in 1777, when the Santa Clara de Asîs Mission (*see below*) was founded, for which the city was named.

Santa Clara de Asís Mission
On Santa Clara University campus.
 From San Jose, follow The Alameda (which becomes El Camino Real) to campus entrance. Open daily sunrise–sunset. Guided tours available by appointment. Closed Dec 26–Jan 1. &P 𝒞408-554-4023. *www.scu.edu/mission.*

Established on the banks of the Guadalupe River in 1777, the eighth California mission was founded as an additional outpost in the vicinity of San Francisco Bay, but was moved in 1781 to its present site on higher ground. Padre Junípero Serra officiated at the laying of the cornerstone for an impressive adobe church that was completed in 1784. Surrounded by fertile lands, the mission prospered until an earthquake destroyed the complex in 1812. A new church, completed in 1814, served first as a mission, then as a parish chapel, until it was destroyed by fire in 1926. The current building resembles the original 1784 adobe.

Visit – Offset by a campanile, the **church** exterior features statues of saints and a roof covered in clay tiles gleaned from the ruins of earlier mission structures. Today encased in redwood, the wooden cross standing in front of the church dates to the 1777 founding of the mission. The painted ceiling of the Victorian-style interior replicates the original design of Mexican artist Augustín Davila.

The simple **St. Francis Chapel** *(behind the main sanctuary)* contains an original wall, ceiling and floor. Left of the church lies a landscaped **quadrangle** where olive trees, roses and wisteria survive from the mission days.

Across from the entrance to the mission lies the **De Saisset Museum** *(*open Tue–Sun 11am–4pm; closed Jul–Sept, major holidays; 𝒞408-554-4528; www.scu.edu/deSaisset)*, a university museum devoted to world art and California history. The main level features temporary exhibits of selections from the museum's permanent collection of 16C–20C European and American art; Asian art and African art.

Triton Museum of Art★
1505 Warburton Ave. at Lincoln St., Santa Clara, 2 blocks north of El Camino Real. Open Tue–Sat 11am–5pm, Sun noon–4pm. &P 𝒞408-247-3754. *www.tritonmuseum.org.*
Ensconced in a tranquil seven-acre park, this modern museum displays an

eclectic collection of Native American and Western art in three skylit galleries. The **Austen D. Warburton Collection of American Indian Art and Artifacts★** spans several centuries of basketry, pottery and other artifacts from California, Southwest and Pacific Northwest tribal traditions. Selections from the permanent collection, displayed in a gallery to the right of the central rotunda, include a 19C Albert Bierstadt landscape, an 18C William Hogarth engraving and a 17C Rembrandt etching. Temporary exhibits emphasize the diversity of contemporary art in the San Francisco Bay Area. A sculpture garden nestles outside the museum walls.

Intel Museum★★
2200 Mission College Blvd., Santa Clara.
➤ *Exit US-101 at Montague Expressway and turn left on Mission College Blvd.*
◷*Open Mon–Fri 9am–6pm, Sat 10am–5pm.* ◷*Closed major holidays.* ♿🅿
℘*408- 765-0503. www.intel.com*
As the world's largest semiconductor company, the Intel Corporation invented the technology—in 1968—that put computer memory on tiny silicon chips rather than in magnetic fields. Interactive exhibits here in the company headquarters walk visitors through the principles of transistor technology, from identification of conductors to chip design and production. Displays showcase the use of these chips in personal computers, as well as future practical applications. To make a silicon chip, sand is chemically purified, converted into crystal ingots, melted with added trace chemicals and cooled, then ground to a uniform diameter and sliced into grooved wafers. A photolithographic etching process forms the multi-layered transistors on a chip; aluminum is patterned on the wafer to make electrical connections that complete the transistor.

♟♟ California's Great America
4701 Great America Parkway, Santa Clara.
➤ *Exit US-101 at Great America Pkwy., 6mi north of San Jose.* ◷*Open mid-Mar –May & Sept–Oct Sat–Sun from 10am;*
Easter week & Jun–Aug daily from 10am. ◷*Closing times vary.* ⊜*$54.99, under 4ft tall $24.99.* ✕♿🅿 ℘*408-988-1776. www.cagreatamerica.com.*
This 100-acre amusement park, originally opened in 1976, is a favorite of roller-coaster fanatics. Its revered coasters include the **Survivor–The Ride**, a "reality roller-coaster" based on the TV show, in which rider are divided into competing tribes and whisked through tropical landscapes studded with 40ft-tall fiery torches. Among other thrill rides are the inverted **Flight Deck** jet-coaster, the 224ft **Drop Tower**, and the **Invertigo** boomerang ride. Snoopy, Charlie Brown and other *Peanuts* characters greet children in more family-oriented areas. There's a full entertainment schedule including IMAX shows and numerous shops and restaurants.

San Carlos
27mi northwest of San Jose.
➤ *Exit US-101 at Redwood Shores Pkwy and drive east; turn right on Airport Rd. and right on Skyway Rd. San Carlos means 'City of Good Living'.*

♟♟ Hiller Aviation Museum
601 Skyway Rd. ◷*Open daily 10am–5pm.* ◷*Closed Jan 1, Easter Sunday, Thanksgiving Day, Dec 25.*
⊜*$12.* ℘*650-654-0200. www.hiller.org.*
Exhibits proceed chronologically through the history of manned flight, with special emphasis on the greater Bay Area. One of the earliest aircraft displayed is the 1883 **Gull,** a fully controllable glider invented by John J. Montgomery, a Santa Clara University engineering professor. Montgomery later was killed testing his third glider prototype in 1911—the same year the **Curtiss-Pusher** landed and took off from the first "aircraft carrier," the USS *Pennsylvania,* in San Francisco Bay. Further exhibits progress from early fixed-wing aircraft to blended and oblique wing designs, and include such innovations as the Flying Platform and the high-altitude Boeing Condor. Many of the aircraft on display have been refashioned by resident craftsmen, whose

projects may be viewed through the windows of the Restoration Workshop.

Fremont

19mi northeast of San Jose.

▶ *Exit I-680 at Mission Blvd (Rte 238).* Fremont was founded from five other towns in 1956. Fremont is now a metropolitan, ethnically rich city with all the conveniences that provides.

San Jose Mission

43300 Mission Blvd. at Washington Blvd., Fremont. ◐*Open daily 10am–5pm.* ◐*Closed Jan 1, Easter Sunday, Thanksgiving Day, Dec 25.* ✆*Donations requested.* ♿ ☎*510-657-1797. www.missionsanjose.org.*

The 14th mission in the California chain was founded by Padre Fermín Lasuén in 1797. The mission's first permanent adobe church was completed in 1809. Before secularization in 1834, San José was one of the most prosperous missions in California.

During the Gold Rush, the mission served as a rooming house and general store for gold seekers. In 1858 the mission complex was returned to the Catholic Church, but a massive earthquake ten years later destroyed the old adobe church, and a wooden Gothic-style structure was erected in its place. In the early 1980s work began on the careful reconstruction of the original adobe that occupies the site today.

Within the simple, unadorned exterior walls, the church interior reflects the 1833–40 period, featuring an ornate gold-leaf replica of the reredos and historic **statuary**. Note the statue of St. Joseph (c.1600) from Spain and that of the Virgin (18C) from Mexico; rear side altars display statues of Christ (early 19C) and St. Bonaventure (1808). The hammered copper baptismal font (1830s) was painted by Augustín Davila, painter of the interior of the original church.

A small garden separates the church from the original adobe **padres' quarters**, which now house a museum featuring Native American and church artifacts.

Don Edwards San Francisco Bay National Wildlife Refuge★

Marshlands Rd., Fremont.

▶ *From I-880 or Rte. 84 at east end of Dumbarton Bridge, take Thornton Ave. to refuge road.* ◐*Visitor center open Tue–Sun 10am–5pm.* ◐*Closed major holidays.* ♿🅿 ☎*510-792-0222. www.fws.gov/desfbay.*

The largest urban wildlife refuge in the U.S. sprawls across 20,000 acres of salt marsh, tidal sloughs, mudflats and rolling hills at the southern end of San Francisco Bay. More than 200 species of waterfowl, shorebirds and migratory birds live, breed and feed in the refuge, dedicated in 1972 and renamed for a former congressman in 1995. From the bluff-top **Visitor Center**👥, an extensive system of trails follows boardwalks and bridges across tidal flats. Within the center are excellent interpretive exhibits on life in the refuge, as well as an auditorium and observation deck. More trails extend through managed wetland habitat from an **Environmental Education Center** (*Los Esteros Rd., Alviso;* ▶ *from Rte. 237, turn right at Zanker Rd. for 2mi;* ◐*open Sat–Sun 10am–5pm; call to verify;* ☎*408-262-5513*).

👥 Ardenwood Historic Farm

34600 Ardenwood Blvd., Fremont, just north of Rte. 84. ◐ *Farm and house open Tue–Sun 10am–4pm (no special programs in winter).* ✆*$3 ($5 Apr–Nov Thu–Fri & Sun).* ◐*Closed Thanksgiving Day, Dec 25.* ✕♿🅿 ☎*510-544-2797. www.ebparks.org/parks/ardenwood.*

Here you can see (and participate in) the common activities of a late-19C farm. George Washington Patterson built a home here in 1857; as his property grew into a prosperous estate, his house was expanded in Queen Anne style in 1889 and surrounded by elaborate Victorian gardens. Many original buildings, including the **house** (☎*visit by guided tour only Apr–Nov;* ☎*510-791-4196*), remain standing. Weekend programs include the planting, tending and harvesting of organic crops, and demonstrations of cooking, farm chores and blacksmithing.

San Mateo County Coast

Untouched by the sprawl of the city to its north or the urbanized peninsula area to its east, coastal San Mateo County is geographically isolated by the San Gregorio and Santa Cruz mountain ranges and protected against development by the lack of a practical commuter route. Route 1 narrows to two lanes as it runs south from Pacifica through the farming and fishing villages of Moss Beach, Princeton, San Gregorio and Pescadero. South of Half Moon Bay, the east side of the highway skirts a undulating landscape of flowers, wholesalers' greenhouses, and rows of artichoke plants; pumpkin patches vividly dot the landscape in the fall. To the west extend ocean beaches, superb spots for strolling, tidepooling and wildlife observation. From January to April, **gray whales** may be seen migrating offshore.

The notorious stretch of highway known as **Devil's Slide** forms a gateway to the coast from San Francisco. South of Point San Pedro, the highway narrows and swerves around steep cliffs dramatically striated with rock layers upthrust from ancient marine sediments. Rock slides have closed the road in recent years, but conservationists fear a tunnel or inland route would encourage development of rural coastal towns to the south.

- **Michelin Map:** See inside back cover.
- **Info:** www.parks.ca.gov (for state parks).
- **Location:** From San Francisco drive south on Hwy. 1 (19th Ave.) or Rte. 35 (Skyline Blvd.), which intersects Hwy. 1 south of Daly City. To return to San Francisco, either retrace the route or take Rte. 92 east from Half Moon Bay, then continue north on I-280. In the driving tour (p298), mileage to each sight is calculated from the preceding sight.
- **Kids:** The fascinating tidepools at Fitzgerald Marine Reserve.
- **Timing:** Plan a leisurely half-day to do the drive itself. You'll need more time if you'd like to relax on a beach or two.
- **Parking:** The car fee at park entrances allows same-day entrance to other state parks.
- **Don't Miss:** Reservations are necessary to visit the wildlife protection areas at Año Nuevo State Reserve during the breeding season from December through March; the spectacle is well worth the effort of advance planning.

SIGHT
CuriOdyssey

1651 Coyote Point Dr., San Mateo. Exit US-101 via Poplar Ave. or Dore Ave. *Open Tue–Sat 10am–5pm, Sun noon–5pm.* *Closed major holidays.* *$8; youth 13–17 $5; children 2–12 $6.* 650-342-7755. www.curiodyssey.org. Geared toward teaching children the natural environment of the Bay Area, this museum offers an interactive walk "from the mountains to the bay" with small animals and an aquarium. A wildlife habitat features more than 40 species of indigenous live animals and a newly renovated 4,000sq ft aviary with more than four dozen native California birds. Eucalyptus- and pine-shrouded Coyote Point offers magnificent views. Adjacent Coyote Point Recreation Area has nature trails, a beach, a saltwater marsh, picnic grounds and a marina.

Santa Cruz beach boardwalk

© Mark Barnes / Santa Cruz County CVC

Santa Cruz

70mi south of San Francisco.

▶ *Take US-101 S. to Mountain View; Rte. 85 S. toward Los Gatos, then Rte. 17.*
The archetypical California beach community (pop. 50,000), Santa Cruz curves around the northern end of Monterey Bay. Founded in 1791 with the Santa Cruz Mission, it became a seaside resort after the railroad arrived in the late 19C.
🛈*Visitor information: ☎831-425-1234; www.santacruzca.org.*

The **Santa Cruz Beach Boardwalk**★★ (👥👤🕐*open Memorial Day–Labor Day daily 11am, Sept–Apr Sat–Sun & holidays noon;* 🕐*closing hours vary;* ✕⚒ ☎*831-423-5590; www.beachboardwalk.com)*, built in 1904, remains the oldest amusement park in California. Its renovated boardwalk features turreted and brightly painted buildings and rides fronting a wide bay beach *(swimming inadvisable because of dangerous currents)*. Both the **Giant Dipper** (1924)—a .5mi-long wooden roller coaster—and the **Looff carousel** (1911)—are national historic landmarks.

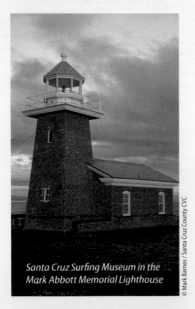

Santa Cruz Surfing Museum in the Mark Abbott Memorial Lighthouse

© Mark Barnes / Santa Cruz County CVC

Nearby, the **Cocoanut Grove Banquet and Conference Center** (1907) is famous for its now-renovated Grand Ballroom, where musicians Artie Shaw and Benny Goodman once performed with their big bands. A few blocks west, the **municipal wharf** is lined with tackle shops and eateries.

North of the waterfront, in the Mark Abbott Memorial Lighthouse *(West Cliff Dr.)*, stands the **Santa Cruz Surfing Museum**, with an informative exhibit on West Coast shark attacks, and various models of surfboards (🕐*open Jul 4–Labor Day Wed–Mon 10am–5pm, rest of the year Thu–Mon noon–4pm;* 🕐*closed Jan 1, Dec 25;* ✺*donations accepted;* ⚒ ☎*831-420-6289; www. santacruzsurfingmuseum.org).*

The **Santa Cruz Museum of Natural History** *(1305 E. Cliff Dr.)*, on a cliff above the bay, covers the natural history of the area and includes an exhibit of artifacts detailing the Ohlone Indians' way of life (○*open Tue–Sun 10am–5pm;* *$2.50;* ✆*831-420-6115; www.santa cruzmuseums.org).*

Santa Cruz Mission and State Historic Park *(Mission Plaza off School St.* ▷ *from Rte. 1 N turn right on Mission St., then left on Emmet St.;* ○*open Thu–Sun 10am–4pm;* ♿ ✆*831-425-5849; www. santacruzstateparks.org) preserves the* site of the original mission (1791). The 12th mission was the smallest of all. After achieving a peak population of 531 neophytes, it declined slowly; only a seven-room **barracks** (1824) remains from the original complex.

The **University of California, Santa Cruz**★ (▷ *follow Bay St. northwest to main entrance on Coolidge Dr.)* is renowned for its architecture and spectacular **setting**★★ in the lush hills amid redwood trees. Eight campuses surround an academic and administrative core that serves 10,000 students. In 1965 the state university system carefully integrated 14 original structures from the 1860s Cowell Ranch into the new campus.

The **Mary Porter Sesnon Art Gallery** (✆*831-459-3606)* at Porter College and the **Eloise Pickard Smith Gallery** (✆*831-459-2953)* at Cowell College mount changing exhibits of contemporary art; the **arboretum** is devoted to exotic flora, particularly from South Africa, Australia and New Zealand *(Empire Grade, .3mi west of main entrance;* ○*open daily 9am–5pm;* ○*closed Thanksgiving Day, Dec 25;* 🅿 ✆*831-427- 2998; www2.ucsc.edu/arboretum).*

Henry Cowell Redwoods State Park

© Greg Pio / Santa Cruz County CVC

Roaring Camp Railroads

© Mark Barnes / Santa Cruz County CVC

Six miles north of Santa Cruz is **Henry Cowell Redwoods State Park**★ *(Rte. 9;* ○*open daily 6am–dusk;* *$6/vehicle;* ⛺♿ ✆*831-438-2396; www.parks.ca.gov). Trails weave* through this 1,760-acre tract, bisected by the San Lorenzo River and notable for its fine stands of coast redwoods. The **Redwood Grove Trail** *(.8mi; begin south of parking lot)* loops past the park's largest trees.

Roaring through the Cowell Redwoods, the **Roaring Camp Railroads** (👥 *Graham Hill Rd., Felton;* ○*open Apr–Nov daily, Dec–Mar Sat–Sun only; call or visit website for schedule;* ✕♿🅿 ✆*831-335-4484; www.roaringcamprr.com) offers two old-time rail* excursions. The narrow-gauge steam-train tour *(6mi, 75min;* *$19.50) snakes through* the redwood forest to the summit of Bear Mountain. The beach train crosses forests, trestles, gorges and a tunnel en route to the Santa Cruz Boardwalk *(3hrs;* *$21.50).*

🚗 DRIVING TOUR

66mi coastal drive south along the West Coast down Hwy. 1.

Sanchez Adobe Historic Site

1000 Linda Mar Blvd., Pacifica, 9mi south of San Francisco via Hwy. 1. ⏰*Open Tue–Thu 10am–4pm, Sat–Sun 1–5pm.* ✆*650-359-1462. www.historysmc.org.*
Reflecting many periods of California history, this adobe was built in 1848 as the home of Don Francisco Sanchez. Artifacts recall the site's prior use as an Ohlone village, a Spanish mission farm and a cattle ranch; it later became a general's residence, a hotel, a Depression-era speakeasy and an artichoke storage facility. Restored in 1953, it has been refurbished and is open for self-guided tours.

Point Montara Lighthouse

5mi south. 16th St. off Hwy. 1, Montara. ⏰*Open daily 8am–sunset.* ✆*650-728-7177. www.parks.ca.gov.*
Built in 1875 as the Point Montara Fog Signal and Light Station, this picturesque beacon house—a naval training base during World War II—has been a youth hostel since 1980.

👥 James V. Fitzgerald Marine Reserve★

2mi south. California Ave. at N. Lake St., Moss Beach, west of Hwy. 1. ⏰*Open daily dawn–dusk.* 🅿 ✆*650-728-3584. www.fitzgeraldreserve.org.*
Extensive shale reefs bridge the expanse between land and sea, creating tidepools richly populated with myriad marine life, including limpets, barnacles, mussels, sea urchins, starfish, anemones, chitons, hermit crabs, sponges and abalone. Rangers help visitors search the wonders of the pools and lead explorations during low tide. A small visitor center identifies specimens.

Pillar Point Harbor

3mi southeast.
A granitic headland extends from the coast here, creating a sheltered harbor that serves as an anchorage for local fishermen. Fresh fish is sold daily from boats and fish markets, and simple seafood restaurants serve up steaming chowder, seafood cocktails and fresh fish and chips. Whale-watching cruises depart from the wharf during the season (⏰*depart late-Dec–Apr Sat–Sun 10am and 1.30pm; round-trip 3hrs; reservations required;* ⊕*$45;* 🅿*Bait & Switch Sportfishing Center;* ✆*650-726-7133; www. baitandswitchsportfishing.com).*

👥 Francis Beach

5mi south. Foot of Kelly Ave. in Half Moon Bay, .6mi west of Hwy. 1. ⏰*Open daily 8am–sunset.* ⊕*$10/car.* ⛺*($35-50)* ♿🅿 ✆*650-726-8819. www.parks.ca.gov.*
The Half Moon Bay State Beach system extends 4mi to the north of this flat, sandy expanse, and includes Venice and Dunes beaches. Francis Beach provides a welcome departure from the coast's typically rocky beaches. Dune grasses fringing the shoreline provide habitat for snowy plovers. Picnic tables overlook the ocean from the day-use area, and a Coastside Trail (3mi) lures hikers and bikers. The skull of a blue whale entangled in a fisherman's net in 1988 is visible near the entry booth. A **visitor center**, with exhibits on regional history and natural resources, is open on Sat–Sun.

San Gregorio State Beach

12mi south. ⏰*Open daily 8am–sunset.* ⊕*$8/car.* 🅿 ✆*650-879-2170. www.parks.ca.gov.*
This broad, sandy beach lies at the mouth of San Gregorio Creek. Walk north at low tide to see dramatic, cavelike erosion at the base of the sandstone bluffs, or stroll atop to spot whales in season.

Pescadero State Beach

4.4mi south. ⏰*Open daily 8am–sunset.* ⊕*$8/car.* 🅿 ✆*650-879-2170. www.parks.ca.gov.*
From the bluffs that loom over this popular beach, views extend west over the Pacific and the San Mateo County coastline. East of Route 1, extensive walking trails penetrate the **Pescadero Marsh Natural Preserve,** a 510-acre freshwater/brackish coastal marsh. Migratory

birds plying the Pacific Flyway stop here to rest, drawing flocks of birdwatchers, especially in late fall and early spring.

👥 Pebble Beach

2.2mi south. ⏰*Open daily 8am–sunset.* *$8/car.* 🅿 ✆*650-879-2170.* *www.parks.ca.gov.*
Breaking waves here deposit glistening, many-colored pebbles onto the beach from an offshore quartz reef *(note: it is illegal to remove pebbles).* This part of the coast bears spectacular displays of **tafoni**—lacy, filigree-like formations wrought by erosion on the face of weathered stone. Pebble Beach is the northernmost unit of **Bean Hollow State Beach**, accessible from here by car or via a 12-station clifftop nature trail *(1mi).*

👥 Pigeon Point Light Station★

3.6mi south. ⏰*Grounds open daily 8am–sunset.* 🚶*Guided tours (30min) Fri–Mon 10am–4pm, weather permitting.* 🚫*Lighthouse closed to the public.* 🅿 ✆*650-879-2120. www.parks.ca.gov.*
Built in 1871, this starkly graceful lighthouse tower was automated in 1926. The lantern room contains the original Fresnel lens, a device consisting of 1,008 glass prisms that shape light from a cen-

Pigeon Point Light Station

© Jeanne Dewey/Dreamstime.com

😎 A Bit of Advice 😎

Though the ocean can look tantalizing on a hot day, swimming is inadvisable along the San Mateo County Coast due to cold water and hazardous surf; beware sneaker (large coastal) waves when venturing close to shore.

tral lamp into a horizontal beam intense enough to be visible many miles out at sea. Although the lighthouse is closed to the public, the point offers lovely views of the coast and surrounding landforms. A self-guided tour of the grounds explains the light station's past. The lighthouse outbuildings today house a unit of the American Youth Hostel Association.

👥 Año Nuevo State Reserve★

7mi south. ⏰*Open daily 8am–sunset. Rookery open Apr–Aug 8.30am–3.30pm; Sept–Nov 8.30am–3pm (visitor permit required; issued at reserve).* ⏰*Closed 1st 2 weeks in Dec.* 🅿 *$10/vehicle, $7 guided tour.* 🚶*Access by guided tour (2hr 30min) only Dec 15–Mar 31 Mon–Fri 9am–5pm, Sat–Sun 9am–3pm; reserve 8 weeks in advance.* ✆*650-879-2025 or 800-444-4445. www.parks.ca.gov.*
This 4,000-acre coastal reserve encompasses a rocky offshore island and a wildly beautiful promontory of bluffs and beaches. The promontory is the largest mainland rookery between Baja and northern California for **northern elephant seals**. From December through March, the seals gradually congregate here, the females coming ashore to give birth to single pups and joining "harems" dominated by massive 2.5-ton alpha bulls. Violent clashes between males over harem control are common. In spring and summer, seals again come ashore to molt.

▷ Continue about 21mi along the Coast Road (Highway 1) until it becomes Mission St. into Santa Cruz. .

Chinatown with Autumn
Moon Festival Decorations
© Ray Laskowitz / Tips Images

Where to Stay

San Francisco is a treasure trove for aficionados of small, European-style "boutique" hotels whose rates range from moderate to pricey. But there is something for everyone here, with nearly 33,000 hotel rooms in the city—small private hotels for the budget traveler, hostels for the backpack crowd, and large luxury hotels, at which rates for standard rooms may start at $300.

Additional hotels are listed throughout this guide. See Index for a complete listing of places to stay.

$$$$$	over $350
$$$$	$250–$350
$$$	$175–$250
$$	$100–$175
$	less than $100

CASTRO DISTRICT

$$ 24 Henry Guesthouse and Village House – *24 Henry St. & 4080 18th St. ☎415-864-5686 or 800-900-5686. www. 24henry.com. 10 rooms.* A largely gay and lesbian clientele frequents these two bed-and-breakfast inns in classic Victorian houses a few blocks from one another in the heart of the Castro. Rates include a complimentary breakfast buffet served in the spacious parlor.

CHINATOWN

$ Grant Plaza Hotel – *465 Grant Ave. ☎415-434-3883 or 800-472-6899. www. grantplaza.com. 72 rooms.* Remarkable value in the heart of Chinatown, this clean, bright inn has rooms with color TVs and private baths. Union Square shopping is just an easy three-block walk away.

CIVIC CENTER/TENDERLOIN

$$ The Inn at the Opera – *333 Fulton St. ☎415-863-8400 or 800-325-2708. www.shellhospitality.com. 48 rooms. Restaurant $$$.* This elegant small hotel is popular among musicians and stage performers, owing to its location a block from the War Memorial Opera House. Tastefully decorated rooms include refrigerators, wet bar areas and

microwaves for après-theater snacking. Rates include a continental breakfast.

$$ Phoenix Hotel – *601 Eddy St. ☎415 -776-1380 or 800-248-9466. www.jdv hotels.com. 44 rooms.* Joie de Vivre's funkiest hotel is a rockers' paradise with its swimming pool fringed by palm trees. Jimmy Buffett would feel right at home amid the tropical island decor of the guest rooms.

$$ Renoir Hotel – *45 McAllister St. ☎415-626-5200 or 800-576-3388. www. renoirhotel.com. 133 rooms.* This ornate, triangular-shaped, historic landmark hotel—built in 1909 at the corner of Market Street—is very popular among European and Latin American visitors. It has seven stories of simple but comfortable rooms.

FINANCIAL DISTRICT

$$$$ Hyatt Regency San Francisco – *5 Embarcadero Center. ☎415-788-1234 or 800-633-7313. www.sanfranciscoregency. hyatt.com. 802 rooms.* An architecturally acclaimed hotel with a 17-story central atrium at the foot of Market Street, the Hyatt is tied to the Embarcadero Center by a pedestrian bridge. Every room is tastefully decorated and has a city or bay view.

$$$$ Mandarin Oriental, San Francisco – *222 Sansome St. ☎415-276-9888 or 800-622-0404. www.mandarin-oriental.com. 158 rooms.* From the hotel's ground-floor entry, high-speed elevators whisk guests to their aeries, located between the 38th and 48th stories atop 345 California Center. Spectacular picture-window views

Lotus Suite, Mandarin Oriental

© Mandarin Oriental San Francisco

await you in your room (binoculars provided), along with Egyptian cotton sheets, CD players and your choice of cotton or terrycloth robes and slippers. If trekking up San Francisco's hills isn't enough exercise for you, try a workout in the hotel's 24-hour fitness center.

FISHERMAN'S WHARF

$ Hostelling International–Fisherman's Wharf – *Bldg. 240, Fort Mason. 415-771-7277. www.sfhostels. com. 160 rooms.* Few youth hostels offer the views afforded by this one, perched on a bluff over San Francisco Bay with the Golden Gate Bridge in the distance.

© Hostelling International USA, Golden Gate Council

Fisherman's Wharf

JAPANTOWN

$$ Kabuki Hotel – *1625 Post St., Japan Center. 415-922-3200 or 800-533-4567. www.jdvhotels.com. 218 rooms. Restaurant $$.* Japanese visitors enjoy the refined and serene rooms here, which feature Asian tea kettles and deep Japanese-style baths. Outside is a Zen-like garden with a koi pond.

NOB HILL

$$$$$ The Huntington Hotel – *1075 California St. 415-474-5400 or 800-227-4683. www.huntingtonhotel.com. 136 rooms. Restaurant $$$.* Overlooking charming Huntington Park and Grace Cathedral on the California Street cable-car line, this quietly elegant 1924 classic entered the 21C by opening its minimalist Nob Hill Spa, one of locals' favorite spots for pampering. Guest rooms are smart and oversized, as the hotel once housed a luxury apartment complex. For the best views, request a

room above the seventh floor. The Big Four Restaurant—named for the railroad barons who built their mansions, and then hotels, on this hill—sits just off the lobby.

$$$ The Ritz-Carlton – *600 Stockton St. 415-296-7465 or 800-241-3333. www.ritz carlton.com. 306 rooms. Restaurant. $$$$.* For pure class, luxury, and service, the Ritz-Carlton reigns supreme. The lobby is decorated with a rich collection of 18–19C antiques and paintings; guestrooms have been carefully restored with European charm and luxury in mind.

$$$$ The Fairmont – *950 Mason St. 415-772-5000 or 866-540-4491. www. fairmont.com. 591 rooms. Restaurant $$$.* This famous grand hotel has a rich history that includes the 1906 earthquake and creation of the United Nations in 1945. Handsomely appointed rooms are in the original main building and in a 1961 tower that offers extensive views across the city. Don't miss happy hour at the exotic **Tonga Room** and **Hurricane Bar** with its thatched umbrellas and simulated rain storms.

$$$ Mark Hopkins InterContinental – *One Nob Hill 415-392-3434 or 877-270-1390. www.intercontinentalmarkhopkins. com. 380 rooms.* **Opened in 1926 on the crest of No**b Hill, this grand, historic hotel stands on the site of the former mansion of "Big Four" Mark Hopkins. Elegantly traditional rooms feature a rich palate of golden yellows and sienna, dark woods and marble bathrooms with black granite vanities. Througout the day, check emails or have a bite at the lobby-level club lounge (nominal fee); come evening, the 19th floor supplies dancing, sweeping views and a 100 Martinis menu at the legendary Top of the Mark lounge.

$$$ The Nob Hill Hotel – *835 Hyde St. 415-885-2987 or 877-662-4455. www. nobhillhotel.com. 52 rooms. Restaurant $$.* Restored in 1998, this neighborhood gem—which dates from 1906—has reclaimed its original marble flooring, alabaster chandeliers and stained-glass windows. Cozy rooms have Victorian furnishings, mini refrigerators, microwaves and coffeemakers. A charming Italian cafe is attached.

NORTH BEACH

$$$ Hotel Bohème – *444 Columbus Ave. 415-433-9111. www.hotelboheme.com. 15 rooms.* Reflecting the bohemian tastes of the Beat Generation in 1950s San Francisco, this quaint boutique hotel at the foot of Telegraph Hill is dedicated to the spirit of Jack Kerouac, Lawrence Ferlinghetti and their cohorts. Colorful rooms occupy a three-story building erected in the 1880s and are equipped with private bathrooms and free Wi-Fi.

$$$ Washington Square Inn – *1660 Stockton St. 415-981-4220 or 800-388-0220. www.wsisf.com. 16 rooms.* A intimate European-style inn at the foot of Telegraph Hill in the heart of bohemian North Beach, this charming bed-and-breakfast offers antique furnishings and afternoon tea, plus evening wine and hors d'oeuvres. Enjoy a complimentary continental breakfast downstairs at an antique table overlooking the square.

$$ Argonaut – *495 Jefferson St. 415-563-0800 or 800-790-1415. www.argonaut hotel.com. 252 rooms.* Perfectly located near Ghirardelli Square, the cable-car turnaround and Fisherman's Wharf, this maritime-themed hotel occupies a 1907 waterfront warhouse at The Cannery. Some rooms offer views of the bay and Alcatraz; all are well soundproofed and have modern amenities, including flat-screen TVs and complimentary high-speed Internet access.

King Exterior Guestroom, Argonaut

© Kimpton Hotels & Restaurants

$ Green Tortoise – *494 Broadway. 415-834-1000 or 800-867-8647. www. greentortoise.com. 40 rooms (110 beds).* Operated by a long-distance budget bus service for backpack travelers, this clean, spacious hostel has private rooms and dorms (some co-ed) with up to eight bunks. Free daily breakfast is included, and a free dinner is served three times a week.

$ San Remo Hotel – *2237 Mason St. 415-776-8688 or 800-352-7366. www.sanremohotel.com. 62 rooms.* Like a European pension, all rooms in in this three-story Italianate Victorian, built in 1906 by A.P. Giannini (founder of Bank of America), share baths, and none have phones or TVs. Accommodations are simple and cozy but charming and neatly kept, with late-19C antiques. The staff is friendly and helpful.

UNION SQUARE

$$$$ Hotel Monaco – *501 Geary St. 415-292-0100 or 866-622-5284. www. monaco-sf.com. 201 rooms. Restaurant $$$.* This Theater District boutique hotel, a remodeled 1910 Beaux Arts classic, offers the warmth and comfort of home in a much grander setting. Baroque-style fireplaces and sumptuous striped armchairs invite conversation in the lobby; Provençal fabrics drape over canopy beds in the guest rooms. The Grand Café offers a bistro-style lunch and dinner. Your four-legged friends are also welcome here.

$$$$ Prescott Hotel – *545 Post St. 415-563-0303 or 866-271-3632. www.prescotthotel.com. 164 rooms. Restaurant $$.* A richly upholstered lobby with a blazing fireplace welcomes guests to this elegant boutique hotel just off Union Square. Room furnishings reflect a European influence with custom-made cherry-wood stylings. Wolfgang Puck's **Postrio** restaurant adjoins the hotel.

$$$$ Taj Campton Place – *340 Stockton St. 415-781-5555 or 866-969-1825. www. tajhotels.com. 110 rooms. Restaurant $$$.* An intimate luxury hotel once popular with the white-gloved "carriage trade" set, Campton Place is the epitome of elegance and service. In guest rooms, fluffy duvets top the beds and bathrooms feature limestone floors. It's a rarefied experience in a discreet location just off bustling Union Square.

$$$$ Westin St. Francis – *335 Powell St.* 415-397-7000 *or* 800-937-8461. *www.westinstfrancis.com. 1,247 rooms. Restaurant $$$$.* Occupying a Renaissance- and Baroque-revival structure built in 1904, this landmark hotel facing Union Square is renowned for its legendary service. A historic charm pervades the rooms in the main building; more contemporary rooms with bay windows and dramatic city views occupy the 32-story tower. All are outfitted with Westin's signature Heavenly Bed™.

$$$ Clift – *495 Geary St.* 415-775-4700 *or* 800-697-1791. *www.clifthotel.com. 363 rooms. Restaurant $$$$.* Dark meets light, antique goes modern, and eccentric cajoles conservative at this high-style hostelry. Built in 1913 and reconceived for the 21st century by Philippe Starck, it features elegantly sleek public areas and guestrooms swathed in quiet tones of foggy gray, beige and lavender. The legendary Redwood Room lounge features original 1933 paneling and a long bar carved from a single tree.

$$$ Serrano Hotel – *405 Taylor St.* 415-885-2500 *or* 866-289-6561. *www.serranohotel.com. 236 rooms.* Don Quixote rides again at this ode to the Spanish renaissance. Rooms are colorful and sophisticated.

$$$ Executive Hotel Vintage Court – *650 Bush St.* 415-392-4666 *or* 888-388-3932. *www.executivehotels.net/vintage court. 106 rooms. Restaurant $$$$.* This Euro-style property creates a cozy atmosphere in its lobby, where guest gather around the fireplace each evening to sample wines of the Napa and Sonoma Valleys. Named after local wineries, guest rooms are decorated in a palette of soft greens and cream, and invite relaxation with fluffy duvets and down pillows. Adjacent to the hotel, **Masa's** serves acclaimed contemporary French cuisine.

$$$ The Handlery Union Square Hotel – *351 Geary St.* 415-781-7800 *or* 800-995-4874. *www.handlery.com. 377 rooms. Restaurant $$.* A four-generation family operation that opened in 1948 (on the site of a 1908 hotel), The Handlery is a gracious, centrally located inn with unpretentious rooms and a mid-city rarity: an outdoor heated swimming pool.

$$$ Orchard Hotel – *665 Bush St.* 415-362-8878 *or* 888-717-2881. *www.theorchardhotel.com. 104 rooms. Restaurant $$.* Perched on the flank of Nob Hill a few blocks above Union Square, this very comfortable, eco-friendly hotel offers modern amenities and conveniences. The updated decor and well-sized guestrooms feature soft pastel colors with warm wood accents. There's a library of DVDs available for borrowing, and the staff garners kudos for friendly, helpful service.

$$$ Sir Francis Drake Hotel – *450 Powell St.* 415-392-7755 *or* 800-795-7129. *www.sirfrancisdrake.com. 416 rooms. Restaurant $$$.* A renovated 1928 classic whose 21st-floor penthouse holds one of San Francisco's longstanding nightclubs, Harry Denton's Starlight Room, the Drake rests on the cable-car line one block from Union Square. Chandeliers hanging from the gold-leaf lobby ceiling lend an atmosphere of grandeur.

$$$ Hotel Triton – *342 Grant Ave.* 415-394-0500 *or* 800-800-1299. *www.hotel triton.com. 140 rooms.* A colorful avant-garde boutique hotel facing Chinatown Gate, this property was labeled "exceedingly groovy" by *Harper's Bazaar* magazine. Designers and artists created cutting-edge accoutrements for the Eco Floor, Zen Dens and suites dedicated to the likes of rock musician Jerry Garcia. Custom armoires hide flat-screen TVs, which include a 24-hour yoga channel. Free in-room Wi-Fi.

$$ Andrews Hotel – *624 Post St.* 415-563-6877 *or* 800-926-3739. *www.andrews hotel.com. 48 rooms. Restaurant $$.* This cozy European-style hotel offers intimacy and personal service three blocks from Union Square. Rooms sport pastel colors and floral prints and are equipped with free Wi-Fi, small TVs and DVD players (complimentary movies are available at the front desk). Each morning, a complimentary continental breakfast—breads, seasonal fruits, coffee, tea—is delivered to the landing on each floor.

$$ Hotel Beresford – *635 Sutter St. ℘415-673-9900 or 800-533-6533. www. beresford.com. 114 rooms. Restaurant $$.* This pleasant, small Victorian hotel attracts British visitors with its English pub, the White Horse Tavern. A similarly priced sister hotel, the Hotel Beresford Arms *(701 Post St.; ℘415-673-2600; 95 rooms)*, is three blocks away.

$$ Hotel Bijou – *111 Mason St. ℘415-771-1200 or 800-771-1022. www.hotel bijou.com. 65 rooms.* Located a block away from cable-car stops, the Art Deco-style Bijou recalls a 1920s movie palace; on its walls hang photos of San Francisco's old movie houses. Bright, jewel-toned guest rooms are named for films shot in the city, which are illustrated in each room by original still photographs. Double features of San Francisco-based films are screened nightly in the small lobby theater. Rates include a complimentary continental breakfast.

$$ Hotel Diva – *440 Geary St. ℘415-885-0200 or 800-553-1900. www.hoteldiva.com. 115 rooms.* Located in the Theater District, the sleek and modern Hotel Diva is the glitziest of several San Francisco hotels in the Personality Hotels group. Rooms feature cobalt blue carpets, sculpted steel headboards and iPod docking stations. Wi-Fi is free throughout the hotel, and rates include morning coffee and tea and an evening wine hour.

$$ Hotel Rex – *562 Sutter St. ℘415-433-4434 or 800-433-4434. www.jdvhotels. com. 94 rooms. Restaurant $$.* The redesign of this intriguing, historic boutique hotel follows the theme of the literary and arts salons rife in San Francisco in the 1920s and 30s. Quotes from regional authors adorn the walls of different floors, and photos and books can be found in the rooms. Appropriately, an antiquarian bookstore adjoins the lobby.

$$ Cartwright Hotel Union Square – *524 Sutter St. ℘415-421-2865 or 800-919-9779. www.cartwrightunionsquare.com. 114 rooms.* Occupying a staid Edwardian building just around the corner from Union Square and the cable car lines, this elegant boutique hotel received a complete overhaul in 2008. Amenities include free Wi-Fi and a fireplace in the lobby. Pets are welcome.

$$ Chancellor Hotel – *433 Powell St. ℘415-362-2004 or 800-428-4748. www.chancellorhotel.com. 137 rooms. Restaurant $$.* Location is everything at this European-style 15-story inn, opened in 1914 on the Powell-Hyde and Powell-Mason cable-car lines, right on Union Square. One of the city's best bargains, the Chancellor boasts amenities like free in-room Wi-Fi and a pillow menu (choose your favorite of 12 styles). Guests have free access to the Club One health club, a block away.

$ Hostelling International–Downtown – *312 Mason St. ℘415-788-5604 or 800-464-4872. www.sfhostels. com. 230 beds.* Five floors of dormitory rooms, none with more than four beds, draw international students to

Guest suite, Hotel Palomar

© Kimpton Hotels & Restaurants

this pleasant hostel, located just one block from Union Square in the Theater District. Amenities include free Wi-Fi, a kitchen, lounges, a TV room and on-site laundry facilities.

YERBA BUENA GARDENS

$$$$ Hotel Palomar – *12 Fourth St. ℘415-348-1111 or 866-373-4941. www.hotelpalomar-sf.com. 195 rooms. Restaurant $$$$.* The Kimpton Group's top-of-the-line venture occupies the fifth through ninth floors of a post-quake, 1908 landmark building at the corner of Market Street. Tailored lines, dramatic lighting and animal-print carpeting offer contemporary elegance throughout. Guests have access to complimentary car service to the Financial District, a 24-hour fitness center, in-room spa services, yoga accessories and free Wi-Fi. The acclaimed **Fifth Floor** restaurant serves some of the city's best contemporary cuisine.

$$$$ St. Regis – *125 3rd St. ℘415-284-4000 or 877-787-3447. www.starwood hotels/stregis.com. 260 rooms. Restaurant. $$$.* Occupying the first 20 floors of a handsome highrise, the historic St. Regis' first incarnation in the City by the Bay epitomizes the look and feel of classic contemporary. A striking 16ft open fireplace greets guests as they enter the lobby, which also features a sleek lounge area. Cool, comfortable, spacious rooms overlook Yerba Buena Park or have expansive city views. Plasma-screen TVs are standard, and a touchscreen on the nightstand controls the room's temperature, curtains and lighting.

$$$ InterContinental San Francisco – *54 Fourth St. ℘415-616-6500 or 888-811-4273. www.intercontinentalsanfrancisco. com. 550 rooms. Restaurant. $$$* San Francisco's newest InterContinental hotel rose on the scene in February 2008, piercing the SoMa skyline with its 32-story blue-glass tower. Boasting LEED Gold certification, the modern hotel's eco-friendly features include floor-to-ceiling windows, organic toiletries, and automatic sensors on lights, sinks and toilets. An indoor infinity-edge lap pool with skylights and a state-of-the-art gym are located on the 6th floor, next to the 10-room

InterContinental San Francisco

© InterContinental San Francisco

I-Spa, with a lovely terrace that wraps around the building. Off the lobby, Luce restaurant features Tuscan cuisine, while the sleek Bar888 offers over 120 grappas to taste.

$$$ Palace Hotel – *2 New Montgomery St. ℘415-512-1111 or 888-627-7196. www. sfpalace.com. 553 rooms. Restaurant $$.* An elegant Market Street landmark since 1875, The Palace—now a Starwood hotel—bridges the gap between the 19C and the 21C. Renovated from head to toe in 1991, the Palace shines again with its centerpiece, the sumptuous **Garden Court**. Decked out with marble pillars, stained-glass domed ceiling and Austrian crystal chandeliers, the Garden Court has hosted many a VIP event over the years. Luxurious rooms are appointed with 14ft ceilings, marble baths, down comforters, windows that open and 37-inch flatscreen TVs. Next to the heated indoor lap pool are a whirpool and eucalyptus sauna.

$$$ Westin San Francisco Market Street – *50 Third St. ℘415-974-6400 or 800-937-8461. www.westinsf.com. 676 rooms. Restaurant $$$.* Towering 36 stories above Yerba Buena Gardens at the heart of the city's dynamic new cultural district, this contemporary hotel boasts marble floors, rich woodwork, and gold-leaf trim. The second-floor business center, full-size desks in the guest rooms, and its location near the Moscone Convention Center make it a good choice for business travelers. In the rooms, floor-to-ceiling windows look out over the stunning skyline.

Where to Eat

Choosing a restaurant in San Francisco can be overwhelming. So great is the variety of eateries here, so outstanding is their quality, that dining has become a recreation in itself. Don't assume you won't be able to get a reservation: hundreds of Bay Area restaurants list their availability on www.opentable.com, a site which allows you to view menus and reserve with a mouse click.

◑*Additional restaurants are listed throughout this guide. See Index for a complete listing of eateries.*

$$$$	over $75
$$$	$50–$75
$$	$25–$50
$	less than $25

CASTRO DISTRICT

$$$ Frances – *3870 17th St. Dinner only. 415-621-3870. www.frances-sf.com.* Contemporary. Chef-owner Melissa Perello's relaxed resto has quickly become one of the hardest reservations to nab in the city. The selective, daily-changing menu of contemporary California fare might feature smoked steelhead trout, ricotta gnocchi, or lamb with butter beans and artichoke.

$ La Méditerranée – *288 Noe St. 415-431-7210. Also at 2210 Fillmore St. 415-921-2956. www.cafelamed.com.* **Mediterranean**. Falafel and Greek spanakopita are favorites; the 10-item *meze* offers greatest value at these friendly cafes.

CHINATOWN

$$ Empress of China – *838 Grant Ave. 415-434-1345. www.empressofchina sf.com.* **Chinese**. A central pagoda is the focal point of this sixth-floor pavilion whose windows overlook the bustling Chinatown street scene. The Empress specializes in traditional Cantonese fare, including dim sum.

CIVIC CENTER

$$$$ Jardinière – *300 Grove St., Civic Center. Dinner only. 415-861-5555. www.jardiniere.com.* **Californian**. Hundreds of bubbles sparkle on the ceiling of the Champagne Rotunda in this renowned two-story restaurant. Chef-owner Traci Des Jardins may start diners with a duck confit salad or a tart of chanterelles and asparagus, then offer herb-crusted loin of lamb with potato gnocchi, followed by blueberry cake with lemon sabayon and apricots.

$$$ Zuni Café – *1658 Market St. Closed Mon. 415-552-2522. www.zunicafe.com.* **Mediterranean**. First opened as a southwestern restaurant, Zuni now offers hearty French and Italian dishes infused with California flavors. The brick-oven-roasted chicken and the Caesar salad are local classics. The wedge-shaped, glass-enclosed space has an oyster-and-champagne bar that's popular for people-watching.

Jardinière

© FrankenyImages.com / Jardinière

\$\$ Max's Opera Cafe – *601 Van Ness Ave.* ☏*415-771-7300*. **American**. This New York-style deli is conveniently located near Civic Center's performing arts venues. If you're not in the mood for a pastrami sandwich, opt for a big salad.

EMBARCADERO

\$\$\$ Boulevard – *1 Mission St. at Steuart St. www.boulevardrestaurant. com.* ☏*415-543-6084*. **Californian**. Belle Epoque accents have transformed the 1889 Audiffred Building, whose windows frame the Bay Bridge. Chef Nancy Oakes melds Asian and Mediterranean elements with classic French techniques. Dishes include pan-roasted fresh fish (sea bass, halibut), and wood-oven-roasted chops, ribs and filets.

\$\$ Fog City Diner – *1300 Battery St.* ☏*415-982-2000. www.fogcitydiner.com.* **American**. Part rural 1930s diner, part urban 40s bar-and-grill, this chrome-and-neon, family-friendly landmark at the foot of Telegraph Hill serves upscale cheeseburgers with fries (choose among white cheddar, Gouda or Point Reyes blue cheese), as well as gourmet seafood and eclectic small plates.

\$\$ MoMo's – *760 Second St., China Basin.* ☏*415-227-8660. www.sfmomos.com.* **American**. Opposite AT&T Park, this favorite of baseball fans offers baked artichokes, pizzas, steaks and chicken. Enjoy fresh Dungeness crab cake with sautéed sweet corn and chipotle aïoli.

\$\$ The Slanted Door – *1 Ferry Building, No. 3.* ☏*415-861-8032. www.slanted door.com.* **Vietnamese**. This trendy cafe in the bustling Ferry Building Marketplace offers fresh, Viet-inspired cuisine and expansive bay views. Crowds arrive early for grapefruit and jicama salad; spring rolls stuffed with pork, shrimp and mint; and fresh Dungeness crab with cellophane noodles.

FINANCIAL DISTRICT

\$\$\$ Plouf – *40 Belden Pl. Dinner only on Sun.* ☏*415-986-6491. www.ploufsf.com.* **Seafood**. A *très français* establishment, this alleyway brasserie offers wonderful steamed mussels in seven styles,

served streetside by day, indoors by night. Other dishes might include a goat cheese-and-walnut croquette, and fine desserts.

\$\$\$ Quince – *470 Pacific Ave. Dinner only. Closed Sun* ☏*415-775-8500. www.quince restaurant.com.* **Italian**. Chef-owner Michael Tusk is a Jersey boy, but his travels after culinary school introduced him to the rustic fare of Southern France and Italy, which provides his inspiration. He sources only the freshest products from a select network of producers, and the menu is updated nightly with original takes on Italian cuisine.

© John A. Benson / Perbacco

Perbacco

\$\$ Perbacco – *230 California St.* ☏*415-955-0663. www.perbaccosf.com.* **Italian.** Northern Italian fare here highlights the dishes of Piemonte. For a quick bite, sit at the marble-topped bar, where you can wash down house-cured meats with a good selection of Italian wines by the glass. Prefer a hearty meal? House-made pastas and the likes of roasted monkfish in porcini *brodo* will do the trick. Perbacco's more casual sister, the eno-trattoria Barbacco, opened next door in 2010.

\$\$ Sam's Grill and Seafood – *374 Bush St. Closed Sat & Sun.* ☏*415-421-0594. www.belden-place.com/samsgrill.* **Seafood**. Founded in 1867 as an open-air market, Sam's is today a no-nonsense cafe serving fresh fish and two-martini lunches to business people. Gruff veteran waiters add to the atmosphere.

FISHERMAN'S WHARF

$$$$ Gary Danko – *800 North Point St. Dinner only. ℘415-749-2060. www. garydanko.com.* **Contemporary**. Celeb chef Danko's culinary creations take center stage at his intimate, posh restaurant near Fisherman's Wharf. Five-course tasting menus ($104) allow you to sample his wizardry in dishes like Moroccan spiced squab over couscous and orange-cumin carrots.

$$ Alioto's – *8 Fisherman's Wharf at foot of Taylor St. ℘415-673-0183. www. aliotos.com.* **Seafood**. Founded as a fish stall in 1925, Alioto's remains a Sicilian family venture. The "fastest crab-cracker on the bay" lures tourists inside, where diners enjoy views of the Golden Gate. Fresh fish are prepared in various styles.

$$ McCormick & Kuleto's – *Ghirardelli Sq. www.mccormickandschmicks.com. ℘415-929-1730.* **Seafood**. Some of the best seafood in the Wharf area is served not on the water but in this attractive restaurant with views toward Alcatraz and rich wood and glass appointments. There's a full oyster bar and a wide-ranging menu of fresh fish.

GOLDEN GATE PARK

$$ Beach Chalet Brewery and Restaurant – *1000 Great Hwy., Ocean Beach. ℘415-386-8439. www.beach chalet.com.* **California**. Built by Willis Polk in 1925 as a tea house, this building now features an upscale restaurant on the top floor (with ocean views) and a Golden Gate Park visitor center and garden cafe on the ground floor. Menu items upstairs, like fried calamari and black Angus steak, are designed to go with the house-made brews. The garden restaurant serves pizza and BBQ specialities.

HAIGHT-ASHBURY

$$ Thep Phanom – *400 Waller St. Dinner only. ℘415-431-2526.* **Thai**. Dishes like ped sawan (boneless duck in honey sauce on spinach) and "The Dancing Lady" (stuffed jumbo prawns with crab meat) result in lines out the door. The gourmet and out-of-the-ordinary dishes appeal to Thai-food lovers looking for something different.

JAPANTOWN

$ Mifune – *1737 Post St., ℘415-922-0337. www.mifune.com.* **Japanese**. This acclaimed noodle house serves 55 hot and cold varieties of udon and soba in a stark, red and black minimalist environment.

MARINA DISTRICT/ COW HOLLOW

$$ Betelnut Pejiu Wu – *2030 Union St. ℘415-929-8855. www.betelnut restaurant.com.* **Asian**. Fashioned after a Southeast Asian beer house, Betelnut serves upscale "street food" in a red-lacquered, bamboo-accented atmosphere. The delicious menu is full of spicy surprises—like Singapore chili crab and coconut chicken— complemented by imported beers.

$$ Greens – *Fort Mason Center, Bldg. A, ℘415-771-6222. www.greensrestaurant. com.* **Vegetarian**. Opened in 1979 by disciples of the San Francisco Zen Center, this gourmet veggie restaurant west of Fisherman's Wharf gets much of its organic produce from the center's Green Gulch Farm in Marin County. Savor such seasonal fare as coconut risotto cakes, wild mushroom ravioli, and broccoli di Ciccio pizza with spring onions, tomatoes, feta, fontina, and Meyer lemon gremolade, along with wonderful view of the marina with the Golden Gate Bridge in the distance.

$$ Mamacita – *2317 Chestnut St. Dinner only. 415-346-8494. www.mamacitasf.com.* **Mexican**. The lighting is low, but the volume is high in this upscale taqueria, where a cool, casual and young Marina crowd gathers nightly for margarita and Mexican fare. Small lacquered wood tables huddle under clusters of Moravian star lanterns, while lively Latin music sets the pace for bold flavors, and changing California-style takes on South of the Border recipes.

$$ Terzo – *3011 Steiner St. Dinner only. ℘415-441-3200. www.terzosf.com.* **Mediterranean**. Locals drop into this casual neighborhood spot with its zinc bar for upscale dining at reasonable prices. Look for the Mediterranean influences at play in dishes like grilled sea bass with garbazo beans, pistachio-

Terzo

© Terzo

crusted goat cheese and slow-cooked Greek chicken.

MISSION DISTRICT

$$ Delfina – *3621 18th St. Dinner only.* ☎*415-552-4055. www.delfinasf.com. Italian.* Craig and Anne Stoll continue to draw enthusiastic crowds to their Mission hotspot—still mobbed after all these years. The ambience is comfortably chic, uplifting and lively (though loud), but the soul-warming Tuscan cuisine is the reason for the masses.

$ Little Star Pizza – *400 Valencia St.* ☎*415-551-7827. Also at 846 Divasadero St.* ☎*415-441-1188. www.littlestarpizza. com.* **Pizza.** This popular pizza spot keeps fans of Chicago deep-dish pie right here in San Francisco, while also offering thin-crust versions. The eponymous "Little Star" combines spinach, onions, garlic, ricotta and feta cheese atop a thick cornmeal crust.

$ La Taqueria – *2889 Mission St.* ☎*415-285-7117.* **Mexican.** Fresh, basic tacos and burritos are dished up with healthy fruit drinks at this tiny neighborhood eatery. The grills are good, the salsa memorable.

NOB HILL

$$$$ Acquerello – *1722 Sacramento St.* ☎*415-567-5432. www.acquerello.com. Dinner only. Closed Sun–Mon.* **Italian.** The sun-soaked colored walls and whispering patrons lend a soothing beauty to this chapel-turned-restaurant. A stylish crowd continues to pour in for Chef Suzette Gresham-Tognetti's upscale, contemporary Italian dinners,

which, depending on your appetite, arrive in 3, 4, 5 or 7 courses.

NORTH BEACH

$$ Rose Pistola – *532 Columbus Ave.* ☎*415-399-0499. www.rosepistola.com.* **Italian.** A wood-burning oven dominates the open kitchen of this busy, family-style restaurant. Try the sweet potato gnocchi, cioppino or fish baked in the sophisticated Ligurian-Genoese style.

$$ The Stinking Rose – *325 Columbus Ave.* ☎*415-781-7673. www.thestinking rose.com.* **Italian.** Tourists flock here for garlic-laden dishes guaranteed to repel vampires. Start with roasted garlic to spread on bread, and end your meal with garlic ice cream. If you don't want to reek from your pores, the lasagna is safe.

PACIFIC HEIGHTS

$$ SPQR – *1911 Fillmore St.* ☎*415-771-7779. www.spqrsf.com.* **Italian.** An outstanding wine list and lovingly prepared Italian-inspired cuisine draw locals to this elegant but comfortable Pacific Heights restaurant. A variety of cold, hot and fried appetizers precedes the list of housemade pastas and elegant main dishes, including trottolone with beans, radicchio and fennel; and pork saltimbocca.

$ Rassellas – *1534 Fillmore St. Dinner only.* ☎*415-346-8696. www.rasselas jazzclub.com.* **Ethiopian.** Spicy African food is served in a dark, exotic atmosphere that doubles as a jazz club after dark.

RICHMOND DISTRICT

$$ Kabuto Restaurant – *5121 Geary Blvd. Dinner only. Closed Mon. ☏415-752-5652. www.kabutosushi.com.* **Japanese**. Little Kabuto does swimmingly with sushi as well as more inventive offerings like fois gras sushi, hamachi pear and sushi mozzarella.

$$ Katia's Russian Tea Room – *600 Fifth Ave. Closed Mon & Tues. ☏415-668-9292. www.katias.com.* **Russian**. This casual, friendly cafe offers piroshki, stroganoff and blini with salmon caviar to homesick Eastern Europeans. Fresh flowers grace every table, and in warm weather full windows open onto the sidewalk.

$$ Ton Kiang – *5821 Geary Blvd. ☏415-752-4440. www.tonkiang.net.* **Chinese**. Clay-pot casseroles (rock cod with tofu; braised oxtail with carrot and celery) and flavorful steamed dim sum speak highly for Asian regional cuisines.

$ Minh's Garden – *208 Clement St. ☏415-751-8211.* **Vietnamese**. Excellent and authentic Southeast Asian food is served at this simple cafe. Multicourse meals are priced under $10 per person.

RUSSIAN HILL

$$$ La Folie – *2316 Polk St. Closed Sun. ☏415-776-5577. www.lafolie.com.* **French**. Fresh produce enhances classic dishes at this bistro, with its white clouds painted on the blue ceiling. The seasonal menu may include quail and foie gras "lollipops," or butter-poached lobster on a salad of squash–sage ravioli.

$$ Pesce – *2227 Polk St. ☏415-928-8025.* **Seafood**. The flavors of Venice inspire small, meant-to-be shared dishes in this relaxed and cozy resto. The menu focuses on the sea (squid-ink risotto, pan-seared scallops in a creamy truffle-laced sauce) but carnivores can still opt for Merlot-braised lamb shank or milk-braised pork with gnocchi, sage and pancetta.

$$ Zarzuela – *2000 Hyde St. Dinner only. Closed Sun. ☏415-346-0800.* **Spanish**. Paellas are served on hand-painted plates at this friendly Madrid-style resto. Dishes include poached octopus and zarzuela, a seafood stew.

SOUTH OF MARKET

$$$ Ame – *689 Mission St. ☏415-284-4040. www.amerestaurant.com.* **Contemporary**. Tucked into the hip St. Regis hotel, Ame has the kind of sleek good looks one has come to associate with SoMa—a handsome, paneled-wood room, Japanese lighting and a custom-designed sushi bar. The fusion fare blends Japanese, Italian and French seamlessly, with a little Asian sensibilty thrown in for good measure.

$$ South Park Cafe – *108 South Park Ave. Closed Sun; Mon lunch only. ☏415-495-7275. www.southparkcafesf.com.* **French**. Latin Quarter ambience pervades this casual sidewalk cafe facing a pretty park. A blackboard menu may feature a sautéed pear and roquefort salad, a chicken liver-and-cognac terrine, couscous with braised vegetables and coriander mint yogurt, or a housemade boudin noir.

UNION SQUARE AREA

$$$$ Fleur de Lys – *777 Sutter St. Closed Sun. ☏415-673-7779. www.fleur delyssf.com.* **French**. French-born chef/

Farallon

© Farallon

owner Hubert Keller adds Pacific Rim accents to classic recipes at his elegant, top-of-the-line restaurant. Diners can't go wrong with venison, lamb, swordfish, prix-fixe tasting menus or special vegetarian selections.

$$$ Farallon – *450 Post St., Union Sq. ℘415-956-6969. www.farallonrestaurant.com.* **Seafood**. Whimsical blown-glass jellyfish chandeliers and octopus stools complement the seafood menu here. Chef Mark Franz prepares such entrées as seared walleye pike with braised fennel and baby artichoke confit and a "hot pot" of seafood, oysters, mushrooms, bok choy and lotus root.

$$$ Postrio – *545 Post St. ℘415-776-7825. www.postrio.com.* **Contemporary**. Wolfgang Puck's spacious and elegant Prescott Hotel eatery serves a changing menu of American, Mediterranean and Asian dishes fashioned from local farm products. Pat Kuleto's splashy, modern decor is a great backdrop for people-watching.

$$ Café de la Presse – *352 Grant Ave. ℘415-398-2680. www.cafedelapresse.com.* **French**. Traditional French fare, including pastries and espresso, is served at this popular cafe beside Chinatown Gate, which overhauled its menu and look in 2005. The all-day menu features classics like warm asparagus salad and duck-leg confit with warm lentils.

$$ John's Grill – *63 Ellis St. ℘415-986-3274. www.johnsgrill.com.* **American**. The true Maltese Falcon, made famous by author-patron Dashiell Hammett and actor Humphrey Bogart, has been at home behind the bar here since 1908. The shrimp Louis and chicken Jerusalem are classics.

$$ Kuleto's – *221 Powell St. ℘415-397-7720. www.kuletos.com.* **Italian**. Shoppers flock to restaurant designer Pat Kuleto's flagship cafe for its stylish setting and excellent food. At the mahogany bar, you can watch chefs prepare fresh fish and grilled meats.

$$ Millennium – *580 Geary St. Dinner only. ℘415-345-3900. www.millennium restaurant.com.* **Vegetarian**. Meat and dairy products are shunned at this gourmet eatery, now tucked in the Savoy Hotel near Union Square. Wild mushrooms, polenta, tofu and bean medleys are staples.

$ Dottie's True Blue Cafe – *522 Jones St. Closed Tue. Breakfast and lunch. ℘415-885-2767.* **American**. A classic 1950s-style diner, Dottie's doles out generous portions of eggs and pancakes for breakfast, vegetarian and other sandwiches for lunch.

$ Sanraku – *704 Sutter St. ℘415-771-0803. www.sanraku.com.* **Japanese.** Regulars rave about this simple, low-key sushi spot, which stands out for its fresh fish in the neighborhood around Union Square. Smiling sushi chefs make conversation while they craft high-quality seafood into maki, nigiri and sashimi.

$ Sears Fine Food – *439 Powell St. ℘415-986-0700. www.searsfinefood.com.* **American**. Though newly renovated, Sears remains a local insitution for its signature dish, 18 delicate Swedish pancakes ($9.95), now served all day. There are also dishes like fish-and-chips, seafood omelets, and a turkey plate complete with cranberry sauce .

YERBA BUENA GARDENS

$$$ Fifth Floor – *12 Fourth St. in the Hotel Palomar. Dinner only. Closed Sun-Mon. ℘415-348-1555. www.fifthfloor restaurant.com.* **French**. This eatery highlights the rustic yet sophisticated cuisine of Gascony. Chef Jennie Lorenzo's kitchen turns out traditional dishes such as roast lamb loin with sweetbreads and fava leaves, and halibut with black trumpet mushrooms and gougere gnocchi.

$$ Fringale – *570 Fourth St. ℘415-543-0573. www.fringalesf.com.* **Basque**. Chef Carmelo E. Lopez mans the stoves at this stylish, intimate corner bistro, known for its mussels and pork dishes as well as its frisée salad, topped with a perfectly poached egg.

$$ Thirsty Bear Brewing Company – *661 Howard St. ℘415-974-0905. www. thirstybear.com.* **Spanish**. Dozens of cold and hot tapas, such as marinated Spanish anchovies with blood oranges and chive oil, highlight a menu that complements 10 different house-made organic brews.

Entertainment

PERFORMING ARTS

The Bay Area is blessed with a great wealth and variety of performing-arts offerings. Nearly 100 live-performance theaters mount stage productions performed by traveling Broadway companies and respected regional and local groups. Acclaimed dance, symphony and opera companies perform at Civic Center venues. The main theater district is centered just west of Union Square, while stages at Yerba Buena Gardens and Fort Mason Center host a variety of music, film, theater and dance events. Popular rock and alternative music performers play at intimate and large-scale nightclubs as well as at stadiums and arenas. A variety of public literary readings light up bookstores, coffeehouses and other locations (check *The San Francisco Bay Guardian* or *SF Weekly* for current listings). For a detailed listing of events, call the SFCVB's information line (☏415-391-2001) or consult www.sfbg.com or www.sfgate.com/entertainment.

TICKETS

As some of the more popular events sell out months in advance, it is wise to buy tickets early. Full-price tickets can be purchased directly from the venue's box office or from one of the brokers listed below (a service charge of $1-$7 may be added to the ticket price). Brokers may have tickets available when the box office is sold out, but expect to pay a substantial service fee. Hotel concierges may also be able to help secure tickets.

TIX Bay Area offers half-price tickets starting at 10am for selected events on the day of the show. Purchases must be made in person from the box office in Union Square on Powell St. between Post and Geary (⏲*open daily 10am–6pm*), online at www.tixbayarea.com or by telephone: ☏415-433-7827. You can also buy tickets through **Ticketmaster** (*www.ticketmaster.com*).

City Box Office offers tickets for classical performances and lectures held at smaller venues (*152 Kearny St.;* ☏*415-392-4400; www.cityboxoffice.com*).

BALLET

San Francisco Ballet
301 Van Ness Ave. ☏*415-865-2000. www.sfballet.org.* Directed by Helgi Tomasson, the company stages classically inspired contemporary ballet works as well as traditional classical repertoire (*Swan Lake, The Nutcracker Suite*) during its February–May season at the War Memorial Opera House.

Oakland Ballet
☏*510-465-6400. www.oaklandballet.org.* Revived in 2007, the company performs a limited repertoire (*The Secret Garden, The Nutcracker*) in the historic Paramount Theatre.

CLASSICAL MUSIC

San Francisco Symphony
201 Van Ness Ave. ☏*415-552-8000. www.sfsymphony.org.* Led by maestro Michael Tilson Thomas, the orchestra performs classical repertoire and 20C and contemporary pieces during its September–June season at Davies Symphony Hall. Families should check out the Music for Families and Concerts for Kids series.

Philharmonia Baroque
401 Van Ness Ave. ☏*415-252-1288. www.philharmonia.org.* The ensemble performs Baroque works (Bach, Corelli, Rameau), on period instruments at the Herbst Theatre and venues in Berkeley, Palo Alto and Contra Costa.

San Francisco Contemporary Music Players
☏*415-278-9566. www.sfcmp.org.* This award-winning contemporary chamber music ensemble showcases new (within the last 10 years) music with its innovative concert series at Yerba Buena Center for the Arts.

THEATERS

Visit **www.theatermania.com** for comprehensive listings of performances throughout the Bay Area.

American Conservatory Theater

415 Geary Blvd. *415-749-2228. www.act-sf.org.* The city's longstanding resident theater company mounts classic and new works (*Speed-the-Plow, Blood Knot, Sweeney Todd*) in the former Geary Theater (1910, Bliss & Faville).

Curran Theater

445 Geary Blvd. *415-551-2000. www.shnsf.com.* Broadway traveling shows (*Hairspray, Wicked, A Chorus Line*) are staged here, at the **Golden Gate Theater** *(1 Taylor St.)* and the **Orpheum Theater** *(1192 Market St.).*

OPERA

San Francisco Opera

301 Van Ness Ave. *415-864-3330. www.sfopera.com.* An active performance repertoire staged at the War Memorial Opera House includes the traditional (*La Bohème, Tosca, Porgy and Bess*) and the groundbreaking (*The Bonesetter's Daugher*, with a libretto by Amy Tan).

Pocket Opera

415-972-8930. www.pocketopera.org. Director Donald Pippin's company makes opera clear, accessible and affordable through small scale productions (*Cosi Fan Tutte, Xerxes, Don Pasquale*) held at various venues.

THEATER FESTIVALS

Shakespeare in the Park

415-558-0888. www.sfshakes.org. The San Francisco Shakespeare Festival's professional troupe mounts free performances on the Main Lawn at the Presidio's Parade Grounds.

NIGHTLIFE

San Francisco's nightlife is as diverse as its population, and ranges from elegant Nob Hill piano bars to clubs offering live music and jazz. Venues blur the line between dance club, bar and live-performance spot, showcasing up-and-coming bands on some nights and celebrity DJs on others.

Though clubs of every stripe can be found throughout the city, Folsom Street and Howard Avenue in the South of Market draw late-night (make that early-morning) crowds to techno/hip-hop dance clubs where bouncers may scrutinize the too-

San Francisco Opera's War Memorial Opera House

© David Wakely Photography / San Francisco Opera

San Francisco Nightlife Websites

+ www.yelp.com
+ www.7x7.com/music-nightlife
+ www.sfweekly.com
+ www.metrowize.com
+ www.sfgate.com/entertainment
+ www.sfstation.com/clubs

casually dressed. The Mission District is home to a slew of hipster dives and DJ dance bars, which draw a young, mixed crowd. The nearby Castro is the city's hub for gay bars. On the other end of the city, North Beach is a mix of smaller dance clubs, comedy clubs, dives and strip clubs. To party with a preppy crowd of affluent young professionals, head to the Marina's mix of sports bars, wine bars and lounges. For swanky lounges, Nob Hill is your neighborhood.

If your venue tastes run posh, or if you want a big dance floor, you can expect to pay for your nightliving: creative cocktails from "mixologists" can start at around $8.00 and cover charges can run as high as $50 for the biggest clubs, although entry fees rarely top $10 for smaller bars and lounges. Proof of age (21) is required to enter most clubs. Many clubs reserve private tables, rooms and VIP lounges for guest list-only entry. Some places serve food (menu may be scaled down to light appetizers after 10 or 11pm).

Consult the arts and entertainment sections of the publications listed above for detailed listings of live performances and events.

BARS

Alembic
1725 Haight St. ℘*415-666-0822. www.alembicbar.com.* The mixologists at this cozy upper Haight haunt are are experts at their art, mixing up sazeracs, pisco sours and Blood and Sands (scotch whiskey, cherry brandy, sweet vermouth and orange juice).

Bin 38
3232 Scott St. ℘*415-567-3838. www.bin38.com.* Social Marina denizens flood this cozy wine bar, which boasts a back patio with a firepit and heat lamps.

Bourbon & Branch
501 Jones St., at O'Farrell ℘*415-931-7292. www.bourbonandbranch.com.* This sultry speakeasy in the Tenderloin has no sign (look for the door below the Anti-Saloon League sign) and you have to ring a buzzer to get in. Make reservations for the main room, or say the password "Books" to gain admittance into the Library bar.

Cantina
580 Sutter St. ℘*415-398-0195. www.cantinasf.com.* Weekend nights find a full house at this Latin-inspired lounge near Union Square, where the cocktail menu is full of caipirinhas, sangrias and mojitos.

Edinburgh Castle
950 Geary St. ℘*415-885-4074. www.castlenews.com.* A laidback bar with Tuesday quiz nights, Edinburgh Castle nestles on the border of lower Nob Hill and the Tenderloin. Fish and chips are served until 11pm.

El Rio
3158 Mission St. ℘*415-282-3325. www.elriosf.com.* A stellar back patio draws diverse throngs to weekend salsa and burlesque shows at this friendly lower Mission bar. Nights brings DJs and live music.

Gordon Biersch
2 Harrison Street. ℘*415-243-8246. www.gordonbiersch.com.* The after-work crowd hangs at this two-level brewpub, with great views of the Bay Bridge, upscale pub fare and a selection of house brews for sampling.

Hotel Biron
45 Rose St. ℘*415-703-0403. www.hotelbiron.com.* Tucked on a Hayes Valley alley, this intimate, hole-

in-the-wall wine bar offers a diverse selection of wine. Small groups and couples gather on comfy sofas beside exposed brick walls, or at the handful of small copper tables.

Nihon Whisky Lounge

1179 Folsom St. ☎415-552-4400. www.dajanigroup.net. Whiskey lovers flock to this intimate SoMa lounge, where a knowledgable staff can helps patrons choose from the extensive selection of whiskeys.

Rickhouse

246 Kearny St. ☎415-398-2827. www.rickhousebar.com. A prime place for post-work mingling, this down-town bar is packed with professionals on weeknights. The small loft often has more breathing room.

La Trappe

800 Greenwich St. ☎415-440-8727. www.latrappecafe.com. Pass through the quiet street-level restaurant and descend the spiral staircase to enter this Belgian beer den, which especially buzzes on weekend evenings.

Toronado

547 Haight St. ☎415-863-2276. www.toronado.com. Beloved by locals, this lower Haight pub has great selection of brews. Bonus: they sell sausages from Rosamunde's next door.

COMEDY

Cobb's Comedy Club

915 Columbus Ave. ☎415-928-4320. Some of the biggest names in standup have headlined at this 400-seat club, which runs two shows nightly. Seating is first-come, first-served, and there's a full dinner menu. Dress is casual.

The Clubhouse

414 Mason St. #705. ☎415-921-2051. www.clubhousecomedy.com. Low cover charges, a BYOB policy and a mission of showcasing local talent draw hipsters in the know to this relaxed spot near Union Square.

The Marsh

1062 Valencia St. ☎415-826-5750. www.themarsh.org. Thought-provoking standup comedy, plays and other performances fill the bill at this intimate theater in the Mission District.

Punch Line

444 Battery St. ☎415-397-7573. www.punchlinecomedyclub.com. The seating is tight, but the cover price is right (plus a 2-drink minimum) at this proving ground for live standup, where big names work out new material.

DANCE CLUBS

Ruby Skye

420 Mason St. ☎415-693-0777. www.rubyskye.com. Four different rooms, a bi-level dance floor and throbbing hip-hop, house and techno music from live bands and DJs make this Union Square-area spot a favored hangout.

Temple

540 Howard St. www.templesf.com. Southeast Asian themes dominate the three main rooms here; dress is strictly club-funk, the better to gyrate to throbbing techno and house music. Brace yourself for a steep cover and a long wait unless you're on a guest list.

Harry Denton's Starlight Room

450 Powell St, in the Sir Francisc Drake Hotel. ☎415-395-8595. www.harrydenton.com. Dress to the nines for your trip to this 21st-floor cocktail lounge, with its breathtaking views, retro feel and sizeable dance floor.

LIVE MUSIC VENUES

Indie and Avant-Garde

Amnesia – *853 Valencia St. ☎415-970-0012. www.amnesiathebar.com.* Red-tinted lighting, and an eclectic array of music ranging from Gypsy to indie make for a funky night at this ultra-laid-back bar and concert space. Fans flock to weekly bluegrass and karaoke nights.

Elbo Room – *647 Valencia St.*
415-552-7788. www.elbo.com.
Head upstairs from the packed bar
area for diverse live shows: Afro-
Cuban, hip-hop, rock, indie rock, jazz,
soul, funk or alternative could be
playing.

The Independent – *628 Divisadero St.*
*415-771-1421. www.theindependent
sf.com.* This spot seems to top everyone's list for great new bands, indie
favorites and a happening crowd.

Red Devil Lounge – *1695 Polk St.* *415
-921-1695. www.reddevillounge.com.*
Local indie, pop and folk bands
frequently take the stage at this
intimate, two-level Nob Hill venue.

Rickshaw Stop – *155 Fell St.* *415-
861-2011. www.rickshawstop.com.*
A younger crowd energizes this
intimate-sized club, which books
up-and-coming bands before they hit
it big. It's warm in there, so dress cool.

FOLK

Slim's – *333 11th St.* *415-255-0333.*
www.slims-sf.com. American roots
music (R&B, jazz, Cajun/Zydeco and
rock) takes the stage at this ever-
popular South of Market nightclub.
Decor is down-to-earth and seating
is limited, but the bands are well
worth it.

Freight & Salvage – *1111 Addison St,
Berkeley.* *510-548-1761. www.the
freight.org.* A Berkeley institution
since the late 1960s, this nonprofit
220-seat venue showcases traditional
music from all over the world; past
headliners include Ricky Skaggs and
Greg Brown. No alcohol is served; kids
admitted for half-price.

JAZZ AND BLUES

Biscuits & Blues – *401 Mason St.* *415
-292-2583. www.biscuitsandblues.com.*
Quality live blues and southern soul
food make an great combination at
this ultrahip belowground club near
Union Square.

Boom Boom Room – *1601 Fillmore St.*
*415-673-8000. www.boomboom
blues.com.* Chicago and New Orleans-
style jazz and blues rule the scene at
this laid-back jazz bar in Japantown.
It's a must for serious music
aficionados.

ROCK AND POP

Great American Music Hall –
859 O'Farrell St. *415-885-0750.*
www.musichallsf.com. Ornate
decor neatly jives with modern
accoutrements at this lovely early
20C music hall in the Tenderloin.
You'll see a variety of bands ranging
from rock to folk.

Bottom of the Hill – *1233 17th St.* *415-
621-4455. www.bottomofthehill.com.*
Advance tickets recommended for the
straight-up rock gigs as well as indie
and punk bands at this smallish club
in out-of-the-way Potrero Hill. White
Snake and Alanis Morissette rank
among the alumni.

Hemlock – *1131 Polk St.* *415-923-
0923. www.hemlocktavern.com.*
The front bar has a pool table, $1 bags
of peanuts and a juke box. In the back
room, underground rock bands and
national touring acts play 5-6 nights
a week.

The Fillmore Auditorium –
1805 Geary Blvd. Made famous by Bill
Graham in the mid-1960s with acts
such The Grateful Dead and Jefferson
Airplane, the Fillmore continues to
draw major rock and pop acts.

Shopping

From large complexes incorporating national chains, restaurants and entertainment venues, to intimate rows of boutiques scattered throughout the city, San Francisco satisfies the most ardent shopper. Most stores accept major credit cards and travelers checks, but not out-of-state checks. Many shops extend their hours during the holiday season (Nov–Dec).

MAIN SHOPPING AREAS

Union Square Area – San Francisco's leading shopping district, this area is home to major city department stores. **Nordstrom** (☎415-243-8500) is in the **Westfield San Francisco Centre** (865 Market St.; ☎415-512-6776), an enormous complex of more than 200 shops and restaurants, including numerous major chains. **Bloomingdale's** (☎415-856-5300) anchors the Westfield's new extension, which also hosts a Burke Williams spa, a movie theater, and a large basement-level food court. Other major Union Square stores include **Macy's** (corner of Stockton & O'Farrell Sts.; ☎415-397-3333), **Neiman Marcus** (150 Stockton St.; ☎415-362-3900), **Gump's** (135 Post St.; ☎415-982-1616), **Saks Fifth Avenue** (384 Post St., The Men's Store at 220 Post St.; ☎415-986-4300), and **Barney's New York** (77 O'Farrell St.; ☎415-268-3500). Designer boutiques and specialty shops like **Emporio Armani** (1 Grant Ave.; ☎415-677-9400) and **Burberry** (225 Post St.; ☎415-392-2200) are found along and around Grant Avenue, Post Street, Sutter Street and Maiden Lane. Also in the Union Square area are major home furnishing chains such as **Crate & Barrell** (55 Stockton St.; ☎415-982-5200) and **Williams Sonoma** (340 Post St.; ☎415-362-9450), and bargain chains selling of-the-moment trends, including **Forever 21** (7 Powell St.; ☎415-984-0380) and **H&M** (150 Powell St.; ☎415-986-4215).

Financial District – The city's major business district boasts the **Embarcadero Center** (next to Justin Herman Plaza; ☎415-772-0700), a 10-acre office-and-retail complex incorporating more than 100 shops and restaurants.
Nearby, the **Ferry Building Marketplace** is home to dozens of specialty food boutiques, as well as **The Gardener** (One Ferry Bldg., ☎415-981-8181) and the newly opened outpost of **Heath Ceramics** (☎415-399-9284).
The Crocker Galleria (50 Post St.; ☎415-393-1505) contains nearly 30 designer and specialty shops. More than 25 fine modern design and **antique** shops, along with numerous art galleries, are located in the Jackson Square Historic District near Jackson and Montgomery Streets (☎415-398-8115; www.jacksonsquaresf.com).

Chinatown – Haggle at an open-air market along Stockton Street, or admire luxurious silks and jades at Grant Avenue shops, in this colorful, bustling micro-city. Pharmacies sell traditional Asian herbal remedies, and a plenitude of restaurants offer *dim sum* and other Chinese delicacies. Grant Avenue is one of the best places in the city to find cheap souvenirs.

Fisherman's Wharf – Four retail centers punctuate this festive strip of souvenir shops and novelty museums. **Anchorage Square** has more than 50 shops and restaurants (☎415-775-6000); **The Cannery** houses a handful of specialty shops and restaurants (☎415-771-3112); **Ghirardelli Square** features more than a dozen shops and restaurants (☎415-775-5500); and **Pier 39** boasts more than 50 specialty and gift shops (☎415-981-7437).

The Marina and Cow Hollow – The shopping scene in the northwest part of San Francisco is dominated by two main streets. **Union Street** from Van Ness Avenue to Steiner Street forms the commercial heart of Cow Hollow, while **Chestnut Street** between Divisadero and Fillmore Streets is the main retail section of the Marina. Both are host to dozens of clothing, jewelry and beauty boutiques, as well as antique stores, salons, cafes and restaurants. Among the most popular womens boutiques on Union Street is **Ambiance** *(1864 Union St.; 415-923-979; also at 1458 Haight St.; 415-552-5095 and 3985 24th St.; 415-647-7144)* offering trendy clothing, shoes and accessories. **Paper Source** *(2061 Chestnut St; 415-614-1585)* offers high-end stationery and craft materials.

Mission District – Valencia Street is the hub of the Mission's shopping district. Here local clothing and jewelry designers such as **Dema** (1038 Valencia St.; 415-206-0500) have set up shop, interspersed with art galleries, small grocery stores, and restaurants. Nearby, the ecletic **BellJar** (3187 16th St.; 415-626-1749) and **Needles and Pen**s (3253 16th St.; 415-255-1534) are great for gifts, with home decor, art, apparel and stationery. The lively area also abounds with vintage and secondhand shops, from large catch-all stores to intimate boutiques with a finely edited selection. Farther down Valencia are unique stores such as **Paxton Gate** (824 Valencia St.; 415-824-1872), which offers everything from garden tools to art to taxidermy supplies, and the pirate supply store at **826 Valencia** (826 Valencia St.; 415 642-5905). Given the neighborhood's ethnic makeup, many stores also sell Latin American imports, including jewelry and clothing.

South of Market – A bargain hunter's dream, this area boasts dozens of outlet centers, resale shops and design showrooms. **Jeremy's** *(2 South Park at 2nd St.; 415-882-4929)* is a huge emporium of deeply discounted designer clothing, while **Rolo Garage** *(1301 Howard St. at 9th St.; 415-861-*

2097) stocks the latest urban fashions, also at a great discount. The **San Francisco Antique & Design Mall** *(701 Bayshore Blvd.; 415-656-3530; www.sfantique.com)* incorporates 200 antiques dealers.

OTHER SHOPPING AREAS

In addition to the areas described above, charming neighborhood shopping areas offer a pleasant mix of small boutiques, specialty shops, bookstores, restaurants and cafes.

♦ **Fillmore Street** (Pacific Heights) *Jackson to Bush Sts. & Union to Greenwich Sts.* Fillmore Street reflects the affluence of Pacific Heights residents, housing numerous fashionable boutiques, with high-end fashions, such as **Heidi Says** *(2426 Fillmore St.; 415- 409-6850)*. Also here are eclectic home furnishing stores like **Nest** *(2300 Fillmore St.; 415-292-6199)* and the modern **Zinc Details** *(1905 Fillmore St.; 415-776-2100)* and **Jonathan Adler** *(2133 Fillmore St.; 415-563-9500)*.

♦ **Haight Street** (Haight-Ashbury) *Stanyan St. to Central Ave.* Haight Street is home to a number of funky clothing boutiques and secondhand shops such as **Crossroads** *(1519 Haight St., 415-355-0555; also at 1901 Fillmore St., 415-775-8885, and 2123 Market St., 415-552-8740)*, as well as music stores like **Amoeba** *(1855 Haight St.; 415-831-1200)*, housed in a former bowling alley. In the Lower Haight, east of Divasdero Street, boutiques become more trendy and artsy, as with **LowerHater** *(597 Haight St.; 415-864-6549)* and **Upper Playground** *(220 Fillmore St.; 415-861-1960)*.

♦ **Hayes Street** (Civic Center) *Franklin to Octavia Sts.* Trendy clothing boutiques like **Azalea**

(411 Hayes St.; ☎415-861-9888) and unique home furnishing shops dominate the small Hayes Valley shopping stretch, supplemented by unique finds like the travel-oriented **Flight001** (525 Hayes St.; ☎415-487-1001) and the beauty supply shop **Nancy Boy** (347 Hayes St.; ☎415-552-3802).

- **24th Street** (Noe Valley) *Church to Douglass Sts.* Noe Valley denizens converge on 24th Street to shop and dine. The small main drag features specialty food shops and a handful of small boutiques.

- **Castro Street** (Castro District) *Market to 20th Sts.* As the city's hub for gay men, it's no surprise that the Castro is home to a number of trendy menswear stores, among them **Diesel** (400 Castro St.; ☎415-621-5557). Also here are numerous novelty shops, such as **Cliff's Variety** (479 Castro St.; ☎415-431-5365).

- **Sacramento Street** (Presidio Heights) *Spruce to Baker Sts.* Sacramento Street caters to a largely local, affluent crowd. Here you will find women's and children's boutiques, as well as high-end home furnishings.

- **Polk Street** (Russian Hill) *Broadway to Filbert St.* The main street of tony Russian Hill, Polk offers a handful of small boutiques, including vintage-inspired **Belle Cose and Molte Cose** (2036–2044 Polk St.; ☎415-474-3494).

ART GALLERIES

San Francisco's greatest concentration of galleries can be found along Sutter, Post and Geary Streets in the blocks north and immediately south of Union Square, especially Sutter between Stockton and Mason Streets. **49 Geary Street** is home to, among

others, the Stephen Wirtz, Jack Fisher, Robert Koch, Shapiro and Fraenkel galleries. Jackson Square, Cow Hollow, Fisherman's Wharf, SoMa and other precincts have smaller concentrations of fine art.

SoMa galleries include the **Catharine Clark Gallery** (150 Minna St.; ☎415-399-1439; www.cclarkgallery.com) and **Crown Point Press** (20 Hawthorne St.; ☎415-974-6273; www.crownpoint.com). Fort Mason is home to the **San Francisco Museum of Modern Art Gallery** (Fort Mason Building A; ☎415-441-4777; www.sfmoma.org).

The San Francisco Gallery Guide, provides a comprehensive listing of exhibits and locations (SF Bay Area Gallery Guide, 1369 Fulton St.; ☎415-921-1600; www.sfbayarea galleryguide.com).

Commercial galleries' hours vary widely, with many of them closing Sundays and/or Mondays. Most open between 10am and 11am and close between 5pm and 6pm. On the first Thursday of the month, many San Francisco galleries stay open later than usual for a casual open house (5.30–7.30pm; www. firstthursdayart.com).

ANTIQUES

In addition to the San Francisco Antique & Design Mall in SoMa and the Crocker Galeria and Jackson Square in the Financial District, a number of antique shops are sprinkled throughout the city, including the following.

African Outlet (Hayes Valley) *524 Octavia St..* ☎415- 864-3576.
Past Perfect (Cow Hollow) *2224 Union St..* ☎415-929-7651.
Schein & Schein (North Beach) *1435 Grant Ave..* ☎415-399-8882. *www.scheinandschein.com.*
Timeless Treasures (Pacific Heights) *2176 Sutter St..* ☎415-775-8366. *www.timelesstreasuressf.com.*

BOOKSTORES

Barnes & Noble (Fisherman's Wharf)
2550 Taylor St.. ℘415-292-6762.
www.bn.com.
Borders Books and Music (Union
Square) *400 Post St.. ℘415-399-1633.*
www.borders.com. Also at 200 King St..
℘415-357-9931.
City Lights Bookstore (North Beach)
261 Columbus Ave. ℘415-362-8193.
www.citylights.com.
A Different Light Bookstore (Castro)
489 Castro St.. ℘415-431-0891.
www.adlbooks.com.
Green Apple Books and Music
(Richmond) *506 Clement St.. ℘415-387-*
2272. www.greenapplebooks.com.
Modern Times (Mission District)
888 Valencia Street. ℘415-282-9246.
www.mtbs.com.
Omnivore Books (Noe Valley) *3885A*
Ceasar Chavez St.. ℘415-282-4712.
www.omnivorebooks.com.
Willam Stout Architectural Books
(North Beach) *804 Montgomery St..*
℘415-391-6757. www.stoutbooks.com.

MARKETS

Farmers' markets abound
throughout San Francisco and the
Bay Area, jam-packed with fresh
(often organic) produce, meats,
breads, cheeses, chocolates, specialty
coffee and prepared foods from local
farmers and producers. Some feature
live music, cooking demonstrations
and craft booths.

Ferry Plaza Farmers' Market
Ferry Plaza, Sat 8am–2pm, Tue &
Thu 10am–2pm. ℘415-291-3276.
www.ferrybuildingmarketplace.com.

Heart of the City Farmers' Market
U.N. Plaza, Civic Center. Sun 7am–5pm,
Wed 7am–5:30pm, Fri 7am–2.30pm.
℘415-558-9455. www.hocfarmers
market.org.

Crocker Galleria Farmers Market
Sutter St. at Montgomery St.,
Financial District. Thur 11am–3pm,
Jun–Sept also Tue 11am–3pm. www.

cafarmersmarkets.com/markets/
category/crocker-galleria.

Castro Farmers' Market
Market Street at Noe Street.
Mid-Mar–mid Dec Wed 4–8pm.
www.pcfma.com.

Alemany Farmers' Market
100 Alemany Blvd., Bernal Heights).
Sat dawn–dusk.

Old Oakland Farmers' Market
Ninth St. at Broadway, Oakland.
Fri 8am–2pm.
www.urbanvillageonline.com.

Berkeley Farmers' Markets
Center St. at M.L. King, Jr. Way.
Sat 10am–3pm.

Adeline St. at 63rd St.
Tue 2pm–6.30pm.

Shattuck Ave. at Rose St.
Thu 3–7pm.
www.ecologycenter.org/bfm.

The **Alemany Flea Market**
(100 Alemany Blvd.; Wed & Sun
8am–3pm) is a favorite with local
bargain-hunters, its tables crammed
with treasures and trinkets of
every kind.

MUSIC

Amoeba Music (Haight)
1855 Haight St.. ℘415-831-1200.
www.amoebamusic.com.
Aquarius Records (Mission District)
1055 Valencia St.. ℘415-647-2272.
www.aquariusrecords.org.
Groove Merchant (Haight)
687 Haight St.. ℘415-252-5766.
Jack's Record Cellar (Haight)
254 Scott St.. ℘415-431-3047.
Rooky Ricardo's (Haight)
448 Haight St.. ℘415-864-7526.
www.rookyricardos.com.
Rasputin Music (Union Square)
69 Powell St.. ℘800-350-8700.
www.rasputinmusic.com.

Sports

SPECTATOR SPORTS

Tickets for professional sporting events can be purchased at the venue, or through Ticketmaster.

AT&T Park

© San Francisco Travel Association photo by Doug Peebles

AT&T Park, home to the San Francisco Giants baseball team, is located at the south end of The Embarcadero within walking distance of the Ferry Building. **Monster Park** (formerly Candlestick Park), home to the San Francisco 49ers football team, lies south of San Francisco in the Candlestick Point State Recreation Area. By **car** take US-101 south to park exit. The "Ballpark Express" **bus** offers service between San Francisco and the stadium *($8 round-trip; MUNI bus 9X, 28X & 47X; ✆415-673-6864).*
☞*Note: park is windy and chilly; bring a jacket or sweater.*
McAfee Coliseum hosts the home games of the Oakland Raiders (football) and the Oakland Athletics (baseball). Next door, **The Arena in Oakland** serves as home to the Golden State Warriors (basketball). By **car** from San Francisco cross the Oakland Bay Bridge and take I-580 to I-980 to I-880 south to 66th Ave. exit. By rail, take the BART Fremont line to the Coliseum stop, where a walkway leads to the stadium.
San Jose Arena is located in downtown San Jose. From San Francisco, take I-280 or US-101 south.

WORKING OUT

The following fitness clubs open their facilities to nonmembers, and have locations throughout the city. Check their websites for hours and addresses.

Club One Fitness

www.clubone.com. $20 per day.
Locations in the Financial District, Nob Hill, Union Square, Yerba Buena Gardens, Fillmore Center and Oakland.

24-Hour Fitness

www.24hourfitness.com. $15 per day.
Locations in Fisherman's Wharf, the Marina District, the Financial District, South of Market, Civic Center, Pacific Heights, the Castro and Noe Valley.

YMCA

www.ymcasf.org. $15 per day non-members; $5 members.
Locations in Embarcadero, SoMa, Chinatown and the Mission District.

SPORT/TEAM	Season	Home Stadium	✆ Information
Major League Baseball	Apr-Oct	(81 home games)	415-972-2000
San Francisco Giants (NL)		AT&T Park	510-568-5600
Oakland Athletics (AL)		McAfee Coliseum	
National Football League	Sept-Dec	(8 home games)	415-464-9377
San Francisco 49ers		Monster Park	800-724-3377
Oakland Raiders		McAfee Coliseum	
National Basketball Assn.	Nov-Apr	(41 home games)	510-986-2200
Golden State Warriors		The Arena in Oakland	
National Hockey League	Oct-Apr	(41 home games)	408-287-9200
San Jose Sharks		HP Pavilion	

INDEX

INDEX

INDEX

INDEX

INDEX

🛏 STAY

🍷 EAT

MAPS AND PLANS

MAP LEGEND

★★★ **Highly recommended**
★★ **Recommended**
★ **Interesting**

Selected monuments and sights

⇥ ▭	Tour with departure point
⛪	Mission
⛪ ⚲	Church, chapel
B	Letter locating a sight
■ ▲	Other points of interest
▪	Statue, monument
☀ ♈	Panorama – View
▬	Building described – Other
▪	Small building
⚑	Lighthouse
◎	Fountain
🛈	Visitor information
▭	Park described – Other
▨	Wooded park described – Other
▦	Cemetery described – Other

Special symbol

▭····	Cable car terminus, line

Additional symbols

▬	Highway, interchange
▬	Toll road, bridge
▭ ⁃⁃⁃	Tunnel with ramp
⟶	One way street
▭	Pedestrian street – Steps
▬	Shopping street
✈ 🚌	Airport – Bus station
⛴ 🚢	Passenger ferry – Cruise
●	Subway station
🎁	Gift shop
🚻	Restrooms
♦	Elevator
🅿 ✉	Parking – Post office
⊶	Gate
► ⟨⟩	Golf course – Stadium
🛡	Interstate Highway
44	US Highway
55	Other Route

All maps are oriented north, unless otherwise indicated by a directional arrow.

COMPANION PUBLICATIONS

MAP 585 WESTERN USA, WESTERN CANADA

Large-format map providing detailed road systems; includes driving distances, interstate rest stops, border crossings and interchanges.
- Comprehensive city and town index
- Scale: 1 : 2,400,000 (1in = approx.38mi)

MAP 761 USA ROAD MAP

Covers principal US road network while also presenting shaded relief detail of overall physiography of the land.
- State flags with statistical data and state tourism office telephone numbers
- Scale: 1 : 3,450,000

INTERNET

Michelin is pleased to offer a route-planning service on the Internet:
www.viamichelin.com
www.travel.viamichelin.com
Choose the shortest route, a route without tolls, or the Michelin recommended route to your destination; you can also access information about hotels and restaurants from *The Michelin Guide*, and tourist sites from *The Green Guide*.

YOU ALREADY KNOW THE GREEN GUIDE,
NOW FIND OUT ABOUT THE MICHELIN GROUP

A better way forward

The Michelin Adventure

It all started with rubber balls! This was the product made by a small company based in Clermont-Ferrand that André and Edouard Michelin inherited, back in 1880. The brothers quickly saw the potential for a new means of transport and their first success was the invention of detachable pneumatic tires for bicycles. However, the automobile was to provide the greatest scope for their creative talents. Throughout the 20th century, Michelin never ceased developing and creating ever more reliable and high-performance tires, not only for vehicles ranging from trucks to F1 but also for underground transit systems and airplanes.

From early on, Michelin provided its customers with tools and services to facilitate mobility and make traveling a more pleasurable and more frequent experience. As early as 1900, the Michelin Guide supplied motorists with a host of useful information related to vehicle maintenance, accommodation and restaurants, and was to become a benchmark for good food. At the same time, the Travel Information Bureau offered travelers personalised tips and itineraries.

The publication of the first collection of roadmaps, in 1910, was an instant hit! In 1926, the first regional guide to France was published, devoted to the principal sites of Brittany, and before long each region of France had its own Green Guide. The collection was later extended to more far-flung destinations, including New York in 1968 and Taiwan in 2011.

In the 21st century, with the growth of digital technology, the challenge for Michelin maps and guides is to continue to develop alongside the company's tire activities. Now, as before, Michelin is committed to improving the mobility of travelers.

MICHELIN TODAY

WORLD NUMBER ONE TIRE MANUFACTURER
- 70 production sites in 18 countries
- 111,000 employees from all cultures and on every continent
- 6,000 people employed in research and development

Moving
for a world

Moving forward means developing tires with better road grip and shorter braking distances, whatever the state of the road.

CORRECT TIRE PRESSURE

RIGHT PRESSURE

- Safety
- Longevity
- Optimum fuel consumption

-0,5 bar

- Durability reduced by 20% (- 8,000 km)

- Risk of blowouts
- Increased fuel consumption
- Longer braking distances on wet surfaces

forward together
where mobility is safer

It also involves helping motorists take care of their safety and their tires. To do so, Michelin organises "Fill Up With Air" campaigns all over the world to remind us that correct tire pressure is vital.

WEAR

DETECTING TIRE WEAR

The legal minimum depth of tire tread is 1.6mm. Tire manufacturers equip their tires with tread wear indicators, which are small blocks of rubber moulded into the base of the main grooves at a depth of 1.6mm.

Tires are the only point of contact between the vehicle and road.

The photo below shows the actual contact zone.

NEW TIRE

WORN TIRE
(1,6 mm tread)

If the tread depth is less than 1.6mm, tires are considered to be worn and dangerous on wet surfaces.

Moving forward
means sustainable mobility

INNOVATION AND THE ENVIRONMENT

By 2050, Michelin aims to cut the quantity of raw materials used in its tire manufacturing process by half and to have developed renewable energy in its facilities. The design of MICHELIN tires has already saved billions of litres of fuel and, by extension, billions of tons of CO_2.

Similarly, Michelin prints its maps and guides on paper produced from sustainably managed forests and is diversifying its publishing media by offering digital solutions to make traveling easier, more fuel efficient and more enjoyable!

The group's whole-hearted commitment to eco-design on a daily basis is demonstrated by ISO 14001 certification.

Like you, Michelin is committed to preserving our planet.

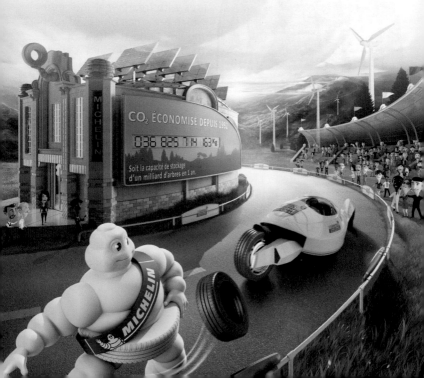

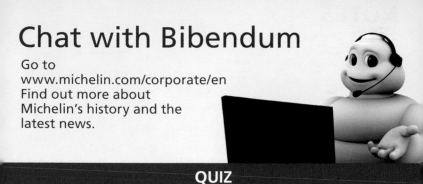

Chat with Bibendum

Go to
www.michelin.com/corporate/en
Find out more about
Michelin's history and the
latest news.

Michelin develops tires for all types of vehicles.
See if you can match the right tire with the right vehicle…

Solution : A-6 / B-4 / C-2 / D-1 / E-3 / F-7 / G-5